N D
AH! QU'IL EST BON LE BON DIEU!
1851
Ex Libris
Notre Dame High School
San Jose

This is a volume in

THE UNIVERSITY OF MICHIGAN HISTORY OF THE MODERN WORLD

Upon completion, the series will consist of the following volumes:

The United States to 1865 *by Michael Kraus*

The United States since 1865 *by Foster Rhea Dulles*

Canada: A Modern History *by John Bartlet Brebner*

Latin America: A Modern History *by J. Fred Rippy*

Great Britain to 1688 *by Maurice Ashley*

Great Britain since 1688 *by K. B. Smellie*

France: A Modern History *by Albert Guérard*

Germany: A Modern History *by Marshall Dill, Jr.*

Italy: A Modern History *by Denis Mack Smith*

Spain and Portugal: A Modern History *by Charles E. Nowell*

Russia and the Soviet Union: A Modern History *by Warren B. Walsh*

The Near East: A Modern History *by William Yale*

The Far East: A Modern History *by Nathaniel Peffer*

India: A Modern History *by Percival Spear*

Australia and the Southwest Pacific: A Modern History *by C. Hartley Grattan*

Africa: A Modern History *by Ronald E. Robinson*

THE UNITED STATES
SINCE 1865

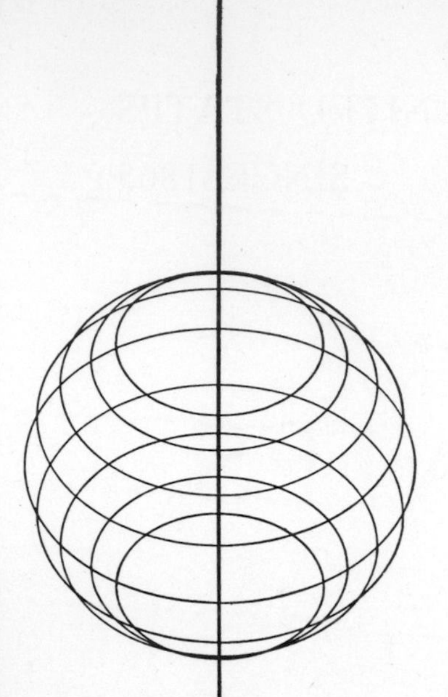

The University of Michigan History of the Modern World

Edited by Allan Nevins and Howard M. Ehrmann

THE UNITED STATES SINCE 1865

BY FOSTER RHEA DULLES

Ann Arbor: The University of Michigan Press

Published in the United States of America by
The University of Michigan Press and simultaneously
in Toronto, Canada, by Ambassador Books Limited

Library of Congress Catalog Card No. 59-62501
Designed by George Lenox
Manufactured in the United States of America by
Vail-Ballou Press, Inc., Binghamton, New York

Contents

MAPS

ACKNOWLEDGMENTS

The lines quoted from "The Hollow Men" by T. S. Eliot are from *Collected Poems 1909–1935,* copyright, 1936, by Harcourt, Brace and Company, Inc.

The lines quoted from E. E. Cummings are copyright, 1926, by Horace Liveright; renewed, 1953, by E. E. Cummings. Reprinted from *Poems 1923–1954* by E. E. Cummings by permission of Harcourt, Brace and Company, Inc.

THE UNITED STATES SINCE 1865

CHAPTER I

The Aftermath of War

★ APPOMATTOX COURT HOUSE

On April 9, 1865—it was Palm Sunday—General Ulysses S. Grant rode through the Union lines to the little village of Appomattox Court House, in Virginia, dismounted from his horse, and walked up the steps of a small house. The door was opened and General Robert E. Lee, who had been awaiting this arrival, rose to his feet. The two generals, commanders respectively of the Union and Confederate forces in the Civil War, greeted each other formally.

They presented a strange contrast: the one heavily bearded, dressed for the field in a soldier's blouse, his boots and breeches spattered with mud, nothing to indicate his rank except the stars on his shoulder straps; and the other tall and imposing, faultlessly garbed in full-dress uniform, a sash of red silk about his waist and a jeweled sword at his side. For a time they chatted, recalling their common experiences in the war against Mexico. "Our conversation grew so pleasant," General Grant was later to recall, "that I almost forgot the object of our meeting."

It was, however, of some moment—nothing less than the surrender of the Army of Northern Virginia. The position of Lee's forces had become untenable and it was the beginning of the end for the Confederacy. The terms were quickly agreed upon. Arms and materiel were to be surrendered, all troops paroled, officers permitted to retain their side-arms, and in order to expedite spring planting, every man claiming a horse or a mule would be allowed to take his animal home. The prolonged and bitter agony of the Civil War was to give way to peace, to re-establishment of the shattered Union, and to the reconstruction of the southern states.

The end of hostilities marked the close of one epoch in the history of the United States and the beginning of another. Certain issues had once and for all been settled. The protracted debate and sectional conflict over the nature of the Union were resolved by the arbitrament of arms. There would be no further questioning of the principle that the United States was "an indestructible union composed of indestructible states." The right of secession had been denied by a stronger force than the polemics of Daniel Webster or the earnest appeals of Lincoln. So too had there finally been decided the crucial problem of slavery. The seal of victory on the battlefield was placed upon the northern contention that human bondage could not exist in the American democracy. The future status of the Negro was still to be determined, and would give rise to no less controversial issues than those which war had solved, but neither slavery nor involuntary servitude would henceforth be countenanced within the United States or any place subject to their jurisdiction.

At the same time, the end of the Civil War meant a great deal more than even the settlement of these issues. At long last the energies of the American people were free to resume the tremendous task of building up a nation without being diverted by the fatal pull of North and South. The historic march across the continent was now to receive a fresh impetus as thousands of settlers poured into the new West that lay beyond the Missouri; while even more importantly, the growth of manufactures in the northern states launched industrial production on a period of phenomenal expansion. An economic revolution already getting slowly underway was immensely accelerated by the profligate exploitation of the country's apparently limitless natural resources, the building of a vast railroad network stretching from coast to coast, and the rapid development of banking, trade and commerce.

"The truth is," wrote Senator John Sherman of Ohio, "the close of the war with our resources unimpaired gives an elevation, a scope to the ideas of leading capitalists far higher than anything ever undertaken in this country before. They talk of millions as confidently as formerly of thousands."

The rise of a gigantic steel industry drawing upon the iron deposits of the Mesabi ore lands in Minnesota and the coal and limestone of Pennsylvania; the growth of oil refineries which followed rapidly upon the discovery of petroleum in Pennsylvania and Ohio; the ever-increasing manufacture of agricultural and industrial machinery; astounding advances in the production of electric light and power—these were the most significant developments to characterize American history in the remaining years of the nineteenth century once the war over the Union had come to an end.

Moreover the face of America was transformed as the old agrarian economy gave way before the advance of the new industrialism.

"Out of his body grows revolving steel," Stephen Vincent Benét would sing more than half a century later in his epic of John Brown—

> Out of his body grows the spinning wheel
> Made up of wheels, the new, mechanic birth,
> No longer bound by toil
> To the unsparing soil
> Or the old furrow-line . . .
>
> Out of John Brown's strong sinews the tall skyscrapers grow,
> Out of his heart the chanting buildings rise,
> Rivet and girder, motor and dynamo,
> Pillar of smoke by day and fire by night,
> The steel-faced cities reaching at the skies

★ THE PROSTRATE SOUTH

The settlement of the West and the growth of industry were outstanding developments, and the heroes of the age were the pioneers who opened up the prairies to wheat and corn, and the captains of industry who built up their empires of coal and steel and oil. But war had created problems as well as solved them: foremost among them in the immediate aftermath of hostilities was that of the status of the South.

How could a lasting reconciliation be effected between the two sections of the country and how could the states that had made up the Confederacy be brought back into a proper relationship with the Union? What were the rights of the newly emancipated Negroes and in what way could they be most effectively safeguarded? How could the South, prostrated by military defeat and with much of its territory laid waste by war, adjust itself to the changed order brought about by the end of slavery?

These basic issues were immediate and urgent. They had to be faced. Closely interwoven in their political, economic and social implications, they demanded statesmanship of the highest order.

In 1865 the conditions generally prevailing throughout the South were chaotic. The Confederate soldiers straggling back to their homes found the country almost everywhere marked by ruin and destruction. Along the line of General Sherman's famous march to the sea through Georgia, the devastation could hardly have been more complete. Towns and cities had been laid waste by fire; railroad lines torn up and destroyed. In many other sections of the South, the countryside had been ravaged by the armies of both sides, and by marauding bands of guerillas.

"A city of ruins, of desolation, of vacant houses, of widowed women, of rotting wharves, of deserted warehouses, of weed-wild gardens, of miles of grass-grown streets, of acres of pitiful and voiceful barrenness—

that is Charleston," wrote one observer. "Columbia is the heart of Destruction," read another report. "Being outside of it, you can only get in through one of the roads built by Ruin. Being in it, you can only get out over one of the roads walled by Desolation. You go north thirty-two miles and find the end of one railroad; southeast thirty miles and find the end of another; south forty-five miles and find the end of a third; southwest fifty miles and meet a fourth; and northwest twenty-nine miles and find the end of still another."

Countless plantations stood deserted. Many of them had been sold under foreclosure proceedings, and in other instances, their owners had been unable to obtain the labor for their cultivation. The land was weighed down by poverty, a helpless poverty from which there seemed no way of escape.

The newly freed Negroes often interpreted their liberty as meaning that they would no longer have to work. Some of them loafed about their cabins in complete idleness, and instead of trying to grow any crops relied upon the rations that were widely distributed by the congressionally created Freedmen's Bureau. Others left their homes and with little thought of the morrow roamed about the country in shiftless enjoyment of their new independence.

A feeling of complete apathy and despair was widely prevalent among members of the old white aristocracy, but there were innumerable individuals who rose above circumstance, valiantly seeking to build a new life amid the ruins of the old. The daughter of Thomas Dabney, a great Mississippi planter, has left a memorable account of the efforts of her father to adapt himself to the changed order. His plantation had been stripped of everything but a few mules and one cow, but he refused to be discouraged. At the age of seventy he took over tasks that had always been left to slaves, cultivating the garden and even doing the family washing.

There were many other examples of men returned from the war who accepted the most humble jobs when they faced the necessity of supporting their families. The story is told of one distinguished Confederate officer selling homemade pies, another hawking fish and oysters, and a third peddling tea and molasses to his former slaves. On one occasion a group of wounded Union soldiers returning to the North asked a raggedly dressed man plowing a field where they could get something to eat. He politely directed them to a nearby plantation house. There they discovered that the man whom they had taken to be a day laborer was a brigadier general who had served as chief of artillery with the Army of Northern Virginia.

Such incidents were symptomatic of the complete disruption of southern life and vividly reflected the widespread poverty. Land values had collapsed; the currency in circulation was almost worthless, and property losses seemed incalculable. Those sustained by plantation owners through the emancipation of the slaves amounted to some $2 billion. For a brief time in the immediate aftermath of war, the towns experienced a hectic flush of postwar prosperity, but the paralysis of agriculture was so widespread that in some parts of the South the crops raised in the first year after Appomattox were little more than a tenth what they had been. "In many whole counties," a press correspondent wrote of conditions in Georgia, "the merest necessaries of life are all any family have or can afford, while among the poorer classes there is a great lack of even these."

★ LINCOLN'S RECONSTRUCTION PROGRAM

The issues created by this appalling economic breakdown and by the complexities of the political situation were overwhelming, but for a time there had been widespread hope that the Union could be effectively reconstituted through moderate and conciliatory policies on the part of the North. This hope was founded on the presence in the White House of a man who during all the bloody years of war had never wavered in the constant expression of his tolerance, his generosity, his magnanimity. But just five days after Appomattox, as he watched a performance of *Our American Cousin* in a Washington theater, Lincoln had been killed by the bullet insanely fired by John Wilkes Booth. All the world mourned. The South knew that it had lost its greatest and most powerful friend among all northern leaders. The problems confronting the country might have been beyond even Lincoln's pre-eminent political skill, but at least he would have approached them with that rare combination of idealistic vision and practical common sense that was the signal mark of his genius. Never has a man been more nearly indispensable to his country. With his passing the nation was to suffer grievously from a tragic failure of leadership.

As early as December, 1863, Lincoln had devised a plan to provide the means for a rapid restoration of normal relations with the southern states. With certain exceptions, he was prepared to grant a general amnesty to all their citizens who would take an oath of loyalty to the Union; and when 10 per cent of the electorate in any one state had taken such an oath, they might establish a new government. As soon as it agreed to abolish slavery and comply with other Union laws, it would be officially recognized. No thought of retribution entered Lincoln's mind. His sole goal was peace and reconciliation. Even before he was struck down, however, it had become clear that powerful forces in the North were unwilling to go along with the lenient policy he proposed.

★ THE RADICAL PROTEST

The so-called Radical Republicans, who had won dominant control over Congress during the war, were prepared to insist upon more effective safeguards than Lincoln proposed against any possible recurrence of secessionist sentiment, and more certain guarantees that the Negroes would be secure in their newly won freedom. They also wanted greater assurance that the old planter aristocracy would not again be able to challenge the program of northern industrial interests in the further evolution of national policy.

In July 1864 they took a first step along such lines with passage of the Wade-Davis bill. It stipulated that a *majority,* rather than 10 per cent, of the citizens of a seceded state would have to take an oath of allegiance before they could form a government, and that new state constitutions should abolish slavery, repudiate state debts and disenfranchise all Confederate leaders. Even more important, this measure provided that Congress rather than the President would then have the power to recognize the reconstituted states.

Lincoln blocked enactment of the Wade-Davis bill through a pocket veto. The Radicals were thus momentarily restrained from interfering with the presidential reconstruction plan and, other than establishment of the Freedmen's Bureau, made only one further move at this session of Congress. This was the approval, in January, 1865, of the Thirteenth Amendment abolishing slavery throughout the Union. It was only three months later, however, that the assassination of Lincoln gave an entirely new complexion to the entire political situation. Deprived of his moderate and conciliatory leadership, the North was to adopt an attitude toward the South that he would never have countenanced. Political passions that might have been modified by his patience and tact were soon fanned into furious and angry flames.

The problem the country faced involved not only re-establishment of the Union and the determination of the status of the Negro. The future balance of political power within the United States was at stake. Even though the war had caused the collapse of the old plantation system in the South and given a tremendous impetus to the growth of manufactures in the North, it had not brought an end to the perennial conflict between the agrarian and industrial interests of the nation. The question was not therefore simply one of offering either harsh or lenient terms of peace to a defeated foe, as it would have been in the case of foreign war. The whole future course of national development appeared to hang in the balance.

Agreement upon policy would have been highly difficult even if circumstances had provided every opportunity for calm deliberation, and every government official and member of Congress had been animated only by the broadest considerations of public interest. Circumstances, however, did not make for calm deliberation and they did not foster patriotic unselfishness. The war had aroused a spirit of intolerance and vengefulness, and encouraged the continued use of suppressive force. When the men who succeeded Lincoln not only allowed themselves to be swayed by wartime passions, but appealed to popular emotions to gain support for their particular policies, the reconstruction of the South was inevitably shadowed by renewed sectional conflict which again gravely imperiled national unity.

★ ANDREW JOHNSON

Lincoln's successor in the White House was Andrew Johnson. The congressional faction scheming to force upon the country a harsh reconstruction policy that would effectively prevent any recovery of political power by the former governing class in the southern states at first thought that he was their man. No one had spoken out more bluntly against the crime of treason. "Johnson, we have faith in you," one of their leaders emphatically declared. "By the gods, there will be no trouble now in running the government." But Johnson was soon to demonstrate that in dealing with the people of the South as a whole, he leaned heavily toward the conciliatory policy favored by Lincoln. The Radical Republicans were appalled, and they grew the more incensed at the President's stand because of their own misinterpretation of his attitude. "Rebellion has vaulted into the presidential chair," Charles Sumner exclaimed bitterly when a long interview convinced him of what he deemed Johnson's soft attitude.

The new President was a onetime Democrat, a former peacetime governor and senator of Tennessee, whose loyalty to the Union had led Lincoln to appoint him the military governor of that important state after its subjection. His nomination for the vice-presidency in 1864 had been a gesture to win the support of other loyal Democrats for Lincoln's re-election, as well as a reward for the outstanding services he had rendered his country. Honest, forthright, and courageous, Johnson was prepared to fight for his principles in war's aftermath just as stubbornly as he had defended them in the dark days of conflict. There was no room for accommodation or compromise in his character. When he came up against the no less intractable stand taken by the Radicals in opposing his reconstruction policies, he was the more determined to have his way.

Johnson was born in North Carolina, of humble origin, and at the age of eighteen moved to the small Tennessee town of Greenville. Forced by poverty to earn his own living while still a boy, he was apprenticed to a tailor, and in Greenville set up his own shop in this useful but unglamorous trade. His interests were broader than tailoring, however. Taught to read and write by his wife, for he had little or no schooling before his marriage, he was soon engaged in politics, and for all his lack of advantages advanced steadily along the road of political preferment from local alderman to the White House.

There was nothing very imposing about Johnson in appearance. He was of medium size, although of a powerful build, and what was described as his "plain weather-beaten face" reflected an essentially simple character. He had a good if somewhat limited mind, was forthright to the point of incredible tactlessness, and was a powerful and eloquent public speaker. His prepared talks were almost invariably well-reasoned and convincing. When he spoke extemporaneously, he was sometimes led into extremes of statement and language that perhaps did him no harm in the rough-and-tumble of Tennessee politics, but were to be highly unfortunate when he spoke as President. Goaded by hecklers, he would become angry and intemperate. "I care nothing for dignity," he once exclaimed. But the presidential office demanded dignity.

One unfortunate episode in his career was to give his enemies an even more effective weapon in attacks on his personal character. Before his inauguration as Vice-President he had been ill, and to fortify himself for the ceremony he had taken enough to drink to become somewhat intoxicated. There was no recurrence of such an incident. Lincoln told those concerned not to worry about vice-presidential decorum—"Andy ain't no drunkard." But the old scandal was revived when the Radical Republicans entered the lists against him and Johnson was luridly portrayed as a chronic drunkard, disgracing the sacred precincts of the White House by his nightly carousing. Thaddeus Stevens sneered at the "drunken tailor," and Sumner talked arrogantly of this "insolent drunken brute in comparison with which Caligula's horse was respectable."

Johnson was on the defensive in respect both to his plebeian origins and to charges of drinking. He was actually self-conscious and timid rather than the coarse, brutal, domineering figure depicted by his foes. Nevertheless he struck back at these attacks in kind, and the intemperateness and violence of his language provided fresh ammunition for further onslaughts upon his fitness for the presidential office.

Before the war, Johnson had been a champion of the small farmers, the workingmen and the "poor whites" of his native state. Known as "the mechanic governor," there was no truer democrat in public life. At the same time, he had a deep and abiding antipathy for the wealthy plantation-owner class. His loyalty to the Union was undoubtedly colored by his conviction that for the class of people whom he represented, secession could bring no possible advantage, and on the same grounds it would have appeared logical for him to support a reconstruction policy directed against the white aristocracy. Where the Radicals made their mistake was in believing that his antagonism toward the planter class would lead him to favor policies that would enable the Negroes to take part in the political life of the former Confederate states. On the contrary, Johnson's attitude toward the Negroes was firmly fixed by his southern background. While he felt that they were entitled to civil rights and some limited form of suffrage, he believed thoroughly in a white man's government. Rather than see the Negroes at once given the vote, as the Radicals were demanding, he was willing to run the risk of having representatives of the old aristocracy recover political power.

His advocacy of a generally lenient policy toward the South was strengthened by his conviction that the stringent controls proposed by the Radicals were primarily designed to protect the interests of northern industrialists. He had no more sympathy for this class than for the southern landowners. Moreover he was also persuaded, and there can be no doubt of his sincerity, that any attempt on the part of the federal government to force either a program of civil rights or Negro suffrage on the southern states was unconstitutional. He retained enough of his democratic heritage of states' rights to believe that such issues should be left to the new state governments, insisting that the problem of the Negro was one that the South itself had to solve.

★ THE NEW PRESIDENTIAL PLAN

Acting upon these principles or convictions, Johnson proceeded to carry out a reconstruction policy that closely conformed to the one projected by Lincoln. He recognized the state governments already set up under Lincoln's 10 per cent plan, extended (again with some exceptions) a general amnesty to citizens of the still unreconstructed states, and provided for their establishment of new governments. He was prepared to recognize such governments upon their repeal of the secession ordinances, repudiation of state war debts, abolition of slavery, and ratification of the Thirteenth Amendment. When the President came before Congress to deliver his first annual message in December, 1865, this process had been completed in every southern state except Texas.

All that remained necessary to mark the full restoration of the Union, Johnson declared, was completion of the process of constitutional amendment: "It reunites us beyond all power of disruption—it heals the wound that is still imperfectly closed." And going beyond the immediate problem of reconstruction, the President pointed enthusiastically to the future. "Where in history," he asked rhetorically, "does a parallel exist to the public happiness which is within reach of the people of the United States?"

★ OPPOSITION OF THE RADICALS

But Johnson reckoned without the Radicals. They had grown increasingly alarmed by a policy which threatened to allow the old South once again to play a major role in national politics through the immediate readmission of its representatives to Congress. At first they bided their time. There was too much popular support for what was being done to make direct interference with the President's program appear advisable. However, Congress set up a Joint Committee on Reconstruction soon after its reassembly to study the entire situation, and the Radicals prepared to mark out the lines of future attack. The new state governments were accepted for the purpose of securing ratification of the Thirteenth Amendment, but further guarantees of loyalty were insisted upon as a condition for recognition of congressional representatives. Congress rather than the President was to be made the judge of southern good faith. Moreover it was soon revealed that the real objective of the Radicals was to prevent the old planter aristocracy's return to power by immediately giving the vote to all Negroes.

As Congress took the first steps to carry out this new policy by broadening the powers of the Freedmen's Bureau to safeguard the interests of the Negroes, and by enacting a comprehensive Civil Rights Bill guaranteeing the Negroes the same civil status as whites, Johnson struck back vigorously through successive vetoes of the proposed legislation. He was not opposed to its objectives but to the means employed. The congressional program was in his opinion not only an entirely unwarranted invasion of states' rights, but a course of action that tended to perpetuate disunion. He attacked the Radical Republicans as a minority faction trying to exercise a power that, if it were not checked, would end in a despotism or in monarchy itself. The gauntlet had been thrown down, and the angry President picked it up without hesitation. In the event, his veto was narrowly sustained on the new Freedmen's Bureau bill, but overridden on the Civil Rights Bill and then on a further Freedmen's Bureau measure.

★ CHARLES SUMNER

Johnson faced a formidable opposition which in Thaddeus Stevens and

Charles Sumner had leaders as determined to have their own way as he was himself. Imperious and self-willed, they were prepared no matter what the cost to push through their own program. The power of the former leaders of the Confederacy was to be crushed beyond any possibility of repair so as to assure both the rights of Negroes and the dominance of northern interests over the national government.

Sumner, the senior senator from Massachusetts, was an idealist and a reformer. An imposing figure, some six feet and four inches in height, his burning eyes proclaimed the zealot who would brook no disagreement with his own intense convictions. In earlier days he had fought valiantly not only for the emancipation of the Negro, but for such other causes as the outlawry of war. No one could have been more certain of his own eternal rightness in defending his principles. On one occasion a friend tried to point out to him in the course of a discussion that he was completely ignoring the other side of the question. "There is no other side," was Sumner's unequivocal answer. His exalted moral fervor and humanitarianism were compounded by his egotism, his dogmatic insistence on his own concepts of justice, and the violent and vituperative scorn with which he assailed everyone who disagreed with him.

He was a firm believer in equal rights for Negroes and completely convinced that unless the southern states were compelled to grant them free schools, free homesteads, and the vote, the purposes for which the Civil War had been fought would be nullified. There could be no temporizing on such a basic issue. And it was within the powers of Congress, in Sumner's opinion, to impose whatever terms of peace it chose upon the southern states. He did not hold with Lincoln's theory that they had been merely out of their proper relationship with the Union. They had committed political suicide. They were to be compelled, by the further display of force if necessary, to acknowledge absolute Negro equality in the enjoyment of all political, economic, and social privileges within a reconstituted southern society.

Sumner was undoubtedly sincere in these views. At the same time he also realized that if the political power of the southern whites was not broken, they might again join with northern Democrats and control Congress. How much his desire to see the suffrage extended to the Negroes was affected by his realization that their votes were essential if the Republicans were to exercise any political influence in the South, is a question that can hardly be answered. But this was a highly important consideration. "Only through him [the Negro]," Sumner once wrote, "can you redress the balance of our political system and assure the safety of private citizens. . . . He is our best guarantee. Use him."

★ THADDEUS STEVENS

Thaddeus Stevens, a representative from Pennsylvania and the dominant member of the Joint Committee on Reconstruction, was fanatically committed to supporting the rights of the Negroes and also animated by a vindictive desire to make the southern states pay the price of rebellion. "The whole fabric of southern society," he declared, "must be changed." There was cold hatred in his attitude toward those Confederate leaders whom he harshly characterized as "proud, bloated, defiant rebels." But while he often appeared to be obsessed with the idea of vengeance for its own sake, there was again the underlying idea of giving the vote to the Negro as a means of guaranteeing "perpetual ascendancy to the party of the Union." Stevens was ready to do anything to avert a new Democratic threat to the Republican program of fostering and promoting the interests of northern industrialists. His concern for the Negro was real and sincere; otherwise there was little of Sumner's idealism about this harsh and angry old man—he was seventy-four—who could bluntly declare: "Throw conscience to the Devil and stand by your party."

With the decline of President Johnson's influence, Stevens was to exercise a measure of control over Congress that made him for a time the most powerful man in the political life of the nation. "He is leader," declared a young member of Congress, Rutherford B. Hayes. There were few, however, to love this brilliant, implacable and sometimes vicious politician. Tall and bent, his long pallid face and beetling eyebrows topped by a dark brown wig, grimly enduring the lameness resulting from a club foot, Stevens was not an attractive figure. During his final illness, with haggard face "scarred by the crooked autograph of pain," he had to be carried daily to his seat in the House. He remained its ruling spirit through an exercise of will that seemed to defy approaching death.

Neither justice nor truth restrained Sumner or Stevens in their charges against a President who they felt was defying Congress and seeking to restore the Democratic party to power by his leniency toward the South. As they prepared to carry the issue to the country in the mid-term elections of 1866, they did everything possible to discredit him as the most effective method of convincing northern voters that their own approach to reconstruction was the only way in which the Union could be safeguarded. "Jefferson Davis is in the casement at Fortress Monroe," Sumner declared, "but Andrew Johnson is doing his work."

★ POLITICS IN THE SOUTH

Events in the South were in the meantime hardly promoting the cause of conciliation. They appeared, indeed, to afford considerable justification for the Radical contention that unless more stringent controls were imposed to guarantee civil rights, the Negroes would be relegated to a status little better than their former slavery. The new state governments that had been recognized by President Johnson adopted a series of laws, known as the "Black Codes," which conferred some privileges upon the freedmen, but continued to draw a marked distinction between their rights and those of the whites. It was only natural that southerners, whose basic conception of the inferior nature of the Negro was not altered by the fact that they had been forced to release him from slavery, should still seek to keep him in a subordinate position. The laws in some of the states, however, went so far in the restrictions imposed upon Negroes that in the eyes of many northerners they looked like an attempt to establish a new peonage.

The severity of these measures was most pronounced in those states that had a large Negro population, especially Mississippi, South Carolina, and Louisiana. In Mississippi, for example, the Black Code declared that all freedmen or free Negroes had to have lawful employment, and they were required to sign contracts binding them to the service of their employers for a full year. Those who were found without work were deemed to be vagrants, subject to being hired out by the sheriff to anyone who would undertake to pay their fines and be responsible for them. "Every civil officer," the law stated in a final punitive section, "shall, and every person may, arrest and carry back to his or her legal employer any freedman, free Negro or mulatto who shall have quit the service of his or her employer before the expiration of his or her term of service without good cause. . . ."

In the confused and chaotic conditions resulting from the freeing of the slaves and in the light of their misunderstanding of what liberty actually meant, there was good reason for stringent legislation in meeting the problem of Negro vagrancy. Many states, moreover, adopted more reasonable and moderate measures than that cited. But the North was aroused by discrimination that all too often was arbitrary and repressive.

"We tell the white men of Mississippi," thundered the Chicago *Tribune,* "that the men of the North will convert the State of Mississippi into a frog pond before they will allow such laws to disgrace one foot of soil in which the bones of our soldiers sleep and over which the flag of freedom waves."

The position of the Radicals was immensely strengthened by such evidence of an unrepentant South, and President Johnson played into their hands when he apparently condoned the policies incorporated in the Black Codes. His vetoes of the measures whereby an aroused Congress tried to protect the Negroes against this legislation were said to be final proof of a treasonable alliance with the southern whites. Johnson cogently presented the reasons for his stand. He declared that the contemplated interference on the part of the federal government with the reserved powers of the states was clearly unconstitutional. To settle this issue, in tacit recognition of the correctness of the President's constitutional position in vetoing the Civil Rights Bill, Congress approved—in June, 1866—the Fourteenth Amendment.

★ THE FOURTEENTH AMENDMENT

This amendment called for the disqualification for political office of all participants in the rebellion who had formerly held any state or federal position, validation of the public debt of the United States and invalidation of that of the Confederacy, and a reduction in the congressional representation of any state in proportion to its denial of the suffrage to any male inhabitants. The amendment's first and most important section, however, dealt with discrimination:

> All persons born or naturalized in the United States, and subject to the jurisdiction thereof, are citizens of the United States and of the State wherein they reside. No State shall make or enforce any law which shall abridge the privileges or immunities of citizens of the United States; nor shall any State deprive any person of life, liberty, or property, without due process of law; nor deny to any person within its jurisdiction the equal protection of the laws.

The Radicals now insisted that the southern states accept the Fourteenth Amendment as a condition for the readmission of their representatives to Congress. In so doing they were asking the leaders of the new state governments both to sacrifice their own political interests, and to accept a civil rights program that ran counter to every southern concept of the Negro's role in society. But the Radical position on these issues was generally supported in the North. Without the guarantees of the Fourteenth Amendment, it was widely believed, discrimination against the Negroes, as reflected in the Black Codes, would be continued. Moreover if congressional representation was not limited in proportion to the extent to which the Negroes were deprived of the vote, the number of congressmen chosen by the white voters of the South on the basis of the states' total population would actually exceed the prewar total.

The southern states were unwilling to approve the Fourteenth Amendment, and at this point Johnson still further strengthened the attacks being made upon his policies by upholding their position. In spite of his own belief in civil equality and limited Negro suffrage, he bluntly reiterated that for Congress to try to compel the South to make such concessions was an unjustified intrusion in matters that should be left to the states. The wide support for the amendment among even moderate northerners did not budge him. Had he been willing to modify his views, he might well have been able to rally the country behind him in opposition to the more extreme aspects of the Radicals' policy. But Johnson would make no concessions. As the President and his foes squared off in the critical congressional elections of 1866, neither side was prepared to give any quarter.

★ VICTORY OF THE RADICALS

The Radicals played up southern refusal to grant civil rights to the Negroes; they attacked the new state governments for opposing the Fourteenth Amendment. Their own political aims and aspirations were seldom brought out as they assailed Johnson for favoring policies that would leave the former Confederate leaders so largely in control throughout the South. Calling for support for their own program as the only way to assure the victory for which so many lives had been lost on the field of battle, they fought the war all over again. They demanded repudiation of the President through the election of a Congress that would uphold the best interests of the Union.

The earlier whispering campaign against Johnson's character came out more and more into the open. The presence of this faithless demagogue in the White House was "the great accident." An entire people had trembled, Sumner declared, "as they beheld a drunken man ascend the heights of power." Stevens denounced him as "an alien enemy, a citizen of a foreign state." Again and again, Johnson was called a traitor whose perfidious betrayal of the Union cause placed him on a par with the southern rebels themselves.

The President bitterly resented these charges and struck back. He countered the vindictive hatred of Sumner and Stevens with equally vicious attacks on their character. The issues at stake were almost forgotten in the clash of personalities. And the extremes to which the President went in assailing his enemies constantly provided fresh ammunition for their innuendoes about his irresponsibility and unfitness for high office. In one embittered speech, Johnson declared:

> I have been called Judas Iscariot and all that. Now my countrymen . . . it is very easy to indulge in epithets; it is easy to call a man Judas and cry out "traitor." . . . Judas Iscariot—Judas. There was a Judas and he was one

> of twelve apostles. Oh, yes; the twelve apostles had a Christ. The twelve apostles had a Christ, and he could never have had a Judas unless he had had twelve apostles. If I have played the Judas, who has been my Christ that I have played the Judas with? Was it Thad Stevens? Was it Wendell Phillips? Was it Charles Sumner? These are the men that stop and compare themselves with the Saviour, and everybody that differs with them in opinion, and to try and stay their diabolical and nefarious policy, is to be denounced as Judas.

Such speeches were quoted and vehemently assailed as "peculiarly indecent and unbecoming in the Chief Magistrate of the United States." It was hard even for his friends to justify them. Granted they were the angry outbursts of a man who felt himself traduced, slandered, and maligned, they were in the worst possible taste. They hardly created the atmosphere in which agreement could be reached on a moderate policy toward the South.

There was actually never much chance that the conciliatory reconstruction policy of the President could win approval in the heated atmosphere created by the congressional campaign. Had Johnson been able to keep his temper and maintain his dignity, had he emphasized the constructive aspects of his program rather than intemperately attacking all his critics, the Radicals might have had a harder time. As it was, everything was in their favor.

"Shall the death of slavery," asked Roscoe Conkling in a discussion in Congress over the readmission of southern congressmen through a system whereby nonvoting Negroes as well as whites formed the basis of state representation, "add two-fifths to the entire power which slavery had when slavery was living? Shall one white man have as much share as three other white men merely because he lives where blacks outnumber whites two to one? Shall this inequality exist, and exist only in favor of those who without cause drenched the land with blood and covered it with mourning? Shall such be the reward of those who did the foulest and guiltiest act which crimsons the annals of recorded time? No sir; not if I can help it."

Couched in these terms, the presidential program for recognizing the southern state governments without compelling them to accept the Fourteenth Amendment seemed indefensible. Johnson was repudiated. The election so strengthened the Radicals' position in Congress that they could completely override the President on every issue.

★ THE SPIRIT OF RECONSTRUCTION

From this point on the spirit in which reconstruction was carried out was often marked by wilful disregard of southern rights and by blind partisanship. This was demonstrated again and again. Yet this was not the whole story. The idea of vengeance against the Confederacy remained coupled with a sincere desire to guarantee the civil rights of the Negroes. The drive to establish the supremacy of the Republican party was allied with an honest concern over democratic ideals threatened by a resurgent southern aristocracy. In their general attitude the seceded states had hardly demonstrated a willingness to accept the full implications of northern victory. It is true that after a postwar tour of the country, General Grant said he was satisfied that "the mass of the thinking people in the South accept the situation of affairs in good faith." Certainly there was little thought of again challenging the indissolubility of the Union or seeking the restoration of chattel slavery. Nevertheless, the Black Codes and disapproval of the Fourteenth Amendment justified in considerable measure the northern feeling that a stricter reconstruction program than Johnson contemplated was essential before the South would be persuaded that it had to respect Negro civil rights.

CHAPTER II

Reconstruction and Recovery

★ CONGRESS AND THE PRESIDENT

While the campaign of 1866 was still underway, President Johnson had issued a proclamation declaring that the "insurrection" was finally over and that "peace, order, tranquility, and civil authority now exist in and throughout the United States." The Radicals felt otherwise. With their electoral victory enabling them to seize complete control over reconstruction policy, they took matters in hand in their own way. Upon the southern states' final rejection of the Fourteenth Amendment, Congress proceeded to act on the assumption that there were no legal governments whatsoever in the South. Dividing former Confederate territory into five districts, it established early in 1867 a system of military rule that completely ignored all constitutional safeguards for states' rights.

All Johnson's attempts to block this program were completely unavailing. His vetoes of the four Reconstruction Acts designed to implement it were overridden, and his influence still further whittled away by the passage of new measures to limit and restrict his executive authority. The President was virtually deprived of command of the army through an act stating that all orders were to be issued through the General of the Army, who was protected from removal, and even his control over members of his own cabinet was undermined by a Tenure of Office Act making their dismissal impossible without senatorial approval. Finally, in blatant disregard of the traditional separation of powers in our governmental system, the Radicals seized upon the ultimate weapon of impeachment. Johnson was brought before the bar of the Senate in March 1868 on a series of trumped-up charges whose political inspiration could hardly have been more transparent.

The pretense for his impeachment was his dismissal of Secretary of War Stanton, who had aligned himself closely with the Radicals. In taking this step Johnson acted on the conviction that the newly adopted Tenure of Office Act was unconstitutional (a contention later upheld by the Supreme Court) and that he was therefore quite within his rights, but the legal aspects of the case were completely overshadowed by politics. The Radicals were out to get the presidency by any means in their power, and their management of the impeachment proceedings could not have been more partisan. The prosecution made every possible appeal to passion and prejudice. Garbled newspaper accounts of Johnson's speeches were quoted to demonstrate his supposed unfitness for office, and much completely irrelevant evidence was introduced in an attempt to discredit his honesty and integrity. He was freely described as "a genius in depravity bent upon the ruin of his country."

Johnson was ably defended by counsel who clearly demonstrated that there were no justifiable grounds for impeachment, but the Radical majority was influenced by neither reason, nor logic, nor law. In the end, under the most dramatic circumstances, the Senate's vote fell just one ballot short of the two-thirds majority required for conviction. The President was saved by the refusal of a group of seven Republicans to sacrifice our whole constitutional system on the altar of political passion. Had a single additional vote been cast against him, Johnson would have been removed from office. A calamitous precedent would have been established whereby any future Congress commanding the necessary votes, would have been encouraged to impeach a President with whom it found itself in disagreement.

Writing some sixteen years after the event, George Julian, one of the seven members of the House committee which prepared the formal charges, candidly expressed his regret over the whole proceedings. "Andrew Johnson was not the devil incarnate he was then painted," Julian wrote, "nor did he monopolize entirely the wrongheadedness of the times. No one will now dispute that the popular estimate of his character did him very great injustice. . . . The idea of making the question of impeachment a matter of party discipline was utterly indefensible and preposterous."

★ THE SITUATION IN THE SOUTH

In the meantime, the congressional reconstruction program was fully underway. Army generals took over command of the five military districts into which the South had been divided, and with an army of occupation at their disposal assumed full responsibility for maintaining law and order. They arbitrarily removed six of the state governors, dismissed thousands of local officials, purged the legislatures of their more conservative elements, and flagrantly disregarded the civil rights of southern whites in preparing the way for the establishment of new state governments, to be chosen through universal suffrage, which would carry out the policies favored by northern Radicals.

In seven of the ten southern states "reconstructed" under such circumstances, so-called "black and tan" constitutional conventions promptly proceeded to adopt the required constitutions. They disenfranchised all Confederate leaders, gave the Negroes the vote, and established complete equality of political and civil rights. This process was completed in 1868; and upon legislative ratification of the Fourteenth Amendment, the seven new governments were at once recognized and their representatives duly admitted to Congress. Two years later the remaining three states had fallen in line; but because of the delay they were also compelled to ratify the Fifteenth Amendment, which provided for Negro suffrage, as well as the Fourteenth, before their representatives could be seated.

The constitutionality of this entire program could be questioned. However, Congress was prepared if necessary to override the Supreme Court and the latter consequently followed a very cautious policy. When Georgia sought an injunction in 1867 against enforcement of the Reconstruction acts, it dismissed the suit on the ground that the Court had no jurisdiction in what was essentially a political question. In another instance where there appeared to be a possibility that the Court might intervene, Congress actually passed a law removing the case under consideration from the Court's jurisdiction.

These developments created what was to become an increasingly embittered political division throughout the South. In every state the conservative white representatives of the old order were in a small minority, and the governing power was transferred to a majority made up of three elements entirely new to southern political life. The Negroes were numerically most important, but of far greater influence were the northern "carpetbaggers," who had descended on the South in droves to reap such harvests as they could from its political and economic chaos, and those few white southerners, derisively known as "scalawags," who had chosen to throw in their lot with the Radicals. A scandalous pursuit of their own selfish interest inspired the activities of many of these politicians, and an equally important obstacle to good government was the inexperience of the Negroes, so suddenly catapulted into political office and such easy victims of the unscrupulous.

Nevertheless, the new state constitutions, modeled to a great extent on those of the North, represented in many ways a significant advance over those which they replaced. They were not only far more democratic but they provided a basis for more efficient government. The abolition of property qualifications for holding office, reapportionment to bring about more equitable representation in the legislature, new provisions for local government, safeguards for the relief of debtors, broader protection of women's rights, and, most importantly, the establishment of universal public education, were among the reforms that represented a constructive advance toward bringing the South more in line with political and social progress in the North.

It was one thing to adopt such reforms, however, and another to carry them out effectively. The new legislatures openly raided state treasuries and with scant consideration of economic or financial realities, floated successive bond issues to meet the resultant deficits. Everywhere there were appalling waste and fraud. Credit was pledged to finance railway construction in return for special favors to the legislators; charters granting unnecessarily broad privileges were secretly awarded to private corporations. The opportunities for bribery and graft were too easily at hand to be avoided even had stricter concepts of public morality prevailed, and the influence of southern conservatives was far too feeble to exercise any effective control. Political chicanery, for which the northern carpetbaggers, aided and abetted by the scalawags, were largely responsible, thrived in an atmosphere in which votes, elections, and even judicial decisions were openly bought and sold.

To meet the mounting costs of government, including the high rates of interest on bonded indebtedness, the southern states also levied ever-higher taxes. They soon rose anywhere from four to fourteen times prewar figures. The levies on property were often so confiscatory that distraught landowners were compelled to put up millions of acres of land at forced sales. Yet there was no holding down the growing burden of debt. It rapidly rose to $21,000,000 in Tennessee, to $32,000,000 in Alabama, to $29,000,000 in South Carolina, to $48,000,000 in Louisiana—in all a total increase for the eleven Confederate states, between 1868 and 1874, of over $100,000,000.

The extravagance and graft that marked financial dealings were not alone responsible for this situation. New expenditures, at whatever cost, were in many instances unavoidable and the high interest rates charged by the North also seriously affected the debt problem. Moreover, corruption in the processes of government was often quite as bad in the North as in the South. The postwar era was a period of such moral laxity that state legislatures, and also municipal governments, in many other parts of the country were quite as adept as those dominated by carpetbaggers and scalawags in looting the public treasury.

★ NEGRO LEGISLATORS

The Negro members of the legislatures were the victims quite as often as they were the beneficiaries of the political corruption of these days. Their sudden transformation from slaves to legislators made them an easy prey to the temptations placed in their way. Their white allies played upon their inexperience, their gullibility, and their natural urge to make the most of their new position in society. And even when there was no question of corruption or graft, the Negroes often acted foolishly. Contemporary descriptions of their casual, carefree, and socially crude conduct of public affairs vividly reveal, in spite of some possible exaggeration, the political atmosphere of reconstruction days.

They were in a majority in the South Carolina legislature and, debauched by white profiteers and spoilsmen, took a huge delight in spending state funds. Operating expenses of the legislature's restaurant, equipped with an elaborate bar open from 8 A.M. to 2 A.M., amounted to over $125,000 for a single session. The lawmakers happily provided themselves with wine, whiskey, and Westphalia hams; plush velvet furniture and Brussels carpets; perfume, gold watches, and ornamental cuspidors. The capitol was completely refurnished at a cost of $200,000, but when the orgy of extravagance and graft came to an end with the election of a new and more conservative legislature, what was left as property of the state was valued at only $17,000.

An account of the South Carolina legislature by James Pike, a correspondent for the New York *Tribune,* is perhaps not wholly reliable, but has validity as reflecting a northern impression of what was happening:

> Yesterday, about 4 p.m., the assembled wisdom of the state . . . issued forth from the State house. About three-quarters of the crowd belonged to the African race. They were of every hue, from the light octoroon to the deep black. They were such a looking body of men as might pour out of a market house or a courthouse at random in any Southern state. Every Negro type and physiognomy was here to be seen, from the genteel serving-man to the roughhewn customer from the rice or cotton field. Their dress was as varied as their countenances. There was the secondhand black frock coat of infirm gentility, glossy and threadbare. There was the stovepipe hat of many ironings and departed styles. There was also to be seen a total disregard of the proprieties of costume in the coarse and dirty garments of the field, the stub jackets and slouch hats of soiling labor. In some instances rough woolen comforters embraced the neck and hid the absence of linen. Heavy brogans and short, torn trousers it was impossible to hide. The dusky tide flowed out into the littered and barren grounds and, issuing through the coarse wooden fence of the inclosure, melted away into the street beyond. These were the legislators of South Carolina.

Pike found that among the 124 representatives there were but 23 white men who stood for the traditions and standards of the old South, while of the 101 remaining, 94 were Negroes. On visiting the legislature in session, he found the handful of conservative whites sitting isolated and alone. "Grouped in a corner of the commodious and well-furnished chamber," he wrote, "they stolidly survey the noisy riot that goes on in the great black Left and Center, where the business and debates of the House are conducted and where sit the strange and extraordinary guides of the fortunes of a once proud and haughty state. . . . This dense Negro crowd they confront do the debating, the squabbling, the lawmaking, and create all the clamor and disorder of the body." Pike graphically described the endless chatter, the gush and babble, the unruly conduct, the complete lack of decorum, and the constant tendency of the legislators, enthusiastically cracking and munching peanuts, to break into heavy guffaws of laughter whenever anything amused them: "They laugh as hens cackle—one begins and all follow."

Yet beneath the surface this northern observer discovered that there was something very real about what these Negroes were doing—all was not sham and burlesque. He felt that they had an earnest purpose which lent a sort of dignity to their proceedings in spite of "the barbarous, animated jargon" in which they indulged:

> Seven years ago these men were raising corn and cotton under the whip of the overseer. Today they are raising points of order and questions of privilege. They can raise one as well as the other. They prefer the latter. It is easier and better paid. Then it is the evidence of accomplished result. It means escape and defense from old oppressors. It means liberty. It means the destruction of prison walls only too real to them. It is the sunshine of their lives. It is their day of jubilee. It is their long-promised vision of the Lord God Almighty.

★ SOCIAL GAINS

For all their extravagance, corruption, and lack of decorum, the legislatures of this unhappy period were, in fact, responsible for a number of constructive things as well as some very foolish ones. However crude its manifestations, democracy was at work. The leveling influence was sometimes carried to an absurd extreme, but against the background of traditional southern society, it was hardly surprising that the pendulum should swing too far. Although many of the whites and almost all of the Negroes were new to their jobs, their record was by no means one of unqualified misgovernment.

Many of the states, however unevenly, continued along the path of progressive legislation marked out by their new constitutions, giving real point and meaning to the theories they embodied. If South Carolina had an unfortunate record, even in that state a good deal was accomplished along the lines of effective social reform. The legislature adopted among other measures laws providing for poor relief, aid to Negro farmers through the distribution of homesteads, and for the establishment of charitable institutions. And again most significantly, South Carolina set up for the first time a system of free public education. Other states also adopted such democratic measures. The new development of schools for both whites and Negroes was of itself a contribution to the welfare of the South that in some measure compensated for the less savory aspects of carpetbag rule.

★ THE CONSERVATIVE REACTION

The fact remained, nevertheless, that the reconstruction governments were not representative of the South, denied the basic tenets of democracy through the disenfranchisement of so many whites, and remained in office only by the power of northern bayonets. It was clear from the very first that if such military support were withdrawn, every state regime based on the Negro vote would be overthrown. An angered people could not have resented more deeply the political revolution brought about by northern intervention, or been more determined to recover for the old Democratic party, representative of the white aristocracy, the power usurped by the unnatural Republican alliance of Negroes, carpetbaggers, and scalawags. The South was not prepared to accept the implications of the Fourteenth Amendment. When the radical state governments then went on to ratify the Fifteenth Amendment, with its definitive provision that no citizens of the United States could be deprived of the vote because of race, color, or previous condition of servitude, a stubborn determination to reassert white supremacy was still further reinforced.

Where the whites had a potential majority, it was possible for them to wage a campaign along accepted political lines to redeem the state governments from Radical control. The excesses of the carpetbaggers and scalawags gradually alienated popular support, and a reconstituted Democratic party began to make heavy inroads upon Republican strength in spite of the continued presence of northern troops. Where the whites were outnumbered by Negroes, as in no less than five states, a different situation prevailed. Here the whites felt compelled to resort to terroristic methods to intimidate the freedmen and prevent them from casting the votes that would have kept the radical legislatures in power.

★ THE KU KLUX KLAN

The Ku Klux Klan was the foremost organization developed to keep the Negroes "in their place" and convince them that they would be wiser not to try to exercise their newly won right to vote. It was first started in Pulaski, Tennessee, a year after the close of the Civil War. A group of young men, wearing sheets and pillow cases for the initiation ceremony of a local social club, discovered by chance how effective such costumes could be in terrifying the more superstitious Negroes. The club promptly seized the opportunity. The Ku Klux Klan was organized as the Invisible Empire of the South, under the direction of a Grand Wizard assisted by Genii, Dragons, Titans, and Cyclops, and throughout the South white-hooded horsemen began to ride about the countryside warning the Negroes to stay away from the polls.

Intimidation was the chief weapon of the Klan, but as self-constituted vigilantes its members soon began to adopt more forcible methods of asserting their power. There was a natural recklessness about the southerner, a tradition of violent action, and the secrecy of the society's activities also began to attract many young hoodlums who saw an opportunity for paying off personal grudges and had no intention of submitting to the authority of Titan, Cyclops, or Grand Wizard. Some of the white-hooded night riders were not long content merely to frighten. They kidnapped, ran out of town, horse-whipped, and on occasion even hanged recalcitrant Negroes. As a reign of violence appeared about to spread through the South, the more responsible leaders of the Klan became alarmed and in 1869 officially disbanded an organization that was getting completely out of control. But while many of the more flagrant crimes of reconstruction days were committed by nonmembers under cover of the society's secrecy, the Klan had encouraged lawlessness by its resort to violence in seeking to re-establish white supremacy.

In a realistic contemporary novel of reconstruction days, Albion W. Tourgée, a well-known carpetbag official, paints a graphic picture of the Ku Klux Klan on the march. He vividly describes the moonlit scene as the masked riders, silent and threatening, invade a little village; its Negro inhabitants, instinctively knowing that the enemy has come, remain indoors awaiting they know not what. There is no disturbance, no excitement, but after a time a whistle sounds, the cavalcade is heard to move off, and the fearful witnesses of this eerie scene see that on one of the horses an inert body is lashed. As the Negroes rush "with chattering teeth and trembling limbs" to the dwellings in the village, they find one where the door has been left open and no one is inside. With the return of the cavalcade to a nearby town another frightened observer describes the final act in this grim drama:

> I heard the noise of horses—quiet and orderly, but many. Looking from the window in the clear moonlight, I saw horsemen passing down the street, taking their stations here and there like guards who have been told off for

duty at specific points. . . . They seemed to have been sent on as a sort of picket guard for the main body, which soon came in. I should say there were from a hundred to a hundred and fifty still in line. They were all masked and wore black robes. The horses were disguised, too, by drapings. . . . Oh, it was a respectable crowd! No doubt about that, sir. Beggars don't ride in this country . . . Plenty of old soldiers in that crowd. Why, everything went just like clockwork. Not a word was said—just a few whistles given. They came like a dream and they went away like a mist. I thought we should have to fight for our lives, but they did not disturb any one here. They gathered down by the courthouse. I could not see precisely what they were at but from my back upper window saw them down about the tree. After a while a signal was given, and just at that time a match was struck, and I saw a dark body swing down under the limb. I knew then they had hanged somebody.

As the terroristic campaign against the Negroes grew in intensity, even though the Ku Klux Klan itself was formally disbanded, the North undertook to restore order by military suppression of the night riders. After passage of the Force Act in 1870 and the Ku Klux Klan Act a year later, federal troops took over the task of policing the country, with suspension of the right of habeas corpus. Thousands of arrests were made and a series of trials was held that, in spite of a relatively small number of convictions, had a marked effect on southerners who sought to take the law in their own hands.

The reimposition of military rule and unseating of a number of the restored Democratic administrations could not, however, permanently block the drive of southern conservatives to recover political power and break the hold of the carpetbag governments. The Ku Klux Klan had largely served its purpose in terrorizing the Negroes, and they increasingly stayed away from the polls. Factional fights among the Radicals further weakened their hold over state legislatures. An aroused South fought its new political battle with fierce tenacity, driving out the carpetbaggers and winning over the scalawags, until the Radicals were everywhere forced into a broadening retreat.

★ THE NORTHERN WITHDRAWAL

By 1872, moreover, the North was beginning to weary of its attempt to impose its rule on the South. Public opinion was no longer willing to approve military support for state governments which could not stand on their own feet. It was increasingly realized that such intervention served only to increase the unrest and dissatisfaction that had often led to riots and disorder. The nation wanted above all else peace and stability. "The whole public," exclaimed President Grant, who had succeeded Johnson in the White House in 1869, "are tired out with the annual autumnal outbreaks in the South and the great majority are ready now to condemn any interference on the part of the government." He did not always maintain the liberal attitude this statement suggested—nor did Congress—but conditions gradually improved from the point of view of conservative southerners.

Congress passed a liberal amnesty act in 1872, the Freedmen's Bureau was allowed to lapse, and the President instructed federal troops not to interfere any further in southern politics. Greatly encouraged by this withdrawal of northern support for the Radical regimes, the "redeemers" pressed their gains in re-establishing the old conservative order, based upon white supremacy, throughout the southern states. By 1876 only three were still under Radical control.

The next year President Hayes recalled all northern troops. This was long thought a part of a bargain whereby the Republican presidential candidate had persuaded the Democrats not to oppose his taking office after the disputed election of 1876 (to which this narrative will return), but actually he had already pledged himself to take this important step.

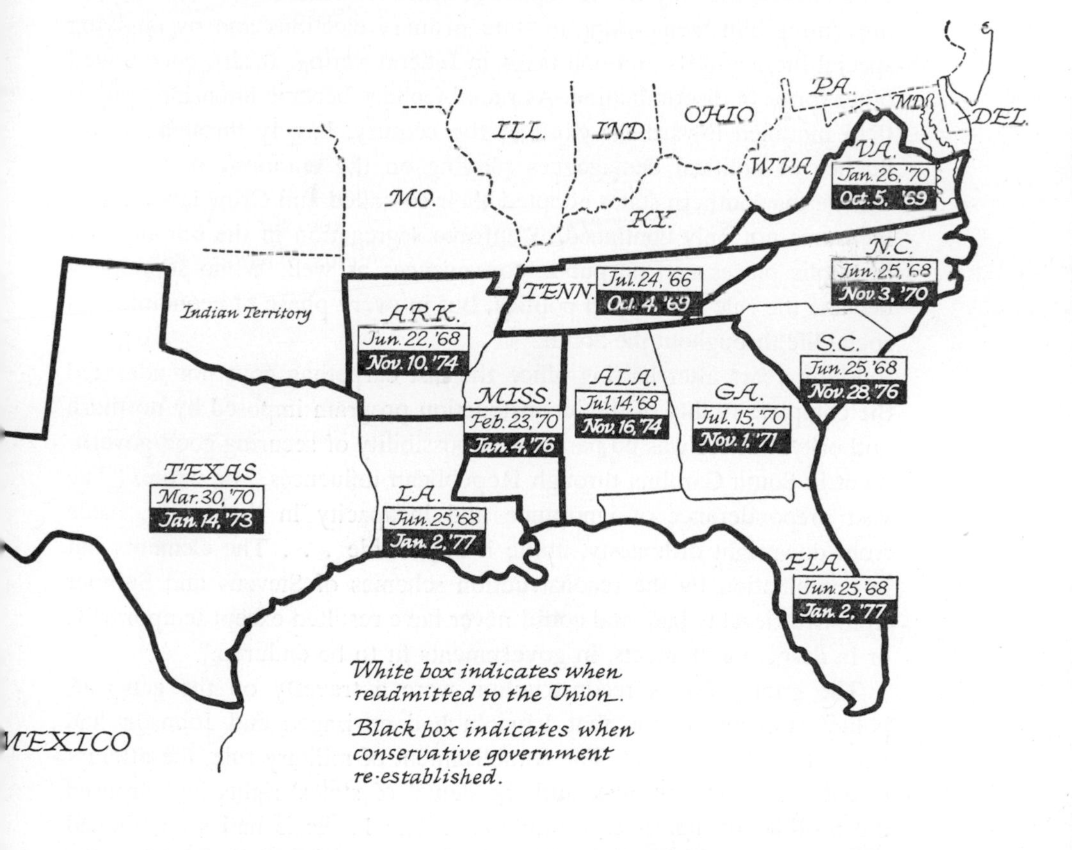

READMISSION of SECEDING STATES to the UNION

It had indeed become imperative as the South gradually succeeded in putting its own house in order and the three remaining radical states—Florida, Louisiana, and South Carolina—in turn bowed to the inevitable.

The carpetbaggers had lost political control both through the insistent pressure of the advocates of white supremacy and because of their own inability to keep the scalawags in line. The latter were finding themselves more and more in disagreement with the states' Negro officials, and a revived racialism led them to cast their lot once more with the conservative whites. Northern businessmen had also lost confidence in the Radical governments. They were now prepared to encourage the redeemers whose conservative principles, for many of them had been prewar Whigs, promised more stable economic as well as political conditions.

Moreover, a series of Supreme Court decisions in the late 1870's and early 1880's further promoted the cause of white supremacy. They established the principle that the federal government could not interfere where state laws imposed limitations on the Negro's exercise of his civil rights. This opened the way to the virtual disenfranchisement of the Negro by preventing him from voting in state primary elections and by applying special literacy tests and poll taxes in federal voting. It also encouraged other forms of discrimination. As racial feelings became intensified rather than modified toward the close of the century, largely through the influence of political demagogues playing on the emotions of the poor whites, the southern states adopted their so-called Jim Crow laws. These measures not only continued to enforce segregation in the schools, but in public places and on public conveyances as well. White supremacy became the rule not only in politics, but in every phase of economic and social life throughout the South.

Many years after leaving office the last carpetbag governor admitted the complete futility of the reconstruction program imposed by northern authority. "There was no permanent possibility of securing good government in South Carolina through Republican influences," he wrote. "The vast preponderance of ignorance and incapacity in that party, aside from downright dishonesty, made it impossible . . . The elements put in combination by the reconstruction schemes of Stevens and Sumner were irretrievably bad, and could never have resulted except temporarily, or in desperate moments, in governments fit to be endured."

The grim years of reconstruction were a travesty on the generous policy of reconciliation that Lincoln had envisaged and Johnson had vainly tried to carry out. The establishment of military rule, the attempt to enforce Negro suffrage, and the denial of states' rights had aroused the hostility of almost all southerners. The Radicals had strengthened their position in Congress by blocking for a time the admission of southern Democrats, but even on this front the long-term consequences of their policy were disastrous. A situation had been created that assured complete Democratic control in every former Confederate state once federal troops were withdrawn. Radical reconstruction committed the entire white South to continuing opposition to the Republican party.

Far from benefiting the Negroes, it may well have set them back on the road to political and social equality. The northern attempt to enforce civil rights by the bayonet could not have had more unhappy results. Racial tensions that might have been gradually modified, if an opportunity had been provided for the education of Negroes in the responsibilities as well as privileges of their freedom, were greatly intensified.

Time would gradually heal the wounds of both war and reconstruction. The road to reunion was long and difficult, but it led ultimately to peaceful reconciliation and to a new nationalism. Still, the problem of the status of the Negro was not resolved, and in politics there remained through the years the unhappy legacy of the Solid South.

★ ECONOMIC PROGRESS

While political reconstruction was going its weary and tragic way, the South was also confronted with the imperative need for economic reconstruction. A first task had been the difficult one of somehow persuading the Negroes that freedom did not mean they no longer had to work and of concurrently setting up a labor system to replace slavery. Many of the freedmen had never left their plantations; others who had restlessly taken to the road returned to their homes. The Black Codes also had a part in restoring more normal conditions. But the question remained as to how the Negroes could be paid. While some plantation owners could afford wages, many of them had no available funds. To meet this situation a system of share-cropping was developed whereby the landlord paid no wages, the worker paid no rent for land, and the two shared the crop which they mutually produced. Even with this system there was often trouble finding the necessary cash for seed, implements, and other supplies. All too frequently it became necessary to borrow money, often from northern lenders, by granting a lien on the prospective crop.

This system obviously had many grave disadvantages, and they were to become greatly accentuated with the passing years, but it at least met the immediate problem of getting the land under cultivation. In many cases share-cropping enabled the Negroes to improve their lot. They were able to enjoy not only the independence heretofore denied them but also a higher standard of living.

There were other plantation owners, however, who could afford neither wages nor share-cropping. Oppressed by the burden of debt, they found themselves either having to sell their land at greatly reduced values or being dispossessed by tax sales and mortgage foreclosures. This led to the parceling out of the land as small farms, both to poor whites, who in previous years had seldom been able to own any land, and in some cases to Negroes. Consequently, the number of small farms greatly increased throughout the South, and more intensive cultivation of the land produced larger yields per acre.

The production of cotton steadily expanded under these new conditions. As early as 1870 the crop was larger than it had been in the last prewar year, and with the prevailing price rising as high as eighteen cents a pound, or nearly twice the costs of production, agricultural recovery for a time made great strides. But the future was not as rosy for southern farmers as this suggested. The new system—both share-cropping and small individual farms—encouraged overproduction with a steady, and ultimately disastrous, decline in prices. By 1890 the production of cotton had doubled, but the price had more than halved—and the end was not yet. There was some diversification of crops during this period, which was a distinct gain, but it was not carried very far. While increases in the production of tobacco, sugar, naval stores, and other products provided the basis for a more stable economy, the average farm throughout a large part of the South at the close of the century was still a cabin, a mule, and a cotton patch.

★ ORIGINS OF THE NEW SOUTH

While the South struggled with its agricultural problems, unhappily finding that share-cropping grew more and more burdensome for Negroes and whites alike, it was also engaged in a concerted effort to build up industry. This new and important departure was especially difficult because of the lack of capital. Largely at the mercy of northern banks and credit agencies, southern businessmen were hard put to find the funds to develop the region's available resources. Nevertheless, they succeeded in making substantial progress.

Sawmills were set up to utilize timber resources, the production of cottonseed oil was promoted, textile mills were established to free the cotton industry from its dependence on the North, newly discovered coal and iron deposits were exploited, and other manufacturing plants were established. Reflecting this economic advance and the further growth of commerce, the cities were rebuilt. Richmond, Atlanta, and Charleston were soon humming with activity. As an even more significant harbinger of the future, a thriving center for iron manufactures arose in Birmingham, whose city site at the end of the war had been a cotton field.

The concept of the "New South" was evolved to encourage activities along these lines. Politicians and newspapers joined forces trying to build up a spirit of hope and optimism to replace the gloomy, discouraged attitude that had been so general when southerners first viewed the overturn of their old way of life after the devastation of war. "If we have lost the victory on the field of battle," the Columbia *Register* declared, "we can win it back in the work shop, in the factory, in an improved agriculture and horticulture, in our mines and in our schoolhouses."

Yet it was one thing to hail industrial progress, as C. Vann Woodward, the historian of the New South, has written, and another to carry it through successfully. For example, only some 3.6 per cent of the people of South Carolina were employed in manufactures as recently as 1900, and 69 per cent remained in agriculture. Moreover the factories in the new mill towns were generally owned by industrial promoters, many of them in the North, who held down wages and still further exploited both white and Negro workers by all the controls and restrictions of company towns. The South was working its way back but it was a long, hard road.

There were other far-reaching changes, apart from the new agricultural system and new industries, in the social and cultural values of the South. Again what might be termed progress in adjustment to a new world was slow, but it was of utmost significance.

The younger sons of the planter aristocracy were compelled by circumstance to seek new ways of making a living without slave labor. They were attracted by the opportunities for trade and commerce, entered into business and the professions, and otherwise began to play their part in the development of an expanding economy. The old feudalistic ideas that had characterized the South in the days before the war gave way to more modern and democratic attitudes. The extension of education, changes in the status of women who had been so carefully protected from reality by the false chivalry of an earlier age, and a generally more forward-looking spirit provided a sounder basis for southern society than had been possible when it was founded upon "the peculiar institution" of slavery.

A nostalgia for old days and old customs would continue to linger on in the South. It would be reflected in much of the literature of post-Civil War days. Thomas Nelson Page, to mention only one popular author, sought to recover the atmosphere of spacious plantation houses, crinolines, mint juleps, and respectful slaves. The social life of the Old South had its faults, he admitted, "but its virtues far outweighed them; its graces were never equalled. . . . It was, I believe, the purest, sweetest life ever lived." Outside of fiction, however, there was a more general recognition that the past was gone, and that southerners had perforce to look ahead, adapting themselves to a new set of values and a new age.

CHAPTER III

The Last Frontier: Gold, Cattle and Wheat

★ THE WESTWARD MOVEMENT

American history for nearly three centuries was dramatically characterized by a constant westward movement. From the days of the early colonial settlements along the Atlantic seaboard, successive waves of pioneers pressed ever farther inland—over the barrier of the Appalachians, into the valleys of the Ohio and the Mississippi, across the Missouri, and along the hazardous trails that led to Oregon and California. "Stand at Cumberland Gap," Frederick Jackson Turner, historian of the frontier, has written, "and watch the procession of civilization, marching single file—the buffalo following the trail to the salt springs, the Indian, the fur trader and hunter, the cattle-raiser, the pioneer farmer—and the frontier has passed by. Stand at South Pass in the Rockies a century later and see the same procession with wider intervals between."

In this historic process that peopled the United States, the vast area of the Great Plains, roughly that territory lying between the 94th meridian and the Rockies, had been passed over in the period before the Civil War. In striking contrast to the forested valleys where the pioneers of earlier days had cleared the land and planted their crops, this country stretched ahead for seemingly endless miles without any protection and without any timber. There was little water, except occasional muddy streams that dried up in the summer heat, and the rainfall was so slight that farming as it was then known seemed completely impractical. The grassland that reached to the far horizon supported great herds of buffalo, but there was no apparent way to plow the tough, matted soil, to build homes or barns or fences, or to contend with the lack of moisture for growing crops. The territory that included what was to become one of the greatest wheat-growing sections in the world—the Dakotas, Nebraska, Kansas—was officially reported in 1850 to be "almost wholly unfit for cultivation" and marked on contemporary maps as the Great American Desert.

The years following the Civil War were, nevertheless, to see the trans-Missouri West finally settled. The Homestead Act of 1862 granted a free quarter section to every settler, a series of bloody wars removed the menace of the Plains Indians, and a transcontinental railroad was pushed to the Pacific coast. As improved methods of farming with modern agricultural machinery were then developed, a new generation of pioneers, thousands of them veterans of the Union and Confederate armies, succeeded in planting the prairies to corn and wheat. Over 400,000,000 acres of land—more than in all America's past—were occupied in the latter half of the nineteenth century. The frontier as it had traditionally existed disappeared. The Great Plains were carved into new states and by 1900 only Oklahoma, Arizona, and New Mexico remained as territories.

The emigrants who had first crossed the Great Plains on their way to the Pacific coast, the prospectors who discovered the mineral resources of the Far West, and the cattlemen who grazed their stock on the Open Range were the forerunners of the homesteaders. In the complex of western settlement they played their important part—as did free land, subduing the Indian, the railroads, and new agricultural developments. Even as the Civil War was being fought, a far western mining kingdom foreshadowed the new expansive forces of a nation freed from the retarding influences of sectional conflict.

★ GOLD!

After the discovery of gold in California in 1849, there were a succession of further strikes and gold rushes in what were to become the states of Nevada, Colorado, Idaho, Montana, and Wyoming. Through the 1850's and after, a hardy, tough race of prospectors, seldom equipped with more than a grub stake, a washing pan, and a pack mule, wandered along the mountain streams in this western country in ever-hopeful search of precious metals. Sometimes their discoveries meant immediate and almost incalculable riches; more often the claims staked out proved to be valueless.

Enthusiastic reports from Colorado in 1859 led to one of the most dramatic of these gold rushes. The prospective miners gathered in the towns along the Missouri that spring, and with the coming of warm weather hundreds of Conestoga wagons made their way along the westward trails headed toward the newest El Dorado. On nearly every one of them was inscribed the slogan "Pike's Peak or Bust." But few of the 100,000 persons estimated to have started for Colorado discovered any gold, however zealously they panned the streams or chipped away at likely rock outcroppings. That summer hundreds of wagons made their way back to the East, and on their canvas sides was now painted, "Busted, by God."

There were gold and silver in the Colorado mountains, however, and those who stayed sometimes hit pay dirt. Important strikes were made at Leadville and somewhat later in the Cripple Creek area near Denver. In spite of the retreat of so many of the Argonauts of 1859, the population of the proposed state of Jefferson, as Colorado was first called, rapidly rose to 35,000. Then the boom spent itself, and further progress awaited the coming of the railroads and the development of farming.

Other parts of the western country were made to yield their riches in the 1860's and 1870's. Among the more important mining areas were the Washoe country in Nevada, where in a canyon of Davidson Mountain the fabulous Comstock Lode was discovered, a number of river valleys in Idaho, the Montana gold fields, where Alder Gulch became Virginia City and Last Chance Gulch grew into Helena, and the Wyoming country along the Sweetwater.

The last great mining rush in the old tradition was that following the discovery of gold in the Black Hills of Dakota in 1875. This territory had been allotted to the Sioux Indians and federal troops were charged with the responsibility of protecting them from any possible incursions by white settlers. But as the news of gold got abroad, prospectors swarmed into the territory, staked out their claims regardless of Indian title to the land, and began placer mining. It was here that Deadwood was founded and Wild Bill Hickok, California Jack, and Calamity Jane had their brief, exciting day.

★ THE MINING TOWNS

The mining towns—whether in the Washoe country or the Black Hills—were all very much alike. Drawn by the lure of easy wealth, the prospectors and miners came from every walk of life. There were seasoned frontiersmen and young graduates of eastern colleges, southern planters and emigrants from New England, reckless adventurers and staid townsmen, good men and bad. Side by side they panned gold out of the mountain streams, shoveled what they hoped was pay dirt into their sluice boxes, and swung their pickaxes at the diggings. Among them were always large numbers of lawless outcasts—gamblers, confidence men, petty thieves, and other assorted jail birds. The few women were those of easy virtue. At every camp there immediately sprang up dance halls, gambling dens, saloons, and bawdy houses where the miners, pockets weighed down with gold dust they were eager to spend, could find all the riotous excitement they desired after a hard day's work. The rapidly growing little towns were wide open. In that reckless, unrestrained, violent atmosphere, it was not surprising that robbery, murder, and general debauchery became characteristic features of the mining frontier's normal life.

Eventually, the more conservative elements in the community would seek to establish some degree of law and order. Rough codes would be drawn up to prevent claim jumping, to settle disputes, and to provide punishment for any disturbance of the peace. Committees subject to the control of community mass meetings, representing democracy in its simplest form, were elected for the enforcement of law, and something like a government was then created with its own rules and regulations. When it was challenged by the lawless, self-constituted vigilantes took matters in hand. They hunted down the ringleaders among the desperadoes, held quick, informal trials, and sentenced the guilty "to stretch hemp."

The mass meetings and vigilance committees were considered temporary expedients. As soon as possible the mining communities set up more formal governments and asked Washington for the establishment of a territory—and ultimately admission into the Union as a state. This became possible as the growing communities attracted not only traders, storekeepers, merchants, and bankers, but also farmers who settled in the surrounding countryside. There were, of course, many mining camps that disappeared as quickly as they had sprung up, but others developed into thriving towns and cities scattered over a great part of the Far West.

The changes that took place in government were accompanied by changes in mining operations. There were sometimes quick profits in placer mining, but the precious metals were for the most part locked in lodes of quartz that might run far beneath the earth's surface. The gold and silver could be obtained only through sinking deep shafts, breaking up the quartz in crushing mills, and then dissolving the metal in large retorts. All this required capital which individual prospectors could not raise, and financiers from California and the East moved in to take over their claims. The day of happy-go-lucky placer mining gave way to an era of organized operations on a huge scale.

The Washoe country in Nevada provides an exciting example of the evolution of a mining community. When news of the discovery of the Comstock Lode got abroad in 1859, thousands of California prospectors made their way over the mountains to stake out their claims, and the principal mining camp at Virginia City rapidly grew into a bustling community of some 15,000 persons living in a never-never land of mounting wealth. If few of the original prospectors made their fortunes, their successors took millions of dollars in gold and silver from the area within a few short years. Then, in 1869 a group of promoters undertook the ambitious project of tunneling through Davidson Mountain—the famous Sutro tunnel—in the belief that the Comstock Lode must somewhere grow wider. They were right. At 1,167 feet they struck the Big Bonanza, and it brought its owners a fortune of $200,000,000.

Virginia City had an early historian in the person of Mark Twain. Accompanying his brother, the secretary of the first governor of Nevada Territory, to the Washoe country, he painted in *Roughing It* one of the classic pictures of frontier life in the Far West.

Virginia City struck him as "the livest town for its age and population, that America had ever produced," and he was fascinated by its carefree, gambling spirit, its color and excitement. "There were military companies," Mark Twain wrote, "fire companies, brass bands, hotels, theatres, 'hurdy-gurdy houses,' wide-open gambling palaces, political pow-wows, civic processions, street fights, murders, inquests, riots, a whisky mill every fifteen steps . . . and some talk of building a church!"

At the peak of its boom days, the town boasted over a hundred saloons, the more pretentious with long mahogany bars, glistening chandeliers, and bright façades of mirrors. Thousands of dollars changed hands nightly at the gambling palaces, and the assorted ladies at the hurdy-gurdy houses were said to rival those of any eastern dance hall. The favorites of the American stage—Junius Brutus Booth, Jr., Lola Montez, Adah Menken—trod the boards of Virginia City's five theaters and six variety houses.

Although not every community was as fortunate as Virginia City, the mines of the Far West produced in the thirty years from 1860 to 1890 over a billion dollars worth of gold and nearly as much silver. The miners had greatly added to the wealth of the nation and, equally important, had helped to open up vast reaches of the western country to more permanent settlement.

★ BUILDING THE RAILROADS

While the miners were establishing scattered communities in the Far West, the railroads were slowly beginning to push out a network of steel rails that eventually spanned the continent. The most dramatic incident in this growth of transportation took place on May 10, 1869. On that day at a point near Ogden, Utah, Leland Stanford and Thomas Durant drove in the golden spikes that finally joined the lines built westward across the prairies by the Union Pacific and eastward over the high ranges of the Sierra Nevadas by the Central Pacific.

It was an occasion that the people of the United States might well celebrate, and celebrate it they did. There was a parade seven miles long in Chicago, proud citizens jubilantly rang the Liberty Bell in Philadelphia, and in New York the buildings were draped in bunting, thanksgiving services were held in Trinity Church, and a hundred-gun salute was fired.

The construction of the Union Pacific was a tremendous engineering feat. As the line was pushed out across the prairies, every item of needed material from wooden ties and steel rails to the daily provisions of the workers had to be brought from the East. Temporary camps were set up at each successive point of advance to store supplies and house the construction gangs. As soon as the tracks were laid some sixty miles farther westward, everything was dismantled and loaded on flat cars to be moved en masse to the next temporary location. The "Big Tent" was always set up first—a mammoth affair with dancing floor, sumptuous bar, and gambling apparatus—and around it soon clustered not only quarters for the workers, but makeshift housing for the women who so faithfully followed them across the continent. The life of these shanty towns was rowdy and dissipated, but during the day the construction gangs worked as feverishly as by night they played. The urge to lay down enough track to get ahead of the Central Pacific, pushing eastward as the Union Pacific pushed westward, made for a lively spirit of competition.

Before completion of this first transcontinental line, covered wagons, stage coaches, oxen-drawn freighters, and the pony express had been the only means of transportation and communication across the Great Plains. They could hardly compete with railroads. As the West began to fill up, additional lines were projected, and huge stock issues were floated to raise the necessary capital. The experience of the Union Pacific had proved, however, that railroad building on a transcontinental scale needed government help. Both Congress and state legislatures undertook to make generous allowances of land along the proposed rights of way, and in many instances granted substantial loans to the railroad companies. Among other lines receiving charters, in addition to the Union Pacific and the Central Pacific, were the Atchison, Topeka and Santa Fé, the Southern Pacific, the Northern Pacific, and somewhat later, the Great Northern Railway.

Open railroad wars, frantic scrambles for government subsidies, wild speculation in railway stocks, failures and bankruptcy characterized this great era of railroad building. Fraud and corruption were widespread in connection with some of the government grants, as well as incredible waste and extravagance. The Crédit Mobilier, a joint-stock company which enabled stockholders of the Union Pacific to draw off immense profits in the construction of this road, caused a malodorous national scandal by offering special favors to congressmen. It was so to conduct its affairs that it received $73 million for construction costs of $50 million. Profits were even larger for the construction companies of the Central Pacific. The American people were to pay a heavy price for their transportation system, many times over its actual cost. Still, the continent was spanned, and an immense impetus given to the economic growth and development of the entire country.

Other railroad lines than the transcontinentals were being built during the same period. The total mileage throughout the country rose from 52,000 to 93,000 between 1870 and 1880, and in another decade it had risen to 163,000. This is even more the story of national economic expansion than western settlement, but without the transcontinental lines, the peopling of the great open spaces of the trans-Missouri West would have been hardly possible.

★ THE INDIAN MENACE

As the railroads reached out across the prairies, the construction gangs grew accustomed whenever an alarm was sounded to throwing down their picks and shovels and seizing their rifles. They were never entirely safe from savage attack. Throughout the entire area, so largely given over to the grazing of buffalo, wandered bands of hostile and daring Plains Indians. They had been driven farther and farther westward by the white man's relentless advance, and now were being remorselessly squeezed into an ever-smaller area by the extension of the mining and railroad frontiers. The treaties that supposedly afforded them some protection were callously broken; land that had been granted them in perpetuity was reoccupied with little compunction. The Indians—some 200,000 in all—were doomed in an unequal struggle that was in actuality a clash between two different civilizations. In the contest for control of the Great Plains, the more advanced, dynamic, industrialized society was bound to conquer.

A government far more concerned with abstract justice than that of the United States proved to be could not for long have effectively safeguarded Indian rights under such circumstances. There could be no controlling the aggression of frontiersmen convinced that the only good Indian was a dead Indian. Nevertheless, even the official policy followed by representatives of what was claimed to be the superior civilization was highly discreditable. President Hayes was to state somberly in 1877:

The Indians were the original occupants of the lands we now possess. They have been driven from place to place. The purchase money paid to them in some cases for what they called their own has still left them poor. In many instances, when they had settled down upon lands assigned to them by compact and begun to support themselves by their own labor, they were rudely jostled off and thrust into the wilderness again. Many, if not most, of our Indian wars have had their origin in broken promises and acts of injustice on our part.

The Plains Indians—the Sioux, Northern Cheyenne, and Arapaho in the North, and the Comanche, Southern Cheyenne, Kiowa, and Apache in the South—were to prove far harder to subdue than the tribes whose Rocky Mountain hunting grounds had been invaded by the trappers and miners. They were skilled horsemen and intrepid warriors, and even without the white man's weapons did not hesitate to challenge his power. Mounted on their swift ponies, they could sweep down upon an unsuspecting emigrant train, railroad gang, or other white encampment, let loose a deadly flight of arrows from their long ash bows, and wheeling in rapid flight dash to safety before the whites could strike back.

Such sporadic attacks flamed up into general border warfare as the thin line of white settlement spread across the plains. Even before the close of the Civil War, the Cheyenne and Arapaho took to the warpath and ravaged the countryside from the North Platte to the Arkansas. There were massacres of white settlers, and in retaliation no less bloody massacres of the Indians. On one occasion a band of tribesmen that thought themselves secure while peace negotiations were underway was treacherously attacked by the Colorado militia in an onslaught that spared neither men, women, nor children.

"They were scalped," a white witness later testified of the fate of these Indians, "their brains were knocked out; the men used their knives, ripped open women, clubbed little children, knocked them in the head with their guns, beat their brains out, mutilated their bodies in every sense of the word."

Reports of such incidents aroused the eastern public to the savagery of the whites as well as that of the Indians, and Congress sought to find some solutions to the problem which would safeguard peace. In 1867 peace commissioners were dispatched with proposals for the establishment of new reservations that would clear the main line of advance across the Great Plains and yet secure reasonable hunting grounds for the Indians and protect them against any further encroachments. Treaties were signed with the northern tribesmen, allotting them land in the Black Hills of the Dakota country; for the southern tribesmen land was set aside in Oklahoma.

"We have now selected and provided reservations for all, off the great roads," General Sherman, the western military commander of government forces reported the next year. "All who cling to their old hunting grounds are hostile and will remain so until killed off. We will have a sort of predatory war for years. . . ."

★ CONTINUING BORDER WARFARE

General Sherman was entirely right in his prediction. The Plains Indians could not be so easily persuaded to abandon their traditional way of life and settle down quietly on small reservations. It was their practice to roam the prairies without restraint in search of the buffalo which provided them not only with food, but with clothing and shelter from the hides, with fuel for their fires, and with sinews for their bows. As the buffalo herds were cut down by white hunters—their slaughter for skins totaling some three million a year until the buffalo was virtually extinct —the young braves chafed more than ever under the restrictions imposed upon them. They were soon ready to take to the warpath once again in order to drive back the encroaching whites. Renewed outbreaks of fighting marked the 1870's, and nowhere was there any real peace.

The savage border warfare of these years, the attacks and counterattacks, the truces concluded and broken make up a sorry and tragic story of treachery, blood, rapine. The Indians, even though they now had fire-arms, could not long withstand the superior force of the army regulars sent against them and only occasionally succeeded in checking the steady extension of the Great White Father's control. One battle among the many of these years, however, has always had a conspicuous place in the history of Indian warfare.

The discovery of gold in the Dakota Black Hills had led in the mid-1870's to an altogether illegal rush into land set aside for the Northern Sioux. When they took up arms under Sitting Bull and Crazy Horse, the government sent troops into the territory to force them into final submission. The campaign was carefully organized and might well have succeeded had it not been for the recklessness of a young and somewhat vainglorious cavalry commander, Colonel George A. Custer. Refusing to wait for the main body of regulars to catch up with him, Custer impetuously attacked an Indian encampment near the Little Big Horn on June 25, 1876, with a troop of 265 men. To his dismay the Indians proved to have a fighting force ten times the strength of his own. They threw a tight ring about the federal troops, and galloping in a rapidly closing circle, poured such a withering rifle fire into the regulars' ranks that within a few hours the battle was over. The Indians had completely wiped out the entire cavalry troop, officers and men.

The Sioux were unable to profit from "Custer's Last Stand." The fresh troops soon thrown against them compelled them to retreat steadily, and they were ultimately caught in a trap that forced the surrender of 3,000 braves. The war came to an end, and the defeated Indians were assigned to a still more restricted reservation. There were further Indian outbreaks—the Nez Percé rose under Chief Joseph and the Apache under Geronimo—but the harsh fate meted out to the Sioux foreshadowed the removal of the other great tribes, such as the Cheyennes, Comanches, and Kiowas, to very limited reservations.

As the long border warfare at last drew to a close and the Indians were confined to their reservations, Congress sought to develop a more comprehensive, long-range Indian policy. It adopted measures to break down the old tribal organizations, thereby making it easier to impose federal control, and tried to encourage the Indians to adopt the white man's way of life. Under the Dawes Act of 1887, Indian lands were divided up and each family given an allotment of 160 acres. These individual holdings were held in trust by the government for twenty-five years, to keep the land from getting into the hands of speculators, and every effort was made to promote agriculture and husbandry. But the promise of this policy was never fulfilled. Some fifty years later—in the 1930's—Congress tried an entirely new approach to the old problem. It approved a program for restoring tribal land-owning, strengthening the bases of the Indians' native culture, and encouraging the development of their own arts and crafts. This was more successful than anything heretofore attempted and the Indian population had expanded by 1955 to some 400,000.

★ THE CATTLE KINGDOM

While the railroads were being built and federal troops were harrying the Indians into the reservations, the Great Plains became for a time a vast cattle-raising area. Immense herds of Texas Longhorns and Kansas Herefords roamed the Open Range from the Dakotas, Nebraska, and Kansas to Montana, Wyoming, Colorado, and New Mexico. Throughout this territory the cowboy was king in the 1870's and 1880's. An important industry was built up, fortunes made, and a legend bequeathed the nation of an exciting Wild West where bronzed, lean horsemen rode the range for lonely weeks, tore up the cattle towns, drank and gambled with carefree exuberance, and always shot straight from the hip.

The Cattle Kingdom had its start when ranchers in Texas, where the cattle on the plains between the Rio Grande and the Panhandle had multiplied enormously during the Civil War, discovered that steers worth three to four dollars a head could be sold for ten times this price in the upper Mississippi Valley. The problem was how to get them to this profitable market. The Long Drive was the answer, and in the spring of 1866 a first experiment was made in herding the cattle northward, grazing as they went, through the Red River country, across the Indian Territory in what is now Oklahoma, over the Ozark Plateau, to the railhead of the Missouri Pacific Railroad at Sedalia, Missouri. This venture was not a complete success, but the profits made on the cattle that survived encouraged further drives. The next year a better trail was laid out, without hills or wooded areas, and the Texans herded thousands of cattle north with fewer losses.

This was the famous Chisholm Trail, and its terminal was the little town of Abilene, Kansas, picked by Joseph G. McCoy, an Illinois meat dealer, as the best possible rail station where northern buyers and southern sellers could meet. Stockyards, pens, and loading chutes were built, and when the advantages of Abilene were advertised, it rapidly became the center for a new industry. As the railroads extended their lines westward, other cow towns sprang up—Newton, Ellsworth, and Dodge City—but Abilene had shown the way. The Long Drive was always a hazardous undertaking for the cowboys who acted as drovers. They had to be constantly on guard against both wolves and rustlers, alert to prevent the longhorns from getting out of control and stampeding, and ever watchful to discover sufficient grazing land and water.

In *The Log of a Cowboy,* Andy Adams has told of an experience on the trail when, after three days without water, a herd grew unmanageable. Their leaders turned back and the cattle milled about aimlessly in a confused mass, lowing pitifully in their fever and thirst:

> No sooner was the milling stopped, than they would surge hither and yon, as ungovernable as the waves of an ocean. After wasting several hours in this manner, they finally turned back over the trail, and the utmost efforts of every man in the outfit failed to check them. We threw our ropes in their faces, and when this failed, we resorted to shooting; but in defiance of the fusillade and the smoke they walked sullenly through the line of horsemen across their front. Six-shooters were discharged so close to the leaders' faces as to singe their hair, yet, under a noonday sun, they disregarded this and every other device to turn them, and passed wholly out of our control. In a number of instances the wild steers deliberately walked against our horses, and then for the first time a fact dawned upon us that chilled the marrow in our bones—*the herd was going blind.*

This was no isolated incident. Everywhere along the Chisholm Trail lay the bones of animals that had not survived the rigors of the Long Drive. However, the millions of steers eventually herded into the stockyards of the Kansas cow towns or turned out on the surrounding prairies to fatten before being shipped to eastern markets continued to bring almost unbelievable profits to their owners.

The custom of letting the cattle graze on the rich buffalo grass near the railheads soon led to experiments in keeping them on the range throughout the winter. It was found that they were hardy enough to withstand the rigors of a more northern climate, and cattle raising on the Great Plains became as practical as it was in Texas. All that the prospective rancher had to do was to buy a small herd, turn it out to graze, and watch the cattle fatten and multiply. An industry whose possibilities were still further enhanced by the development of refrigerator cars and a growing eastern demand for beef soon began to attract big-time capital. In the late 1870's, eastern investors and many English and Scottish speculators formed large cattle-raising companies with holdings of hundreds of thousands of acres and thousands of head of cattle.

No phase of our national history is more familiar than this period in the settlement of the West. Innumerable are the accounts—magnified and romanticized in western melodrama—of Indian skirmishes, cattle wars, and desperate fights with rustlers and badmen. The gambling and drinking of the cow towns rivaled that of the mining camps and gave the West an exciting flavor that—with the aid of dime novels, Hollywood, radio, and finally television—has ever since gripped the imagination of the country.

★ HOME ON THE RANGE

The cowboy was actually a hardworking ranch hand whose picturesque qualities were the consequence of a necessary adaptation to a very special way of life. His horse provided the only means of transportation on the range, and his six-shooter was essential to defend both himself and his cattle in a lawless land. His broad-brimmed sombrero, knotted handkerchief, leather chaps, high-heeled boots, and jingling spurs were completely functional in protecting him from the elements and making it easier for him to ride and control his horse. The cowboy also had a very special air about him, marked by his pride in costume and equipment. Little wonder that small boys of succeeding generations have prided themselves on cowboy suits, and visitors to dude ranches have insisted on every item of the traditional outfit. The cowboys were a unique and romantic breed of men—independent, vigorous, fearless. "We felt the beat of hardy life in our veins," wrote Theodore Roosevelt as a temporary member of the clan, "and ours was the glory of work and the joy of living."

The West has left a far more authentic record of its life in folk songs and ballads than that portrayed by movies, pulp magazines, radio, and television. The cowboy often sang to quiet the cattle on the Long Drive or to cheer his own loneliness while riding the range. "The Home I

Ne'er Will Live to See," "Oh, Bury Me Not on the Lone Prai-rie," and "I'm a Poor, Lonesome Cowboy" expressed a nostalgic feeling that has little to do with a roistering night of whiskey, poker, and gunplay. Then there were "The Old Chisholm Trail," "Ten Thousand God-Damn Cattle," "The Little Black Bull," and "Little Dogies"—

> Whoopee ti yi yo, git along, little dogies;
> It's your misfortune and none of my own.
> Whoopee ti yi yo, git along, little dogies;
> For you know Wyoming will be your new home.

Many of these songs have lived. Their continuing popularity reflects the appeal of what now seems such a far-off and distant day.

By the 1880's the Cattle Kingdom was thriving, with five million steers being fattened for eastern markets on the Great Plains. Nevertheless, the profit possibilities had led to overexpansion, and experienced ranchers realized that with the pasturage becoming exhausted, something had to be done to restrict the number of cattle on the open range. The problem was solved, disastrously, during the winters of 1886 and 1887. Bitter cold weather and the worst blizzards the West had ever known struck the plains. The cattle could not get down to the grass, and hundreds of thousands either starved or froze to death. The herds were so depleted that relatively few of the large ranching outfits were able to remain in operation.

Cattle raising did not come to an end with this disaster, but when the industry was revived, it was placed on an entirely different basis. Cattle and pasturage had to be kept in balance, and this meant an end to the Open Range. The new ranchers enclosed the land, sometimes brazenly appropriating the public domain, and used some of it for grazing and some for growing hay. The cowboy soon found himself transformed into a farm hand.

★ COMING OF THE HOMESTEADERS

On the trail of the buffalo, the Indian, and the cattle raiser, came the pioneer farmer. Even while the longhorns still thundered by, the homesteader with his steel-molded plow, his barbed-wire fences, and his new farming methods was persistently advancing on the Open Range and beginning to plant the rich grasslands to wheat and corn. For a time there was to be fierce warfare between cattlemen and farmers, but the latter's ultimate victory could not be long postponed.

Cheap land was the greatest lure for western settlement. The Homestead Act, granting 160 acres to every prospective settler undertaking their cultivation, was important, but the land being offered for sale by the transcontinental railroads soon became even more of an inducement.

Lying along or near the railway's right of way, and therefore within easy reach of transportation, it was highly desirable in every way. And the railroads, whose federal grants from the public domain made them the nation's largest landowners, were anxious to sell. Settlement meant future business. Thousands upon thousands of acres were consequently sold to pioneer farmers at anywhere from one to eight dollars an acre.

The railroad companies set up land departments, widely advertised the advantages of farming in the territory through which they provided transportation, and circulated elaborate brochures painting glowing pictures of the fertility of the soil, awaiting only the plow to yield incredible harvests. One pamphlet sought to attract women to the new West with the suggestion that "when a daughter of the East is beyond the Missouri she rarely recrosses it except on a bridal tour."

Nor were the railroads content to appeal only to native Americans. The message of opportunity in the New World was carried overseas, and branch land offices in England, Holland, Germany, and the Scandinavian countries were wonderfully effective in stimulating immigration. Steamship companies anxious for steerage passengers readily co-operated in such promotion, and everything possible was done to facilitate the long journey from Europe to the western prairies.

Cheap land was not in itself enough to make possible the settlement of the Great Plains. Just as important were the development of new farming techniques, experimentation with hardy varieties of wheat adaptable to the plains, and the introduction of new machinery that enabled the pioneers to overcome the natural obstacles that had for so long blocked their path. Chilled-iron and steel plows provided means to break up soil that defied wooden plows. Strong-tooth harrows, self-binding harvesters, steam threshers, and other machinery for the first time made possible the cultivation of staple crops on an economically feasible scale. Deep wells operated by windmills proved an effective means for combatting the scarcity of water in such a generally arid country. And finally, the invention of barbed wire furnished material for fencing.

The development of the barbed-wire fence, indeed, has been shown by the historian Walter P. Webb to have been one of the most interesting examples of how modern invention came to the aid of settlement on the Great Plains. The need to protect the farms on the fringe of the Cattle Kingdom from being constantly overrun by wandering steers became a vital issue as early as the 1870's. Bringing in wood to the timberless prairie lands of western Kansas and Nebraska was so expensive that it was estimated that the cost of fencing a single homestead might run as high as $1,000. A fortune awaited anyone who could solve this problem, and it was won by Joseph F. Glidden, an Illinois farmer, who devised a method of twisting two strands of wire together with pointed barbs at close intervals. Three million pounds of barbed wire were sold in 1876; four years later, the figure had risen to eighty million.

★ THE HOMESTEADERS' WAY OF LIFE

The new farming frontier of the Great Plains differed very much from earlier frontiers in the history of national expansion. Nevertheless, it made exacting demands on the pioneers who first turned over the tough prairie sod, sank their deep wells to obtain water, and fenced in their acreage with barbed wire. In the early days many settlers housed their stock and themselves in makeshift sod-houses. Distances were long, and there could be little contact between widely separated homesteads. The bareness of the plains and their limitless fields of waving grass often gave rise to a depressing sense of loneliness and isolation.

"How will human beings be able to endure this place?" asked the pioneer wife in O. E. Rölvaag's vivid account of western settlement,

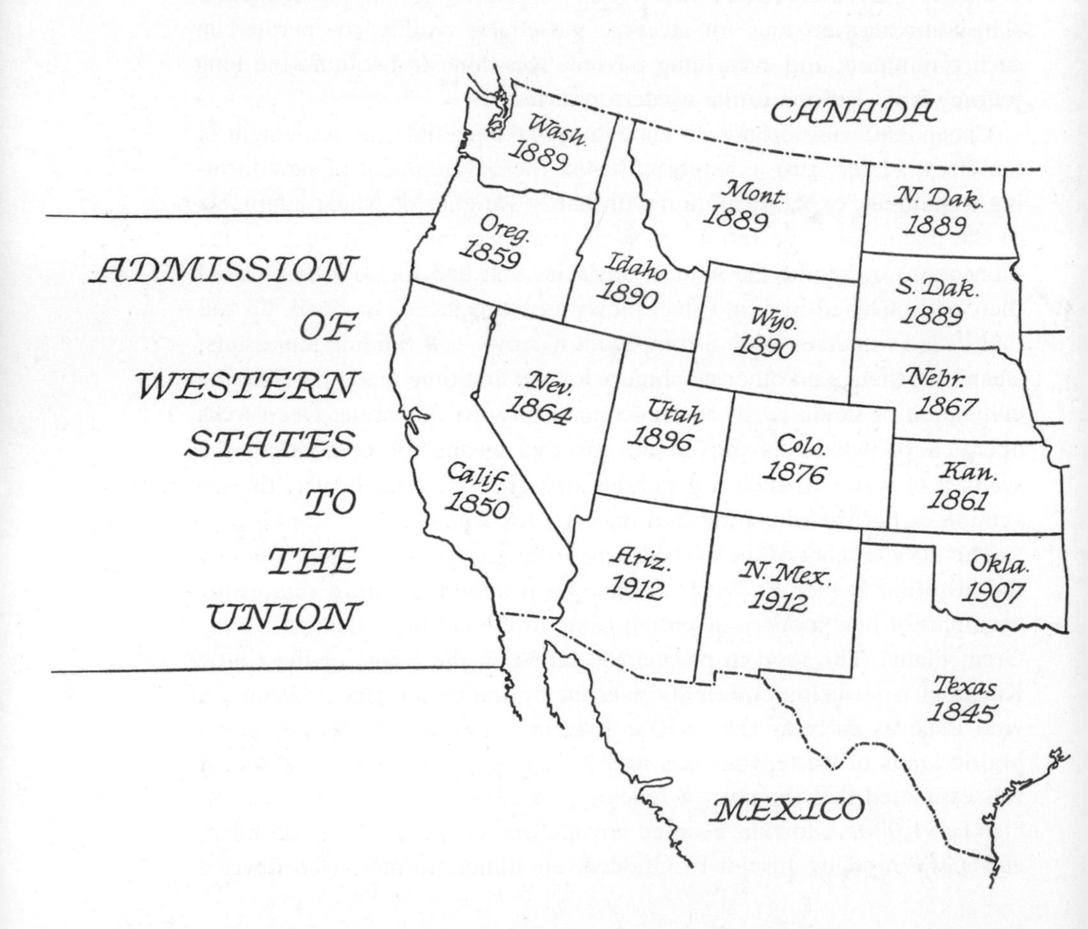

Giants in the Earth. "Why, there isn't even a thing that one can hide behind!"

The life was one of unremitting toil. There was little variety in the homesteader's daily tasks, and the unrelieved drudgery broke the spirit of all but the hardiest souls. While a sense of excitement and adventure might enliven the first stages of settlement, it was soon replaced by a monotony of work that had no parallel among farmers in any other part of the country.

Large profits could be made when all went well and harvests were good, but the weather proved to be disastrously variable. The winters could be bitterly cold, and there were summers of such intolerable heat and persistent drought that the crops dried up and the livestock sickened and died. In one year alone 30,000 newcomers in western Kansas gave up and returned to the more temperate East. The scenes enacted on Colorado's mining frontier nearly three decades earlier were recalled in the 1880's as many of the emigrants' prairie schooners headed back home with the scrawled inscription on their sides: "In God we trusted, in Kansas we busted."

"They had seen it stop raining for months at a time," William Allen White wrote of this exodus. "They had heard the fury of the winter wind as it came whining across the short burned grass and cut the flesh from their children huddling in the corner. These movers have strained their eyes, watching through the long summer days for the rain that never came . . . They have tossed through hot nights, wild with worry, and have arisen only to find their worst nightmares grazing in reality on the brown stubble in front of their sun-warped doors."

Plagues of grasshoppers were at one time even more devastating than heat and drought. They descended on the farms in great clouds that blotted out the sun and quickly devoured every green, living thing—the young grain, the vegetable gardens, the corn stalks, the leaves on the trees. They covered the walls of the houses and sometimes worked their way indoors to feast on the curtains. Absolutely nothing could be done under such circumstances. The farmers would go into town and loaf about hopelessly, afraid to face their haggard wives whose only desire was to climb on their wagons and strike back for home.

Yet in spite of all such difficulties and hardships, the greater number of the settlers survived the bad years and clung tenaciously to their new land. There was always the strong faith that luck would change, conditions improve, and the next year bring a fine harvest. And this happened often enough to keep things going.

After Kansas and Nebraska were occupied, the pioneers turned northward into the Dakotas, where the Great Northern Railroad encouraged settlement so successfully that there was a tremendous Dakota boom, and they then followed the railroads into Wyoming, Montana, and Washington. As these territories filled up, the demand arose for statehood. In 1889 an omnibus bill provided for the organization of North Dakota, South Dakota, Montana, and Washington as states, and their admission into the Union was followed in the next year by that of Wyoming and Idaho.

★ THE "BOOMERS"

At the same time, settlement was proceeding apace in the Southwest, and as the available free land was exhausted, so-called "boomers" began to look hungrily upon the fertile acres of the Oklahoma District of Indian Territory. Congress finally succumbed to this insistent pressure, and still another Indian treaty was torn up. The Creeks and the Seminoles were compelled to surrender their lands, federal troops that had been protecting the territory were withdrawn, and it was announced that Oklahoma would be opened for settlement at noon on April 22, 1889.

This was to be one of the last great land rushes in American history. On the appointed day, thousands of prospective settlers and land speculators crowded the border of the Oklahoma District, and fifteen special trains of the Sante Fé, whose line crossed the Indian Territory, waited with steam up to carry still others to the promised land. At noon the stampede started. Horsemen galloped ahead in a mad scramble to stake out their claims, followed by careening wagons, carriages, and hacks. The special trains pushed ahead farther within the territory, and as they approached each possible town site, the passengers plunged from the car platforms in a frantic rush to mark off the best lots.

Within a few hours, nearly two million acres of the Oklahoma District had been occupied. Oklahoma City had a tent population of 10,000, and Guthrie nearly 15,000. The boomers—perhaps 100,000 strong—had descended on the land like locusts and in twenty-four hours laid the foundation of what was to become a new state. The population of Oklahoma rose to nearly 800,000 in the next ten years, but continued problems in adjusting Indian claims delayed its admission as a state until 1907.

In the two decades that followed the beginnings of permanent settlement in the Great Plains, the population of all the western states grew by leaps and bounds. Between 1870 and 1890 it multiplied fourfold in Kansas, eightfold in Nebraska, fourteenfold in Washington, and fortyfold in the Dakotas. Throughout the trans-Mississippi West, there was an increase from 6,877,000 to 16,775,000. No such rapid and extensive expansion in the settled territory of the United States had ever before occurred.

★ THE END OF THE FRONTIER

When in 1890 the director of the census announced that the country's unsettled area "has been so broken into by isolated bodies of settlement that there can hardly be said to be a frontier line," there were few to recognize the deep significance of what had taken place. There was still a vast area of free land in the public domain, and actually more homesteads were settled in the next two decades than in the previous twenty years, but the disappearance of the frontier in a traditional sense was to have a profound impact on our national economy and on many phases of American life. The opportunity for what had seemed to be almost unlimited growth and expansion was significantly curtailed, and time was soon to demonstrate the need for far-reaching and difficult readjustment.

Through all the years in which westward expansion had been such an integral factor in our national growth, the frontier exercised an immensely powerful influence upon the character of the American people. It symbolized opportunity; it was in no small part responsible for the buoyancy, the confidence, and the unquestioning faith in the future that foreign visitors so often singled out as national characteristics. At one and the same time it fostered a community spirit in meeting common problems—the log rollings, the house raisings, the "changing works" of harvest days—and emphasized a spirited individualism which stood out stubbornly against hampering social controls. It promoted nationalism, pride in country, and sometimes a chauvinistic boastfulness.

The frontier's role in American development and in molding American character has undoubtedly been exaggerated at times. Frederick Jackson Turner, to whom is so often attributed "the discovery" of the frontier's influence, certainly overstated the case when he wrote that "American democracy is fundamentally the outcome of the experiences of the American people in dealing with the West." Other things must be taken into account. Most importantly, there can be no denial of the enduring influence of our European heritage. Nevertheless, the frontier was of tremendous importance in shaping both national ideals and national institutions.

CHAPTER IV

The Growth of Industry

★ INDUSTRIAL TRIUMPH

However important the gradual emergence of a New South from the dim shadows of reconstruction and the rise of a New West with the settlement of the Great Plains, the industrial boom in the northeastern states was of even greater moment in the growth of the United States during the latter half of the nineteenth century. The spread of railways over the entire continent, the expansion of old industries and the establishment of new ones, steadily increasing trade and commerce, and the rise of cities marked the emergence of modern America. A new industrial civilization was coming into being that pointed the way toward that position of world leadership that the United States would attain in the twentieth century.

The forces that made this industrial growth possible were released by the Civil War, but they were bound in any event to have made their influence felt. An economic revolution was taking place throughout the western world, and in no other country, except possibly Russia, was such a wealth of natural resources waiting to be tapped. The United States was almost unbelievably rich. Its coal and iron reserves, its mineral deposits and newly discovered petroleum, its vast forest areas, the great potential of its agricultural lands provided all the essential raw materials for economic advance. Moreover, the nation was young, confident, and forward looking. Once its energies were harnessed to the development of its resources, there was no halting its dynamic progress.

"The old nations of the earth creep on at a snail's pace," Andrew Carnegie wrote enthusiastically in his *Triumphant Democracy* in 1886, "the Republic thunders past with the rush of the express. The United States, the growth of a single century, has already reached the foremost rank among nations, and is destined soon to outdistance all others in the race. In population, in wealth, in annual savings, and in public credit; in freedom from debt, in agriculture, and in manufacture, America already leads the civilized world."

Three years later President Harrison rejoiced that American prosperity was "so magnificent in extent, so pleasant to look upon, so full of generous suggestions to enterprise and labor. . . . God has placed upon our head a diadem and has laid at our feet power and wealth beyond definition and calculation."

★ RESOURCES AND THEIR EXPLOITATION

It is difficult to relate in any proper sequence the events that marked the dramatic transformation of the United States, within so short a time, from a relatively simple agricultural society to a highly complex industrial state. The progress made along so many fronts was closely interrelated. Without natural resources little could have been done, and yet they were not enough in themselves to assure economic advance.

The march of science carried us into the machine age. Inventions from electric dynamos to adding machines, together with those technological developments that constantly emphasized mass production and the assembly line, were basically essential factors in building up our manufactures. An ample labor force, continually replenished, provided the necessary manpower that underlay all production. A transportation system furnishing the means to assemble essential raw materials and distribute finished products was also of the utmost importance. Without a continually increasing population, spread over a vast territory completely free of all trade barriers, industry and manufacture would have lacked the constant stimulation of an ever-expanding market.

Moreover, these factors so important for industrial advance—raw materials, technology, labor, transportation, and mass markets—needed some sort of catalytic agent for the full realization of their potentialities. Men of vision and imagination, power, and drive were necessary to take over and direct the immense task of creating the new industrial commonwealth. The country did not have long to wait for their appearance. The postwar years were to see the rapid rise to power of a new class of railroad magnates, captains of industry, and financial barons. Neither soldiers nor politicians nor statesmen were the leaders of America in this period. This role was played by the men who built up the new empires of railroading, industry, and finance.

"After all business is the biggest thing in this country," a contemporary newspaper commented. "Politicians may talk, but businessmen will act, control, and dominate the destinies of this common-sense country."

The foresight and daring of these industrial leaders were often matched by a wasteful greed that overrode all considerations of public interest. The years following the Civil War were a period of unrestrained and profligate exploitation. Just as the western mines had been made to disgorge their gold, silver, and copper to build up the fortunes of individual investors and speculators, and the prairie lands had been overgrazed to swell the profits of absentee ranch owners, so were other sources of wealth drained in a fierce first come, first served rush to take part in what has been called "the great barbecue."

Nor were natural resources alone exploited. The industrialists of that day considered labor a commodity to be bought like any other as cheaply as possible, drawing upon the steady stream of Old World immigrants to build up a labor force that they needed pay only the barest subsistence wage. Between 1860 and 1900, some fourteen million persons crossed the Atlantic to the Land of Promise, and in the latter years of the century they included an increasing number of ignorant, penniless, unskilled workers from southeastern Europe who sought not western lands but jobs in mines, mills, and factories. Italians, Poles, Serbs, Croats, Slovenes, Hungarians, and Bohemians worked long hours under the whip lash of economic necessity to help build up American industries and the fortunes of those who established them.

The "public be damned" was a widely prevalent attitude among those engaged in constructing railroads, consolidating industrial enterprise, and speculating in stocks and bonds. Waste and extravagance, ruthless suppression of competition in the creation of manufacturing monopolies, a casually indifferent attitude toward the people as consumers were all a part of the crude process of economic growth.

In the years immediately following the Civil War—a period to which Mark Twain has given the name of the Gilded Age—the railroad magnates provided the outstanding examples of lawless arrogance. Charles Francis Adams wrote in 1871:

> These modern potentates have declared war, negotiated peace, reduced courts, legislatures, and sovereign States to an unqualified obedience to their will, disturbed trade, agitated the currency, imposed taxes, and, boldly setting both law and public opinion at defiance, have freely exercised many other attributes of sovereignty. . . . The strength implied in all this they wielded in practical independence of the control of both governments and individuals; much as petty German despots might have governed their principalities a century or two ago.

Their example was soon followed by the men who set up monopolies in steel and oil, meat packing, sugar refining, distilling, and tobacco manufactures. They bought up state courts and legislatures and sent their representatives to Congress. It was generally expected that the latter, especially in the Senate, would promote the interests of their industrial overlords rather than those of the people.

Yet for all this exploitation of natural resources and of labor, and callous disregard of public welfare, the fact remains that the dynamic drive and magnificent audacity of these railroad barons and captains of industry were largely responsible for the nation's amazing economic development. Looking back upon the latter years of the nineteenth century, Franklin D. Roosevelt attempted in 1932 to assess the good and the evil that resulted from allowing them freedom of all restraint or control in pursuing their own selfish interests:

> So manifest were the advantages of the machine age . . . that the United States fearlessly, cheerfully, and, I think rightly, accepted the bitter with the sweet. It was thought that no price was too high to pay for the advantages which we could draw from a finished industrial system. The history of the last half century is accordingly in large measure a history of a group of financial Titans, whose methods were not scrutinized with too much care, and who were honored in proportion as they produced the results, irrespective of the means they used. . . . As long as we had free land; as long as population was growing by leaps and bounds; as long as our industrial plants were insufficient to supply our own needs, society chose to give the ambitious man free play and unlimited reward provided only that he produce the economic plant so much desired.

★ THE RAILROAD BARONS

Whatever else may be said of these Titans in praise or blame, they were colorful figures who stamped the imprint of their vivid personalities deeply on the pages of history. Some of them were no more than gamblers and speculators; others were imaginative and constructive industrial statesmen.

An unholy trio was that made up of Jim Fisk, Daniel Drew, and Jay Gould—railroad manipulators who sometimes conspired together to milk the public, sometimes conspired against each other, but who were always animated by the grasping motive of personal gain. Fisk was a huge, jovial, vulgar libertine, whose greed and dishonesty were unabashed. "Nothing is lost save honor!" he exclaimed cheerfully upon the conclusion of one sensational deal involving the stock of the Erie Railroad. Daniel Drew, a tall, thin, dried-up figure, who founded Drew Seminary in pious exculpation of a lifetime of rascality, applied to the issuance of new securities that practice of "watering stock" that he had first learned when as a drover he had let his cattle fill up on water at every passing stream in order to increase their market weight. His sometime partner, Jay Gould, cold, astute, and unscrupulous (his one redeeming trait a love of gardening), was even more successful in winning control of railroads and hurrying them into bankruptcy through ruinous rate wars. At one time he virtually owned the Union Pacific, already floating on a sea of watered stock, but he managed to leave it even worse off than he found it.

More important was Commodore Cornelius Vanderbilt, no less a master of the arts of bribery and corruption, but a stock manipulator and gambler with vision. He started life as a ferryman, went on to build up a fortune in steamboats, and then sensing the potentialities of railroad development, made the New York Central into a great railway linking the resources of the Middle West with the Atlantic seaboard's leading port. Nothing was allowed to stand in the way of his ambition. "What do I care for the law? I got the power ain't I?" he once declared. He was reputed to have read only one book in a lifetime of eighty years—and that was *Pilgrim's Progress*.

There were other railroaders far removed from Fisk and Gould and Drew who helped to develop such important trunk lines as the Pennsylvania, the Baltimore and Ohio, and the Illinois Central. The greatest of them was James J. Hill. His creation of a new railroad empire in the Northwest was one of the outstanding achievements of the entire period.

When Hill won control in 1878 of the little St. Paul and Pacific, later to become the Great Northern Railway, the day of extravagant federal subsidies was over. He realized that if he were to achieve his ambition of constructing a line through the still undeveloped country of Minnesota, the Dakotas, Montana, and Washington, he would have to do so by new methods. To make his railroad a paying proposition, he was consequently prepared to develop the territory by attracting settlers, encouraging the introduction of scientific farming methods, and otherwise seeking to meet community needs. "We consider ourselves and the people along our lines as co-partners in the prosperity of the country we both occupy," Hill declared in a statement that would have made little sense to Daniel Drew or Jay Gould. "The prosperity of the one should mean the prosperity of both, and their adversity will be quickly followed by ours."

Skillful, conservative management enabled him to carry his program through successfully. The Great Northern was extended to Winnipeg, then pushed out across the Dakota plains and to the headwaters of the Missouri, cut through the Rockies, and finally brought to the Pacific shore at Seattle. Hill also obtained partial control of the Northern Pacific Railroad, with connections with Chicago, and ultimately added to his railway holdings steamship lines both through the Great Lakes and across the Pacific.

★ ANDREW CARNEGIE

Among the industrialists, two men especially stand out, different in many ways but both representative of the forces at work in economic expansion. They were Andrew Carnegie and John D. Rockefeller—the one built an empire of steel, and the other an empire of oil. There were other important figures: Armour and Swift in meat packing, Pillsbury in flour milling, Havemeyer in sugar, Weyerhauser in lumber—but Carnegie and Rockefeller were pre-eminent.

Carnegie, a keen, sharp-eyed, little Scotsman, came to this country a penniless immigrant, getting his first job as a bobbin boy in an Allegheny, Pennsylvania, cotton mill at $1.20 a week. He had a glowing faith in the possibilities of America, tremendous ambition, and a passion for thrift and efficiency. "Aim for the highest," he once said in a talk to young men, "never enter a barroom; do not touch liquor, or if at all only at meals; never speculate; never indorse beyond your surplus cash fund; make the firm's interest yours; break orders always to save owners; concentrate; put all your eggs in one basket, and watch that basket." Here was the road to success that he followed. His basket was the steel industry, and he watched it with calculating shrewdness to take advantage of every possible break.

Steel was the basis for the new economy. It provided the stuff from which the railroads fashioned their transcontinental network, industry manufactured its machines, farm equipment, and household appliances, and the cities constructed their new buildings—"the steel-faced cities reaching at the skies." The story of steel was the story of American industry, and the story of Carnegie was the story of steel.

Bringing together Minnesota's iron ore and Pennsylvania's coal and limestone marked the start of the modern industry, but equally important was the development of the Bessemer and open-hearth processes in converting iron into steel. Carnegie was neither a pioneer nor an inventor. Once he was convinced of the practicality of any new scheme, however, he developed it for all it was worth. In 1875 he entirely made over the steelworks that he had already acquired in Pittsburgh to utilize the Bessemer process, and thereafter steadily built up the Carnegie Steel Company to a dominant position in the rapidly expanding industry.

He had daring and imagination, resourcefulness, and business acumen. He showed unexampled skill in choosing his associates and lieutenants, always allowing them full freedom to develop their own capacities. His own particular forte was promotion and salesmanship, combined with unremitting industry. Largely through such qualities he pushed the fortunes of his company (greatly aided, also, by the high tariffs on foreign steel) until in one year it reported profits of $40,000,000, of which over half were for Carnegie's own personal account. The wealth he accumulated and then largely gave away in charity—for at the peak of his career he sold out his holdings to set up his various philanthropies—was estimated at the huge figure of $350,000,000.

The sale of the Carnegie Steel Company upon its founder's retirement led to a merger with a number of other companies—iron ore and coal producers, transportation systems, and finished-steel plants—which under the direction of J. P. Morgan became the United States Steel Corporation. Capitalized in 1901 at $1,400,000,000, or more than half the total estimated wealth of the country a century earlier, United States Steel symbolized not only the position the nation was gaining in the production of this basic commodity, in which it now led all the world, but its growing pre-eminence in all industry.

★ JOHN D. ROCKEFELLER

While Carnegie was building up steel manufacture, Rockefeller was doing the same thing in oil. There was no business leader in all the country who kept his attention fixed more carefully on the main chance than this efficient, calculating, and acquisitive promoter. From the day when as a boy he bought candy by the pound and sold it to friends and members of his family by the piece, he never allowed anything to divert him from his single-minded pursuit of wealth. "Don't be a good fellow—don't be convivial," Rockefeller once advised. "Be moderate. I haven't taken my first drink yet." There was to be no careless waste of energy, no dissipation or heedless fun in his well-ordered life.

Rockefeller was a quiet and methodical man but one also possessed of great acumen, often daring in his business operations, and imaginatively far-sighted. His appearance was not particularly prepossessing—medium-sized, thin, a rather long nose, large eyes, pale bony cheeks covered with reddish sidewhiskers in his early days, and a thin mouth that one unfriendly biographer has described as "a slit, like a shark's." Nevertheless, the general impression he apparently made was that of a man of great power. He was always deeply religious. His Sunday-school teaching was perhaps his favorite activity outside of his business concerns and from his earliest days he practiced the philanthropy that would become so closely associated with his name. Always certain that he would be successful, he believed that he came by his riches through the Lord's interposition and that he consequently held his wealth in trust—it was "God's gold."

His business tactics, however, were to raise considerable doubt in the public mind as to any such divine origin for his wealth. Rockefeller built up what was to become the great Standard Oil Trust by sharp practices that enabled him to win increasingly tighter control over that highly competitive industry. He introduced many improvements in marketing, executed a series of bold business strokes, and as a "sublimated bookkeeper" constantly increased the efficiency of his operations. Yet these were not the factors primarily responsible for his success. Secret rebates from the railroads, occasional drawbacks from the major lines on his rivals' transportation charges, choking off other companies' crude supplies, and constant price manipulation enabled Rockefeller to force the Cleveland refiners to sell out to him under threat of bankruptcy. And these tactics were then carried to other parts of the country until the Standard Oil monopoly was nationwide.

Rockefeller was, of course, doing what was also being done in the development of other trusts and business combines in a score of industries. In the circumstances of the time there could be no denying the benefits achieved for the American economy as a whole through such consolidations. The trust movement which Standard Oil symbolized helped to limit the cut-throat competition, the ceaseless price wars, the incessant struggles over railroad rates that were in that day leading to what appeared to be increasingly chaotic economic conditions. For his own part Rockefeller was able to introduce many economies in the refining of oil, carry through a program of vertical integration in his company operations, and develop the manufacture of countless byproducts from machine oil to paints. What appeared most striking about his activities in the public eye, however, was the creation of a monopoly that did not so much mean lower prices or better services for consumers, but the accumulation of immense profits for the owners of Standard Oil stock—and particularly John D. Rockefeller.

In 1879 the Hepburn Committee reported that the Rockefeller interests completely controlled the pipe lines of the oil-producing regions, shipped 95 per cent of the oil produced, dictated terms and rebates to the oil-carrying railroads, and through its superior transportation facilities could undersell in the markets of the entire world. "Thus it has gone on buying out and freezing out all opposition," the report continued, "until it has absorbed and monopolized this great traffic."

The immense profits realized through such controls were revealed in a distribution of dividends between 1882 and 1906 averaging some $22,000,000 a year. And John D. Rockefeller owned approximately one-fourth of all Standard Oil assets.

★ J. P. MORGAN AND FINANCE CAPITALISM

Toward the close of the century, a new phase of the process of economic growth was the gradual shift from industrial to finance capitalism as banks and bankers began to exercise an increasing influence over general business activity. The outstanding symbol of this new finance capitalism was John Pierpont Morgan. Long before he undertook the formation of the United States Steel Corporation, he had been active in the consolidation and merger of railroads. Wresting control from such buccaneers as Fisk, Drew, and Gould, whom he did not hesitate to combat with their own weapons, Morgan sought to stabilize and place on a firmer financial foundation the major railway systems in the East. He did so with conspicuous success, and then moved on to do very much the same thing with steel and other industries. He became a power in the financial world such as this country has never known before nor since. Not only railroads and industries relied upon him; the government called on his aid in 1895 during a threatening gold crisis.

A son of an Anglo-American banker, J. P. Morgan represented an entirely different strain in life from the more humbly born Carnegies and Rockefellers. An aristocrat who utilized his wealth to live in princely style, there was something about Morgan which awed both those who came into direct contact with him and a public who only read about him. He had a commanding presence: shaggy brows, piercing eyes, a very prominent and rubescent nose, and an abrupt, dictatorial manner that could easily terrify. He was a man of tremendous vigor and energy, with the power of instant decision, and could be equally violent in his likes and dislikes. Distant and aloof in most of his personal relationships, he was a friend of the great both here and abroad.

His social activities, a great interest in the Episcopal Church, and a passion for yachting and art collecting showed him to be no slave to business. Although finance was a constant preoccupation, his horizons seemed broader than those of Carnegie or Rockefeller. His outstanding success was primarily due to his unshakeable faith in the future of America, absolute and unquestioned integrity, and a measure of financial genius that has seldom been equaled. An individualist above everything else, he was not endowed with any great sense of social responsibility. "Men owning property should do what they like with it," Morgan once stated. "I owe the public nothing." He left a fortune of $68,000,000 and an art collection valued at $50,000,000.

The over-all growth of American industry, as built up by such men as Carnegie and Rockefeller, and further encouraged by such a banker as Morgan, can be set forth only through comparative statistics. Between 1850 and 1900, the aggregate total value of all manufactures rose from one to thirteen billion dollars, and in the latter year was twice that of all farm products. As industry spread westward from New England and New York into Pennsylvania, Ohio, and Illinois, dominating an ever-larger area of the country, the Census Bureau reported, in 1900, the following values for specific manufactures: iron and steel products $800,000,000, slaughtering and meat-packing products $800,-000,000, foundry and machine shop products $645,000,000, lumber products $560,000,000. As the foremost industrial nation of the world, with its great potentialities still only partly realized, the republic was indeed thundering past with the rush of an express.

★ THE GROWTH OF MONOPOLY

The process of industrial development, as suggested by the story of Standard Oil, was marked by a steady trend toward corporate growth, mergers and combinations, and ultimately monopoly. The nationalizing of business, as within each industry the more powerful companies reached out to control national sources of raw materials and national markets, was perhaps inevitable. Only through large-scale operations could the necessary capital be obtained, mass production be successfully developed, and sales promoted in the volume that was essential for profitable operation under modern conditions. This process was carried through, however, by methods that often stifled small business enterprise in other industries than oil refining. And while monopoly might again mean tremendous economy in operation, this was seldom reflected in any lowering of prices for the consuming public.

Edward Bellamy, outstanding social critic, acutely diagnosed what was happening in his popular Utopian romance, *Looking Backward:*

> The small capitalists, with their innumerable petty concerns had in fact yielded the day to the great aggregations of capital, because they belonged to a day of small things and were totally incompetent to the demands of an age of steam and telegraphs and the gigantic scale of its enterprises. To restore the former order of things, even if possible, would have involved returning to the day of stage coaches. Oppressive and intolerable as was the regime of the great consolidations of capital, even its victims, while they cursed it, were forced to admit the prodigious increase of efficiency which had been imparted to the national industries, the vast economies effected by concentration of management and unity of organization, and to confess that since the new system had taken the place of the old the wealth of the world had increased at a rate before undreamed of. To be sure this vast increase had gone chiefly to make the rich richer, increasing the gap between them and the poor; but the fact remained that, as a means merely of producing wealth, capital had been proved efficient in proportion to its consolidation. The restoration of the old system with the subdivision of capital, if it were

possible, might indeed bring back a greater equality of conditicns, with more individual dignity and freedom, but it would be at the price of general poverty and the arrest of material progress.

Apart from such huge industrial combinations as the Standard Oil Company and the United States Steel Corporation, other trusts or corporations formed as this movement reached its climax at the turn of the century included the Amalgamated Copper Company, the American Sugar Refining Company, the American Tobacco Company, the United States Rubber Company, the United States Leather Company, the International Harvester Company, and the Pullman Palace Car Company, each with an individual capitalization of $50,000,000 or more. There were 185 large corporations in 1900 with total assets of more than $3,000,000,000. These combinations, with those that had been organized in mining, communications, transportation, and banking dominated the industrial scene. Local enterprise and small-scale manufacturing were completely overshadowed. Big business had arrived.

The growth of monopoly had the further effect of bringing about an increasing concentration of wealth, with the amassing of tremendous personal fortunes. There had been but some nineteen millionaires in 1865; there were several thousand in 1900. And this concentration of economic power in the hands of the few, as already noted, emphasized the increasing concentration of political power. The corporations' control over public affairs threatened the bases of democratic government. President Cleveland and somewhat later President Theodore Roosevelt bore witness to this dangerous development. The former declared that corporations, "which should be carefully restrained creatures of the law and the servants of the people, are fast becoming the people's masters." The latter stated that "the power of the mighty industrial overlords of the country had increased with mighty strides while the methods for controlling them on the part of the people, through the government, remained archaic and therefore practically impotent."

★ GOVERNMENTAL POLICIES

Government policy had fostered rather than restrained such developments. Just as railroad expansion had been aided through land grants, loans, and subsidies (the federal land grants alone totaled 155,000,000 acres, or nearly the equivalent of the area of Texas), so had other forms of assistance, direct or indirect, encouraged the growth of industrial monopolies. In the years following the Civil War, no national policy was maintained more consistently than that of tariff protection. It was considered essential if American industry was to meet the competition of European manufactures, especially in the case of steel and wool, and vigorously upheld by the Republican party as the keystone in the arch of industrial enterprise. With every effort to bring about a downward revision in existing rates defeated, protection continued to foster the growth of monopoly well into the twentieth century.

However justified such a policy may have been to aid young and struggling industries, its value to the nation certainly became dubious when American industry was more than able to stand on its own feet. Abram S. Hewitt, an ironmaster second only to Carnegie, stated that the duty on steel rails, which he himself opposed, enabled the manufacturer to add so much to the sales price that within a few years fifty million dollars was "transferred from the great mass of the people . . . to the pockets of a few owners." Even President McKinley, the leading proponent of protection who gave his name to the high tariff bill of 1890, finally admitted that under such circumstances, there was no longer any warrant for continuing a policy that had outlived its usefulness so far as the public interest was considered.

Even though government's tacit encouragement of monopoly was helping to create an irresponsible economic power overshadowing its own political power, members of Congress showed little alarm. Too many of them were willing to accept the thesis that government was little more than an appendage of industry. Whatever helped business helped the country, according to prevailing theory. Anything the government could do in promoting still further industrial expansion was a paramount obligation—without the need for too much concern over how this might affect the farmers, the workers, or the little businessmen who fell victim to monopolistic practices.

★ LAISSEZ FAIRE

The theory underlying this attitude was the economic doctrine of laissez faire: a hands-off attitude so far as any measure of government control or regulation was concerned. It stemmed from the principles developed by Adam Smith and John Stuart Mill in reaction to the controls that had been exercised over trade and commerce in England's mercantilist era. Political economists believed, with considerable justification under conditions existing in the eighteenth and early nineteenth centuries, that laissez faire would promote competition, encourage business enterprise, and increase national wealth. The doctrine had a natural appeal for Americans with their ingrained belief in freedom. It was fostered by the individualistic spirit of the frontier and strengthened by the new Darwinian theories of evolution. If it was inevitable and right that the fittest should survive in nature's struggle for existence, the same thing should hold true in the economic sphere. Free competition, with the government holding aloof, would enable the most efficient business to survive, thereby promoting the national economy in the most effective way.

Whatever the effect of a laissez faire policy in a day of small business enterprise, its consequences were not so clearly in the public interest in an era of big business, especially when government actually denied its basic tenets through subsidies, loans, and a protective tariff. Laissez faire in the 1890's tended to kill off competition. The small steel companies were absorbed by the United States Steel Corporation; the small refiners were crowded to the wall by the Standard Oil Trust. And when monopoly dominated the scene, the concentration of power in the hands of the few threatened the liberty and freedom of the many.

★ THE GOSPEL OF WEALTH

This situation was justified by careful cultivation of the idea that economic and political power should rightfully be concentrated in the hands of a privileged minority. The old Hamiltonian theory that the rich, the good, and the wise should rule was revived, and the industrial leaders of the day easily interpreted these terms as interchangeable. They had strong support in other than business circles. "In the long run," Bishop Lawrence of Massachusetts stated, "it is only to the man of morality that wealth comes. . . . Godliness is in league with riches." What more natural than that men who had climbed the ladder of business success, men of riches and wealth, should exercise economic and political power in behalf of people who looked to them for leadership? They would exercise a trusteeship or stewardship in which the successful protected the interests of the less fortunate through benevolent paternalism.

Thus, there was developed a new Gospel of Wealth which won wide acceptance among those who found themselves in the select group of the rich, the good, and the wise. It was not a doctrine that would ever have interested the Goulds, the Drews, and the Vanderbilts. They were content to let the public be damned. But it had a very real appeal for the more responsible leaders in railroading, industry, and finance. Its foremost exponent was Andrew Carnegie, and no one could have expressed more succinctly the ideas involved.

The man of wealth, Carnegie said, should consider himself an agent for his poorer brethren, and should bring to their service his superior wisdom, experience, and ability to administer. He could do for them much better than they would or could do for themselves. "Thus is the problem of the Rich and the Poor to be solved," Carnegie continued. "The laws of accumulation will be left free; the laws of distribution free. Individualism will continue, but the millionaire will be but a trustee of the poor. . . . Such, in my opinion, is the true Gospel of Wealth."

For one Carnegie or Rockefeller prepared to expend wealth in a spirit of trusteeship, there were scores of Goulds and Fisks. Too often the Gospel of Wealth was the Gospel of Greed. And even when the rich did distribute some part of their money through public philanthropy, the question still remained of how adversely the public interest might have been affected by the means through which they had acquired it. A theory that sought to justify a system that actually increased the chasm between the rich and the poor, substituting charity for a more equitable division of income, soon aroused criticism and resentment. Years later Woodrow Wilson would recall the attempt to develop this Gospel of Wealth, categorically stating that he was "one of those who absolutely reject the trusteeship theory, the guardianship theory."

★ THE PROTEST AGAINST LAISSEZ FAIRE

While the philosophy of laissez faire generally prevailed throughout the entire period from the Civil War to the close of the century, there were to be repeated attacks upon it, a strong popular movement of protest, and ultimately a successful assault upon its major tenets. Farmers and industrial workers grew increasingly unwilling to accept a concept of government's role that provided aid and comfort for business while refusing any sort of regulation of its activities. Economic and social critics—as we shall later see—also took up arms against a theory of economic development that encouraged both the growth of monopoly and the consequent increase of economic power in the hands of the few.

The beginnings of this popular revolt may be traced back to the Granger movement of the 1870's. The farmers of the Midwest became especially indignant over the arbitrary and arrogant attitude of the railroads which held them so completely at their economic mercy through their unregulated control of the only agency for the transportation of crops. Matters reached such a pass, it was reported on one occasion, that no one dared to engage in any activity in which transportation played a substantial role without first securing permission of the railway managers. The farmers insistently demanded, through the Granges in which they combined for political action, that state legislatures bring to an end exorbitant traffic charges, rate discrimination, secret rebates, and other unfair practices in which railroads engaged.

In response to such pressure, a number of states enacted regulatory laws. The railways challenged their constitutionality on the ground that such legislation actually deprived them of their property, as guaranteed by the provision of the Fourteenth Amendment which stated that no person (a corporation was a person in the eyes of the law) could be deprived of property without due process of law. The Supreme Court upheld the constitutionality of the new laws in the case of *Munn* v *Illinois,* in 1876, and stated that legislatures could in the exercise of their police power regulate any business "affected with a public interest."

It was soon demonstrated, however, that state regulation of the railroads was largely ineffective. The local governments were too much under the influence of the railroads or other business interests to make strict enforcement feasible, and in a further series of railway rate cases, the Supreme Court began to limit very strictly the application of the principle that it had set forth in *Munn* v *Illinois.* It assumed the right to review the regulatory activities of the states and itself decide whether they were reasonable or constituted an unwarranted infringement of property rights. The conservative nature of its decisions had already largely nullified the laws when the Court struck an even heavier blow at them. In the Wabash case, in 1886, it declared that the states could not regulate any state railroad rate that involved interstate commerce since such regulation was a function of the federal government. The relationship between intrastate and interstate commerce was so close that this clearly meant—and the Supreme Court implied—that any effective regulation must be provided by Congress.

As a result of the continuing demand for railroad regulation, the revelations of an investigating commission, and the Wabash decision, Congress finally felt compelled to act. It passed in 1887 the Interstate Commerce Act. This important law outlawed many of the discriminatory practices of the railroads and set up an Interstate Commerce Commission with authority to pass upon the reasonableness of rates applying to the broad area of commerce among the states.

At the same time that the drive for railroad rate regulation was coming to a head, a comparable movement arose for control of the trusts. This led to attempts at regulation on the part of the states, and their ineffectiveness demonstrated that what had become a national problem could only be met by national action. After considerable debate Congress passed, in 1890, the Sherman Anti-Trust Act. It specifically declared that any combination, trust, or conspiracy in restraint of trade, so far as this applied to commerce among the states, was illegal and provided penalties for any infraction of the statute's provisions.

★ THE BREAKDOWN OF THE I.C.C. AND THE SHERMAN ACT

These two laws were an entering wedge in breaking down the laissez faire policies so long pursued by government. On their face, they appeared to provide the means for bringing both the railroads and the trusts under some measure of control. In reality, in spite of the popular pressure that had led to their adoption, there was little more support for their enforcement than there had been in the case of state legislation. Government proponents of laissez faire were far more concerned with nullifying the new laws than with enforcing them.

This point of view was clearly revealed in the attitude of Richard Olney, Attorney General in President Cleveland's cabinet. In correspondence with a railroad president, he advised him not to be unduly concerned over the Interstate Commerce Commission. "It satisfies the popular clamor for government supervision of the railroads," Olney wrote, "at the same time that that supervision is almost entirely nominal. Further, the older such a commission gets to be, the more inclined it will be found to take the business and railroad view of things. It thus becomes a sort of barrier between the railroad corporations and the people and a sort of protection against hasty and crude legislation hostile to railroad interests. . . . The part of wisdom is not to destroy the Commission, but to utilize it." On another occasion, when suit was brought against a trust charged with restraint of trade under the Sherman Act, Olney expressed his gratification rather than his disappointment when the government was defeated. He was not really surprised, he wrote, because he had in fact assumed "the responsibility of not prosecuting under a law I believed to be no good."

Moreover the Supreme Court, in continued defense of the principles of laissez faire, rendered the enforcement of both laws virtually impossible. It declared that while the Interstate Commerce Commission could protest unreasonable railroad rates, it could not establish reasonable ones. The burden of proof as to reasonableness lay with the government, and such barriers were placed in the way of the I.C.C. that having lost case after case, its members by the close of the century admitted they were powerless. As to the Sherman Act, the Supreme Court emasculated its provisions in 1895 through its decision *E. C. Knight Company* v *the United States.* While this company had a monopoly in sugar refining, the Court decreed that such manufacture was something quite distinct from commerce, and its operations could not be restrained because the federal government's power did not extend to what was an intrastate rather than interstate activity.

Whatever the validity of these interpretations of constitutional law, the effect was to throw the powerful influence of the Supreme Court behind the protection of property interests and against legislative efforts for control or regulation. Little could be done under the circumstances. Those who profited from uncontrolled exploitation of the country's natural and human resources exercised too powerful an influence. The forces of reform could not combat them effectively until the people as a whole were sufficiently aroused to compel a basic change in policy.

Industrial expansion, uncontrolled and unregulated, remained the most important aspect of the American scene until after the close of the nineteenth century. Economic growth continued to have its counterpart in an increasing concentration of wealth. Trusts and monopolies were the order of the day. The tremendous gain in national income and a general rise in the standard of living were widely accepted as justifying prevailing policies. They appeared more important than either the glaring paradox of progress and poverty or the possible threats monopoly presented to political democracy.

CHAPTER V

Agriculture and Labor

★ THE EXPANSION OF FARMING

While industry appeared largely to dominate the national scene, the economy remained equally dependent upon the forces of agriculture and of labor. The farmers throughout the country and the army of workers in mines, factories, and workshops were always a factor to be reckoned with even though the managers of industry so often called the tune. They constituted the great bulk of the American people; they were ultimately to make their voice heard increasingly in the economic as well as political evolution of the nation.

At the close of the century some two-thirds of the population still lived in rural areas—for all the spectacular growth of the cities. In his famous "Cross of Gold" speech at the Democratic convention in 1896, William Jennings Bryan was dramatically to remind his audience of the nation's continued dependance on agriculture. "Burn down your cities and leave our farms," he declared, "and your cities will spring up again as if by magic; but destroy our farms and the grass will grow in the streets of every city in the country."

Between 1865 and 1900 agricultural production underwent a period of phenomenal growth. The settlement of the western plains, and also to some degree expansion in the South, had brought vast new areas of land under cultivation—the addition, as already noted, of some 430,-000,000 new acres. For the most part this was immensely fertile territory, especially the prairie land in what was to become the great agricultural states of the Midwest. Here production was to grow apace in wheat and corn, beef and pork. There was a mounting demand for such products both within the United States, consequent upon the steady rise of population, and in foreign markets. Political disturbances abroad and a series of poor harvests in Europe accounted for increased overseas exports that appeared to be making America the bread basket of the world.

At the same time revolutionary new developments continued in the techniques of farm production. The agricultural machinery that had been first introduced before the Civil War was being constantly improved, and with it went new scientific methods in the selection of seed, the use of fertilizers, and crop rotation. Agriculture was becoming a business enterprise, with highly significant consequences for the farmer's general way of life.

He faced constantly increasing costs in maintaining production and had to borrow from banks, very often eastern banks, at a high rate of interest. In addition to payments that had to be made on the inevitable mortgage on his land, there were now the payments on combines, harvesters, and other machinery, on equipment and tools, and on expensive fertilizers. Moreover, there was always the burden of taxation which fell more heavily on farmers than on industrial entrepreneurs because land lent itself more easily than other forms of wealth to the imposition of taxes.

Increasing production consequently did not always mean increasing profits, and the farmer remained completely at the mercy of prices determined in a world market over which he had no control. Immediately after the Civil War there had been a short-lived boom, and following the depression of the early 1870's another period of agricultural prosperity, but by the late 1880's prices had started on a downward course that would continue until almost the close of the century. In the difficult period of the 1870's the farmers had first rebelled against the railroads whose arbitrary and discriminatory transportation charges weighed so heavily upon them, but their problems were to prove even more serious as time went on.

★ DECLINING PRICES, MOUNTING DEBT

The period of marvelous growing seasons that in the 1880's gave rise to exaggerated conceptions of the inexhaustible productivity of the land was followed by those years of drought and insect plagues that greatly discouraged many of the early pioneers of the West. Watching their crops wither and die from lack of rain, or seeing the fields of waving wheat totally destroyed by the thick clouds of locusts darkening the limitless skies, debt-burdened homesteaders often felt they had no alternative to giving up and returning to the East. Without a successful harvest, they had no way of meeting their mortgage payments, and foreclosure left them stranded and helpless.

More important in the long run than a succession of bad years, however, was what had become the persistent price decline. Conditions at home and abroad were responsible for this development. There had been overproduction in this country so far as world markets were concerned, for the late 1880's and 1890's witnessed recovery in European farming and the development of new growing areas, especially for wheat, in such countries as Canada, Australia, and the Argentine. As a consequence, the price of wheat fell from ninety-five cents a bushel to fifty cents between 1880 and 1895, while in the same period corn prices declined an approximate 50 per cent and cotton 37 per cent.

Even these figures do not clearly indicate what was happening to the farmer. There was no corresponding decline in prices of the things he had to buy. He purchased his agricultural machinery, equipment, and tools in a market protected by high tariffs and monopoly controls. Nor was there any relief in his burden of taxation or in interest payments on his debt. As prices fell for what he sold, and the cash payments he had to make remained the same, if they did not increase, he was caught in a remorseless squeeze. Even to hold his own, he had somehow to increase his annual yield. A farmer who contracted debts—mortgages and equipment charges—when wheat was at a dollar a bushel found that his debt had in effect doubled when wheat fell to fifty cents. His interest payments called for twice as much production as when he had first borrowed the money.

This steadily rising burden of debt remained largely in the hands of bankers, mortgage companies, and insurance companies in the East. When the farmer sought to meet his problems by again expanding his acreage, and still further increasing production, he sank still deeper into the morass. Producers of almost all staple crops found themselves in this situation, and by the close of the century nearly a third of the nation's farms were heavily mortgaged. The interest rates ranged from 7 to 10 per cent, and they were nearly doubled by special charges and exactions. Absentee mortgageholders held the whip hand.

Even those farmers who had survived the worst years of drought and insect plague were caught up by the mounting interest charges. The rate of foreclosures rose alarmingly; there was a steady increase in farm tenancy. As agrarian distress spread through the Middle West and the South, where the holders of crop liens were forcing the share-croppers more and more into debt, resentment rose against eastern mortgage holders. The farmers felt they were being compelled to pay an intolerable tribute to a voracious money power which completely controlled the nation's economy.

★ HARSH TIMES

The statistics of declining prices and rising debts, however, do not tell the whole story of what was happening on the farms of the prairie states. There were aspects of agrarian unrest other than the financial contest between the debtor West and the creditor East. The developing contrast between rural and urban life, and the feeling among farmers that they were being cut off from the social as well as economic advantages of an industrial society, were also important contributing factors to their discontent. The toil, the drudgery and the monotony of farm life became all the harder to bear when compared with the change and variety of urban living.

The national emphasis upon industry and manufacture, upon getting ahead in the urban world, was indeed causing a subtle change in the social status of the farmer. As the more enterprising young people were drawn to the city, with all it represented in the way of opportunity, culture, and more expansive living, those who stayed behind found themselves cast in the role of laggards in the march of progress. In popular estimation they were no longer the stout yeomanry whom Thomas Jefferson had called the pride of the nation and the only true repositories of democracy. They had become "rubes," "mossbacks," and "hayseeds."

The dispirited atmosphere born of economic failure and social isolation was reflected in the writings of many contemporary midwest authors; Hamlin Garland, the author of *Main-Travelled Roads* and *A Son of the Middle Border,* is specially revealing of what was taking place in the prairie states in the early 1890's:

> All about me as I travelled, I now perceived the mournful side of American "enterprise." Sons were deserting their work-worn fathers, daughters were forgetting their tired mothers. Families were everywhere breaking up. Ambitious young men and unsuccessful old men were in restless motion, spreading, swarming, dragging their reluctant women and their helpless and wondering children into unfamiliar hardships.

His own father, successful by all ordinary standards, nonetheless felt helpless and hopeless under existing circumstances. Garland quotes him as saying:

> I am farming nearly a thousand acres this year and I'm getting the work systematized so that I can raise wheat at sixty cents a bushel—if I can only get fifteen bushels to the acre. But there's no money in the country. We seem to be at the bottom of our resources. I never expected to see this country in such a state. I can't get money enough to pay my taxes. Look at my clothes! I haven't had a new suit in three years. Your mother is in the same fix. I wanted to bring her down, but she had no clothes to wear. . . .

★ THE CURRENCY ISSUE

There were many phases of what was ultimately to become a full-fledged agrarian revolt. The growers of staple crops in the Midwest, who had first rebelled against the railroads in the Granger movement, extended their attacks along a broad front against industrial monopoly, the banks, and other agencies of eastern control. But as debtors, suffering more and more from the downward trend of agricultural prices, they instinctively felt that their difficulties stemmed primarily from the dearness of money. The currency problem became of engrossing concern. Convinced that only an inflationary monetary policy could halt or reverse the down trend of prices in wheat and corn and cotton, they insistently demanded the expansion of the currency.

This demand first found expression as early as the 1870's, when the farmers, joining forces with labor, called for the additional circulation of the greenbacks that had been issued during the Civil War. A Greenback-Labor Party was formed to carry the issue to the people and force congressional support for its program. It failed. The more conservative advocates of a hard-money policy, fearful of the inflationary effects of the issuance of greenbacks, succeeded in carrying through Congress their program for government resumption of specie payments and then, in 1875, a measure for the redemption of the greenbacks in gold. With this restriction of the currency—and dearer dollars of course meant lower prices for agricultural produce—the farmers turned to silver as another inflationary device.

Traditionally, both gold and silver had served as a basis for the currency, with consequent difficulties due to changes in their relative market value, but in 1873 Congress had enacted a measure that prohibited any further coinage of silver. Although this bill was later to be violently attacked as the "crime of 1873," it was not so judged at the time. On the basis of the existing sixteen to one ratio in the official value of gold and silver, the latter was being driven out of circulation as currency because it was worth more in the open market. With the immense increase in the production of silver in the late 1870's, however, this situation changed. The market price of silver declined and the western miners thereupon insisted that its free and unlimited coinage be resumed at the old rate. The farmers promptly gave such proposals their support as a means of increasing the currency and thereby stimulating a rise in farm prices. Silver producers and midwestern farmers thus joined hands in a strenuous campaign for currency revision.

Their combined forces won a partial victory when they prevailed upon Congress in 1878 to pass the Bland-Allison Act. It called on the

Secretary of the Treasury to purchase from two to four million dollars of silver each month for official coinage at the ratio of sixteen to one. But the effect of this measure on prices was disappointing. The West continued to press for completely free and unlimited silver coinage as the only effective way of overcoming the currency stringency which was held responsible for falling prices.

In 1890, again under the combined pressure of the mining and farming interests, Congress took a further step. It passed the Sherman Silver Purchase Act. This measure called upon the Treasury to purchase 4,500,000 ounces of silver each month, the entire estimated output of the nation's mines, for its currency reserves. This silver was not necessarily to be coined, but since it was to be paid for by Treasury notes redeemable in either gold or silver, it in effect provided for an increase in the currency that went far beyond previous measures. Yet this was still something less than the free and unlimited coinage of silver. Agrarian unrest was anything but mollified; it began to take on a more active political complexion.

★ THE ORIGINS OF POPULISM

The first definite move along political lines was the formation, in the West and the South, of a number of Farmers' Alliances. They were to become grouped in two organizations generally known as the Northern Alliance and the Southern Alliance, and by 1890 they found themselves deeply involved in the politics of their respective regions. Their basic complaint was that farmers everywhere were being subject to unjust discrimination that deprived them of the prosperity which they saw being enjoyed by other elements in the population—the rising industrialists, the bankers, the businessmen. It was the West and the South against the East. The farmers were ready to take up arms not only on the silver issue, but against the continued impositions of the railroads, the stranglehold of monopoly and the rule of the money power. Their leaders believed that government action was necessary to satisfy their well-founded grievances against the existing economic system, and they were prepared to organize the power of the agricultural community to force Congress to meet their demands.

This was the beginning of what was to become the Populist movement—the emphatic political expression of agrarian revolt—that dominated the political scene through the 1890's. It was to challenge the whole concept of a laissez faire economy, for a time split the country asunder as it had not been divided since the Civil War, and come to an exciting climax in the bitterly fought election of 1896.

"On the one hand," a spokesman of the farmers declared passionately at this time, "stand the corporate interests of the United States, the money interests, aggregated wealth and capital, imperious, arrogant, compassionless. . . . On the other side stand an unnumbered throng . . . work-worn and dust-begrimed, they make their mute appeal, and too often find their cry for help beats in vain against the outer walls, while others, less deserving, gain ready access to legislative halls."

To the further story of Populism we shall return, but the farmers were to have allies among the nation's industrial workers in the struggles of the 1890's, and there must now be some accounting of what was happening to labor in the post-Civil War period. For here—in the ranks of labor—were great changes and a mounting protest against the industrial interests that so generally controlled the national economy.

★ THE STATUS OF INDUSTRIAL WORKERS

The growth of industry had meant a great increase in the numbers of industrial workers, and the technological developments making possible the establishment of new manufactures created entirely new conditions of work. As the use of machines increased, the worker's position underwent a complete transformation. Skilled craftsmen gave way to unskilled industrial workers, and as more and more of them were drawn into factories, mills, and foundries, they tended to lose the independence and freedom that laborers had once enjoyed. More and more they became virtually helpless pawns in the hands of corporations which considered labor, like any other commodity, as something to be bought as cheaply as possible.

In the face of this deterioration in economic and social status, the workers of the country sought some means for the better protection of their interests. They tried to organize, as industry was organized, in order that labor and capital should be able to meet on more equal terms. They wanted to increase their economic power in the ceaseless struggle for higher wages and better working conditions, and when other means failed, they were ready to strike to enforce their demands.

While labor was also to co-operate in some measure with agriculture in what appeared to be a common cause at the time of the Populist uprising, it is important to note that in the long run the labor movement in this country was to be primarily economic rather than political-minded. Moreover, the conditions of life in the United States—a young, expanding country with all the opportunities for individual advancement symbolized by the frontier—forestalled the class struggle, or even the hardening of class lines that generally developed in Europe. The American worker accepted the basic tenets of capitalism. The ever-present possibility of his becoming a capitalist himself left him cool to the blandishments of socialism and communism, or any other form of political radicalism. The impact of the industrial revolution drove home the importance of some form of concerted action to protect the workers' interests, but the labor movement remained fundamentally conservative.

It was to find itself almost helpless against the industrial forces arrayed against it in the latter half of the nineteenth century. The workers' repeated efforts to develop effective labor unions were invariably met by the concerted opposition of management. Again and again their embryonic organizations were smashed by employers who had behind them the general support of public opinion. As conditions constantly deteriorated, in spite of general economic advance, a sense of frustration and the feeling of unrest always simmering beneath the surface led to frequent strikes and labor uprisings. This industrial strife was to come to a climax in the 1890's, but labor still found itself too weak to meet the opposition of employers, government, and courts. The great mass of unskilled workers representative of the new industrial economy could not maintain any really effective defense of their interests.

★ THE NATIONAL LABOR UNION

In the first year following the Civil War, a group of leaders of existing labor unions which had grown up in the 1850's among ironmolders, machinists, miners, building-trades workers, and other groups took a first step toward national organization. Meeting at Baltimore, they formed the National Labor Union and issued an address which called upon the workingmen of the United States "to rise in the majesty of their strength" and challenge the employing class to acknowledge labor's rights. Legislation establishing an eight-hour day was set forth as "the first and grand desideratum of the hour"; other goals were the formation of co-operatives, currency revision to break the power of nonproductive capital over productive labor, the restriction of immigration, and establishment of a federal Department of Labor. The National Labor Union, in other words, appeared to rely more upon political than economic action to better the conditions of the working people. It paid little heed to the modern approach to labor problems based upon union recognition, collective bargaining, and the strike.

With such general and theoretical aims the National Labor Union failed to achieve any very concrete results. Nevertheless, it has a very real place in the history of the labor movement. It first emphasized the need for action on a national front, brought together for consideration of their common problems the representatives of an important group of national unions and local trades' assemblies, and created a new popular interest in industrial relations. Moreover, in William H. Sylvis, president of the National Labor Union, there appeared for the first time a national labor leader.

Sylvis, the son of a wagonmaker in Armagh, Pennsylvania, had served an apprenticeship in a local iron foundry. He early became interested in labor organization and almost singlehandedly built up the Iron Molders' International Union into one of the strongest and most closely knit labor unions in the country. He traveled thousands of miles back and forth across the continent enrolling members. "He wore clothes until they became quite threadbare and he could wear them no longer," his brother was later to write. "The shawl he wore to the day of his death . . . was filled with little holes burned there by the splashing of molten iron from the ladles of molders in strange cities, whom he was beseeching to organize." When he attended in 1868 the meeting of the National Labor Union at which he was chosen president, the New York *Herald* singled him out especially among labor leaders commended for their statesmanlike views on industrial questions and stated that his "name is familiar as a household word."

Although Sylvis continually emphasized the importance of union activity in organizing the ironmolders, a succession of unsuccessful strikes ultimately convinced him that the broader program of the National Labor Union was more hopeful than such economic pressure. "Let our cry be REFORM," he demanded in his first pronouncement as president, "Down with the monied aristocracy and up with the people." He threw himself behind the drive for a legislative eight-hour day, co-operatives, and currency reform with the same zest and enthusiasm with which he had formerly urged union organization. His devotion and energy were phenomenal, but, unhappily for the National Labor Union, he died within a year of his election to the presidency at the age of forty-one.

The Union did not long survive the death of Sylvis. Its reformist tendencies drew it toward political activity increasingly more remote from labor's immediate interests. All contact with the workers themselves was gradually lost, and in 1872 the union was reorganized as the National Labor Reform Party. As it became more and more deeply involved in an unsuccessful program of currency reform, the country's first national labor organization quietly folded up.

★ THE KNIGHTS OF LABOR

In the meantime another society was slowly rising over the labor horizon and in another ten years or so would achieve a far greater prominence than the National Labor Union. By the 1880's, indeed, this new organization of the Knights of Labor appeared so powerful that the conservative elements of the country were fearful that organized labor would take control from the business community, elect a president, and transform the entire social and economic system. Discussing the importance of the Knights' executive board, a contemporary writer in the New York *Sun* stated:

> Five men in this country control the chief interests of five hundred thousand workingmen, and can at any moment take the means of livelihood from two and a half million souls. . . . They can stay the nimble touch of almost every telegraph operator; can shut up most of the mills and factories, and can disable the railroads. They can issue an edict against manufactured goods so as to make their subjects cease buying them, and the tradesmen stop selling them. They can array labor against capital, putting labor on the offensive or defensive, for quiet and stubborn self-protection, or for angry, organized assault as they will.

These fears were greatly exaggerated. The Knights of Labor never attained the disciplined organization this article suggested, and their leaders were far from exercising complete control over the forces of labor. At this very time the Grand Master Workman, Terence V. Powderly, was nervously contemplating their growth and wondering what he should do. "The position I hold," he ruefully commented, "is too big for any ten men. It is certainly too big for me. . . ." The Knights of Labor nevertheless exerted a profound influence before it too began to break up and go the way of the National Labor Union.

It was founded in 1869 by nine journeymen tailors, members of a local Garment Cutters' Association, who had a new idea for the organization of workingmen. In terms of "the great brotherhood of toil," they considered trade unionism unduly narrow and circumscribed. They hoped to bring "all branches of labor into a compact whole" through a single organization in which workers of all categories, skilled and unskilled, could co-operate to bring about "the complete emancipation of the wealth producers from the thralldom and loss of wage slavery." The leader of the group was Uriah S. Stephens, a garment cutter who had originally been educated for the Baptist ministry, and he imparted a certain mysticism to the organization of the Knights which found expression in the secret rituals that for long were part of the membership procedure. Although Stephens was to drift away in a few years, his influence was important. His concept of labor solidarity and union membership without distinction of nationality, color, creed, or sex was a lasting contribution to labor history. The ideal expressed in the Knights of Labor's slogan: "An injury to one is an injury to all," could hardly be realized, but it created a new feeling of common interests among the nation's workers and helped to impress upon them the potentialities of national association.

The Knights were organized in local assemblies, at first largely made up of individual workers in separate crafts but later including all branches of labor. These local groups then sent delegates to district assemblies that were representative of all worker members, skilled and unskilled, in the territory covered. The district assemblies in turn sent delegates to a General Assembly which became the supreme authority for all Knights of Labor throughout the country. The constitution as adopted in 1878 opened membership to all wage earners and former wage earners (except lawyers, doctors, bankers, and liquor dealers), and called for concerted action to check the alarming aggression of wealth which threatened "the pauperization and hopeless degradation of the toiling masses." While the Knights' primary aim was to raise wages and shorten working hours, they also asserted a much broader ultimate goal. "Strikes at best afford only temporary relief," it was stated, "and members should be educated to depend upon thorough education, co-operation and political action, and through these the abolition of the wage system."

Theory and practice were never successfully reconciled. The Knights of Labor embodied much of the reform spirit that had animated such earlier organizations as the National Labor Union, and they in some measure foreshadowed the industrial unionism of the twentieth century. They at once sought to minimize strikes and became deeply involved in them. There was increasing confusion over the scope and purposes of political activity. The workers themselves wavered back and forth so far as policies adopted by the General Assembly were concerned, and while on paper the organization was highly centralized, the local assemblies actually went very much their own way.

These inner contradictions were reflected in the indecisiveness of the Knights' leadership. Powderly had had considerable experience as a labor agitator when he was elected Grand Master Workman in 1879, but he never grew up to his job. An eloquent and persuasive speaker, as well as an indefatigable letter writer, he lacked the dynamic qualities essential for effective leadership. Even his appearance was against him. He was slender and of medium height, with wavy, light brown hair, blond drooping mustache, and mild, bespectacled blue eyes. "English novelists take men of Powderly's look," a labor journalist commented, "for their poets, gondola scullers, philosophers and heroes crossed in love."

Nevertheless, Powderly performed yeoman's service for a time in building up the Knights of Labor. Between 1881 and 1885 enrollment rose to over 100,000, and a series of successful strikes then drove it up to a peak of 700,000. The workers were as excitedly gratified as the employers were fearfully alarmed. "Never in all history," one labor leader exulted, "has there been such a spectacle as the march of the Order of the Knights of Labor." "It is an organization in whose hands now rests the destinies of the Republic," exclaimed another. "It has demonstrated the overmastering power of a national combination among workingmen."

This sudden increase in membership, however, had been a forced growth, with workers rushing to join the organization faster than they could be absorbed. The hapless Powderly, far from ruling his followers with the firm control attributed to him, hardly knew which way to turn. At least four hundred thousand of the new members, he was plaintively to complain, came in from curiosity and caused more damage than good.

This may well have been true. The fresh recruits soon began to drop away, and when the Knights became involved in another series of strikes, this time without repeating their earlier victories, the retreat became a rout. Membership dropped within two years to less than a third of the former total. By 1893 it was down to 75,000.

John Swinton, a leading labor journalist of the day, was among those now forced to realize that while it had for a brief time appeared as if labor's Golden Age were at hand, the workers "had been deceived by the will o'-the wisp." Strikes had been crushed and union members blacklisted under the direction of Jay Gould—"the enemy's generalissimo"—and there was no way for the workers to combat the employers' aggressive counterattack. "The money power had swept all before it," Swinton wrote discouragedly, "and established its supremacy beyond challenge."

It is easier to explain the collapse of the Knights of Labor than to account for their brief day of glory. In trying to bring all workers in the fold of a single organization, they were attempting the impossible under the circumstances of the times. The skilled workers had some bargaining power. If they went out on strike, their employers could not completely ignore their demands. The great mass of unskilled workers, on the other hand, could not exert any such economic pressure. If they went out on strike, they could be too easily replaced from the vast reservoir of immigrants who annually swelled the labor force. Under such conditions the members of craft unions were unwilling to tie their fortunes to those of the unskilled workers. The solidarity of labor could not possibly be maintained in the face of stubborn employer refusal either to recognize or deal with the Knights of Labor.

There were other factors in the situation. A reckless resort to strikes without adequate preparation, unsuccessful experiments with co-operatives and other reform activities, and Powderly's weak and vacillating leadership all militated against success. But the fundamental reason for the failure of the Knights of Labor was the impracticality of trying to draw all the unskilled, industrial workers of the nation into a single organization.

★ FOUNDATIONS OF THE A.F. OF L.

As the Knights of Labor faded out of the picture, the remaining trade unions, largely made up of skilled workers in the various crafts, finally took those steps that were to make national labor organization possible on a more permanent basis. It was in the very year that saw the Knights at the peak of their membership and prestige—1886—that these unions, with a membership of some 150,000, came together to form the American Federation of Labor. While its growth was anything but phenomenal, membership was on a more substantial basis than had been the case in any previous labor organization. "It is noteworthy," the Federation's president was proudly able to state after the panic of 1893, "that while in every previous industrial crisis the trade unions were literally mowed down and swept out of existence, the unions now in existence have manifested, not only the powers of resistance, but of stability and permanency."

Samuel Gompers was the principal architect of the A.F. of L., and from the very first he was to impress upon the organization his own down-to-earth, pragmatic labor philosophy. He was a fervent disciple of the "new unionism" which sought to get away from the utopian ideals, vague reforms, and tendency to become involved in politics that had plagued both the National Labor Union and the Knights of Labor. Gompers believed in a program of organization and collective bargaining, backed up by the strike, which strictly limited itself to the practical goals of higher wages, shorter hours, and better working conditions for union members.

"We have no ultimate ends," one spokesman for the new unionism stated at a senatorial hearing. "We are going on from day to day. We fight only for immediate objectives—objects that can be realized in a few years."

That was to be the consistent policy of the A.F. of L., and under Gompers' leadership nothing was allowed to divert its energies from such simple and direct aims. There were to be no political involvements, no flirting with the idea of a labor party. The A.F. of L. asked nothing of government except freedom to organize, freedom to strike, and freedom to boycott in support of labor's rights. It maintained a nonpartisan political attitude based on the principle that labor's vote should be cast, regardless of party, to reward its friends and punish its enemies.

The principal difference between the A.F. of L. and the Knights of Labor, however, was that the new federation did not try to organize the unskilled workers who lacked the potential bargaining powers of the skilled. It drew together, in a loose federal structure, such national trade unions as those of the carpenters, furniture makers, typographers, ironmolders, journeymen tailors, journeymen bakers, coal miners, metalworkers, and cigar makers. The autonomy of each trade was carefully observed, in contrast with the mixed assemblies of the Knights, and the unskilled workers in the great mass industries had no place whatsoever in the new organization. Craft unionism was the basic feature of the A.F. of L. and was to remain so until the 1930's.

For many years the Federation was almost entirely Samuel Gompers. Setting up his headquarters in a tiny eight-by-ten office, with a kitchen table, some crates for chairs, and a filing case made out of tomato boxes, he step by step built up what was originally little more than a blueprint into a powerful and vital organization.

Gompers was ambitious only for labor. Short, thickset, sturdy—seeming to justify his boast that all his family were "built of oak"—his stubborn jaw revealed the tenacious force of his character. There would be no wavering in his determination to defend, as he thought they should be defended, the interests of the class of which he was always proud to be a member. In time Gompers became the friend and confidant of captains of industry, Wall Street bankers, senators, and presidents, but he never lost touch with the workers themselves. He apparently enjoyed himself most with a group of "the boys" in the back room of a saloon—a big, black cigar firmly gripped in his strong teeth and a foaming stein of beer on the table beside him. The rank-and-file of union labor gave him their support and followed his leadership for over a quarter century.

★ THE RAILWAY STRIKES

For all the progress made in the organization of labor during post-Civil War days, contemporary society was primarily affected by the strikes that more dramatically revealed the mounting discontent of the workers themselves. They began to take on a scope and a violence that gave a new and alarming significance to industrial relations. The national labor organizations were not necessarily involved in these outbreaks. They were for the most part almost spontaneous revolts on the part of the workers themselves, sometimes acting through unions and sometimes independently.

The first such uprising on a national scale was that of the railway workers in 1877. It developed originally in protest against a wage cut by the Baltimore and Ohio, and the strike then spread to the Pennsylvania, the New York Central, and other railroads throughout the country. There were attacks upon railroad property, and bloody clashes with the troops summoned to maintain law and order. In the course of one pitched battle in Pittsburgh, in which some twenty-five persons were killed, an infuriated mob drove the troops into the railway shops and then pushed blazing freight cars into the buildings. When the soldiers finally escaped under a hail of bullets, the rioters proceeded to tear up the tracks, break up freight and passenger cars, and burn what could not be carried away. The Union Depot was gutted by the spreading flames and some 2,000 freight cars and 125 locomotives destroyed. "Pittsburgh Sacked—The City Completely in the Power of a Howling Mob" read the next day's headlines in the New York *Herald*.

President Hayes ordered out all federal troops in the Atlantic Department to cope with the emergency. As they took over control in Pittsburgh and other cities, the strikers realized that they were defeated. Although there had been some public sympathy for them at the initial stage of the uprising, their excesses had alienated all popular support. The railroad men went glumly back to work at their old wages, order was restored, and within a few days the trains were once again running on schedule.

The country had never witnessed such an outbreak of rioting and mob violence. New fears were aroused in the business community of what might happen should the industrial workers really get out of hand. Labor was also awakened to a new realization of its potential strength, but even more to the need for organization and discipline to forestall the intervention of government troops. While President Hayes was widely hailed for his prompt action in suppressing disorder, thoughtful observers recognized the need for more careful consideration of the basic causes for industrial unrest.

★ HAYMARKET SQUARE AND HOMESTEAD

Nine years after what many newspapers had termed "the labor revolution" of 1877, a riot at Chicago's Haymarket Square again underscored the dangers inherent in the still troubled industrial situation. This riot was only indirectly connected with strike activity, however, and all segments of organized labor quickly disassociated themselves from the events that led up to it. What happened was this: A protest meeting against a fatal attack on some strikers at the McCormick Harvester Company was about to break up when a police detachment arrived at Haymarket Square and ordered the workers still remaining to disperse. Suddenly, someone threw a bomb into the ranks of the police. They at once opened fire, and there were answering shots from the workers. Seven police were killed and sixty-seven injured; four workers were killed and fifty or more injured.

The meeting had been addressed by a number of known anarchists who had distributed inflammatory leaflets urging the workers to avenge the deaths of the strikers at the McCormick plant. Jumping to the conclusion that anarchists must therefore be responsible for the bomb outrage, the Chicago police at once scoured the city to arrest every known anarchist leader. In a paroxysm of hysterical fear, the press of the entire country thereupon called for their immediate trial and conviction on charges of murder. Whether they had even been at the scene of the riot was immaterial. "Convict these men, make examples of them, hang them," the state's attorney urged at their trial, "and you save our institutions."

The jury agreed. The anarchist leaders were found guilty. Seven—two of whom were subsequently given life terms—were sentenced to death, and an eighth to fifteen years imprisonment. It was a shocking miscarriage of justice, and Governor Altgeld of Illinois, who later pardoned the three men not executed, assailed the presiding judge for his "malicious ferocity." In not a single case had there been any direct evidence connecting the convicted men with the actual bombing. Hysteria had triumphed over every guarantee of civil rights.

The repercussions of the Haymarket Square riot affected organized labor through the suspicion cast on every activity that could possibly be labeled radical. The Knights of Labor tried in every way to demonstrate that their organization had no sympathy with anarchists. "Better that seven times seven men hang," it was said, "than to have a millstone of odium around the standard of this Order in affiliating in any way with this element of destruction." Labor's foes were, nevertheless, able to tar all union organization with the brush of anarchism and communism. They pointed to the dreadful example of the Haymarket Square riot as demonstrating what might happen again if all radical organizations were not rigidly suppressed.

Violence was begetting violence in labor relations, and the country soon witnessed another shocking defiance of law and order. A strike broke out at the Homestead, Pennsylvania, plant of the Carnegie Steel

Company in the early summer of 1892, and when the management called in Pinkerton guards something like open warfare broke out. The first clash took place on July 6. Early that morning two barges packed with three hundred Pinkerton men armed with Winchester rifles were towed up the Monongahela River to Homestead. As they drew alongside the steel mill, there was an exchange of shots. The forewarned strikers had barricaded themselves behind steel billets and now assailed the guards deployed against them with heavy rifle fire and a small cannon. The Pinkertons fought back, but as the raging battle swirled along the river front, they suffered heavy losses. The strikers then poured barrels of oil into the river and set it afire. The battle did not last very long. Hopelessly trapped, the Pinkertons soon surrendered and were promptly run out of town by the infuriated workers. Both sides had suffered heavy casualties.

The strikers won this first round, but they could not hold out. The state militia, mobilized at the request of Carnegie Company officials, took control of Homestead and established martial law. Under the protection of the troops, the company brought in strikebreakers. The workers who had attempted to defy their employer by demanding higher wages either submitted to his terms or lost their jobs.

This was industrial warfare: a private army in the pay of employers fighting it out with armed strikers. The Chicago *Tribune* gave over its entire first page to what it described as "a battle which for bloodthirstiness and boldness was not excelled in actual warfare." The entire nation was aroused. Popular support went to the company rather than to the strikers. If the Homestead employees did not want to work for the wages offered them, ran the popular argument, they could quit; there was no warrant for their seeking to protect their jobs or trying to prevent other men from taking their places. The *Independent* declared that men talked "like anarchists or lunatics when they insist that the workmen at Homestead have done right." There was general approval for the role played by the state militia in making it possible for the Carnegie Company to oust the discontented workers from the struck plant.

★ THE PULLMAN STRIKE

Homestead was to take its place in the annals of labor history as one of the great battles for workers' rights. Two years later an even more epochal struggle was fought, again unsuccessfully, by railway employees in the famous Pullman strike. This outbreak was universally characterized as a "rebellion," and in the person of its leader, Eugene V. Debs, the conservative press found a hapless victim for their most vicious assaults on all labor activity. The *New York Times* assailed Debs as "a lawbreaker at large, an enemy of the human race"; the Chicago *Herald* asserted that "short work should be made of this reckless, ranting, contumacious, impudent braggadocio . . ."

Debs was brought into the strike when the workers of the Pullman Palace Car Company, seeking some reconsideration of wage cuts ranging from 25 to 40 per cent while the company was still paying high dividends, called for assistance from his independently organized American Railway Union. Earnest and sincere, sensitive and warm-hearted, inspiring greater loyalty and affection than perhaps any labor leader the country has ever known, Debs was anything but the anarchist, lunatic, and madman that the conservative press delighted to call him. He was actually very reluctant to come to the aid of the Pullman workers, fearing the possible repercussions of their strike. However, when their employer stubbornly refused arbitration or any other adjustment of the wage issue, he felt in honor bound to do so. The members of his union were instructed not to handle any Pullman cars and to cut them out of any trains they were operating. At the same time Debs counseled moderation and restraint and gave rigorous orders that there should be no injury to railway property.

The railroads were prepared to back up the Pullman Company. Cooperating through the General Managers' Association in Chicago, they called for the discharge of all workers refusing to handle Pullman cars, swore in special deputies to protect strikebreakers in trying to keep the trains running, and defied the American Railway Union to do its worst. Under such circumstances, the strike soon caused a general paralysis of railway traffic in Chicago and disrupted the country's entire transportation system. "The struggle," Debs declared in a ringing manifesto, "has developed into a contest between the producing classes and the money power of the country. We stand upon the ground that the workingmen are entitled to a just proportion of the proceeds of their labor." Again there was little sympathy for the strikers. The nation's press stood almost solidly behind the General Managers' Association. The New York *Herald* expressed the general sentiment when it stated emphatically that the strike had become "war against government and against society."

The tense situation in Chicago, where the railroad managers were inciting violence by the most provocative tactics, led to violent clashes between strikers and railway guards in spite of Debs' strenuous efforts to maintain order. This was what the General Managers' Association had been awaiting. It promptly appealed to President Cleveland for federal troops to restore order, safeguard the mails, and protect interstate commerce. While Governor Altgeld protested against any such move, stating that the railroads were paralyzed not because of the strikers' obstructive tactics but because the companies could not get men to operate the trains, Cleveland acceded to the request for intervention. He ordered troops to Chicago.

"If it takes every dollar in the Treasury and every soldier in the United States to deliver a postal card in Chicago," the President was reported as saying, "that postal card should be delivered."

The use of federal troops precipitated further violence. Ray Stannard Baker recalled in his *American Chronicle,* an autobiographical record of those days, one incident when the trainmen and their sympathizers, goaded on by the use of strikebreakers, were retaliating against the railroads by overturning freight cars and coaches:

> Suddenly I heard what seemed to me firecrackers exploding. A moment later a spectator, who was standing near me, slumped to the ground, and I saw blood spurt from his breast. Then another man fell. I looked up the track and saw a locomotive moving slowly down upon the mob. Blue-clad soldiers covered the fender, and the running boards, and the top of the cab. They had rifles lifted and were firing directly at us.
>
> Instantly there was a panic, men running and women screaming.

There could be no effective resistance against such use of armed force—in this particular clash Baker reported that the casualties were all among spectators—but for a time the strikers' ranks held firm and there were sympathetic turnouts on the part of engineers, firemen, and other workers in many parts of the country. The General Managers' Association then took the further step of applying in the federal court for an injunction against all strike leaders on the charge of conspiracy to obstruct the mails and interfere with interstate commerce. Its application was granted. When the strike still continued, Debs and his principal aids were thereupon arrested for contempt of court and sent to prison. Deprived of leadership, the railway workers realized their cause was lost. They gave up what had become a hopeless struggle and gradually drifted back to work.

Government by injunction, enforced by federal troops, had won a first dramatic victory. Without any consideration of the issues in dispute, or any attempt to encourage mediation, all the weight of the national government had been thrown behind the employers and against the striking workers. President Cleveland's vigorous action, for which he was widely hailed as the savior of the country, completely crushed the strike regardless of labor's possible rights. Moreover when Debs' case was appealed, the Supreme Court upheld the use of the injunction as a rightful exercise of federal power and, at least tacitly, as a legitimate means of safeguarding interstate commerce. It was unexpectedly revealed that in the Sherman Anti-Trust Law, which had been adopted to prohibit corporate conspiracies in restraint of trade, industry had a weapon that could be effectively used to combat as conspiracies the strikes or boycotts of union labor.

One further indirect consequence of the Pullman strike was that Eugene V. Debs, thinking over the course of events while in prison, became a socialist. The railway workers' defeat convinced him that socialism alone held any promise for labor in a society where employers were able to call upon the government to enforce their dictate, "work for what we want to give you, or starve." Acclaimed by great masses of people as the victim of judicial lynch law, he embarked upon a campaign to promote his socialist ideas that would end only with his death.

"While there is a lower class I am in it," Debs once stated. "While there is a criminal element I am of it, while there is a soul in prison I am not free."

Homestead and Pullman, as well as other contemporary strikes which ended disastrously for the workers, had a profound effect on American labor. While very few union members were prepared to follow Debs into the socialist camp, the workers generally became convinced that there was little hope of protection for what they considered their rights as long as government, both state and federal, so vigorously supported industry. Moreover, their discontent increased as the depression of the early 1890's further accentuated their grievances and led to spreading unemployment. Industrial armies, made up of the unemployed, marched on Washington to demand relief. Congress paid no heed to their demands, however, and the workers seemed to have nowhere to turn. The power of the Knights of Labor was by now completely broken; the American Federation of Labor was not yet strong enough to lead a united labor movement. It was under these circumstances that labor began to look toward possible alliance with the discontented farmers combining under the banners of Populism.

CHAPTER VI

The Changing Pattern of American Life

★ THE GROWTH OF CITIES

Every phase of American life reflected the growth of industry during the latter half of the nineteenth century. While a rural atmosphere remained predominant in that midwestern region known as the Valley of Democracy, cities were becoming the controlling factor in the new civilization. The Age of Steel was also the Age of Metropolis. The great, sprawling, congested, urban communities, attracting every year more recruits to their busy ranks of businessmen and tradespeople, white collar workers, and wage earners, were already beginning to provide a cultural pattern for industrial America.

In 1850 there had been only eighty-five cities with a population of more than 8,000. Fifty years later, there were almost seven times as many. The urban population doubled in the last two decades of the century, rising to some thirty million; even more remarkable was the dynamic growth of individual communities. New York became a financial, commercial, and manufacturing metropolis of well over three million, Chicago had a population of a million and a half, Philadelphia boasted more than a million, and St. Louis, Boston, and Baltimore half a million or more. The lure of the city seemed almost irresistible. In parts of New England, abandoned farms and overgrown fields bore mute witness to this urban movement, and there were sections of Missouri, eastern Iowa, southeastern Indiana, and western Illinois where the countryside was almost depleted as the more restless or ambitious young men and women made their way to the thriving manufacturing cities of the Midwest.

"Sloven farms alternate with vast areas of territory half forest, half pasturage," wrote a New England traveler in 1892: "Farm buildings, partly in ruins, testify at once to the former prosperity of the agricultural industry, and to its present collapse." Another visitor commented on the abandoned churches, dismantled academies, and moribund lodges in sections where so many of the inhabitants had fled "to the manufacturing villages, to the great cities, to the West."

The urban population was also swelled by the throngs of immigrants who were pouring into the country at an ever-increasing rate. The cities took on a strangely polyglot character. At the century's end New York reported half as many Italians as Naples, as many Germans as Hamburg, as many Jews as Warsaw, and twice as many Irish as Dublin. The foreign-born in Chicago exceeded its total population of a decade earlier. Its busy streets were crowded with Germans, Swedes, Norwegians, Italians, Poles, Lithuanians, Hungarians, and Slovenes. And in varying degrees much the same thing could be said of other urban centers from Boston to St. Louis.

A shocking contrast could be found in every metropolis between the business and residential areas, and the crowded slums where so many of the newly arrived immigrants were compelled to live. New York had not only its Fifth Avenue, its Wall Street, and its Broadway, but also its Shantytown and its notorious Bowery; Chicago had not only its north shore and beautiful lake front, but the tenements clustered about its noisome stockyards. "Having seen it," the visiting Rudyard Kipling was to say of the "splendid chaos" of Chicago, "I urgently desire never to see it again."

★ TECHNOLOGICAL ADVANCES

Inventions and technological advance contributed to the rise of cities and in turn were further stimulated by the pressing needs created by rapid urban growth. As the century drew to a close new buildings of steel and stone were beginning to arise, electric street railways (and then elevated trains and subways) were innovations in transportation, gas lighting gradually gave way to electricity with invention of the arc lamp, and telephone poles lined almost every street as evidence of new means of urban communication. And not only were cobblestone or brick roads repaved with asphalt, but suspension bridges and underriver tunnels were built. New York took the lead in much of this construction. John A. Roebling designed the majestic sweep of the Brooklyn Bridge, and President Arthur and his entire cabinet attended its formal opening in 1883.

Traffic congestion was already a serious problem in spite of broader streets and new bridges. "The visitor is kept dodging, halting and shuffling to avoid the passing throng," one observer wrote, "the confusing rattle of 'busses and wagons over the granite pavement in New

York almost drowns his own thoughts, and if he should desire to cross the street a thousand misgivings will assail him." The addition of horse cars and then electric cars added still more to the confusion and to the general atmosphere of bustle and activity.

Amid the phaetons, broughams, landaus, gigs, and hansom cabs that cluttered city streets in the late 1890's, there were already a few automobiles. But there was neither then nor for a good many years afterward any such confidence in their future as in that of streetcars or electric lighting or the telephone. "The ordinary 'horseless carriage,'" it was pontifically stated by one editorial writer of the day, "is at present a luxury for the wealthy, and although its price will probably fall in the future, it will never, of course, come into common use."

The progress of science, or rather of the labor-saving devices, conveniences, and gadgets made possible by new developments, was also transforming the urban home. The miracle of modern lighting had been realized with Thomas Edison's invention of the incandescent bulb, and electricity soon began to be used in many other ways to ease the housewife's traditional burdens. In the 1880's and 1890's, hot-air furnaces were first introduced, gas stoves began to replace coal ranges, refrigerators (although not until the 1930's would they be mechanized) became increasingly common, and modern plumbing was rapturously hailed as one of the great triumphs of American civilization.

New-fangled washing machines and flat irons with detachable handles were to be found in the laundry, while aluminum ware, steam cookers, egg beaters, and asbestos stove mats were welcome innovations in the kitchen. Factory-made products filled the larder in city homes. Baker's bread was increasingly popular, packaged cereals were widely advertised and widely bought, and canned goods proved a popular substitute for fresh vegetables. "Housekeeping is getting to be ready-made, as well as clothing," a magazine contributor noted happily in 1887.

All these innovations were still largely confined to the cities, and the traditional divergence between urban and rural ways of living was sharply accentuated. The future, indeed, belonged to the city and ultimately its culture would invade even the most isolated country areas. Nor was this culture entirely based upon business and moneymaking, for all their noisy predominance. The urban communities were the centers of the intellectual, artistic, and literary life of the nation to an ever-increasing degree. Here were most of the large universities, the great libraries and museums, the theaters and symphony halls and opera houses. The advances made along these lines were not always as readily apparent as the paving of streets or improvement in communications, but they were of lasting and profound significance.

★ THE WORLD OF FASHION

A conspicuous feature of urban social life was the extravagance of the very rich. They went their own way, a way that directly reflected the emphasis on wealth. "The dollar is the measure of every value," wrote William Dean Howells, "the stamp of every success." Those who had arrived wished to advertise their success and sought to do so through ostentation in their homes, their amusements, and their social activity. The advance of the *nouveaux riches,* who had made their money out of the mining ventures, railway building, and new industrial undertakings of the 1870's and 1880's, was aptly described as "the Gold Rush."

Coaching was one highly fashionable display. At the annual coaching parade in New York, four-in-hand drags and tally-hos bowled down Fifth Avenue in the crisp autumn air with beautifully matched horses. The bright lights of metropolitan society rode atop these elegant equipages, the men in striped waistcoats and toppers, the ladies holding parasols over their immense picture hats. Yachting was also in vogue among those who could afford it. J. P. Morgan set a standard that could hardly be rivaled when he built the first "Corsair" at an expense that unanswerably demonstrated his pre-eminence in the world of finance. The wealthy also took up fox hunting and polo, and ownership of a stable of thoroughbred race horses was always an effective way of publicizing one's place in society.

The balls and entertainments of the era became increasingly elaborate and fantastic. On one occasion a banquet room was filled with cages of rare songbirds and half a dozen swans swam on a miniature lake; on another, the guests ate while on horseback, their steeds' hoofs covered with soft pads to protect the waxed floor. For the most famous of all these gala events the ballroom of New York's Waldorf Astoria was converted into a replica of Versailles and decorated with rare tapestries while the guests came in costumes and jewelry worth fortunes. The press of the entire country reported this extravagance and even the London *Chronicle* congratulated New York society: "It has cut out Belshazzar's feast and Wardour Street and Mme. Tussaud's and the Bank of England. There is no doubt of that."

The Metropolitan Opera House was built in New York in 1883 to satisfy this urge for conspicuous display even more than to present operas. Its Golden Horseshoe was its most prominent feature. "The Goulds and the Vanderbilts and people of that ilk," the New York *Dramatic Mirror* reported on the occasion of the formal opening, "perfumed the air with the odor of crisp greenbacks. The tiers of boxes looked like cages in a menagerie of monopolists."

★ THE URBAN POOR

In sharp and glaring contrast with all this was the life of the very poor. Something like one-tenth of the population of our large cities lived in slums in the closing years of the century, and it was estimated that in New York 43,000 tenements housed over 1,500,000 people. These buildings were closely packed together, five or six stories high, with little light and less ventilation. Plumbing facilities were primitive. The rooms were small, halls and stairways always dark, and fire was a constant danger.

The death toll among people living under such conditions, and especially of children, was far higher than among other city residents. Tuberculosis, the great white plague of the era, was widespread, as were typhoid, scarlet fever, smallpox, and diphtheria. There could be no escape from the dirty, fetid, infectious atmosphere of the tenement house except the street, and there was nothing about street life to promote the health and well-being of the children playing on dirty pavements alongside filth-ridden gutters. The slums were breeding places not only for disease, but for immorality, drunkenness, and crime.

Jacob Riis, a newly arrived immigrant himself, has left a series of depressing vignettes of New York tenement life in his *How the Other Half Lives*. Describing one visit to the slums, he wrote:

> All the fresh air that enters these stairs, comes from the hall door that is forever slamming and from the windows of dark bedrooms that in turn receive from the stairs their sole supply of the elements that God meant to be free but man deals out with such a niggardly hand. That was a woman filling her pail by the hydrant you just bumped against. The sinks are in the hallway, that all tenants may have access—and all be poisoned alike by their summer stenches. Hear the pump squeak! It is the lullaby of tenement house babes. In summer, when a thousand thirsty throats pant for a cooling drink in this block, it is worked in vain. But the saloon, whose open door you passed in the hall, is always there. The smell of it has followed you up. . . .
>
> Come over here. Step carefully over this baby—it is a baby, spite of its rags and dirt—under these iron bridges called fire escapes, but loaded down, despite the incessant watchfulness of the firemen, with broken household goods, with washtubs and barrels, over which no man could climb from a fire. This gap between dingy brick walls is the yard. The strip of smoke-colored sky up there is the heaven of these people. Do you wonder the name does not attract them to churches? That baby's parents live in the rear tenement here. She is at least as clean as the steps we are now climbing. There are plenty of houses with half a hundred such in. The tenement is much like the one in front we just left, only fouler, closer, darker—we will not say more cheerless. The word is a mockery. . . .

A tenement house commission found that the slums in New York were a good deal worse in 1900 than they had been fifty years before. Continued overcrowding made for more disease, more vice, more crime. The saloons and the brothels multiplied; juvenile delinquency and gangsterism were the rule. There was no more disgraceful blot on American civilization than the urban slums, and no tragedy deeper than the thwarted lives of so many of their residents. Numerous Americans were to struggle out of the tenement to eminence in various walks of life, but the environment all too often bred pauperism and crime.

A middle class in the cities, living neither in luxury nor in the slums followed a mode of life more nearly corresponding to that of comparable people in the small towns. Their homes were comfortable, with the gradual acceptance of new conveniences and gadgets, and on quiet side streets they were often able to escape from the bustle and excitement of the metropolis. Although behind only New York and Chicago in size, Philadelphia was specially known as the city of small homes. While its rows of brick houses, with their white wooden shutters, may have lacked the broad verandahs and deep yards of small-town residences, they otherwise provided very much the same living conditions. Nevertheless, it remained true that the urban world was most distinctively characterized by the two extremes—ostentatious wealth and grinding poverty.

★ THE NEW IMMIGRATION

As already suggested, an important factor both in the growth of cities and in the creation of their swarming slums was the tremendous influx of immigrants. In the 1870's and early 1880's these newcomers were following an earlier pattern and largely sought out the new land being opened up in the West. The steamship companies and railroads, which combined forces to encourage such settlement, sometimes offered transportation rates from Europe to the Middle West as low as $25 per passenger. Immigrants from northwestern Europe, particularly Germany and the Scandinavian countries, played an outstandingly important role in the growth of the prairie states. In the last two decades of the century, however, the immigrants no longer took up land along the moving frontier. They sought out jobs in the mines, the steel mills, the textile factories, and the manufacturing establishments that were the mark of the new industrialism. They stayed in the cities along the eastern seaboard and in the Midwest and created those foreign enclaves that became characteristic of all urban centers.

During the 1870's immigrants were reaching American shores at the rate of nearly 300,000 annually. In the 1880's the figure rose to 500,000, and after a slight decline in the 1890's it was, in the first decade of the new century, to average nearly 900,000 a year. Of a total population of 76,000,000 in 1900, some 10,000,000 were foreign-born, and 26,-000,000 were of foreign parentage. The United States was indeed "a nation of nations," and the consequences of this engulfing flood were felt in every phase of national life—in industry, in politics, in social and cultural attitudes. The immigrants made continuing and vital contributions to the civilization of which they became a part, but also by the sheer weight of their numbers, they created highly complex problems of assimilation. They were at once welcomed by industry in search of cheap labor and resented by union members who feared the depressing effect upon industrial wages.

However, it was not only the increase in immigration that began to disturb the country toward the century's close. Its character was sharply changing. Until the mid-1880's, the great majority of immigrants had come from northwestern Europe; thereafter, an increasing majority were from southeastern Europe. The "new immigration" was made up of peasants from the submerged peoples of Russia and Poland, from the various territories of the old Austro-Hungarian empire, from Italy and the Balkan states. They were not Irish, Germans, and Scandinavians, but Russian Jews, Poles, Czechs, Hungarians, Italians, and Greeks. Their racial background, their religion, their social customs appeared to make the whole process of "Americanization" much more difficult than in the case of their predecessors. This problem was further accentuated by the overcrowding in the cities to which they came and by the immigrants' natural inclination to group together in national blocs that cut them off from a normal intermingling of races.

The new immigrants sought out America because of population pressures in the Old World and the opportunity that the New World still symbolized. Other factors sometimes entered the picture—religious persecution in the case of the Jews, the want of political freedom for the oppressed minorities in Russia and Austro-Hungary, the restrictions based on caste lines almost everywhere in Europe—but the primary impulse for the transatlantic passage was economic. America was the promise of a job, of a higher standard of living, of opportunities that might be realized by the immigrants' children if not by the immigrants themselves.

These promises were not always fulfilled. The immigrants who found work often labored at wages that provided little more than the barest subsistence, and the conditions under which they both worked and lived were no better—perhaps even worse—than those from which they had fled in the old country. Unable to speak the language of their new home, unaccustomed to American ways of living, they were beset by many baffling problems which added a sense of frustration and helplessness to their economic suffering. Their loyalties were divided. As Oscar Handlin has so graphically described in *The Uprooted,* they were often torn by inner conflicts that made America anything but the realization of the bright dreams with which they had embarked on the long sea voyage to the New World. Moreover, these conflicts could be heightened when the immigrants' children, seeking to adjust themselves to American life, turned against their tradition-bound parents who continued to follow old ways in their pathetic inability to adapt themselves to such a wholly strange environment.

As this tide of immigration mounted and the foreign colonies in the cities continued to expand, a movement developed to restrict immigration. It was to take on ever-gathering momentum and finally come to a climax in the 1920's. It was already significant, however, in the 1890's. The immigrants were held responsible not only for depressing the wages of American labor but for causing the conditions that made for the disease, the vice, the crime associated with urban slums. Their poverty, their illiteracy, their ignorance of democracy were held against them and said to make assimilation almost impossible. The peoples of eastern and southern Europe, as contrasted with those from northwestern Europe, racial purists maintained, were an inferior breed who threatened to contaminate the predominantly Anglo-Saxon stock that had heretofore gone into the making of the American people.

This intolerant antiforeignism found virulent expression in such a poem as Thomas Bailey Aldrich's "Unguarded Gates":

> Wide open and unguarded stand our gates,
> And through them presses a wild motley throng—
> Men from the Volga and the Tartar steppes,
> Featureless figures from the Hoang-Ho,
> Malayan, Scythian, Teuton, Kelt, and Slav,
> Flying the Old World's poverty and scorn;
> These bringing with them unknown gods and rites,
> Those, tiger passions, here to stretch their claws.
> In street and alley what strange tongues are loud,
> Accents of menace alien to our air,
> Voices that once the Tower of Babel knew!
>
> O Liberty, white Goddess! is it well
> To leave the gates unguarded?

★ MUNICIPAL REFORM

The problem of the immigrant was the problem of the city. Little attention was paid to the possible alleviation of slum conditions by those who most feared the "motley throng"; the world of wealth and fashion ignored the whole situation. But there were those who grew highly concerned over what could be done to combat urban vice and disease. Realizing that philanthropy and reform faced a challenge that had somehow to be met, they began to organize the hit-or-miss charitable activities of the day on a more efficient basis. By the close of the 1890's, at least one hundred well-organized societies were in operation. Professional social workers were taking over tasks previously left to the well-intentioned but sometimes inept efforts of informal church groups and women's clubs.

Jane Addams and Julia Lathrop founded Hull House in 1889 to provide aid for the Polish Jews, Italians, Bohemians, Germans, and Irish in one of Chicago's most congested slums. Under their direction men's clubs were formed as a counterattraction to the district's overabundant saloons, day nurseries set up to help care for the children, sports and recreational activities encouraged to keep young men off the street, and an employment agency to find jobs for those out of work. The undertaking was so successful that scores of similar enterprises were established in other cities, including New York's well-known Henry Street Settlement.

Other organizations took up the problems of special groups within urban society in a continuing battle with the slums. The Salvation Army had an important role as early as the 1890's. A number of agencies developed special Americanization programs for the newly arrived immigrants and extended aid to the Negroes who were beginning to move North in search of jobs in factory or mill. Child welfare programs were also adopted in the large cities with special attention paid to juvenile delinquency; concerted reform efforts were directed against commercialized vice in the hope of cleaning up red light districts.

The churches played an increasing role in such activities as ministers of all faiths grew increasingly aware of the need for a new social gospel to meet the problems of the day. By the 1880's there were to be found in many congested urban areas so-called institutional churches. With programs very comparable to those of the settlement houses, they maintained day nurseries, social clubs, reading rooms, and gymnasiums that were open throughout the week to the entire community. One of the early leaders in this movement was Henry Codman Potter, who made Grace Church in New York a center for social work with workingmen's clubs, missions, and day nurseries. Another important figure was Washington Gladden who somewhat later developed a similar program in Columbus, Ohio, and was known throughout the country as a spokesman for the social gospel.

One special aspect of reform was reflected in the temperance movement. Rural rather than urban in its inspiration, it represented a phase of the country's revolt against the wicked ways of the metropolis and was promoted by a part of the nation which was to become known as the Bible Belt with almost fanatical zeal. It was in the cities, however, that the real battle had to be fought. Here such organizations as the Women's Christian Temperance Union, the Anti-Saloon League, and the Methodist Church waged a relentless war against the liquor traffic and the saloon. One of the dramatic crusaders in this cause was the famous Carrie Nation, who resorted to direct action by smashing up saloons with her little hatchet. The more customary technique of the temperance advocates was to try to persuade people, and especially children, to sign abstinence pledges. Little headway was made against the city saloon during these years, however, and in New York alone there were estimated to be nearly eight thousand in busy operation. Local option laws were in effect in many parts of the country at the century's close, but only three states were completely dry.

★ RECREATION AND AMUSEMENTS

"The social civilization of a people," Lord Lytton has written, "is always and infallibly indicated by the intellectual character of its amusements."

On this premise, the recreational life of the American people in the late nineteenth century may not have shown very great promise of intellectual advance. The changes that were taking place in what is always one of the most interesting illustrations of how people live—for certainly the use of leisure time is significant—nevertheless reflected clearly the impact of urban life on the national scene. City dwellers cut off from the simple, outdoor activities of village life, and in many cases unable to enjoy the traditional social affairs of the small town, were compelled to seek out new amusements. There was a rising demand for commercial entertainment which would suit both the tastes and the pocketbooks of the great masses of urban workers.

The theater had always been popular in the United States, but the serious plays of the legitimate stage were becoming more and more overshadowed by melodrama, burlesque shows, and vaudeville. Every city had its large popular playhouses, with admission at ten, twenty, or thirty cents, to which immense audiences were attracted by glowing advertisements of "entertainment of the more democratic type."

The usual themes of the melodramas presented in these theaters were the pitfalls the big city presented for the innocent country girl or the blood and thunder heroics of the Wild West. *Under the Gaslight, Only a Working Girl,* and *Nellie, the Beautiful Cloak Model* were popular examples of the former type of play. Virtue inevitably proved triumphant in spite of the wiles of insidious city slickers. "An honest shop girl," the honest shop girl would sententiously proclaim, "is as far above a fashionable idler as heaven is above earth." Among the westerns were *The Gambler of the West, The Scouts of the Plains,* and *The Red Right Hand; or The First Scalp for Custer*. One authentic hero was the famed Buffalo Bill, who toured the country with his own Wild West, Rocky Mountain and Prairie Exhibition, staffed by Indians, cowboys, and Annie Oakley in person.

The advertisements for burlesque in the 1890's had a titillating appeal. One company's billboards announced "50—Pairs of Rounded Limbs, Ruby Lips, Tantalizing Torsoes—50"; another's declared that while the show's merry maidens were clothed in "close-fitting, flesh colored silk tights," this was really far more attractive than no costume at all. Anthony Comstock, "the Roundsman of the Lord," had long since founded his Society for the Suppression of Vice, but he could make scant headway against burlesque.

Vaudeville, the offspring of the old-time minstrel show, the circus, and the variety stage, had been made over into entertainment for all the family by the 1880's, and it became immensely popular with its dancing and acrobatic acts, trained animals, jugglers, and magicians. Among vaudeville headliners were Montgomery and Stone, Weber and Fields, Lillian Russell, and the Cohan family, whose little boy, the George Cohan of later Broadway fame, played the lead in *Peck's Bad Boy*. Keith and Proctor developed a nationwide circuit, introduced the continuous show, and by staging their "refined vaudeville" in small towns as well as cities, provided entertainment for millions.

In the 1890's some of the vaudeville theaters experimented with a new feature known as the vitascope. A sort of peep show invented by Thomas Edison, where one put a nickel in the slot of a small machine and saw through a tiny aperture uncertain figures jerkily moving against a dim background, had been developed to the point of throwing "living pictures" on a screen. However, the novelty of the vitascope soon wore off and it was relegated to penny arcades. Not until well into the new century did moving pictures embark on the career that was to make them the leading form of popular entertainment, completely eclipsing melodrama, burlesque, and vaudeville.

The crowded city and the electric street railway combined to give rise to another form of amusement. Trolley parks were built on the outskirts of almost every urban center and attracted increasing Sunday and holiday throngs with their roller coasters, merry-go-rounds, ferris wheels, dance halls, and band concerts. At Coney Island, where New York had long since had such an amusement center, George C. Tilyou opened his famed Steeplechase Park toward the close of the century, and trolley parks everywhere were soon following his lead with ever new attractions for fun-seeking excursionists. It was also at Coney Island about this time that an observer was puzzled by a new concoction sold on the boardwalk. He described it as "a weird-looking sausage muffled up in two halves of a roll." Here in all its glory was the hot-dog.

The trolley parks, *Harper's Weekly* declared, were "the great breathing-places for the millions of people in the city who get little fresh air at home." Another contemporary magazine stated that their pastimes yielded far more enjoyment "than all the courtly balls and fashionable dissipation indulged in by fortune's favorites."

★ SPECTATOR SPORTS

One further aspect of the recreational scene was the rise of so-called spectator sports. Unable to play games themselves because there were so few public parks or recreational facilities, urban dwellers enjoyed watching them.

Professional baseball came into its own. The National League had been formed in 1876, and some twenty years later the American League. Countless thousands attended their games. "Let me say," Cardinal Gibbons said in 1896, "that I favor Base Ball as an amusement for the greatest pleasure-loving people in the world. . . ." It was played on sandlots, in country villages, and on school and college diamonds, as well as at urban parks, but its growth as a commercial sport was more significant. Baseball cut across all class lines and invaded every part of the country. It was already the national game.

Prize fighting was its only possible rival in popular interest, for while few people actually saw the championship bouts of the 1880's (they were banned in most states), millions read about them. John L. Sullivan, the Strong Boy of Boston, was the great sports hero of his day. When he finally went down to defeat before the flailing fists of Gentleman Jim Corbett in 1892, an incredulous public found it hard to believe the sad news even though it was emblazoned in newspaper headlines from coast to coast:

> John L. has been knocked out! the people all did cry
> Corbett is the champion! how the news did fly,
> And future generations, with wonder and delight,
> Will read in hist'ry's pages of the Sullivan-Corbett fight.

Although football was still played at relatively few colleges, the games of Princeton, Yale, and Harvard—the "Big Three" of the 1890's—were attracting crowds of as many as thirty thousand persons and were given wide coverage in the newspapers' pioneer sports pages. And already there were charges of professionalism. No one had any conception, one irate sports critic wrote in *Harper's Weekly* in 1895, "of the rottenness of the whole structure through the middle and far West. Men are bought and sold like cattle to play this autumn on 'strictly amateur' elevens."

However true this may have been, the atmosphere of the big games corresponded very much to that of later years even though the huge stadiums of today were still in the future. After one Princeton-Yale game the *New York Times* reported:

> The air was tinged with the blue and the orange and the black as the great throngs poured through the city over the bridges, invaded Brooklyn and swept like a rising tide into Eastern Park. They came by the railroads, horse-cars, drags and coaches and afoot. Coaches, drags and tally-hos decorated with the blue or the orange and the black wound through the thoroughfares and quiet side streets in a glittering procession, freighted with jubilant college boys and pretty girls, who woke the echoes of the church bells with cheers and tooting of horns. In an almost endless procession they inundated the big enclosure, and when it was 2 p.m. the sight was that of a coliseum of the nineteenth century, reflecting the changes and tints of a panoramic spectacle.

★ TOWN AND COUNTRY

In the small town recreation was generally along more traditional lines than in the cities—playing games rather than watching them and informal parties rather than commercial amusements. However, the theater and the new vaudeville were brought to local opera houses throughout the country by traveling companies. Such favorites as *Uncle Tom's Cabin, East Lynne,* and *The Old Homestead* were seen by countless thousands from coast to coast, even though the actual performances of the plays often left something to be desired. "Doubtless there are worse theatrical companies than those which visit Kansas," William Allen White wrote in 1897, "but no one has ever described them."

Other small-town entertainment was centered to a great extent about the lodge, the social club, or the church. There was a phenomenal increase in fraternal orders. Masons, Oddfellows, Knights of Pythias, and Elks were joined by Shriners, Good Templars, Druids, and Gophers in such profusion that the land seemed to be covered with temples, camps, clans, castles, and conclaves. The United States proved itself to be a "nation of joiners." The conventions and balls, picnics and sociables of the myriads of new clubs and societies were an enlivening addition to the traditional church suppers.

Music had an important part at many of these affairs. The talking machine had been invented and already foreshadowed a new era of record playing, but this was still a day of local band concerts, home-talent piano recitals, family sings, and barbershop quartets. Reflecting as they always do the temper of the times, popular songs revealed a strongly sentimental strain in the society of the 1890's. The generation that saw the triumph of capitalism and fierce outbreaks of industrial strife sang the traditional favorites from "Old Black Joe" to "Annie Laurie," such new songs as "On the Banks of the Wabash," "O Promise Me," "Wait Till the Clouds Roll By," "After the Ball Is Over," and also "The Sidewalks of New York" and "The Bowery."

The countryside was still cut off from amusements and recreation to an extent that can hardly be realized in a world of macadam highways, automobiles, moving pictures, radio, and television. Its great occasions for social activity were the Grange meeting, the Fourth of July picnic, the annual county fair, and the coming of the circus. Barnum and Bailey's—"The Greatest Show on Earth"—led every other circus in the land, but there was many a smaller road show which proudly offered its "grand centralization of genius, concentration of merit, monopoly of equestrian stars, avalanche of attractions."

"Each year one came along from the east," Hamlin Garland has written in nostalgic memory of his own boyhood, "trailing clouds of glorified dust and filling our minds with the color of romance. . . . It brought to our ears the latest band pieces and taught us the popular songs. It furnished us with jokes. It relieved our dullness. It gave us something to talk about."

Recreational life could hardly have varied more from metropolis to small town to country. But under the impact of the times it was soon to become far more uniform and more commercialized. Over the horizon was a great amusement industry on which the public would annually spend billions of dollars to compensate for the changes wrought by an urban civilization.

★ THE STATUS OF WOMEN

A further consequence of the changing conditions of nineteenth-century life, again more marked in the city than in the country, was the altered status of women. Time and opportunities for activities outside the home made for a new independence and self-reliance on the part of the American female. The inventions that introduced the typewriter, the cash register, the adding machine, and the telephone into the business world opened up an entirely new area of job opportunities for young women and girls. While women had always been a part of the industrial labor force, having been employed in the first textile mills established in New England, they were now to play a more important role in the office than in the factory.

There was still among most middle-class families a widespread prejudice against women trying to support themselves, and Victorian conventions had a strong hold in matters of deportment, dress, chaperoning. But new winds were stirring and the young women who became salesgirls, secretaries, typists, and telephone operators could no longer be governed by rules based on the premise that woman's place was in the home. Manners and morals, general ways of life, could not fail to be affected. And as always such changes affecting women were considered a dangerous threat to the sanctity of the home and family life.

"The great fault of the girl of today," one writer declared in the *Ladies' Home Journal* in 1890, "is discontent. She calls it by the more magnificent sounding name of ambition, but in reality she is absolutely restless and dissatisfied with whatever may be her position in life."

The period also saw the flowering of women's clubs ranging from Browning and Shakespeare "circles" to less culturally-minded Ladies' High Jinks. "We have art clubs, book clubs, dramatic clubs, pottery clubs," one contemporary wrote. "We have sewing circles, philanthropic associations, scientific, literary, religious, athletic, musical, and decorative art societies."

Fashions further reflected the changing role of women in American society. Most noteworthy perhaps was the popular vogue for tailored suits and shirtwaists, so much more suitable for business wear than earlier clothing styles. But one of the strongest influences for dress reform was the new sport of bicycling. Sweeping the country in the 1890's, it appealed to women no less than to men, and obviously compelled a modification of conventional costume. "Her windage is multiplied," a sports handbook pointed out in respect to the too-amply skirted, "and so is the exertion she needs to bring to bear on her riding. Added to that, her mind is continually on the strain that her skirt may be preserved in a position of seemliness." Shorter skirts were a necessity, and the very fact that under such circumstances the "female cyclists" were tolerated was a sign of woman's emancipation no less significant than acceptance of her role as clerk or stenographer. Moreover the new style was encouraged for street wear. "A few years ago," a magazine writer commented in 1895, "no woman would dare venture on the street with a skirt that stopped over her ankles. . . . The bicycle has given to all American womankind the liberty of dress for which reformers have been sighing for generations."

Finally, there was a developing movement in support of broader civil rights and woman suffrage. The western states newly admitted in the 1890's gave women the vote and everywhere, except perhaps in the South, there was mounting interest in equality between the sexes. Nevertheless, the general cause of woman suffrage, to which we shall return, was not to gather very much headway until after the turn of the century.

★ POPULAR EDUCATION

Directly or indirectly affecting every phase of American life, as important as any single social or cultural development from the Civil War to the end of the century, was expansion in the field of popular education. There was not only a tremendous growth in the number of public schools and in student enrollment, but an extension of both ends of the educational spectrum—kindergartens and graduate schools. The greatest advance was at the high-school level. While the total school population doubled between 1870 and 1900 to a total of 15,000,000, the number of high schools rose from 500 to over 6,000.

Statistics tell only a part of the story. The mounting interest in education was accompanied by broadened curricula and improved teaching as the more prosperous states (the South continued to lag far behind the rest of the country) placed an increased emphasis upon teacher training. The "little red school house" with pupils of all grades in one room—concentrating primarily on the three R's—for long remained the most characteristic feature of popular education, but town and city schools were year by year becoming larger, more highly organized, and more advanced.

In thousands of elementary schools throughout the country the basic texts that carried over from earlier days were the *McGuffey Readers,* once described by the novelist Herbert Quick as "the most influential volumes ever published in America." Their carefully chosen selections from English novelists and poets, pious tales of exemplary children, and edifying verse were read by countless children. They extolled all the virtues; they belabored all the vices. As attested by the interesting reminiscences later brought together by Mark Sullivan in *Our Times,* they formed the mind of a generation. Between 1836 and 1900 their circulation is estimated to have totaled one hundred million.

The *McGuffey Readers* taught obedience and industry; they inculcated patriotism and temperance. No story was told without pointing a moral lesson, and no poem reprinted which did not serve to foster virtue. Perhaps the best-known story for whose universal acceptance the *McGuffey Readers* were responsible was that of the stalwart honesty of the little George Washington:

"George," said his father, "do you know who killed that fine cherry-tree yonder in the garden?"

This was a hard question; George was silent for a moment; and then, looking at his father, his young face bright with conscious love of truth, he bravely cried out: "I can't tell a lie, father; you know, I can't tell a lie. I did cut it with my hatchet."

"Come to my arms, my dearest boy!" cried his father, in transports; "come to my arms! you killed my cherry-tree, George, but you have now paid me for it a thousandfold. Such proof of heroic truth in my son is of more value than a thousand trees, though they were all purest gold."

If this reflected primarily the tone and atmosphere of the one-room school houses, a broader range of studies and less traditional texts were being introduced into city schools. History and geography—later to be termed social studies—supplemented reading, and writing, and arithmetic, and the high schools reached out with a range of courses that embraced both vocational training and preparation for college.

An increasing number of high school students went on to college. And to the already well-established private institutions were added not only hundreds of comparable new colleges, but those great state universities that were the outgrowth of federal land grants under the terms of the Morrill Act of 1862. This measure had extended subsidies to the states for the formation of colleges that were intended primarily for instruction in "agriculture and the mechanical arts." Some sixty-nine land grant colleges were set up in the post-Civil War years and a number of them were to evolve into such outstanding state universities as those in California, Wisconsin, Illinois, and Ohio. This significant development affected the whole pattern of higher education.

The state universities, attracting thousands of students who could not meet the tuition charges of the private colleges, provided a constantly expanding program of studies that included the liberal arts but also embraced vocational training. They in effect extended the principle of free education (or almost free education) to higher levels than had ever before been contemplated. While these new colleges and universities hardly came into their own until after the turn of the century, their tremendous potentialities for the future were clearly apparent as they constantly strove to raise their educational standards.

These advances in popular education (we shall turn in the next chapter to higher education and its contribution to increasing the world's knowledge) had their counterpart in the growth of public libraries and various cultural programs for adults. The number of libraries, with the help of funds made available by Andrew Carnegie, rose to some 9,000, while far and away the most important cultural institution was Chautauqua. The latter's lecture series were interlarded with xylophone orchestras, Swiss yodelers, and college-girl octettes, but education remained the keynote. Among the speakers who carried the message of culture to the hinterlands—Chautauqua was described as "a cross between a camp meeting and a county fair"—were William Jennings Bryan and P. T. Barnum, Mark Twain and Viscount Bryce, and every president from Grant through McKinley. A contributor to the *Atlantic Monthly* wrote:

> Any man who loves knowledge and his native land must be glad at heart when he visits a summer session of Chautauqua: attends the swiftly successive Round Tables upon Milton, Temperance, Geology, the American Constitution, the Relations of Science and Religion, and the Doctrine of Rent; perhaps assists at the Cooking School, the Prayer Meeting, the Concert, and the Gymnastic Drill; or wanders under the trees among the piazzaed cottages, and sees the Hall of Philosophy and the wooden Doric Temple shining on their little eminences.

Here was a highly significant demonstration of the intellectual interests of middle-class America.

★ THE READING PUBLIC

All this meant a tremendous increase in the reading public, and great gains were scored in the publication of books, in the number and circulation of magazines, and in newspaper coverage. America had become a "land of readers," one observant foreign visitor declared. To what extent this actually meant any rise in intellectual standards is another question. In considering popular literature, it must be remembered that for all the educational advance of these years, school attendance at the close of the century still averaged only some five years per pupil for the country as a whole.

To the more serious literature of the day we shall return in another chapter, but so far as popular fiction was concerned (it represented one-fourth of all books published), the great majority of readers were women. One skeptical critic described the omnipresent female reader as "the Iron Madonna who strangles in her fond embrace the American novelist." Among the most widely read authors of the latter half of the nineteenth century, in any event, were Mrs. E. D. E. N. Southworth and the Reverend E. P. Roe, whose sentimental and moralistic effusions had a tremendous appeal, while further escape from the problems of the day was afforded in the 1880's and 1890's by such still remembered historical novels as *Quo Vadis, Ben Hur, The Prisoner of Zenda,* and *When Knighthood Was in Flower*. The best seller in 1900 was to be

Mary Johnston's romantic *To Have and To Hold,* a triumph of heart-throbbing romance which was bought in a brief twelve months by nearly a quarter of a million readers.

Among younger readers the books of Horatio Alger, such as *Strive and Succeed* or *Bound to Rise,* monotonously retelling how the poor boy made good in the best accepted tradition of American success stories, were always popular. In a somewhat different vein, the goody-goody tales that Martha F. Finley spun out endlessly in the *Elsie* books appealed mightily to little girls.

The note of sentimentality and religious morality in such children's books was typical of middle-class culture. But while it may have had some influence on the attitudes of young people, much more to their taste—at least that of boys—were the memorable dime novels. These popular little paper-backed books, best known through *Beadle's Pocket Library,* drew primarily upon the dramatic atmosphere of the Wild West for their blood-and-thunder stories. Deadwood Dick, Mustang Sam, Bronco Billy, Calamity Jane, and a host of outlaws, cattle rustlers, and gamblers shot their way through hundreds of pages of exciting adventure, keeping alive the legends of the frontier which were then handed on to the pulp magazines, the movies, and the radio and television. The rising cities, however, provided the background for equally thrilling stories of crime and detection, and the Old Sleuth and Old Cap Collier became figures hardly less admired than the heroes of the western plains.

Among other dime novel series—and there were hundreds of them—were *Pluck and Luck, The Liberty Boys of '76, New York Detective Library, Wild West, Secret Service,* and *Nick Carter's Weekly.* This whole school of fiction was vigorously condemned by the moralistic Anthony Comstock as "boy and girl devil-traps," but whether the young reader was ripping through the pages of *Big Foot Wallace, The Lariat King, Jay Gould's Office Boy, Diamond Dick's Slashing Blow,* or *The Terrible Mystery of Car No. 206* he could be assured that eventually right would triumph and that the fortitude and bravery of his hero would be rewarded.

★ MAGAZINES AND NEWSPAPERS

Whatever their category, books were always outnumbered by magazines, and before the close of the century the circulation of the latter rose to the then tremendous total of three million. At the top of the list were such staid and respectable publications as the *Atlantic Monthly, Harper's, Century,* and *Scribner's Monthly;* and there were the *Nation,* a leading review of opinion, the *Independent,* and *Harper's Weekly,* a well-illustrated family magazine. More significant innovations were the new women's magazines and the cheap, popular monthlies.

The former were best represented by the *Ladies' Home Journal,* which under the able editorship of Edward W. Bok broke fresh ground with its special homemaking departments, advice columns, serialized fiction, and profuse illustrations. The new vogue of the popular monthlies was started when *McClure's* came out at fifteen cents a copy, shortly followed by the *Cosmopolitan* and *Munsey's* at ten cents. Then in 1897 Cyrus H. K. Curtis bought the old *Saturday Evening Post* and, opening up its pages to the best as well as the most popular writers, launched it on its spectacularly successful career.

Magazines became highly profitable as their circulation boomed, and additional revenue was obtained through the increased sale of advertising space heretofore largely restricted to patent medicines. The nationalization of business and the standardization of products forced manufacturers to try to reach the largest possible number of potential buyers, and the magazines joined forces with the advertising agencies in building up a new, nationwide market. Together with such other media as billboards, they gave increasing currency during these years to many immemorial slogans: "Ivory Soap—It Floats," "Castoria—Children Cry for It," "Schlitz—the Beer that Made Milwaukee Famous," and "Eastman Kodak—You Push the Button; We Do the Rest." As early as 1876 a foreign visitor commented that advertising in the United States was "playing upon the brain of man like a musician does upon a piano," but it was hardly on the threshold of its tremendous expansion.

Among newspapers, the greatest growth and largest circulation were found among weeklies rather than dailies. The former's readers were estimated in 1900 to have reached a total of 42,000,000, in comparison with a circulation for the latter of 15,000,000. Nevertheless, the daily of the 1890's mirrored much more faithfully the basic changes taking place in American society. It became the spokesman for the new urban culture, and both reflected and further encouraged the increase in the reading public.

The outstanding papers in the country were in New York—most notably the *Times,* the *Tribune,* the *Herald,* and the *Sun*—and in this city there also took place that further popularization of the daily press which led to increasing emphasis on current news and human interest stories rather than political reports. This trend in news writing, with the introduction of such features as sports pages, women's pages, Sunday rotogravure sections, and special columns from Finley Peter Dunne's "Mr. Dooley" series to Dorothy Dix's advice to the lovelorn, spread gradually throughout the country. New printing and publishing techniques, such as Linotype machines, rotary presses, and photo-engraving, further served to improve the appearance of the papers and to make it possible to get out late editions—the popular "extras"—much more quickly.

Sensationalism also pervaded newspaper columns and was particularly pointed up during a dramatic circulation race in New York between the *World* and the *Journal.* A new era of publishing was introduced when Joseph Pulitzer, who had arrived in this country as a penniless immigrant from Hungary, bought the *World* in 1883 from Jay Gould. Emphasizing all reports of crime and scandal with banner headlines, lurid detail, and dramatic illustrations ("X marks the spot"), he rapidly built up the *World's* circulation to over a million. Twelve years later, even Pulitzer's sensationalism was overshadowed by William R. Hearst, the son of a wealthy Californian. Taking over the *Journal,* he recklessly played up still more lurid crime stories and more titillating scandals in a frankly emotional appeal to reader interest.

One phase of the developing rivalry between Pulitzer and Hearst was a battle over rights to a popular colored comic strip, known as the "Yellow Kid"—precursor of the "Katzenjammer Kids," "Happy Hooligan," "Buster Brown," and "Mutt and Jeff." From this incident the term "yellow journalism" was derived to describe the new departures in sensationalism. The rivalry between the *World* and the *Journal* then came to a climax in their hysterical reporting of the Cuban insurrection and the Spanish-American war. "Nothing so disgraceful as the behavior of these two papers," the irate editor of the *Nation* declared, "has been known in the history of American journalism."

There was no question of the unfortunate influence of the Hearst and Pulitzer tactics, yet at the same time they helped to make newspapers more real and vital than they had ever been. Many special features, even including the advice to the lovelorn columns, had legitimate reader appeal. Able journalists of the school of Richard Harding Davis raised the standards of reporting in a number of instances. And the publishers' crusading zeal, however colored by the desire to gain circulation through sensational exposures, was to play a significant part after the turn of the century in arousing the public to some of the evils in contemporary society so urgently calling for reform.

CHAPTER VII

Literary and Intellectual Trends

★ THE GENTEEL TRADITION

The literary scene has always reflected the lights and shadows, the interplay of divergent forces, in our national life. For a time after the Civil War, writing appeared to be largely negative and inconsequential against the background of the country's economic advance and industrial progress. Many of the prewar figures lived on—Emerson and Lowell, Holmes and Whittier—but their best work was done and literary New England was entering upon its long Indian Summer. Its novelists and poets were out of touch with the fresh, new winds stirring American life and blind to the significance of the underlying forces of a resurgent democracy.

"Do you call these genteel little creatures American Poets?" Walt Whitman asked. "Do you term that perpetual, pistareen, paste-pot American art, American drama, taste, verse? I think I hear, echoed as from some mountaintop afar in the west, the scornful laugh of the Genius of these States."

In the 1880's Thomas Bailey Aldrich sought to rule the world of polite letters from his eminence as editor of the *Atlantic Monthly* and may be taken as representative of the literary school Whitman deplored. While he seldom considered social questions in his own writing, he watched with affrighted concern everything that threatened the established order of his Brahmin world. "Personally I must confess," he wrote in 1899, "that I have never been very deeply impressed by the administrative abilities of what we call the lower classes. The Reign of Terror in France is a fair illustration of the kind of government which the masses give us when they get the happy opportunity." Yet he knew almost nothing of these people whom he feared and his horizon scarcely extended beyond the Hudson. When his refined and delicate verses, in which decorum and gentility went hand in hand, occasionally strayed so far as to consider something other than romance, they almost invariably viewed with timid alarm.

Yet for all such pallid writers, there were other voices in the land and they were making themselves heard. A period which found Walt Whitman writing some of his most magnificent poetry, Mark Twain telling his classic stories of an America far removed from Aldrich's genteel circle, Henry James composing his subtle novels on "the international situation," and William Dean Howells encouraging a new school of realistic writers was hardly inconsequential. The scepter had passed from New England. Literature was becoming far more representative of the country as a whole through the books of both a vigorous group of local colorists and of other writers who could more nearly speak for the nation.

★ WALT WHITMAN

Whitman, who had been dismissed from a government post in 1865 when he was discovered to be the author of the "scandalous" *Leaves of Grass,* was the great poet of Democracy, far and away the most authentic spokesman of the new America coming into being. He celebrated every phase of life and every part of the country. But the materialism of the age awoke in him, as in the minds of so many thoughtful observers, a very real foreboding of what might lie ahead for the nation. In his *Democratic Vistas* he wrote warningly in 1871:

> I say that our New World democracy, however great a success in uplifting the masses out of their sloughs, in materialistic development, products, and in a certain highly deceptive superficial popular intellectuality, is, so far, an almost complete failure in its social aspects, and in really grand religious, moral, literary and esthetic results. . . . It is useless to deny it: Democracy grows rankly up the thickest, noxious, deadliest plants and fruits of all—brings worse and worse invaders—needs newer, larger, stronger, keener compensations and compellers. . . . Even today, amid these whirls, incredible flippancy, and blind fury of parties, infidelity, entire lack of first-rate captains and leaders, added to the plentiful meanness and vulgarity of the ostensible masses—that problem, the labor question, beginning to open like a yawning gulf, rapidly widening every year—what prospect have we? We sail a dangerous sea of seething currents, cross and undercurrents, vortices,—all so dark and untried. . . . In vain do we march with unprecedented strides to empire so colossal, outvying the antique, beyond Alexander's, beyond the proudest sway of Rome. In vain we annexed Texas, California, Alaska, and reach north for Canada or south for Cuba. It is as if we were somehow being endowed with a vast and thoroughly appointed body, and then left with little or no soul.

Yet in spite of his admission of all the charges that might be made against democracy, he could still retain a noble conception of "the majesty and reality of the American people *en masse*" and a clear faith in the ultimate fruition of democracy on the grand scale which he envisaged. "The older I grow," he once said, "the more I am confirmed in my optimism, my democracy."

It was a note that entered into many of the poems that he added to his *Leaves of Grass,* first published in 1855, in the years following the Civil War. For this was the period in which he wrote "Passage to India," "Pioneers! O Pioneers!," "Thou Mother with Thy Equal Brood," and a great part of "Whispers of Heavenly Death." He would continue to sound his "barbaric yawp over the roofs of the world," and while there were relatively few either to read or appreciate his verse, his stature steadily grew as poet and prophet both here and abroad.

Whitman had much the same faith as Lincoln, and no one paid more eloquent tribute to the nation's great war leader than the poet of whom Lincoln himself once said, seeing Whitman pass in the street, "Well, he looks like a *man.*" His most grand elegy was not "O Captain! My Captain!"—memorized by so many generations of schoolboys—but the lovely and moving "When Lilacs Last in the Dooryard Bloom'd":

> When lilacs last in the door-yard bloom'd,
> And the great star early droop'd in the western sky in the night,
> I mourn'd, and yet shall mourn with ever-returning spring.
>
> O ever-returning spring! trinity sure to me you bring;
> Lilacs blooming perennial, and drooping star in the west,
> And thought of him I love.
>
> O powerful, western, fallen star!
> O shades of night! O moody, tearful night!
> O great star disappear'd! O the black murk that hides the star!
> O cruel hands that hold me powerless! O helpless soul of me!
> O harsh surrounding cloud, that will not free my soul!

Whitman lived on to the close of the century—a familiar figure in his Camden haunts, with baggy suit, open collar, slouch hat, and long white beard. There has been no one like him, before or since.

★ MARK TWAIN

In some measure *Democratic Vistas* had its counterpart in *The Gilded Age* that Mark Twain wrote in 1873 in collaboration with Charles Dudley Warner. For this novel, accepted as the classic expression of the period to which its name has been given, probes deeply into the excesses, the crudities, the spirit of grab and conquest, which marked the postwar era. Yet it also reflects much of the vitality and enthusiasm, the zestful drive that animated American society. Mark Twain differed from Walt Whitman, however. He was ultimately to turn his back on the America that had nourished him, the frontier of which he was the product, and ally himself more and more with the respectable and wealthy classes of the East. His own life was a success story, but disillusionment and a sense of frustration were to shadow his later years. The arresting personality that was so often seen on New York's lower Fifth Avenue, a sprightly white-clad figure with a heavy crest of disorderly hair, thick eyebrows and mustache, had unhappily lost all faith in "the damned human race."

Much has been written of the reasons for Mark Twain's surrender to the conservatism, conventions, and artificialities of the life he led in Hartford and New York, and of the transformation of the infectious humor of his early writing to the sometimes savage satire of his later works. Perhaps he was irretrievably caught up in the complexities of the age in which he lived, perhaps it was a reaction to the influence of his wife and his cautious literary mentors, perhaps it was merely a consequence of growing old.

No one has ever drawn a picture of phases of American life long past to compare with *Life on the Mississippi* and *Roughing It.* He caught the spirit of frontier days, with all their gusto and rough humor, their love for tall tales, and made them alive and exciting. But far more deeply embedded in the memory and affection of countless readers than these books are *Tom Sawyer* and *Huckleberry Finn.* Their place in American literature stands assured, however widely Mark Twain's other books may or may not be read. His later writings, indeed, ran an unusual course, from the often hilarious travel record of *Innocents Abroad,* through such dissimilar excursions into the past as *A Connecticut Yankee in King Arthur's Court* and *Personal Recollections of Joan of Arc,* to the embittered *The Man That Corrupted Hadleyburg* and *The Mysterious Stranger.*

Discussing Mark Twain's contribution to our literature, Vernon Louis Parrington has written:

> He is a mirror reflecting the muddy cross-currents of American life as the frontier spirit washed in, submerging the old aristocratic landmarks. To know Mark Twain is to know the strange and puzzling contradictions of the Gilded Age. With unconscious fidelity he reveals its crudity, its want of knowledge, discipline, historical perspective . . . and he reflects with equal fidelity certain other qualities that go far to redeem the meanness: a great creative power; an eager idealism, somewhat vague but still fine; a generous sympathy; a manly independence that strove to think honestly; a passionate hatred of wrong and injustice and an honest democratic respect for men as men.

It was William Dean Howells who called Mark Twain "the sole, the incomparable, the Lincoln of our literature . . . the very marrow of Americanism."

★ EMILY DICKINSON AND EDWIN MARKHAM

Walt Whitman and Mark Twain were of their time authentic spokesmen of the vigor and failings of democratic society. No one could have been more unlike them than Emily Dickinson, the sheltered recluse who wrote her hundreds of poems in a private world of the spirit that had no direct association with the shrinking frontier, the new metropolis, or even the sprawling factory towns of her own New England. It is true that she saw far beyond the narrow horizons of her own personal life and was well aware of the outside world, but she rarely ventured into the market place. Unknown to her own generation, it was left to a later age to discover her as an authentic poetic genius.

The other poets of the day were lesser figures, but a number of those writing toward the close of the century mirrored the changing times. Their mood was one of questioning and growing revolt against the consequences of an industrial expansion that seemed to be progressively widening the gulf between the rich and the poor. They seldom reached a wide audience and except for scattered verses in the anthologies are not much read today.

A poem that is an exception to such a generalization is "The Man With the Hoe," inspired by Millet's painting, in which Edwin Markham voiced in vigorous tones his warning against the continued exploitation of labor, not only on the farm but even more in factory and mine:

> Bowed by the weight of centuries he leans
> Upon his hoe and gazes on the ground,
> The emptiness of ages in his face,
> And on his back the burden of the world . . .
> Through this dread shape the suffering ages look;
> Time's tragedy is in that aching stoop;
> Through this dread shape humanity betrayed,
> Plundered, profaned and disinherited,
> Cries protest to the Judges of the World,
> A protest that is also prophecy.

★ HOWELLS AND THE NEW REALISM

Toward the end of the nineteenth century, and well on into the twentieth, there was no figure in American letters so generally honored as William Dean Howells. His own novels introduced a new note of realism into American literature, and even more importantly, he welcomed and encouraged many young writers who were breaking away from traditional and conventional forms. Greatly influenced by Tolstoi, Turgenev, and the French realists, Howells believed that literature should look to "the work-worn, care-worn, brave kindly face" of the everyday world rather than "the romantic, the bizarre, the heroic." Convinced also that fiction should be a great civilizing force, he became at once the historian of the commonplace and a crusader for social justice.

Neither the realism nor the crusading of Howells, however, had a very sharp cutting edge. His social novels of the 1880's and 1890's reflected the rise of capitalism and its effects on modern society. No one painted the contemporary scene with greater fidelity. But his own hopeful temperament led him always to emphasize what he cheerfully called "the more smiling aspects of life that are the more American." He avoided the ugly and the unduly depressing, and he treated everything concerning sex gingerly. Nevertheless, he was alive to the main currents of the age, courageously took his stand against exploitation and injustice, and sympathized with all those movements for reform that were beginning to stir the country. In *The Rise of Silas Lapham* he wrote shrewdly of the career of a self-made man against the background of Boston society; in *A Hazard of New Fortunes* he told a story of New York life in which he introduced the somber note of industrial strife for almost the first time in American literature.

His own social views were most expressly stated in his utopian novel *A Traveller from Altruria* which set forth a mild Fabian socialism. Its constant emphasis is upon the extent to which the America of his day worshipped material prosperity and ignored the unequal distribution of its benefits. "I don't think there is any doubt," he has one of his characters say, "but the millionaire is now the American ideal. It isn't very pleasant to think so, even for people who have got on, but it can't very hopefully be denied. It is the man with the most money who now takes the prize in our national cake-walk."

His books invariably showed the highest qualities of literary craftsmanship, and if they did not always penetrate too deeply beneath the surface they could not be matched for their verisimilitude and sharp delineation of character. Howells' reputation began to wane somewhat even before the end of the century, but his role as dean of American letters was enthusiastically recognized at a dinner on his seventy-fifth birthday in 1912 by none other than President Taft.

"I have traveled here from Washington," Taft stated, "to do honor to the greatest living American writer and novelist. Easily at the head of living literary men of the nation, Mr. Howells is entitled, on this celebration of his seventy-fifth birthday, to this tribute of respect."

This was, however, an older generation honoring a man who had himself long since confessed that he was growing old—"tired easily, mind as well as body; I am losing my incentive." But whereas Howells himself became convinced that he was "comparatively a dead cult with my statues cut down and the grass growing over them in the pale moonlight," it may well be that future generations will turn with appreciation to the finely written novels of this author who stood at the dividing point between the new and old in American literature.

Among the young writers who came to see Howells and were greatly aided by his encouragement was Hamlin Garland. This "son of the middle border," as he would later entitle his autobiography, never really fulfilled the early promise of his writing during the 1880's. While he had sincerity and an evangelical passion, there was little grace to his style. Nevertheless, his grimly realistic stories of life on midwestern farms were a significant contribution to the literature of the day. In *Main-Travelled Roads,* published in 1891, he depicted in somber and realistic hue, with little of the afterglow of color and beauty that he would later give to the story of his own boyhood, the harsh, unremitting toil of the farm:

> The Main-travelled road in the West (as everywhere), is hot and dusty in summer, and desolate and drear with mud in fall and spring, and in winter the winds sweep across it; but it does sometimes cross a rich meadow where the songs of the larks and bobolinks and blackbirds are tangled. Follow it far enough, it may lead past a bend in the river where the water laughs eternally over its shallows. Mainly it is long and weariful, and has a dull little town at one end and a home of toil at the other. Like the main-travelled road of life it is traversed by many classes of people, but the poor and the weary predominate.

The realism that Garland applied in writing of rural life was adapted to the urban world by Stephen Crane. This young writer, who was also welcomed by Howells, at whose home he once dined respectfully in a borrowed suit, is perhaps best known for *The Red Badge of Courage.* This was a Civil War story in which Crane described the reaction of men under fire—their fears, their cowardice, their bravery—with startling realism even though he had himself never had such an experience. It was in *Maggie: A Girl of the Streets,* however, that he most clearly foreshadowed a later trend. Writing with blunt and startling honesty of the brutalizing effect of life in the city on a young girl, he did not hesitate to deal candidly with such a social issue as prostitution, for all the outraged horror of the conventional-minded.

Realism—characterized by Aldrich as a "miasmic breath blown from the slums"—was to become more generally characteristic of American literature with the turn of the century when it was re-enforced by the work of a new, naturalistic school owing much to Zola and other French novelists. Its followers portrayed the individual in modern society as the almost helpless victim of mechanistic forces which he could neither control nor influence. Theodore Dreiser published his *Sister Carrie* in 1900, first of a long line of novels; Frank Norris wrote *The Octopus* in 1901, a memorable story of California farmers crushed within the tentacles of the railroad that completely dominated their lives; three years later with *The Jungle* Upton Sinclair began a writing career that extended past the middle of the twentieth century; and Jack London won both popularity and critical acclaim with his Darwinian glorification of force in *The Sea Wolf* and *The Call of the Wild*.

★ HENRY JAMES

While these authors dealt vigorously with the varied aspects of an American scene that they knew intimately and well, Henry James, whose novels cover a period from the 1870's through the early 1900's, sought escape from the strident democracy that pressed too closely upon him by living abroad. The crudities, vulgarities, and acquisitive instincts of his fellow countrymen deeply depressed him, and from his ivory-towered vantage point in England, he often drew an ironic picture of American travelers whose cultural deficiencies stood out glaringly against the age-old background of Europe. It has been said that as a novelist James would have been greatly improved "by a few whiffs from the Chicago stockyards," but that would have made him a different writer altogether. His world was largely a world of high society, and he wrote about the intricate personal relationships of the men and women who inhabited it with both keen psychological insight and the most delicate and superb artistry.

A major theme in his writing was the relationship between America and Europe and many of his best novels dealt with this "international situation." Again and again he posed the problem of American innocence—often personified by the young American girl—confronting the sophistication, the guile, and the corruption of Europe. For all his residence abroad and often critical attitude toward his own country, James remained fundamentally American in attitude and spirit.

He was a prolific writer—novels, short stories, criticism—and opinion will always differ as to which were his most important books. Among them would certainly be included, however, *The American, Daisy Miller,* and *The Portrait of a Lady* among his earlier novels dealing with the problem of the expatriate in Europe, the eerie short story *The Turn of the Screw,* and in later years *The Ambassadors* and *The Wings of the Dove*. He was more of a writer's writer than a popular author.

There are many other writers that might be noted. Two quite disparate figures that were highly popular were Bret Harte and George W. Cable. And apart from the novelists, a number of historians and biographers were winning distinction in their more specialized branches of literature. Henry Adams, who was later to become even better known through *The Education of Henry Adams,* wrote his *History of the United States* in this period, and Frederick Jackson Turner first published his influential essay on "The Significance of the Frontier in American History" in 1893.

★ THE ADVANCE IN HIGHER EDUCATION

Paralleling the rise of such authentic new voices in American literature, there was widespread ferment throughout the intellectual world in the latter decades of the nineteenth century. Fresh currents were disturbing traditional patterns of thought and the horizons of knowledge were being steadily pushed back. The colleges and universities had a first part in these developments. The progress that was being made in popular education (as previously discussed) was more than matched by that in the field of higher education. The actual expansion in this area—the number of colleges and universities rose from 350 to 500 between 1878 and 1898 and their enrollment from 58,000 to 100,000—was not nearly so important as the new spirit animating the academic world. Research, study, and writing in a score of different fields which embraced the humanities, the new social studies, and the physical sciences had taken on entirely new dimensions by the century's close.

"Nothing more strikes a stranger who visits American universities," James Bryce wrote in 1888, "than the ardour with which the younger generation has thrown itself into study, even kinds of study which will never win the applause of the multitude."

This activity throughout the entire field of higher education and the broad realms of academic scholarship was being fostered and promoted by an unusual group of great college presidents. Charles W. Eliot at Harvard, Daniel Coit Gilman at Johns Hopkins, James B. Angell at Michigan, William Rainey Harper at Chicago, Nicholas Murray Butler at Columbia, Andrew D. White at Cornell—these are the enduring names associated with a period which continues to stand out pre-eminently in the whole history of intellectual America.

One interesting and important feature of higher education in these years was the mounting interest in education for women. A few private colleges had pioneered with coeducation before the Civil War, and the foundation of Vassar in 1865 marked the beginnings of the movement for special women's colleges. While the latter were soon to include Bryn

Mawr, Smith, Mount Holyoke, and Radcliffe (associated with Harvard), the acceptance of coeducation in the great state universities of the Midwest and West was to prove even more significant for women students and scholars. By the century's close it was reported that four out of every five colleges and universities throughout the country were prepared to accept women. Experience had demonstrated—in spite of the contemporary misgivings of Victorian society—that young men and young women could take the same courses and compete on equal terms. As President Angell told a visiting English social worker, none of the young ladies at the University of Michigan "had found the curriculum too heavy for their physical endurance."

The changes in college curricula were in the direction of an ever-widening choice of courses. President Eliot had taken the epochal step of introducing the elective system at Harvard and students there were encouraged to branch out from the traditional studies in the classics and philosophy to courses in literature and modern languages, social studies, and laboratory courses in the physical and biological sciences. Harvard's example was followed by other colleges, and the elective system soon became almost universal.

Graduate education was an even more revolutionary development. Johns Hopkins, founded in Baltimore in 1876, led the way in this field and patterned its course of study largely on the experience of the German universities, where hundreds of young Americans were studying in the 1880's. It rapidly began to attract an array of young scholars who were to make the most notable contributions to the world of learning—Woodrow Wilson, John Dewey, Josiah Royce, Frederick Jackson Turner, and John R. Commons, among scores of others. Harvard and Yale, Columbia, Chicago (which had been created almost overnight in 1892 through the beneficence of John D. Rockefeller), and a number of the state universities were now inspired to give more emphasis to graduate work, and advanced degrees gradually became the essential qualification for all university teaching. The whole pattern of higher education changed with the availability of more highly trained scholars and their insistence upon rigid standards of work at every level.

There were comparable developments in the professional schools—in teacher-training colleges, in medicine, in engineering, and in law. Perhaps most important was the transformation of the medical schools, where Johns Hopkins and Harvard were again the leaders. For the first time they began to insist upon a liberal arts college degree for their entering students and provided a three-year course of study which included both laboratory and clinical work. Somewhat lagging for a time in these developments in professional training were the law schools. Until after the turn of the century they rarely required entrance examinations (Harvard and Columbia were notable exceptions to this generalization) and offered only two years of study. But they gradually tightened up on their standards and introduced the case method in the general study of law.

The rapid development of both graduate and professional schools was accompanied by a great increase in the number of students enrolled. Between 1878 and 1898, for example, those in the nonprofessional graduate schools rose from a little over 500 to more than 5,000. At the same time great improvements were effected in the physical plant of these institutions, especially in the case of libraries, as a result of funds largely contributed through private benefactions. Scholars and scientists also began to pool their knowledge as they had never before been able to do. The last quarter of the nineteenth century saw the formation of countless new learned societies—the American Historical Association, the American Physical Society, the Modern Language Association, the Geological Society, the American Society of Electrical Engineers, the American Psychological Society.

"Amply equipped for the first time with tools of research-laboratories, instruments of precision, libraries, museums, observatories, hospitals," the historian Arthur S. Schlesinger has written, "scholars and scientists in the United States were enabled to make a contribution to the world's learning comparable to that of the first nations in Europe."

★ NEW CURRENTS OF THOUGHT

Under the impact of such research and study, and in reaction to the sharp changes effected in American society through technological and industrial advance, minds were in transition off college campuses as well as on them. Philosophers and educators, historians and political scientists, economists and sociologists were inspiring a new approach to the problems of society. There was everywhere a questioning of accepted values and an eager search for new means of adaptation to a rapidly changing economic and social environment.

The evolutionary theories of Charles Darwin had a tremendous influence in leading to such questionings of man's place in the world, in arousing conflict between science and religion, and in the development of what was called Social Darwinism. In the field of philosophy, William James, the brother of Henry James, advanced the ideas that were to take shape and form as pragmatism. A long line of social critics, from Henry George to Thorstein Veblen, assailed the doctrines of laissez faire and in some instances called for far-reaching reforms in the entire structure of American society.

The theory of evolution struck a hard blow at conventional religious ideas and called for an entirely new interpretation of the Biblical story. The concepts of "natural selection," "struggle for existence," and "survival of the fittest" could hardly be approved by fundamentalists. They obdurately refused to accept them or the new historical criticism of the Bible and waged unceasing war against evolution for many years. More liberal thinkers, however, soon found ways to reconcile religion and science. Among them the historian and popular lecturer, John Fiske, was immensely influential in developing the thesis that evolution was actually a marvelous proof of the divine will of Providence. It demonstrated, he wrote, the long travail whereby God had finally brought to consummation His greatest handiwork, the human soul.

Darwinism also had its influence on more abstract phases of philosophical thought. It is impossible here to go into the interplay of ideas that reflected this, or such other aspects of contemporary American philosophy as the influence of Hegelianism in the writings of Josiah Royce, foremost among American idealists. The growth of pragmatism, so generally associated with William James, psychologist as well as philosopher, nevertheless had an impact that can hardly be ignored. It turned away from abstractions and fixed principles and was largely concerned with facts and action. "The true is the name of whatever proves itself to be good in the way of belief," James wrote, "and good, too, for definite, assignable reasons." And another time: "The ultimate test for us of what truth means is the conduct it dictates or inspires. . . . The effective meaning of any philosophical position can always be brought down to some particular consequence."

In oversimplified form such statements seemed to mean that whatever worked was good and true. Such concrete, realistic thinking had an immense appeal to the American spirit. Moreover, in sustaining a basic belief in democracy and in upholding the life of action, this "philosophy of practicality" re-enforced all the popular beliefs of a people naively certain of their own great destiny.

The basic concepts of William James were carried forward in the 1890's and into the new century by John Dewey who developed them into his own system of instrumentalism. Even less interested than James in the abstract, he sought the application of pragmatic principles in attempting to govern life which should not be accepted passively, according to his views, but could be shaped and altered by man. Dewey was a critic of the prevailing system of laissez faire and a vigorous proponent of reform, but his greatest influence was in the field of education. He was convinced that the schools could be made into effective instruments to promote democracy and social justice, and he became the great champion of educational "progressivism." These ideas were to become the cause of continuing and often bitter controversy in educational circles for many years, and their reverberations had not wholly subsided in the mid-twentieth century.

★ SOCIAL DARWINISM

Well before the full development of either pragmatism or instrumentalism, the views of another philosopher, the Englishman Herbert Spencer, had exercised both directly and indirectly a remarkable influence on American thinking through his interpretation of Darwinism in social terms. Spencer found in the evolution of society and social institutions a parallel to the biological evolution of man—the same competitive struggle and the same survival of the fittest. Moreover, Spencer believed—and such American disciples as John Fiske enthusiastically supported him—that social evolution constituted not merely change but progress and would ultimately lead to the disappearance of evil and immorality.

Social Darwinism, so appealing to the American spirit, was widely preached and widely accepted. It fortified the laissez faire concepts to which business was so thoroughly committed and also the Gospel of Wealth as set forth by such men as Andrew Carnegie. The application of evolutionary ideas to economic practice, postulating the survival of the most fit in the struggle for business success, obviously precluded any interference by government. William Graham Sumner, sociologist and political economist, became one of the foremost proponents of this realistic acceptance of Social Darwinism. He opposed everything in the way of government aid for the poor, had only scorn for reformers who would seek to make over society, and believed that the rich were the rightful products of natural selection.

"Society needs first of all to be free from these meddlers—that is, to be left alone," Sumner wrote in vigorous attack upon all reformers, "Here we are, then, once more back at the old doctrine—laissez-faire. Let us translate it into blunt English, and it will read, Mind Your Own Business. It is nothing but the doctrine of liberty. Let every man be happy in his own way."

His individualism and his consistency carried him at times beyond what his fellow conservatives were willing to accept or approve. Sumner opposed tariff protection as a handout for big business which could no more be justified than special help for farmers, workingmen, or the poor. Still, he had few rivals as an outstanding defender of the existing order in the terms first advanced by Herbert Spencer.

★ CRITICISM AND DISSENT

The Social Darwinists by no means had everything their own way in the field of social debate. From the 1870's on the voice of protest was raised, frequently and often eloquently, against these concepts that shored up laissez faire and an acquisitive society. One earlier dissenter was Henry George, economist and reformer, who completely rejected everything about Social Darwinism and expressed his basic view of the course of American economic development in the title of his most important book, *Progress and Poverty*.

Vividly describing the shocking contrast between the ever-increasing concentration of wealth in the hands of the few and the economic distress of the great masses of the poor, George gave both an analysis and a solution of this overriding problem. He believed the whole trouble stemmed from a system of land ownership that enabled property owners to profit from the increasing social value of the land without necessarily doing anything themselves to improve it. They were not entitled to this unearned increment, he argued, and it should be returned to the people whose presence in the community had accounted for the land's increase in value. This was to be done through a "single tax" on land. George was convinced that it would minimize the difference between the poor and the rich, make all other taxes unnecessary, and usher in a new golden age. *Progress and Poverty* was written so persuasively that it had great influence, not only in this country but throughout the world. Even though the single tax was never adopted, George's ideas gave an impetus to economic and social reform which continued well into the twentieth century.

Even more widely read in the 1890's was Edward Bellamy's *Looking Backward*. This popular utopian romance, published in 1888, was in effect a plea for the radical reform of American society through a system of what was virtually state socialism. Bellamy accepted the growth of trusts and monopoly as a necessary phase of economic development, but he then proceeded in his idyllic description of what society might be like in the year 2000, to carry this development through to its logical conclusion. One gigantic state-controlled trust would govern the entire economy. The wage system was abolished in his utopia, every man and woman served in an all-inclusive national labor force, and payment was made for their work through equal credit cards that were exchangeable for whatever goods or services the recipient desired. The result was a society in which security, comfort, and happiness replaced the grim struggle for existence.

While such a socialistic panacea appeared to run counter to every tenet of American individualism, Bellamy wrote so well and gave such a delightful picture of the world in the year 2000 that *Looking Backward* not only sold in the hundreds of thousands, but inspired the creation from coast to coast of Nationalist clubs designed to carry its program of reform into effect. The Bellamyites never used the word "socialism," which had connotations highly repugnant to the average American, but nevertheless urged public ownership of railroads and utilities and a host of other socialistic measures.

Without advancing any such definite reform as either George or Bellamy, Henry Demarest Lloyd was another contemporary writer who took up the problems of an industrial society. His *Wealth Against Commonwealth* was a forerunner of the muckraking literature of the early 1900's, factually demonstrating just what was happening to our economy as a result of the application of laissez faire philosophy. Lloyd took the Standard Oil Company as his example of the unhappy consequences of trust-building, but drew from a study of Rockefeller's techniques and practices a much broader lesson of the ill effects of such concentration of economic power.

The sociologist Lester Ward was still another rebel against the consequences of laissez faire. He flatly asserted his conviction, in *The Psychic Factors of Civilization,* published in 1893, that competition in the economic sphere, far from assuring the survival of the fittest, often had a quite opposite effect. Without adopting any socialist panacea for the ills of society, he was a foremost advocate of economic planning. He was prepared to welcome the intervention of government in controlling monopoly. He believed that in the long run only broader controls throughout the entire economic sphere could assure the great masses of the people of either security or liberty.

These constant re-evaluations of contemporary society and the incessant questioning of its philosophic bases, whether by the Social Darwinists or by their critics, were a natural consequence of the vast changes wrought by a new industrial order. In this age of vast manufactures, growing cities, millionaires, and paupers, older values appeared to be in constant danger. "We call ourselves the masters of machinery," wrote the Congregational minister Josiah Strong, "are we quite sure that machinery is not mastering us?" "What shall we do with our great cities?" asked another contemporary. "What will our great cities do with us?" And Woodrow Wilson, a professor at Princeton University, observed that "haste, anxiety, preoccupation, the need to specialize and make machines of ourselves, have transformed the once simple world."

This was in the 1880's and 1890's, not the twentieth century. Later generations have often looked back upon the latter decade as the Golden

'Nineties or the Gay 'Nineties. They were actually years of harsh depression among the farmers and embittered industrial strife for the workers, as well as a period marked by the ferment of new ideas and intellectual questioning. Whether in the field of literature, where the new realism was replacing the genteel tradition, or of philosophy and social criticism, where pragmatism and a new spirit of reform were coming into vogue, dynamic changes were foreshadowed in American thought and life that would only come to full fruition with the new century.

CHAPTER VIII

The Political Scene

★ POLICIES AND BUSINESS

"No period so thoroughly ordinary had been known in American politics," Henry Adams once wrote of the post-Civil War era, "since Christopher Columbus first disturbed the balance of American society."

There were many other contemporary observers to confirm this caustic view, and historians have almost universally agreed that during these years something like a low point was reached in the evolution of political democracy. Once Republican policy toward the South had been settled by Grant's election to the presidency in 1868, there would be no real consideration of the fundamental issues confronting the country until 1896. A great deal was made of tariff policy, the currency, civil service reform, and pensions for Civil War veterans, but the relationship between the growing power of business and traditional democratic principles was largely ignored. Elections were little more than periodical struggles between the "ins" and the "outs." Moreover, there is slight reason to believe that American history during this politically barren era would have been importantly affected by any shift in the political complexion of the successive administrations. Whether Republicans or Democrats were in office made little difference. The few legislative acts of any significance—such as the Interstate Commerce Act and the Sherman Anti-Trust Act—were not a consequence of party policy, but calculated gestures to appease public opinion on the part of a Congress highly reluctant to depart from the prevailing principles of laissez faire.

Presidential campaigns awoke widespread interest and excitement. The era was one of flamboyant oratory, enthusiastic flag waving, industrious band playing, and gaudy torchlight parades. The two major parties co-operated in putting on a grand show every four years, but the issues dragged out for public debate were generally superficial. Neither Republicans nor Democrats had the courage to take a decisive stand on the possible regulation or control of monopoly, the plight of the farmers, the status of industrial labor, or the emerging problems of foreign policy. The issue was squarely drawn between the minority rule of privilege and the democratic aspirations of the great masses of the people in 1896; until that great struggle, elections were largely sham battles.

In part a cause and in part a consequence of this state of affairs was the mediocrity of political leadership. There were no Clays or Calhouns or Websters, let alone a Lincoln, to debate what were the really important controversial questions. There were as yet no Bryans, La Follettes, Roosevelts, or Wilsons. The succession of presidents from Grant through McKinley (with the possible exception of Cleveland) never exercised any real qualities of leadership and scarcely made a mark on history. And the men who sat in the Senate or the House remained representatives of the principalities and powers in the world of business, or spoilsmen entirely engrossed in the plums of office, rather than spokesmen for the people who sent them to Washington. There were exceptions to such a general indictment of course, men of integrity and social conscience, but the adjective "ordinary" could be applied to the general run of politicians quite as accurately as to the period's political manifestations.

James G. Blaine, the most popular figure of the day, stood only for partisanship and was not above accepting favors from the railroad interests he so warmly defended. The senior senator from New York, the elegant, showy Roscoe Conkling, epitomized the cynical attitude of the spoilsman, scornfully dismissing all advocates of reform as "the man-milliners, the dilettanti and carpet knights of politics." His understudy, "Me Too" Platt, was even more unprincipled, devious and furtive in all the ways of political chicanery. And then there were Senator Quay, Pennsylvania's expert legislative juggler, and Senator Foraker, whose personal political machine became the "Ohio Gang."

The explanation for the role played by such men was found in the domination of big business and the extent to which the railroad magnates, the industrial overlords, and the financial tycoons were able to see to it that members of Congress were their henchmen. They exercised a controlling influence in the high councils of both major parties and cared little for meaningless labels. "The sugar trust is democratic in a democratic state and republican in a republican state," its creator declared. Concentrated wealth had become the fount of political as well as economic power, and never was America more nearly transformed into an unabashed plutocracy.

Wrote Frederick T. Martin, a member of this hierarchy of wealth who had become highly critical of his own class in society:

> It matters not one iota what political party is in power or what President holds the rein of office. We are not politicians, or public thinkers; we are the rich; we own America; we got it, God knows how, but we intend to keep it if we can by throwing all the tremendous weight of our support, our influence, our money, our political connections, our purchased Senators, our hungry Congressmen, and our public-speaking demagogues, into the scale against any legislation, any political platform, any Presidential campaign, that threatens the integrity of our estate.

Some politicians were sufficiently honest and candid to admit frankly that their major concern was the interest of the business community rather than that of the people as a whole. They believed in the rule of privilege, sometimes mitigated by the Gospel of Wealth, and forthrightly took the attitude that they owed nothing to the public, their primary obligation being to safeguard railroads, industrial monopolies, and utility corporations from any control or regulation. Accepting the thesis that government existed primarily to protect, encourage, and fortify business, they wore the collar of business with a stubborn pride.

★ PRESIDENTIAL ELECTIONS

Grant had been elected President in 1868 when the Republicans, fearful of the possible rise of a resurgent Democratic party, had nominated the great war hero as the best possible vote getter whose services they could command. It was an eminently shrewd move. The colorless and inconsequential Horatio Seymour, named by the Democrats, had little chance against the folk-hero which Grant had already become. When the votes were counted, the Republicans had carried all but eight states. They had consolidated their hold upon both the presidency and Congress and were to remain in power for another sixteen years.

Yet the remarkable aspect of this campaign was not that Grant was elected, but that with such a weak candidate, the Democrats made as good a showing as they did. For Grant's victory was far from being the overwhelming triumph it appeared to be. His popular majority was only 300,000 out of a total of six million, and this included the Negro vote in the South. His sweep in the electoral college was largely owing to Republican control of the states undergoing reconstruction. The party that had so recently been that of secession and rebellion was far from eliminated in national politics.

Subsequent elections would also show how closely the country was divided in its political allegiance. While Grant was re-elected four years later by an even greater majority in the electoral college than in 1868, the Democrats' inept nomination of Horace Greeley in the hope of profiting from a split between radicals and liberals within the Republican party made this almost inevitable. To this and later elections we shall return, but it may be noted at this point that not until 1896 would the Republicans again obtain a popular majority. They won three out of the five intervening elections, but in one instance by the narrowest possible plurality and in two cases with an actually smaller popular vote than that given the Democratic candidate. Their political supremacy was far more precarious—even disregarding the two Democratic victories scored by Cleveland in 1884 and 1892—than the returns of the electoral college would suggest.

★ THE GRANT ADMINISTRATIONS

Although Grant came into office on a wave of popular enthusiasm as "the Savior of the Union," he was to prove to be one of the most sorry failures as President that the country has ever known. The qualities that had made him a great leader of men during the war seemed to evaporate in the unfamiliar atmosphere of the White House. Completely out of his element, he was an easy prey to the scheming importunities of political sycophants. In the exacting role of President, this "dumb, inarticulate man of genius" was discovered to be indirect and irresolute, prejudiced and vindictive, incapable of making sound judgments about either men or affairs. It was not only that he lacked any real political aptitude and let himself be used by men whose sole concern was their own interests. He was seemingly unable to understand the responsibilities and obligations of the presidency.

"Let us have peace," Grant declared in accepting his nomination, but the magnanimity of the victor at Appomattox became a foil for the vengefulness of the Radical Republicans. They interpreted his willingness to accept their views as a conversion. "He is a bolder man than I thought him," Stevens exclaimed; "now we will let him into the church." Grant followed without knowing where he was led; he was the victim of pressure groups whose real motivation he never dimly appreciated. His friends, to quote Henry Adams once again, "could never measure his character or be sure when he would act. They could never follow a mental process in his thought. They were not sure that he did think."

The most important aspect of Grant's first administration was of course the reconstruction policy being pursued in the South under the domination of the Radicals. Congress also wrestled with the currency issue, passing an act for the redemption of all government bonds in gold coin or its equivalent, a resumption act which provided for specie payments on all paper money, including the Civil War greenbacks. These victories for hard money advocates outraged the farmers and workers, as we have seen, but they met the needs of the business community. Taxes were also substantially reduced and existing tariff rates somewhat lowered. There was a beginning of the long struggle for some sort of civil service reform. Congress authorized a commission to investigate the situation, with the appointment of George W. Curtis, the able editor of *Harper's Weekly,* as its chairman—and then conveniently neglected to provide it with any funds.

This was not an inspiring record and other consequences of the President's political leadership were even more discouraging to liberal elements within as well as without his own party. The unhappy situation created by the reconstruction program, repeated surrender to the business interests demanding and receiving special favors from government, a scandalous affair involving operations in the gold market in which the President was at least indirectly involved, open encouragement of the spoils system, and, finally, spreading rumors of corruption in high government circles led to a widespread revolt against what came to be called "Grantism." A deep split in Republican ranks appeared to give the Democrats a very real chance for victory in the elections of 1872.

Breaking away from the party organization, a resurgent group of Liberal Republicans planned to put forward a candidate on whom both the reform element in their party and the Democrats could unite in common opposition to Grant. But their nomination of Horace Greeley, the hard-hitting Yankee editor of the New York *Tribune,* could not have been more ill-advised. For while Greeley was a militant champion of the underprivileged and a friend of reform, he was also a high tariff man, a life-long foe of the Democrats, and throughout the Civil War, he had been almost vindictively partisan. The Democrats accepted him, but with such reluctance that the results of the election were a foregone conclusion. A stronger candidate might have defeated Grant, but Greeley, carrying only six states, went down to ignominious defeat.

While the unfitness of the war hero for the presidency had already been demonstrated, his second administration was to plumb new depths of incompetence, irresponsibility, and corruption. With a bold-faced effrontery that shocked the country, Congress carried through with Grant's full approval one of the most egregious salary grabs on record. It doubled the President's pay and voted its own members a 50 per cent increase, retroactive for two years. Various undercover activities on the part of government officials also became gradually known. The disclosure of widespread fraud in the building of the Union Pacific, which its promotors had sought to conceal through generous grants of stock to key congressmen, gave rise to the notorious Crédit Mobilier scandals. The Secretary of War was found to have sold trading posts on Indian reservations for personal profit. Investigation revealed the operations of a Whiskey Ring in St. Louis that had defrauded the government, with the collusion of both Treasury officials and the President's private secretary, of millions of dollars in internal revenue.

The circumstances were very much the same as those that would lead to the Harding scandals half a century later. In the aftermath of war there was a startling letdown in both public and private morals. It was not only in the carpetbag governments in the South, as previously suggested, that corruption often ran rampant. Throughout the country local political machines, of which the best known was the Tweed Ring in New York, were mulcting the public without let or hindrance. Nor was the Union Pacific the only railroad or business concern that was looting the public treasury and bribing legislators. What was happening in Washington was a reflection of what was happening elsewhere, but the evidence of corruption among persons so closely associated with the national government was a shattering demonstration of how far things had gone.

"Let no guilty man escape," Grant declared when popular protest swelled to nationwide proportions. "Be especially vigilant against all who insinuate that they have high influence to protect them." But the Augean stables were never fully cleansed.

★ THE ELECTION OF 1876

The Democrats naturally hoped to capitalize on Republican corruption in the election of 1876, and their chances for capturing control of the government appeared to be further enhanced by hard times. The country had fallen on evil days, partly because of the extravagance and speculation that marked the Gilded Age, and there was everywhere severe economic distress. A financial panic had brought in its sorry wake price declines, farm mortgage foreclosures, business failures, dwindling factory production, wage cuts, and unemployment. From every point of view a change in administration seemed in order, with a complete repudiation of everything for which Grantism had come to stand.

The Republicans were again divided, this time into two camps known as the Stalwarts, who would have liked to see Grant run again, and the derisively named Halfbreeds who represented a faction supporting James G. Blaine. Neither group could nominate their candidate, and the convention finally chose Rutherford B. Hayes. He had three times served as Ohio's governor without hint of scandal, and his selection could be interpreted as indicating that the Republicans were seeking to turn over a new leaf. The Democrats had even more internal differences than their rivals, but they hopefully resolved them in the conviction that by avoiding the mistakes of 1872 they were certain to sweep the polls. Their candidate was Samuel J. Tilden who had proved himself to be an able administrator as governor of New York.

Both men were reform candidates. Born on an Ohio farm, Hayes had struggled hard to obtain an education, taken up the practice of law, served in the Civil War. Skillfully combining party loyalty with conscientious concern for the public welfare, he played a notable role in the postwar politics of his home state. His seriousness of purpose could be traced to his boyhood, when he had confided to his diary his determination "to use what means I have to acquire a character distinguished for energy, firmness, and perseverance."

Tilden had carved out quite a different career. The son of a storekeeper in New Lebanon, New York, he too had studied law and, moving to New York City, had become an outstanding corporation attorney and financier, building up one of the largest fortunes in the country. In spite of chronic ill health and a sensitive, aloof nature, he had become a power in politics. It was largely through his work in smashing the Tweed Ring that he was elected New York's governor as a vigorous advocate of reform and social justice.

There was a good deal of shrewd infighting during the campaign. Hayes sought particularly to win over the old Whig-minded southerners, while Tilden tried to hold the Solid South as well as northern Democrats in line. But the election of 1876 has a unique place in American history, not because of the personalities or tactics of the opposing candidates, but because of the disputed returns. Tilden won a popular majority and had apparently also obtained a majority in the electoral college. The Democrats enthusiastically celebrated their triumph. However, the votes of the three remaining carpetbagger states, Louisiana, Florida, and South Carolina (together with one vote in Oregon), were in question because of rival returns from Republican and Democratic election boards. If the disputed votes were awarded Hayes, he would win the contest by the close electoral college count of 185 to 184. The Republicans swung into action, telegraphing their boards in the doubtful states to hold the line, and declared that Hayes had won.

The election was thrown into Congress and amid wild talk of possible insurrection, it sought to meet this unprecedented crisis by setting up a special electoral commission made up of five senators, five representatives, and five justices of the Supreme Court. Dividing completely along partisan lines, the commission upheld by one vote the Republican contention that Hayes was the victor. For a time there was a question whether the Democrats would accept this verdict. There had been probable fraud on both sides in the disputed returns, but since Tilden had received a popular majority, the Democrats could hardly help feeling their man was the rightful president. A conference among party leaders, however, cleared the way for certifying Hayes' election.

While at the time it was believed that agreement had been reached on the basis of an earlier pledge by Hayes to withdraw the remaining federal troops from the South, adoption of a more generous policy toward southern Democrats was primarily responsible for their acquiescence in his election. Commitments were made in regard to political favors, patronage, and subsidies to southern railroads that seemed designed to bring to an end the embittered postwar feelings between North and South. They were not all to be kept. But while the Republicans would soon be again waving "the bloody shirt" in their political feuding with the Democrats, the truce enabled Hayes to take over the presidency without further opposition.

The nation had in this same year—1876—happily celebrated the centenary of national independence. It had cause for pride in this triumph of the principles of orderly government which had been adopted as the basis for our political system.

★ THE HAYES ADMINISTRATION

Hayes was most certainly an improvement over Grant. While he was neither a great leader nor an imaginative statesman, he was honest, an astute and skillful politician, and a reasonably able administrator. "I shall show a *grit* that will astonish those who predict weakness," he noted in his diary on taking office, and in a limited measure he did. He successfully brought to an end the final phase of military reconstruction in the South; as a convinced hard money man, he vigorously supported the movement for resumption of specie payments and combatted with at least partial success the drive for free silver (it was during his administration the Bland-Allison Act was passed), and he worked conscientiously for civil service reform.

Beyond such developments—and the surface was only scratched so far as civil service reform was concerned—there is actually little to record of his administration. In spite of severe depression, Hayes passively accepted all the implications of a laissez faire philosophy. But while he hardly advanced the cause of either democratic or economic reform in the face of the new industrial overlordship, his term of office was at least a respectable contrast with "the great barbecue" that had led to such flagrant exploitation of the nation's resources in the days of Grant.

★ GARFIELD AND ARTHUR

Hayes refused renomination in 1880 and internal dissension among the Republicans led to another quarrelsome division between Stalwarts and Halfbreeds. But this was only a temporary embarrassment; there was no real change in party alignments. The election came and went with the usual shadow-boxing over largely artificial issues. James A. Garfield, another Ohio politician with little more than his availability to recommend him, was brought forth as a dark horse Republican candidate and elected President over the even less impressive Democratic nominee, General Winfield Scott Hancock. After only a few months in office, Garfield was assassinated by a disappointed office seeker. Vice-President Chester A. Arthur then took his place in the White House.

A machine politician closely allied with the Stalwart faction in New York, there was nothing about Arthur's record to promise a constructive administration. It was both feared and expected that he would discourage further civil service reform and reopen the doors to all the practices that were associated with Grantism. Arthur, however, confounded his critics. He broke away from the spoilsmen, revealed an unexpectedly independent spirit, and staunchly supported Congress in the passage of a bill which for the first time provided a practical basis for civil service reform.

This latter measure, the Pendleton Act of 1883, placed under civil service regulations some 14,000—or more than 12 per cent—of the 110,000 employees then in government service and established a three-man Civil Service Commission. This was a modest start, but it pointed the way toward further improvement and the ultimate end of the spoils system as it had heretofore existed. Other than a new tariff law, so confused as a result of logrolling and lobbying that it was known as the "Mongrel Tariff," the Pendleton Act was about all that could be claimed for another undistinguished administration.

President Arthur himself was an impressive figure. Tall, well-built and handsome, with gorgeous sidewhiskers, always meticulously dressed, he could be described as would another incumbent of the White House some forty years later—Warren G. Harding—as "a man who looked like a President." He gave a dignity to his high office that it had not recently enjoyed and renewed old customs of generous hospitality that gave a new tone to Washington social life. A man of varied interests, with the reputation among other nonpolitical attributes of being the best fly fisherman in the country, Arthur was always well-liked by his associates if not too popular with the public.

These personal qualifications were not enough to assure his leadership of the Republican party. His past associations continued to make him unacceptable to the more liberal reformist element; his support for civil service did not endear him to the regulars. Under these circumstances the next election found the Republicans passing him by and finally awarding the nomination to the man who had for long been their most popular leader—James G. Blaine.

★ "THE GENTLEMAN FROM MAINE"

The "gentleman from Maine" was in many ways the outstanding political leader of this entire period. While he never succeeded in attaining his lifelong ambition of the presidency, he completely overshadowed the Hayes, the Garfields, the Arthurs, and the Harrisons who did reach the White House. A past master at the art of politics, which he lived and breathed, he exercised a tremendous influence through his exceptional oratorical powers, political acumen, and a magnetism that evoked more personal loyalty and enthusiasm than any of his contemporaries of either party.

Blaine, however, stood for nothing very constructive. He accepted all the implications of the close alliance between the Republican party and big business and had a very easy conscience about the favors that business offered to cement that alliance. As was said of other members of Congress, in which Blaine served for many years, first as Speaker of the House and then as a member of the Senate, he may have been helping in his public role to make the desert blossom like the rose, but as a private citizen he was busily garnering the blossoms at handsome prices. A constant need for money to maintain his expansive way of life involved him in a number of very questionable transactions, and he was never able to clear himself completely of the charge of political corruption.

With his fine dark eyes and flashing smile Blaine was a marked man in any assembly. He dominated without giving the impression of domination. There was no resource of parliamentary strategy which was not at his command, and he exercised a wonderful control over any political gathering. He was generous and open-handed, had a memory that never forgot a face, and was always thoroughly charming. But these personal gifts were prostituted to the pursuit of his own political ambition. "When I want a thing," he once said, "I want it dreadfully."

Principle was all too easily sacrificed for expediency. While Blaine had a strong sense of the national destiny of America and would perform very real services to the country as Secretary of State under both Garfield and Harrison, no one more cynically kept alive sectional conflict by waving the bloody shirt in partisan appeal to the passions and prejudices of the Civil War. He was something more than a wholly selfish spoilsman, and yet his scruples were always conveniently elastic.

On one occasion that most famous of orators, Robert G. Ingersoll, grandiloquently referred to Blaine as the "Plumed Knight." In the hearts of millions of people, he remained the Plumed Knight through all the vicissitudes and disappointments of his spectacular career. He was viciously attacked by his political foes, and the scandals associated with his term as Speaker of the House were continually being revived, but he never lost his general popularity among the Republican rank-and-file.

★ THE ELECTION OF 1884

Blaine's opponent in the election of 1884 was a man of a quite different stripe. In Grover Cleveland, the Democrats had found a candidate who stood for something and who had vigorous strength of character. Trained as a lawyer, he had been a county sheriff, a reform mayor in Buffalo, and an able governor of New York. His stubborn honesty stood in sharp contrast with the compliant conscience of Blaine. With such a nominee, the Democrats were able to win the support of the reformist elements among Republicans—former Liberal Republicans who were equally opposed to Stalwarts and Halfbreeds and were now called the Mugwumps. Unable to accept Blaine, they came out strongly in Cleveland's behalf. The Democrats at long last saw the dawn of political preferment.

The campaign was bitter and hard-fought, largely on the plane of personalities. The old charges of corruption were brought up against Blaine, with special reference to some correspondence in which he had made the guilty statement, "burn this letter." It was revealed that Cleveland had an illegitimate child, which he admitted with forthright candor, and all the changes were rung upon this moral lapse.

The Democrats sang in their torchlight parades:

> Blaine, Blaine, James G. Blaine,
> The continental liar from the State of Maine
> *Burn this letter!*

And when the Republicans countered:

> Ma! Ma! Where's my pa?

they gleefully answered

> Gone to the White House,
> *Ha! Ha! Ha!*

The personal scandal nevertheless somewhat disconcerted the reformers who had thrown their support behind Cleveland. They met the issue by pointing to a significant contrast between their candidate's unfortunate mistake and the backsliding attributed to his rival.

"From what I hear," one of the Mugwumps said at a meeting hastily summoned to meet the crisis, "Mr. Cleveland has shown high character and great capacity in public life, but in private life his conduct has been open to question, while, on the other hand, Mr. Blaine in public life has been weak and dishonest while he seems to have been an admirable husband and father. The conclusion I draw . . . is that we should elect Mr. Cleveland to the public office which he is so admirably qualified to fill and remand Mr. Blaine to the private life he is so eminently fitted to adorn."

The voters may not have thought things out along these lines, but this is exactly what they did. Blaine saw the prize snatched from his eager grasp, and Cleveland became the first successful Democratic candidate since Buchanan. Moreover, while Cleveland was to be defeated for re-election four years later, he again reversed the field in 1892 and was then chosen for a second term.

★ GROVER CLEVELAND

Although Cleveland favored tariff reduction and recognized the dangers inherent in monopoly, he was basically conservative in his general attitudes and almost completely lacking in imagination. He was not the man to lead any crusade against the rule of privilege. "I feel . . . that the vast business interests of the country," the ineffable Jay Gould wrote him shortly after his election, "will be entirely safe in your hands." Cleveland lived up to Gould's trust in his policy toward business, but there was nevertheless no question of his personal and political integrity, his sound moral judgment on men and affairs, his stubborn determination to pursue those policies that he felt best for the country. He wore no man's collar. When Cleveland defended industry it was because of his unshakable conviction that he was doing the right thing. It is perhaps slight praise of a President to single out honesty as an outstanding quality. Anyone aspiring to that high office might well be expected to be honest. But in a period when a Blaine could approach so close to the White House, this attribute had a significance that warranted special emphasis.

Cleveland's integrity was matched by a certain austerity in manner; he had none of Blaine's magnetism and social grace. He was a rough, outdoors man, anything but averse to a drink, and yet not given to easy conviviality. Large and heavily built—his two hundred and forty pounds were to set something of a record until William Howard Taft entered the White House—he had the appearance of a benevolent walrus. A drooping mustache hung down over a strong jaw which gave way to several fat, receding chins. He rarely smiled, although when he did so it completely transformed his rather immobile face. He was never the man to seek public acclaim for its own sake, to go out of his way to win popularity, or to deviate for some expedient advantage from the principles in which he believed. He obeyed the stern dictates of duty, as he felt God had revealed them to him, whatever the possible consequences. Cleveland sailed through American history, it has been said, "like a steel ship loaded with monoliths of granite."

The political events of his first administration centered about civil service reform, pensions, tariff revision, and fiscal policy. Cleveland fought valiantly against the spoilsmen, even though circumstances compelled him to make many political appointments, and he urged new legislation to expand the civil list. He took a strong stand against the greed of Civil War veterans, who were backed by all the political influence of the G.A.R., and in spite of his acceptance of a number of private pension bills, had the audacity to reject a great many more. When Congress adopted one measure that would have granted outright pensions to all veterans suffering disabilities, whether or not they had been incurred during the war, he risked his entire political future with his ringing veto. It was also during his administration that Congress passed the Interstate Commerce Act, but this was none of his doing.

Cleveland's greatest fight was for downward tariff revision. He admittedly knew little of this problem when he first entered the White House, but he soon became convinced that high rates were a mistaken policy, not only because there was no longer any real need for protection but because of the unusual circumstance of there being a mounting surplus in the national treasury. Something had to be done to cut down revenue so as to protect Congress from the temptation of reckless and corrupt extravagance and to protect the financial system. In his annual message to Congress in 1887 Cleveland took the bull by the horns. In the face of warnings to ignore so dangerous an issue, he bluntly demanded immediate tariff cuts regardless of high-spun ideas about protection or free trade. "It is a condition which confronts us," he stated, "not a theory."

★ THE HARRISON ADMINISTRATION

Congress failed to enact the tariff legislation that Cleveland demanded, and he thereupon insisted upon making it the principal issue in the presidential election of 1888. The Republicans seized upon it happily.

Having nominated the conservative Indiana lawyer Benjamin Harrison, a grandson of President William Henry Harrison, as their candidate, they campaigned vigorously not only for business support, but also for that of farmers and workers, on the ground that Cleveland's "free trade" policy would impoverish the country. Harrison was elected, but it was a very close call. He had a margin of only sixty-five ballots in the electoral college, and actually lagged 100,000 behind Cleveland in the popular vote.

Back in power with their conservative leadership strongly entrenched in Congress, the Republicans proceeded to deal with the tariff in their own way. Through the passage of the McKinley Act of 1890 they raised existing rates to new high levels, broadening and emphasizing protection in the name of "the safety and purity and permanency of our political system." The support that westerners gave this new measure was partly repaid by eastern votes for the Silver Purchase Act and the Sherman Anti-Trust Act, both passed this same year, but events were soon to demonstrate that this compromise on the silver issue and half-hearted gesture to control the trusts hardly placated the rising tide of agrarian opposition to Republican conservatism.

The problem of revenues over and above the government's real needs was met by the give-away appropriations of what came to be called "the billion dollar Congress." It opened wide the doors of the Treasury to the hungry veterans. "God help the surplus," was the exclamation of the new Pension Commissioner, and his boast—or lament—was to be fully justified. A new disability measure was so generous that even the G.A.R. was satisfied.

"While not just what we asked," its pension committee reported, "it is the most liberal pension measure ever passed by any legislative body in the world, and will place upon the rolls all of the survivors of the war whose conditions of health are not practically perfect."

Harrison was highly conscientious. However, he had almost no appreciation or understanding of what might be at stake in tariff and pension legislation and easily let himself be controlled by members of his party who knew just what they wanted and why they wanted it. A high tariff strengthened the bonds between the business community and the Republican party; pensions won the further support of the great army of war veterans. Nor did Harrison have the strength, if indeed any great inclination, to resist the pressure of other groups seeking to share in governmental bounty. He had nothing to do with passage of the Sherman Anti-Trust Act and made no real effort to see that it was enforced.

Few presidents have made a slighter impression on their own times or been more nearly forgotten by posterity than this "rather circumspect, erudite, self-willed, dainty little aristocrat." Enjoying the distinction of being the last bewhiskered Civil War general to sit in the White House, Harrison was greatly obsessed with the dignity of his position and tried to hold himself aloof from the rough and tumble of politics. He was a little pompous and a little cold. For all his goodwill a casually coined epigram, "a cheap coat makes a cheap man," betrayed a fundamental lack of sympathy and understanding for those elements of the population outside his own aristocratic circles.

★ CLEVELAND'S RETURN: CURRENCY AND THE TARIFF

In spite of such limitations Harrison was renominated by the Republicans in 1892, only briefly challenged by the aging and now rather pathetic Blaine. The Democrats again named Cleveland. His position had been greatly strengthened by the unpopularity of a tariff too high for even a protection-minded country, and the rising tide of agrarian protest, born of the unhappy situation in the agricultural West and South which has been already noted and to which we shall again return, further cut into Republican strength. With the candidate of the Populists polling a million votes, the Democrats were able to stage a decisive comeback marked by a plurality of nearly 400,000 over their Republican opponents. Cleveland found himself once again in the White House.

He was confronted, almost immediately after his second inauguration, with the bleak fact of economic depression. The panic of 1893 caused an epidemic of railroad, banking, and commercial failures even more disruptive of the national economy than the depression of the 1870's. Cleveland was prepared to renew his demand for a reduction in the tariff, but he first felt called upon to cope with a fiscal and currency crisis that he believed to be at least partly responsible for hard times.

He was quite as much a hard-money man as any Republican, fully convinced that temporizing with silver was weakening the currency, destroying business confidence, and causing a loss of gold to foreign countries (the cheaper money driving out the dearer) that was dangerously depleting the Treasury's reserves. Summoning a special session of Congress, he consequently called for immediate repeal of the Silver Purchase Act. Congress approved such a measure in October, 1893, but the gold reserves continued to shrink. Cleveland then felt compelled to call upon J. P. Morgan and other banking interests in New York for help. They loaned the Government $62,000,000 in gold, at least half obtained from foreign sources, and this move was so successful in restoring confidence that the further loss of reserves was halted. Cleveland was strongly criticized for going to Wall Street for aid (the bankers made a profit of some $7,000,000), but it was probably the only way in which the immediate financial crisis could have been met.

The President then took up the tariff, only to discover that on this issue he could not control Congress. The Senate so manhandled the bill for downward revision introduced with his approval that as ultimately passed in 1894 under the title of the Wilson-Gorman Act, only a nominal dent was made in the protective system built up so carefully over the past years. Nor were Republicans entirely responsible for the defeat of Cleveland's program. Democratic senators were no less concerned with safeguarding the industrial interests of the states they represented. The extent to which tariff reform as debated in political campaigns was a specious issue could hardly have been more clearly demonstrated.

Cleveland denounced the Wilson-Gorman Act as "party perfidy and party dishonesty." He declared that "the livery of Democratic tariff reform has been stolen and worn in the service of Republican protection." Nevertheless, he allowed the measure to become law without his signature.

There was one provision in the new bill, however, that had greater significance than any individual tariff rate. It incorporated a federal income tax. This levy did not represent what later generations would consider a very excessive burden. The rate was a flat 2 per cent on incomes over $4,000 a year. Nevertheless an income tax of any sort at once aroused the most violent opposition on the part of business interests, and they promptly challenged the law's constitutionality. When the issue was carried to the Supreme Court, the opposing lawyers vehemently assailed the whole idea as an unwarranted attack upon property. The principles underlying an income tax, Joseph H. Choate declared, were "communistic, socialistic—what shall I call them?—as populistic as ever have been addressed to any political assembly in the world."

Opponents of the measure found a completely sympathetic attitude among a majority of the learned brethren on the bench. A Supreme Court that had already given evidence of its acceptance of all the implications of a laissez faire philosophy through its decisions on both railroad regulation and antitrust suits was again prepared to do everything possible to safeguard property interests. Upon very narrow legal grounds, it declared the income tax unconstitutional in *Pollock* v. *Farmers Loan and Trust Company,* decided in 1895 by a five to four decision. Not until the sixteenth amendment was adopted two decades later was the government able to draw upon what has since become its principal source of revenue.

"The present assault upon capital," Associate Justice Field declared in a statement that was patently based upon his own social and economic views rather than constitutional principles, "is but the beginning. It will be but the stepping stone to others, larger and more sweeping, till our political contests will become a war of the poor against the rich." If there was some justification for his fears, the challenge of the people to the continued rule of privilege could hardly be answered by such a simple expedient as denying the government the power to tax incomes.

★ DEEPENING DEPRESSION

Apart from currency and tariff legislation, neither of which contributed materially to basic economic recovery, there was no more idea in the 1890's than in the 1870's of any direct government action to combat the continuing depression. Business and industry might collapse, banks fail, farm mortgages be foreclosed, millions of workers lose their jobs, but the general laissez faire attitude of the times precluded interference with what was considered the normal course of the economic cycle. The advisability of such a hands-off policy while the national economy gradually adjusted itself, whatever the immediate cost in human suffering, was not even questioned. Cleveland was conforming to accepted practice, as well as following his own conservative tendencies, in ignoring the depression except so far as fiscal policy might be affected.

The mid-1890's, however, were one of the most critical periods in domestic affairs through which the country has ever passed. Events appeared to be giving ever greater validity to Henry George's aphorism of progress *and* poverty. "From the same prolific womb of governmental injustice," cried the outraged Populists, "we breed the two great classes—tramps and millionaires." On the one hand Homestead and Pullman, the march of Coxey's army of unemployed on Washington; and on the other, Cleveland's deal with J. P. Morgan, and the Supreme Court—in a single year—emasculating the powers of the I.C.C., nullifying antitrust legislation in the Knight case, and blocking an income tax. These were the background and circumstances of the Populist revolt and the election of 1896.

CHAPTER IX

Populism and the Election of 1896

★ THE RISE OF POPULISM

If the election of 1896 provided the occasion for a final dramatic eruption of popular discontent, the tide of agrarian and labor revolt had been rising steadily. It was in 1891, the year before Cleveland's second election, that the dissident Farmers' Alliances, with some support from workers' organizations, began to coalesce with formation of the People's Party. As the political arm of Populism, it constituted a direct challenge to all those principles that Cleveland, no less than his Republican predecessors, was seeking to maintain in defense of a laissez faire economy and the overlordship of business and industry.

The aim of Populism was to assert the rights of the producing classes throughout the nation, win redress for their grievances, and break the hold of monopoly capitalism over the nation's economic life. The Populists were to throw their full weight behind the old agrarian demand for currency reform, insisting upon the imperative necessity for the free and unlimited coinage of silver, but this demand was more a symbol of what they sought than its real substance. Entering the presidential campaign of 1892 with their own candidate, General James B. Weaver, they adopted a ringing declaration of rights. It called for an end to government by vested interests, an end to protection and monopoly, an end to social privilege in all its forms. It demanded a return of political power to the plain people and a new rule of social justice. The Populist platform declared:

> We have witnessed for more than a quarter of a century, the struggles of the two great political parties for power and plunder, while grievous wrongs have been inflicted upon the suffering people. We charge that the controlling influences dominating both these parties have permitted the existing dreadful conditions to develop without serious effort to prevent or

> restrain them. Neither do they now promise us any substantial reform. They have agreed together to ignore, in the coming campaign, every issue but one. They propose to drown the outcries of a plundered people with the uproar of a sham battle over the tariff, so that capitalists, corporations, national banks, rings, trusts, watered stock, the demonetization of silver and the oppressions of the usurers may all be lost sight of. They propose to sacrifice our homes, lives and children on the altar of mammon; to destroy the multitude in order to secure corruption funds from the millionaires.

They had not elected their candidate in 1892. Nevertheless, in winning more than a million votes for him, they served notice upon the country that here was a determined and fighting third party. Conservatives who had been alarmed by their platform, which they assailed as little short of communism, could no longer ignore this strident voice of popular discontent. Moreover, the Populists were far from discouraged by their election showing. They promptly rallied their forces for an even more aggressive campaign in the mid-term elections in 1894. In that bleak year of discontent, which was described as the darkest the country had known for thirty years, they campaigned with a vigor that everywhere throughout the Midwest and South fanned the flames of unrest to even greater fury.

Populist orators carried their message of revolt to Grange meetings, farm picnics, county fairs, and political assemblies. Men and women who had driven long miles over dusty country roads from their lonely farms wildly applauded the speakers who told them that all their troubles stemmed from the grasping greed of eastern bankers and money lenders. The post-Civil War law that had demonetized silver in 1873 was called the most gigantic crime of this or any other age; the "gold-bugs" who insisted that the only sound currency was one based upon gold were hotly denounced. "We Are Mortgaged. All But Our Votes"—this was the slogan unfurled on Populist banners.

Among others who have borne witness to the fanatic fervor of the Populists and their emotional hysteria is William Allen White. Recalling in later years their campaign in 1894, he wrote:

> Sacred hymns were torn from their pious tunes to give place to words which deified the cause and made gold—and all its symbols, capital, wealth, plutocracy—diabolical. . . . Far into the night the voices rose—women's voices, children's voices, the voices of old men, of youths and maidens, rose on the ebbing prairie breezes, as the crusaders of the revolution rode home, praising the people's will as though it were God's will and cursing wealth for its iniquity.

It did not matter where reason lay in all this vehement discussion of the silver issue. A popular pamphlet of the day, *Coin's Financial School,* declared that the demonetization of silver was a crime because it had confiscated millions of dollars of property, made thousands of tramps, and "brought this once great republic to the verge of ruin, where it is now in imminent danger of tottering to its fall." Carried away by their feelings, the Populists again and again singled out gold as the personification of the enemy—of banking greed, of the oppressive policies of the railways, of the paralyzing grip of monopoly. Their voices may have been shrill, hysterical, and charged with emotion, but they were clamorous for public attention.

★ POPULIST LEADERS

The leaders of Populism were men—and women—of all sorts and kinds. There were sincere, impassioned reformers and political demagogues, plain dirt farmers overcome with a sense of grievance, and radical fanatics riding the crest of a popular revolt that they hoped perhaps to divert to their own ends. Many of them had been Greenbackers or supporters of earlier reform movements, bound together in a burning zeal to improve the lot of the underprivileged and the exploited. Although Populism had its lunatic fringe, its leaders also provided a healthy contrast to the general run of careful and cautious politicians who were so assiduously serving the interests of aggregated wealth.

The Populist presidential candidate of 1892, General Weaver, gave an air of respectability to the movement which not all his followers promoted. A man of about sixty, once nominee of the Greenbackers, he had a dignified and commanding presence which was accentuated by his impressive white hair. Even more influential as the author of the Populist platform was Ignatius Donnelly. Known to his fellow citizens of Minnesota as "the Sage of Nininger," he had a wider reputation as "the Prince of Cranks." There was almost no reform that Donnelly had not sponsored at one time or another, and among his literary effusions were a colorful account of *Atlantis: the Antediluvian World,* and a discursive elaboration of the Baconian theory, entitled *The Great Cryptogram,* in which he once and for all settled, at least to his own satisfaction, the question of Shakespearian authorship. Ready to take up any new cause with an enthusiasm that nothing could dampen, he threw himself heart and soul into Populism. His eloquence, wit, and humor made him a favorite speaker among farm audiences.

Then there were "Pitchfork Ben" Tillman and "Bloody Bridles" Waite. The former had been governor of South Carolina. A dark, savage-featured, irascible southern extremist, he campaigned for the Senate on a program of white supremacy and agrarian reform which whipped up immense enthusiasm among the poor whites of his state. "Send me to Washington," he shouted in one speech denouncing Cleveland, "and

I'll stick my pitchfork into his old ribs." David H. Waite was the Populist governor of Colorado, and a no less impassioned and violent defender than Tillman of what he declared were the interests of the people. His nickname was derived from a campaign statement that it was better "that blood should flow to the horses' bridles rather than that our liberties should be destroyed."

Kansas, however, furnished Populism with more leaders than any other state. Senator William A. Peffer, who had originally been a Republican, headed the new party's more conservative wing but nevertheless provided the stock figure for newspaper caricatures of the Populists because of a long, wavy beard which he continually combed with his fingers as he delivered his interminable, tedious, senatorial harangues. "A well-meaning, pinheaded, anarchistic crank" was one cruel characterization of this earnest, if somewhat confused, reformer.

"Sockless Jerry" Simpson, another famous figure, hardly deserved the name fastened upon him by a casual comment that while his opponents might wear silk socks he was quite content to wear none. Far from being the clown he was depicted, he was self-educated, well read, and a sincere proponent of Populism. He had himself been caught in mortgage foreclosure proceedings and thoroughly sympathized with the plight of the farmers.

Finally, there was the redoubtable Mary Ellen Lease, a powerful influence in Kansas, whose platform eloquence and lovely voice could hardly have contrasted more with her unfeminine appearance. Six feet tall, with a thick torso and heavy jowls, her hair invariably combed in an unlovely knot, a contemporary emphatically declared, "She had no sex appeal—none!" As she whirled across the Kansas plains calling upon the farmers "to raise less corn and more Hell," her enraptured audiences nevertheless saw her as an inspired goddess.

Looking out upon the strange and wonderful doings in his own state, William Allen White first won nationwide prominence by a notable editorial (later regretted) which he was to publish in the Emporia *Gazette* in 1896:

> What's the matter with Kansas?
>
> We all know; yet here we are at it again. We have an old moss-back Jacksonian who snorts and howls because there is a bathtub in the statehouse; we are running that old jay for governor. We have another shabby, wild-eyed, rattle-brained fanatic who has openly said in a dozen speeches that "the rights of the user are paramount to the rights of the owner"; we are running him for chief justice, so that capital will come tumbling over itself to get into the state.
>
> . . . Oh, this is a state to be proud of! We are a people who can hold up our heads. . . . Give the prosperous man the dickens! Legislate the

thriftless man into ease! Whack the stuffing out of the creditors! . . . Whoop it up for the ragged trousers; put the lazy, greasy fizzle who can't pay his debts on the altar, and bow down and worship him. Let the state ideal be high. What we need is not the respect of our fellow men, but the chance to get something for nothing. . . .

★ POLITICAL TIDES

The Populist revolt was in full swing as the presidential campaign of 1896 approached. For all the sarcasm of William Allen White and the attacks of eastern newspapers, the farmers of the Midwest were rallying determinedly behind the banners of free silver and social reform. They were incensed by the repeal of the Silver Purchase Act and embittered by what they considered Cleveland's surrender to eastern banking interests; they were indignant with the lax enforcement of both the Interstate Commerce Act and the Anti-Trust Act and felt all the more hopeless of redress for their grievances because of the conservative position of the Supreme Court. In the South discontent with existing conditions was forcing a radical reorientation of the Democratic party. The traditional control of the conservatives gave way as candidates for office found themselves compelled to accept the basic tenets of Populism to command any support from distressed farmers. Demagogic leaders who combined agrarian reform with a renewed appeal for white supremacy were in full control.

Eastern workingmen were also increasingly responsive to the new party's pledge to work for their interests. While Samuel Gompers tried to hold the A.F. of L. on its nonpartisan course ("These Middle Class issues," he stated in explaining why the workers should ignore free silver, "simply divert attention from their own interest"), other organized labor groups fell in line. The surviving assemblies of the Knights of Labor, the followers of Henry George, and the Nationalist clubs organized by the Bellamyites, all made the Populists' cause their own.

The threat to the two major parties had become a very real one, and the immediate question was what stand they would take on the issue of free silver. For the Republicans the choice was an easy one in spite of some protest by dissident elements. They were prepared to continue their support of the country's business interests and could be expected to uphold the gold standard as representing everything that was stable, respectable, and fitting in American society. Their convention duly nominated William McKinley, a former governor of Ohio and as a congressman, the safe and conservative author of the McKinley tariff of 1890.

The Democrats were more divided. Cleveland was strongly opposed to the financial heresy of free silver, as he clearly demonstrated in his insistence upon repeal of the Silver Purchase Act and his strenuous efforts to safeguard the country's gold reserves, but he had lost control of his party. A powerful pro-silver faction was determined to swing the Democrats over to support of monetary reform as the only way of capturing the vote of the discontented farmers and workingmen. Unless the Democrats stole the Populists' fire by adopting free silver as their own cause, this group argued, they were lost.

"All the silverites need," the New York *World* stated as the Democrats prepared to meet in their national convention, "is a Moses. They have the principle, they have the grit, they have the brass bands and the buttons and the flags, they have the howl and the hustle, they have the votes, and they have the leaders, so-called. But they are wandering in the wilderness like lost sheep, because no one with the courage, the audacity, the magnetism and the wisdom to be a real leader has yet appeared among them."

It was only a few days later that a young Nebraskan, who had already won a wide reputation for political campaigning in the Midwest, mounted the convention rostrum to speak on the proposed Democratic platform. When his eloquent and emotional appeal for a free silver plank came to its exciting peroration, the Democrats had found their Moses. William Jennings Bryan became the spokesman for the resurgent army of agriculture and labor, for all those forces of reform that were assailing capitalist domination of the government.

In the eyes of such a spokesman of business and banking interests as the New York *Tribune,* Bryan was "a wretched rattle-pated boy, posing in vapid vanity and mouthing resounding rottenness." To farmers and workers, storekeepers and clerks, especially in the Midwest, he was an ardent knight fearlessly crusading for the people's cause. While conservatives feared him for the heresies he preached, the discontented masses believed that he held the key to their salvation. He was one of them, and yet a leader and a prophet who could put in burning words their own grievances and their own hopes and aspirations.

★ WILLIAM JENNINGS BRYAN

Bryan was born in a small town in southern Illinois, to which his family had moved from Ohio, and attended Illinois College in Jacksonville, where he first showed his interest in oratory and debate. After reading and practicing law for a time he moved to Nebraska and entered politics. He served one term in the House of Representatives and, after being defeated in an attempt to go on to the Senate, took up journalism and became an editor of the Omaha *World-Herald*. Caught up in the free silver movement, which he accepted lock, stock, and barrel, he was soon writing and speaking on this issue to the exclusion of everything else. Before he came to the Democratic convention he was already widely known, but few people other than Bryan himself considered him a possible candidate for the presidential nomination.

Bryan's ideas were extremely simple and far more the product of feeling than of thought. He was never to show any real intellectual growth, and thirty years later would be saying very much the same things he said in 1896. Economic and social problems were fundamentally religious and moral problems, as he conceived them, and free silver became in his mind a symbol of righteousness over against the powers of evil represented by the gold standard. He saw himself as the voice of plain-living, God-fearing, rural America, calling for an end to the wicked ways of the urban aristocracy and industrial magnates of the Atlantic seaboard. An idealist, with an intuitive and unswerving faith in the people, he also had a very shrewd political sixth sense. It enabled him to appeal directly to the interests of the men and women in his audiences and play upon their emotions with tremendous effect. He had great vitality, unusual personal magnetism, and an unstudied charm. He was to command both the loyalty and the affection of millions of his countrymen.

Life was in a measure to pass Bryan by. After so many of the reforms he unsuccessfully advocated in his early career were taken over by others, he had nothing more to offer. He turned back to the religious faith that was always so basic in his approach to public questions, soberly practiced as well as eloquently preached, and on the lecture platform he undertook to deny the implications of the modern scientific thinking that he had never even tried to understand. The Bryan of later years became a pathetic figure, futilely sparring against evolution in a dogmatic defense of fundamentalism that served only to expose his own intellectual weaknesses.

H. L. Mencken, the iconoclastic critic of democracy in the 1920's, was fatuously to call him "a charlatan, a mountebank, a zany without sense or dignity." But in doing so Mencken merely revealed his own pretentious scorn for democratic leadership. Even though his reach always exceeded his grasp, Bryan's early role in voicing the aspirations of the common people, in which he so earnestly and sincerely believed, had a profound effect upon national history.

Thirty-six years old in 1896, Bryan looked even younger than he was. Tall, agile, with a high brow and thick mop of dark hair, he was impressively handsome. This was not the fat-jowled, stooped old man, with the Panama hat, black string tie, alpaca coat, and baggy trousers of later years. The young Bryan had a platform presence that matched the eloquence of his wonderful voice.

★ "THE CROSS OF GOLD"

When Bryan faced his audience at the Democratic convention in 1896, he immediately commanded their attention. It would be presumptuous to present himself against the distinguished gentlemen whom they had already heard, Bryan declared, but the humblest citizen in all the land, when clad in the armor of righteousness, is stronger than all the hosts of error. And he was speaking, the youthful Nebraskan continued, as the voice of the plain people who had already rendered their judgment upon the issues facing the convention:

> We do not come as aggressors. Our war is not a war of conquest; we are fighting in the defense of our homes, our families, and posterity. We have petitioned, and our petitions have been scorned; we have entreated, and our entreaties have been disregarded; we have begged, and they have mocked when our calamity came. We beg no longer; we entreat no more; we petition no more. We defy them! . . .
>
> And now, my friends, let me come to the paramount issue. If they ask us why it is that we say more on the money question than we say upon the tariff question, I reply that if protection has slain its thousands, the gold standard has slain its tens of thousands. If they ask us why we do not embody in our platforms all the things that we believe in, we reply that when we have restored the money of the Constitution, all other necessary reform will be possible; but that until this is done, there is no other reform that can be accomplished. . . .
>
> You come to us and tell us that the great cities are in favor of the gold standard; we reply that the great cities rest upon our broad and fertile prairies. Burn down your cities and leave our farms, and your cities will spring up again as if by magic; but destroy our farms, and the grass will grow in the streets of every city in the country. . . .
>
> Having behind us the producing masses of this nation and the world, supported by the commercial interests, the laboring interests, and the toilers everywhere, we will answer their demands for a gold standard by saying to them: You shall not press down upon the brow of labor this crown of thorns; you shall not crucify mankind upon a cross of gold.

As Bryan concluded, the audience of twenty thousand men and women broke into thunderous applause and the convention hall became bedlam. "The tumult," wrote a contemporary observer, "was like that of a great sea thundering against the dykes." It was the greatest speech Bryan—or perhaps any political leader of his era—ever made. It won him the Democratic nomination and also that of the Populists, who now gave up all idea of naming a separate presidential candidate. As he went forth under this joint sponsorship, swinging back and forth across the country with inexhaustible energy throughout a hot summer, he again and again awoke the same response as he had at the convention. He made free silver glimmer miraculously before millions of his countrymen as the token of escape from all their troubles.

★ THE REPUBLICANS

Bryan's fighting campaign awoke among Republicans forebodings of disaster that were voiced in a rising crescendo of alarm. The threat to the stability of our national institutions which seemed implicit in the possible triumph of free silver was called the greatest danger the country had faced since the Civil War. The Democratic platform, which had incorporated many other Populist planks as well as the free coinage of silver, was said to have been drawn up in a spirit that would "organize sedition, destroy the peace and security of the country."

"I speak with the greatest soberness," the young Theodore Roosevelt was quoted as saying, "when I say that . . . the sentiment now animating a large part of our people can only be suppressed, as the Commune in Paris was suppressed, by taking ten or a dozen of their leaders out, standing them against a wall, and shooting them dead. I believe it will come to that. These leaders are plotting a social revolution and the subversion of the American Republic."

Roosevelt was to deny having made this statement and term it a "tissue of falsehood"—and well he might, for not many years later he would have taken over a large part of the Democratic program as his own. But whether or not he actually made it, it was highly typical of the hysterical fears that at the time were sweeping through the East. Farm revolt upon the heels of the Debs' rebellion did not promise too well for continued popular acceptance of a laissez faire economy.

The Republican high command was prepared for all-out measures to repel the Democratic-Populist onslaught upon the citadels of high finance and big business. Never was a political campaign more carefully organized. It was under the direction of Mark Hanna, wealthy Cleveland industrialist and economic power in Ohio, who epitomized the businessman in politics. He had been largely responsible for McKinley's nomination and his astute, efficient, and unscrupulous management of the campaign was to pay high dividends. Hanna believed sincerely, and was not afraid to say so with forthright candor, that government existed to protect, encourage, and fortify business. He had what has been described as "a cash register conscience," and while himself a man of the utmost integrity—direct, forceful and self-reliant—he accepted all the implications of the need for business control of government. The election of McKinley became for him an all-important issue, and he was prepared to do whatever was necessary to bring it about.

McKinley completely accepted Hanna's guidance. To avoid any possible mistakes, campaign strategy called for him to remain at his home at Canton, Ohio, rather than follow the magnetic Bryan about the country. There McKinley received on his comfortable front porch selected delegations of citizens from all over the nation, carefully coached in the questions they should ask, and he spoke to them soberly of the dangers facing the country according to a prepared script. The Republicans were playing it safe so far as campaign oratory was concerned.

The real job Hanna undertook was to collect campaign contributions from the banks, the insurance companies, the railways, and the industrial corporations. "In 1896 Hanna incorporated McKinley," one commentator has written, "and every business house in the United States . . . subscribed for McKinley stock." With contributions reported at over $3,000,000, but probably running to five times this figure, the Republicans flooded the country with pamphlets and tracts (including "What's the Matter with Kansas?"), and sent out thousands of speakers to carry throughout the land the message that a vote for Bryan and free silver spelled disaster. Corporations were prevailed upon to put messages in their employees' pay envelopes, telling them to vote for McKinley as the only way to hold their jobs. The forces of eastern conservatism could not have been more effectively arrayed to turn back the radical agrarianism of the West and South.

★ ELECTION RESULTS

When the votes were counted, McKinley had been elected. His majority in the Electoral College was 271 to 176, but the election was actually closer than this suggests. He polled about 500,000 more votes than Bryan, of a total of some 13.5 million. Had the election been held earlier in the summer, the Democrats might well have won a popular majority. More than any other cause, rising farm prices and improved economic conditions, affording some substance to the slogan that McKinley was "the advance agent of prosperity," gave the triumph to the Republicans.

Sang Vachel Lindsay:

> Election night at midnight:
> Boy Bryan's defeat,
> Defeat of western silver.
> Defeat of the wheat.
> Victory of letterfiles
> And Plutocrats in miles

With dollar signs upon their coats
Diamond watchchains on their vests
And spats on their feet.
Victory of custodians,
Plymouth Rock,
And all that inbred landlord stock.
Victory of the neat.
Defeat of the aspen groves of Colorado valleys,
The blue bells of the Rockies,
And blue bonnets of old Texas,
By the Pittsburgh alleys.
Defeat of alfalfa and the Mariposa lily.
Defeat of the Pacific and the long Mississippi.
Defeat of the young by the old and silly.
Defeat of tornadoes by poison vats supreme.
Defeat of my boyhood, defeat of my dream.

The Populist cause had indeed failed. The fundamental issue in the great contest, as Henry Adams was later to write, had been between an agrarian and a capitalistic economy. It had come to a head "on the single gold standard, and the majority at last declared itself, once for

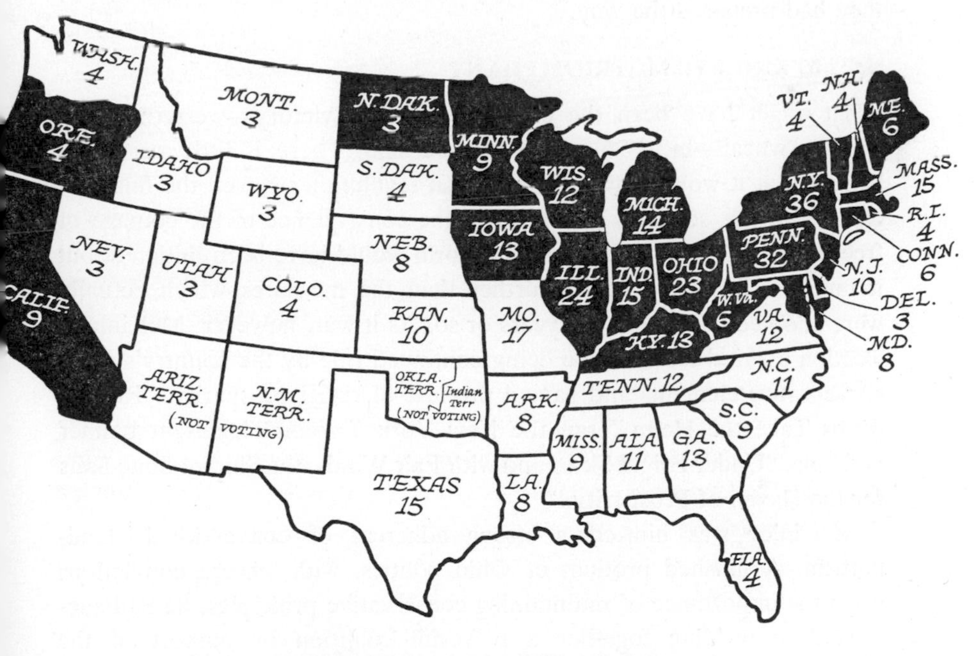

ELECTION OF 1896

	ELECTORAL VOTE	POPULAR VOTE
McKinley	271	7,111,607
Bryan	176	6,509,052

Numbers in each state show electoral vote

all, in favor of the capitalistic system with all its necessary machinery." Yet this was not the whole story. The Populists had overreached themselves. They had not been able to command the support of the less radical elements, especially among the white collar class, who feared the intemperate tone of their attacks upon capitalism. But their campaign gave a tremendous impetus to the reforms which were to bring the new capitalist order into greater harmony with political democracy.

The Democratic-Populist coalition had called for the initiative and the referendum, and the direct election of senators to restore political power to the people; it had demanded effective regulation of the railroads, control of the trusts, and an income tax on great wealth, in order to equalize economic opportunity. The conservative defenders of the *status quo* had overwhelmingly rejected these new proposals—as well as free silver—by returning the Republicans to office, but it was laissez faire's last victory. With the turn of the century the seemingly radical ideas of the Populists were to become the program of the Progressives. The latter's broader appeal for popular support, enlisting the middle class in their ranks rather than solely embattled farmers and workers, was to win a measure of success that had evaded the Populists but for which they had prepared the way.

★ MC KINLEYISM TRIUMPHANT

What might have been the effect of a Bryan victory—western silver, western wheat—in 1896 can hardly be said. There is little reason to believe that it would have caused social revolution or even the financial chaos that was so freely predicted as the consequence of the coinage of free silver. Political and economic reform would have been initiated, but it might well have gone no further than the measures which actually were adopted in another ten years or so. As it was, however, McKinley's election assured for the time being continued rule by the country's more conservative elements and gave a promise of rising prosperity. "Republicans Take the Helm," ran the New York *Tribune*'s exultant banner headline. "Under Bright Skies and with Fair Winds, the Ship of State Sails for the Haven of Prosperity."

McKinley was himself a strong adherent of conventional standpattism. A finished product of Ohio politics, with sincere convictions upon the importance of maintaining conservative principles, he had succeeded in welding together a powerful coalition in support of the policies for which he stood. He would continue to uphold the business interests of the country at every turn.

He was personally a kindly, amiable, unassuming gentleman, industrious and reliable in administrative work, and always highly dignified in his formal Prince Albert coat, white vest, and meticulously tailored trousers. He appeared to stand under the shadow of Mark Hanna, with whom he remained on the most friendly and cordial terms, and while he actually led more often than he followed, it was not with any dramatic impact. He was above everything else eminently safe. McKinley was to serve as president in a time of momentous events, but like those earlier post-Civil War presidents who had their brief day in the White House, he lacked the essential qualities of really effective leadership.

Fortune smiled on the Republican party after his election. The discovery of gold in both the Klondike and South Africa made available the reserves for a substantial increase in the currency, and at the same time there were serious crop failures abroad. The result was a quick rise in wheat and cotton prices and new prosperity for the American farmer. The demand for the coinage of free silver rapidly subsided as the producers of staple crops found themselves better off than they had been for many years, and while the Republicans had in no way been responsible for these happy developments, they were quick to claim all credit for the return of good times. After some further vague investigation of the possibilities of international bimetallism, definitely blocked by Great Britain, it proved possible in 1900 to enact legislation placing the country definitely on the gold standard. When Bryan once again tried to raise the silver issue in the presidential election of that year, it fell absolutely flat. The agricultural West was no longer concerned.

On other counts as well, the McKinley administration was with even greater expedition successful in promoting traditional Republican policies. At a special session in 1897, Congress adopted the Dingley Tariff Act. Its rates were so high, substantially above those of the McKinley tariff, that imports declined some $25 million during the first year they were in effect. This was protection with a vengeance. Other legislation was unimportant, and the regulatory provisions of both the Interstate Commerce Act and the Sherman Anti-Trust Act remained conveniently forgotten. Prosperity was giving a new sanction to the theory and practice of laissez faire, and it appeared to underscore ever more heavily the beneficence of the Gospel of Wealth.

McKinley had hardly been inaugurated, however, before he had to come to grips with a problem of quite a different sort. The forces making for American overseas expansion had been slowly gathering momentum during these years of domestic crisis. Insurrection in Cuba was to start an unexpected train of events that was suddenly to impose upon the United States an entirely new role in world affairs.

CHAPTER X

Imperialism

★ THE BREAK WITH THE PAST

Throughout the period from the close of the Civil War until the 1890's, the American people had been so largely absorbed in domestic issues, found such full play for their energy and enterprise in the settlement of the West and the development of industry, that foreign affairs were almost completely ignored. They excited at best, in Henry Cabot Lodge's phrase, "only a languid interest." Nevertheless, a number of almost isolated developments foreshadowed the possibility of a more assertive foreign policy, and with the changing conditions of national life at the close of the century, a groundswell of imperialistic ambition swept the country. The American people hardly realized what was happening in 1898 and 1899 before they discovered, to their often amazed bewilderment, that the nation had finally broken away from the moorings of the past and become—almost in spite of itself—a world power with far-flung overseas possessions that carried the American flag even to the coasts of Asia.

The circumstances were dramatic. In the 1880's the United States had no clear-cut foreign policy of any sort; its navy was inferior not only to that of every principal European power but even to that of Chile; it had no insular possessions. The people as a whole could hardly be said to look beyond their Atlantic and Pacific barriers. Yet by 1900 all this was changed. A successful war had been fought with Spain, a decisive stand had been taken in support of what were deemed to be vital American interests in both Latin America and eastern Asia, and a new, modern navy had been created. Having become an empire with possessions and protectorates in both great oceans, the United States had been irresistibly drawn into the main current of international affairs.

Almost half a century was to pass before the American people accepted the full implications of these momentous developments. "In foreign affairs," Theodore Roosevelt was soon to write, "we must make up our minds that, whether we wish it or not, we are a great people and must play a great part in the world. It is not open to us to choose whether we will play that great part or not. We have to play it. All we can decide is whether we shall play it well or ill." To state such a proposition remained easier, however, than to find the answer to the questions it raised. Over against the challenge of new responsibilities was the constant pull of the continental self-sufficiency that had served the nation so well throughout the nineteenth century. Internationalism and isolationism were to contest for popular support until World War II.

★ POST-CIVIL WAR DIPLOMACY

Immediately after the Civil War, there had, it is true, been a brief flurry of interest in foreign affairs. On the initiative of Secretary of State Seward, the United States successfully combatted French intervention in Mexico for the protection of the empire set up in that country under Archduke Maximilian of Austria; purchased from Russia what was to become the territory of Alaska; entered into tentative negotiations for the annexation of the Danish West Indies and Santo Domingo, and even looked far overseas toward the possible acquisition of naval bases in the Pacific. Here were presaged those later moves which so greatly changed our role in both Latin America and eastern Asia.

In the late 1860's, however, popular support for such a vigorous foreign policy was not forthcoming. The purchase of Alaska was the only annexationist project conceived by the imperialistic Seward that was carried through successfully. And it was consummated only because of his stubborn determination. When Russia offered to sell Alaska, as a consequence of pressing financial needs and a belief that the territory was a strategic liability, Seward singlehandedly negotiated the agreement for its purchase at a price of $7,200,000.

He was then called upon to exercise all possible influence to win approval for what he had done from a reluctant Congress. In the popular mind the purchase of Alaska—"Johnson's Polar Bear Garden" and even more derisively "Seward's Folly"—was a bad bargain, a willful extravagance, and a foolish mistake. "Have the people desired it?" one irate congressman demanded. "Not a sensible man among them had ever suggested it. The whole country exclaimed at once, when it was made known to it, against the ineffable folly, if not the wanton profligacy, of the whole transaction." But Seward won out. The years to come were to demonstrate his far-sighted vision and in 1959—nearly a century later—Alaska was to become the forty-ninth state in the Union.

Backing was refused, however, for Seward's other ambitious schemes—the Hawaiian Islands, the Danish West Indies, Santo Domingo—and the country quickly reverted to its traditional isolationist policy. "The desire for the acquisition of territory," the Secretary of State wrote rather mournfully, "has sensibly abated. . . . We have come to value dollars more, and dominion less." It was not so much dollars though. The American people were so absorbed in the immense domestic tasks they had undertaken that they had no time or thought for overseas expansion or foreign adventure.

Only one positive diplomatic move need perhaps be recorded for these years. This was the settlement through negotiations with Great Britain of the so-called "Alabama" claims, arising out of the depredations of Confederate cruisers operating out of British ports during the Civil War. In 1869 an agreement for arbitration was concluded only to be emphatically rejected by the Senate. Charles Sumner irately claimed that the United States was entitled to damages of some two billion dollars because of the prolongation of the war. Two years later, however, the Treaty of Washington, in which Great Britain acknowledged that her action in allowing the "Alabama" to get to sea, violated the laws of neutrality, smoothed the way to mutual acceptance of arbitration. A five-man tribunal—its members nominated by the United States, Great Britain, Italy, Brazil, and Switzerland—met soon thereafter in Geneva and awarded the United States $15,500,000.

The Treaty of Washington also adjusted a number of other minor issues and gave evidence of a basic desire on the part of the United States and Great Britain to settle whatever disputes arose between them by peaceful means. The flare-up over the "Alabama" claims was by no means the last Anglo-American quarrel, but the resort to arbitration in this instance pointed the way to better understanding.

About this time, it should also be noted, new ties were formed with both Hawaii and the Samoan Islands, growing out of trade interests in those Pacific outposts. Nevertheless, it was not until the close of the century that a gradually reviving public interest in foreign affairs and in possible overseas expansion set the stage for the exciting events that led to empire.

★ "LOOKING OUTWARD"

In a broad sense, the history of the United States has always been one of persistent expansion—across the Alleghenies, down the Ohio and into the broad valley of the Mississippi, over the western plains, and across the Rockies. We fought Mexico to secure our territorial aims in the Southwest, quarreled with England over Oregon, and have at times looked toward Canada or Cuba with a possessive gleam in the national eye. Once territorial United States was settled and the free land exhausted, it was almost inevitable that the American people should question whether their long history of progressive settlement in new territories had come to a final close. "Whether they will or no," Captain Alfred Thayer Mahan, naval strategist and historian, was writing in the *Atlantic Monthly* in 1890, the very year in which the Census Bureau declared that there was no longer a land frontier, "Americans must now begin to look outward."

It was a sentiment that found increasing expression as the 1890's advanced and was perhaps nowhere stated more clearly than in a contemporary article in the *Overland Monthly:*

> The subjugation of a continent was sufficient to keep the American people busy at home for a century. But now that the continent is subdued, we are looking for fresh worlds to conquer; and whether our conservative stay-at-homes like it or not, the colonizing instinct which has led our race in successive waves of immigration . . . is the instinct which is now pushing us out and on to Alaska, to the isles of the sea,—and beyond.

Nor was it only the disappearance of the frontier that awoke an interest in overseas extension which Secretary of State Seward had been unable to evoke in the 1860's. The growth of industry and the consequent increase in foreign trade and commerce (exports had quadrupled since 1865 to a total value of over a billion dollars) gave a new urgency to the question of foreign markets. If the United States was to dispose profitably of the steadily increasing production of farms, mines, and factories, it was considered imperative to make every possible effort to develop and promote new commercial outlets.

This did not necessarily mean political control of foreign markets and therefore did not of itself involve actual overseas expansion. But the European powers, seeking new markets from the same incentives as animated the United States, were aggressively extending their possessions. They had taken the lead in both Africa and eastern Asia, and appeared to be casting covetous glances toward South America, in carving out special spheres of interest, setting up protectorates, and acquiring colonies. The United States was confronted by the competition of powers that had already fully embarked upon an imperialistic course.

Such circumstances seemed to compel action. If the United States were to protect its interests in an imperialistic world, ran the expansionist thesis, it too would have to seek out overseas colonies. The tradition of expansion that had played such an important part in the American past was to be newly invigorated by a realization of what was now being done by Great Britain and Germany, France and Italy. The United States was gradually to accept imperialism through surrender to what John Hay would call a "cosmic tendency."

These pragmatic arguments for possible overseas expansion were further re-enforced in the 1890's by the American people's strangely interwoven concepts of duty and destiny. The United States had attained a position, according to such concepts, which placed on it the immense responsibility of extending to other peoples, perhaps to other lands, the benefits of its own freedom and democracy. There was in fact no way of escaping the fulfillment of such an obligation: it was the American mission, both duty *and* destiny. In the view of the imperialists of the 1890's, moreover, the case for expansion was all the more unanswerable because of the innate superiority of the Anglo-Saxon race. It was fated to provide for the backward people everywhere a rule of law and order of which they were themselves incapable.

"This race of unequalled energy," wrote Josiah Strong in *Our Country,* a book which reached hundreds of thousands of readers, "with all the majesty of wealth and numbers behind it—the representative, let us hope, of the largest liberty, the purest Christianity, the highest civilization—having developed peculiarly aggressive traits calculated to impress its institutions upon mankind, will spread itself over the earth." And Strong further believed that the seat of Anglo-Saxon power had been transferred to the United States, and that from this new base it was already prepared to move down "upon Mexico, down upon Central and South America, out upon the islands of the seas, over upon Africa and beyond."

One more factor making for expansion in the situation of the 1890's might be cited. The tumult and confusion of domestic conditions, the seemingly impossible problems posed by the plight of farmers and the restless demands of industrial workers, caused many Americans to look outward as a form of escapism. Some of their leaders encouraged a jingoistic, imperialistic spirit, sought to whip up patriotic fervor for a more aggressive foreign policy, in order to divert attention from the Populists' demands for reform.

★ THE MAHAN SCHOOL

The most convinced and also the most persuasive of the imperialist-minded was neither politician nor businessman. Captain Alfred Thayer Mahan was a naval strategist whose historical studies had convinced him of the supreme importance of naval power and of the imperative necessity for the United States to strengthen its position in a highly competitive world. His arguments for overseas expansion were drawn from every possible source, but what he did most effectively was to link commercial supremacy and naval power together in a carefully elaborated system of mercantile imperialism. Mahan called upon his countrymen to realize that because of its geographic position and immense resources, the United States was bound to be "one of the frontiers from which, as from a base of operations, the Sea Power of the civilized world will energize."

This country, to simplify Mahan's thesis, needed foreign trade, markets, and a great merchant fleet. A powerful navy was necessary for their protection. It in turn could not operate safely in distant waters except insofar as the United States also controlled the naval bases and coaling stations upon which it would be dependent. Consequently, there was no alternative to overseas expansion. Mahan then happily foresaw that with such distant outposts, we should need a still larger fleet, which in turn would demand additional bases, and then for their protection, more ships. It was an apparently endless proposition.

Urging the annexation of the Hawaiian Islands in 1890, Mahan justified such a move on the very ground that it would not be a "mere sporadic effort, irrational because disconnected from an adequate motive." On the contrary, he saw our acquisition of this Pacific base as "a first-fruit and token that the nation in its evolution had aroused itself to the necessity of carrying its life—that has been the happiness of those under its influence—beyond the borders which heretofore have sufficed for its activities."

Among his converts to imperialist expansion were both Henry Cabot Lodge, senator from Massachusetts, and Theodore Roosevelt, soon to become Assistant Secretary of the Navy.

"From the Rio Grande to the Arctic Ocean," the former wrote enthusiastically, "there should be but one flag and one country. . . . We should control the Hawaiian Islands and maintain our influence in Samoa. . . . The great nations are rapidly absorbing for their future expansion and their present defense all the waste places of the earth. It is a movement which makes for civilization and the advancement of the race. As one of the great nations of the world the United States must not fall out of the line of march."

Roosevelt was even more ambitious and belligerent. In these days he was ready to fight any nation which sought to establish colonies in those parts of the world where he felt American influence should be supreme. "If I had my way," he wrote Mahan on one occasion in relation to the problem of Hawaii, "we would annex those islands tomorrow. If that is impossible I would establish a protectorate. . . . I believe we should build the Nicaragua Canal at once . . . and should build a dozen new battleships."

★ THE VENEZUELA CRISIS

This was the heady atmosphere—"the taste of Empire is in the mouth of the people," one newspaper editorial declared—in which the first steps toward overseas expansion were taken. Even before war with Spain provided an actual opportunity to obtain colonies, however, a clash with Great Britain revealed the changing temper of the country.

The dispute arose from Great Britain's attitude in refusing mediation of a long-standing controversy over the boundaries between Venezuela and British Guiana. The discovery of gold in the unsettled area claimed by both countries heightened the conflict, and Cleveland's Secretary of State, Richard Olney, sought in 1895 to settle the issue by reminding Great Britain of the Monroe Doctrine, and suggesting that even apart from the unwarranted pressure being placed upon Venezuela, there was little logic in England having any colonies at all in Latin America. Moreover, he stated the position of the United States in reference to South America in words that he would himself later describe as the equivalent of blows.

"Today the United States is practically sovereign on this continent," Olney bluntly informed the British Foreign Office, "and its fiat is law upon the subjects to which it confines its interposition. . . . Distance and three thousand miles of intervening ocean make any permanent political union between a European and an American state unnatural and inexpedient."

Great Britain took its time in answering this provocative statement, and when it did so, it totally rejected the idea that the Monroe Doctrine could apply to its quarrel with Venezuela. President Cleveland promptly called upon Congress to provide the funds for a commission to determine the actual boundary line of British Guiana, and declared that in the meantime, the United States was prepared to resist any attempt by Great Britain to occupy territory rightfully belonging to Venezuela. For a brief time a war spirit swept the country and in some quarters there was actually a hope that England would challenge Cleveland's forthright stand. "The clamor of the peace faction," exclaimed the bellicose Theodore Roosevelt, "has convinced me that this country needs war."

Great Britain's dangerous world involvements and her overwhelming desire to maintain peace with the United States militated against any further building up of the crisis, and wiser counsels than those of Roosevelt soon prevailed in this country. With an agreement finally reached for arbitration of the dispute, the danger of war was averted.

★ HAWAII AND SAMOA

In the meantime, the opening moves had been made toward annexation of Hawaii and American Samoa, and the course firmly set toward that overseas expansion in the Pacific which had been Seward's bright, particular dream in the 1860's. He had strongly felt that this area of the world had the greatest potentialities for future development. European commerce, politics, thought, and activity were destined to sink in relative importance, Seward once told the Senate, "while the Pacific Ocean, its shores, its islands, and the vast regions beyond, will become the chief theater of events in the world's great hereafter."

The desire to secure control of Hawaii grew out of considerations of both trade and strategy, and opportunity seemed clearly at hand when in 1893 a revolution against the islands' native sovereign, Queen Liliuokalani, brought into power the local American faction that favored annexation in large part to escape United States duties on sugar. A treaty providing for this move was promptly concluded between the Harrison administration and the new Hawaiian government. Before it had been approved, however, President Cleveland came into office and he withdrew it from consideration. American marines had landed in Hawaii at a critical moment during the revolt, and our minister in Honolulu had clearly shown his sympathy for the revolutionaries. The new President was convinced that the United States had wrongfully intervened in Hawaii's internal affairs, and he was unwilling to condone actions based on the premise that there was one law for a strong nation and another for a weak one.

Withdrawal of the treaty nevertheless left him in a difficult predicament. When Queen Liliuokalani was asked what her policies would be if the United States restored her to her throne, she promptly answered that she would behead all the leaders of the revolt. Cleveland could not quite accept this proposal, and he consequently allowed the government representing the American elements in Hawaii to remain in power. When it officially established the Republic of Hawaii, the United States and the other powers extended formal recognition.

Annexation, however, had been merely postponed. Upon the return of the Republicans to office with the election of McKinley, his Secretary of State promptly concluded a new treaty comparable to that of 1893. Sentiment had grown in favor of this move, and even though anti-imperialists argued strongly against it in the Senate, McKinley was able to state with considerable justification that "annexation is not a change; it is a consummation." Nevertheless, final action was to be delayed until after the outbreak of war with Spain. On July 7, 1898, Hawaii was then at last annexed through a joint resolution of Congress.

Cleveland could never be reconciled. "Hawaii is ours," he wrote gloomily to Olney. "As I look back upon the first steps in this miserable business and as I contemplate the means used to complete the outrage, I am ashamed of the whole affair."

The acquisition of Samoa also grew out of questions of trade and strategy. Ever since the Civil War American naval officers had coveted Pago Pago as the best harbor and potential naval base in the South Pacific, and a treaty to bring it under American control was negotiated with native chieftains in 1878. Twelve years later, in order to accommodate the rival claims of Great Britain and Germany in the archipelago, the United States entered into a tripartite agreement which in effect placed the Samoan Islands under the three powers' joint protection. This was a highly significant undertaking, in spite of the relative unimportance of Samoa, for it marked a first departure from our traditional policy of avoiding all entangling alliances. But the tripartite protectorate worked none too well, and during the days of imperialistic fervor at the close of the century, the United States concluded a new agreement with England and Germany which left it free to assume complete control over the desired naval base. It annexed American Samoa in 1899 as a part of its general program of Pacific expansion.

★ REVOLT IN CUBA

The Venezuela episode, moves to annex Hawaii, tightening bonds with Samoa, were but first-round preliminaries to the main bout, staged in Cuba and the Philippines after the outbreak of hostilities with Spain. War gave the expansionists the real opportunity for which they were looking. It enabled them to promote a policy that was to carry the country even farther along the imperialistic road than they had ever envisaged. In spite of the strong expansionist urge that provided the background for war with Spain, however, this was not the immediate cause for that conflict. The American people embarked on martial adventure in 1898 because their emotions had been whipped up to a pitch of hysteria by the call to free the people of Cuba from Spain's oppressive rule. Only after the war had come to an end were the possibilities that it provided for American empire fully realized.

The Cuban people had long been struggling for independence. They had fought a bloody and unsuccessful ten years' war in 1868–78, and when they again took up arms in 1895, American sympathy was naturally extended to the revolutionary cause. Cuba's geographical position and rich resources had always made the island an object of special interest, and earlier ties were now strengthened by an increased stake in the Cuban sugar industry. American investments amounted to some $50,000,000 and our annual trade totaled twice this figure. Pro-Cuban sentiment, that is, had a substantial economic as well as ideological basis. Nevertheless, the anti-imperialist Cleveland, and for a time McKinley, sternly rejected the demands that were voiced in some quarters for immediate American intervention, not only to drive out the Spaniards but to provide an opportunity for our own annexation of Cuba. On taking office in 1897, indeed, McKinley stoutly declared that there would be "no jingo nonsense" during his administration and pledged his opposition to any annexation of territory—whether Cuba, Hawaii, or Santo Domingo.

Interventionist forces were to prove too strong for the easy-going McKinley. As reports reached the United States of the cruel tactics being employed by the Spaniards in their efforts to suppress the Cuban revolt, public opinion became more and more inflamed. "Torn from their homes, with foul earth, foul air, foul water, and foul food or none," Senator Proctor reported of the tragic plight of the Cuban people herded into concentration camps by the Spanish military authorities, "what wonder that one half have died and that one quarter of the living are so diseased that they can not be saved?" How could the United States stand by passively while such horrors were being enacted off its very shores? The demand for action gathered irresistible momentum.

It was immensely stimulated by yellow journalism. The New York *World* and New York *Journal* were locked in a great competitive struggle, and atrocity stories from Cuba paid rich dividends in added circulation. Pulitzer and Hearst each tried to outdo the other with more inflammatory articles, more lurid eye-witness stories, more sensational headlines. The *Journal* fixed upon the Spanish commander the name of "Butcher" Weyler—"the devastator of haciendas, the destroyer of families, and the outrager of women. . . . There is nothing to prevent his carnal, animal brain from running riot with itself in inventing tortures and infamies of bloody debauchery." The *World* refused to be outdone. "Blood on the roadsides, blood in the fields, blood on the doorsteps, blood, blood, blood!" its correspondent in Cuba telegraphed. "Is there no nation wise enough, brave enough, and strong enough to restore peace in this bloodsmitten land?"

As sensation piled on sensation, an incident whose origin has never been explained furnished new inflammatory fuel. The United States warship "Maine," anchored in the harbor of Havana, blew up on February 15, 1898, with the loss of over 250 officers and men. The immediate assumption, never proved, was that the explosion had been caused by treachery. "Intervention is a plain and imperative duty," the *Journal* declared, while the *World* screamed "The Only Atonement —Free Cuba." A popular slogan swept the country:

Remember the Maine!
To hell with Spain.

The McKinley administration did not want hostilities. While the business community which it represented was not immune to the expansionist impulses underlying popular belligerency, it feared the disturbing effects of war on the national economy. This attitude outraged such excitable jingos as Theodore Roosevelt. "We will have this war for the freedom of Cuba," he is said to have shouted at Mark Hanna, "in spite of the timidity of the commercial interests." Nevertheless, President McKinley made every possible diplomatic effort to discover some way of re-establishing peace in Cuba, and early in April negotiations through our minister in Madrid appeared to be making very real headway. On the ninth, the Spanish government indicated its willingness to meet the American demand for granting the Cuban insurgents an armistice. "I hope that nothing will now be done to humiliate Spain," the American minister cabled McKinley, "as I am satisfied that the present Government is going, and is loyally ready to go, as fast and as far as it can."

In the meantime, however, a Congress reacting to the popular clamor for war fostered by the yellow press and other jingoistic elements was preparing to take matters into its own hands. The political-minded McKinley, worrying more and more about the fortunes of the Republican party if he stood out any longer against the popular demand for action, finally gave in. Virtually ignoring Spain's conciliatory move, he went before Congress on April 11 with what was in effect a war message. Both houses responded with alacrity. After adoption of a self-denying ordinance to the effect that once Cuba was pacified, the United States would withdraw, authorization was given the President to employ armed force in meeting the emergency. A formal declaration of war followed on April 25 and an excited country enthusiastically took up arms to free Cuba and drive Spain from the New World.

★ "A SPLENDID LITTLE WAR"

In comparison with the great conflicts that were to engulf the country two and four decades later, the Spanish-American War was no more than a casual skirmish. The United States was totally unprepared, except for such progress as had been made in building up the new navy, and the bungling and inefficiency that marked the mobilization, training and operations of its military forces would, under other circumstances, have been disastrous. Spain, however, was even less prepared and more bungling. She was so much weaker in every respect, and so incapable of offering any effective resistance to American arms, that within a brief ten weeks she had capitulated on land and sea.

There was little to mar the ardor and gaiety with which the volunteer troops marched off to combat, or the sense of excitement with which the country then sat back to read the thrilling reports of frontline action. The American people, the *Outlook* soberly reported, "had been moved to battle by the demand of an awakened conscience answering the call of outraged humanity." More typical of the spirit of 1898 were the stirring strains of the martial music to which the troops had marched off—"The Stars and Stripes Forever" and "There'll be a Hot Time in the Old Town Tonight."

The campaign which finally got underway in Cuba in mid-June was not altogether smooth going. The troops lacked proper equipment, fought under the hot Cuban sun in heavy garrison uniforms, and hardly enjoyed the "embalmed beef" that was their dietary staple. Yet in spite of these hazards and a great deal of confusion in landing operations, the fighting was soon over. A force of some 17,000 American troops was thrown against the Spanish in the region of Santiago and decisively defeated them at the battles of Las Guasimas, El Caney, and San Juan. The victory was won with relatively few casualties and brought fame to many heroes, perhaps most conspicuously Theodore Roosevelt and his Rough Riders. The toll taken among army troops was to prove heavy before the war was over, more than 5,000 deaths, but they were largely accounted for by sickness and disease.

The army went on after its conquest of Cuba to mopping-up operations in Puerto Rico; greater laurels were to be won by the navy. As our victorious land forces merged on Santiago, the Spanish fleet trapped in that port attempted on July 3 to escape. An American squadron under Admirals Sampson and Schley (dispute over who was responsible for the victory would echo down the years) realized a Heaven-sent opportunity and closed in for the kill. Within a few hours every Spanish vessel had been either sunk or beached at the cost of only minor damage to our fleet and one casualty. The American people had momentous news when they read their papers on that memorable Fourth of July following the battle at Santiago—news which signaled the final downfall of what had once been imperial Spain's expansive rule in the New World.

In the meantime there had been even more astounding developments in the far-off Philippines—a Spanish colony that most Americans had not known existed until they suddenly discovered that the islands were about to fall into their hands. Upon the outbreak of war, Commodore Dewey had sailed with the Pacific squadron from Hongkong for Manila on secret orders. There on May 1 he engaged the Spanish fleet in an epochal battle. "You may fire when you are ready, Gridley," was his historic order, and the American squadron majestically sailed back and forth across Manila harbor while its guns poured a withering fire into the hapless Spanish vessels. When the smoke finally lifted, the enemy force had been totally destroyed and a white flag flew from the badly raked shore batteries. As at Santiago (two months later), the Americans had suffered only a single casualty—an engineer who died of a heat stroke. So the battle of Manila Bay became history.

After defeat in the Philippines had been followed by defeat in Cuba, total and complete, Spain was forced to sue for peace and the sweeping armistice terms imposed upon her marked the beginning of a new epoch in world history. "It has been a splendid little war," wrote John Hay in an often quoted comment, "begun with the highest motives, carried on with magnificent intelligence and spirit, favored by the fortune which loves the brave."

★ FRUITS OF VICTORY

What were the fruits of victory of the Spanish-American war?

The United States stood by its pledge to secure the Cuban people in their liberty, but according to the Platt Amendment, which was incorporated in the Cuban constitution at the insistence of the American Congress, it asserted the right to intervene should either foreign danger or domestic insurrection threaten Cuban independence or government stability. For over thirty years Cuba was consequently to remain only a thinly disguised American protectorate. Puerto Rico was annexed, and while given a considerable degree of self-government, was held directly as a colony subject to congressional control. The mid-Pacific island of Guam, which United States troops had taken over en route to the Philippines before an amazed Spanish governor even knew his country was at war, also became an American possession. And most importantly, Spain was compelled to cede (in return for $20,000,000) the entire archipelago of the Philippine Islands.

The United States may have entered the war in answer to the call of outraged humanity, but its reward was the establishment of a colonial empire with firm control of the Caribbean, and overseas possessions in the western Pacific. Having caught the vision of world power, moreover, the American people were ready to embrace still further opportunities to demonstrate their imperial coming of age. The pronouncement of the Open Door policy in China followed almost immediately upon acquisition of the Philippines, a newly assertive policy was soon adopted toward the countries of Latin America, and within a few years American engineers would be building the Panama Canal.

★ THE PHILIPPINES

The decision to accept what were for a majority of Americans such unexpected results of the campaign to free Cuba was not reached without vigorous debate and prolonged controversy in both Congress and the press. The basic issue was whether or not the United States should retain control of the Philippines. Although Spain had little to say about what the United States should do, the problem was immensely complicated by the quite apparent reluctance on the part of the Filipinos to accept American domination in place of that of Spain. They wanted independence. While the great debate over the Philippines raged in the United States, the island people fought bitterly under the leadership of Emilio Aguinaldo against the American occupation forces. The campaign to subdue the Filipinos was more hard fought, more costly, and more bloody than that which had been waged against the Spanish forces in Cuba. They were reduced by force rather than reconciled by persuasion in the sanguinary process of establishing American rule.

After the battle of Manila Bay the United States had dispatched troops to the Philippines and on August 13, 1898, they had finally invested Manila and taken over control of the government. The armistice terms concluded with Spain provided for the continued occupation of Manila pending final settlement of "the control, disposition and government of the Philippines." For a time the policy of the McKinley administration appeared to look no further than a possible demand for retention of an American naval base. But from the moment of Dewey's dramatic victory at Manila Bay, public appetite was whetted. "The whole policy of annexation," Senator Lodge was happily writing Roosevelt on June 15, "is growing rapidly under the irresistible pressure of events."

The commercial and business interests that had originally opposed war with Spain became increasingly anxious, once hostilities were over, to make the most of the new opportunities which victory presented. The Philippines, from their point of view, were a base of operations that would enable the United States to compete more successfully with the European powers in the exploitation of China. "If it is commercialism to want the possession of a strategic point giving the American people an opportunity to maintain a foothold in the markets of that great Eastern country," Mark Hanna declared with characteristic bluntness, "for God's sake let us have commercialism."

His sentiments were echoed in almost all the journals of trade and commerce, in many popular publications. The Philippines were considered the key to the Orient, and an equivalent for the spheres of influence which England and France, Russia and Germany, were carving out for themselves on the Asiatic mainland. Having fallen almost gratuitously into our hands, the argument ran, such a rich prize could not possibly be abandoned.

Nor were the strategic implications of American possession of the Philippines ignored. There were many converts to the views Captain Mahan had long since been advancing.

"It is from no general policy of 'annexation' or 'colonization,' or 'imperialism'—which, in spite of the deceptive use of those terms, we neither seek nor need—that the acquisition of the Archipelago is to be urged," the editor of the *Journal of Commerce* wrote. "The one all-controlling reason is that we have an imperative need for an impregnable defensive position in the Pacific, and that we have no other way of getting it than by keeping these Islands, and cannot calculate upon another opportunity if this be neglected."

From another unexpected quarter an additional reason for holding the Philippines was advanced. Church and missionary groups argued that the United States had a moral obligation, forced by the dictates of humanity, to extend the beneficent rule of the United States to the downtrodden Filipino people. Totally ignoring the fact that the great majority were already members of the Roman Catholic Church, it was said to be our duty to Christianize the natives. Brushing aside their desire for independence, the religious press maintained that the United States could not turn its back upon this opportunity to bestow upon the islanders our own laws, institutions, and moral standards. "To refuse the responsibilities thrust upon us," one journal declared, "would be to render the nation guilty of a great crime in the sight of high Heaven."

Finally, the pertinent question was raised of what would be the fate of the Philippines if the United States withdrew. There was little likelihood that with the collapse of Spanish authority the islands would be allowed to maintain their freedom. Germany would be only too glad, a number of political writers pointed out, to take over Spanish responsibilities, and any such dislocation of the delicate balance of power in the Pacific might have dangerous repercussions. The United States was considered the one power whose extension of authority in this part of the world would not constitute a threat to peace.

Subject to such pressures, the American people were drawn irrevocably along the imperialistic path, and nowhere were the ironies of this situation more aptly pointed out than by the inimitable Mr. Dooley—fictional creation of Peter Finley Dunn:

"I know what I'd do if I was Mack," said Mr. Hennessy, "I'd hist a flag over the Ph'lippeens, an' I'd take in th' whole lot iv' thim."

"An' yet," said Mr. Dooley, " 'tis not more thin two months since ye larned whether they were islands or canned goods."

President McKinley was to follow the lead of the commercial interests, the naval strategists, the missionary societies, the proponents of a Pacific balance of power—and Mr. Hennessy. His ultimate decision was that "the march of events rules and overrules human action." The United States could not be unmindful, he declared, of "new duties and responsibilities which we must meet and discharge as becomes a great nation on whose growth and career from the beginning the Ruler of Nations has plainly written the high command and pledge of civilization." On September 16, 1898, he had instructed his peace commissioners in Paris to demand the island of Luzon; on October 26 it was the entire archipelago; and when Spain hesitated, her envoys found themselves, on November 21, facing an ultimatum.

Fortunately for the historian, McKinley has left on record just how he arrived at this conclusion, and thereby threw all the influence of his administration behind a course of action that was to lead to our increasing involvement in the Far East. He explained his decision to a group of visiting clergymen:

I walked the floor of the White House night after night until midnight, and I am not ashamed to tell you gentlemen, that I went down on my knees and prayed God Almighty for light and guidance more than one night. And one night late it came to me this way—I don't know how it was, but it came: (1) That we could not give them back to Spain—that would be cowardly and dishonorable; (2) that we could not turn them over to France or Germany—our commercial rivals in the Orient—that would be bad business and discreditable; (3) that we could not leave them to themselves—they were unfit for self-government—and they would soon have anarchy and misrule over there worse than Spain's was; and (4) that there was nothing left for us to do but to take them all, and to educate the Filipinos, and uplift and civilize and Christianize them, and by God's grace do the very best we could by them, as our fellow men for whom Christ also died. And then I went to bed and went to sleep and slept soundly.

★ THE IMPERIALIST DEBATE

However soundly McKinley slept, there were many persons in the country whose rest was badly disturbed by the idea that the United States was prepared to become a colonial power, governing against their will an alien and distant people. The President was to win both congressional and popular support for the policy he so naively justified in his talk with the visiting clergy. The treaty ensuring the freedom of Cuba and cession of the Philippines, Puerto Rico, and Guam was duly ratified by the Senate on February 6, 1899, and generally endorsed by the American people. But at the same time, an anti-imperialist bloc crossing party lines vigorously fought the whole idea of overseas expansion. Its members attacked annexation of the Philippines on grounds of strategy, expense, dangerous involvement, but most importantly in the conviction that by accepting colonialism, the United States was denying its democratic heritage and those basic principles of liberty and self-government for which it had always stood.

Former President Cleveland and Andrew Carnegie, William Jennings Bryan and Charles Francis Adams, President Eliot of Harvard and Samuel Gompers, Senator Hoar and Speaker Reed, Mark Twain and William Vaughn Moody were among this stalwart band of dissenters. The last named appealed eloquently to the spirit of those who had died for the preservation of American liberties:

> For save we let the island men go free,
> Those baffled and dislaureled ghosts
> Will curse us from the lamentable coasts
> Where walk the frustrate dead.

But the anti-imperialists were combatting the trend of the times. They could not influence a public that was far more stirred by the glorious prospects of overseas expansion than disturbed over any possible conflict with democratic ideals. The opponents of annexation might talk of "this modern swamp and cesspool of imperialism," but the public listened more happily to the expansionists who told them that the United States had embarked upon "a great, a difficult and a noble task."

The election of 1900 confirmed the decision that the President had reached and the Senate duly approved. The Republicans renominated McKinley and the Democrats again named Bryan. While the latter sought desperately to make imperialism the major issue and argued eloquently against retention of the Philippines, the former sought to ignore it and stressed the country's returning prosperity. The fact that the Filipinos themselves were bitterly resisting American occupation forces, an insurrection that would last for three years, might have been expected to provide a basis for stronger support of Bryan's cause, but it could make little headway against the McKinley symbol of "the full dinner pail." The Republican victory was greater than that in 1896, and while the verdict could hardly be considered a specific endorsement of imperialism, it at least showed that the American people were quite prepared to accept overseas expansion rather than run any risk of disturbing prosperity by the election of Bryan.

The new, expansive spirit of the times generally welcomed the role that the United States might now play in world affairs. Nowhere was it expressed more eloquently than in a speech, made during the campaign of 1900, by the young senator from Indiana, the imperialist-minded Albert J. Beveridge:

> The Philippines are ours forever. . . . And just beyond the Philippines are China's illimitable markets. We will not retreat from either. We will not repudiate our duty in the archipelago. We will not abandon our duty in the Orient. We will not renounce our part in the mission of our race, trustee, under God, of the civilization of the world. . . . This island empire is the last land left in all the oceans. If it should prove a mistake to abandon it, the blunder once made would be irretrievable. If it proves a mistake to hold it, the error can be corrected when we will. Every other progressive nation stands ready to relieve us. But to hold it will be no mistake. Our largest trade henceforth must be with Asia. The Pacific is our ocean . . . and the Pacific is the ocean of the commerce of the future. Most future wars will be conflicts for commerce. The power that rules the Pacific, therefore, is the Power that rules the world. And, with the Philippines, that Power is and will forever be the American Republic.

There were some questionable aspects to this glowing prophecy of the future. The Philippines would not prove to be the commercial asset that Beveridge envisioned, and the imperialistic fervor of the country was to subside almost as rapidly as it had arisen. Yet from this time on, the United States was not to abandon what the Senator from Indiana was pleased to call "our duty in the Orient." Nor has the final word been said of the significance of the Pacific in the history of the United States and in that of the world.

★ CHINA AND THE OPEN DOOR

The ink was hardly dry on the peace treaty with Spain when the developing situation in China, where the European powers were encroaching more and more upon that helpless country, led President McKinley's new Secretary of State, John Hay, to make a move no less significant than acquisition of the Philippines. This was the dispatch, in September, 1899, of his famed Open Door notes asking of the powers some guarantee of equality of trade within the Chinese Empire. They did not add up to very much in themselves. They did not even question the powers' existing spheres of influence. But they set in motion a train of events that, after a long period of successive advance and retreat, would lead to Pearl Harbor.

The European advance in China—Russia in Manchuria, Germany in Shantung, Great Britain in the Yangtze Valley—had already aroused American concern, but the actual instigation for the Open Door notes came from within the State Department rather than from either Hay or McKinley. Even though their tone was moderate and mild, they did not particularly please European capitals. Secretary Hay's great feat was to interpret the powers' somewhat ambiguous answers to his demarche as a full-fledged acceptance of his proposal that there should be no discrimination within any power's existing sphere of influence against the trade of nationals of other countries. He formally declared that the principle of commercial equality had been universally accepted.

A year later internal revolt flared up within China and fanatical antiforeign bands known as Boxers ravaged the countryside and finally besieged the legations in Peking. The powers appeared intent upon using the occasion for further demands upon China, and the old empire's very existence seemed to be threatened. The United States joined forces with an allied military expedition to raise the siege of the legations, which was successfully achieved under the most dramatic circumstances, but Hay now took a further step to uphold the Open Door and prevent any possible political division of China. He announced that it would be American policy to respect Chinese territorial and administrative independence, as well as the principle of trade equality, in all its dealings with the Chinese Empire. To what extent this pronouncement may have been responsible for the preservation of China's independence in 1900 may be questionable, but the United States had taken a strong and decisive stand in its support. Moreover, it continued to exercise a restraining influence on the powers in the settlement of claims arising out of the Boxer Rebellion and returned to China part of the payments made on its own claims.

These two phases of American policy toward China—insistence upon trade equality and respect for Chinese sovereignty—have ever since 1900 been linked together in popular understanding as the Open Door policy. This policy has commanded a measure of interest and support over the years second only to that accorded the Monroe Doctrine. Neither the European powers nor Japan, however, ever fully accepted its implications. Their apparent willingness to acknowledge China's independence in 1900 was perhaps more due to their inability to agree on how the country could be divided than to anything else. The United States was to find itself hard pressed to maintain the Open Door, first against encroachments on the part of Russia and then on the part of Japan. It was again and again compelled to retreat from the position

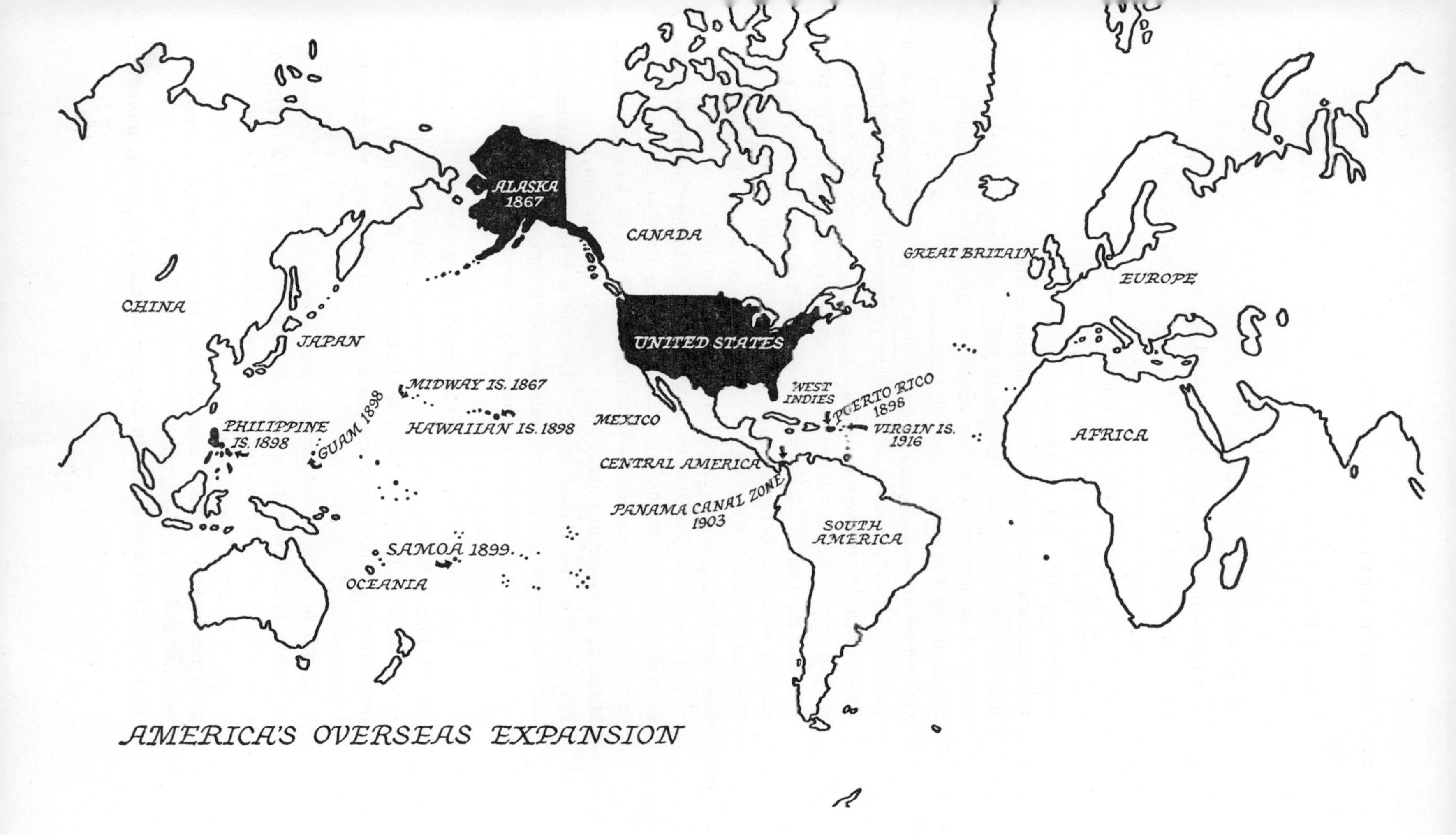

AMERICA'S OVERSEAS EXPANSION

taken in 1900 until the issue came to a final climax in the Pacific war forty-one years later.

★ COLONIAL POLICIES

The important role assumed by the United States in eastern Asia with pronouncement of the Open Door policy was a direct consequence of overseas expansion. As for our new colonial possessions themselves, they would present many and difficult problems even after the final suppression of revolt in the Philippines. The constitutional issue of their assimilation under our republican form of government was the first important question. It was not practical to treat them as territories, with all the rights and privileges of self-government which had been extended to territories in the course of continental expansion. The people of the Philippines were of a different race, with a different social and cultural background, and in their religion predominantly Roman Catholic. Much the same thing could be said of the inhabitants of Puerto Rico. Moreover, on highly pragmatic grounds, a protection-minded country had no desire to allow the entry of these islands' products into the United States free of all tariff controls. Yet at the same time, it would have run counter to all our national traditions to rule Filipinos or Puerto Ricans as completely subject people, without benefit of the basic liberties accorded by the constitution.

The solution, as eventually set forth by the Supreme Court in a series of decisions in the Insular Cases, beginning in 1901, was to make the new possessions "unincorporated territories," or as was specifically stated in reference to Puerto Rico, "territory appurtenant to . . . but not a part of the United States." Through a highly complicated and sometimes vague process of reasoning, their inhabitants were consequently said to be entitled to enjoy certain fundamental rights—freedom of speech, freedom of religion—but not necessarily all the privileges extended to citizens of the continental United States. Our new possessions, for example, were to be subject in matters of tariff regulations to such special duties as Congress might see fit to impose. To the hotly debated question of whether the constitution followed the flag, the Supreme Court answered: only in part.

In spite of certain ambiguities in this colonial system and continuing difficulties in administration, originally undertaken by the War Department, it may nevertheless be said that the United States provided the people in its new possessions with a degree of self-government they had never before known. They were also helped out through generally enlightened policies in respect to education, sanitation, transportation, and other aspects of social life. In the case of the Philippines, moreover, freedom was promised "as soon as a stable government can be established."

President McKinley sent William Howard Taft to the islands in 1900 in charge of a commission to prepare the way for self-government and other reforms. Within a few years, the Filipinos were electing the lower house of their legislature, and the Jones Act of 1916 then gave them almost complete control over domestic affairs, except for an appointed governor. After considerable delay and protracted debate, the Tydings-McDuffie Act of 1934 finally made definite provision for complete independence within a ten-year period. The Filipinos themselves accepted the law's provisions two years later, and in spite of the interposition of World War II, an independent Philippine Republic was proclaimed on July 4, 1946.

Whatever its record as a colonial power, the more important consequence for the United States of the imperialist upsurge of the closing years of the nineteenth century was the nation's dramatic emergence upon the stage of world politics. The complacent aloofness of the nineteenth century had come to an abrupt end. However long it might be before the American people were fully ready to accept the responsibilities of a new international role, they could never again completely ignore them.

Once more Mr. Dooley may perhaps be given the last word as he viewed these developments, not from the vantage point of the middle of the twentieth century, but from his contemporary post of observation:

> I sigh f'r th' good old days befur we became what Hogan calls a wurruld power. In thim days our fav'rite spoort was playin' solytare, winnin' money fr'm each other, an' no wan th' worse off. Ivry body was invious iv us. We didn't care f'r th' big game goin' on in th' corner. Whin it broke up in a row we said: 'Gintlemin, gintlemin!' an' maybe wint over an' grabbed somebody's stake. But we cuddn't stand it anny longer. We had to give up our little game of patience an' cut into th' other deal. An' now, be Hivens, we have no peace iv mind.

That peace of mind in the realm of foreign affairs would be even more elusive a half century later.

CHAPTER XI

The Spirit of Progressivism

★ THE NEW CENTURY'S CONFIDENT OUTLOOK

The opening of the new century found the United States strong, prosperous, and confident. The nation's imperialistic ventures, however skeptically viewed in some quarters, were an expression of mounting power deeply satisfying to most Americans. International prestige was greatly enhanced with overseas possessions, and it was gratifying to have the European powers acknowledge the new role of the United States in world affairs.

It is true that the tremendous changes wrought in modern society by industrial growth and development were a cause for concern among some of those who thought more deeply. A growing absorption in materialistic values, at the apparent expense of those simple republican virtues associated with an earlier day, was deeply disturbing to moral philosophers. The American people generally, however, were certain that all would be well in a world that had so far been so kind to them. Their attitude was exemplified in Theodore Roosevelt's buoyant declaration that "we think the greatest victories are yet to be won, the greatest deeds yet to be done, and that there are yet in store for our people and the cause that we uphold, grander triumphs than have yet been scored."

Ample justification for such optimism appeared to be at hand. The re-election of President McKinley in 1900 promised the continuation of government policies directed toward fulfillment of the Republican slogan of "the full dinner pail." Business and industry were forging ahead with this new assurance that there would be no attempt to restrain their expanding activities. Good times had returned for the farmer with bumper crops and higher prices. Even labor could look to a brighter future as the embittered industrial warfare of the 1890's gave way to efforts for co-operation in what contemporaries called a honeymoon period of capital and labor. "An air of contentment and enthusiastic cheerfulness," William Graham Sumner wrote of the twentieth century's dawn, "characterized the thought and temper of the American people."

The country experienced a sudden shock when President McKinley, attending the Pan-American Exposition at Buffalo, was shot by a half-crazed anarchist on September 6, 1901. His death brought Theodore Roosevelt, who had been elected vice-president, to the White House, and no one knew what this young, impetuous man so unexpectedly called to national leadership might do. It was whispered about that J. P. Morgan, symbol of triumphant American capitalism, had collapsed when he heard of McKinley's death, and that Mark Hanna was in a frenzy as he realized that "that damn cowboy" was the new President. But hastily summoned to Buffalo from the Adirondack wilderness where he had been vacationing, Roosevelt was reassuring. "I wish to say," he stated solemnly as the oath of office was administered, "that it will be my aim to continue, absolutely unbroken, the policy of President McKinley for the peace, the prosperity, and the honor of our beloved country."

★ BACKGROUND OF PROGRESSIVISM

There was a certain irony in this pledge. Roosevelt's assumption of the presidency was actually to usher in a new period in American history that was to witness far-reaching changes in the policies for which McKinley had stood. The Progressive era, which may perhaps be dated from that memorable day when Roosevelt took the oath of office and was to extend to the eve of our entry into World War I, was marked by a shift in popular attitudes that spelled the eclipse of the laissez faire philosophy that had dominated national life throughout the nineteenth century. The roots of these far-reaching changes may be easily traced back to the 1890's and still earlier periods of protest and dissent, but the Progressive era has a distinct identity. It was to witness the Square Deal, the New Nationalism and the New Freedom, which were in turn antecedents of the New Deal, and the growth of popular reforms that greatly transformed the role of government in the sphere of economic legislation.

The new principles adopted in these years were in large part those that had been put forward by the Populists and for which Bryan had unsuccessfully campaigned in 1896. They represented the acceptance of responsibility on the part of state governments, and even more notably on the part of the national government, for more effective regulation of business and industry. The Progressive movement was a drive to restore to the people as a whole the political power that had been usurped by the business community. It was an attack upon privilege and "invisible government"—a campaign to control the railroads, the trusts, and the money power in the national interest. Where Populism had failed to break through the ramparts of embattled industry, Progressivism breasted them successfully. The aims of its leaders were by no means fully realized, but the bases of democracy were strengthened. A broad program of social and economic reform accounted for a very considerable advance along the endless road to social justice.

Progressivism succeeded where Populism failed because it had a much broader foundation, less radical connotations, and reached out far beyond distressed farmers and discontented workingmen. However much it actually borrowed from this earlier movement, it couched its demands in less revolutionary language and relied on more responsible leadership. "Populism shaved its whiskers, washed its shirt, put on a derby," William Allen White wrote, "and moved up into the middle of the class —the upper middle class."

There were a number of reasons why the middle classes who had feared Populism should now endorse Progressivism. They saw it leading to their own recovery of political power and believed this to be essential if small businessmen, members of the professions, and white collar workers generally were to hold their own in the face of the economic pressures being exerted by big business on the one hand, and by the new strength of industrial labor on the other. The changing pattern of national life was seriously affecting these groups not only in respect to their economic position but also their social status. They felt the role they had once played in society was somehow being denied them, and that they were menaced almost equally by the lower classes and the upper classes. "From above come the problems of predatory wealth," one contemporary wrote. "From below come the problems of poverty and pigheaded and brutish criminality." The middle class supported progressive reforms, especially in the political sphere, to safeguard their freedom and liberty and to recover the social status they appeared to be losing.

The Progressives believed firmly in democratic capitalism, were certain that they could eliminate the abuses which had made poverty the handmaiden of progress, and never doubted that they could solve the problems facing twentieth-century America. They were embarked on a crusade which drew its strength from the deep wellspring of the liberal and humanitarian sentiments of the American people. While Progressivism differed as the times differed from earlier manifestations of the defense of popular rights, it was in the tradition of such democratic uprisings as those associated with Jefferson, Jackson, and Lincoln.

Having said this much, it must nevertheless be added that from the perspective of another age, Progressivism had its conservative—sometimes even reactionary—aspects as well as its liberal impulses. It was torn between a desire to try to re-create the conditions of the past, especially in the realm of business competition, and the urge to build up a new highly nationalistic state with far-reaching economic controls. It failed to understand or generally support the cause of organized labor and retained a very skeptical attitude toward the role of unions. It was strongly marked by attitudes of racial superiority which found expression in support for the colonial rule of subject peoples, discrimination against Negroes, and intolerance toward the new immigrants from southeastern Europe. The progressive mentality was a compound of many curious elements, as George E. Mowry has written in a recent analysis of "the progressive profile," and one of these elements was "a rather ugly strain of racism."

The frontal assault that the Populists had directed against monopoly and the money power alarmed many moderates, as has been suggested, quite as much as the captains of industry and finance. Progressivism's goal was always to conserve rather than to destroy. Drawing its support from so many walks of life and from every part of the country, it was neither sectional nor partisan. Both major parties, seeking as they always must to appeal to the largest possible number of voters, were compelled to subscribe to its major tenets. Jumping nimbly aboard the bandwagon of reform, Senator Beveridge wrote in 1905:

> I have been carefully studying the present unrest and interviewing numbers of people about it. I am coming to the conclusion that it is not a passing whim, but a great and natural movement as occurs, in this country, as our early history shows, about every forty years. It is not like the Granger episode or the Debs episode. The former . . . affected only the farmers; the latter only the workingmen. The present unrest, however, is quite as vigorous among the intellectuals, college men, university people, etc., as it is among the common people.

What was happening in the United States, it should also be pointed out, was not peculiar to this country. Throughout the western world a fresh impetus had been given to an almost universal drive for social welfare. In Great Britain and Germany, in France and Italy, social and humanitarian legislation was being enacted. Conservative as well as liberal governments felt the need for such measures, if for no other reason than to silence a rising socialist demand for a complete overhauling of the capitalist state. The immense changes wrought by the industrial revolution no longer permitted governments to accept the laissez faire doctrines of the nineteenth century. These changes demanded intervention in the economic and social sphere to adjust more equitably the conflicting interests of capital and labor, business and agriculture, producer and consumer. The universal trend was already pointing toward the welfare state. It would in time be carried to arbitrary extremes where the tradition of democracy was not strong enough to defend individual liberties. The United States was conforming to a general pattern of reform when its citizens insisted that government pay more attention to the needs of the common people.

★ PROGRESSIVE LEADERS

The leaders of Progressivism came from both parties and widely separated regions. Bryan still found the presidency beyond his reach, but he continued to do yeoman service invigorating principles for which he had been a forthright spokesman long before they had become respectable. From Wisconsin came forth a doughty champion of the people's cause in the person of Robert La Follette, governor and senator, a stubborn, implacable fighter who also hoped, as Bryan hoped, to make his way to the White House. There was no one who at once had a more realistic understanding of economic problems and showed a more impassioned zeal for reform than "Fighting Bob" La Follette.

Of far greater importance in the opening years of the century was Theodore Roosevelt. Never one to head an unpopular cause, he sensed intuitively that the times demanded new policies. Sound and fury characterized his dynamic career. After one of his explosions it was often difficult to discover whether anything at all had happened. Yet in the popular mind, he came to symbolize Progressivism. Even La Follette, who became his political foe, declared that Roosevelt had crystallized public sentiment and made the people ready "for the greatest work that any nation ever did."

And then there was Woodrow Wilson, the austere and lonely idealist. He signally lacked the common touch, but his growing conviction that entirely new adjustments were necessary to meet the needs of modern economic society, and his abiding faith in democracy, were eventually to give form and substance to the New Freedom.

Behind these men stood others: Tom Johnson of Cleveland, called the best mayor of the best-governed city in the United States; "Golden Rule" Jones who fought corruption and provided free kindergartens and free concerts in Toledo; such progressive state governors as Charles E. Hughes in New York, Hiram Johnson in California, Joseph W. Folk in Missouri, and Albert B. Cummins in Iowa; and among the senators in addition to La Follette, George W. Norris, Albert Beveridge, Joseph L. Bristow, Jonathan P. Dolliver and William E. Borah, men who wore the badge of no special interest but represented the people. In the ranks marched a citizen army that gave Progressivism its force and strength.

★ THE MUCKRAKERS

How universal was the awakening of the people to the need for reform —what one contemporary writer called the "bracing of the moral sense of the country"—is revealed in the newspapers, the magazines, the fiction of the day. Philosophers and journalists, economists and novelists were alike in challenging the rule of plutocracy and demanding the return of political power to the people and the promotion of social justice. The criticism of the economic order, if not the proposed solutions, which had been advanced by Henry George, by Edward Bellamy, by Henry Demarest Lloyd, by Lester Ward was now bearing fruit.

And other leaders of thought were taking up their burden. John Dewey continued to exemplify Progressivism in education and social philosophy; in the realm of economics, Thorstein Veblen mordantly assailed a system that encouraged waste and extravagance through its emphasis upon "conspicuous consumption"; the sociologist E. A. Ross ably exposed "the sins of society" in the framework of a new, impersonal, corporate business structure. Church leaders too lent their influence to reform, talking less of the Gospel of Wealth and more of the Social Gospel.

The general public was even more stimulated by the books and articles of a group of magazine writers who were to become collectively known as muckrakers, a term derived from *Pilgrim's Progress* which Roosevelt fastened upon them in a moment of exasperation. Lincoln Steffens wrote a memorable series of articles published under the general title of *The Shame of the Cities* which ruthlessly exposed the graft and corruption so prevalent in municipal politics. His attack was leveled not so much against the businessmen who bribed the politicians, or the bosses who betrayed the people, as against a system that encouraged the purchase and sale of special privileges, fraud in street railway franchises, and police protection for saloons and brothels. From another angle, Ida Tarbell graphically exposed in her *History of the Standard Oil Company* the practices and policies that encouraged industrial monopoly. Her presentation was precise, factual, and carefully documented, and once again there was no attempt to single out villains. Miss Tarbell let the record speak for itself.

The publication of these series of articles began with the October 1902 issue of *McClure's Magazine*. It had taken the lead in reducing the price of the popular monthly magazine to attract a wider audience, and somewhat to the surprise of its editors, "muckraking" struck a very responsive chord. The circulation of *McClure's* zoomed. Other magazines were quick to profit from its experience, and comparable articles began to appear in almost every popular monthly. The *Cosmopolitan, Everybody's, Collier's* and later *The American Magazine* were soon exploiting the literature of exposure. Millions of readers who had been only vaguely aware of the implications of the tie-up between big business and politics, the corruption so widespread in municipal government, and other abuses in our national life, became thoroughly aroused. Muckraking, or at least the literature of exposure, was not entirely new; what was new was that the magazines printing such articles had a mass circulation.

Ray Stannard Baker took up an old grievance in *The Railroads on Trial;* Charles Edward Russell attacked the meat-packers in *The Greatest Trust in the World;* Burton J. Kendrick wrote his revealing *Story of Life Insurance,* based upon investigations in New York; and Thomas Lawson, a onetime spectacular plunger in stocks, told in *Frenzied Finance* the inside story of the organization of the Amalgamated Copper Company. Going beyond the sphere of local or even state politics, David Graham Phillips traced the unsavory trail of fraud and corruption to Washington itself, and startled the nation with his outspoken account of *The Treason of the Senate.*

"Now when I pick me fav'rite magazine off the floor," the irrepressible Mr. Dooley was quoted as saying, "what do I find? Everything has gone wrong. The world is little better than a convict's camp. All the poems by the lady authoresses that used to begin, 'O Moon, how fair,' now begin: 'Oh Ogden Armour, how awful'. . . . Here you are. Last edition. Just out. Full account of the crimes of Incalculated. . . . Graft everywhere. Graft in the insurance companies, graft in Congress, graft in the Supreme Court. Graft by an old Grafter."

Mr. Dooley moreover recognized the influence of the muckrakers. In his observations upon the power of the press, he told his countrymen that "th' hand that rocks th' fountain pen is th' hand that rules th' wurruld."

★ MUCKRAKING FICTION

The muckraking articles had their counterpart in the novels of the day. The new school of realistic writers took up the same problems and the same issues. Frank Norris' exposure of railroad practices in *The Octopus* was a case in point. The domineering role of the business magnate, going his imperious way with scant consideration of the public interest, was Theodore Dreiser's theme in *The Titan* and *The Financier*. The more popular novels of Winston Churchill (the *American* Winston

Churchill), such as *Coniston* and *Mr. Crewe's Career,* were revelations quite as explicit as those in nonfiction of the course of political preferment in a business civilization.

An unusual but striking illustration of the muckraking novel promoting the cause of reform was Upton Sinclair's *The Jungle.* It was written to expose the ruthless exploitation of workers in the Chicago stockyards, but it happened to be published in 1906 at the climax of a nationwide drive for federal meat inspection and pure food laws. Sinclair's gruesome portrayal of the prevalence of tuberculosis among the meat handlers, the dirt and filth of the cutting rooms, and the completely unsanitary conditions of life in "Packingtown" did more to arouse support for the proposed legislation than any other single factor. One passage read as follows:

> There was never the least attention paid to what was cut up for sausage; there would come all the way back from Europe old sausage that had been rejected, and that was mouldy and white—it would be dosed with borax and glycerine, and dumped into the hoppers, and made over again for home consumption. There would be meat stored in great piles in rooms; and the water from the leaky roofs would drip over it, and thousands of rats would race about on it. It was too dark in these storage places to see well, but a man could run his hand over these piles of meat and sweep off handfuls of the dried dung of rats. These rats were a nuisance, and the packers would put poisoned bread out for them; they would die, and then rats, bread, and meat would go into the hoppers together.

Among the readers of *The Jungle* was President Roosevelt, and Mr. Dooley gave his readers a picturesque description of the scene he imagined to have taken place at the White House:

"Tiddy was toying with a light breakfast an' idly turnin' over the pages iv the new book with both hands. Suddenly he rose from th' table, and cryin': 'I'm pizened,' began throwin' sausages out iv the window. . . . since then th' President, like th' rest iv us, has become a viggytarian."

The story was perhaps closer to fact than fancy. In any event, Roosevelt was persuaded to give his full support to the meat inspection and pure food bills. In spite of the shrill outcries of diehard opponents of business regulation, they became law.

★ LOCAL POLITICAL REFORMS

In response to the popular pressure aroused by muckrakers and reformers, the Progressive era saw city after city, state after state, seeking to deal more effectively with the economic and social sores that had for so long been festering in American society. The movement for municipal reform was in many cases short-lived and ephemeral. It was too often an uprising to throw the rascals out, rather than the basic attack urged by Lincoln Steffens on a system that created rascals. Nevertheless, the adoption of home rule won greater freedom for urban democracy over a larger part of the country, and in a number of cases the establishment of a commission form of government, or appointment of a city manager, provided the basis for lasting reform. At least a beginning was also made in the more efficient handling of traffic and sanitation problems, slum clearance and low-cost housing, fire and police protection. It was finally realized that urban government and city planning demanded a modern and scientific approach.

In the sphere of state activity, the Progressives launched a twofold drive to break the power of machine politics and secure the enactment of needed social legislation. What had been happening was most pointedly revealed, not by some wild-eyed reformer, but by so stalwart a conservative as the Republican statesman, Elihu Root. At the New York constitutional convention in 1915, he said:

> They call the system . . . invisible government. For I don't know how many years Mr. Conkling was the supreme ruler in this State; the Governor did not count; comptrollers and secretaries of state and what not did not count. . . . Then Mr. Platt ruled the State; for nigh upon twenty years he ruled it. It was not the Governor; it was not the Legislature; it was not any elected officers; it was Mr. Platt. . . . The ruler of the State during the greater part of the forty years of my acquaintance with the State government has not been any man authorized by the Constitution or by the law.

In attacking this "invisible government," the Progressives campaigned vigorously and with success, in state after state, for the secret ballot, direct primaries, the initiative and referendum, and the recall of elected officials. Wisconsin and Oregon were leaders in this movement, both Roosevelt and Wilson paying tribute to the effectiveness of their new laws. The former spoke of the two states' "wise experimental legislation aiming to secure the social and political betterment of the people as a whole"; the latter declared that the effect of their reforms was "to bring government back to the people and to protect it from the control of the representatives of selfish and special interests."

The Progressives were too sanguine in their estimation of the value of these reforms. There was no smooth path to the establishment of political democracy. The party bosses were not easily discouraged and managed in many instances to retain a firm control. Tinkering with the machinery of politics was no substitute for that continued public participation in government which alone could assure responsible leadership and honest administration. But the Progressive drive worked immediate improvements and set higher standards for political life. It changed the prevailing atmosphere to the extent that the bosses were put on the defensive and could no longer rule with the effrontery that had been their wont.

★ CONSTITUTIONAL AMENDMENT

Associated with this movement for political democracy were the nationwide campaigns for the direct election of senators and for woman suffrage. They naturally transcended local and even state boundaries. They grew up from the grass roots, but could be fully realized only through constitutional amendment.

The contention of reformers, as originally set forth in the Populist platform, was that the reactionary influence of the Senate could only be broken by having the people vote directly for senators instead of having them chosen by state legislatures. They also believed that, given the franchise, women would exercise a liberalizing influence on government and provide strong support for social legislation. Experience would appear to indicate that while direct elections have given the Senate a greater sense of public responsibility, woman suffrage, for all its influence on local issues, has had little perceptible effect on national politics.

The movement to revise the method for election of senators began in the 1890's when the conservatism of the Senate, as indeed the Founding Fathers had intended, became an increasingly powerful barrier to liberal legislation. It had proved itself long since to be the stronghold of the business interests of the country, derisively known as "the millionaires' club." Moreover, there had been all too frequent occasions when these business interests secured the election of men they wanted through bribery or other forms of corrupt pressure upon the state legislatures. While all earlier attempts to amend the constitution had been defeated by the Senate itself, changing conditions were now to compel it to fall in line with the popular demand. More than half the states, in fact, had adopted various forms of preferential primaries in the early 1900's whereby the state legislatures no more than endorsed candidates already chosen by the people. In these circumstances, Congress finally approved the proposed reform in 1912 and a year later it was ratified by the states to become the Seventeenth Amendment.

In the case of woman suffrage, there had been continued agitation in its favor since the middle of the nineteenth century. By its close, four western states had adopted constitutions with equal suffrage, and women also voted to a considerable extent in local elections in other parts of the country. Not until 1910, however, did the vigorous campaigning of the suffragettes under such able leaders as Carrie Chapman Catt and

Anna Howard Shaw begin to make real headway. Washington, California, Arizona, Kansas, and Oregon then set an example in extending the vote that soon became a stampede. Younger members of the National American Woman Suffrage Association were at once encouraged to press the demand for federal action through constitutional amendment, and the more militant among them began to stage mass demonstrations and great woman suffrage rallies, even picketing the White House to draw public attention to their cause.

Entry into World War I then gave a further impetus to the entire movement, with so many women taking up war work and going into munitions factories, and President Wilson finally gave it his formal endorsement in January 1918. The equal suffrage amendment—the nineteenth—was approved by Congress the next year and duly ratified by the required three-fourths of the states in 1920.

The two other amendments of this period, the sixteenth, which as adopted in 1913 legalized an income tax, and the eighteenth, which established Prohibition in 1920, are discussed under later headings.

★ SOCIAL AND ECONOMIC LEGISLATION

The adoption of political reforms was partly the means to an end for the Progressives; they wanted popular support for state social legislation. Attacking the prevailing concepts of laissez faire, they demanded laws that would do away with child labor, safeguard the position of women in industry, enforce workmen's compensation, and otherwise protect the interests of the factory workers. Their concern over such issues was humanitarian in its origins rather than inspired by organized labor. Under Samuel Gompers' leadership, indeed, the A.F. of L. upheld the principles of laissez faire as applied to social legislation quite as vigorously during these years as did business leaders. The Federation insisted upon labor's freedom to organize, strongly attacking the use of injunctions and enforcement of yellow dog contracts. It also believed in workmen's compensation and was sympathetic toward legislation in behalf of better working conditions for women and children. However, proposals for maximum hour or minimum wage laws that would apply to labor as a whole—let alone any idea of unemployment insurance—found no support whatever among organized labor's high command. Writing in the *American Federationist* in 1915, Gompers asked:

> Whither are we drifting? If wages are low, a law or commission is the remedy proposed. What can be the result of such a tendency but the softening of the moral fibre of the people? Where there is unwillingness to accept responsibility for one's life and for making the most of it, there is a loss

> of strong, redblooded, rugged independence and will power. . . . We do not want to place more power in the hands of government to investigate and regulate the lives, the conduct and the freedom of America's workers.

The advances made in social legislation, which steadily weakened the concept of laissez faire so far as state governments were concerned, were nonetheless very important. Factory codes were stiffened, child labor greatly restricted, maximum working hours for women prescribed in almost every state, and through workmen's compensation laws employers were made liable for benefit payments in the case of the death or injury of their employees regardless of accident responsibility. In some instances, maximum hour laws were extended to all employees, and a tentative—but unsuccessful—beginning was also made toward minimum wage legislation.

★ THE ATTITUDE OF THE COURTS

Many of these laws faced a difficult hurdle in the Supreme Court's interpretation of that clause in the Fourteenth Amendment stating that no person could be deprived of life, liberty, or property without due process of law. While the real intent of this amendment had been to safeguard the civil rights of the Negroes, the Court gave it a broader meaning, as it already had in the state railway regulation cases, in judging wage and hour legislation. It laid down the principle that maximum hour laws, enacted under the states' police power for the protection of public health, were an unconstitutional restriction of freedom in that they interfered with the right of both employer and employee to agree upon any terms of employment they might choose. A fallacy in this reasoning, quickly pointed out by the reformers, was that in a highly industrialized age the individual worker did not in fact have any "liberty of contract." He had to take the terms his prospective employer offered him—or go without the job. He did not meet the employer on a basis of equality and could not effectively protect his own interests.

Nevertheless, in the notable case of *Lochner* v *New York,* involving a law limiting the hours of work in bakeries, the Supreme Court flatly stated in 1905 that there was no reasonable foundation for holding such a statute necessary or appropriate as a health law, and that it was invalid as a violation of both freedom of contract and property rights. The opinion underscored the Court's opposition to social reform, and Justice Oliver Wendell Holmes, whose attitude on such issues was to win him a lasting reputation as "the great dissenter," took strong exception to the majority opinion. He declared that the Constitution did not embody any particular economic view, whether of paternalism or laissez faire, and that the states were free to experiment with social legislation even though the members of the Court might find such laws injudicious or even tyrannical. "The accident of our finding certain opinions natural and familiar, or novel, and even shocking," he warned, "ought not to conclude our judgment upon the question of whether statutes embodying them conflict with the Constitution of the United States."

It was not until well into the new century that the Supreme Court, in such cases as *Muller* v *Oregon* and *Bunting* v *Oregon,* finally faced the realities in this situation and first for women, and then for all industrial employees, acknowledged the power of the states to limit working hours. But when minimum wage legislation was then proposed on the same grounds—that is, as representing a legitimate exercise of the police power to protect public health and morals—the Supreme Court again balked. It divided equally in a first case, *Stetler* v *O'Hara,* but then in *Adkins* v *Children's Hospital,* decided in 1923, emphatically denied the constitutionality of a congressional law that sought to establish minimum wages for women in the District of Columbia. The New Deal was well established before there was judicial admission that a power sustained in the case of maximum hour legislation was equally valid in the establishment of minimum wages.

While no attempt was made to block the abolition of child labor by the states, the conservatism of the Supreme Court on economic issues was again conspicuously revealed when it denied the federal government any right to legislate in this field. Two attempts were made to eliminate child labor on a national basis. Congress first passed a law banning the transportation in interstate commerce of goods manufactured by companies employing children and then sought to impose a heavy federal tax on such goods. In both instances, as decided in *Hammer* v *Dagenhart* in 1918 and *Bailey* v *Drexel Furniture Company* in 1922, the Supreme Court declared the laws in question unconstitutional on the ground that congressional powers over interstate commerce had been exceeded. There was a sharp dissent on the part of the minority, but the child labor decisions held good until the mid-1930's.

In spite of judicial hesitations in sustaining social legislation, the record made by the states in doing away with child labor, safeguarding women in industry, setting up workmen's compensation, and otherwise trying to meet the problems of the factory age was a notable one. In flat contradiction of the nineteenth-century concept that government should hold completely aloof from any interference in the economic sphere, a broad responsibility to protect public health, safety, and morals was now widely accepted. Even though the new laws were still limited to the states, they had won for society important and far-reaching gains.

★ A NATIONAL PROBLEM

The problems with which the Progressives were seeking to cope rose in every instance out of the industrial background of modern America. Their program represented a belated recognition of the popular demand for something more than those governmental controls that had sufficed in the far simpler days of the nineteenth century. The many ugly manifestations of an age of corporate enterprise, in which individual ethical standards were not applied to business management or industrial relations, were a challenge that democracy had to face.

There was a minority element that saw the only solution to "the sins of society" in the substitution of socialism for capitalism. Some of the muckrakers and contemporary novelists believed in the assumption by government of complete control over the country's basic industries—beginning with the public utilities, the railroads, and coal mining. Under the dynamic leadership of Eugene V. Debs, whose honesty and sincerity won general respect, the Socialist party was stronger than in any other period of our history. But in spite of some fears that it might attract a really significant popular following, its doctrinaire tenets were unacceptable to a people who so greatly prized free enterprise. Socialism made very slight headway even among labor groups. There was no important movement, as there was in contemporary England, for the formation of an independent labor party favoring the nationalization of industry.

The Progressives remained firmly committed to the preservation of the capitalist system. It was in this conservative spirit that they campaigned so vigorously in asserting popular rights and in pushing forward their program of social and economic legislation in the states. At the same time it was fully recognized that many of the fundamental problems facing the country were, in the final analysis, national problems. Big business was national; organized labor was national. If effective controls were to be set up to regulate the railroads, the trusts, and the money power, only the national government could do this successfully.

Among the publicists of this era was Herbert Croly, subsequently the editor of the *New Republic.* There were others, but he was the leading exponent of this national approach. In *The Promise of American Life,* published in 1909, he declared that the movement for progressive reform should be lifted above the level of local governments as rapidly and as effectively as possible. He was convinced that some measure of social planning was necessary to adjust the inequalities of American life and secure for the masses of the people greater economic as well as political freedom. "The problem belongs to the American national democracy," he asserted, "and its solution must be attempted by means of official national action."

Croly believed that with such an approach the problems confronting the country could be solved. No one expressed more emphatically the hopeful and confident spirit of Progressivism. He saw grave abuses casting "a deep shadow over the traditional American patriotic vision." He felt that it was no longer enough merely to proclaim one's belief in "an indubitable and a beneficent national future." But he was superbly confident that if works were added to faith, the American dream would surely be realized.

Roosevelt accepted this thesis. It lay at the basis of his New Nationalism. Wilson supported it though in somewhat different form. It was intimately related to his concept of the New Freedom. Municipal and state reforms were in some measure only preliminaries to what these presidential exponents of Progressivism accomplished on the national stage.

CHAPTER XII

The Roosevelt Era

★ T.R.: BACKGROUND AND CHARACTER

"Do you know the two most wonderful things I have seen in your country?" the British statesman, John Morley, asked rhetorically during the administration of the first Roosevelt. "Niagara Falls and the President of the United States, both great wonders of nature."

Theodore Roosevelt was by every count one of the most colorful, energetic, and popular presidents ever to live in the White House. He was not invariably the great reform leader that he was so often considered to be by his contemporaries. Fundamentally conservative in his thinking, as his position during the campaign of 1896 had revealed, he was swept along by the progressive current of the times. He favored such reforms as he did, not so much from the conviction of a Bryan or a La Follette, but to avert the dangers he saw in the demands of organized labor, the rising tide of socialism, and the popular reaction to the disturbing revelations of the muckrakers. "How I wish I wasn't a reformer, oh, Senator!" he once wrote Chauncey Depew. "But I suppose I must live up to my part, like the Negro minstrel who blacked himself all over!"

And live up to his part he did. He struck out magnificently against the "malefactors of great wealth" and the "mighty industrial overlords." He convinced the public that he was always the fearless champion of the people, the foe of monopoly, and the great trust buster. The noise of his incessant efforts to defend the common cause filled the land:

> T.R. is spanking a Senator,
> T.R. is chasing a bear,
> T.R. is busting an awful Trust
> And dragging it from his lair.
> They're calling T.R. a lot of things—

The men in the private car—
But the day-coach likes exciting folks
And the day-coach likes T.R.

When the dust raised by his prodigious exertions—Henry Adams once characterized Roosevelt as "pure act"—settled down, the scene had not always greatly changed. The trusts actually multiplied during his term of office more than during the McKinley administration. The drive to regulate the railroads, some of his critics felt, was slowed down by his willingness to compromise. The movement for tariff reform was stalemated. "Whence comes this demand for tariff tinkering?" Speaker of the House Cannon asked. "Aren't all our fellows happy?" Roosevelt took his advice. "For the last two years," he wrote Cannon in 1907, "I have accepted your view on just what we should say on the tariff—or rather as to what we should not say. . . ."

Nevertheless, as even La Follette admitted in praising his role in arousing the people to the need for reform, Roosevelt gave the country the national leadership that it had long lacked. He wielded the "big stick" in foreign affairs to build up national prestige, resolutely asserted the political power of the federal government against the rival forces of capitalism, and vigorously set forth the authority of the Chief Executive. He was convinced that it was not only the right but the duty of the President to do anything, unless expressly forbidden in the Constitution, that the needs of the nation demanded. He was often ready to act first and then seek authority for what he had done. Whatever else may be said of Theodore Roosevelt, he instilled new life and vigor in national affairs.

He came to the presidency with a background and experience that differed sharply from that of any of his predecessors since the Civil War. Inherited wealth, Harvard, close association with the social aristocracy of the Atlantic seaboard were unusual points of departure on the road to the White House. His friends were never really able to understand why he entered politics. But Roosevelt had ambition, an utter scorn for mere wealth-making, a keen desire for a full and active life, and a sincere if somewhat vague feeling of public dedication. Politics were a natural outlet for him. He fought the party bosses as an assemblyman in New York, served on the Civil Service Commission during the Harrison administration, made a name for himself as an energetic and unpredictable president of New York City's Board of Police Commissioners, and went to Washington as assistant secretary of the Navy. When he resigned the latter post to sail for Cuba with the Rough Riders, he sprang into national prominence. Rewarded as a war hero with the governorship of New York, he was then elected Vice-President on the Republican ticket in 1900.

He was forty-three—the youngest man ever to assume the presidency—when McKinley's assassination suddenly elevated him to the highest office in the land. But he never doubted his ability to lead the nation. The touchstone for his policies, at home and abroad, was his own conception of righteousness and the moral law. Roosevelt sought to maintain a balance between the opposing forces of what he judged to be the selfish reactionary interests and demagogic radicalism. He was for neither the rich man nor the poor man, but "the upright man, rich or poor." Whatever the issue at stake, he acted on the moral principles that he had convinced himself would promote the best interests of the country.

"How do you know that substantial justice was done?" he was once asked. "Because I did it," he answered, "because . . . I was doing my best."

Other men following what so often appeared to be tactics of compromise and accommodation would have been charged with weakness. It was Theodore Roosevelt's particular genius that no matter what he did he endowed his policy with all the attributes of fearless independence. He struck out so fiercely in his attacks upon plutocracy that few people stopped to realize that words were not always commensurate with deeds.

It has been suggested that the impulses behind his political beliefs were essentially negative—inasmuch as he favored reforms only to avert what he considered the graver dangers of "socialistic action." Negativism, however, was something the public could never associate with Roosevelt. He was "a very Goliath of a personality." His immense enthusiasms, his inexhaustible energy, his exuberant vitality, and his easily aroused combativeness were outstanding characteristics.

No President has had broader or more catholic interests. From his youthful days on a ranch on the Dakota plains, when he was seeking to build up his health, he always maintained a close association with the West. He was as anxious to go to war, to lead troops in battle, at the close of his life as he had been when he rushed off to Cuba. He was an omniverous reader on almost every subject under the sun, and a sufficient critic to recognize the genius of the poet Edward Arlington Robinson to whom he gave a political sinecure. He was a historian, and in *The Winning of the West* wrote an exciting chapter in national history. Cowboys and ward heelers, prizefighters and clergymen, Rough Riders and diplomats were equally welcome guests in his informal entertaining at the White House. Always the proponent of the "strenuous life," he took up sports—boxing, tennis, big game hunting—with a zest that was part of everything he did.

The youthfulness that he never outgrew, however deplored by some of his friends, helped to endear him to the public. Responsibility could not crush the perennial boy. He was forever charging up San Juan Hill, forever waving his victorious sombrero, and the wonderful show he put on never failed to command an audience. He was never pompous. He was no stuffed shirt. Talking with effervescent enthusiasm, gesticulating wildly, shaking his clenched fist as he assailed his foes, gnashing the gleaming teeth that were the perennial delight of cartoonists, "Teddy" awoke immense enthusiasm as he strutted across the national stage.

For all those who sometimes laughed at his posturing, feared him or despised him, there were many, many more who greatly admired him, knowing that he always had at heart, a brave and generous heart, what he believed to be the best interests of the country. While his actions might sometimes fall short of his promises, he nevertheless gave voice to the hopes and aspirations of the common people, and contributed immensely to the growth of the progressive spirit.

★ THE ANTITRUST CAMPAIGN

When Roosevelt became President, a letter from Mark Hanna advised him "to go slow." Roosevelt promptly answered that he was prepared to follow what he believed could not possibly be wiser advice. His first message to Congress dealt with the vital issue of the trusts, but he cautiously avoided taking an extreme position. There was a need for regulation, but care should be taken not to disturb the delicate adjustment of the country's economic machinery. "On wan hand I wud stamp them undher fut," Mr. Dooley quietly satirized, "on th' other hand not so fast." But events were soon to show that Roosevelt was ready for action.

A first sign of his intentions was a dramatic order to his Attorney General, in 1902, to bring suit under the antitrust laws against the Northern Securities Company, a railroad holding company formed under the astute direction of J. P. Morgan. The business community was shocked and alarmed. Morgan himself hurried to Washington to discover what Roosevelt had in mind, and whether any other interests of his were likely to be attacked. The President assured him that there would be prosecution of other companies only if "they have done something that we regard as wrong," and with that meager reassurance the country's leading banker had to be content. Roosevelt made it clear, as he would do on later occasions, that entirely apart from the economic implications of the trust issue, there could never be any question of the paramount authority of the federal government. It did not bargain with J. P. Morgan.

The Northern Securities case was prosecuted successfully, the Supreme Court exhibiting a greater willingness to enforce the antitrust laws than it had in any previous litigation. Roosevelt was later to claim that his initiative in securing a reversal of the former narrow interpretation of the Sherman Act rendered in the E. C. Knight case was entirely responsible for establishing the government's power to deal effectively with monopoly. This was an exaggeration. Yet it is true that the whole antitrust movement, as it has been spasmodically carried on ever since 1902, largely stems from Roosevelt's successful suit against the Northern Securities Company.

A number of other antitrust suits, including actions to dissolve both the Standard Oil Company and the American Tobacco Company, were also started about this time. Roosevelt's position, however, was not one of opposition to all trusts. He recognized that there were possible social values in monopoly. In keeping with his basic philosophy, he sought to draw a distinction between "good" trusts and "bad" trusts whereby the benefits of monopoly might be maintained while its abuses were eliminated. In its final decisions in the Standard Oil and American Tobacco cases, the Supreme Court was itself to reflect this point of view. It laid down the so-called "rule of reason." Only such practices as could be interpreted as unreasonable restraint of trade were held subject to government prosecution under the antitrust laws. For the determination of such abuses Roosevelt created the Bureau of Corporations, later to become the Federal Trade Commission.

The trust-busting campaign, as it was soon called, awoke great public interest. It suggested that at long last effective steps were being taken to break the power of uncontrolled monopoly in American business. But while Roosevelt's original drive was unquestionably of great significance in asserting the government's right to hail these "subjects without a sovereign" into court, its permanent results, as already indicated, hardly bore out the claims made for it. Through the formation of new holding companies, trusts which had supposedly broken up were soon doing business at the old stand. "Don't be downhearted," a contemporary cartoonist depicted a group of trusts encouraging a new victim of government attack. "Dissolution gives you that nice legal feeling."

The problem of monopoly would continue to baffle all attempts made to deal with it; it has remained seemingly insoluble. Since the Progressive era, trusts have been in some measure on the defensive, constantly forced to defend themselves against government prosecution, but the consolidation of capital has by no means been halted.

★ THE COAL STRIKE

Apart from these activities, the only other important development of Roosevelt's first term was his intervention in the coal strike of 1902. Under the leadership of John Mitchell, of the United Mine Workers, some 150,000 men had quit work, and their strike dragged on through the summer and early fall without any sign of settlement. The miners were always ready to negotiate, but the operators refused to deal with them. One of the latter, George F. Baer, arrogantly set forth their position in a statement that did more than anything else to arouse popular sympathy for the miners. "The rights and interests of the laboring man," he wrote a correspondent who had urged a peaceful settlement of the strike, "will be protected and cared for not by the labor agitators, but by the Christian men to whom God in his infinite wisdom has given the control of the property interests of the country."

The strike soon began to threaten a serious coal famine and pressure mounted for some sort of governmental action to bring it to an end. Roosevelt summoned both Mitchell and the coal operators to the White House and proposed arbitration. Mitchell agreed; the operators adamantly refused. Faced with an emergency not unlike that confronting Cleveland at the time of the Pullman strike, Roosevelt now followed a quite different course of action. He laid plans for government seizure of the coal mines and, with this threat in the background, exerted the pressure upon J. P. Morgan that persuaded him to exercise his decisive influence in convincing the coal operators that they had better accept the President's proposals for arbitration. After some haggling over the proposed arbitral commission, they did so, and the strike came to an end with the miners eventually winning a considerable wage increase.

For the first time the federal government had intervened in a labor dispute not just to protect property, but to assure a strike settlement in the public interest that took both labor's and management's rights into consideration. Roosevelt's forthright stand contributed greatly to his popularity and his stature.

★ ELECTION OF 1904

For the rest Roosevelt followed a rather cautious line. He was anxious for election and did not want to alienate any possible support. He sought at once to keep the progressive-minded in his camp and also the more conservative business interests. There was never any real question of his renomination, which he duly won, but he could not be too certain of the attitude of the country as a whole on his continued occupancy of the White House.

The Democrats played into his hands. Their candidate in 1904 was not Bryan, who might have commanded a good deal of the liberal vote. They made the blunder of nominating for the presidency a colorless conservative, Judge Alton B. Parker, of New York. They somehow hoped to capitalize on the doubts of the business community as to just where Roosevelt really stood—"a little loose in the relations of capital and labor, on trusts and combinations," Senator Platt had phrased it—and win over timid Republican voters. They miscalculated doubly: conservatives did not trust the Democrats, whomever they nominated, and the country as a whole had become far more receptive to progressive principles. Roosevelt was able to borrow many of Bryan's old planks and at the same time maintain an unbroken Republican front.

The attitude of eastern conservatives was perhaps best exemplified in the single-line editorial with which the New York *Sun* stated its position: "Theodore! with all thy faults. . . ."

Roosevelt was elected in his own right by an overwhelming popular majority—7,623,000 to 5,077,000—and an electoral college vote giving him every state outside the Solid South. He was now free to set his own pace. Both at home and abroad he was prepared to provide the leadership which he felt the country demanded. While he did not break with the Old Guard within the Republican party, he showed a greater degree of independence than he had during his first term and pushed ahead vigorously with the policies in which he believed. Foreign affairs were always highly important—and this narrative will return to Panama, the Caribbean and the Far East—but he was also aggressively active on the domestic front.

★ RAILROADS AND CONSERVATION

Roosevelt had singled out monopoly in his first message to Congress; he now turned to the railroads. He demanded such strengthening of the Interstate Commerce Act "as shall summarily and effectively prevent the imposition of unjust rates." While this was a popular move from the public's point of view, railroad rate regulation nevertheless precipitated a battle royal in Congress and the proposed bill was strongly contested throughout the spring of 1906. Rather than see it killed by the powerful conservative bloc in the Senate, Roosevelt again demonstrated his willingness to compromise. He came to an understanding with the regulatory measure's opponents whereby the proposed power of the Interstate Commerce Commission to prescribe maximum railroad rates on its own responsibility was made subject to broad judicial review by the courts. This concession was a blow to liberals of both the Republican and Democratic parties. They had counted upon the President's continued backing for the more rigid rate controls originally contemplated. But while some of them aggrievedly felt that he had betrayed them, Roosevelt secured the bill's passage.

Moreover the Hepburn Act, as this new railroad measure was called, greatly bolstered the position of the Interstate Commerce Commission. Even though its decisions were made subject to judicial review, it now had the authority to compel the lowering of unreasonable rates, and the burden of proving that such reductions were unjustified rested with the railroads. Government regulation had been placed on a solid foundation, and in spite of the skepticism of critics of the new law, rate reductions ordered by the Interstate Commerce Commission were generally sustained by the courts. The Hepburn Act started the Interstate Commerce Commission along the path which finally enabled it to do away with those abuses in railway management that had first aroused the Grangers thirty years earlier.

Over and beyond trust and railroad regulation, and his support for the Pure Food and Drug Act, also passed in 1906, the most effective service performed by Roosevelt was his sincere and zealous leadership of the conservation movement. No one in public life more clearly recognized the immense importance of the problem created by the ruthless plundering of our forest reserves, the unrestrained exploitation of mineral wealth, and the reckless exhaustion of soil fertility. Roosevelt saw as a whole the interrelated issues of river control, flood prevention, the reclamation and irrigation of arid land, the preservation of timber reserves, and the prevention of erosion. Here he was not only a determined leader, but an impassioned prophet, seeking to arouse the American people to the necessity of safeguarding their heritage for posterity.

He wrote in his *Autobiography:*

> The idea that our natural resources were inexhaustible still obtained, and there was as yet no real knowledge of their extent and condition. The relation of conservation of natural resources to the problems of national welfare and national efficiency had not yet dawned on the public mind. The reclamation of arid public lands in the West was still a matter for private enterprise alone; and our magnificent river system, with its superb possibilities for public usefulness, was dealt with by the National Government not as a unit, but as a disconnected series of problems, whose only real interest was in their effect upon the re-election of a congressman here and there.

Roosevelt gave to conservation something of the driving force of his own dynamic personality. He promoted measures that authorized the use of money obtained from the sale of public land for reclamation and irrigation projects in sixteen western states, supported such impressive undertakings as the impounding of the waters of the Salt River at the Roosevelt Dam, breathed new life into the creation of forest reserves and national parks, and backed the formation of an Inland Waterways Commission to investigate the interrelationship between forests, water power, river navigation, and soil erosion.

He summoned in 1908 a national conference, attended by cabinet members, congressmen, governors, federal officials, and public-spirited citizens that went still further into the problems of conservation. After prolonged sessions it issued a declaration of principles which called for the protection of all forest lands, the regulation of private timber cutting, the improvement of navigable streams and safeguarding of their watersheds, and the retention by the federal government of all public land containing coal, phosphate rock, oil, natural gas, and water-power sites. Shortly after this meeting, a National Conservation Commission was created, and forty-one states soon fell in line with establishment of as many state conservation commissions.

★ WILLIAM HOWARD TAFT

Roosevelt was on record as disavowing a possible third term, but as his administration drew to its close, his undisputed party leadership enabled him to choose his successor. He named his Secretary of War—William Howard Taft. Although the Democrats belatedly returned to the liberal fold and nominated Bryan, there was never much doubt of the outcome of the election of 1908. It was a rather apathetic campaign—in spite of Roosevelt's admonition to Taft to "hit them hard, old man!"—and the Republicans were returned to office by a popular majority considerably less than in 1904 but still decisive—7,679,000 to 6,409,000. It was another Roosevelt victory. The country voted as it did in the belief that his policies would be faithfully pursued by the heir apparent.

For a time at least, this seemed to be the case. As Roosevelt tactfully bowed out of the picture, sailing for Africa on a big-game hunting expedition followed by a royal tour of Europe, Taft sincerely tried to carry forward a program of progressive reform. But he was slow-moving and very scrupulous over constitutional issues. He entirely lacked Roosevelt's gift to dramatize whatever he did. The liberal elements within his own party became increasingly restless, and a number of fumbling blunders soon strengthened their conviction that Taft was betraying Progressivism. Needled by insistent demands to move faster than he was prepared to do, the new President then began to swing more and more to the right. By the time Roosevelt returned from his foreign travels, there was a dangerous rift within Republican ranks and the new administration seemed about to fall apart.

Taft was unsuited for the presidency. A man of strong, definite convictions, an able administrator, and as Roosevelt affectionately called him, a "big, generous, high-minded fellow," he lacked the driving force and aggressive leadership that the times demanded. His state papers were well-reasoned, forthright documents, but he made little effort to force Congress to accept his views. He was too easy-going, too deliberate, too much a man of peace, to enjoy a political fight. His earlier positions in the government had all been appointive—solicitor general, federal judge, governor of the Philippines, secretary of war—and partisan quarrels always worried him. His judicial temperament was in striking contrast with his predecessor's blithe impetuosity.

Taft was, indeed, especially handicapped by falling under Roosevelt's shadow. Shortly after the inauguration, he confessed rather plaintively that every time he heard someone say, "Mr. President," he looked around for Roosevelt. He could never escape that unseen presence, and he was thoroughly aware that the country was always contrasting his calm, moderate conduct of affairs with the Rooseveltian fireworks. The change-over, Elihu Root once commented, was "a good deal like that from an automobile to a cab." Taft would have agreed with him. "It is a very humdrum, uninteresting administration," he said himself, "and it does not attract the attention or enthusiasm of anybody."

The new President was personally popular. He had the qualities that are usually associated with a fat man—Taft was six foot two and tipped the scales at nearly three hundred pounds—and was a lovable person. Senator Dolliver once described him, however, as "a large, amiable island, surrounded entirely by persons who knew exactly what they wanted." When political storms broke out with the growing conflict between the two wings of his party, he could not have been more unhappy. "I am not so constituted," he wrote ruefully, "that I can run with the hare and hunt with the hounds." His drift into the conservative camp was in a measure the line of least resistance. It also reflected a growing impatience with the liberals that more and more brought out his innate conservatism.

★ THE LEGISLATIVE RECORD

His administration, as has been often pointed out, actually had a more effective record for trust-busting than that of Roosevelt. It initiated and prosecuted more cases, some forty-six in all, and placed effective antitrust action on a stable basis. Further progress was also made with railroad regulation, most notably the Mann-Elkins Act of 1910. At least one contemporary political commentator declared that Taft managed to produce more results "than anybody else who has sat in his chair since the Civil War." Two highly publicized developments, however, greatly overshadowed his achievements and largely accounted for a ruinous loss of prestige.

Taft was unable to avoid, as Roosevelt had so skillfully, the tariff issue, and under strong pressure he called a special session of Congress in 1909 to undertake the popularly demanded downward revision of existing rates. The protectionists rallied and fought this move with such dogged tenacity that, as in the case of the revision sponsored by Cleveland some fifteen years earlier, the Payne-Aldrich bill that finally emerged from the struggle saw prevailing duties firmly re-established, if not actually raised. A gesture to the proponents of downward revision was an expanded free list, but it was a palpable fraud. Mr. Dooley explained it graphically:

> Th' Republican Party has been thru to its promises. Look at th' free list if ye don't believe it. Practically ivrything nicessary to existence comes in free. Here it is. Curling stones, teeth, sea moss, newspapers, nux vomica, Pulu, canary bird seed, divvy-divvy, spunk, hog bristles, marshmallows, silkworm, stilts, skeletons, an' leeches. Th' new tariff puts these familyar commodyties within th' reach iv all.

Taft signed the Payne-Aldrich Act on the ground that it was a sincere effort at downward revision, but there was immediate and widespread public indignation over its provisions. He might have ridden out the storm, for it was evident that he was trying to make the best of a bad bargain, but with amazing political ineptitude he was not content to stop at this point. In a later speech he declared that the new law was "the best tariff bill that the Republican Party ever passed."

The second incident that served even more to convince Progressives that Taft had surrendered to conservatism was his dismissal of Gifford Pinchot, a zealous and enthusiastic advocate of conservation whom Roosevelt had made Chief Forester. This move grew out of an internal quarrel within the administration which had led Pinchot to charge Secretary of the Interior Ballinger with protecting private interests at the expense of public rights. Taft was convinced on legal grounds that Ballinger had acted properly, and he felt forced to take a stand following the dictates of his conscience. "If I were to turn Ballinger out, in view of his innocence," he stated sharply, "I should be a white-livered skunk. I don't care how it affects my administration. . . ." But Pinchot's adherents, not so concerned with legalities as with their cause, could never become reconciled to what they interpreted as an overt attack upon the whole conservation movement.

Nor was Taft's attitude on tariff and conservation the only thing about his administration which served in the eyes of Progressives to nullify his achievements in the field of trust-busting. In a struggle over the speakership in the House of Representatives he fully supported the reactionary Joseph G. Cannon. He allied himself more and closely with the conservative bloc in the Senate. He showed little concern for the interests of farmers and workers and appeared to accept more and more the views of the business community. An innate conservatism was increasingly overshadowing his more progressive impulses.

★ REPUBLICAN INSURGENCY AND THE NEW NATIONALISM

When Roosevelt returned from his travels on the eve of the mid-term elections in 1910, he did not hide his disappointment that his successor had not carried forward his policies more aggressively. Taft's course, he let it be known privately, appeared to him "absolutely inexplicable." For a time he stood on the political sidelines, but his inner conviction that he alone was really capable of carrying forward the banners of Progressivism soon persuaded him that something had to be done. He had no alternative—Roosevelt rather easily let himself be persuaded—other than to contest the Republican presidential nomination with his onetime protégé. Responding to a call for his return to active politics carefully engineered by seven Progressive governors, Roosevelt was to announce dramatically in February, 1912, "My hat is in the ring."

There had in the meantime arisen among liberal Republicans in Congress an insurgent movement, largely inspired by Senator La Follette, which was also prepared to challenge the continued leadership of Taft. Looking to the forthcoming election, this group had thought in terms of the Wisconsin senator as their candidate for the presidential nomination, and La Follette, who had so long and so valiantly battled for reform, was led to believe that he could count upon Roosevelt's support. By entering the race himself, Roosevelt was consequently not only deserting Taft, but also undercutting La Follette's candidacy. With all the makings of "an elegant row," the country looked forward with somewhat mixed emotions to what might be the final consequences.

The program on which Roosevelt was prepared to make his bid for the Republican nomination had already been set forth in a fighting speech, delivered at Osawatomie, Kansas, shortly after his return from abroad in 1910. It was a more radical Roosevelt than the Roosevelt of the presidency. There were still to be close ties with conservative business interests, but in current phraseology, he had swung to the left. At Osawatomie he outlined his views with a new intensity:

> I stand for the square deal. But . . . I mean not merely that I stand for fair play under the present rules of the game, but that I stand for having

those rules changed so as to work for a more substantial equality of opportunity and reward. . . . The betterment which we seek must be accomplished, I believe, mainly through the National Government. The American people are right in demanding that New Nationalism without which we cannot hope to deal with new problems.

In subsequent addresses he would further develop the thesis to which he referred as the New Nationalism, and which owed no little to those ideas set forth by Herbert Croly in *The Promise of American Life*. It meant the abandonment of laissez faire and the assumption by government—the national government—of new responsibilities. It was the acceptance of the old Hamiltonian conception of a strong government, but it postulated the exercise of governmental power toward the Jeffersonian goal of a broader democracy which would promote the well-being of the entire people.

In more particular reference to the relationship between government and business, Roosevelt was prepared to accept the inevitability of bigness and concentration in industry. But government should be able to control and regulate the large corporations through an effective trade commission which would assure the exercise of their power for the public good. Whether dealing with business, agriculture, or labor, Roosevelt wanted government to act as an effective instrument for economic and social justice.

At the Republican convention, Roosevelt threw himself into the struggle with all his old zest and fervor. He felt "like a Bull Moose," he told reporters, and he was determined to overcome the forces of reaction that he now identified completely with Taft and his conservative supporters. Once again he was battling for righteousness. "Our cause is the cause of justice for all in the interests of all," he told his enthusiastic followers. "We stand at Armageddon, and we battle for the Lord."

Taft had neither the crusading spirit nor the eloquence to combat such fervor, but as President he controlled the party organization. And he had now become convinced, however reluctantly, that Roosevelt's new radicalism was a threat to the nation. He had to take up the challenge. "I am a man of peace," he stated. "I don't want to fight. But when I do fight, I want to hit hard. . . ." The party machine swung into action, with those steam roller tactics that Roosevelt himself had employed to control the convention four years earlier, and the office holders and other stalwarts were carefully brought into line. Taft was named Republican candidate on the first ballot.

Roosevelt and his followers refused to accept the convention verdict. They abstained from the final vote. They were ready to split the party and carry the issue to the country. The very night that Taft was nominated, amid charges of theft, brigandage, and treason, they met to plan formation of the Progressive party—popularly known as the Bull Moose party—and soon proceeded to name Roosevelt as their presidential candidate. Had either Taft or Roosevelt a chance for election under these circumstances? "The only question now," one Republican leader commented sardonically, "is which corpse gets the most flowers."

★ THE ELECTION OF 1912

Sensing the opportunity that the split within Republican ranks represented, the Democrats battled almost as fiercely over their nominee as had the Republicans. The leading candidate was Champ Clark, Speaker of the House of Representatives, but challenging his claims was a newcomer in Democratic politics, Woodrow Wilson, the former president of Princeton University, who had served a highly successful term as a progressive governor of New Jersey. There was a long embittered struggle at the Baltimore convention, but when Bryan withdrew his support from Clark, due to charges that the latter was being backed by the vested interests, the nomination of Wilson was assured. He was finally named on the forty-sixth ballot.

The election of 1912 was a three-cornered race, but its most significant aspect was the degree to which it reflected the generally liberal and progressive spirit of the country. As the nominee of the regular Republicans, Taft represented a more conservative viewpoint than his rivals, but his administration had advanced Progressivism in spite of the attacks of the insurgents. The Democratic platform called specifically for additional antitrust legislation, more stringent railroad regulation, revised banking and currency laws, and a lower tariff. Wilson was to campaign, vigorously and eloquently, for what he called the New Freedom.

The Progressive party differed from the Republicans and Democrats only in that its campaign promises, as embodied in the New Nationalism, were more sweeping and included every possible reform. In addition to measures favored by the other two parties, it called for the popular election of senators, woman suffrage, the eight-hour day, minimum wages for women, social insurance, direct primaries, the recall of judicial decisions, and anti-injunction laws. While there appeared to be something for everyone, one significant omission revealed the fine hand of Roosevelt's conservative backers from the business community. There was no pledge of downward revision of the tariff.

What most distinguished the Bull Moosers, apart from their popular and dynamic candidate, was their crusading fervor. The western insurgents and eastern liberals, the social reformers and visionary Utopians, who were brought together under the magic of Roosevelt's spirited personality, had transformed their political convention into something more nearly resembling a revival meeting. Its theme song was "Onward Christian Soldiers" and the army of righteousness enthusiastically closed ranks behind a new messiah:

> Follow! Follow!
> We will follow Roosevelt,
> Anywhere! Everywhere!
> We will follow on.

The conventions provided the political fireworks of 1912 rather than the campaign itself. Roosevelt expounded his program of the New Nationalism; Wilson eloquently outlined the New Freedom. There were certain basic differences here: on the one hand, the emphasis upon a strongly nationalistic policy, with government regulation of trusts; and on the other, greater concern for state rights, with an apparent hope of restoring earlier conditions of free competition that would eliminate trusts altogether. Yet both programs appeared to be too much alike in their support for broad progressive reforms to enable the general public to distinguish very much between them.

As it became increasingly evident that the split in Republican ranks made a Democratic triumph virtually certain, the voters lost interest. Taft soon realized that he was ruled out of the race because of a reputation for conservatism that did him no good in a progressive year. Roosevelt manfully kept his hopes alive, but as the months passed his supporters found their faith somewhat dimmed. Wilson looked forward to victory with sober confidence.

When the results were in, informed predictions were fully verified. With 6,293,000 votes Wilson had a slight popular plurality which, translated into the votes of the electoral college, became a decisive majority. Roosevelt was a respectable second with 4,119,000 votes, and Taft ran third with 3,484,000. The combined Roosevelt and Taft vote was actually less than Taft's had been in 1908, while Wilson's was smaller than Bryan's in any of his three campaigns. The Bull Moosers had made a disastrous blunder in trying to launch a third party; popular indifference rather than any great outpouring of votes was the sorry consequence.

Roosevelt's star had set. He recognized the finality of his defeat and the futility of the third-party movement. "There is only one thing to do," he told a friend, "and that is go back to the Republican Party." He could never accept his rival's victory—Wilson was "purely a demagogue," "a doctrinaire," and "an utterly selfish and cold-blooded politician." There could have been no more bitter experience for Roosevelt than to stand aside while a Democratic president carried the progressive movement to fruition and then led the nation into war.

CHAPTER XIII

The New Freedom

★ WILSONIAN POLICIES

The program that Wilson set forth during the campaign of 1912 as the New Freedom may not have differed greatly from the proposals of Roosevelt, but it was far more important because Wilson was to attain the position which enabled him to carry his ideas into effect. And he was to do this with exceptional success. "Our program with respect to business is now virtually complete," he felt able to tell Congress a little more than a year after his inauguration. "The road at last lies clear and firm before business."

In keeping with the underlying spirit of Progressivism, the New Freedom called for the return of the machinery of political control to the hands of the people. "The government of the United States at present," Wilson declared, "is a foster-child of the special interests. It is not allowed to have a will of its own. It is told at every move: 'Don't do that; you will interfere with our prosperity.' And when we ask, 'Where is our prosperity lodged?' a certain group of gentlemen say, 'With us.' The government of the United States in recent years has not been administered by the common people of the United States."

Wilson had not always had progressive views. His early conservatism was quite as pronounced as that of Roosevelt had been. In the 1890's he showed no sympathy for labor and vigorously attacked the Populists. He publicly criticized Bryan as "foolish and dangerous in his political beliefs," privately proposing "to knock him into a cocked hat." In keeping with the trend of the times, however, this attitude was gradually modified, and Wilson became increasingly liberal and increasingly forthright in the expression of his views. He was in no sense a radical. But he called for a reconstruction of society that would restore for individual Americans the freedom that had been submerged by a ruthless economic system.

What the United States needed above everything else, Wilson stated, was a body of laws "which will look after the men who are on the make rather than the men who are already made." Believing that the creative energy of the nation arose out of the ranks of the unknown, he was convinced that it was the role of government to provide a maximum of opportunity for those who were the potential leaders in politics, business, and the professions. This concept of the people as a great reservoir of leadership was re-enforced by a fervent faith in their individual capacities. "I believe, as I believe in nothing else," Wilson said, "in the average integrity and average intelligence of the American people." He resolutely refused to accept the theory that there was any one group which should exercise a trusteeship for the people as a whole.

His program to free the people from domination by the special interests and provide full equality of opportunity was set forth in specific terms. Wilson asked for the revision of tariff duties to meet radical alterations in the condition of economic life, the reform of an antiquated and inadequate banking and currency system, the further promotion of conservation as the only answer to problems of water-courses undeveloped, forests untended, and waste places unreclaimed, the strengthening of the antitrust laws to strike down monopoly and restore free competition, passage of labor legislation to satisfy the new needs of the nation's workers, and such further action as would provide for the health and well-being of men, women, and children whose vitality was sapped through the working of great industrial processes over which they had no control.

Wilson accepted his election as a popular mandate for the execution of these policies. The split within Republican ranks that contributed so importantly to his victory did not enter into his public analysis of the election results. His triumph, as he declared in his inaugural address, in March, 1913, was a triumph of principle:

> It means much more than the mere success of party. The success of a party means little except when the nation is using that party for a large and definite purpose. No one can mistake the purpose for which the nation now seeks to use the Democratic Party. It seeks to use it to interpret a change in its own point of view. . . . Our duty is to cleanse, to reconsider, to restore, to correct the evil without impairing the good, to purify and humanize every process of our common life without weakening or sentimentalizing it. . . . The nation has been deeply stirred, stirred by a solemn passion, stirred by the knowledge of wrong, of ideals lost, of government too often debauched and made an instrument of evil.
>
> The feelings with which we face this new age of right and opportunity sweep across our heartstrings like some air out of God's own presence, where justice and mercy are reconciled and the judge and the brother are one. . . .

> This is not a day of triumph; it is a day of dedication. Here muster not the forces of party but the forces of humanity. Men's hearts wait upon us; men's lives hang in the balance; men's hopes call upon us to say what we shall do. Who shall live up to the great trust? Who dares fail to try? I summon all honest men, all patriotic, all forward-looking men, to my side. God helping me, I will not fail them, if they will but counsel and sustain me!

His speech was enthusiastically received. While opposition would develop later, he had an unusually good press from newspapers of every political persuasion. The New York *Mail* declared that the inaugural address expressed a spirit "to which the whole country can respond"; the New York *Tribune* at least momentarily set aside its Republican loyalties to say that "the nation is hungry for leadership like that," and as a spokesman for the Democratic South, the Louisville *Courier-Journal* commented colloquially: "Assuredly the new president has the right pig by the ear."

★ WOODROW WILSON: THE MAN

What manner of man was this who spoke so eloquently to the American people, with such intense fervor, such strong faith, such a sense of dedication?

The most significant factor in Woodrow Wilson's background was that among his forebears on both sides of the family was a long line of Presbyterian ministers. He inherited their stern Calvinistic faith and their firm moral convictions. It has been said that Wilson judged men and events from a lofty plateau where he walked alone with God. He felt it to be his task to regenerate the spirit of the American people—and later that of the world—and he held to the ideals and principles that he professed with what sometimes became a stubborn and self-willed intractability. Tolerance was not a virtue to which he attached undue importance.

Intellectual rather than emotional, unable to feel much warmth or affection toward people except in the case of his family and a few close personal friends, scornful of showmanship and demagogy, Wilson nevertheless won a strong hold over the minds and hearts of the American people. He did not have the colorful and exciting personality of Roosevelt. He seemed cold and reserved. But his eloquence and sincerity enabled him to reach the populace in ways even more effective. "I have a sense of power in dealing with men collectively," he once wrote, "which I do not feel always in dealing with them singly." With such conscious acceptance of his ability to lead, he never doubted that he could obtain any goal he set for himself. But he was influenced not so much by personal ambition, as by a moral compulsion for service to his country and mankind.

Wilson's early career did not point toward the White House. After graduating from Princeton, briefly studying law, and then taking up further graduate work at Johns Hopkins, he went into college teaching. He held appointments at Bryn Mawr, Wesleyan, and Princeton, rapidly climbing the academic ladder as he proved to be a stimulating and popular instructor and a brilliant interpreter of American history and politics. His demonstrated ability, his several books on government, and his wide recognition in academic circles then led, in 1902, to the presidency of Princeton. His democratic ideals soon involved him in a fight for greater democracy on the college campus, largely directed against Princeton's exclusive club system, and his reputation grew with the publicity given this struggle and his public addresses upon political issues.

Wilson's southern background, for his family had lived in Virginia and Georgia, South Carolina and North Carolina, drew him naturally to the Democratic party, and he first allied himself with its more conservative eastern wing. He had had no previous experience of direct participation in politics, however, when in 1910 it was proposed that he run for the New Jersey governorship. The party bosses wanted a man who was respectable, whose views reasonably conformed to the progressive sentiment of the day, and whom they felt they could control. Wilson appeared to be their man. When he accepted their offer, they threw the full strength of the party organization behind his campaign.

On accepting the nomination for governor, Wilson stated his intention to retain complete independence of action. This had not been taken too seriously. Upon election, however, he at once demonstrated that he meant exactly what he had said. He refused to accede to the dictates of party bosses. He would follow no course of action other than that which he himself believed to be in the best interests of the people of New Jersey. More and more committed to progressive principles as his ideas broadened and grew, his administration proved to be surprisingly successful. He began to be looked upon by liberals throughout the country as a potential national leader. This was an idea anything but displeasing to a political novice whose energies had so recently been directed toward nothing more important than a campaign against the Princeton club system. Wilson viewed his new role with characteristically self-conscious gravity.

"There are serious times ahead," he wrote in April, 1911. "It daunts me to think of the possibility of my playing an influential part in them. There is no telling what deep waters may be ahead of me. The forces of greed and the forces of justice and humanity are about to grapple for a bout in which men will spend all the life that is in them. God grant I may have strength to count, to tip the balance in the unequal and tremendous struggle!"

His presidential nomination and victory over Taft and Roosevelt brought to the White House a man whose slight experience in practical politics was more than compensated for by his unusually strong political convictions. Wilson was determined to be the spokesman both of his party and of the nation and to look for support from neither bosses nor congressmen but from the people themselves.

"The country craves a single leader," he had once written, and it was his ambition to play this unifying role. It was to set him more than ever apart from friends and associates. On leaving the White House his gregarious predecessor had expressed no regrets. "I'm glad to be going," Taft declared, "this is the loneliest place in the world." Wilson was to find this even more true, partly of his own making; in time that loneliness would have tragic consequences for the country and the world.

When he delivered his first message to Congress, shattering a precedent maintained since the days of John Adams by appearing in person, the assembled representatives and senators saw a man of medium height, well set up, dignified and handsome, with the assurance that came from a confident belief in his own ability to meet the challenge of his post as President of the United States. If they had any idea that the professor in politics would prove too impractical to give effect to the principles he eloquently voiced, they were soon disillusioned. He was at once idealist and dreamer and an audacious man of action. There was to be no temporizing in carrying out his broad and comprehensive program.

"We have itemized with some particularity the things that ought to be altered," Wilson had said. He now called upon Congress to take up the first item on his agenda; downward revision of the tariff. And he was prepared to use all his executive authority, take every advantage of party patronage, and if necessary appeal to the people over the heads of Congress, to make certain that his campaign pledges were redeemed.

★ TARIFF REVISION

There was little question that the country wanted tariff reform. Protection had long since outlived its usefulness, as even McKinley had come to admit before his death in 1901. The failure of the Taft administration to satisfy the popular demand on this score, as has been indicated, was one of the reasons for its growing unpopularity. Wilson had the nation behind him when he demanded the abolition of "everything that bears even the semblance of privilege or of any kind of artificial advantage." He had almost universal support when he declared that "the object of the tariff duties henceforth laid must be effective competition, the whetting of American wits by contest with the wits of the rest of the world." But this did not mean that the special interests that had for so long profited from the protection accorded by a high tariff were prepared to surrender their privileges.

The Underwood bill, embodying Wilson's demand for reductions in existing duties and a broad extension of the free list, was quickly approved in the House. But it met stiff resistance in the Senate. Tariff lobbyists descended upon Washington in droves. In the time-honored fashion that had accounted for the defeat of downward revision during the Cleveland and Taft administrations, they sought by secret pressures and logrolling to safeguard the industries they represented. Spokesmen for the woolen manufacturers and the beet sugar growers, the lumber industry and the steel companies, the textile trades and the cement makers, brought all possible influence to bear upon the harassed senators. As one of the latter stated:

> By telegram, by letter, by resolutions of commercial and industrial associations and unions, by interviews, by threat, by entreaty, by the importunities of men and the clamor of creditors, by newspaper criticism and contention, by pamphlet and circular, by the sinister pressure of a lobby of limitless resources, by all the arts and power of wealth and organization, the Senate has been and will be besieged, until it capitulates or the Underwood bill shall have been enacted.

The influence of these lobbyists was withstood. After weeks of wearing debate during all the rigors of a hot Washington summer, the Senate finally accepted the House measure. In September 1913 it became law as the Underwood Tariff Act.

Wilson was primarily responsible for this victory. He held the Senate relentlessly to its task, used pressure where it was needed, and repeatedly struck out against the undercover activities of high tariff advocates who would sacrifice the well-being of the country for their private profit. "There is every evidence," the President declared, "that money without limit is being spent to sustain this lobby and to create an appearance of a pressure antagonistic to some of the chief items of the tariff bill. . . . It is of serious interest to the country that the people at large should have no lobby, and be voiceless in these matters." He made himself their spokesman and carried the day.

The Underwood Act not only revised the tariff downwards—for the first time since the Civil War—but it incorporated a new measure of even more lasting significance. A sixteenth constitutional amendment, authorizing the levy of an income tax, had been ratified in February, and the new tariff measure imposed a graduated levy, ranging from one to six per cent, on all incomes over $4,000.

★ CURRENCY AND BANKING

His tariff bill enacted, Wilson turned to currency and banking reform. The control of money had been subject to repeated attack since the days of Populism, and Republicans as well as Democrats fully realized that remedial measures were long overdue. As a candidate for the presidency, Wilson had declared that "the great monopoly in this country is the money monopoly." He now stated even more bluntly: "The banking system of the country does not need to be indicted. It is convicted. . . ."

Certain steps looking toward reform had already been taken and a National Monetary Commission established to investigate the entire situation further. But the Wilsonian drive for more effective action was at this point greatly re-enforced by the disclosures of the so-called Pujo Committee, established by the House.

The star of its hearings was J. P. Morgan who put on a dramatic public show. He appeared thoroughly to enjoy himself. Fixing his questioners with his frighteningly piercing eyes, he repeatedly banged on the table for emphasis in making his replies, and chuckled happily whenever a sharp rejoinder caught the committee counsel off guard. Asked whether he did not have an advantage in competing for deposits with other banks, he answered with typical arrogance: "I do not compete for any deposits. I do not care whether they come. They come." On the major issue of financial monopoly, his impatient testimony was that there could be no such thing. "All the money in Christendom and all the banks in Christendom," Morgan declared, "could not control money; there could be no money Trust."

Other financial witnesses told a somewhat different story. They candidly admitted that control over the nation's credit was dangerously concentrated in Wall Street. The Pujo Committee obtained evidence showing that through affiliated banks and trust companies, as well as insurance companies, three financial institutions in New York almost completely dominated the money market: J. P. Morgan and Company, the First National Bank, and the National City Bank. The directors or firm members of these institutions, through the directorships they held in other companies, exercised dominating influence in the affairs of over a hundred subsidiary banks, insurance companies, railroads, public utilities, and other corporations with a total capitalization of over $22,000,000,000. An aroused public was convinced that there was if anything understatement in the committee's final report of a "great and rapidly growing concentration of the control of money and credit in the hands of a few men."

Determined to remedy this situation, Wilson supported a new banking law to set up a Federal Reserve System. His purpose was to preserve private banking under such government control as would best protect the public interest. Addressing Congress on this issue, the President stated:

We must have a currency, not rigid as now, but readily, elastically responsive to sound credit. . . . Our banking laws must mobilize reserves; must not permit the concentration anywhere in a few hands of the monetary resources of the country or their use for speculative purposes in such volume as to hinder . . . more legitimate uses. And the control of this system of banking and of issue which our new laws are to set up must be public, not private, must be vested in the Government itself, so that the banks may be the instruments, not the masters of business and of individual enterprise and initiative.

The Federal Reserve Act, finally passed in December, 1913, divided the country into twelve districts, with a Federal Reserve Bank in each to act as a fiscal agent for the member banks of that area, gave general supervisory control over their operations to the Federal Reserve Board, and authorized the issuance of Federal Reserve notes to be secured by commercial and agricultural paper, as well as 40 per cent gold reserves, in order to give greater elasticity to the currency. The new system won the support of the nation's banks and was generally successful in promoting the financial stability of the country. It was the most important and significant reform in our national banking laws ever adopted.

★ THE CLAYTON ACT

The third phase of Wilson's attack on privilege was amendment of the Sherman Anti-Trust Law. The Democratic party was fully committed to more stringent legislation to prevent the growth of trusts, and its platform backed up Wilson's own position by stating that any private monopoly was "indefensible and intolerable." "If I had my way," Champ Clark, Speaker of the House, stated, "I would fill the penitentiaries and jails of the United States so full of trust magnates that their arms and legs would stick out of the windows."

Several months were spent in consideration of what might be done, with continued debate in Congress and in the country. There was marked conflict between the old progressive idea of a strong, independent commission with full authority to regulate the trusts, and the Wilsonian concept of more limited action which would proscribe unfair trade practices by statute and thereby create the conditions that might restore normal competition. The two measures that finally evolved from this discussion have been described as marking a distinct shift from the New Freedom to the New Nationalism. That is, they tended to fall more in line with Roosevelt's ideas on trusts than those originally held by Wilson, and were the forerunner of Wilsonian support for other moves in the direction of more centralized government authority. However that may be, the final upshot of the debate was the passage, in the fall of 1914, of the Federal Trade Commission Act and the Clayton Act.

The former set up a new regulatory body to investigate any violations of the trust laws, with authority to issue "cease and desist" orders whenever warranted; the latter outlawed such monopolistic practices as unwarranted price discrimination, interlocking directorships in competitive corporations, and stock acquisitions that lessened competition. Individuals suffering damage from violation of the laws could bring suit for triple damages.

Senator Cummins of Iowa, echoing the views of a number of other liberals, expressed the opinion that some of the clauses in the Clayton Act did not have enough teeth in them to masticate milk toast. Wilson was far more hopeful that a way had been found not only to combat monopoly, but to "check and destroy the noxious growth in its infancy." His confidence was not fully justified. Experience was to prove that the Clayton Act was not much more successful than the original Sherman Act in meeting adequately the basic problem of trusts. Yet its passage represented a sincere effort to regulate business more effectively.

It was at this point, in any event, that the President felt justified in making the statement that his program of legislation with respect to business was virtually complete. The effect of these laws and several other measures on labor is still to be considered, but passage of the Underwood Tariff Act, the Federal Reserve Act, and the Clayton Act marked the fulfillment of the major objectives that Wilson had outlined in the New Freedom.

★ LABOR POLICIES

The Clayton Act, apart from its provisions affecting business, also carried forward—at least in theory—the idea that the laws respecting the organization of workers should be modified to give them "freedom to act in their own interest." Labor had for long been chafing under antitrust suits brought against unions on the ground that strikes and boycotts were conspiracies in restraint of trade. While the Sherman Act was supposedly designed to break down industrial monopoly, it was being enforced against unions more vigorously than against corporations. To meet this situation a number of specific labor clauses were proposed for the new trust legislation, and while they were watered down in the process of debate, they were finally accepted.

This section of the Clayton Act stated that the labor of a human being was not to be considered a commodity or article of commerce, that the antitrust laws should not be construed as forbidding the existence of unions, that in promoting their lawful aims such labor organizations should not be held to be engaged in illegal conspiracies in restraint of trade, and that court injunctions should not be granted in labor disputes unless necessary to prevent irreparable injury to property or property rights. *The Wall Street Journal* bitterly commented that in adopting such provisions, Congress had shown itself to be "a huddled mob of frightened cowards . . . watching for the labor boss to turn down his thumb." President Gompers of the A.F. of L. joyfully hailed the new law as "Labor's Charter of Freedom."

Just as events demonstrated that the Clayton Act's provisions for strengthening the antitrust laws against corporations were not as effective as anticipated, so they showed that its labor clauses were a good deal less than a complete guarantee of freedom for unions. The interpretation of the new law by the courts, which indicated little sympathy for labor organization, left the door open to injunctions against strikes and boycotts in innumerable instances. The bitterly contested "yellow dog contracts," whereby many coal operators and industrial corporations insisted on agreement not to join a union as a condition for employment, continued to be enforced. Labor was soon to become completely disillusioned over what it had interpreted as a great victory. It vigorously campaigned from this time on for those further guarantees of its right to organize which were finally recognized in the Norris-La Guardia Act of 1932 and subsequent legislation under the New Deal.

While the high promise of the Clayton Act was not realized, a number of other measures were adopted—although in some instances without the support of the administration—which were very much in labor's interest. The La Follette Seamen's Act, passed in March 1915, raised the safety requirements on American ships and also served in some measure to limit the tyrannical control traditionally exercised by ship masters over their crews. The Adamson Act, approved a year later, established an eight-hour day, with time and a half for overtime, for all employees on interstate railways. The latter measure grew out of emergency wartime conditions, but it nevertheless set a new precedent for the exercise of federal authority in improving conditions for union labor. Congress also passed in this period the Child Labor Act, which the Supreme Court was later to declare unconstitutional, and more successfully established workmen's compensation for all federal employees.

Although the record was uneven, the course of events during the Wilson administration revealed a new approach toward the problems of labor that reflected a slowly growing realization that the workers were entitled to protection in their rights.

★ THE BALANCE SHEET OF PROGRESSIVISM

In spite of such later measures as those just noted in relation to labor, and a significant Federal Farm Loan Act providing rural credits, the basic drive for reform which characterized the Progressive era appeared to have largely spent itself in 1914. The temper of the country seemed to favor the consolidation of such gains as had been made rather than the establishment of further controls over the economic life of the nation. Regardless of any such considerations, moreover, events over which the American people had no control dramatically shifted the focus of public attention from domestic affairs to world affairs. War broke out in Europe. The United States became increasingly absorbed in what was to prove an unsuccessful attempt to maintain its neutrality in the bloody conflict raging overseas.

Intervention in war and the reaction against Wilsonianism that marked the postwar years in some measure undermined the achievements in national politics associated with Progressivism. The establishment of the Federal Reserve System proved to be a permanent gain, but tariff policies were reversed with new triumphs for protection, the attempt to eliminate monopoly was largely nullified by a tacit encouragement of the further concentration of capital, and administrative policy in the 1920's was generally unfriendly to agriculture and labor. The spirit of reform faded away. William Jennings Bryan, Robert La Follette, Theodore Roosevelt, and Woodrow Wilson had battled strenuously to do away with capitalistic abuses, but their immediate successors largely ignored them.

Nevertheless, the principles for which the Progressives stood and which they had so deeply impressed upon the country did not lose their validity. Even though laissez faire appeared to receive a new lease on life after World War I, it could never again hold such undisputed sway as it had in the 1890's. The first steps had been taken in establishing the right and the obligation of government to intervene in the economic sphere in order to protect the interests of the people as a whole. Neither banks, nor railroads, nor industrial corporations could henceforth defy the power of the state with the impunity with which they had in the last quarter of the nineteenth century. And if the measures that sought to recover for the people the political power usurped by big business were not as effective as their proponents hoped, government had become far more responsive to the popular will.

The Progressive reforms were sometimes superficial because of a failure to understand the realities of the industrial age. They went only part way in meeting some of the basic economic problems they were supposed to solve. But substantial progress was made toward broadening the bases of American democracy and providing conditions that made for greater economic equality.

The excitement of the New Nationalism and the New Freedom gave to the Progressive era a unique quality. It was a period of high endeavor and hopeful achievement. With complete faith in the democratic process and in the tremendous potentialities of the American nation, a prosperous country was trying to strengthen the basis of its prosperity in the common interest. Wrote William Allen White:

> Those were surely Cromwellian times—from 1901 to 1917. What a lot of liberty we bought "with lance and torch and tumult" in those days from Roosevelt to Wilson! In those days the America of *laissez-faire*, the Jeffersonian America, passed. The morality of the people restated itself in the laws and institutions needed by a complex civilization. If ever our land had a noble epoch, America enjoyed it in those days of the Great Rebellion.

CHAPTER XIV

Social and Cultural Change

★ THE TEMPO OF THE TIMES

"To stay where you are in this country," a contemporary magazine writer observed about 1908, "you must keep moving."

The dynamic drive that generally characterized the era associated with Theodore Roosevelt and Woodrow Wilson had countless manifestations. The mounting rapidity of technological advance as invention crowded upon invention, the swifter tempo of life resulting from the increased use of machinery, and the continued growth of cities provided the background not only for social and economic reform, but for often startling departures in every phase of our national culture.

The rise of organized labor, largely dominated by the American Federation of Labor, raised new issues in the field of industrial relations, and there were distant reverberations of radical protest from an aggressive I.W.W.—the Industrial Workers of the World. At the same time, the ranks of wage earners were more than ever swelled by the continuing influx of immigrants from southeastern Europe. Urban authorities no less than employers had to cope with the problems created by such a situation. A new impetus was given earlier campaigns to assimilate the newcomers into an alien culture and clean up conditions in the densely congested slum areas where they usually congregated. In keeping with the humanitarian spirit of the times this required renewed efforts to improve health conditions, provide parks and playgrounds, combat juvenile delinquency, control prostitution and the white slave traffic, and eliminate the saloon.

The technological progress of this era was most conspicuously manifest in the revolution brought about in transportation with the development of the automobile. But an event in an allied field, even though it had little immediate impact on society, was to have consequences of incalculable importance. This was the successful experiment in aviation conducted on the beach at Kitty Hawk, North Carolina, by Orville and Wilbur Wright. When these two brothers succeeded in December 1903 in flying for the first time a heavier-than-air machine (their first epochal flight lasted just twelve seconds), man had realized an age-old dream. Although their achievement went almost unnoticed at the time, perhaps no single happening of these years was of greater significance.

Also of great importance were discoveries in the field of medical science. Persistent work in the laboratory developed the means for materially reducing the death rate in such diseases as typhoid, tuberculosis, diphtheria, and scarlet fever. The identification of what the press called "the germ of laziness" led to a spectacular drive to eradicate hookworm in the southern states. X-ray and radium experiments, among many others, held out further hope for the alleviation of suffering and the prolongation of human life.

Once again there were interesting developments in such a sharply contrasting area of activity as recreation. Technology was making an important contribution here, but until moving pictures swung into leadership, vaudeville remained the most popular commercial amusement. While baseball was still the national game, winning fresh prestige with the establishment of the World Series in 1903, other spectator sports increasingly caught public attention. Jack Johnson won the world's heavyweight boxing championship ("He said he'd bring home the bacon," exclaimed his rapturous mother, "and the honey boy has gone and done it"); American athletes took all honors in track events at the Olympic games, and intercollegiate football became of such major concern that when a high rate of fatalities (forty deaths in one year) threatened its abolition, President Roosevelt came to the rescue.

On the eve of the war, a dancing craze swept the country with the introduction of ragtime—precursor of jazz. "Everybody's Doin' It" seemed to have a literal application as the vogue grew for the fox trot, the bunny hug, and the one-step. The mania awoke nervous alarm over the degeneration of society. "Are we going to the dogs by the ragtime route?" the New York *Sun* asked censoriously. Another critical observer characterized the new dances as "a substitute for the Turkish bath and the masseuse." Such comments had no effect, however, as the music blared forth invitingly:

> Come on and hear, come on and hear
> Alexander's ragtime band;
> Come on and hear, come on and hear,
> It's the best band in the land.

Women's fashions went through amazing transformations between 1900 and 1914. Perhaps the most spectacular, although the contemporary press reported "hot debate over corset," was the famed hobble skirt. Soon the Gibson Girl of the opening of the century was only a nostalgic memory. Men's clothes maintained a staid conservatism, with advertisements stressing Arrow collars, B.V.D.'s, and Hart, Schaffner & Marx ready-made suits.

Among the popular songs were "The Trail of the Lonesome Pine," "My Wife's Gone to the Country," "Oh, You Beautiful Doll," and "Give My Regards to Broadway."

The fads of the Progressive era, as well as its concern with social and economic reform, reflected for the most part the interests of urban society. They expressed in their different ways the vitality and restless drive of the city. Along a thousand Main streets in the hinterland, and in countless villages in the rural sections of the country, life retained much of the simplicity, quiet leisure, and tranquility associated with the nineteenth century. There were still small towns with dusty, elm-shaded streets and comfortable houses set back in carefully tended yards. Neighbors visited in the long, cool evenings; boys courted girls on wide, spacious porches—white flannels and summery dresses, mandolins, and lemonade. Here was an atmosphere far removed from the nervous excitement of the city, its bitter contrasts of poverty and wealth, the hectic rush of an urban civilization.

The cities, however, were setting the pace for American living even more than they had in the 1890's. The new means of communication and transportation were soon to spread urban standards, customs, and fashions over all the land.

★ ORGANIZED LABOR

Organized labor made very considerable gains between the opening of the twentieth century and American entry into World War I. Wage rates rose and there was some decline in average working hours. Factory conditions improved. However, a *rapprochement* with capital at the beginning of this period, symbolized by the organization of the National Civic Federation with Mark Hanna as president and Samuel Gompers as vice-president, did not last very long. Alarmed at the progress unionized labor was making, industry opened a powerful counterattack which, in the name of the "open shop," sought to block further union organization. The Springfield *Republican* declared that capital should make up its mind on the need for co-operation, prophetically forecasting that "the law is more likely to compel the unionization of labor than it is to outlaw the labor union," but the country's industrial leaders were still far from accepting the principle of collective bargaining. They were ready to employ any means to break up labor boycotts and smash strikes.

An indication of a more sympathetic attitude on the part of government was the action taken by President Roosevelt in the coal strike of 1902 and the later labor legislation of the Wilson administration. There was still little response to labor's insistence on really effective safeguards for its right to organize, to strike, to boycott.

Throughout this period the leaders of the A.F. of L.—representing the great bulk of organized labor—consistently adhered to the conservative line that Gompers had laid down in the 1880's. No important attempt was made to organize the workers in the mass production industries, and the federation emphasized craft unionism rather than industrial unionism. While union membership as a whole rose to some 3,000,000 by 1917, or four times the total at the opening of the century, something like 90 per cent of the labor force, largely unskilled, immigrant labor, was wholly outside the organized labor movement.

The A.F. of L., although Samuel Gompers and other labor leaders campaigned for Wilson in 1912, maintained its official policy of political nonpartisanship. It presented a Bill of Grievances in 1906 which embraced such familiar demands as freedom for unions from prosecution under the Sherman Act, an end to the use of injunctions in industrial disputes, and the outlawing of yellow dog contracts, but its program remained one of supporting labor's friends and opposing its enemies. Nor was labor beguiled into the socialist camp even though Eugene Debs, running every four years for president on the Socialist party ticket, steadily built up his strength to a total of nearly 900,000 votes in the election of 1912.

★ THE I.W.W.

In these circumstances the A.F. of L.'s conservative attitude, both in respect to the organization of unskilled industrial workers and political activity, almost inevitably led to discontent on the part of leftwing radicals among American workers. The I.W.W. was organized in 1905. Its members were prepared by sabotage and violence to seek the overthrow of the entire capitalist system. "Instead of the conservative motto, 'A fair day's wage for a fair day's pay,' " the ringing manifesto of the I.W.W. declared, "we must inscribe on our banner the revolutionary watchword, 'Abolition of the wage system.' It is the historic mission of the working class to do away with capitalism."

The I.W.W. never had a membership of more than sixty thousand. Largely made up of migratory workers in the western wheat fields, lumberjacks, metal miners, and some few newly arrived immigrants in eastern textile mills, it made little headway among the more stable elements in the organized labor movement. Under the fiery leadership of "Big Bill" Haywood, onetime cowboy, homesteader, and miner, the "Wobblies" nevertheless won a national reputation for aggressive violence. Their strikes and free speech fights for a time awoke widespread alarm.

They entered the struggle for workers' rights with a zest, enthusiasm, and reckless bravado that welcomed combat. The songs sung at union meetings, in harvest and lumbering camps, and on the picket line, reflected their fighting spirit: "Dump the Bosses Off Your Back," "Paint 'er Red," "Tie 'em Up," "The Red Flag," and "Hallelujah! I'm a Bum!"—

O! I like my boss,
He's a good friend of mine,
And that's why I'm starving
Out on the picket line!
Hallelujah! I'm a bum!
Hallelujah! Bum Again!
Hallelujah! Give us a hand-out
To revive us again.

In their invasion of the East, the I.W.W. won a great strike of textile workers at Lawrence, Massachusetts, and then were defeated in another spectacular strike in the silk mills of Patterson, New Jersey. Thereafter, their influence began to decline, and when they adopted a strong anti-war stand in 1917, their doom was sealed. Their leaders were arrested, tried and convicted under the Sedition Act. Many of the Wobblies found a postwar haven among the communists, but the I.W.W. disintegrated.

★ IMMIGRATION

While this radical movement welcomed the immigrants when it tried to organize eastern workingmen, these newcomers to the United States, so generally unskilled, ignorant, poverty-stricken, found few to defend their interests. The A.F. of L. unions generally ignored them. Employers beat down their wages. Politicians were only concerned in trying to buy their votes. Left to themselves, the immigrants continued to crowd the slums of coal towns, steel centers, and other industrial cities of the eastern seaboard and Midwest. Packed into Hungarian, Bohemian, Polish, Italian, or Greek tenement districts, the first generation of immigrants appeared to stand apart from the main stream of American life. For many of them, as Anzio Yezierska wrote in *Hungry Hearts,* the New World was a bitter disillusionment:

I looked about the narrow street of squeezed-in stores and houses, ragged clothes, dirty bedding oozing out of windows, ash-cans and garbage cans cluttering the sidewalks. A vague sadness pressed down my heart, the first doubt of America.

"Where are the green fields and open spaces in America?" cried my heart. "Where is the golden country of my dreams?"

I looked out into the alley below, and saw pale-faced children scrambling in the gutter. "Where is America?" cried my heart.

As the number of immigrants annually landing on our shores continued to increase, approximately a million every year to a total of some 14,500,000 from 1900 to 1915, the doubts of those who arrived as to the advantages of the New World were more than ever matched by the misgivings of native Americans as to whether they favored further immigration. The questions first asked in the 1890's were renewed. Could the country continue to absorb these alien hordes? Could it assimilate these people whose culture was so different from our own? The new immigrants from Russia, Poland, Hungary, Italy, the Balkans were blamed more than ever for the overcrowding of the cities and the alarming prevalence of urban disease, vice, and crime. Many of those Americans who had once thought of their nation as a huge melting pot, in which those foreign elements could be fused into a unified and homogeneous whole, now convinced themselves that the melting pot was in imminent danger of boiling over. The movement to restrict immigration gained a new momentum.

The arguments over this issue waxed violent. There was perhaps no more eloquent defender of the immigrants and their place in American life than Mary Antin, who had herself migrated to this country from Russia in 1894. She stoutly defended their role in building America—"our brains, our wealth, our ambitions flow in channels dug by the hands of immigrants." The alien could hardly be held responsible for the slums, Miss Antin wrote, or why even worse slums in London? He was not the real source of municipal corruption. The greater responsibility was that of the party boss and the ward heeler so willing to buy his vote. And on the positive side, Miss Antin stressed the burning idealism of so many immigrants who found in America the liberty they were seeking, for all the economic exploitation of mines and mills and factories, and became the most staunch defenders of Americanism.

On the other side of the question, Henry Pratt Fairchild took the lead in vigorously attacking what he termed the myth of the Melting Pot. He bluntly stated that unrestricted immigration "was slowly, insidiously, irresistibly eating away the very heart of the United States. What was being melted in the great Melting Pot, losing all form and symmetry, all beauty and character, all nobility and usefulness, was the American nationality itself."

The Progressives generally, as already noted, favored the restriction of immigration, and they were prepared to support a literacy test as the most effective means of doing so. It would have the twofold effect, its proponents argued, of cutting down the total number of aliens admitted, and favoring the old immigration from northwestern Europe. In the face of all objections that a literacy test was a measure of lack of opportunity, rather than of intelligence or of any other quality desired for American citizenship, the drive in favor of restriction along these lines gathered increasing headway. Earlier bills embodying a literacy test had been defeated by vigorous presidential opposition, but in 1917 Congress finally passed such a bill over President Wilson's veto.

It was a first important step toward bringing to an end the historic process whereby the United States had been peopled and grown to greatness. Linked with the passing of the frontier and the disappearance of free land on the western prairies, immigration restriction was ultimately to mark the closing of an epoch in American history.

★ THE STATUS OF THE NEGRO

A not unrelated problem was that of the status of the Negro in American society. There was already a beginning of that northward migration, to become so much more pronounced in the 1920's, and a consequent development of segregated Negro districts in many eastern and midwestern cities. The North was not actually to prove much more tolerant in its attitude on race relations than the South. The conception of white superiority was sustained by Progressives no less than by other more conservative elements in contemporary society. The South was largely responsible for the tragic toll of lynchings during this period, over a thousand between 1900 and 1914, but there were violent anti-Negro riots in northern as well as in southern cities. One of the worst occurred in Springfield, Illinois—within a half mile of Lincoln's home.

An outstanding Negro leader of the day was Booker T. Washington. Born a slave in Franklin County, Virginia, he was educated at Hampton Institute, rose to an unexampled position as a leader of his race, and inaugurated and encouraged a program of vocational education for Negroes that at the time appeared to hold out high hopes for racial peace. He advised his fellow Negroes in the South to ignore politics and set as their goal becoming teachers, farmers, and tradesmen rather than striving for social or political equality. President Roosevelt entertained him in the White House, to the outraged consternation of many southerners, and praised his work.

There were other elements among northern Negroes, however, who were unwilling to abide by such a moderate program. Under the leadership of William B. B. DuBois, a Harvard graduate, they called for a more militant campaign to achieve complete equality for their race. Members of this group and a number of white sympathizers organized, in 1909, the National Association for the Advancement of Colored People. In revolt against the so-called Washington Compromise, it was prepared to work for the abolition of all aspects of segregation, North and South.

★ THE PROHIBITION MOVEMENT

Among the reform movements dealing with the problems of urban congestion, the most spectacular was the renewed warfare against "the demon rum." The temperance movement of the 1890's now became a determined, fanatical drive for prohibition. Its strength was still largely derived from the rural areas of the country, where a puritanical attitude toward drinking generally prevailed, but the new attack was more than ever centered on the city saloon.

The Anti-Saloon League, the Women's Christian Temperance Union, and the Temperance Society of the Methodist Church remained in the forefront of this campaign. Under zealous and untiring leadership, dedicated members of these groups worked ceaselessly to arouse public opinion to the necessity of outlawing the liquor traffic. Drinking was held responsible for the degradation of municipal politics, the vicious life of the slums, and the country's high rate of industrial accidents. The saloon itself was luridly depicted as the source of all evil in what was becoming a degenerate urban society.

This movement, gathering so much support from the rural church-going elements of the population, did not entirely fit into the pattern of the more general reforms associated with the Progressivism of these years. "It was linked," Richard Hofstadter has written in a recent study of *The Age of Reform,* "not merely to an aversion to drunkenness and to the evils that accompanied it, but to the immigrant drinking masses, to the pleasures and amenities of city life, and to the well-to-do classes and cultivated men. It was carried about America by the rural-evangelical virus: the country Protestant frequently brought it with him to the city when the contraction of agriculture sent him there to seek his livelihood." But this does not tell the whole story. In the South large landholders favored prohibition to keep liquor from their Negro farm hands; in the North manufacturers similarly sought to protect their employees. There was also a conservative urban element which did not necessarily feel very strongly about drinking itself, but was ready to support any movement that would do away with the recognized evils of the old-time saloons that were so often directly owned or controlled by the brewery interests.

The advocates of prohibition often had a dogmatic, intolerant attitude toward moderate drinkers that had not characterized the proponents of temperance. They gave a highly moralistic tone to their campaign, but were never greatly concerned over the means they employed to stamp out the liquor traffic. The Anti-Saloon League in particular was to develop pressure politics to a point that was the envy of all other lobbying groups, whether in state capitals or in Washington. Its one criterion for support of a candidate for public office was his publicly announced stand (not his personal convictions or his personal drinking habits) on the single issue of prohibition.

Working in season and out, the prohibitionists succeeded in having their way in state after state during these opening years of the twentieth century. On the eve of American entry into World War I, some twenty-six states had antisaloon laws in one form or another, and thirteen were absolutely bone dry. A federal law—the Webb-Kenyon Act—was passed in 1913 forbidding the transportation of liquor into states where its sale was illegal. After nearly three-quarters of a century of active agitation, the reformers appeared to be in sight of the promised land—an arid land where all drinking would be forbidden.

While some three-fourths of the American people were living in counties dry by local option or state law in 1913, it was nevertheless only after the war that the final victory for prohibition was won through the adoption of the Eighteenth Amendment, going into effect in January 1920. It was then to be charged that prohibition was something that had been "put over" on the country while the nation was absorbed by larger issues, and while the boys were overseas. Yet the momentum gained during prewar years suggests that prohibition was steadily winning popular support and would have soon been adopted, war or no war.

★ THE AUTOMOBILE

Labor organization, the melting pot, the status of the Negro, and prohibition were important social problems. The revolution in transportation had an even more general impact, as the "horseless carriages" of the 1890's became the motor cars of the 1900's. The city and the country were linked together as never before, the old isolation of the farm disappeared, and an avid public found itself endowed with a mobility that appeared to be nothing short of miraculous. The United States dramatically emerged from the horse-and-buggy era into the age of the automobile.

There were already eight thousand cars on the country's roads as the new century opened. Olds and Duryea, Haynes and Ford, among a host of other tinkering mechanics, had been putting together new machines, tearing them apart, building them up again, and dreaming of a practical automobile to be economically manufactured, dependable for efficient service, and sold to the public at a reasonable price. Such progress had been made along these lines by 1900 that a new industry was coming into being, and the first tentative steps toward mass production and the assembly line foreshadowed its glowing future.

It was nevertheless still taken for granted by most people that the automobile was destined to remain a fad and plaything for the wealthy. The magazine *Life* poked fun at the new "automobility" in parodying "The Charge of the Light Brigade":

> Half a block, half a block,
> Half a block onward
> All in their automobiles,
> Rode the Four Hundred.
> 'Forward!' the owners shout,
> 'Racing car!' 'Runabout!'
> Into Fifth Avenue
> Rode the Four Hundred.

A few years later, in 1907, Woodrow Wilson condemned what he considered the snobbery of motoring. "Nothing has spread socialistic feeling in this country more," he wrote, "than the use of the automobile. . . . a picture of the arrogance of wealth, with all its independence and carelessness."

Fortunately, fears of socialism did not lead to the outlawing of the automobile. Even as Wilson spoke, such improvements and economies in the production of cars were underway as to make them available for a public far larger than the Four Hundred. While prices for the more elaborate machines were as high as $7,000, runabouts could be bought for a tenth of this sum. Moreover, the price trend was downward. Ford's famous Model-T was soon selling at $780, then at $490, and ultimately at $290. The five-hundred-thousandth Ford of this design came off the assembly line in 1912. Their enterprising manufacturer was said to be planning to paint the cars yellow—so that they could be sold in bunches like bananas.

Motoring remained hazardous throughout this prewar period. Frequent mechanical breakdowns, tire trouble, and constant danger of being stuck in muddy roads made every trip an adventure. Motorists in linen dusters, visored caps, and goggles (swathed in veils if women) went prepared for any emergency. A successful hundred-mile run was a great triumph. There had to be a good deal of "sprinting" to make such a record, and the effect of driving as fast as thirty miles an hour was described at the time as very much like that derived from "drinking several cups of coffee." The pace was even more disturbing for the horse-drawn conveyances and pedestrians that such a "scorcher" might encounter. The states soon passed laws limiting speed to ten miles an hour in congested areas, twenty miles an hour in the open country. Night driving was rare (motorists were advised to stop at once on meeting a carriage and throw a lap robe over their acetylene headlights), and cars were invariably put away for the winter.

The improvements that were to make motoring practical at all times came about gradually. Cloth tops and windshields were added (the closed car was largely a product of the 1920's), tires greatly improved, electric headlights developed, and the self-starter introduced with its revolutionary effect of making driving as feasible for women as for men. At the same time motoring inspired a good roads movement, and a beginning was made in the construction of those surfaced highways that later crisscrossed the entire country.

With some two million cars in operation in 1914, the automobile had passed the pioneer stage. The expansion of production and motoring that marked the 1920's still lay in the future, but the tremendous influence of the automobile was every day more apparent. In addition to bringing town and city within easy distance of the rural dweller and opening the country to the townsman, the motorcar helped to develop the suburbs, contributed to the substitution of combined schools for the little one-room schoolhouses, and importantly served the purposes of business and industry. For hundreds of thousands of people, if not yet millions, motoring had also become a popular form of recreation.

★ MOVING PICTURES

The development of moving pictures paralleled that of the automobile. But they were from the very first, as seen in their introduction in music halls during the 1890's, an amusement for the great masses of the people rather than a plaything of the wealthy. They were a cheap and popular form of entertainment that provided an escape from the dull routine of everyday life.

It was some time before they began to attract an audience which could afford more sophisticated and expensive amusement. After the novelty of the early films—seldom depicting more than a man sneezing, a girl dancing, a baby being given its bath—wore off, they were in fact demoted from the music halls to the penny arcades. Their appeal was largely limited to the working class, especially immigrants, in the large cities. It was not until about 1905 that they were so improved that they began to be exhibited in pioneer moving picture theaters, known as nickelodeons. Two years later, *Harper's Weekly* described what was taking place in an article entitled "Nickel Madness":

> In almost every case, a long, narrow room, formerly used for more legitimate purposes, has been made over into what is called a 'nickelodeon.' At the rear a stage is raised. Across it is swung a white curtain. Before the curtain is placed a piano, which does service for an orchestra. Packed into the room as closely as they can be placed are chairs for the spectators, who number from one hundred to four hundred and fifty. Directly above the entrance is placed the moving picture machine, which flashes its lights and shadows upon the white curtain dropped in front of the stage. Many of the machines are operated by means of a tank filled with gasoline or some similarly inflammable material.

The films shown in the nickelodeons were far better than those exhibited in the penny arcades. Longer sequences had become possible, and endless variations were presented on the chase motif: cowboy heroes hunted down western bad men, city sleuths pursued bank robbers. Then with the production of a film called *The Great Train Robbery* the movies first began to tell a complete story (producers were willing to pay $15 to $30 for a good plot) and elaborate their scenes. But the performances were still dismissed by casual critics as "a harmless diversion of the poor" or "an innocent amusement and a rather wholesome delirium." Occasionally, a sterner note was heard, in part growing out of Anthony Comstock's fears of what might be going on in the darkened movie house. "There is no voice raised to defend the majority of five cent theatres," the Chicago *Tribune* asserted, "because they cannot be defended. They are hopelessly bad."

Still the movies marched on. They borrowed from the theater and further developed their own plots. They experimented with travelogues and news pictures. They discovered romance and, in time, sex. They introduced the star system. Soon "Little Mary" films enshrined Miss Pickford as America's sweetheart; John Bunny was convulsing nationwide audiences with his antics, and Tom Mix thundered across the prairies in a series of exciting westerns. Serials were presented and an ever-growing audience flocked to the movies every week to gasp over the latest hair-raising exploits of Pearl White in *The Perils of Pauline.*

By the time of World War I, the movies were coming of age with the camera's handling of distant scenes, switch-backs, fade-outs and close-ups marking a tremendous advance in photography. When D. W.

Griffith produced *The Birth of a Nation* in 1914 (it was to earn more than $18,000,000 with an original production cost of $100,000), they had, indeed, risen far above the lowly level of the nickelodeons. They now demanded more formal presentation and could command higher admission prices. In the larger cities elaborate moving picture palaces began to be built, with pipe organ music and complete orchestras. Even in smaller communities more comfortable accommodations were provided, though the accompanying music usually remained a tinkling piano.

Before the war was over production costs had begun to skyrocket, Mary Pickford signing a million-dollar contract for two years' work as early as 1917. An industry which had moved to Hollywood to take advantage of California's sunny climate was doing a land office business. Some ten thousand moving picture theaters, spread over the length and breadth of the land, were attracting over ten million persons weekly —a greater volume of business than all the legitimate theaters, variety halls, dime museums, lecture bureaus, concert halls, carnivals, and circuses combined.

★ FICTION AND POETRY

The continued increase in educational facilities—schools, high schools, colleges, and universities—meant still further growth in the reading audience whose great expansion in the 1890's has already been noted. This led to ever-wider circulation of newspapers, magazines, and books. If the exposures of the more unsavory aspects of American life in the muckraking articles had an unexpected effect in boosting magazine sales, popular fiction relied much more heavily on sentiment and romance. So far as its taste in such literature went, the generation of the early 1900's would appear to have been sentimental above everything else.

Three of the most popular books of this period were *Mrs. Wiggs of the Cabbage Patch, Freckles,* and *Pollyana.* Gene Stratton Porter, the author of *Freckles,* confessed that God had given her "a taste for sweets and the sales of the books I write prove that a few other people are similar to me in this." With her five books selling over eight million copies, her statement was more than justified.

Then there were the Graustark novels of George Barr McCutcheon and the heady and exciting romances from the prolific pens of Rex Beach, Stewart Edward White, Harold Bell Wright, and Zane Grey. The latter's record in exploiting the Wild West was phenomenal. With his sixty-three novels, he was constantly on the best-seller lists, and his total sales ran to nineteen million copies. In 1914 Edgar Rice Burroughs introduced *Tarzan of the Apes.* This book and its innumerable sequels were ultimately to exceed even Zane Grey's sales record.

If these years accounted for larger fiction sales than would be made again until the 1920's, the more serious writers—with one or two exceptions—fared less well. As already noted, almost every one of the nonfiction muckraking exposures of the day had its counterpart in the field of the novel, but such books were unable to compete in popularity with sentiment or romance. Nevertheless, Theodore Dreiser and Frank Norris, Jack London and Upton Sinclair were important exemplars of the new realistic approach to fiction.

Dreiser's naturalistic approach, even more than in the case of Norris or London, offended all the prejudices of polite society, and not until the 1920's was he widely read or critically recognized to any very great extent. His first novel, *Sister Carrie,* had been promptly withdrawn after publication in 1900 because of its frankness in dealing with the experience of a young girl adrift in Chicago. In his later political stories, *The Financier* and *The Titan,* he created a character, Frank Cowperwood, who embodied all those dominating and rapacious characteristics that marked the business tycoon of that era. Dreiser had at best a difficult style, but his writing had sincerity and strength. While his condemnation of the existing economic order reflected the journalistic muckraking of the day, he dug much deeper beneath the surface than most of his contemporaries. His best book, *An American Tragedy,* was not to be published until 1925.

Among other distinguished writers of the period were Sherwood Anderson, who published in 1919 his remarkable collection of realistic sketches of a small town, *Winesburg, Ohio,* and two of the country's most talented women novelists, Ellen Glasgow and Willa Cather, whose writing like that of Anderson would carry over into the postwar decade. Ellen Glasgow was well started, however, on her long account of the struggles of the emerging middle class in Virginia and was bringing a new realism to descriptions of the southern scene. Willa Cather, a superior artist, first revealed her talent in the years which saw publication of *The Song of the Lark* and *My Antonia.* Her books depicted the lonely life of settlers in the prairie states, their children's struggles in the larger world, with unusual honesty and beauty. And then there was also Edith Wharton and her novels of sophisticated urban society.

It has been commented by the literary historian Robert Spiller that "sometime between 1910 and 1920 American literature 'came of age.'" Certainly, a ferment of new ideas, a sharp rejection of tradition and genteelism, and a certain literary radicalism marked the Progressive era. But so far as this movement, if it may be so called, manifested itself before World War I, it was more significant in poetry than in the novel. There was, indeed, a "little renaissance" which foreshadowed the further literary flowering of postwar years.

Vachel Lindsay was started on his memorable career with "General Booth Enters into Heaven" and "The Congo." In the Midwest Carl Sandburg was celebrating the glories of an industrial metropolis in his "Chicago":

> Hog Butcher for the World,
> Tool maker, Stacker of Wheat,
> Player with Railroads and the Nation's Freight Handler;
> Stormy, husky, brawling,
> City of the big shoulders.

Robert Frost caught the integral spirit of New England, its rugged landscape, and its rugged characters, in *A Boy's Will* and *North of Boston.* Edgar Lee Masters published his *Spoon River Anthology* with its sharp, scathing portraiture of midwestern village life.

Edward Arlington Robinson, suffering himself from poverty, obscurity, and misunderstanding, sought to discover the enigma of life in exploring other men's lives. He never found the answers: "We come, we go: and when we're done, we're done." In this early period, he wrote *Children of the Night* and *The Man Against the Sky*. The latter found him confessing, lonely and frustrated,

> We lack the courage to be where we are:—
> We love too much to travel on old roads,
> To triumph on old fields.

This was also the theme of a shorter and more popular poem, "Miniver Cheevy," whose hero also loved the days of old, sighed for what was not, cursed the commonplace, scorned the gold he could not do without:

> Miniver Cheevy, born too late,
> Scratched his head and kept on thinking;
> Miniver coughed, and called it fate,
> And kept on drinking.

About the same time that the voices of Sandburg and Lindsay, Frost and Masters, were joined by that of Edward Arlington Robinson, other proponents of "the new poetry" were carrying on experiments with impressionism and imagism. In the pages of *Poetry,* a little magazine started in Chicago by Harriet Monroe, appeared the often startling verse of such newcomers as Amy Lowell, Ezra Pound, and T. S. Eliot.

★ ART AND ARCHITECTURE

The excitement and fervor of the Progressive era affected other phases of cultural and artistic activity. There was an ever-increasing interest in music, with a growing number of opera companies, symphony orchestras, and civic music federations. At least in the field of semi-classical forms and light opera, American composers—of whom Victor Herbert and Sigmund Romberg were best known—were beginning to make their mark. Achievement in music was slight, however, compared with what was happening in art and architecture, and not until the 1920's would American contributions become important in the general world of music.

American painting was still to a considerable extent dependent on that of Europe, but in the latter half of the nineteenth century, a number of artists had developed styles that were both distinctive in themselves and distinctively American. The outstanding names in this earlier period had been Winslow Homer, whose Civil War illustrations for *Harper's Weekly* afforded training for his later paintings of the sea and sky, the pre-eminent portrait painter John Singer Sargent, and perhaps most widely recognized, James M. Whistler, an expatriate in art like Henry James in literature, but nonetheless American. Also, spanning the turn of the century, there may be noted Albert Ryder, Thomas Eakins, and Mary Cassatt. These were memorable artists. With the new century, however, discovery of the revolutionary ideas and techniques being developed in Europe caused the world of art to go through a period of great change and ferment.

A revolt against tradition, and more specifically against the National Academy, broke out among a group of young artists under the leadership of John Sloan. A number of them, who were to become collectively known as the Ash Can School, boldly chose subjects for their painting that the traditionalists roundly condemned as entirely unsuitable, and the public considered as somehow subversive. "To paint drunks and slatterns, pushcart peddlers and coal mines, bedrooms and barrooms," complained one young painter, "was somehow to be classed among the socialists, anarchists, and other disturbers of the prosperous equilibrium." Yet these were the subjects that the Ash Can School spread upon their canvases.

Other painters, including such members of the advance guard as Alfred Henry Maurer and John Marin, studied abroad and were greatly influenced by French impressionism and postimpressionism. These new styles also continued to be looked upon askance, and a popular sensation was caused when, together with cubism and futurism, they in effect crossed the Atlantic for the memorable New York Armory show in 1913. At this exhibition many European painters such as Cézanne, Picasso, Matisse, Van Gogh, and Gauguin were seen for the first time by the American public.

Although many critics wrote scornfully of this "Ellis Island art" and condemned such crazy, ignorant, incompetent painters, the Armory show itself was an immense success. Thousands of people flocked to see the enigmatic cubist drawing entitled "Nude Descending a Staircase," even though they could make out neither the staircase nor the nude. Yet if the general public was baffled by the new "isms," the European invasion was a greatly stimulating experience for American painters.

Sculpture was represented by a number of outstanding artists after the turn of the century. It has been claimed that they were responsible for as much good work in the next few years as had been produced in America during the previous hundred. Augustus Saint-Gaudens, George Grey Barnard, Daniel Chester French, and Frederick William MacMonnies were at the height of their powers.

American artistic talent was perhaps to achieve even finer expression in architecture than in either sculpture or painting. There was a distinct break from the imitative and derivative styles that had covered the United States with pallid and sometimes grotesque reproductions of Greek, Gothic, Romanesque, Renaissance, Queen Anne, and Georgian buildings. The closing years of the nineteenth century had seen American architecture "wallowing in turrets, pinnacles, gables, columns, braces, jigsaw brackets, iron balustrades, mansard roofs, stained-glass windows, tortured moldings and fanciful arches." With the new century, there was a growing insistence upon greater honesty and simplicity in both homes and public buildings.

A pioneer in these new developments was Louis Sullivan, a Chicago architect who emphatically stressed the relationship between form and function, insisting that architecture could have no significance except so far as it faithfully reflected the life of a people. He experimented with structural steel in the building of skyscrapers, designed stores and factories, and created public monuments of lasting and permanent beauty. His successor and disciple was Frank Lloyd Wright, but the field in which the latter was most to distinguish himself at this time was in building private homes. He sought to harmonize and adopt the structure to its environment, ignored tradition with bold experimentation, and made full use of new materials and the techniques of modern engineering.

Wright had little use for the skyscraper. It had no integral relation to its surroundings, in his opinion, and was nothing more than a commercial exploit—a social and architectural catastrophe. But the skyscraper was becoming during these years increasingly important. It found its finest early expression in the Flatiron Building in New York, built in 1902, and was then further developed until it reached a prewar peak in the nearly eight hundred feet of the Woolworth Building. The impressive skyline of New York became a thing of fantastic beauty. However much the skyscraper may be condemned for adding to the density and congestion of urban life, it has continued to stand forth as a distinctive American contribution to world architecture.

CHAPTER XV

The Road to War

★ AUGUST, 1914

The outbreak of war in Europe in August 1914 caused stunned surprise throughout the United States. In his inaugural address only a little over a year earlier, President Wilson had spoken of "a growing cordiality and sense of community interest among the nations, foreshadowing an age of settled peace and good will." While foreign affairs were not ignored as they had been before the exciting days of America's own imperialistic ventures, the American people had been paying little attention to the complicated political maneuvering among the European powers. War was a rude awakening from any complacent feeling that the enlightened twentieth century had outgrown the barbarism of employing military force for the settlement of international disputes.

The President's immediate announcement of neutrality and declaration that "we must be impartial in thought as well as in action . . . a nation that neither sits in judgment upon others nor is disturbed in her own counsels," struck a responsive chord. If Europe chose to fight, that was her affair. We would have none of it. Separated from the battleground by the protective expanse of the Atlantic Ocean, the public generally had little fear that the United States would in any way be involved in hostilities. There is much evidence that Wilson himself in these days did not have the feeling of impartiality he enjoined upon the nation, but he was determined to maintain American neutrality in the conviction that this was best both for the country and for the world.

There was certainly little to suggest at this time that some thirty months later a reluctant President would call upon Congress to take up the challenge that had been presented by the attacks of German submarines on our commerce. By April 1917, however, the American people had become convinced that war could no longer be avoided.

They applauded Wilson's solemn declaration that "the right is more precious than peace" and that the United States must perforce go to war, not for any selfish end but in defense of the principles for which it stood.

But before considering the events that led to this sharp change in opinion and the decision to intervene in Europe's quarrel, the pages of history must be turned back. What had been the course of American foreign policy since 1900?

★ ROOSEVELT AND PANAMA

The imperialistic fervor of the 1900's had subsided after the acquisition of Puerto Rico, Hawaii, Samoa, Guam, and the Philippines. Nevertheless the United States continued to play that larger role in world affairs initiated by overseas expansion. If it still generally held aloof from Europe, for the most part ignoring the shifts and changes in the Old World's precarious balance of power, interest in both Latin America and eastern Asia brought the nation into increasing contact with the rival forces of world imperialism.

In the opening years of the new century, Theodore Roosevelt became an outspoken advocate of a strong foreign policy and brandished the "big stick" with magnificent aplomb in compelling respect for what he considered American rights and American interests. A first example of his vigorous action was the cavalier way in which he treated Colombia when that little country appeared to be blocking his plans for the construction of the Panama Canal. It was one of those occasions when Roosevelt acted first, and then sought to find arguments of morality and righteousness to justify his policy.

The canal project was an old one, but not until after the Spanish-American war were definite steps taken to bring it to fruition. First, a new treaty was concluded with Great Britain, the Hay-Pauncefote Treaty of 1901, abrogating certain rights that country had long held in respect to a possible canal and providing for its construction and fortification by the United States. Then after serious consideration of Nicaragua as a possible site, negotiations were started with Colombia for the cession of the necessary territory across the Isthmus of Panama, then a province of Colombia. The proposed treaty, ceding a six-mile wide canal zone to the United States upon a cash payment of $10,000,000 and a $250,-000 annuity, was concluded in March 1903. At this point Colombia balked, its senate withholding approval of what was called the Hay-Herran pact.

Roosevelt was incensed. The Colombians, he exploded, were "contemptible little creatures," "jack rabbits," and "homicidal corruptionists." It was no more possible to reach an agreement with them, he declared, than to nail currant jelly to the wall. He was impatient for action—and suddenly things began to happen.

A revolution broke out in Panama at the beginning of November. The United States had no part in it, but by a coincidence that was never fully explained an American cruiser happened at this opportune moment to be at Colón, the port on the Atlantic side of the Isthmus of Panama. On the basis of an old treaty granting the United States the right to control communications across the isthmus, its commander denied transit to the Colombian troops seeking to cross the isthmus and quell the revolt. The patriotic Panamanian forces, consisting largely of members of the local fire brigade and section hands of the Panama Railroad, were quickly able to establish the independence of their little country. The new Republic of Panama was then immediately recognized in Washington and within two weeks—on November 18, 1903—a treaty was concluded granting the United States, on exactly the same terms as those Colombia had refused, the desired territorial concessions. Roosevelt had his canal zone!

The story is told that on one occasion the President was attempting to explain to his cabinet just how these transactions were carried through with such unusual dispatch. "When he had finished," an account of this episode runs, "he glared around the table, finally fixing his eye on Secretary of War Root. 'Well,' he demanded, 'have I answered the charges?' 'You certainly have, Mr. President,' Root suavely replied. 'You have shown that you were accused of seduction and you have conclusively proved that you were guilty of rape.' "

However questionable such precipitate action may have been—and Roosevelt was later to state frankly, "I took the Canal Zone"—the way was cleared for building the canal. The President proceeded "to make the dirt fly." Constructed at a cost of $367,000,000, the Panama Canal was a stupendous engineering achievement. It was opened to traffic on the eve of World War I and was to prove an immense boon for world commerce in linking the Atlantic and Pacific oceans.

★ THE MONROE DOCTRINE

Once the canal was underway, Roosevelt felt it to be essential for the United States to do everything possible to safeguard its security by strengthening American political influence in the Caribbean. He undertook to amplify our traditional policy toward European intervention in the Western Hemisphere by serving notice that the United States would not tolerate any outside interference in the affairs of the little republics of Central America on any pretext whatsoever. This new policy, which

The UNITED STATES in the CARIBBEAN, 1916

was to be known as the Roosevelt Corollary to the Monroe Doctrine, was set forth in 1904:

> Chronic wrongdoing, or an impotence which results in a general loosening of the ties of civilized society may in America, as elsewhere, ultimately require intervention by some civilized nation, and in the Western Hemisphere the adherence of the United States to the Monroe Doctrine may force the United States, however reluctantly, in flagrant cases of such wrongdoing or impotence, to the exercise of an international police power.

The immediate cause for this pronouncement was a developing crisis in the Republic of Santo Domingo that was a result of its inability, after prolonged civil war, to meet the interest payments on its foreign debt. Roosevelt feared that its default might lead to intervention by the European powers and a consequent threat to American interests. A similar situation had arisen a few years earlier in Venezuela and in an attempt to enforce debt collection, German warships had bombarded a Venezuelan town. At that time Roosevelt had protested, declared his intention to uphold the Monroe Doctrine, and by a threat of possible naval action induced Germany to accept arbitration. He was determined to avoid a recurrence of any such dangerous situation. To forestall trouble in Santo Domingo and satisfy the legitimate claims of the European powers against its government, he concluded an agreement in January 1905 whereby the United States would take over control of Dominican customs, earmarking 45 per cent of the funds received for the needs of local government and the remainder for payment on Santo Domingo's foreign debt.

In keeping with pronouncement of the Roosevelt Corollary and this precedent, the United States was henceforth prepared to intervene in any of the Central American republics to assure debt collection, the maintenance of law and order, and the general peace of the Caribbean. The Monroe Doctrine had been given a new meaning whose importance was not lost upon either Europe or Latin America.

★ DOLLAR DIPLOMACY

Taft followed the general lines of the policy initiated by Roosevelt. His approach was a little different. He urged American banks to take over the loans of the Central American republics, thereby eliminating European influence at the source, and promised them the protection of the State Department. If he often seemed to lack Roosevelt's verve in foreign affairs, as in domestic policy, his "dollar diplomacy" was effective. Its most important application was in Nicaragua where after a series of revolutionary outbreaks, the United States landed marines, appointed a receiver-general for the customs, and occupied the country for several years.

Wilson proved no less susceptible to the protective impulses which determined Latin American policy during this period. While the Democrats had been severely critical of both the Roosevelt and Taft administrations on this score, once in office they went even further in some respects in seeking to make the Caribbean an American lake. The *New York Times* observed sarcastically that the dollar diplomacy of Wilson was making that of Taft "more nearly resemble ten-cent diplomacy."

Whatever the economic and strategic gains from such developments—added to our protectorate over Cuba and the annexation of Puerto Rico—arbitrary interference in the internal affairs of supposedly independent countries hardly made for cordial relations with Latin America as a whole. South of the Rio Grande there was a growing resentment of what was universally interpreted as Yankee imperialism. As one Latin American leader declared:

> The Monroe Doctrine is not a doctrine of America for the Americans, but of America for the North Americans. It has served as an admirable instrument for the United States to separate Europe from America and to establish its hegemony over the latter. The United States has been at all times preoccupied in obtaining concessions of every kind at the cost of the sovereignty of the rest of the American states. The doctrine is dangerous because it is North American imperialism hidden under a principle of international law.

Not until well into the 1920's would the United States realize how heavy a price it was paying in Latin American ill-will for its predominance in the Caribbean. Only then were the first steps taken toward restoring the independence of the Central American republics, giving up our professed right to interfere in their internal affairs, and withdrawing the marines. Another Roosevelt would finally substitute for his predecessor's forceful extension of a one-sided Monroe Doctrine the policy of the Good Neighbor.

★ EASTERN ASIA

While these developments were taking place in Latin America, the United States was also seeking to expand its influence in eastern Asia through support of the Open Door policy. It was none too successful. Czarist Russia particularly showed little disposition to respect China's independence, and her steady advance in Manchuria first brought the United States into conflict with that formidable power. But nothing could be done to block Russian imperialism in a part of the world in which the American people did not yet feel they had any vital interest.

Secretary Hay fulminated helplessly over trying to deal "with a government with whom mendacity is a science." He finally gave up trying to defend the Open Door in Manchuria. "I take it for granted," he stated, "that Russia knows as we do that we will not fight over Manchuria, for the simple reason that we cannot. . . ."

When Japan, whose interests in Manchuria were considered vital to her national security, was driven to take up this challenge of Russian aggression in the Russo-Japanese War of 1904–5, American sympathies were entirely with the island kingdom. "The organization and control of the millions of China by Russia," one magazine editorial declared in words which had a prophetic implication for the situation nearly half a century later, "is far more dangerous to the rest of the world than would be their control by the Japanese." Roosevelt firmly believed that "Japan is playing our game." He later stated that had either Germany or France intervened in the Russo-Japanese War, he was prepared to go to whatever lengths were necessary to uphold Japan.

The spectacular victories Japan won over Russia on land and sea eventually awoke some misgivings in the President's mind. He was led to offer his good services for peace in the conviction that a too decisive Japanese triumph would not be in this country's interests. Primarily interested in the maintenance of Chinese sovereignty and the Open Door to trade, Roosevelt exerted his influence in favor of a "balanced antagonism" between Russia and Japan that would prevent either power from dominating China. When a Russo-Japanese peace treaty was signed in August 1905 at Portsmouth, New Hampshire, there were elements of compromise in the agreed-upon settlement—most notably lack of an indemnity—that the Japanese public attributed to American interference. Japan nevertheless took over Russian interests in both Manchuria and Korea. Almost overnight she had become a world power, with a position on the Asiatic mainland that enabled her to exercise increasing influence in the future developments of the Far East.

The rivalry between the United States and Japan that led to the Pacific war dates from this early period. American support for Chinese independence and the Open Door came into direct conflict with Japanese ambitions to dominate China and all eastern Asia. Moreover, at this same time, there developed a bitter dispute over Japanese immigration into the United States as a consequence of various anti-Japanese measures adopted on the West Coast. For a time it appeared to threaten war and was resolved only by the skillful negotiation of a Gentleman's Agreement whereby the Japanese government itself undertook to restrict the passage of its subjects to America.

In dealing with these issues it was Roosevelt's constant aim, in spite of all the charges brought against him for wielding "the big stick," to seek out compromise. In 1908 he sent the fleet on a voyage around the world primarily to impress upon Japan the country's naval strength, but he carefully avoided any threatening gesture. He realized that Japan had special interests on the Asiatic mainland. In return for her reaffirmation of the principles of the Open Door, he agreed to recognize them and also to accept Japanese annexation of Korea. There was a basic contradiction in this policy, but in all his dealings with Japan, the President showed a surprising—and thoroughly realistic—spirit of accommodation. He set forth his long-term views on eastern Asia in a letter to President Taft in 1910:

> I do not believe in our taking any position anywhere unless we can make good; and as regards Manchuria, if the Japanese choose to follow a course of conduct to which we are adverse, we cannot stop it unless we are prepared to go to war, and a successful war about Manchuria would require a fleet as good as that of England, plus an army as good as that of Germany. The Open Door policy in China was an excellent thing and I hope it will be a good thing in the future, so far as it can be maintained by general diplomatic agreement; but, as has been proved by the whole history of Manchuria, alike under Russia and Japan, the Open Door policy, as a matter of fact, completely disappears as soon as a powerful nation determines to disregard it, and is willing to run the risk of war rather than forego its intention.

Taft tried another approach to resolve the differences between American and Japanese policy. His Secretary of State, Philander C. Knox, proposed the internationalization of the railroads in Manchuria as a means of ending all rivalry in that part of the world. It never received serious consideration, and other efforts to strengthen the American position in China through financial investments and a form of Far Eastern dollar diplomacy were largely ineffective. At one point agreement with the Chinese government for a huge currency loan seemed to promise a great increase in the influence of the United States. "Dollar diplomacy is justified at last," exulted the agent of the banks involved. But the revolution that in 1912 overthrew the old Manchu dynasty and led to creation of the Chinese Republic caused the abandonment of this project.

When Wilson succeeded Taft in the presidency, he withdrew government support from all further ventures along these lines and sought to maintain a hands-off policy in eastern Asia. But he too became involved when Japan tried to extend her influence over China through the notorious Twenty-One Demands, made on that hapless country in 1915. The United States strongly protested and was partly successful in persuading Japan to moderate her extreme position.

American influence in eastern Asia, as in Latin America, had increased during the Progressive era, but effective defense of the Open Door policy had not proved feasible. China was not dismembered; she remained theoretically independent. However, the encroachments of foreign powers on her sovereignty had by no means been halted, and the United States found itself more and more seriously challenged by the rising imperialism of Japan.

★ THE ALGECIRAS CONFERENCE

Another development in American policy during these years did not at the time appear highly significant, but it interestingly foreshadowed the future. This was participation in a European conference, held in 1906 at Algeciras, Spain, for the settlement of a dispute over conflicting French and German claims in Morocco. The United States had only the slightest interest in Morocco, but at the instigation of Germany, President Roosevelt dispatched the experienced diplomat Henry White to this meeting in order that American influence might be exercised to help keep Europe "on an even keel." Here was a startling departure from the traditional isolationist policy of nonintervention in European affairs. It reflected Roosevelt's strong conviction that the United States could not ignore its responsibilities as a great power and was bound to do everything it could to prevent the Moroccan dispute from bringing on European war.

In the event, American mediation had a very helpful influence in working out a compromise settlement of the issues at stake, and the immediate threat to peace was averted. The conference had, nevertheless, dramatically revealed the growing rift between Germany on the one hand and England and France on the other. There was never any question where American sympathies lay—or perhaps more accurately those of Roosevelt, for the public was not greatly interested—but skillful diplomacy succeeded in bridging the gap between the contending powers without sacrificing official American neutrality. Upon the conclusion of the General Act of Algeciras, which for the time sustained commercial freedom in Morocco, both Germany and France expressed appreciation to Roosevelt for the part he had played in the conference's success.

Few realized that this agreement was but a temporary truce between the emerging European power blocs represented by the Triple Alliance of Germany, Austro-Hungary, and Italy, and the Triple Entente of Great Britain, France, and Russia. There was even less understanding that the role played by the United States presaged intervention on the side of the Triple Entente when war did break out. One statement made at the time, however, accurately predicted a future that went even beyond World War I. "We have got to support France against Germany and fortify the Atlantic System beyond attack," wrote Henry Adams, "for if Germany breaks down England or France, she becomes the center of a military world, and we are lost. The course of concentration must be decided by force—whether military or industrial matters not much in the end." It was somewhat ironical, indeed, that in approving the General Act of Algeciras, the Senate expressly stated that American participation should not be construed as marking any departure from our historic policy of noninvolvement in European affairs.

Roosevelt was very happy over the consequences of his policy. It was not only that he had aided in keeping the peace but that, as he wrote at the time, he had stood the Kaiser "on his head with great decision."

★ WILSON IN MEXICO

There was no further intervention on the part of the United States in European affairs in this prewar period in spite of further crisis in Morocco and war in the Balkans. Both Taft and Wilson reverted to traditional policy. But a problem nearer home developed in which this country was to become dangerously involved. Revolution broke out in Mexico in 1911 against the dictatorial regime of Porfirio Diaz, and in the ensuing struggle of rival groups for power, American interests in Mexico appeared to be gravely threatened. There was a clamorous demand for intervention for their protection.

When Wilson came into office in 1913, the chaotic conditions in Mexico and actual attacks upon American property and American lives made his position very difficult. He wanted if possible to avoid intervention and maintain peace. In spite of mounting criticism, he insisted on maintaining what he termed a policy of "watchful waiting," and in October took the occasion of a speech at Mobile, Alabama, to outline what he considered the principles that should govern our entire policy toward the countries of Latin America. "We must show ourselves friends," he declared, "by comprehending their interest whether it squares with our interest or not. It is a very perilous thing to determine the foreign policy of a nation in the terms of material interest."

Affairs in Mexico had in the meantime gone from bad to worse. Diaz' successor, Francisco Madero, was overthrown and assassinated in a new revolt, and another military chieftain, Victoriano Huerta, came into power. In these new circumstances Wilson refused to recognize a regime that had been established through such violent means, and he was prepared to throw American support behind still another Mexican faction, the so-called Constitutionalists, headed by Venustiano Carranza.

The situation could not have been more complicated. As the Mexicans continued to fight among themselves, with increasing danger for Americans, the demand grew for active American intervention. Wilson still refused to accede to it. "I have to pause and remind myself," he told his secretary, "that I am the President of the United States and not of a small group of Americans with vested interests in Mexico." Yet his own policy of watchful waiting had in fact given way to an attempted exercise of pressure to force Huerta out of office, and it approached closer and closer to the intervention he deplored. The impulse behind his entire approach to the Mexican problem was an idealistic belief that he could further the cause of democracy; his policy has not inaptly been called "missionary diplomacy." But it involved him in contradictions that to his critics appeared to make his idealistic pronouncements hypocritical and self-seeking.

The crisis came when Huerta's forces arrested a boatload of sailors who had landed from an American vessel at the port of Tampico on April 9, 1914. While Huerta promptly apologized for the incident, he refused to authorize the formal salute to the American flag insisted on by the naval officer in command. The country was incensed. "I'd make them salute the flag," shouted one outraged senator, "if we had to blow up the whole place." Wilson supported the naval commander at Tampico. He believed that at all costs he should uphold the dignity and the honor of the United States. Moreover, he went before Congress to ask authority to compel Huerta to redress the injury done the United States, and when word was received of a German merchant ship about to land arms for the Mexican dictator's government, he ordered the occupation of Vera Cruz by American forces.

Did this mean the active intervention that Wilson had so long opposed? Happily the envoys of Argentina, Brazil, and Chile at this point offered their services to mediate the dispute and Wilson promptly accepted this escape from his dilemma. Negotiations were started but had hardly settled the issue when affairs in Mexico took another turn. The increasing pressure upon Huerta, unable to maintain a stable regime, forced him to resign. He was succeeded in August by the American-backed Carranza.

Events seemed to have paid off. The succession of Carranza to the presidency was characterized by the *New York Times* as "such a triumph for President Wilson's much misunderstood policy as to astonish even the staunchest supporters of the President." Yet the issue was not settled. Carranza, to whom the United States had extended *de facto* recognition, found it as hard to maintain order as had Huerta, and a new revolt flared up in the northern states of Mexico under the leadership of General Villa. He systematically attacked American citizens, on one occasion taking eighteen from a train and shooting them in cold blood, and another time staging a raid across the border in which seventeen residents of Columbus, New Mexico, were killed. The old demand for intervention flared up once again, and to meet the new crisis, President Wilson, with Carranza's grudging consent, dispatched General John J. Pershing in March 1916 on a punitive expedition after Villa.

Further friction between the United States and Mexico grew out of this unnatural situation, and there seemed greater danger than before of the outbreak of war. The militia were called out and stationed along the border, and plans made for possible hostilities. It was at this point, however, that the far more threatening crisis developed in our relations with Germany. Wilson recalled General Pershing from Mexico and renewed the diplomatic contacts that had been broken off with the Carranza government. As the border troubles gradually subsided early in 1917, the United States prepared to take up the challenge of Germany's submarine warfare.

★ WAR AND NEUTRALITY

The war in Europe had dragged on for two and a half years by this time, and ever since its outbreak Wilson had persistently tried to avoid American involvement. There was a basic contradiction, however, in his concept of neutrality and his insistence upon freedom of the seas. For in asserting the right of the United States to maintain overseas trade—as early as February 1915 the State Department declared that Germany would be held to "a strict accountability" for submarine attacks on American ships—the President was in effect insisting that we should be allowed to continue to supply the Allies with the economic sinews of war.

For Great Britain controlled the seas, and our wartime trade was necessarily with the Allies. Germany's only means of cutting off the flow of American munitions which enabled her enemies to go on fighting was submarine warfare directed against all cargo ships, regardless of nationality. Sooner or later she was certain to accept the risk of being held to account by the United States by turning her U-boats loose. To allow the constant re-enforcement of the Allies was to accept defeat.

The continuing controversy over neutral rights was consequently marked, until the close of 1916, by a German retreat whenever the United States protested attacks upon merchant shipping, and then another aggressive test of our attitude. At last the strength of the U-boat fleet inspired the German Admiralty with the hope that sufficient cargo vessels could be sunk to starve Great Britain out, even if the United States retaliated against submarine warfare by taking up arms.

William Jennings Bryan, whom Wilson had made Secretary of State, recognized from the first the implications of economic support for the Allies under these circumstances. He tried to block the extension of credit for England's purchase of arms in the United States, favored measures that would have kept American ships and American citizens out of the war zone, and finally resigned his office when Wilson's notes on the sinking of the "Lusitania" set forth what he considered an untenable position for a neutral nation. He was convinced that we had embarked upon the road to war without just cause or provocation.

Wilson continued to assert our neutral rights to trade as embraced in the historic concept of freedom of the seas. He was prepared to protest when Great Britain infringed upon them, as she repeatedly did by arbitrarily hauling ships bound for neutral ports into harbor and seizing their cargoes, but he was far sterner in his attitude toward Germany. He drew a sharp distinction between British infractions of international law limited to cargo seizures, and Germany's more flagrant sinking of unarmed cargo vessels. In the one case there was a violation of property rights; in the other, the sacrifice of the lives of men, women, and children. Wilson reflected the general popular attitude of the time in judging unrestricted submarine warfare as not only an invasion of neutral rights, but as a shocking crime against humanity.

The sinking of the "Lusitania" in 1915 called forth the first American protests, and, while they were sufficiently firm to cause Bryan's resignation, an increasingly belligerent pro-Ally faction vehemently criticized the President for not going far enough. Roosevelt again took the lead in attacking Wilson. Although he had not originally had any such idea, the former Rough Rider by this time was convinced that the United States should come actively to the support of the Allies. He bitterly castigated the "note-writing professor" in the White House as a "mollycoddle" and "flapdoodle pacifist." But Wilson stood his ground as he had when assailed for watchful waiting toward Mexico. He would go no further than note-writing. And while Germany's replies were highly equivocal, an apparent cessation of submarine attacks (secret orders had actually been issued to U-boat commanders to spare large liners) appeared to mark a victory for American diplomacy.

The hope that there could be any such easy solution to the problem of neutrality soon proved illusory. Within three months another liner, the "Arabic," was sunk, and the pattern of American protest, temporizing negotiations, and German retreat was repeated. This time the German Foreign Office said it had all been a mistake and declared that new orders given to submarine commanders would make the recurrence of such an incident as the sinking of the "Arabic" impossible. An uneasy calm now reigned on the seas for nearly seven months, and Germany made no new attacks on passenger vessels. But in March 1916 the truce was again broken when a submarine torpedoed an unarmed channel steamer, the "Sussex," causing eighty casualties.

The American protest this time was an ultimatum:

> Unless the Imperial Government should now immediately declare and effect an abandonment of its present methods of submarine warfare against passenger and freight-carrying vessels, the Government of the United States can have no choice but to sever diplomatic relations.

Germany had not yet reached the point where she was prepared to run the risks of retaliation. She consequently reaffirmed her earlier pledges that submarines would not attack merchantmen without warning and promised that every effort would be made to provide for the safety of passengers and crew. This time, however, there was a string to her pledge. Should the United States fail to persuade other belligerents to observe "the laws of humanity" (which simply meant compel Great Britain to lift her naval blockade), the German government reserved complete liberty of action. A diplomatic break had been temporarily avoided, but it was clear that whenever she felt it to be her interests to do so, Germany would openly resort to submarine warfare.

★ THE ELECTION OF 1916

As this international situation grew increasingly tense, with preparedness measures belatedly adopted to build up our national defense, the presidential election of 1916 gave the American people their first opportunity to pass judgment on Wilson's policies. Nominating Charles Evans Hughes, former governor of New York and an associate justice of the Supreme Court, the Republicans campaigned with the vague slogan, "America first and America efficient." They were critical of Wilson's policy as not going far enough in upholding our neutral rights, but they were not ready to go so far as to urge breaking off relations with Germany. The Democrats renominated Wilson and made "he kept us out of war" their rallying cry, but the President was candid enough to state that the time might come when the choice would be between peace and national honor, and the country could not expect of him "an impossible and contradictory thing."

Domestic issues also entered the campaign. The liberal Wilsonian policies won the support of Progressives, the Bull Moose party of 1912 having completely collapsed, and while Hughes sought to win over Roosevelt's followers, his position was basically conservative. There was a more clear-cut popular division over the fundamental question of reform—with a good deal of crossing of party lines—than in any campaign since 1896.

It was an exciting, hard-fought election with the result very much in doubt. Early morning newspapers on the day after the balloting announced a victory for Hughes. But the returns from California were not yet in, and they narrowly tipped the scales in Wilson's favor. The final popular vote was 9,128,000 for the Democrats and 8,534,000 for the Republicans. The President accepted the verdict as an endorsement of his reform policies at home and as a mandate to continue doing everything possible to keep the country out of war so long as this was possible with respect for American rights.

★ WILSON'S PEACE PROGRAM

Wilson had by now become convinced, however, that Germany would not for long allow the United States to maintain its neutrality. The only possible way to avoid being drawn into war was to persuade the belligerents to lay down their arms. There had been earlier efforts to exert American influence in behalf of peace. In the spring of 1915, and again early in 1916, the President had sent his close friend and confidant, Colonel Edward M. House, on unofficial overseas missions to explore the possibilities of peace by negotiation. Although nothing had come of them, Wilson felt he had no alternative other than to try again. On December 18, 1916, he dispatched identical notes to the warring powers suggesting immediate negotiations on the ground that "the objects which the statesmen of the belligerents on both sides have in mind are virtually the same. . . ."

His pro-Ally advisers were shocked. Their idea had been that the only justification for American intervention in the war, regardless of the issue of neutral rights, would be to assure a complete Allied victory. In suggesting that there was no distinction between the Allied and German cause, Wilson had in their opinion betrayed the basic principles for which the United States had always stood. This opposition, however, did not shake the President's conviction that only an immediate cessation of hostilities could rescue the United States from an impossible dilemma and enable it as a great and powerful neutral to exercise a dominant influence in the establishment of peace. When once again neither the Allies nor Germany showed any disposition to enter into negotiations, he made one more last desperate effort to summon the power of world public opinion to support his cause.

In a speech before the Senate on January 22, 1917, he called for a "peace without victory." This memorable address was the embodiment of all Wilson's idealistic and moralistic concepts in regard to international relations. He envisaged a new world order based upon government only with the consent of the governed, freedom of the seas in times of war as well as in times of peace, and the end of all entangling alliances in favor of "a peace made secure by the organized major force of mankind." Any settlement that violated the basic principles of international morality and represented an attempt on the part of a victor to impose his will upon the vanquished, the President declared, could not possibly endure. "It would be accepted in humiliation, under duress, at an intolerable sacrifice," he prophetically proclaimed, "and would leave a sting, a resentment, a bitter memory upon which terms of peace would rest, not permanently, but only as upon quicksand. Only a peace between equals can last."

His gesture was a futile one. There could be no breaking down the resolve of either the Central Powers or the Allies to fight to complete victory. Already the German government had made the fateful decision that caught Wilson in the trap of his own making. Nine days after the "peace without victory" speech, Germany announced that all merchant ships, armed or unarmed, would be sunk on sight in the war zone. In view of his earlier statements that the United States would hold Germany to a strict accountability should she resort to unrestricted submarine warfare, the President now had no choice but to break off diplomatic relations. He did so on February 3, 1917.

There were to be frantic efforts to avoid the next step. Wilson stoutly declared that "war can come only by the willful acts and aggressions of others," and tried to meet the immediate issue by arming American merchantmen so as to discourage submarine attacks. But events were beyond his control. They now succeeded each other in dramatic sequence and led inevitably to war.

★ THE GATHERING CRISIS

On February 25 the report was received of an intercepted note that the German Foreign Minister, Alfred Zimmerman, had sent to the German minister in Mexico. It proposed that in the event the United States and Germany found themselves at war, Mexico should ally herself with Germany in return for the reward of her "lost territory in Texas, New Mexico and Arizona" and should also invite Japan to join the anti-American coalition. A few days later the first Russian revolution broke out, and the overthrow of the autocratic government of the czars appeared more than ever to identify the Allied cause with democracy. And finally on March 12, Germany made good her threat of unrestricted submarine warfare by sinking an unarmed American merchantman, the "Algonquin," and six days later three more ships were torpedoed.

There could now be no quieting the popular demand for war. The Zimmerman note seemed to threaten national security, the Russian revolution strengthened the concept that the war was one to overthrow autocracy, and the sinking of American ships was both a direct attack on lives and property and a seemingly unforgivable assault upon our national honor.

"From the quixotic adventure of imposing upon the Old World a 'peace without victory,' " the Boston *Transcript* declared in a typical editorial, "we are brought up with a sharp turn by the imperative necessity of defending American honor, American rights, American lives, and American property—against a war without quarter with which Germany has threatened, not the New World only, but the whole world."

Still Wilson hesitated. Feeling gravely the responsibility for a crisis that had in large part grown out of his own policies, he appeared to be torn by doubt and indecision. But his cabinet agreed with the general editorial opinion that Germany's challenge had to be accepted, and the President reluctantly summoned Congress to meet in special session to "receive a communication by the executive on grave questions of national policy." His mind must now have been made up, but there is evidence of his searching vainly, even at this last moment, for some way out other than a declaration of war. At one o'clock on the morning of the day Congress was to meet, Wilson told a White House visitor that he had never been so uncertain about anything in his life, and asked plaintively, "What else can I do?"

When he faced Congress on April 2, 1917, however, there was no equivocation in his words or manner. Nor were there any traces of that old concept of peace without victory. Accepting the challenge of submarine warfare as one that violated the most sacred rights of the nation and left the United States only one course of action, Wilson asked Congress to declare the recent acts of the German government to be nothing less than war against the government and people of the United States. He made it clear that there would now be no temporizing with an autocratic government which could not be trusted to keep faith. Tyranny must be overthrown; freedom restored in a world made secure against war. In the hushed silence that greeted his message, he concluded:

> . . . To such a task we can dedicate our lives and our fortunes, everything that we are and everything that we have, with the pride of those who know that the day has come when America is privileged to spend her blood and her might for the principles that gave her birth and happiness and the peace which she has treasured. God helping her, she can do no other.

★ ECONOMIC INTERPRETATIONS

Germany's adoption of unrestricted submarine warfare was the direct and immediate cause for American entry into World War I. Underlying factors in the situation, however, must be examined to account for the position in which the United States found itself early in 1917. For it was defending policies that were no longer neutral in any real sense of the term. The struggle for freedom of the seas had become in actuality a struggle to keep a flow of supplies going exclusively to England and France, and the total of this trade with the Allies had risen from $825,000,000 in 1914 to $3,214,000,000 in 1916. Moreover, it was being largely financed through American loans. The United States had a financial stake in Allied victory and its economic well-being had become to a substantial extent dependent on the continuance of an expanding commerce in munitions and food supplies.

There was a vociferous group in Congress that had always strongly opposed this entire program of trade and loans. They had long since become convinced that it was carrying the nation closer and closer to hostilities, and now stated that the protection of banking and commercial interests, rather than those of the American people, was the real reason leading the administration and Congress to plunge the country into war. They condemned the Allies for following a course quite as militaristic and imperialistic as that of Germany and declared that the United States had neither cause nor reason for coming to their aid. This was a minority view. The country as a whole appeared convinced that the United States had every right on its side—and an overpowering national interest—in upholding freedom of the seas, and that to retreat in the face of Germany's challenge would be incompatible with national honor.

There was a period in the 1930's when perhaps most Americans accepted the economic explanation of why the United States entered the war which the opponents of this move—such as Senator La Follette of Wisconsin and Senator Norris of Nebraska—first advanced in 1917. The country became convinced that matters of trade and finance had been almost solely responsible for American policy, and going even further, singled out the munitions makers and international bankers as the villains of the day. Such business influence, according to this popular interpretation born of the disillusionment of the postwar years, forced the Wilson administration's hand. On one occasion Ambassador Page had cabled from London: "Perhaps our going to war is the only way in which our pre-eminent trade position can be maintained and a panic averted. The submarine has added the last item to the danger of a financial world crash." Here was the significant explanation, it was maintained, of

Wilson's abrupt shift in policy from peace without victory, to an all-out demand for Germany's complete defeat.

This was an oversimplification of the record. There is no evidence that Wilson was directly influenced by such considerations in making his fateful decision for war. Nevertheless, it would be wholly unrealistic not to recognize that economic ties forged with the Allies between 1914 and 1917 had a part in convincing the American people that an Allied victory was essential for their own welfare and that the challenge of German submarine warfare threatened the national interest.

Our wartime trade had brought a prosperity to the country by no means limited to bankers and munitions makers; it was universally reflected in high business profits, mounting wages for labor, and increased income for farmers. To have suddenly sacrificed that trade by abandoning our defense of neutral rights, withdrawing protection from our shipping, and acquiescing in Germany's right to sink merchant ships at sight would have had consequences the Wilson administration could hardly have faced. It was the fear of dangerous repercussions for the national economy that blocked every early effort to embargo the sale of munitions, to prevent the floating of Allied loans in this country, or otherwise to restrict our thriving commerce. The arguments that loans and munitions sales to the Allies were inconsistent with the true spirit of neutrality could not hold their own in the face of an increasing dependence upon wartime trade. "We need it," the editor of one business magazine stated bluntly, "for the profits it yields."

★ SENTIMENT AND PROPAGANDA

But while the influence of such economic factors cannot by any means be wholly disregarded, this is only a part of the story. Principle and sentiment were far more important in building up American sympathy for Britain and France, and in persuading a formerly indifferent and complacent people that an Allied victory over Germany was greatly in the national interest. They had become convinced that it was the Allies who were fighting for liberty, for freedom, and for a peaceful world against the aggressive designs of an autocratic and imperialistic Germany. Rightly or wrongly they had come to believe that Germany was primarily responsible for starting the war, that her invasion of neutral Belgium was a flagrant violation of international morality, and that submarine warfare was a crime against all civilization. From this point of view victory for a government guilty of such sins could only be a threat to peace-loving nations everywhere. America could not afford to stand by and see it happen.

The economic determinists explained this growing sympathy for the

Allies and mounting opposition to Germany entirely on the basis of Allied propaganda. And it was true that this propaganda was both pervasive and effective. The British spoke our language, largely controlled the sources of news, and were extremely adept in presenting their case to the American public. They skillfully played upon popular emotions, not only drawing a somber picture of German ruthlessness, but in some instances manufacturing lurid atrocity stories that won widespread credence. They knew the strength of American idealism and constantly appealed to it by pointing out Allied concern over democracy and the rights of small nations. But for all the influence of such propaganda, its importance could be greatly exaggerated. It was only deepening the channels in which public opinion already ran.

What turned the American people against Germany was not so much what the Allies said but what the Germans actually did. The invasion of Belgium and the sinking of the "Lusitania" were indisputable facts. In commenting on the latter, the *Nation* described it as "at once a crime and a monumental folly . . . She [Germany] has affronted the moral sense of the world and sacrificed her standing among nations." A later generation, accepting all the implications of submarine warfare, may find it difficult to understand this popular reaction, but the world of 1915 had not yet become inured to total war. It still expected observance of those traditional rules of international law that sought to safeguard civilians—and especially women and children—from any military or naval operations.

Whatever propagandists might or might not say, moreover, there was a natural sympathy for Britain born of the ties of race and lauguage, the heritage of a common culture, and a growing feeling of community interest. As the war went on, with its awful toll of lives, this feeling became stronger. Those whose backgrounds were either German or Irish naturally felt no such bonds, but the general sense of kinship with the British people overshadowed all other national ties. There was also a highly sentimental feeling of friendship for France which propaganda may have deepened but which grew out of the long traditions of the past. Criticism of the Allies was never entirely stilled, but it did not undermine the growing belief that their victory was essential in re-establishing a peaceful and democratic world.

National security was not greatly stressed in 1917. Certainly, most Americans felt that they would be safer in the event of an Allied rather than a German victory. When the hope of a negotiated peace faded, new fears were aroused of Germany's devotion to militarism and of her imperialistic ambitions. They seemed to be confirmed by her willingness to risk conflict with the United States rather than abandon submarine warfare. But while it has been said that the American people "intuitively" realized that a German victory would gravely imperil national security, contemporary comment clearly suggests that sympathy for the Allied cause and a determination to uphold American rights, rather than any such fears, created the attitude of mind that made any retreat in the face of German submarine warfare impossible.

★ THE GREAT CRUSADE

Whatever the relative importance of the various factors that finally carried the United States into war, Wilson succeeded amazingly—once the die had been cast—in convincing the American people that they had taken up arms not only as defenders of their own honor, lives, and property, but as the disinterested champions of right. He lifted them to the heights represented by his own determination to transform the struggle into a great crusade that would make the world safe for democracy and end all wars. He had lost the fight to maintain a neutrality that would have enabled the United States to exercise a moderating influence on the eventual peace. Now only a complete victory for the forces of righteousness could justify the stand he had finally taken.

"For us there is but one choice," Wilson declared. "We have made it. Woe be to the man or group of men that seek to stand in our way in this day of high resolution. . . . Once more we make good with our lives and fortunes the great faith to which we are born, and a new glory shall shine in the face of the people."

It was in this spirit of dedication to a great cause that the American people as a whole took up arms in April 1917.

CHAPTER XVI

The Great Crusade

★ THE HOME FRONT

Active intervention forced the United States to take every possible measure for the mobilization of its economic and military resources. The country was called on to provide further support for the Allied war effort and to raise, equip, and prepare to send overseas an expeditionary force that could take its place beside the Anglo-French armies ranged against Germany on the western front. This twofold task was to be carried through successfully. The American contribution to final victory in 1918 was decisive. The alternative to participation in the war might well have been a German victory.

The preparedness measures of 1916 had achieved little, however, and it was a full year before the United States was in any position to marshal its full strength. The American people had no experience with modern warfare. They had not known since 1861–65 what it was to fight, for the Cuban adventure of 1898 hardly counted, and consequently they learned the lessons of what had to be done through bitter experience. There were mistakes of both commission and omission, much fumbling and incompetence, before an effective war machine was hammered out on the anvil of necessity. "The military establishment of America has broken down. . . . It has almost ceased functioning," the chairman of the Senate Committee on Military Affairs stated discouragedly as late as January 1918. Yet before the year was out, the nation had dramatically demonstrated the almost incalculable potential of its military and economic might.

The pattern of economic organization was very much the same as that which would be generally adopted during World War II. An over-all industrial command was set up in the War Industries Board, headed by Bernard M. Baruch, and through its allocation of raw materials, establishment of priorities, and exercise of other regulatory powers, all manufacture and production were directly harnessed to the national war effort. The conversion of factories was not carried as far as it was in 1941–45, and direct rationing and price controls were avoided. Nevertheless, industrial activity was largely concentrated on meeting the needs of the armed forces. Plants from coast to coast were soon pouring out guns, tanks, small arms, and ammunition in stupendous quantity, and an entirely new industry was established—although hardly in time for effective production—in the manufacture of airplanes.

It was not enough just to produce the sinews of war. Provision had to be made for transporting supplies to the Atlantic seaports and carrying them overseas. One step was taken that went beyond the controls exercised during World War II. The inability of the railroads to meet the demands made upon them in a day when there was almost no supplementary transportation by trucks, compelled the government to set up a Railroad Administration, under the direction of William G. McAdoo, to take over the railroads in order to co-ordinate all traffic, eliminate nonessential services, and generally quicken freight deliveries.

Additional shipping for the trans-Atlantic passage was also necessary, and a United States Shipping Board was formed to provide the vessels that would assure overseas deliveries. For a time in mid-summer 1917, the German U-boats were sinking Allied cargo ships at a rate three times faster than they were being built, and the Shipping Board consequently launched a construction program that was one of the most impressive of wartime activities. It let contracts for hundreds of ships of every kind—steel ships, wooden ships, composite ships, even concrete ships—and within a year they were coming off the ways in almost unbelievable numbers. On July 4, 1918, one hundred new vessels were launched simultaneously to celebrate the national holiday. This program was no more than really underway, however, before the war came to an end. Of the 9,000,000 tons of shipping that were ultimately placed under government control through purchase, charter, seizure, or construction, only some 500,000 tons were newly built. This great merchant fleet met all demands upon it. As the submarine menace was gradually averted by naval operations, transportation between the home front and the battlefields of France was maintained with only nominal losses.

Almost as important as supplying materials of war was the provision of food supplies. The Allies looked to the United States to meet needs they could not themselves fulfill, and "Food Will Win the War" was a slogan placarded throughout the country. A Food Administration was established under the leadership of Herbert Hoover, an engineer whose first wartime service had been as director of the Belgian Relief Commission. The Food Administration undertook to increase production, with the aid of legislative authority guaranteeing the nation's farmers a price of over two dollars a bushel for wheat, and to curtail consumption through a voluntary program of wheatless and meatless days. The public response to Hoover's appeals for co-operation was wholehearted and enthusiastic. The Gospel of the Clean Plate was preached the length and breadth of the land, substantially helping to avoid waste and to free additional supplies for shipment abroad.

Another comparable wartime agency was the Fuel Administration, charged with the conservation of coal, gas, and petroleum. It was found necessary to close down all nonessential industries for one brief period in order to make emergency coal supplies available for cargo ships, railway engines, and munitions plants, and fuelless Mondays were subsequently enforced over a nine-week period. The relative unimportance of automobile transportation in 1918, however, obviated the need for any such restrictions on the use of gasoline as marked the days of World War II. The Fuel Administrator went no further than to call for "gasless Sundays" that were observed in the same voluntary spirit as the meatless and wheatless days requested by Hoover.

The inevitable labor shortage of war days was for a time a serious problem. Women took the place of many men called from the assembly line for war service, a far more spectacular development in 1918 than it would be a quarter of a century later, and they crowded into the munitions plants. For a time strikes threatened to interfere with the production program, especially those by members of the I.W.W. Governmental action helped to smooth out labor relations, however, and this situation improved rapidly with establishment in April 1918 of a National War Labor Board, and somewhat later of a War Labor Policies Board, providing new means for the settlement of industrial disputes and the standardizing of wages and hours. In return for assurances that labor's right to organize and bargain collectively would be respected, responsible union leadership agreed on a no-strike pledge for the duration of hostilities.

The war effort was financed through increased taxation, with the adoption of many special excises as well as higher income taxes for both corporations and individuals, and through the sale of government securities. Four Liberty Loan drives and a final Victory Loan campaign raised a total of over $21,000,000,000, or approximately two times the total obtained through taxation. The total cost of the war to the American people amounted to some $35,000,000,000, and a public debt that had approximated $1,000,000,000 prior to 1914 had consequently risen six years later to $26,000,000,000. Although such figures are only about one-tenth those of expenditures during World War II, the increase in indebtedness appeared at the time extremely alarming.

★ PUBLIC OPINION AND CIVIL LIBERTIES

There was at no time any doubt of general public support for the war effort. The American people co-operated fully in observance of the new industrial controls, accepted the voluntary restrictions on food consumption, and generously subscribed to both Liberty Loan drives and Red Cross campaigns. But the patriotic response was not altogether spontaneous. A Committee on Public Information, headed by George Creel, did everything possible to maintain war sentiment at a fever pitch and to persuade every citizen "to do his bit." Seventy-five thousand "four minute men" volunteered to speak in support of the draft, the Liberty Loan drives, and other phases of wartime activity. Millions of pamphlets and loyalty leaflets, printed in every language, were distributed to keep the fires of patriotism burning.

This zealous campaign was sometimes marked by an almost hysterical note and a mounting intolerance toward any Americans who might, however vaguely, be suspected of latent sympathies toward Germany or who dared criticize any phase of the war effort. The very fact that there was a small minority who questioned our participation in the war and who opposed such measures as the draft intensified this intolerance to an extent that would not be repeated when a more closely united country faced the challenge of Germany and Japan in 1941. There were cruel attacks in 1917 on thoroughly loyal German-Americans, whose only sin was their place of birth, and anti-German feeling was sometimes carried to absurd lengths. The teaching of German was banned in some state school systems, orchestras were not allowed to play German music, and anything with a German name came to be looked at askance. There were even attempts to rename sauerkraut "liberty cabbage" and German measles "liberty measles!"

A dangerous expression of the superpatriotism encouraging this war spirit was an often completely unjustified infringement upon individual liberty and free speech. Congress passed an Espionage Act in June 1917 and a year later a Sedition Act to combat possible subversion; popular feeling encouraged their enforcement with the greatest severity. Hundreds of persons suspected of spying, sabotage, or aiding the enemy were arrested, and more than forty given prison sentences as high as twenty years on charges of obstructing the draft or otherwise interfering with the war effort. Eugene Debs received a ten-year sentence for a speech in opposition to the war; other critics of national policy went to jail for unfavorable comment on the Liberty Loan drives, the operations of the Red Cross, and even the Y.M.C.A. program. A considerable number of conscientious objectors paid the price of wartime adherence to their principles. Moreover, the prevailing hysteria enabled self-constituted patriots to extend this suppressive campaign to all radical opponents of capitalism—even some of its liberal critics—in the name of One Hundred Per Cent Americanism. Anyone out of step with majority opinion was in constant danger of denunciation, arrest, and conviction for supposed subversive behavior.

President Wilson had foreseen this reaction. "Once lead this people into war," he had said on the eve of intervention, "and they'll forget there ever was such a thing as tolerance. To fight, you must be brutal and ruthless, and the spirit of ruthless brutality will enter into every fiber of our national life, infecting Congress, the courts, the policeman on the beat, the man in the street."

Yet for all such instances of intolerance, the fundamental basis for national unity remained the determination of the people as a whole to see the job through. A popular readiness to make the sacrifices demanded by the war effort was almost everywhere apparent. Moreover, the suppression of individual liberties when patriotism spilled over into intolerance did not prove fatal. The Constitution that Wilson thought might be sacrificed under the impact of war successfully survived the strain. Time would see the reassertion of democratic freedom.

★ THE A.E.F.

The mobilization of the home front was, of course, a means to an end, and that end became most importantly the unremitting support of the expeditionary force that was to fight America's battles overseas. There had originally been some idea that the contribution to the war might be largely limited to naval action and additional supplies for the Allies, but the need to back up the Anglo-French armies with military force became quickly apparent. They were hard pressed in the spring of 1917, and a spirit of defeatism was making dangerous headway. "Let the American soldier come now," was the dramatic appeal of Marshal Joffre, the French commander, and the United States hastened to meet his request for immediate aid on the fighting front. As plans were made for the American Expeditionary Force, President Wilson announced that a first contingent of army regulars would sail for France "at as early a date as practical" under the command of General Pershing, fresh from his foray into Mexico.

The national guard had been called out as soon as war was declared, but far more important was the decision to rely upon a draft to build up a new army. The Selective Service Act was passed in May 1917 and by midsummer over 9,000,000 men had registered and the first contingents of draftees were making their way to the camps and cantonments set up for their training. Ultimately, the number registered—men from eighteen to forty-five—totaled over 24,000,000, and nearly 3,000,000 of them were inducted into the service. With the addition of national guardsmen, regulars, volunteers, and navy personnel, the United States had 4,800,000 men and women under arms in November 1918.

There were no precedents for building this modern army. The construction of cantonments, the procurement of military supplies, the care and transportation of troops, and the actual training program presented formidable problems with which the military authorities in 1917 had no experience. Yet haberdashers and farmhands, brokers' clerks and shoe salesmen, factory workers and college boys, had somehow to be hammered into an effective fighting force in the shortest possible time. The job was done, and something more accomplished than merely training and equipping the millions of inexperienced draftees. The citizen army of World War I was imbued with an offensive spirit that was to stand it in good stead when it took over its frontline positions from the battle-weary Allied troops.

The A.E.F. was a youthful army, confident and eager. Its members were hardly prepared for the disillusioning experiences of actual war when they sailed for France in 1917 and 1918. For many of them it was high adventure. Others strongly felt a sense of dedication born of Wilson's eloquent summons to make the world safe for democracy. While they were ready to accept danger, wounds, and even the risk of sudden death, few foresaw that war also meant continual discomfort, tedium, loneliness, and trench fever.

Once abroad and in the front lines, the American troops, however raw and untried, acquitted themselves well. Their crusading spirit gave way to a more realistic attitude. They wanted to get through with the job as quickly as possible and then shake the dust of Europe off their feet. They were not interested in conquest or glory. Homesickness pervaded the ranks and overshadowed all other emotions. America was not a militaristic nation.

The spirit of the A.E.F. was reflected in its songs, and never perhaps has an army sung so much. In the camps and cantonments at home there had risen a universal chorus:

> And we won't be back till it's over,
> Over there.

In France, apart from the ever-popular "Mademoiselle from Armentières," most of the songs were sentimental and nostalgic—"The Long,

Long Trail," "It's a Long Way to Tipperary," and "K-K-K-Katy, Beautiful Katy." The bored, wearied, mud-covered, cootie-infested doughboy of World War I wanted above everything else to get back to "the girl that he adored":

> And when the moon shines
> Over the cowshed,
> I'll be waiting at the k-k-k-kitchen door!

★ VICTORY ON THE WESTERN FRONT

Before the A.E.F. reached France, the American navy had waged a critical campaign in the Atlantic in combatting the German submarines. The adoption of a convoy system rapidly cut down the losses by sinkings, while a North Sea mine barrage and intensified antisubmarine warfare by destroyers and gunboats soon began to take an increasingly heavy toll of the U-boats. These measures, taken in co-operation with the British navy, made possible the safe convoy overseas of American troops and supplies.

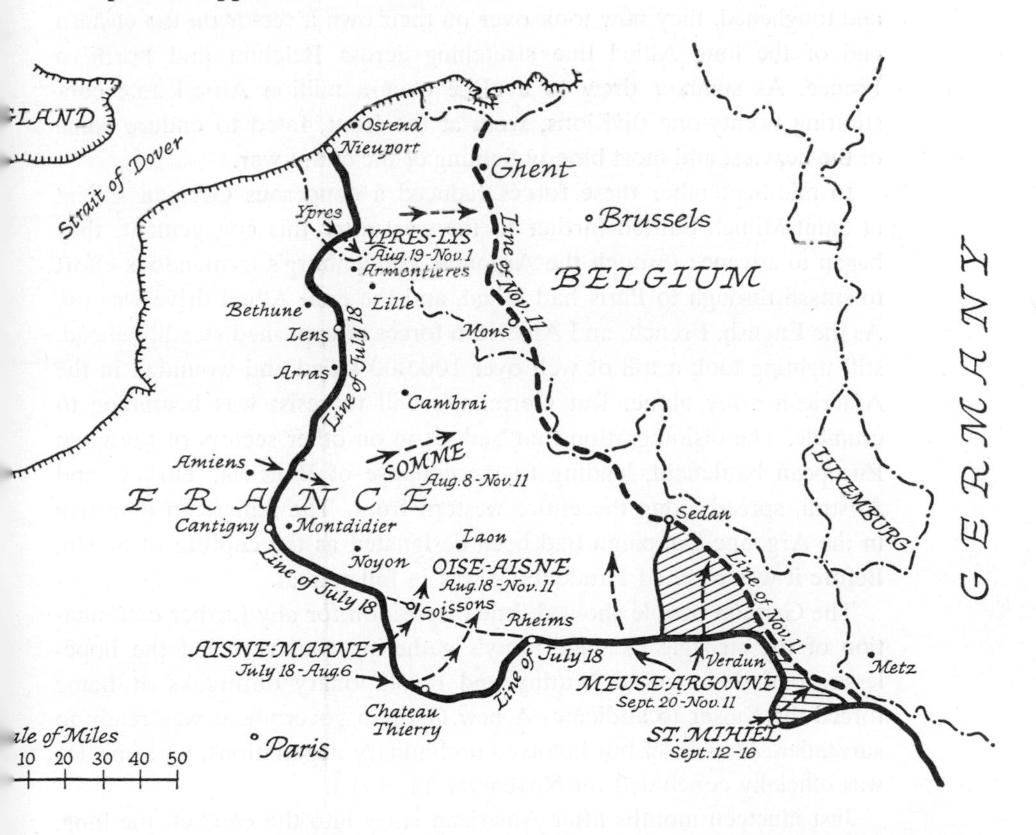

THE AMERICAN ARMY IN FRANCE, 1918

The original plan for the A.E.F. had been to brigade the troops with the English and the French. General Pershing was convinced, however, of the importance of creating an independent command. As early as October 1917 a first contingent of American troops consequently took over a quiet sector of the French front near Toul. The reverses suffered by the Allies during the great German offensive early in 1918 then necessitated a temporary change in plans. The fresh American forces had to be used to stiffen the broken Allied lines. Once the enemy advance had been checked, with a rallying of the Anglo-French forces under the unified command of Marshal Foch, Pershing returned to his original idea. Provision was made for the creation of a separate American army, eighteen divisions strong, which could take a major responsibility in the great counteroffensive that was being set up at Allied headquarters.

The American troops had proved their worth in the earlier fighting under Allied command on the Aisne and on the Meuse, at Chateau Thierry, and at Belleau Wood. Six divisions had won their spurs backing up the French in desperate defense of the Marne. Battle-hardened and toughened, they now took over on their own a sector on the eastern end of the long Allied line stretching across Belgium and northern France. As summer drew to a close over a million Americans, constituting twenty-one divisions, were at the front, fated to endure some of the heaviest and most bloody fighting of the entire war.

In mid-September these forces reduced a dangerous German salient at Saint-Mihiel. Shifted farther to the west after this engagement, they began to advance through the Argonne. Hindenburg's tremendous effort to smash through to Paris had failed, and the final Allied drive was on. As the English, French, and American forces now pushed steadily ahead, stiff fighting took a toll of well over 100,000 killed and wounded in the American army alone. But Germany's will to resist was beginning to crumble. The disintegration that had set in on other sectors of the great European battlefield, leading to the collapse of Bulgaria, Turkey, and Austria, spread along the entire western front. The American objective in the Argonne campaign had been designated as the capture of Sedan. Before it was reached Hindenburg was in full retreat.

The German people showed little disposition for any further continuation of the struggle as their army's gathering rout revealed the hopelessness of their cause. Mutiny and revolutionary outbreaks at home forced the Kaiser to abdicate. A new German government was ready to surrender. After brief but involved preliminary negotiations, an armistice was officially concluded on November 11, 1918.

Just nineteen months after American entry into the conflict, the long, gruelling, bloody struggle on the battlefields of Europe had come to an end with complete Allied victory. The news of the armistice was greeted with wild and boisterous excitement throughout the United States. The war had been won; Germany was crushed and helpless.

★ MAKING THE PEACE

President Wilson had not forgotten his peace aims. Early in 1918 he set forth in his famous Fourteen Points the objectives for which the United States was fighting. They were at once cleverly contrived propaganda to break down German resistance and keep Russia, which had undergone its Bolshevik revolution in the fall of 1917, in the war, and also a sincere expression of the President's own views on the kind of world that peace should bring into being. The Fourteen Points embraced freedom of the seas, the removal of economic barriers, the reduction of national armaments, the evacuation and restoration of all conquered territory, the impartial adjustment of colonial claims, autonomy for the peoples of Austria-Hungary, and the creation of an independent Poland. Finally and most importantly, they called for "a general association of nations . . . for the purpose of affording mutual guarantees of political independence and territorial integrity to great and small nations alike."

There was to be nothing vindictive or punitive about the peace which would be concluded within the framework of these terms. "We have no jealousy of German greatness," the President stated, ". . . nor do we presume to suggest to her any alteration or modification of her institutions."

The Allies accepted the Fourteen Points reluctantly and with reservations, but Wilson was determined to see the principles set forth, and especially the proposed association of nations, incorporated in the treaty with Germany. To this end he undertook to represent the United States at the peace conference and in December 1918 sailed for Paris as head of the American delegation. There were already ominous undertones in the political reaction to his policy among some segments of the American public, but Wilson was to be hailed in Europe as the avowed champion of mankind. The common people everywhere appeared to have placed in him all their hopes for a peace that would demonstrate beyond doubt that the struggle they had endured was in truth "the culminating and final war for human liberty."

"No one has ever had such cheers," wrote one foreign correspondent. "I, who heard them in the streets of Paris, can never forget them in all my life. I saw Foch pass, Clemenceau pass, Lloyd George, generals, returning troops, banners, but Wilson heard from his carriage, something different, inhuman or superhuman."

The peace conference was to prove a tragic letdown. The Allies, already committed through a series of secret treaties to a traditional distribution of the spoils of war, soon came to resent the high-minded idealism of the American war president. "Mr. Wilson bores me with his Fourteen Points," Premier Clemenceau cynically commented on one occasion, "why, God Almighty has only ten." Neither the astute and wily Lloyd George, Great Britain's prime minister, nor Italy's suave Premier Orlando showed very much more enthusiasm for proposed settlements that ran counter to their own tough-minded concepts of how to deal with a defeated enemy.

Clad in the armor of righteousness, Wilson battled valiantly for his ideal of a new world order. Again and again he was compelled to give ground and compromise. Not always. When Clemenceau, disregarding every idea of that right of self-determination on which Wilson set such store, insisted upon either permanent occupation of the Rhineland or its establishment as an independent buffer state between France and Germany, the President threatened to return home and ordered steam up on the "George Washington." He did, however, accede to territorial concessions to Italy that directly violated the principle of self-determination, and in another crisis allowed Japan to retain certain former German rights in the Chinese province of Shantung. The Fourteen Points were not entirely disregarded, but neither could they be said to have formed the real basis for the treaty finally concluded in the fierce heat of controversy and dispute.

Germany had no voice in the proceedings, and the terms finally presented to her were an Allied ultimatum. They included acknowledgment of German war guilt as a basis for still undetermined reparations payments, the restoration of Alsace-Lorraine to France, the surrender of all overseas colonies, and complete disarmament. Yet they were probably not nearly so harsh as those which a victorious Germany would have imposed upon the Allies. They fell far short of the territorial dismemberment that was demanded by Frenchmen who felt that German military potential, at whatever cost, should once and for all be completely crushed.

The settlements in eastern Europe were in some measure even more significant than those applying to Germany. The old Austro-Hungarian Empire was broken up entirely, and recognition accorded Poland, Czechoslovakia, and Yugoslavia as independent states. But while these arrangements theoretically conformed to the Wilsonian principle of national self-determination, large blocs of alien peoples were included within the boundaries of the succession states. The seeds were planted for new national and international rivalries that boded ill for the stability of eastern Europe.

Apart from the merits or demerits of the political settlements, the most grievous error of the peacemakers was their failure to give any real consideration to the economic aspects of international relations. The third of Wilson's Fourteen Points had called for the removal, so far as possible, of all economic barriers. It was completely ignored. The Allied attitude toward German reparation payments, and toward the trade and fiscal questions confronting the succession states in eastern Europe, was entirely governed by political considerations. "The fundamental economic problems of a Europe starving and disintegrating before their eyes," John Maynard Keynes, the British economist, wrote, "was the one question on which it was impossible to arouse the interest of the Four." Although Wilson had himself stated that the war had been in its inception a commercial and industrial conflict rather than a political war, he made no effort to reach to the heart of such problems. From this point of view there was no real change in the circumstances out of which the war had arisen.

Wilson's concessions at the Paris peace conference were compensated in his own eyes by one outstanding and dramatic triumph. In spite of the lukewarm support or scarcely concealed opposition of European statesmen, a League of Nations was established. Moreover, it was so definitely embodied in the Versailles Treaty that it became an integral part of the postwar settlements as a whole. The former Allies stood pledged to refer all future disputes to this new organization for peaceful settlement, to take collective action against any nation which refused to abide by the League's decision, and to uphold the territorial integrity and political independence of all member nations against aggression from any quarter. This was the realization of Wilson's dream of world security.

Time was to demonstrate the bitter irony in the sacrifices made to assure acceptance of the League covenant, but Wilson was above everything else determined on its incorporation in the peace treaty. Far more important in his view than the actual terms of peace was the creation of this world organization to provide the means to redress all wrong and injustice without resort to war. "The settlement may be temporary," Wilson declared, "but the processes must be permanent." He was prepared to place all his bets on the League of Nations. He returned home completely confident that the ultimate victory at the Paris conference was his—a new world order that would banish war.

★ THE LEAGUE OF NATIONS ISSUE

Had President Wilson not gone to Paris, the League Covenant might well have been omitted from the Versailles Treaty. The trip abroad, often criticized as a blunder, was not necessarily one. Where Wilson more clearly failed in 1919 was in assuming that the American people were prepared to go as far as he was in accepting international responsibilities. He had never let himself get too far ahead of them in domestic policies, but in dealing with international issues he forgot the vital importance of leading the public step by step along the unknown road of collective security. Superbly certain of the rightness of his own views, he came more and more to condemn those who opposed or even questioned his policies as being either fools or knaves. The conciliatory spirit that had contributed so much to his earlier triumphs of statesmanship gave way to a stubbornness that would not admit the need for compromise.

A series of missteps also played into the hands of those who were prepared to put party advantage ahead of any disinterested concern over foreign policy. Wilson unduly stressed partisan politics by calling for the return of a Democratic Congress in the mid-term elections of 1918; he failed to provide acceptable Republican representation on the peace commission, and when disgruntled members of the Senate expressed their opposition to the inclusion of the proposed League in the peace treaty, he arrogantly defied them to do their worst. "When that treaty comes back," he stated, "gentlemen on this side will find the covenant not only in it, but so many threads of the treaty tied to the covenant that you cannot dissect the covenant from the treaty without destroying the whole vital structure."

In spite of the senatorial opposition aroused by these unfortunate moves, however, the great majority of the American people still seemed prepared to accept the League when Wilson returned from Paris and presented the Treaty of Versailles to the Senate. Thirty-two state legislatures endorsed it; as many governors went on record as favoring it. But time was to work against the President. As the country turned to take up the old tasks of peace, a growing indifference to foreign affairs began to replace the flaming enthusiasm with which the country had embarked on its crusade to make the world safe for democracy. Idealism gave way to apathy and disillusionment. The political opponents of Wilsonianism saw their chance to deprive the President of his final triumph. Purposely delaying action on the peace treaty, they worked assiduously to encompass the League's defeat in the Senate.

The leader in this conspiracy, for it was little more than that, was Henry Cabot Lodge. This suave, scholarly, distinguished Republican leader had conceived a bitter political hatred for Wilson, and it was to govern his entire attitude toward foreign policy. He had originally been in favor of some sort of a league, but there would be no acceptance of any world association sponsored by Wilson. The senator from Massachusetts, coldly cynical about every move he made, was relentless in his stern opposition to this "evil thing with a holy name."

Lodge's program was to block approval of the treaty through reservations, involving endless and protracted debate, while the anti-League forces did everything they could to arouse the public to the dangers of the policy commitments involved in American membership. Every effort was made to convince German-Americans that the peace settlements to be guaranteed by the League were unjust, appeals were made to the prejudice of Irish-Americans on the ground that the League was an instrument of British imperialism, and countless statements were issued for the benefit of timid isolationists on the grave risks of departing in any way from the traditional policy of no entangling alliances. The Hearst press played a leading role in this campaign. It sounded a terrifying note of alarm on the perils of creating a superstate and zealously spread the slogan of One Hundred Per Cent Americanism as an answer to all foreign commitments.

The opposition to membership in the League of Nations became much broader than political partisanship, however. The entire postwar settlement, which it was felt the League would be constrained to uphold, was widely assailed as betraying the purposes for which the United States had taken up arms. Its failure to uphold consistently the principle of self-determination, the concessions made to Japan in allowing that country to take over economic control of Shantung, the reparations clause, the failure to come to grips with colonial problems—all were described as a betrayal of the democratic cause. "The European politicians who with American complicity have hatched this inhuman monster," declared the *New Republic,* always in the past a strong supporter of Wilson, "have acted either cynically, hypocritically, or vindictively, and their handiwork will breed future cynicism, hypocrisy, and vindictiveness in the minds of future generations."

★ DEFEAT OF THE LEAGUE

Wilson finally felt compelled to stump the country to counteract these attacks, and in September 1919 he embarked on a western tour to revive confidence in his leadership and stress the importance of American membership in the League. In speech after speech he declared that unless the covenant was ratified, the whole movement for international peace would collapse and our wartime sacrifices would have been made in vain. The effort taxed his physical strength, unduly strained by his work in Paris, beyond the limit. He broke down, suffered a paralytic stroke, and was never again fully to recover his health. Whatever chance there might still have been of winning senatorial approval of the League was lost. The forces working for treaty ratification were deprived of effective leadership, and indecision and uncertainty came to characterize the general conduct of national affairs.

The wildest rumors spread through the country in respect to Wilson's condition as he remained for long months confined to a sick room from which all visitors were barred. Finally, a congressional delegation was admitted, and its report at least dispelled the idea that he might have lost his mind. There was, indeed, good evidence that his mental faculties were still keen. As the delegation was leaving Senator Fall, one of Wilson's arch foes, turned back to say: "Well, Mr. President, we have all been praying for you." Wilson looked up: "Which way, senator?"

In the meantime the fight over ratification continued in the Senate with Lodge stubbornly holding out for a series of reservations that would almost certainly have led to a reopening of the whole League question among the signatories of the Versailles Treaty. The President refused to accept them. He was unable to believe that the American people would not insist upon approval of his entire program. He made no effort to find a possible middle ground that without too seriously weakening the organization's basic structure might have met the objections of sincere critics of the League Covenant.

When the treaty first came up for vote without reservations on November 19, it was rejected by the combined forces of Lodge's followers who favored reservations and those isolationists who would not have approved of any league under any circumstances. The vote was thirty-nine to fifty-five. Submitted immediately afterwards with reservations it again went down to defeat, thirty-eight to fifty-three, Wilson's cohorts now voting against it in unhappy alliance with these same irreconcilables. "The greatest victory since Appomattox," the League's foes exulted.

One more attempt was to be made to secure approval with the League's supporters making renewed and desperate efforts to rally popular support behind their cause. It was now clear, however, that the only chance for favorable action was approval with some form of reservations, and yet there was still no persuading the obdurate President that he should try to meet the opposition half way. None can say whether concessions at this point would have saved the day for American membership in the League. The fact remains, however, that Wilson's insistence that his followers reject even modified reservations blocked favorable action. The final Senate vote on the issue, in March 1920, showed twenty Democrats deserting the President to combine with Lodge's followers in favor of the treaty with reservations, but this was not enough. The forty-nine to thirty-five count fell seven votes short of the necessary two-thirds majority.

Wilson's final word had in effect been all or nothing. He showed an intransigency that contrasted sharply with the concessions he had made at the Paris peace conference. His position was nevertheless honest and forthright. "Either we should enter the League fearlessly," he wrote in his concluding statement on the issue, "accepting the responsibility and not fearing the role of leadership which we now enjoy . . . or we should retire as gracefully as possible from the great concert of powers by which the world was saved."

Again, no one can say whether a tentative and reluctant membership in the League, under the conditions prevailing in 1920, would have made any great difference in the future course of collective security. The outcome of the bitter duel between Wilson and Lodge over League membership was not so important as the incontrovertible fact—which the Senate debates reflected—that the American people let the issue be settled by default. They had already turned their backs on Europe in shortsighted absorption in their own affairs.

★ THE ELECTION OF 1920

The election of 1920 confirmed American withdrawal from further participation in the world peace movement. Wilson was unable to do anything more than stand on the sidelines, but he had already called for a "great and solemn referendum" on the treaty, and when the Democrats nominated Governor James M. Cox of Ohio for president, with Franklin D. Roosevelt of New York as his running mate, he persuaded them to make membership in the League the principal campaign issue. It was a forlorn cause. The Republicans felt it advisable to placate important pro-Leaguers within their ranks by vaguely declaring themselves in favor of some new association of nations, but this was only a gesture. The country as a whole showed itself indifferent to foreign affairs and anxious to forget everything for which Wilsonianism had come to stand.

The Republican candidate was Warren Gamaliel Harding, senator from Ohio, and his carefully contrived nomination in "a smoke-filled room" symbolized what was to become the postwar degradation of national politics. "America's present need," Harding declared after ambiguously straddling the League issue, "is not heroics but healing; not nostrums but normalcy. . . ." It was no time for turning back on history, even if that were possible, but Harding's phrase struck a responsive chord among a people disillusioned by the quarreling, disputes, and bitterness that appeared to be the first fruits of the great crusade for democracy. They voted overwhelmingly for the Republican ticket. Harding was swept into office with a majority of over 7,000,000 votes—16,152,000 to 9,147,000—and carried every state outside the South.

★ ISOLATIONIST RETREAT

The United States had taken up arms in the war against Germany in the confident belief not only that the enemy would be defeated, but that victory on the battlefield would ensure a stable world from which war would finally be eliminated. Wilson's idealistic faith largely permeated the nation. All such hopes were dashed to the ground and the high promise of our entry into the war was denied when the League of Nations was rejected. The retreat to isolationism was a fatal blow to the prospects of collective security that no excuses or attempted self-justification could soften.

The American people repudiated "a fruitful leadership for a barren independence," declared the broken statesman in the White House. "They will have to learn by bitter experience just what they have lost. . . . We had a chance to gain the leadership of the world. We have lost it, and soon we shall be witnessing the tragedy of it all."

There is little profit in trying to single out any special villain as responsible for rejection of the League. The American people as a whole demonstrated that they had not yet attained the political maturity to realize and accept international responsibilities in the twentieth-century world. They seemed to believe that the defeat of Germany was all that was necessary to make the world safe for democracy; the further task of helping to make democracy safe for the world was not even considered. They tried to reshape the old pattern of life in almost complete disregard of how isolationism might affect both the political and economic course of events in other countries.

CHAPTER XVII

Foreign Policy in the 1920's

★ THE REPUBLICAN PROGRAM

When President Harding was inaugurated in March 1921 he solemnly declared that the United States sought "no part in directing the destinies of the world." The wheel had come full cycle since Wilson had first called for "such a concert of free peoples as shall bring peace and safety to all nations and make the world itself at last free." In withdrawing from world co-operation to follow a policy of narrow nationalism the American people were prepared to put their own immediate interests ahead of everything else.

Having refused to join the League of Nations, the United States tried to ignore its very existence. Communications from Geneva were not even acknowledged. The issue of our membership, it was officially stated, was "as dead as slavery." At the same time Congress raised tariff rates to block any further influx of foreign-made goods, insistently demanded the payment of the war debts, and erected new barriers against European immigration into the United States. These economic measures, indeed, were more significant and were to have more far-reaching consequences than rejection of the League. Nothing could have more effectively hampered any concerted action to combat the dislocations caused by war.

It was impossible, however, for the United States to hold itself completely aloof from world events. Theodore Roosevelt's statement that it was no longer a question of whether we would play a great part in the world, but only whether we would play that part ill or well, was even more valid in the 1920's than it had been in the early 1900's. The Harding administration was soon taking important steps in the realm of foreign policy in spite of itself. As the years went by the United States actually drew further and further away from political isolationism, however grimly it clung to economic nationalism. It did not join the League of Nations. Foreign policy remained subordinate to domestic policy. But the decade that opened with the great retreat was marked by a slow, reluctant, but nonetheless steady advance toward a broader participation in world affairs. There could be no return to the happy innocence of the nineteenth century.

★ SOVIET RUSSIA AND THE RED SCARE

One phase of foreign policy, whose significance was not generally appreciated at the time, involved relations with Soviet Russia. The Bolshevik Revolution, Russian withdrawal from the war in early 1918, and the triumph of Lenin in establishing communism both astounded and alarmed the American people. There was at the same time little realization of the permanent repercussions of these events on world society. Abhorring everything about a political philosophy that ran counter to the basic religious, economic, and political tenets of American democracy, the United States sought to ignore the Soviet Union as in quite a different way it tried to ignore the League of Nations.

Toward the close of the war Wilson had been drawn, with grave misgivings, into support for Allied intervention in both north Russia and Siberia. This policy was promoted to encourage the possible recreation of an eastern front against Germany, and in the circumstances then existing in Russia it inevitably led to open assistance to those elements still fighting the Bolsheviks. This support for the so-called White Russians was sporadically continued even after the Armistice, as Allied hostility to the Bolsheviks mounted and bitter civil strife nursed the illusory hope that the Soviet government might still collapse. The American troops were recalled in 1919 and 1920, but intervention nevertheless left an unhappy legacy of mutual distrust to poison future Russian-American relations.

Suspicions of Soviet Russia and fears of the possible spread of ideas inimical to democratic capitalism were at this same time further magnified by the formation of the Communist International. There was no danger of Russian aggression. The Soviet Union was far too weak to challenge the western democracies as it would in the tragic aftermath of another war. But the communist program of world revolution was considered a grave menace to democratic institutions in 1919. The country was swept by a great Red Scare which caused a hysterically excited people to see the hand of Moscow in every instance of domestic radical activity.

A wave of strikes marked this first postwar year. Their real basis was the determination of labor to maintain its wartime gains and secure wage advances to meet a spiraling rise in the cost of living. The public widely believed, however, that labor unrest was communist-inspired. Conservative employers, seeking to break the power of the unions, did everything to encourage such suspicions, and all supposed Bolsheviks —that is, radical agitators or leftwing critics of capitalism—were ruthlessly hunted down.

An American Communist Party that had been formed on the example of that in Russia was driven underground, a series of raids was dramatically staged by the Department of Justice for the arrest of alleged communists, syndicalists, and other radicals, and aliens suspected of subversive tendencies were taken in custody, with 150 summarily deported to Russia. In scores of cases the rights of free speech and free assembly were entirely ignored in frantic efforts to stem further communist infiltration.

"No one who was in the United States, as I chanced to be, in the autumn of 1919," a British journalist later wrote, "will forget the feverish condition of the public at that time. It was hag-ridden by the specter of Bolshevism. . . . Property was in an agony of fear, and the horrid name 'Radical' covered the most innocent departure from conventional thought with a suspicion of desperate purpose."

The Red Scare was to have grave consequences for civil liberties; its effect on foreign policy was to re-enforce a determination to have nothing to do with Soviet Russia. The United States withheld recognition from the communist regime in the ill-founded hope of thereby weakening its position. Other nations entered into diplomatic relations with Moscow, accepting the demonstrated fact of the Soviet government's political stability, but throughout the 1920's the United States adamantly refused to consider any renewal of normal ties. Under no circumstances, Secretary of State Kellogg declared on one occasion, could the United States recognize "a governmental entity which is the agent of a group which hold it as their mission to bring about the overthrow of the existing political, economic, and social order throughout the world."

In time this policy came to be considered in many quarters as completely unrealistic. It was argued that whatever we thought of communism, and however much we disliked the Soviet regime, refusal to accept the established Russian government could have no other effect than to build up ill-will between two nations which had somehow to discover a way to live in peace and friendship. It was not only liberals who favored recognition. American business interests became increasingly anxious to trade with Soviet Russia, for all their fears of communism, and they began to exert strong pressure for a diplomatic accord. But Harding, Coolidge, and Hoover refused in turn to make any change in the nonrecognition policy initiated by Wilson.

The effect of this attitude on subsequent events can hardly be evaluated. The different political and economic philosophies of Soviet Russia and the United States would not have been reconciled—as they were not reconciled when recognition was finally accorded—by an earlier resumption of normal relations. Nevertheless, the ill-will engendered during these years did not help to smooth the path toward co-operation during World War II; it may well have contributed to the later collapse of the wartime alliance.

★ LATIN AMERICA

In another part of the world postwar foreign policy followed a quite different course and ultimately served to improve international relations. While a nationalistic spirit that in some measure seemed to mark a revival of imperialism governed our attitude toward Latin America during the early 1920's, vigorous efforts were being made by the decade's close to strengthen the basis for a friendly *rapprochement.*

Before the adoption of this new policy, on a number of occasions the United States exerted a pressure on the smaller Latin American countries that could hardly be reconciled with a reasonable respect for their independence. President Coolidge was prepared to act on the principle that it was the duty of the United States to afford protection to the persons and property of its citizens wherever they might be. What this often meant in practice was that the State Department held the threat of economic retaliation—or more forceful measures—over any government south of the Rio Grande that did not provide full security for American banking loans and American trade.

Nicaragua was a case in point. The marines that had long since been stationed in that country to maintain what was in effect a fiscal protectorate were recalled in 1925, but when revolutionary disturbances broke out again the next year, they were promptly sent back. The United States refused to recognize the faction that had won control of the country, although it was accepted by other Latin American countries, and threw its support behind an opposition party that was more pro-United States in its sympathies. Coolidge stoutly declared that "we are not making war on Nicaragua any more than a policeman on the street is making war on passers-by," but the other Latin American nations gave a different interpretation to American policy. While order was eventually re-established in Nicaragua when a mission led by Henry L. Stimson succeeded in negotiating an agreement among the quarreling political factions, the continued presence of American marines kept alive the old charges of Yankee imperialism.

When difficulties arose soon afterwards with Mexico over her expropriation of foreign oil properties, the United States moved more carefully. Secretary of State Kellogg was at one time to charge that Mexico had embraced communism and that the influence of Moscow accounted for the policies followed by President Calles, representative of the radical wing of the revolutionary party, but more sober counsels prevailed among other Washington leaders. President Coolidge rejected the demand of oil companies and the Hearst press for active intervention in support of American property rights, and initiated negotiations for the peaceful adjustment of the issues at stake. A settlement was shortly concluded and more friendly relations were established between the United States and Mexico than had existed for many years.

President Hoover undertook on a far broader basis to restore Latin American faith in our good intentions. He explicitly stated in his inaugural address that far from having any desire for territorial expansion or economic domination over other peoples, the United States was dedicated to a policy of Latin American friendship. Shortly afterwards a State Department document definitely repudiated the old Roosevelt Corollary to the Monroe Doctrine, wherein the United States had asserted a right to intervene in Latin American affairs as a self-constituted international policeman. The groundwork was laid for that further elaboration of a generous interest in Latin American countries to which Franklin D. Roosevelt was to give the name of the Good Neighbor policy.

★ THE WASHINGTON CONFERENCE

More important than the negative aspects of relations with Soviet Russia or a slowly maturing friendship with Latin America were developments in the Pacific and Far East. Even as the United States turned its back on Europe, it projected its influence farther afield in eastern Asia. The basis for this policy was support in its broadest sense for the Open Door in China. In the fall of 1921 President Harding summoned an international conference to meet in Washington with the twofold objective of reaching new political settlements in the general area of the Pacific and bringing to a halt a threatening naval race among the United States, Great Britain, and Japan.

The Washington Conference appeared at the time to be eminently successful. The Pacific powers agreed in a Nine Power Treaty to respect the territorial integrity of China and to accept the principle of equality of trade in all their dealings with her. "The Open Door in China," the American delegation at the conference reported, "has at last been made a fact." A Four Power Treaty, wherein the United States, Great Britain, France, and Japan undertook to respect one another's insular possessions in the Pacific, replaced the Anglo-Japanese Alliance as a further guarantee of Pacific security. Finally, and in part as a result of these political accords, an agreement was reached on naval limitation in a highly significant Five Power Treaty. This pact set a ceiling of 525,000 tons for the capital ships of the United States and Great Britain, 315,000 tons for those of Japan, and 175,000 tons for those of France and Italy. It was also stipulated in this naval treaty that (except for Hawaii in the case of the United States) the signatory nations would not further fortify their island possessions in the Pacific.

There were some few contemporary critics who pointed out that in waiving its right to develop naval bases in the Philippines, Guam, Samoa, and the Aleutian Islands, the United States had in effect surrendered control of the Western Pacific to Japan. "Anybody can spit on the Philippines," Admiral Sims exploded, "and you can't stop them." More generally, however, the Washington Conference treaties were hailed as a spectacular victory for the peace and security of the Pacific. On the face of things, the United States had certainly won a notable diplomatic triumph. In accepting the Open Door policy as set forth in the Nine Power Treaty, Japan seemed to have forsworn such imperialistic ambitions as she might have harbored for expansion on the Asiatic mainland. Naval limitation was considered sign and symbol of a new Pacific order that held out the best possible guarantee for continuing peace in a part of the world where international rivalries had always been a dangerous menace.

For ten years the promise of the Washington Conference seemed to be fulfilled. Relations between the United States and Japan were on the whole thoroughly cordial. There was a flare-up of resentment in the latter country when the new immigration laws of the 1920's excluded Japanese from entry into the United States—an insult to racial pride that the Japanese would not forget—but on other issues there was general agreement. In confronting the most important development in eastern Asia during this period, the rise of Chinese nationalism and an embittered outbreak of antiforeign feeling among the Chinese people, the United States and Japan followed generally parallel policies. After some hesitation they both recognized the new nationalist regime of General Chiang Kai-shek.

When subsequent events shattered the peaceful accord established by the Washington Conference, once again bringing American and Japanese policy in eastern Asia into direct and dangerous conflict, it became customary to denounce the agreements concluded in 1921–22 as a needless sacrifice of naval strength in the Pacific and a totally unjustified betrayal of American interests. Writing in the 1940's, the newspaper columnist Walter Lippmann apologized for having at the time been too weak-minded to have taken a stand against "the exorbitant folly" of the Washington Conference, and for having hailed as "a triumph" what was in effect "a disaster." The Washington Conference was nevertheless in itself an outstanding victory for the cause of peaceful negotiation and disarmament. Its early success was not sustained because the accords did not go far enough, rather than because they went too far. Had the political and naval treaties included effective provision for their enforcement, with a guarantee of collective action should any one of the powers violate its obligations, the future history of the Pacific might have followed a more peaceful course.

★ JAPAN IN MANCHURIA

Japan's sudden and unprovoked attack upon Manchuria in the fall of 1931—which comes in at this point even though it carries us beyond the 1920's—was the first move to destroy the peaceful stability of eastern Asia. Re-establishing its political dominance, in eclipse at the time of the Washington Conference, the military party in Tokyo set in motion a program of imperialist aggression which, time was to show, aimed at nothing less than the conquest of all China. The Manchurian incident was a brutal violation of Japan's international obligations, especially as a signatory of the Nine Power Treaty.

The United States entered a vigorous protest against the Japanese attack, and even went so far as to express a willingness to co-operate with the League of Nations should it undertake to apply sanctions against a nation so clearly guilty of willful aggression. But nothing was done. The League failed to take any effective measures whatsoever; the United States was not prepared to act alone. There was talk of a possible boycott of Japanese trade, but President Hoover strongly believed that any such move might lead to war. He refused to risk further involvement in the Far East. His policy had a strongly realistic basis in the circumstances, for the American public would not have supported any action that held out even the most remote possibility of conflict with Japan. While the Philadelphia *Record*'s pungent assertion that "the American people don't give a hoot in a rain barrel who controls North China" may have been exaggerated, isolationist sentiment in the United States was much too strong to have permitted the government to take a forthright stand against Japanese aggression in such a distant part of the world.

The failure of either the United States or the League of Nations to act during the Manchurian crisis spelled the complete collapse of all postwar concepts of collective security. When Japan was allowed to violate her treaty obligations with complete impunity by attack in Manchuria, notice was served that no aggressor nation need fear concerted restraint by the peace-loving nations. This was a lesson taken to heart not only by the Japanese militarists, who soon renewed their forward drive on the Asiatic mainland, but also by the fascist nations in Europe. The year 1931 marked a tragic turning point on the road to a second world war.

The United States did take one step to make clear its own position, even though it was unable and unwilling to go so far as direct intervention. In February 1932 it dispatched identical notes to China and Japan in which it explicitly stated that the United States would refuse to recognize any situation, treaty, or agreement in the Far East which impaired American rights or was brought about by resort to force. While this statement of principle, popularly known as the Stimson Doctrine after Hoover's secretary of state, kept the record straight, it had no effect whatsoever on Japan, which continued to ignore all protests against its policy, whether from the United States or from the League. It ruthlessly forced China to submit to its demands and set up a puppet state in Manchuria that was to serve as a springboard for subsequent war and conquest.

There was little popular realization in the United States of the implications of the Manchurian incident. Secretary Stimson noted in his diary, however, that renewal of the rivalry between the United States and Japan in their Far Eastern policies, supposedly settled at the Washington Conference, could not fail to have the most dangerous consequences. He felt that it was almost impossible that an armed clash could be permanently avoided. But Stimson was determined that the American position, based upon the original Open Door notes and reaffirmed in the Nine Power Treaty of 1922, should be steadfastly maintained. There could be no surrender on the principles involved, in his opinion, unless the United States was prepared to retreat entirely from the western Pacific and acquiesce in Japanese control over all eastern Asia.

"If at any time the United States had been willing to concede to Japan a free hand in China," Stimson was to write in later years, "there would have been no war in the Pacific. The lines of division laid down so clearly in February 1932 led straight to Pearl Harbor."

★ THE KELLOGG-BRIAND TREATY

While the realities of international politics—as involvement in the Far East so strongly emphasized—drew the United States steadily away from the extreme isolationism represented by rejection of the League of Nations, it was still unwilling to make any commitments that would have a binding effect upon future policy. Out of this confusion there had arisen, before the Manchurian episode, a vague movement to outlaw war by the force of public opinion. This led in August 1928 to signature of the Kellogg-Briand Anti-War Treaty, sometimes known as the Pact of Paris. Fifteen powers, with the subsequent adherence of other nations bringing the total to sixty-two (including Japan, Italy, and Germany), solemnly agreed that they would not resort to war as an instrument of national policy.

The conclusion of the Kellogg-Briand pact was hailed by happy optimists as the most significant move ever made to promote world peace. It was considered an advance beyond even the League of Nations. The treaty, however, did not give any consideration to the issues which made for war or include any provisions for its own enforcement. Realists were quick to point out that the pact was actually no more than the expression of a pious hope. In a contemporary article in *Foreign Affairs,* Franklin D. Roosevelt wrote: "It does not contribute in any way to settling matters of international controversy."

The complete futility of the treaty was first revealed at the time of Japan's attack on Manchuria; as the mounting tension in Europe during the 1930's foreshadowed even more dangerous conflict, it was entirely forgotten. Sumner Welles, onetime under-secretary of state, has taken the position that the Kellogg-Briand Treaty was not only a useless gesture, but one which had a gravely unfortunate influence upon public opinion in this country. "It lulled to sleep," he has written, "any still lurking feeling of national obligation. It blinded the American people to the danger to their own security in an increasingly unstable world."

It may be doubted whether the treaty had any influence, positive or negative, on the actual course of events. The claim might be made that in theory if not in practice it marked a further step in developing a new principle of international morality, but little was heard of this at the time. The American people were not so much lulled to sleep by this vague affirmation of peace as satisfied that the expression of their ideals freed them from any further necessity to implement them. While the United States took an increasing part in the nonpolitical activities of the League of Nations, it continued to hold itself aloof from any closer collaboration. In spite of the urging of every president during the 1920's, the Senate even refused to approve America's membership in the World Court, set up by the League for the adjustment of international disputes by judicial process.

★ TRADE AND WAR DEBTS

When economic depression overwhelmed the world at the close of the first postwar decade, it was graphically revealed that the American attitude toward international trade and finance had had more serious consequences than any of the moves that the United States made in the realm of international politics. The high tariff that had been consistently maintained since 1921—to be raised still higher with the adoption of the Hawley-Smoot tariff in 1929—directly contributed to the choking up of the normal channels of foreign commerce. The insistence on war debt payments, even though substantial reductions were allowed in the amounts originally owed, made immensely more difficult the normal operations of foreign exchange. No such gesture as the Kellogg-Briand Treaty could in any way compensate for the failure of the United States to accept on a realistic basis the economic responsibilities of what had become the most powerful nation in the world.

In discussing postwar tariff policy, President Wilson had gravely warned against any return to the protectionist principles of the nineteenth and early twentieth centuries. "If there ever was a time when America had anything to fear from foreign competition," he stated, "that time has passed. If we wish to have Europe settle her debts—government or commercial—we must be prepared to buy from her. Clearly this is no time for the erection of high trade barriers." When the Hawley-Smoot tariff was under consideration, a thousand economists joined forces (which was something of a miracle in itself) to echo Wilson's views. They advised President Hoover that the proposed act would disastrously curtail the market for European exports, deprive foreign countries of the exchange to purchase American exports, provoke retaliation in the form of additional worldwide trade restrictions, and otherwise increase the burden upon our own economy. All such advice was ignored. Throughout the 1920's the United States was actually a leader in promoting those parochial tariff policies that contributed substantially to world depression.

The debt issue provided an equally flagrant example of economic nationalism. A basic factor in this situation was that during the war the United States had been transformed from a debtor to a creditor nation. With the money owed by our wartime associates amounting to over $10 billion, there was no way under existing circumstances, even with the cancellation of all interest, in which this sum could be repaid so long as the United States shut off its markets from European trade. The terms originally concluded for settlement of the debts were from one point of view very generous. The period for their discharge was extended over some sixty-two years, based upon supposed ability to pay, and the interest rates were variously scaled down to what amounted to an average of 2.1 per cent. But even such liberal terms did not meet the situation because of the impossibility of our onetime allies acquiring foreign exchange. A totally unrealistic approach to the problem was perhaps best exemplified by President Coolidge's typically laconic comment: "They hired the money, didn't they?"

The debt problem was interwoven with that of reparations. The United States had not sought any such payments from Germany. It refused to become officially involved (though American citizens gave their names to both the Dawes Plan and the Young Plan) in the efforts of the Allies to work out a practicable solution for demands that went far beyond Germany's capacity to pay. It was unwilling to accept any direct link between reparations and war debt payments and remained deaf to all requests for debt cancellation.

Only additional American loans prevented a complete breakdown in foreign exchange transactions during the 1920's. They were extended to private and governmental units in Germany to a total of some $2,600,000,000 between 1924 and 1930. Germany in turn paid the Allies $2,000,000,000 in reparations, and the Allies forwarded to the United States about $2,600,000,000 on the war debts. This was a regular ring-around-the-rosy. When the depression made the extension of American loans no longer feasible and Germany defaulted on those already made, the entire system collapsed. President Hoover was driven by events to propose a complete moratorium on all international payments, but this move was too late to save the day. When the United States then sought to make some arrangement for further payments, the answer of the debtor nations was complete repudiation of all their obligations. Having for so long been assailed by Europe as "Uncle Shylock," the United States ultimately found itself unpaid, without the goodwill that might have been won by voluntarily freeing its debtors from an impossible obligation.

★ THE FAILURE OF DISARMAMENT

Apart from the debt moratorium, Hoover was to make a number of other moves in the field of international politics that revealed the gradual growth of a more co-operative attitude on the part of the United States in world affairs. Strongly pacifist in his own convictions, he continually sought to promote disarmament as a means for averting the menace of future war. The United States participated in another naval conference held in London in 1930 to further the work begun at Washington ten years earlier and sent a delegation to the World Disarmament Conference summoned by the League of Nations to meet in Geneva in 1932.

Some further progress was made at London in limiting the naval powers' strength in cruisers and smaller craft, and a warm reception was accorded American proposals at Geneva for the reduction by one-third of all existing land armaments. The net result of these efforts at disarmament, however, was to demonstrate that the nations of the world were far from ready to surrender their weapons. A deep-seated feeling of political insecurity made any effective action impossible. Moreover, an important factor in the failure to reach such settlements of underlying international issues as might have encouraged disarmament was the continued refusal of the United States to make any commitments as to where it stood on the enforcement of peace.

American participation in the World Disarmament Conference underscored the impossibility of our remaining completely aloof from world affairs. The United States was playing a broader and broader international role in spite of nonmembership in the League of Nations. Yet Hoover did not in any real sense break away from the economic nationalism that was so strongly emphasized in our stand upon tariffs and war debts, and he was unwilling to commit the United States even to consultation in the event of any threat to world peace. Nor was there to be any immediate change in policy upon the election of Franklin D. Roosevelt in 1932. The early years of the latter's administration, indeed, were to witness a reversal of the trend toward greater world collaboration that had seemed to be gathering momentum. The forces of political isolationism and economic nationalism hardened into the neutrality legislation of the mid-1930's.

This new development, however, carries us beyond the chronological limits of this chapter. As the United States turned its back on Europe and sought to go its own way politically and economically in the early 1920's, what was happening on the home front? What was the significance of the first postwar decade so far as the domestic life of the American people was concerned?

CHAPTER XVIII

A Business Civilization

★ THE CLIMATE OF THE 1920's

The 1920's were one of the most confusing and colorful periods in all American history. They were marked by the ominous retreat from international co-operation, the absorption of the country in a heightened materialism, the utter bankruptcy of politics, and the slow building up of the forces making for depression and ultimate war. They witnessed a "revolt" on the part of the younger generation, exciting new movements in art and literature, turbulent violence associated with prohibition and gangsterism, and zooming prosperity symbolized by a runaway stock market. The decade has been given many names: the jazz age, the roaring 'twenties, the prohibition era, the golden 'twenties, the aspirin age. In the perspective of mid-century, there seems to have been something hectically artificial about the contemporary scene, and an ironic contradiction between its surface manifestations and the deep undertow of little understood historical forces.

"Prosper America first," was Harding's admonition to his countrymen; Coolidge declared that "the business of America is business," and Hoover pontifically stated toward the period's close that if the country went forward with the policies of the previous eight years, "we shall soon, with the help of God, be in sight of the day when poverty will be abolished from this nation." The American people accepted such pronouncements in good faith. They could hardly have been less prepared for the crashing debacle of depression that was so soon to overwhelm them and all the world.

The contrast between the 1920's and either the preceding or following decade was sharp and decisive. The Progressive era saw a ferment of reform and an idealistic spirit that drew to its climax in the great crusade to save the world for democracy. A new awakening of social conscience characterized the 1930's as under the impact of depression the New Deal assumed a broadened responsibility for the welfare of the people as a whole. But between 1919 and 1929 the liberalism which had largely accounted for the country's successive advances on the long road leading to political and economic democracy seemed to be almost dormant. One recent historian, Arthur S. Link, has stressed "the survival of progressivism" during the decade and stated that as "an articulate expression of social and economic aspiring" it actually widened its horizons. Yet all too often the continuing protests of those who recognized the limitations of social justice in contemporary America appeared to be drowned or brushed aside as un-American.

"There is only one first-class civilization in the world today," the *Ladies' Home Journal* complacently stated on one occasion. "It is right here in the United States."

The majority of the people seemed highly content. They ignored the unpalatable fact that the prevailing prosperity did not actually reach all classes in society. The plight of unemployed coal miners, distressed southern share-croppers, and many notoriously underpaid workers was conveniently overlooked. To raise any question about the beneficent working of the capitalist system was immediately to arouse the suspicions of the American Legion, the Chamber of Commerce, and the local Rotary club. The paradox of unquestioning faith in capitalism and timid fears of any criticism of the existing system was at times confusing, but uniformity in every phase of national life appeared to be the conventional goal of the 1920's. In some ways it was more nearly realized than ever before.

Foreign visitors who had often emphasized the diversity of the American scene—one Englishman in the 1890's had called the United States the "Land of Contrasts"—were now more generally impressed by what they termed its monotonous sameness. As towns and cities continued to grow, they became more and more alike. A thousand Main streets appeared almost indistinguishable. Middle-class mores dictated much the same way of life from Maine to California. Mass production and national advertising, the latter given new coverage by the radio, prescribed how people should furnish their homes, what they should wear, what they should eat, and how they should enjoy their leisure. They saw the same movies, heard the same radio programs, read the same best sellers, and worshipped at the altars of the same journalistic-created gods. There remained sharp differences beneath the casual surface of social life, but standardization and conformity were becoming increasingly characteristic of the American scene.

The conservatism which such popular attitudes reflected was a negative quality. As the country prospered, nothing but harm seemed likely to result from any interference by government in the economic sphere. Just as the nation had turned its back on internationalism, so did it turn its back on any further domestic reform. Apart from their own individual concern with making money, raising their standard of living, and getting ahead, the American people sometimes seemed to have few serious interests. The problems of the twentieth century had become even more acute as a result of the economic dislocations caused by war, but the public was largely indifferent toward efforts for their possible solution. It was absorbed in "tremendous trifles," the vagaries of the younger generation, the worship of sports champions, the excitement of the rising stock market—General Electric at 396, Montgomery Ward at 466, Radio at 505.

★ ECONOMIC GROWTH

The course of the stock market, however false the mirage created by rising prices, had at least a greater relevancy to the basic forces operative in the 1920's than the ballyhoo over so many other superficial happenings. The outstanding development of this astounding decade was economic growth and progress. Recovering quickly from a brief but sharp postwar depression, industry made a phenomenal advance between 1922 and 1929. The Frenchman André Siegfried, visiting the United States in the middle of this period, believed that America had finally come of age, but as "a materialistic society, organized to produce things rather than people." On this count at least there could be no doubting national success. The annual value of the products of American industry reached what then appeared to be the incredibly high figure of $70,000,000,000. The over-all record of American economic history had always been marked by continued expansion, but never before had mines, mills, and factories reported such tremendous gains.

The rise of new industries was largely responsible for this economic advance, and outstanding among them was the automobile industry. On the eve of World War I, half a million cars were being produced annually. By 1930 the number had increased tenfold. Automobile production had become the most important of all industries, and a tremendous stimulant to other manufactures. It absorbed immense quantities of steel, copper, plate glass, rubber, and fabrics, and directly or indirectly accounted for the employment of 4,000,000 workers. Operation of the millions of cars turned out every year called for further services creating additional economic activity. The production of gasoline and the building of hard-surfaced roads, the establishment and management of filling stations, roadside stands, and tourist camps were all offshoots of this dominating industrial enterprise whose influence was felt throughout the entire country.

The basic industries—coal, steel, machinery and machine tools, flour and bread, meat, clothing—also expanded. There was a great increase in the production of electric power and in the manufacture of all kinds of electrical equipment. Other pioneer enterprises grew up through the development of new kinds of consumer goods. But automobile manufacture was the sign and symbol of the decade's industrial prosperity.

Its development also reflected all the principal features of the new economy. No industry more clearly revealed the continuing trend toward monopolistic integration (three companies accounted for 90 per cent of all automobile manufacture); the importance of mass production and the assembly line; the influence of advertising, modern salesmanship, and installment buying; the upward spiral of manufacturing and selling profits; and the furor over speculation in common stocks. When General Motors replaced Ford as the leader in its field, ranking eighth among all American corporations, it was earning more than $200,000,000 annually. By 1929 it had made a millionaire out of everyone who eight years earlier had invested as much as $25,000 in its common stock.

★ LABOR AND AGRICULTURE

Industrial advance meant a larger national income and an improved standard of living. But while the American people as a whole profited from the economic gains made during the 1920's, income was still anything but equitably distributed. The business community and the professional classes directly or indirectly associated with business enterprise were favored far more than either industrial workers or farmers. Labor was rewarded with some increase in real wages during these years, but the gain fell far short of the increase in productivity. The moderate improvement registered for a time in farm income was more than offset for most individual farmers by higher mortgage debts, higher taxes, and higher operating costs.

The immediate effect of prosperity upon labor as an organized group was somewhat paradoxical. Wage increases served to raise the standard of living for many workers—with such notable exceptions as coal miners, textile mill operatives, and garment workers—and at the same time sapped the strength of the unions. Never before had they failed to gain in good times, but at the close of the 1920's their membership had fallen from over 5,000,000 to less than 3,500,000. The wage earners of the nation appeared to have accepted the thesis of ever-continuing prosperity with the same assurance as other members of society. They sacrificed their militancy in the belief that union activity was no longer necessary to protect their interests. Though there were intermittent strikes throughout the period, industrial peace never seemed more assured than on the eve of the depression.

Two other factors also contributed importantly to the decline in the strength of organized labor. One was the vigorous campaign of employers to break the unions by force, and the other their even more effective efforts to kill with kindness. At the urging of such organizations as the National Association of Manufacturers and the National Industrial Conference Board, industry employed all the weapons in its arsenal—yellow dog contracts, injunctions, labor spies, strikebreakers—to suppress union activity, and succeeded in identifying the Open Shop, which was still a synonym for an anti-union shop, with the period's One Hundred Per Cent Americanism. At the same time it developed more conciliatory policies. Company unions were encouraged as a substitute for bona fide unions, profit-sharing and pension schemes were introduced to win employee loyalty, and elaborate welfare programs adopted as a means of further strengthening the bonds of industrial cooperation.

Where it was not crushed by forceful anti-union activity, organized labor widely succumbed to these mild blandishments of welfare capitalism. Under the conservative leadership of William Green, who succeeded Samuel Gompers in 1924, the American Federation of Labor often appeared to be operating almost as an adjunct of the N.A.M. Little effort was made to establish or build up new unions. The great body of unskilled workers in the mass production industries—automobiles, steel, electrical equipment, rubber, agricultural machinery—remained as unorganized as they had been in the early 1900's. The power of industry was steadily increasing, but that of union labor was relatively declining. So long as prosperity continued and wages rose, this did not seem to be of any great concern. Labor was to suffer a rude awakening when depression suddenly swept away all the benefits of welfare capitalism. The workers discovered that in allowing union strength to be undermined, they had lost the means to protect their own interests.

The farmers did not enjoy any such illusion as to their place in the national economy. They had suffered severely in the sharp depression of 1921, and in spite of subsequent gains they never fully recovered their wartime or even prewar prosperity. Although the prices for their products were for a time well above previous levels, a persistent decline in the export demand for such staples as wheat and cotton soon began to drag them downward. Farm income was at the high figure of $10,-000,000,000 at the decade's close, but the decline in the relative proportion of such income to total national income was far more significant. Between 1919 and 1929 it fell from 22.9 per cent to 12.7 per cent. The rapid increase in the ratio of debt to farm property, the constantly larger proportion of farm income that had to be set aside to meet fixed charges, and the steady increase in mortgage foreclosures and farm tenancy were the really important facts in this unhealthy situation.

The farmers were not sharing in the general prosperity, and they saw even graver dangers ahead. Some sort of government aid was clearly necessary. For all the exertions of a powerful congressional farm bloc, however, almost nothing was done in the way of practical agricultural relief until the end of the decade. Then it was much too late to avert depression.

The bases of the prosperity of the 1920's would without doubt have been greatly strengthened had the country's leaders sought to bring about a more equal distribution of the national income. So far as industrial workers and farmers were cut off from their proportionate share of the benefits of an expanding economy, just so far were they once again limited in playing their role as consumers of the goods industry was so plentifully producing. The restriction of their purchasing power not only held down the workers' and farmers' standard of living, but by severely curtailing the domestic market for all the new automobiles, radios, washing machines, and refrigerators, it could not fail in time to have the most adverse effects on industry itself. The essential balance between production and consumption was dangerously threatened. Nevertheless, the superficial signs of what appeared to be a universal prosperity dazzled almost everyone in those halcyon days which were to see a chicken in every pot and two cars in every garage. Nowhere did there appear to be any realization that thought should be taken for the morrow or that anything could possibly be wrong with the principles on which our prosperity was based.

★ THE REVIVAL OF LAISSEZ FAIRE

Those principles were a virtual throwback to the laissez faire doctrines of the nineteenth century. The conservative postwar reaction had brought to an abrupt halt the trend toward government control and regulation of business that was underway during the Progressive era. Hoover was to deny that he believed in a laissez faire philosophy, but the "rugged individualism" which he preached and fostered was very much the same thing. Industry should be left entirely free to direct its own development, according to prevailing theory in the 1920's as in the 1890's, and there was persistent opposition to every move that could be interpreted as direct government intervention in the economic sphere. The further regulation of industry, aid for the farmers, legislation in support of organized labor, and control of electric power production were all condemned by the Republican leadership of the 1920's—and would probably have been equally condemned by the Democrats had they been in power—as endangering the very foundations of the Republic. They were viewed as steps that would inevitably lead to state control and state operation of all business. Hoover stated his views explicitly on one occasion:

> Even if government conduct of business could give us more efficiency instead of less efficiency, the fundamental objection to it would remain unaltered and unabated. It would destroy political equality. It would increase rather than decrease abuse and corruption. It would stifle initiative and invention. It would undermine the development of leadership. It would cramp and cripple the mental and spiritual energies of our people. It would extinguish equality and opportunity. It would dry up the spirit of liberty and progress.

Hoover's attack was an attack upon anything that remotely savored of socialism, and he saw in every proposal for government regulation of business a step toward the socialist state. But just as it had been possible for the nineteenth-century advocates of laissez faire to support government aid for industry while condemning regulation, so did their prototypes in the 1920's fail to see any contradiction in a willingness to provide at least indirect assistance for big business while preaching the virtues of rugged individualism. The antitrust laws were virtually suspended. The Federal Trade Commission encouraged the formation of trade associations even though they tended to strengthen rather than weaken monopolistic controls over industry, and the Interstate Commerce Commission fostered rather than sought to prevent further railway consolidations. Commenting upon this apparent shift in the original purpose of these regulatory commissions, Senator Norris caustically asked why trusts, combinations, and big business should not run the government directly.

The government also manipulated fiscal policy primarily in the interests of industrial enterprise rather than in the interests of the larger tax-paying public, and other substantial benefits were extended to business through the generosity of the terms under which it surrendered wartime controls over shipping and the railroads. Even more significant was the era's high tariff policy. The protection afforded American manufacturers in meeting foreign competition was once again a form of aid for which farmers and workers received no equivalent.

The revival of laissez faire doctrines so far as they applied to bans on economic controls was graphically demonstrated in the attitude of the courts as well as in that of government. The trend toward approving legislation regulating the conditions of labor, for example, was sharply reversed when in 1923, as previously noted, the Supreme Court rejected a law establishing minimum wages for women employees in the District of Columbia. The majority opinion in *Adkins* v *Children's Hospital* not only stated that such an act violated the constitutional safeguards of liberty of contract, but peremptorily dismissed all arguments on the social need for protecting the health of women workers as "interesting, but only mildly persuasive." The decision could hardly have been a more eloquent defense of laissez faire.

The Supreme Court bore down heavily on labor. It virtually abrogated the provisions of the Clayton Act exempting unions from prosecution under the antitrust laws and consistently upheld the use of injunctions against both strikes and labor boycotts. In *Truax* v *Corrigan,* a case decided in 1921, the Court said that an Arizona law prohibiting the use of injunctions in industrial disputes was invalid. This decision was on the ground that to take from an employer the right to enjoin his employees from striking was to deprive him of a legitimate safeguard for his property interests.

Even such a conservative as William Howard Taft, now Chief Justice, dissented in the minimum wage case, strongly opposing what he considered arbitrary restrictions upon the legislative power. Yet in spite of all warnings that the judges had no warrant to inject their own economic philosophy into their decisions, the antilabor verdicts were sustained. The Supreme Court majority continued to act upon the assumption that social or economic legislation arbitrarily interfered with the liberty of workers to labor for as long hours or at as low wages as they might individually choose. Conservatism was once again entrenched in the courts, as it was in the executive and legislative branches of government.

Public opinion generally endorsed such an attitude; popular support for industry was as widespread as it had been thirty years earlier. The apotheosis of big business, which continued under such protection to grow bigger every year, went even further than it had in the 1890's. The popular magazines featured success stories as they once had played up muckraking articles. One of the most extreme examples of this glorification of business was the attempt of a New York advertising man, Bruce Barton, to give it a new religious sanction.

In a book he entitled *The Man Nobody Knows*, Barton declared that Jesus might well be called the founder of modern business and had won his success through becoming the world's outstanding executive. "He picked up twelve men from the bottom ranks of business," Barton wrote, "and forged them into an organization that conquered the world. . . .

Nowhere is there such a startling example of executive success as the way in which that organization was brought together." The significant aspect of this strange interpretation of the career of Jesus was that *The Man Nobody Knows* was for two years the country's nonfiction best seller.

★ SUPPRESSION AND INTOLERANCE

The other side of the coin in respect to popular support for business was the attempted suppression of all criticism of the capitalist system. While the hysteria of the Red Scare of 1919 gradually subsided, a vigorous campaign to stamp out radicalism and heresy persisted throughout the decade. Five protesting members were summarily expelled from the New York state assembly because they were socialists; on two occasions a socialist duly elected to Congress was denied the right to take his seat. Such patriotic organizations as the National Security League and the National Civic Federation set themselves up as self-constituted guardians of Americanism, and their Red-baiting literature kept alive nationalist fears of subversive foreign influences. Criminal syndicalism laws, teachers' loyalty oaths, the denial of citizenship to pacifists, and the censorship of history textbooks reflected the popular belief that it was un-American to question the validity of existing institutions, let alone advocate radical reform.

The rights of free speech continued to be gravely endangered under such circumstances, and the Supreme Court often appeared to subscribe to popular fears. It repeatedly upheld convictions under both federal and states laws dealing with sedition or syndicalism with what appeared to be a willful disregard of constitutional guarantees. Justice Oliver Wendell Holmes, the dissenter in so many cases nullifying social legislation laws, argued eloquently—if often futilely—in defense of civil liberty. In *Schenck* v *United States,* a case decided in 1919, he had laid down the basic principle that there should be no restraint upon free speech except when the words uttered were of a nature to create "a clear and present danger" to national security. He soon found himself, together with Justice Brandeis, sharply dissenting from the court majority, and in *Abrams* v *United States,* a case upholding an inconsequential conviction for alleged sedition, took occasion to set forth his basic ideas:

> When men have realized that time has upset many fighting faiths, they may come to believe even more than they believe in the very foundations of their conduct that the ultimate good desired is better reached by free trade in ideas —that the best test of truth is the power of the thought to get itself accepted in the competition of the market, and that truth is the only ground upon which their wishes can be safely carried out. That at any rate is the theory of

> our constitution. It is an experiment, as all life is an experiment. Every year if not every day we have to wager our salvation upon some prophecy based upon imperfect knowledge. While that experiment is part of our system I think that we should be eternally vigilant against attempts to check the expression of opinions that we loathe and believe to be fraught with death, unless they so imminently threaten immediate interference with the lawful and pressing purposes of the law that an immediate check is required to save the country.

In time the nation was to recover its sense of balance, but for long this assertion of the right of free speech fell on deaf ears. Latent fears of communism continued to be played upon by reactionary forces to stifle the minority protest against the decade's ultraconservatism.

The famous trial of Nicola Sacco and Bartolomeo Vanzetti, two Italian workmen accused in 1921 of murdering a paymaster at South Braintree, Massachusetts, revolved about this conflict of ideas. The two men had evaded military service and were anarchists, and it soon became evident that the hostility created by their militant radicalism gave them little chance of a fair trial on the murder charge. When they were found guilty, in spite of evidence that appeared fully to substantiate their innocence of the murder, liberals throughout the nation—and throughout the world—rallied to their support in the conviction that they were being condemned for anarchism rather than on the charge for which they were being tried. Sacco and Vanzetti became a dramatic symbol of the struggle to uphold justice and human rights. While the popular outcry compelled a review of the case, the court's verdict of guilty was upheld. The two Italian workers, whose final message was "this is our career and our triumph," went to their death widely hailed as martyrs in the cause of freedom.

A further manifestation of rabid intolerance was the revival of the Ku Klux Klan. Its professed goal in the 1920's was to make America safe for white, Protestant, native-born Americans, and in what was a horrible travesty on the boosters' drive for conformity, it launched a campaign of terrorization directed against all minority elements within the community. Negroes, Catholics, Jews, and foreigners were brutally persecuted—taken from their homes and beaten up, tarred and feathered, sometimes killed. Membership in the Klan eventually rose to over 4,000,000, and masquerading under the flag of patriotism this iniquitous organization exercised an intimidating influence in the politics of the South and in many states in the East and Midwest.

The Ku Klux Klan operated in secrecy. Its members were bound by special oaths as in reconstruction days, and through a chain command of mysterious kleagles and goblins, took their orders from an imperial wizard. Midnight meetings brought together hordes of these white-hooded fanatics. The fiery glow of burning crosses, symbol of their warped and twisted concept of Americanism, spread a baleful light over the national horizon. It was not until about 1929 that shocking revelations of political intrigue, corruption, and lawlessness finally led to the Klan's downfall.

★ HARDING AND THE POLITICAL SCENE

Against the background of economic growth, the revival of laissez faire, and a conservatism on occasion spilling over into ugly intolerance, the role of government during the 1920's remained relatively inconsequential. In wry comment on Coolidge's conduct of public affairs, the columnist Will Rogers once stated that "he didn't do anything, but that's what the people wanted done." It was a valid expression of the government's waiver of any responsibility for the general welfare.

The successive Republican administrations of these years commanded wide support. There was an unsuccessful insurgent uprising in 1924, when Senator La Follette bravely unfurled the old banners of Progressivism, but otherwise there were few notes of popular protest. The Democrats hungered for office, but they did not propose any radical change in the handling of public affairs. Their leaders appeared as willing as those of the Republican party to subscribe to the tenets of laissez faire and pay obeisance to the desires of big business.

Harding came into office in 1921 with no definite policies and no specific program. The sharp reaction to Wilsonian idealism created an atmosphere in which purposeful leadership was, indeed, the last thing the country wanted. Americans were content to let Congress take over the direction of affairs, and few objections were raised even when it was demonstrated that left to their own devices the nation's representatives allowed themselves to be pushed about freely by powerful pressure groups. The result was not only special interest legislation, however. The official corruption in the Washington of Harding's day had its only counterpart in that earlier postwar era in which Grantism covered such a multitude of sins.

Secretary of the Interior Fall went to jail on being convicted of accepting bribes in the disposal of government oil lands—the leasing of Elk Hills in California to the oil interests of Edward L. Doheny and of Teapot Dome in Wyoming to Harry F. Sinclair. The Attorney General, Harding's good friend Harry M. Daugherty, was tried upon charges of conspiracy to defraud the government as a result of shocking revelations of corrupt practices in the Department of Justice. The administrator of the Veterans' Bureau was sentenced to Leavenworth for robbing the government of thousands of dollars in handling medical supplies, and the Alien Property Custodian was found guilty of fraud in the sale of properties under his control.

The record was a sorry one, and its greatest significance lay in its revelation of the sad state of civic morality. When these unhappy scandals were finally unveiled, the public for the most part followed the trials with cynical complacency. It almost appeared as if the major mistake of these thoroughly corrupt businessmen and public officials, leagued in conspiracy to rob the government, was that they had been caught.

Harding was not directly involved. Easy-going, affable, well-meaning, he simply let his personal loyalty to his friends blind him to the possibility that they might betray his trust in them. His sense of public responsibility was atrophied. A small-town newspaper publisher who had successfully—and sometimes too shrewdly—played the political game in Ohio, he never rose above his background and could hardly have been less suited for the high office he attained.

His senatorial career had been notably undistinguished. Standing for nothing, except perhaps party regularity, his lack of convictions on the issues of the day was shown in an entirely negative voting record. William Allen White wrote caustically of this period in Harding's life:

> He played some poker, drank some liquor, was a conspicuous ladies' man, ran with the gay crowd, took orders, talked when talk was needed, voted when votes were required. His arm was ever on the shoulder of some colleague; his feet were ever running errands. . . .

Harding had no illusions about his capacity for leadership. Once in the White House, he casually let "the Ohio gang" take over. The revelation that trusted friends were betraying him was to drive him to his death, but he could not bring himself to call them to account while there was still time. He lacked both the executive talent and the moral stamina that would have enabled him to take the drastic steps that were necessary to restore a spirit of public responsibility to his administration.

It has been said that one of the factors pointing toward Harding's availability for the Republican nomination in 1920 was his personal appearance—"he looked like a president." Tall, dignified, with a commanding presence, he was unusually handsome and invariably dressed with meticulous care. Moreover, he was a natural mixer: a Mason, a Rotarian, an Elk. He was friendly and unassuming in his contacts with people from all walks of life, and what was described as his "warm and endearing humanity" had a popular appeal all the greater for its contrast with Woodrow Wilson's aloof austerity. The American people welcomed the arrival in the White House of a man who could give apparent dignity to the office of the presidency and at the same time be so genuinely "just folks."

Nor were they disappointed that Harding made no pretense to intellectualism, again in contrast with his professorial predecessor. Actually, he had few ideas of any sort, and while he could present his conventionally conservative views with a certain oratorical flair, he lacked any real facility of expression. His speeches were once described, albeit by a political rival, as leaving "the impression of an army of pompous phrases moving over the landscape in search of an idea." A public weary of ideas that called for action and sacrifice listened happily to his comfortable platitudes.

Harding died after two years in office in August 1923. There was little of a positive character during this brief period to counterbalance the shady record of Teapot Dome, the Department of Justice frauds, and malfeasance in the conduct of veterans' affairs. Yet that little projected the major pattern of legislative activity for the entire decade. The Fordney-McCumber tariff, which generally continued the high rates of the immediate postwar tariff measures, was the measure of the decade's protectionism. Revenue acts that progressively reduced the income tax, especially in the higher brackets, were characteristic of its fiscal policy. Prosperity was to make it possible to cut the federal debt from $26,000,000,000 to $17,000,000,000 by 1930, in spite of tax reductions, but the failure to place heavier levies upon corporations and upon the wealthy contributed, as did also tariff policy, to that economic imbalance that was ultimately to result in depression.

Whatever may be placed on the credit side of the ledger for the Harding administration was primarily the work of those "best minds" whom the President had invited to join his cabinet in frank recognition of his own limitations. As Secretary of State, Charles Evans Hughes brilliantly conducted negotiations at the Washington Naval Conference, Andrew Mellon, Secretary of the Treasury, directed fiscal policy with astute skill, and Herbert Hoover worked strenuously to promote foreign trade as Secretary of Commerce. But if these men represented Harding's right hand, they completely ignored what his left hand was doing in the persons of Attorney General Daugherty and Secretary of the Interior Fall. The Harding administration had envisaged the return of the country to normalcy; on the historical record it was a normalcy that little profited the American people.

★ PRESIDENT COOLIDGE

The news of Harding's death on August 2, 1923, reached Vice President Calvin Coolidge while he was visiting his family home in Plymouth,

Vermont. In the early hours of the next morning, the new chief executive was dramatically sworn into office by his father, a notary public, with only a half dozen persons present, including his wife, a stenographer, and his chauffeur. This simple ceremony, performed in the flickering light of a kerosene lamp, typified the background of the homely, unassuming Vermonter who became the thirtieth President of the United States. At the same time, it could hardly have contrasted more vividly with the strident, boom times over which he was called upon to preside.

Calvin Coolidge's outstanding attributes, insofar as there was anything outstanding about a man whose character was so generally negative, were personal integrity, an unquestioning conservatism, abiding caution, and a keen, native shrewdness. He had none of Theodore Roosevelt's vigorous enthusiasm, Wilson's flaming idealism, nor Harding's generous goodfellowship. He was to command the respect of his countrymen, for he promised an end to official corruption and embodied their ideas of a laissez faire governmental policy. He could never awaken their admiration or their affection.

There was at times something slightly ridiculous about his awkward attempts to cast himself in the uncongenial role of sportsman or good fellow in order to portray human qualities that he really lacked. Newspaper photographs of Coolidge posing in Indian headdress or tossing a baseball at the season's opening game show a serious, hatchet-faced little man with sharp Yankee nose and pointed chin, conscientiously doing what he was told to do. There was no joy of living in his make-up; there would be no convivial backroom parties during his stay in the White House. A contemporary described the familiar expression of his features as "that curiously characteristic disdain which gives one the impression that he has just encountered a bad smell."

His taciturnity became a myth, although with a few intimates he could be loquacity itself. A careful husbanding of energy which led him to take a nap every afternoon, his feet comfortably resting on the presidential desk, inspired countless stories. "He slept more than any other President, whether by day or by night," H. L. Mencken once wrote. "Nero fiddled but Coolidge only snored."

The path which had led this little man from his Vermont village to the nation's capital was straight and undeviating. A graduate of Amherst College, he had entered public life while practicing law in Northampton, Massachusetts, and from that day on he gingerly climbed the ladder of political preferment without a single misstep—assemblyman, mayor, lieutenant governor, governor, vice-president, and president. It seemed an almost automatic advancement, but was in reality due to the consummate skill with which Coolidge played his cards. He was at once intensely ambitious and yet so cautious that it could always be said of him that he was pre-eminently safe. "Keep Cool with Coolidge" was a satisfying slogan in an era that had no desire for dynamic, and therefore disturbing, presidential leadership. The good luck that marked every stage of his political career did not desert him when, after election to the presidency in 1924, he cryptically stated that he did not choose to run again in 1928. In making this decision he stepped out neatly from beneath the impending economic crash that his own negative policies had done much to precipitate.

While Coolidge napped in the White House, the nation was engaged in an orgy of speculation, spending, and extravagance. He did nothing about it. His main concern was not to interrupt business growth and expansion. At the same time he completely failed to recognize the importance of sustaining the purchasing power of farmers or workers. While believing thoroughly in the protective tariff, his answer to any move for agricultural aid, governmental control over power resources, or other regulatory legislation was invariably an emphatic veto. Coolidge simply sat tight as around him swirled the pleasing excitement of boom times, mounting corporation profits, and a soaring stock market.

★ THE ELECTIONS OF 1924 AND 1928

The measure in which the country was prepared to accept the political philosophy of Coolidge, as representative of the close alliance between the Republican postwar administrations and big business, was shown by his return to office in 1924.

Coolidge was the obvious choice of his party for the nomination and the Democrats selected an almost equally conservative candidate in the New York corporation lawyer, John W. Davis. This was too much for the more liberal and progressive elements in the country. As already noted, they succeeded in setting up a third-party candidate, sponsored by the Conference for Progressive Political Action, in the person of Robert La Follette. The platform as well as the candidate was a direct carryover from prewar days, but La Follette had no chance whatsoever in the atmosphere of the 1920's. He succeeded in winning nearly 5,000,000 votes, in spite of wild charges of radicalism, but carried only his own state of Wisconsin. The vote for Davis was not so very much larger, 8,386,000, but Coolidge received 15,725,000 votes, more than his rivals' combined total. The election was primarily an endorsement of Republican conservatism. The President was perhaps justified in his complacent statement that the public mood revealed "a state of contentment seldom before seen."

The election of 1928 was to give even more graphic evidence of this spirit. When Coolidge did not choose to run, the Republicans nominated Herbert Hoover, who had continued to serve as Secretary of Commerce. The Democrats named Alfred E. Smith, the hard-hitting, able and popular governor of New York. Yet in spite of the latter's progressive ideas on many subjects, there was no very clear-cut distinction—except on the critical issue of prohibition—between the general policies he proposed and those Hoover advocated. The degree to which the Democrats felt compelled to follow a basically conservative course was shown not only by an innocuous platform, but by their naming the vice-president of General Motors as their campaign manager.

The election was not fought on basic issues. "Al" Smith was a product of New York's East Side, a member of Tammany Hall, a Roman Catholic, and an uncompromising Wet. No one could have overcome such handicaps in the prejudiced atmosphere of an era in which the Ku Klux Klan was powerful. An undercover campaign of personal vilification, in which Hoover himself had no part, cut sharply into such strength as Smith might otherwise have commanded. The Republican landslide was a terrific one. With a popular majority of 21,391,000 to 15,016,000, Hoover carried all but two northern states and five states of the Solid South, winning an electoral college victory of 444 to 87. The results could only be interpreted as a decisive popular mandate in favor of the policies of the previous eight years.

This was demonstrated not so much by the Democratic debacle as by the complete lack of any protest vote. While four years earlier La Follette had won his nearly 5,000,000 votes inveighing against "the control of government and industry by private monopoly," all such signs of popular dissent had now disappeared. The Socialists polled less than 300,000 votes, little more than a quarter of their total in 1920; the Communists tallied fewer than 50,000. There was no real opposition to a governmental program the success of which appeared self-evident in the country's continuing prosperity.

CHAPTER XIX

Social Developments

★ THE CHANGING SCENE

In spite of a national background of absorbed interest in business and of general conformity, social change marked the 1920's—and the entire period between wars—perhaps even more significantly than in earlier epochs. As characterized by that noisy revolt of the younger generation against the morals and conventions of their elders, something of the aura of the jazz age still seems to shroud the immediate postwar years in a hazy glamor. And for all the heavy weight of predominantly conservative forces, the times inspired excited discussion over the many "isms," old and new, that were perennially disturbing the accepted patterns of a business-oriented civilization.

There was sharp debate over the unhappy manifestations of nationalism. Many people were deeply disturbed over the mounting threat to democratic values in communism and fascism, religious leaders found themselves locked in a new struggle over fundamentalism, social analysts were aroused by the implications of Freudianism, artists experimenting with abstract forms talked of modernism, and literature was still fighting the battle of naturalism.

Apart from the issue of government's role in the economic sphere and the status of labor, it is indeed interesting to note the extent to which the 1920's actually provided the basis for the continuing social pattern of American life, extending even through another war and postwar period. They witnessed the final culmination of the movement to restrict immigration, the beginning and also the end of prohibition, the triumph of what contemporaries called "the emancipation of women," the climactic stage in the revolution in transportation, the development of mores in popular recreation and popular entertainment that have not materially changed in succeeding years.

This chapter will try to deal with some of these social developments and controversies, both as they took shape in the 1920's and as they carried over into the 1930's. The atmosphere of the latter decade, under the impact of depression, differed sharply from that of the 1920's. Economic issues inevitably became of dominant concern for a people plagued and harassed by dwindling incomes and unemployment. In spite of want and distress, however, further growth and development were slowed down rather than halted. Technological advances were in some instances stimulated by the depression; the questioning of many prevailing concepts was accentuated by its impact on the economy.

★ THE RESTRICTION OF IMMIGRATION

The adoption of a literacy test over President Wilson's veto in 1913 had not brought the immigration issue to a settlement. While the tide of alien arrivals had completely subsided during the war, the desire of hundreds of thousands of Europeans to escape their own ravaged countries soon threatened an influx greater than that of the early years of the century. Nearly a million immigrants crossed the Atlantic in 1921. The doubts and misgivings as to whether the United States could absorb such large numbers, so widely prevalent during the Progressive era, were not only reborn, but greatly intensified in an atmosphere of revived nationalism. The demand grew for more effective restriction than any such relatively mild measure as a literacy test.

The result of this agitation was the adoption of a program that set a specific annual total for all European immigrants and controlled the number to be accepted from each country through a carefully devised quota system. The scales were weighted in favor of the "old immigration" from northwestern Europe as opposed to the "new immigration" from southeastern Europe in the traditional belief that the people from the former countries could be more easily assimilated. It was argued, as it had been in the days when the literacy test was under consideration, that immigrants from Great Britain, Germany, and the Scandinavian countries would strengthen the forces of Americanism, while those from Italy, Poland, and other eastern European countries would dangerously weaken them.

The legislation carrying this policy into effect, far and away the most important of the entire period, originally provided for specific quotas for each country based on the number of its nationals in this country, first as of 1910 and then later as of 1890. The National Origins Act of 1924, however, set up a somewhat more complicated system, to go into effect in 1929, that has generally governed immigration policy ever since. This law established a total over-all figure of 150,000 for all immigrants from Europe and gave each country of origin a quota based on a proportion of this figure corresponding to the proportion of persons of such national stock in the American population as of 1920. This meant in practice, for example, that the quota of the United Kingdom was 43 per cent of 150,000, or approximately 65,000, on the ground that 43 per cent of the people in the United States were of British stock. The annual quota from Italy was under 6,000, since it was estimated that only about 4 per cent of the population was of Italian racial origin. Immigration from Latin America was not affected by the new restrictions, but included in the Immigration Act of 1924 was a ban on entry of persons of non-Caucasian stock, a provision directed primarily against the Japanese.

The results of this legislation were seen in an immediate and drastic drop in immigration: to about 164,000 in 1925 and to an average of less than 100,000 annually in the 1930's. In terms of previous history this brought the transatlantic passage to a virtual end. There were many years between the two world wars when the number of aliens leaving the United States actually exceeded the number arriving. This affected both the rate of national growth and the character of the population. The problem of the Melting Pot had been solved by refusing to add any new ingredients, and as the proportion of foreign-born in the country steadily declined, old issues involving conflicting loyalties and other aspects of assimilation tended to disappear.

There still remained inscribed on the base of the Statue of Liberty towering over New York harbor the oft-quoted lines written by Emma Lazarus:

> Give me your tired, your poor,
> Your huddled masses yearning to be free,
> The wretched refuse of your teeming shore,
> Send these, the homeless, tempest-tost to me;
> I lift my lamp beside the golden door.

Now the door was all but closed: America no longer welcomed the "huddled masses" of the Old World. A great epoch in our national history, the peopling of a continent by European immigrants, had come to an end.

★ ENFORCING PROHIBITION

Paralleling the early drive to control immigration during the Progressive era there had also been, as we have seen, a powerful movement for prohibition, not unaffected by the influence of the new immigrants on national drinking habits. This issue now came to a climax. After ratification of the Eighteenth Amendment, Congress passed the Volstead Act to prohibit throughout the country the sale, manufacture, or transportation of all intoxicating beverages and in January 1920, prohibition came into effect throughout the United States. It was not, however, to have the finality of immigration restriction. The country endured the rigors of a dry regime for only a few years before it began to repent of such radical reform, and a gradually rising tide of popular protest set the stage for repeal.

Prohibition had a far-reaching effect upon the manners and morals of the nation during the years in which the federal government and most of the state governments were endeavoring to enforce the Volstead Act. But not along anticipated lines. The attempt to impose such stern restraints on individual liberty bred a widespread disrespect for law, and among some people the Volstead Act appeared to encourage the very practices that it was supposed to forbid. When prohibition finally broke down completely and the Eighteenth Amendment was repealed, drinking had paradoxically enough become respectable among many middle-class elements of society that had formerly frowned on it. Women began to drink in public with little of the stigma of pre-prohibition days; the cocktail party became an accepted social institution.

The disrespect for law that was a notorious consequence of prohibition was never so widespread as sensational newspaper reports or popular literature sometimes suggested. The majority of the people certainly remained law-abiding. Among a large segment of the population, especially city dwellers and suburbanites, however, there was little compunction about disobeying the Volstead Act. Drinking became a conspicuous symbol of the younger generation's revolt in the reckless days of the Jazz Age. What had supposedly been outlawed became for that very reason all the more popular. The speakeasy flourished throughout the land; the hip flask became a token of sophistication.

To meet the demand for illegal liquor, bootlegging rapidly became big business. Rum runners anchored off the Atlantic coast until their cargoes could be surreptitiously smuggled ashore, truckloads of beer rumbled across the Canadian border with the connivance of customs inspectors, and moonshiners everywhere operated secret stills to produce immense quantities of dubious illegal whiskey. Those who could not afford to patronize bootleggers or speakeasies bravely experimented with bathtub gin and other concoctions that suggested an insatiable thirst, proof against any niceties of taste.

The drinking of the noisy, self-conscious minority represented by the college and country club sets, especially in the East, largely set the tone of the prohibition era. Such people took delight in flouting the law; they found something very intriguing about the speakeasy. As expressed in a verse appearing in an editorial page column in the New York *World:*

> Prohibition is an awful flop.
> We like it.
> It can't stop what it's meant to stop.
> We like it.
> It's left a trail of graft and slime,
> It's filled our land with vice and crime,
> It can't prohibit worth a dime,
> Nevertheless we're for it.

The worst aspect of prohibition was its encouragement of gangsterism. Bootleggers operating with the corrupt protection of law enforcement officers soon set up a highly organized system of liquor distribution. According to accepted business practice, this development promptly led to attempts to establish monopolies—only monopolies so completely outside the law were not interested in mildly unfair price manipulation. They resorted to intimidation, threats, and violence to crush their rivals. The trade competition of hijacking liquor dealers often became open warfare, fought with sawed-off shotguns.

In Chicago an especially notorious gang, dominated by "Scarface Al" Capone, sought to control the bootlegging activities of that thirsty city and would tolerate no invasion of its territory. When another liquor-selling gang tried to do so, henchmen of Capone, disguised as policemen, trapped seven members of this rival gang, lined them up against the wall in a deserted garage, and shot them down in cold blood. It seemed a far cry from this brutal massacre, that took place on St. Valentine's Day, 1929, to the cocktail parties of country club society. Every purchase of liquor during the prohibition era, however, helped to support an underworld of crime and violence. It was an ironical aspect of this situation that when the government finally caught up with Capone, he was jailed on the charge of income tax evasion.

The profits of bootlegging soon led the gangsters to expand their sphere of operations. They moved to new rackets and began to levy tribute upon gambling, race tracks, dance halls, and houses of prostitution. They combined forces in some instances with labor racketeering to compel legitimate business enterprises to buy protection. The country experienced a reign of lawlessness that grew increasingly alarming.

As these unexpected consequences of prohibition made themselves felt, the issue entered politics. The Drys insisted upon larger federal appropriations for enforcement of the Volstead Act; the Wets demanded repeal of the law and a return to state control of the liquor traffic. Party lines were completely disregarded and local conditions largely determined the attitude of individual congressmen. Under the intensive pressure of the Anti-Saloon League, many of them who were privately convinced that prohibition was a failure and who themselves disregarded the law continued to support it for fear of political retaliation.

By the close of the decade the breakdown of enforcement had become too widespread to be overlooked, and there was increasing skepticism over the validity of what Hoover still hopefully called "an experiment noble in motive and far-reaching in purpose." Even the report of a special commission appointed by the President to investigate the entire situation admitted that, in spite of its feeling that prohibition should be maintained, enforcement was practically impossible. In the presidential campaign of 1932 the Democrats came out candidly for immediate repeal; the Republicans called for revision of existing laws. Roosevelt's election settled the issue. A new Congress promptly adopted the Twenty-first Amendment, repealing the Eighteenth, and with its ratification in December 1933 prohibition came to an inglorious end.

★ THE EMANCIPATION OF WOMEN

A third prewar movement carried on during the 1920's with increasing vigor finally led to the general acceptance of the political and social equality of women. Its most conspicuous triumph was the adoption of the Nineteenth Amendment in 1920, giving women the vote, but the economic and social gains scored in the long battle for sex equality were actually far more significant. The call on women and girls to enter war plants in 1917–18 had far-reaching effects in breaking down any lingering Victorian ideas as to the role of the female in modern society. It became universally accepted that young women graduating from high school and college—and an increasing number went to college—should go out and get jobs. It is true that such an attitude had long prevailed in families where economic necessity compelled women to work; postwar change was in the spread of such ideas to all classes of society. A job often proved only a temporary occupation before undertaking the duties of wife and mother, but business and professional women became much more numerous.

With this broader participation in the economic life of the community went the successful assertion of equality in almost every phase of social activity. It was dramatized once again by the younger generation's postwar revolt against conventional mores, but had a much more substantial basis in permanent changes in customs and manners. These changes were manifest in women's fashions—short skirts, bobbed hair, sports clothes, and ultimately shorts and slacks, the complete disappearance of chaperones in recognition of the new female independence, and increasing participation in athletics and many other forms of outdoor activity.

In the new relationship between the sexes there was further manifest the influence of Freudianism. The teachings of the Viennese psychoanalyst, Sigmund Freud, had spread rapidly throughout the country. They were often misinterpreted. But as suggesting that a cause of individual maladjustment in contemporary society was the suppression of sexual desires, they brought into question many accepted conventions and made for a freer and franker acceptance of sex. Among the more sophisticated elements of society this often led to endless and ill-informed discussions of the need for free expression of the libido, and in later years to a popular craze for psychoanalysis, but Freudianism was of immense significance in creating a new and often more rational approach to all sex problems.

The new freedom for women worried many observers of the contemporary scene. It seemed to further a number of developments, first noted during the Progressive era, that were highly disturbing. The divorce rate continued to rise until the ratio of separations to marriages was about one to six, and the increasing practice of birth control led to smaller families. What such phenomena meant in regard to the possible deterioration of family life was not always agreed on, but that old ways were changing was clearly evident.

Still another aspect of this situation was the degree to which women appeared to be accepted, at least from the point of view of many foreign observers, as "superior beings." One German visitor declared that America was a two-caste country in which the higher caste was made up of females. "Her inspiration and influence," he wrote of the American woman, "stand behind all American educators, as it stands behind all American prohibitionists. Her influence accounts for the infinity of laws and rules. She directs the whole cultural tradition. She also dictates in the field of moral conduct."

Other contemporary writers stressed the important place women held in society, the extent to which they set national standards, and the measure of control they exercised over the wealth of the country. The United States was sometimes described as a matriarchy. While the men made the money and the laws, it was said, women dominated the home, the schools, and most social activity. There may have been some substance in such views, but any realistic analysis of women's more general role suggests that in many fields equality was still far from realized.

★ THE AUTOMOBILE AND THE AIRPLANE

The revolution in transportation that had been started in the 1900's came to a climax between the world wars with the great expansion of the automobile industry and the gradual growth of commercial aviation. On a comparative basis, motoring was well ahead—and would remain ahead—of anything happening in Europe, but flying lagged far behind developments overseas until almost the eve of World War II.

There were an estimated 20,000,000 automobiles in the country by the close of the 1920's. Commuting to work by car had become commonplace, and trucks and busses were playing an important role as rivals to the railroads, but motoring for pleasure—whether a brief spin in the country, weekend trips to beaches and holiday resorts, or summer vacations—accounted for the largest proportion of the use of automobiles. "Tell the family to hurry the packing," full-page advertising spreads in the magazines urged car owners, "and be off with smiles down the nearest road—free, loose, and happy—bound for green wonderlands." And over the macadam and concrete roads which now crisscrossed the entire country, millions of motorists took such advice.

Improvements, most notably the closed car, made driving a year-round activity, and the annual introduction of new models inspired automobile owners with a great zest "to keep up with the Joneses." Something of a sensation was created in 1927 when Henry Ford, acknowledged leader in the industry, closed his factories, completely retooled, and brought out a replacement for the old Model-T to meet the popular demand for a more ornate, luxurious car. Thousands of people stormed the showrooms of Ford dealers throughout the country to see the new Model-A as presented to the public with a sensational barrage of publicity and advertising.

The mushroom growth of filling stations, roadside stands, tourist cabins, automobile courts and motels has already been noted in discussion of the automobile industry itself. Florida, perhaps the most popular tourist state, was reported as early as the mid-1920's to have tourist camps whose overnight cabins could accommodate 600,000 people. The automobile also made the national parks more accessible, so that the few hundred thousand campers who annually visited them before the war increased to between twenty and thirty million.

Not even the depression was to persuade the average American to give up his car. When Robert and Helen Lynd made their sociological survey of Middletown—a typical American community—in the mid-1920's, they found an automobile considered more important than a telephone, electric lighting, a bathtub, or even ownership of one's own home. "The car is the only pleasure we have," was a typical worker's comment. America had become so automobile-minded that motoring was as distinctive a phase of social life as the great industry which had made it possible was representative of the nation's industrial achievement.

In the field of aviation the United States had got off to a very belated start during the years of World War I, in spite of the pioneering experiments of the Wright brothers, and with the end of hostilities the wartime plane factories were largely dismantled. Commercial aviation consequently developed slowly. Not until 1925 did the Post Office Department let contracts for carrying the mail to private airlines, and even then progress remained somewhat hesitant. In 1929 only some 50,000 passengers flew over regularly established air routes.

The 1930's were to witness, in spite of the depression, the beginnings of the real expansion in flying. The very first year of this decade, in fact, would see a ninefold gain in passengers carried in comparison with figures for the previous year. Conditions still remained relatively primitive and experimental, but with rapid technological advance, there was a corresponding improvement in all operations. By 1934 twenty-four American air lines were carrying half a million passengers over 51,000 miles of established air routes.

This was still a long way from what would take place during and after the Second World War. For most people flying remained a novel and rather frightening experience. It had not as yet made any great impact on the nation's transportation system as a whole and neither the railroads nor the automobile felt its competition. Soon far safer, far faster, far larger and far more comfortable planes would greatly change this general picture.

★ MOVIES AND THE RADIO

The movies continued to expand their role in popular recreation, and the postwar years found Hollywood coming into its own. The films reflected the spirit of the Jazz Age, especially its self-conscious flouting of convention and extravagant pursuit of pleasure. *Flaming Youth* and *Sinners in Silk, Women Who Give* and *The Daring Years* were boldly announced in the garish posters of ten thousand moving picture houses. "Brilliant men, beautiful jazz babies, champagne baths, midnight revels, petting parties in the purple dawn," advertised the producer of *Alimony,* "all ending in one terrific, smashing climax that makes you gasp." As postwar nerves steadied, there was an inevitable reaction from such sensationalism. Hollywood began to soft-pedal the jazz babies and red-hot kisses. A moral czar was appointed to control the situation; he soon announced that the moving picture industry held its Supreme Purpose to be Service.

If the realization of this goal remained somewhat problematic, good films were produced as well as tawdry ones. *The Gold Rush, The Covered Wagon, The Three Musketeers,* and *The Ten Commandments* were a great improvement over prewar pictures. Mary Pickford remained the nation's sweetheart, but she had many rivals including Constance Talmadge, Lillian Gish, and Gloria Swanson. The muscular Douglas Fairbanks, William S. Hart, and Harold Lloyd were leading male stars, while Rudolph Valentino became the idol of millions of lovelorn maidens. Above all others, however, Charlie Chaplin was universally recognized as the screen's greatest artist.

The outstanding producer of the 1920's was Cecil de Mille, who specialized in the supercolossal films that demonstrated Hollywood's tremendous urge for the spectacular and extravagant. *Ben Hur* was produced at a cost of $6,000,000. In other films lavish expense helped to give a thoroughly unrealistic—and often vulgar—representation of American life. The movies created a fabulous and completely false world reflecting the contemporary emphasis on wealth and riches. Critics were more concerned over the artificiality of such pictures than over Hollywood's lack of respect for conventional moral standards, shuddering to think of the impression created abroad.

The close of the decade witnessed a new departure when the talkies were introduced and promptly drove out the silent films. Within little more than a year of Al Jolson's appearance in the *Jazz Singer* in 1927, the audiences had so increased under the stimulus of the new pictures that something like 100,000,000 people went to a movie every week. Feature films were now made of successful stage plays, established classics, and best-selling novels, as well as from the original effusions of Hollywood script writers. There was a whole new generation of stars.

As the movie industry developed the technical possibilities of the new films, introducing Technicolor in 1935, Hollywood embarked on what one historian has called its "golden decade." It was not only that the new pictures set higher standards than ever before—in such epic films as *Gone with the Wind*—but they dared to deal with important social questions, and also included so-called documentaries. In the first category was *The Grapes of Wrath* and in the latter *The River,* both films that clearly reflected the impact of economic depression. Another distinctive development of the 1930's was the animated cartoon which Walt Disney brilliantly used in *Snow White and the Seven Dwarfs.* Other memorable films among the many that might be noted were *It Happened One Night, Citizen Kane,* and *Mutiny on the Bounty,* while the new stars included Gary Cooper, Charles Laughton, Walter Huston, and

Paul Muni. The movies had become more than ever the country's most popular form of entertainment, a tremendous boon in a time when so many people desperately needed some way to escape from the drab atmosphere of their own lives.

The radio had been introduced in the 1920's and was to become a rapidly growing rival to the movies. The first permanent commercial broadcasting station to go on the air was KDKA, in East Pittsburgh. On November 2, 1920, it broadcast to a handful of listeners (many of whom had been provided with free receiving sets) the news of Harding's election. Twelve years later, over some thirty million receiving sets, a nationwide audience heard the results of Franklin D. Roosevelt's first presidential campaign.

While news broadcasts were to become an important function of radio, popular entertainment was the principal concern. The air waves became crowded with what one commentator described as "the greatest single sweep of synchronized and syncopated rhythm that human ingenuity has yet conceived." Orchestras throughout the land hammered away night and day at "Mister Gallagher and Mister Shean," "Yes, We Have No Bananas," "Barney Google," and "Valencia." Rudy Vallee stirred millions of feminine hearts as he crooned "I'm Just a Vagabond Lover," while husky-toned torch singers made their appeal to the opposite sex with "Moanin' Low" and "Am I Blue?" And there were Amos n' Andy, Blondie, Little Orphan Annie, Buck Rogers, Uncle Don, the Lone Ranger, and the Quiz Kids.

Soap operas soothed the nerves of harassed housewives; radio drama lightened the cares of tired breadwinners. These programs, from symphony concerts to hillbilly bands, from vaudeville skits to sports announcements, did not enter the homes of the American people without interruption. National advertisers had quickly discovered the more practical uses to which the air waves could be put. Entertainment and information were interlarded with the commercials that insistently praised the unique value of special brands of soap, toothpaste, automobiles, mattresses, electric refrigerators, watches, ginger ale, or cough drops. Radio was business as well as entertainment.

★ SPECTATOR SPORTS

Another part of the amusement industry, as in earlier periods, represented commercial sports. Millions of Americans enjoyed sport for its own sake. They fished and hunted, went on camping trips, played golf and tennis, crowded the bathing beaches, and otherwise enjoyed themselves on their own. But spectator sports were so highly developed that the impression was given of an entire country spending most of its leisure time in the bleachers or at ringside watching professionals perform.

The sports champions were the nation's heroes. Babe Ruth, the sultan of swat; "Big Bill" Tilden of the tennis courts, and Bobby Jones, the incomparable golfer, were far better known than any congressman or cabinet member. Jack Dempsey and Gene Tunney attracted million-dollar gates for their world championship prize fights. In the short autumn season of intercollegiate football the famed Four Horsemen of Notre Dame, the Praying Colonels of Centre College, and Red Grange, the Galloping Ghost of Illinois, took over the headlines.

Spectator sports continued to attract the crowds during the days of depression, but hard times caused many people to seek ways of participating rather than watching professionals. This trend was encouraged by the extension of parks, playgrounds, and other public recreational facilities under the auspices of the New Deal's public works program. With the gradual return of more prosperous times, spectator sports once again began to break attendance records, and they were also promoted through the sponsorship of radio and, later, television.

They had become an integral part of the American scene as a consequence of urbanization and increasing leisure. The shorter workday and the five-day week gave the American people more time for recreation and amusement than any people had ever before known. Yet in some ways the 1920's marked the heyday of spectator sports, or at least in no other period did they excite such great interest or produce such a galaxy of stars.

★ THE GROWTH OF EDUCATION

In another area of social development, the further expansion of public education, especially at its higher levels, should be noted. In the two decades from 1910 to 1930, to cite a few basic statistics, enrollment in the public schools rose from 18,000,000 to 25,000,000, and total expenditures for education increased from $426,250,000 to $2,317,000,000. The gains were greatest at the high-school level, where enrollment increased some 400 per cent. In the following two decades public-school enrollment declined somewhat, under the impact first of depression and then of war, but was to spiral upward again in the 1950's.

The changes in the schools centered largely around the new ideas that John Dewey had been advancing since the opening of the century, and educational progressivism had a very considerable impact throughout the country. Dewey urged that teaching should concern itself more with the interests of the child and encourage his individual initiative, and yet at the same time—somewhat paradoxically—he placed great emphasis upon the child's adjustment to the group and to society. His own formula was "no indoctrination, no orthodoxy, no absolutes," but overzealous disciples often carried his system a good deal further. They appeared to be primarily using education as a means to promote group welfare and democracy rather than to teach the familiar reading, writing, and arithmetic, and critics also charged them with sacrificing subject matter for methodology.

There was perhaps nothing that more clearly reflected the cross currents and confusions of the years between wars than this continuing and often embittered battle over progressivism in the schools. In later years its influence would be held responsible for many of the manifest deficiencies of American education.

The increase in enrollment in high schools reflected a trend toward vocational training even more than preparation for college. At least relatively, the courses necessary for students going on with their education did not expand as much as those in more practical subjects. The high-school curriculums, embracing the interests of girls as well as boys, more and more included courses in manual training, home economics, typewriting, and agricultural science.

Another outstanding development in education was the greatly expanded attendance at colleges and universities. Between 1910 and 1930, enrollments grew from 266,654 to 924,275. They declined somewhat during the depression years, although the National Youth Administration was to help many students to stay in college who would otherwise have had to leave, but with the war and postwar developments of the 1940's, they shot up spectacularly to a total of more than 3,258,000 in 1958.

Neither basic curriculums nor teaching techniques at the college level underwent any very unusual changes. The number of courses, which was a longterm outgrowth of the introduction of the elective system, expanded enormously. This was especially true in the large state universities which felt the compulsion to provide vocational as well as cultural training. Their catalogues listed hundreds of courses which ranged from the traditional scientific and humanistic studies to business organization, farm management, teachers' training, and other highly specialized vocational subjects. From a quite different point of view, a number of private colleges sought to develop restricted honors courses, tutorial systems, conference meetings instead of lectures, but expense remained in many cases a prohibitive factor.

At the beginning of the 1920's—the days of the Red Scare—grave fears were felt for the maintenance of academic freedom. Numerous instances occurred of interference by conservative legislatures with the operation of state universities and by reactionary trustees with faculty control of private institutions. But such pressures gradually subsided. Whether the colleges and universities, as well as the country's secondary schools and high schools, were really doing the job they should remained as always a question on which there was wide disagreement.

★ POPULAR READING

A direct consequence of educational advance, which between 1910 and 1930 reduced illiteracy from 7.7 per cent to 4.3 per cent of the population, was the steady increase in the reading public and the sharp gains recorded in all manner of reading material—books, magazines, newspapers. At some levels the taste of the reading public emphasized anew a question that had persisted for a century: what price schools and colleges and universities? In spite of westerns, true confession magazines, and comic books, however, circulation of newspapers and serious magazines increased enormously, and the general public was reading more omniverously than ever before. To the distinct literary revival that characterized the years between the wars we shall turn in the next chapter, but here something should be said of more popular books, and, of even greater importance, of the new styles—first introduced in the 1920's—in newspaper reporting and in magazines.

In the realm of popular fiction, the spirit of the times was reflected in a vogue for daring expositions of sex (as they contemporaneously appeared to be), and for romance and adventure. Among the best sellers of the 1920's could be found such books as Edith M. Hull's *The Sheik,* Michael Arlen's *The Green Hat,* Vina Delmar's *Bad Girl,* Rafael Sabatini's *Scaramouche,* and—reflecting quite a different taste—*The Book of Etiquette.* Somewhat later, in the 1930's, the flamboyant historical novel had a new flowering with the phenomenal sales of *Anthony Adverse* and *Gone with the Wind.* Detective stories and mystery tales were another, and often even more widely read, form of escapist fiction.

The sale of books was greatly stimulated by the formation of the new book clubs. The Book of the Month Club and the Literary Guild pioneered in this field in the mid-1920's and soon had a host of imitators. It was estimated that before the formation of these clubs, only about one million persons bought books regularly. The club membership was to rise in twenty years to three times this figure, with over 20,000,000 books distributed annually. Cheap reprints and paper back books had not yet come on the market in the 1920's, but they would eventually increase book sales even more. One publisher was to claim at the close of the 1940's that in eight years he had sold nearly 200,000,000 books, or more "than the combined sales of all best sellers published since 1880."

The influence of the book clubs was hotly debated by critics. It was maintained that they concentrated sales on a few titles to the exclusion of other and better books and led to still further regimentation of the American mind. But in creating a wider audience for books they played an important role in the growth of American culture. In spite of the frothiness of many of the titles they helped to place on the best seller lists, a very considerable number of highly significant books by serious writers were given a far greater audience through their support than would otherwise have been possible.

★ NEWSPAPERS AND MAGAZINES

The same influences that were at work to popularize books affected the field of newspaper and magazine publishing. The daily press went through changes which sharply distinguished it from the prewar press. While the total number of newspapers substantially declined as a result of mergers and consolidations paralleling those in the business world, circulation increased at a more rapid pace than ever before. The papers reflected the demands of a public primarily interested in entertainment. Such conservative organs as the *New York Times,* which remained the country's leading newspaper, observed a reasonable restraint in handling the news, but the great majority tried to outdo the old yellow press, represented at the turn of the century by the New York *World* and New York *Journal,* in playing up crime and sex. The new tabloids set the pace. Lurid photographs, further freeing its subscribers from any undue intellectual strain, enabled the New York *Daily News* to build up rapidly a circulation of over 3,000,000.

That part of the public which could not attend world series baseball or championship prize fights was regaled with endless copy on sports, and particularly in the 1920's every out-of-the-ordinary event in this realm of activity was promoted with great fanfare. Gertrude Ederle was welcomed on her return from swimming the English Channel, the first woman to perform this unusual feat, with tremendous ballyhoo. Day-by-day accounts of nationwide dance marathons and flagpole sitting contests, to say nothing of illustrated descriptions of the annual Atlantic City bathing beauty contests, were also front-page news.

Murder cases were covered so sensationally as to provide a Roman holiday for the reading public. When a local minister and a member of his church choir were mysteriously slain in a small New Jersey town, an army of reporters sent out 5,000,000 words of lurid copy on what became known throughout the country as the Hall-Mills case. Almost equal publicity was given the famed Scopes "monkey trial" in Dayton, Tennessee, which found the aging William Jennings Bryan pathetically battling to justify his fundamentalist opposition to the teaching of evolution. Of all the newspaper stories of the decade, however, one was preeminent—Charles Lindbergh's solo flight across the Atlantic in 1927. The nation's press made the youthful flier a legendary figure, and all records were eclipsed by an aroused public's enthusiastic welcome for a returning hero. New York's street cleaners collected some eighteen tons of ticker tape, torn-up telephone books, and waste paper after Lindbergh triumphantly paraded up Broadway.

The front page, the sports section, and the stock market reports were about all most subscribers bothered to read, but other changes were taking place in newspaper make-up that continued into the 1930's and 1940's. Editorials were increasingly subordinated to special columns and features. The public got its opinions, so far as the newspapers contributed at all to national thinking, from sources that had little association with the local community. Some of the columnists were penetrating observers of the contemporary scene, writing better than the average editorial writers, but syndicate distribution of what were sometimes specially tailored views made for uniformity and gave little scope for individual criticism of existing ways of thought.

The magazines underwent a transformation somewhat comparable to that of the newspapers. Their articles revealed little of the muckraking fervor which had once given such impetus to political and social reform. The *New Republic* and the *Nation,* it is true, kept the fires of progressivism burning; the *Atlantic* and *Harper's,* among others, continued serious discussion of current issues, and the *American Mercury* reached a highly sophisticated audience. The more popular magazines, however, flourished on the success stories whose pattern was set by the *Saturday Evening Post,* the *American Magazine,* and *Collier's.*

The most important development in the field of magazine publishing in the 1920's and 1930's was the founding of a number of periodicals which broke completely fresh ground. The *Reader's Digest,* which undertook to make every type of magazine article easily available to men and women who read as they ran, attained a phenomenal circulation; *Time,* and somewhat later *Newsweek,* successfully introduced the weekly news-review; *Life* pioneered in still another field with its weekly summary of current events in pictures, and *The New Yorker* developed a new brand of humor, literary stories and profiles for the sophisticated. These magazines were to experience great growth in future years, but what stands out particularly was that they were all started in the same between-wars period.

The advertising in many of them (the *Reader's Digest* was for long an exception) played a double role: it won reader interest and was also an important source of revenue. The automobile companies, electrical equipment concerns, and manufacturers of the thousand-and-one new products that were the triumph of modern technology spread their wares before the public in beguiling advertisements that immeasurably stimulated national buying. Ingenious copywriters exercised a tremendous influence on customs and manners which went even beyond their important role in promoting automobile travel, the spread of radios, the introduction of new gadgets into the home.

This was, of course, nothing new. No one can say how much the old slogan, "Good Morning, Have You Used Pear's Soap?" inculcated new habits of national cleanliness. But the advertising copy first introduced in the 1920's reached a much broader public. It encouraged women to smoke cigarettes ("slenderizing in a sensible way" by reaching for a Lucky instead of a Sweet), ruthlessly exposed the horrendous consequences of B.O. ("Often a Bridesmaid but Never a Bride"), stimulated culture ("They Laughed When I Sat Down at the Piano"), and awoke new concepts of gallantry ("Say It with Flowers"). These are only casual samples. "Measured in dollars and cents," wrote one economist, "advertising is the most important form of education in the United States."

Edward E. Cummings, poet and novelist, wrote caustically:

> take it from me kiddo
> believe me
> my country, 'tis of
>
> you, land of the Cluett
> Shirt Boston Garter and Spearmint
> Girl With The Wrigley Eyes(of you
> land of the Arrow Ide . . .

The magazines that carried such advertising and were designed through their articles and fiction to reach the more important segment of the consuming public had their counterpart in another group on a lower intellectual level. Bernarr Macfadden developed a gold mine in *True Story* with its intriguing tales, supposedly authentic, of betrayed virgins, unhappy wives, and broken marriages. Emphasis on sex was its chief stock in trade and other magazines—*True Confessions, Secrets, I Confess*—were soon carrying this successful formula even further. Other so-called pulp magazines, to distinguish them from "the slicks" printed on coated paper, published endless pages of romance and adventure stories. The newsstands were crowded with such titles as *Ranch Romances, Love Stories, Spy Stories,* and *Amazing Stories.* And then the popular comic strips of the newspapers began to be reproduced in comic books. They were supposedly written for children but appealed also to a surprisingly wide adult audience.

The extent to which newspapers and magazines became unabashed entertainment for the masses should not be interpreted as meaning that journalism had completely abandoned its function of interpreting the political and social scene. The coverage of news, both at home and abroad, was more extensive than ever before, and many of the leading writers of the day contributed to the better magazines. There was good fiction as well as trash in the popular weeklies, and the literary and artistic achievements of the 1920's were often reflected in the nation's press.

The literary output of this period, indeed, marked an exciting revival of American letters whatever may be said of the more popular best sellers, magazine fiction, or newspaper sensationalism. An entirely new group of writers came to the fore immediately after the war to give a new vitality and new significance to the literature of the twentieth century. Often in revolt against the blatant materialism of the day and the conventions of contemporary society, their novels, plays, and poetry—and the extent to which many of them were read—were a paradoxical denial of the cynical assumption that all Americans were interested only in making money and seeking cheap entertainment. Turning to these authors, one finds reflected in the contemporary literary scene an amazing degree of life and vigor.

CHAPTER XX

Literature and the Arts Between Wars

★ THE LOST GENERATION

"Here was a new generation . . . grown up to find all Gods dead, all wars fought, all faiths in man shaken."

So wrote Scott Fitzgerald, novelist of the Jazz Age, whose vivid prose has left an enduring picture of "flaming youth" in its cynical, disillusioned revolt against the betrayal of idealism that was the aftermath of war. In *This Side of Paradise,* that first gay and sometimes flippant novel which so shocked contemporary society, and then in *The Beautiful and Damned,* he wrote engagingly of the sad young men and the effervescent flappers with their petting parties, their drinking, their madcap escapades.

Beneath the surface of these and other Fitzgerald stories, however, there was always the feeling of futility, the sense of frustration, that was so poignantly to mark his own life. He was continually aware of a "misty tragedy behind the veil" and burned himself out in his hectic, feverish efforts to find himself. The new generation of which Fitzgerald wrote with intimate knowledge settled down in time to the staid virtues of middle age—the force of its revolt was soon spent—but though he lived until 1940, this brilliant portrayer of the early 1920's was never to grow up, never outlive the glitter and tinsel of his youth, never find salvation.

Fitzgerald possessed a unique talent, if not a great one. He rebelled against the currents of his time, and yet in spite of his individualistic spirit was caught up by them. He was attracted by the riches and conspicuous display that were the life of the people of whom he wrote, even while he showed that riches were the illusion of happiness. The hero of *The Great Gatsby,* that intriguing figure who obtained, by whatever means, wealth and position only to find himself ultimately deserted amid the garish trappings of his success, commanded all his creator's sympathy. This was Fitzgerald's best book (some critics called it the best book of the decade), and it remains a deeply symbolic record of the atmosphere of the early 1920's and a vivid portrayal of their gaudy materialism.

Fitzgerald's sense of disillusionment was shared by many of his contemporaries. Ernest Hemingway, who was numbered for a time among the group of writers who fled to Europe because they found the climate of the United States so intellectually barren, depicted in *The Sun Also Rises* the futile search of the expatriates for something in which they could believe. The young John Dos Passos, who was later to assail so vigorously many facets of contemporary American society in *U.S.A.*, expressed in these early years his contemporaries' reactions to war in *Three Soldiers*.

This was "the lost generation" which did not know where to turn in the face of what they believed to be the "majestic and terrible failure of the life of man in the western world." But even more than in Fitzgerald, Hemingway, or Dos Passos, this sense of frustration is found in quite a different literary figure—the T. S. Eliot of the 1920's. The very title of his major poem of these years, *The Waste Land,* is sign and symbol of the despair that seized upon the postwar literary generation. And this terrifying exposure of what Eliot thought to be the emptiness of life was carried still further when he wrote "The Hollow Men":

> Those who have crossed
> With direct eyes, to death's other Kingdom
> Remember us—if at all—not as lost
> Violent souls, but only
> As the hollow men
> The stuffed men.

It was a bitter poem and came to a bitter climax:

> This is the way the world ends
> Not with a bang but a whimper.

★ FROM PROTEST TO AFFIRMATION

If Eliot was expressing the spirit of intellectual defeatism in his early poems, his attitude soon underwent a marked change. Taking up residence in England, he found a refuge in the Anglo-Catholic church and turned so sharply to the right politically that he was to declare himself a royalist. His poetry under such influences became positive rather than negative, but whatever his new philosophy owed to tradition, he continued to write in nontraditional forms. *Ash Wednesday* first expressed the affirmations of his new faith, and *Murder in the Cathedral* was a further development of his idea of Christian law. In the *Four Quartets,* published in 1943, he again took up his deeply religious concepts of "how man lives both in and out of time. . . ." A decade later another T. S. Eliot, more assured and more optimistic, was still writing.

Eliot's poetry was often difficult and abstruse, characterized by great erudition and a bewildering wealth of literary allusions, but it also contained wonderful passages of great lyrical beauty. His position as both poet and critic became one of undisputed eminence in the literary world and his influence on other poets and writers was tremendous.

While Eliot found an answer to disillusionment by joining the Anglican Church, Hemingway and Dos Passos were also to undergo significant if not as dramatic changes in point of view. They at least grew beyond Fitzgerald, who would always continue, as he confessed shortly before his death, to look back nostalgically to the Jazz Age. If there was to be no complete reconciliation with their times, Hemingway and Dos Passos ultimately appeared to discover something in which they could believe. While it is true that the former continued to have an abiding preoccupation with death and the latter long held to complete defeatism, both of them struck a more affirmative note in their writings of the 1930's and after.

Hemingway's first widely popular book was his moving and poignant *A Farewell to Arms,* with its realistic descriptions of war and its romantic love story. Soon after its publication, he embraced a new cult of blood and violence. His absorption in bull fighting was an expression of this philosophy, most notably developed in *Death in the Afternoon,* and it was also reflected in many of his short stories. They contained much of his best writing, and the short, staccato Hemingway style was used with great effectiveness. In such a brief episode as that related in "The Killers," he gave a brutally vivid picture of the gangster spirit of the 1920's unsurpassed in its stark realism. Such other stories as "The Snows of Kilimanjaro" and "The Short Happy Life of Francis Macomber" have become minor classics.

It was the Civil War in Spain in the mid-1930's that inspired a far more positive novel than anything Hemingway had heretofore written and the depiction of a hero who had found something in life—a sense of values if not a cause—for which he could live and for which he could die. *For Whom the Bell Tolls,* published in 1940, was an important book in the development of Hemingway's philosophy, and in its reflection of new attitudes of mind that had greatly changed since the 1920's. Whatever the judgment on his still later novels in the 1940's and 1950's—and few critics were very enthusiastic—this book was widely acclaimed.

The outstanding book of John Dos Passos was *U.S.A.,* whose three parts were published as a unit in 1938, and the general impact of its picture of American society was devastating. Dos Passos did not tell the whole story, although perhaps no other writer has ever tried to be so comprehensive; he cruelly exposed the ambition, ruthlessness, and vulgarity that he found in the business world. His characters were a good deal more than symbols and yet they were cast in much the same mold, and it was as an unrelenting moral critic that Dos Passos described their self-centered search for the means to gratify their ambitions and their passions. More interesting in some ways than his note of radical protest—it has been said that he transferred the defeatism of the lost generation from the individual to society—were his style and experiments in form. His lively "biographies" of actual people and his impressionistic "newsreels" of actual events contained some of his best writing, while in the short sections he called "the camera eye" he gave his own unhappy conclusions upon what he believed to be the disintegration of American society.

U.S.A. did not give a pleasant picture of the country, which was in effect the hero of the novel, and as he wrote Dos Passos seemed to grow more and more cynical as to any redemptive qualities among the American people. His scorn and bitterness were perhaps expressed with least restraint when he turned the "camera eye" upon the Sacco-Vanzetti case:

> They have clubbed us off the streets they are stronger they are rich they hire and fire the politicians the newspaper editors the old judges the small men with reputations the college presidents the wardheelers (listen businessmen college presidents judges America will not forget her betrayers) they hire the men with guns the uniforms the police cars the patrolwagons
>
> all right you have won you will kill the brave men our friends tonight
>
> America our nation has been beaten by strangers who have turned our language inside out who have taken the clean words our fathers spoke and made them slimy and foul . . . all right we are two nations

Dos Passos appeared despairing and yet his very summons to meet the problems of the day, as with other naturalistic novelists, was a denial of his despair. Ultimately, he shifted his ground from radical protest against a capitalistic society to a new conservatism. In *The Ground We Stand On,* written in 1941, he re-examined the traditions of the past—trying to rediscover "the clean words"—as the foundation for an entirely new approach to life. His further writing, however, did not approach the intensity and depth of *U.S.A.* and seemed steadily to deteriorate in substance and in style.

★ OTHER LITERARY TRENDS

The writer is perhaps always somewhat in revolt against the spirit of his times, and this appeared to be more than ever the case in the 1920's. But while the novelists of the "lost generation" were forever inveighing against what they considered the false values of contemporary society, their attitude differed very much from that of the muckrakers of the early 1900's. They were not concerned with basic economic or social problems; they showed little or no interest in farmers and industrial workers. Their revolt was largely directed against what they considered the materialistic standards and hypocritical conventions of a bourgeois society.

There were exceptions to this somewhat superficial attitude. In 1925, for example, Theodore Dreiser wrote *An American Tragedy,* which dealt somberly with the individual helplessly caught in the meshes of a mechanistic social order. This powerful novel was not in the usual pattern of the 1920's, however, and other contemporary writers remained more generally concerned with manners and morals.

"Where the novelists of the Bryan-Roosevelt era had found it intolerable that a virtuous people should suffer," the historian Henry Steele Commager has written, "the literary rebels of the twenties found it intolerable that virtue should be so dull."

The high priest of many young intellectuals in the 1920's was for a time H. L. Mencken, and the *American Mercury,* which he edited, became their bible. The "bad boy" of Baltimore enjoyed himself hugely attacking the "booboisie" and assailing conventional morality, prohibition, fundamentalism, One Hundred Per Cent Americanism. A flippant attitude which barely concealed a sourly antidemocratic point of view somehow carried enormous weight. From a broader perspective it is difficult to understand how Mencken could have set the tone for so much of the writing of the day, but he had great influence. His disciples were so thoroughly indoctrinated that they generally agreed that little of any value could possibly be found in contemporary society: there was nothing in the United States to satisfy the artistic, intellectual or cultural needs of an educated man.

In *I'll Take My Stand* twelve southern writers railed hopelessly against the ugliness of an industrial society. Harold Stearns, the editor of another symposium, *Civilization in the United States,* summed up its contributors' general impressions by stating that "the most amusing and pathetic fact in the social life of America today is its emotional and aesthetic starvation." Mencken asked himself why he stayed in the

United States if he found so much that was unworthy of reverence and answered scornfully, "Why do men go to zoos?"

★ THE DRAMA

Eugene O'Neill, the outstanding dramatist of the period between wars and probably the greatest this country has ever produced, first attracted attention with *The Emperor Jones* in 1921. Thereafter, a long succession of plays revealed his profundity of purpose, his originality and imagination, his zest for constant experimentation. Dealing in various ways with the deep frustrations of the human spirit, and the everlasting problem of man's relationship to something outside himself, O'Neill brought a note of Greek tragedy to the American stage. This was most notably expressed in *Mourning Becomes Electra,* but other plays as well made a deep impression and further established his pre-eminent place among dramatists—*Anna Christie, Beyond the Horizon, Desire Under the Elms,* and *Strange Interlude.*

There were Freudian undertones in a great deal of O'Neill's writings —indeed Freud greatly influenced almost all the literature of the period —and always a deep concern with moral values. "The playwright of today," O'Neill once wrote, "must dig at the roots of the sickness of today as he feels it—the death of the old God and the failure of science and materialism to give any satisfactory new one for the surviving primitive, religious instinct to find a meaning for life in and comfort its fears of death with." This was a recurrent theme, however different its expression in his many plays.

While O'Neill was almost alone among significant serious dramatists in the 1920's, the theater was soon to have a distinct revival. The little theater movement encouraged experimentation and new dramatic forms, and the changed social scene of the 1930's inspired a number of plays with distinctive content. An example of the former was Thornton Wilder's *Our Town* and of the latter, Clifford Odets' *Waiting for Lefty.* Another new writer for the theater was Maxwell Anderson, whose most distinguished play of this period was *Winterset.*

★ MORE NOVELISTS AND POETS

Returning to the novel of the 1920's, the criticism of prevailing middle-class mores reached something of an all-time high in the work of Sinclair Lewis, social historian extraordinary. His books skillfully uncovered the cant and hypocrisy, the false values, that were often to be found in the towns and cities of contemporary America. At the very time that President Harding was declaring that if he could plant a Rotary club in every city and hamlet, he would "rest assured that our ideals of freedom would be safe and civilization would progress," Lewis was making Rotary a symbol of flamboyant flag waving, intolerance, and a cheap booster spirit.

Babbitt, the hero of his book of that name, was in many ways a savage portrait of the average businessman. But Babbitt's daily activities and daily thought were so faithfully reproduced, with such fascinating detail, that hundreds of thousands of Mr. and Mrs. Babbitts hugely enjoyed reading about themselves—or rather seeing in Babbitt their friends and neighbors. It was not, however, altogether surprising that Lewis was so widely read by those whom he most devastatingly criticized. In spite of his satire, he had no little sympathy for the people at whom it was aimed. He was never a true cynic. He believed thoroughly in the ideal values of American life, however scornful of its actual values.

His most important book was *Main Street,* published as early as 1920, and it was an immediate popular success. Neither its story nor its delineation of character accounted for its huge sales, but rather the memorable picture it presented of the life of Gopher Prairie. It was followed by *Babbitt,* and then by a number of other books which tried to do for members of other professions what *Babbitt* had done for the businessman. The most successful artistically was *Arrowsmith*—whose main character, a dedicated scientist, is sympathetically drawn—and the most unpleasant *Elmer Gantry*—whose go-getting and promiscuous clergyman was presented with cruel exaggeration.

Later novels fell away from the standards Lewis first set himself; no new ideas really caught his imagination. His books grew progressively more dull. "The village atheist ended his tirade," Alfred Kazin has written, "and sighed, and went on playing a friendly game of poker with the local deacons." Nevertheless, Lewis stood out as one of the most powerful novelists of the period, recognized and rewarded abroad by bestowal of the Nobel Prize. No one could have more faithfully—or devastatingly—recorded the surface manifestations of American life.

William Faulkner was a quite different author whose first books were published in the 1920's, although he then went on to write even more memorably, and with broadening recognition, in later decades. His novels and short stories were largely centered about the life story of the people in the mythical Mississippi county of Yoknapatawpha, where traditions of the past, represented by a decayed aristocracy, were in constant conflict with the materialism of the newcomers to southern society whose only interest was making money and getting ahead. There is a note of despair in his treatment of the descendants of the great pre-Civil War families giving way before the advent of the new commercial classes. Faulkner felt they were paying the incalculable debt of their own past—their selfish exploitation of the land, the Indians and the Negroes. He saw little hope for the South, although remaining in bondage to its traditions. His world often appeared to be one of revolt and denial, degradation, chaos, and death.

Among his books in the 1930's were *The Sound and the Fury,* sometimes considered his greatest artistic achievement; *Light in August,* a symbolic story of the contrasts between the Old and New South; *Absalom, Absalom!,* and *The Wild Palms.* This was his most productive period. Faulkner was forever experimenting in form, as were so many writers of these years, and there were stories within stories in much of his writing. His style could also be amazingly subtle and complex, sometimes nearly incomprehensible to the general reader. He wrote with such power, feeling, and beauty that he won a unique place in American literature that gave every indication of permanence. Later books, for Faulkner continued writing and was awarded the Nobel Prize in 1950, included *Intruder in the Dust* and *A Fable.*

Apart from the modern and experimental writers who tended to hold the center of the stage, a number of other literary craftsmen drew on past tradition for their subject matter and wrote in a style that owed a great deal to discipline and control. Contemporary critics sometimes damned them with faint praise, seeing little more in their work than a reflection of older traditions, but there was an enduring value to some of their books which outlasted the age.

Ellen Glasgow and Willa Cather remained in the forefront of such writers, superb artists in portraying those facets of American life in which they found their inspiration. In such books as *Barren Ground* and *The Sheltered Life,* Ellen Glasgow continued to write of post-Civil War days and the break-up of southern feudalism with keen and penetrating irony. Willa Cather turned from the re-creation of the life of the West to new themes dealing with the influence of Catholicism on the early history of the continent. *Death Comes for the Archbishop* and *Shadows on the Rock,* the one centered in New Mexico and the other in Quebec, both won critical acclaim and were widely read.

Of other authors who might be noted, Sherwood Anderson continued to examine what was called the revolt from the village, and Ring Lardner was a humorist with a great deal more than humor in his biting irony. Nor was T. S. Eliot by any means the only significant poet. Frost and Sandburg continued to gain in stature, Edward Arlington Robinson wrote during these years his notable Arthurian trilogy, and then there were Ezra Pound, Robinson Jeffers, Hart Crane, Wallace Stevens, and Stephen Vincent Benét.

Pound belonged to the school of imagists, lived abroad, and during the 1920's and 1930's and later wrote his long series of *Cantos.* Jeffers was a poet of violence and despair, rejecting social progress in what has been described as his unconscious worship of force. Crane, a tragic victim of his own personal insecurity, reflected the influence of Eliot and yet tried to find an answer to the latter's early disillusionment in the tenuous affirmations of *The Bridge.* At once far better adjusted to his times and less of a poet in the deeper sense than either of these three men, Benét produced the most widely read poem of these years. *John Brown's Body,* published in 1928, was a noble evocation of America's past, and while there were critics who considered it "a cinema epic," it remains a moving and lyrical treatment of the Civil War.

★ THE SPIRIT OF THE 1930'S

While many of the writers of the 1920's, as already noted, continued their work along familiar lines in later years, there was a change in the literary atmosphere, as in the general social climate, during the depression. This was seen in a greater concern with economic and social problems and in a growing sympathy with contemporary efforts to promote social reform. The writers of the 1930's were for the most part distinctly New Deal in their sympathies, and some of them flirted with communism as the literary world grew increasingly aware of the contemporary challenge to our democratic way of life. Ultimately, a strong note of affirmation was sounded, which definitely cut off the 1930's from the 1920's. The novelists broke away from their obsession with manners and morals. Some of them ruthlessly exposed the poverty, ignorance, degeneration of Southern "poor whites" or northern slum dwellers, uncompromising in their hard-boiled realism. Others with a broader vision saw the country more nearly whole.

The books of John Steinbeck were among those which dealt most directly with the contemporary scene of strikes, depression, drought, and unemployment. While he wrote somewhat in the tradition of Norris and London, his naturalism was modified by a deep sense of sympathy and a belief that something could be done to remedy the evils of society. He had faith in people.

Grapes of Wrath, his most significant book, was an account of the impact of drought and depression on the lives of the small farmers and sharecroppers of the southwestern dust bowl. This record of the tragic migration of the Okies, forced by circumstance to abandon their own land and seek out the promised security of California, is an eloquent and moving document that relates as no other book of the time the dire consequences of depression:

There is a crime here that goes beyond denunciation. There is a sorrow here that weeping cannot symbolize. There is a failure here that topples all our success. The fertile earth, the straight tree rows, the sturdy trunks, and the ripe fruit. And children dying of pellagra must die because a profit cannot be taken from an orange. And coroners must fill in the certificates—died of malnutrition—because the food must rot, must be forced to rot. . . .

In the eyes of the people there is a failure, and in the eyes of the hungry there is a growing wrath. In the souls of the people the grapes of wrath are filling and growing heavy, growing heavy for the vintage.

Steinbeck's novel was at once grimly realistic in its detailed treatment of the story of the Joad family and suffused with a deep feeling that sometimes threatened to spill over into sentimentality. *Grapes of Wrath* was one of the most widely read books of the period, and in its social impact has been compared to *Uncle Tom's Cabin.* Steinbeck continued to write on into the 1950's but none of his later books had the power of this significant depression novel.

Thomas Wolfe stood out even more prominently among the new novelists. Sometimes considered "the central spokesman for the artistic beliefs of the 1930's," his concern was not with immediate social and economic problems, but with the fundamental issue of personal insecurity in a world whose values appeared to be so greatly changing. He poured forth his doubts and questioning—"lost, lost, forever lost"—in four tremendous books, a full million words, that were amazing self-revealing autobiographies. The first and in many ways most notable was *Look Homeward Angel,* long, diffuse, inchoate, and disorganized, but written with great emotional power, compelling sincerity and poetic beauty.

Wolfe was in some measure a prose Walt Whitman in his celebration of his country. His aim has been said to have been to "set down America as far as it can belong to the experience of one man." There were many passages in *Look Homeward Angel,* as well as in his later books, that have been seldom equaled in their power to evoke a compelling response:

'Promised, promised, promised, promised, promised,' say the leaves across America. . . . And everywhere, through the immortal dark, something moving in the night, and something stirring in the hearts of men, and something crying in their wild unuttered blood, the wild, unuttered tongue of its huge prophecies—so soon the morning, soon the morning: O America.

He was always the young man in search of understanding and certainties that seemed to elude his grasp, but he also had abiding faith. If he believed that we were lost here in America, he was also convinced that we would one day be found. "I think that the true discovery of

America is before us," he wrote shortly before his death in 1938, "I think the true fulfillment of our spirit, of our people, of our mighty and immortal land, is yet to come."

There was another school of writers in the 1930's, the so-called "proletarian writers," who under the impact of the depression had become socialists, communists or vague "fellow travelers." There was often a bitter tone to their writing and some of them appeared more than willing to sacrifice artistic integrity on the altar of Marxist propaganda. Others succeeded—James T. Farrell with his Studs Lonigan series placed against the background of Chicago tenement life, the Negro writer Richard Wright in such a powerful novel as *Native Son*—in voicing their protest without sacrifice of literary style.

More important than the proletarian writers were those other novelists, poets, playwrights and critics who were not swept off balance by the depression, but found fresh sources for their hope in society and in individual man. This new approach was evident in the later books of Sinclair Lewis and John Dos Passos, even if they were poor books. But there was still Robert Frost in poetry; Maxwell Anderson and Robert Sherwood were writing memorable drama; Archibald MacLeish was inveighing against "the irresponsibles" in his own rediscovery of the American spirit, and other former critics of the contemporary scene—Van Wyck Brooks, Lewis Mumford—were turning back to the wellsprings of American history.

Paradoxically finding their faith renewed as the world's time of troubles deepened, these writers and others echoed Wolfe's evocation of the spirit of America. They looked about them and found in spite of depression and the impending shadow of war, values that had been overlooked in the 1920's. Some whose earlier books were said to have reflected "a literary fallacy" in their failure to interpret the real spirit of America, now faced more squarely the basic issues confronting the world. Again and again they turned to the past, to the past of their own country, to find courage for the future.

"Here in this body of writing," Alfred Kazin has written of the literature of the 1930's, "is evidence of how deeply felt was the urge born of crisis to recover America *as an idea*—and perhaps only thus to prepare a literature worthy of it."

In *The People, Yes,* Carl Sandburg eloquently expressed this new vision:

> And across the bitter years and howling winters
> The deathless dream will be the stronger
> The dream of equity will win.

★ AMERICAN MUSIC

Very much the same air of new discovery and eager experimentation that distinguished literature also characterized the development of other arts between wars. The materialistic spirit that so generally prevailed in the era of the Big Money seemed, paradoxically enough, to create an atmosphere conducive to artistic expression, and the depression then provided still further stimulation of a somewhat different order. It may have been the very fact that the artist felt himself to be a rebel that inspired him to ever greater creative activity.

This was to be true of music. America had no strong musical tradition and had produced no great composers, but the 1920's and 1930's were to witness a widening popular appreciation of classical music, in which both the phonograph and the radio played an important part. The rise of a number of serious composers and the more interesting development of distinctively American musical forms were to attract worldwide attention. At the same time there was continued growth in symphony orchestras, chamber music groups and choral societies throughout the country. With some 35,000 youthful orchestras reported in 1930, music was winning a place for itself even in the nation's schools.

Among the orchestral composers was Aaron Copland, who wrote in 1925 his very well received *A Dance Symphony,* and in the operatic field there were Deems Taylor, music critic as well as composer, and Howard Hanson, director of the Eastman School of Music. Both wrote operas that were produced at the Metropolitan Opera House in New York and won the general acclaim of critics. The former's *The King's Henchman* was first performed in 1927, and the latter's *Merry Mount,* based upon an old colonial story, in 1934.

But undoubtedly a more significant American contribution to music than anything in symphonic or operatic form was jazz. Its origins are lost in the folk history of the Negro, but in the opening years of the century jazz became a highly popular musical feature of night life in New Orleans, especially in its notorious red-light district. In the early years of the war it made its way northward to Chicago, and then in the postwar period swept the country—and ultimately the world—by storm. The intermixture of ragtime tunes and blues ballads, the syncopated rhythm, the spontaneous embroidering of themes, the constant improvisation, sometimes by all an orchestra's players and sometimes by individual instrumentalists, gave jazz a unique and exciting quality. Negro bands were the customary performers, both in night clubs and at concerts, but it was taken up by other musicians and orchestras. The band leader Paul Whiteman gave a jazz concert in Carnegie Hall, New

York, in 1924, and George Gershwin took over jazz's syncopated rhythms in such popular symphonic compositions as *Rhapsody in Blue* and *An American in Paris.*

This was not a temporary craze, as many people at the time thought. Jazz continued to have its enthusiastic devotees, especially among young people, the length and breadth of the land. During the 1930's and 1940's such name bands as those of Louis Armstrong, Duke Ellington, and Count Basie were in constant demand, and Benny Goodman was widely hailed as the "King of Swing." The recordings of their performances had phenomenal sales.

The sophisticated and the intellectual became greatly interested in jazz, and it became a cult among music enthusiasts. It went through many progressive changes and refinements—swing, boogie-woogie—always with further exploration of its complex harmonies and rhythms.

Another uniquely American development was the composing and staging of a new form of musical play that went far beyond anything attempted by the old operettas. A first and most successful team of composer and lyricist was Jerome Kern and Oscar Hammerstein II. With their staging of *Showboat* in 1927, they originated a succession of musical plays that for life, vitality, and tuneful songs were comparable to nothing ever before seen on the American stage. Gershwin entered this field with the incomparable *Porgy and Bess* (that two decades later would tour Soviet Russia), and Richard Rodgers, teaming up with Oscar Hammerstein, in the 1940's, produced in succession such immensely popular shows as *Oklahoma!, South Pacific,* and *The King and I.*

★ ART AND ARCHITECTURE

Something of a revival in art also stemmed from the 1920's with constantly mounting popular interest in painting and to some extent in sculpture. In 1929 the Museum of Modern Art was founded in New York, and two years later, giving particular encouragement to American painting, the Whitney Museum. The well-attended exhibitions of the Independent Artists Society, and later of the American Artists Congress, further reflected a new popular awareness of painting, while the great fairs held in Chicago, San Francisco, and New York provided an unusual opportunity for the exhibition of both painting and sculpture. At the New York World's Fair in 1939, some 25,000 entries were submitted for an exhibition of "American Art Today."

Equally important in the 1930's was the influence given to all artistic endeavor by the Arts Division of the Works Progress Administration, established by the New Deal in meeting the problem of depression unemployment. It provided encouragement that the nation had never before extended to its artists. The paintings, murals, and sculpture commissioned by the WPA for public buildings, however mediocre many of them may have been, provided the impetus for something of an artistic renaissance. These projects stimulated particularly the growth of a school of regional painters who drew their inspiration from the contemporary scene.

In sculpture, even more than in painting, there was a marked trend in this period between the two wars toward the abstract. The new younger sculptors broke away from the traditional forms exemplified in the work of such men as Augustus Saint Gaudens and Daniel Chester French. Gutzon Borglum, the best known of the realists, continued his work and was commissioned to chisel the massive portraits of American heroes on Mount Rushmore in South Dakota. But more representative of the new era were such sculptors as William Zorach and Gaston Lachaise. Commenting on the trend that was making sculpture more and more abstract, one critic declared that it meant the abandonment of all traditional aesthetic standards and subjects. He nevertheless recognized the value of such sculpture as an "attempt to achieve a full expression of the modern complex mind."

In painting there were a dozen schools. They cannot be closely defined and their members shifted and changed their loyalties—and their styles—with the passing years. The realistic tradition exemplified by the prewar Ash Can School was carried forward in the paintings of such men as Edward Hopper and George Bellows; among the impressionists were John Marin, Charles Sheeler, Georgia O'Keeffe, and Yasuo Kuniyoshi; painters in what is sometimes classified as the independent group were Alexander Brook, with his delicate portrait figures, Reginald Marsh, who painted scenes and characters from New York's Fourteenth Street and Coney Island, and Charles E. Burchfield. Then there was the surrealist Peter Blume.

Two distinctively American schools of the 1930's, born of the depression, were the radical exponents of social discontent and the regional painters of the contemporary American scene. The former were sometimes communist-oriented and reflected in their work a bitter rebellion against fascism, war, and social injustice, while the latter turned to rediscover America and the American tradition as did many writers of the 1930's.

The radicals included such painters as William Gropper, Ben Shahn, and Joseph Hirsch. Their themes were often degradation and poverty, not as pictorial compositions, but as savage protest against contemporary conditions. They painted scenes of industrial strife, police oppression, riots, and lynchings. Their leftwing sympathies sometimes exceeded their artistic skill, and one critic and art historian, Oliver W. Larkin, has written that the energy these paintings possessed "was simply one of the nerves and muscles."

Among the regional painters, John Steuart Curry, Grant Wood, and Thomas Hart Benton stood out prominently. They came from the Midwest, and their paintings were of prairie landscapes, scenes in the small towns of Kansas, Iowa, and Missouri, and of farmers and ordinary people of this so typically American part of the country. There were a host of other regionalists, many of them getting their start with the WPA. Their paintings and murals were of New England countrysides, decaying southern plantations, western deserts, and the life of people in villages, towns, and cities.

Architecture went through a period of startling developments. The 1920's and 1930's saw the gradual acceptance of the functional school in which Louis Sullivan and Frank Lloyd Wright had pioneered, and modern ideas increasingly influenced the construction of both public and private buildings. The new skyscrapers in New York and other cities, garden-apartment houses, experimental styles for private homes (especially the popular ranch-type houses), reflected a fresh approach to architecture that added a new note to the American scene. New materials—especially glass and glass brick—were being skillfully employed as well as new structural designs in steel and masonry. The New York World's Fair in 1939 provided an occasion for experimentation in public buildings that stimulated a fresh interest in all architectural forms.

There was later to be something of a movement away from what one critic called "the unchanging and silent façades of cruel smooth steel and glass" that characterized so much urban building. While such construction continued to typify many modern factories, as well as city office buildings, architecture became increasingly characterized by fresh innovations, and to some extent by the attempt to modify the purely functional with decorative and romantic elements.

Frank Lloyd Wright, who has been characterized as "the immense, unique genius" of American architecture, continued to inveigh against every trend other than those he himself inspired. America had no culture, he stated in one newspaper interview, because other than "water closets, washbowls, and radiators," it had no indigenous architecture. Yet even Wright would ultimately admit that the country appeared to be waking up and that American architecture was coming into its own. Throughout the country, indeed, new office buildings and factories, schools and churches, museums, auditoriums, public buildings, apartment houses, and private homes reflected the vitality that ever since the 1920's appeared to animate American architecture.

All this activity—in literature, music, art, and architecture—not only greatly enriched the artistic heritage of the American people but dramatically revealed that this country had at long last freed itself from its artistic dependence on Europe. Throughout the nineteenth century and even in the opening years of the twentieth, American art and literature were largely derivative. We borrowed from abroad; we slavishly followed European models. By the 1920's and 1930's Europe had to recognize that the United States had attained a cultural independence, and in many areas a level of cultural achievement, that it had never before approached.

CHAPTER XXI

Prosperity to Depression

★ THE OUTLOOK IN 1929

When President Hoover was inaugurated in March 1929, the future appeared bright for a prosperous America. The triumphs of a business civilization were thought to be secure. Throughout his campaign the Republican candidate had reiterated his confident prediction that by continuing to follow the policies of the previous eight years, the United States should be able to abolish poverty and spread the benefits of an inspiring economic progress the length and breadth of the land.

He was prepared to summon Congress into special session to meet the imperative demand of the farmers for some form of agricultural relief and to reconsider tariff policy. The fact that the farmers were not sharing in the general prosperity had to be recognized, and the sharp wave of agrarian discontent could no longer be ignored. President Coolidge had twice vetoed, in 1927 and 1928, the farm bloc's program for assistance embodied in the McNary-Haugen bill, and something had to be done. But this problem was not considered insoluble. Hoover proposed to help the farmer through a program whereby the government would hold surplus crops off the market and thus stabilize prices. The one serious defect in the functioning of the industrial system would be eliminated, and the nation would enjoy an even better-balanced economy.

Otherwise, he felt there was no need for modification of the "American system of rugged individualism" that had served the country so well. For what had been the consequences of this system? "Our country has become the land of opportunity to those born without inheritance," Hoover declared, "not merely because of the wealth of its resources and industry but because of this freedom of initiative and enterprise. . . . By adherence to the principles of decentralized self-government, and freedom to the individual, our American experiment in human welfare has yielded a degree of well-being unparalleled in all the world."

It was just half a year after the inauguration of the new President, however, that the sudden crash of the New York stock market in the fall of 1929 heralded an economic collapse more widespread, more prolonged, more devastating in its nationwide consequences, than anything the country had ever experienced. Business and industry were prostrated, trade and commerce almost completely dried up, agriculture was laid waste. Millions of men and women were thrown out of work. As unemployment mounted steadily in the ensuing years, the long dreary lines of people waiting sullenly at food stations and soup kitchens became a tragic commentary on the hopeful promise of poverty abolished. The bands of frustrated men and boys eking out an existence in the tumble-down, tin-roofed shacks of tramp jungles, ironically known as Hoovervilles, were doleful evidence of the failure of rugged individualism.

What had happened to American prosperity? What were the factors that so insidiously undermined national well-being? Why had our economic system broken down with such catastrophic consequences?

★ CAUSES OF THE DEPRESSION

There were few economists who foresaw or even dimly realized at the beginning of the Hoover administration that the country was headed for hard times. The experts generally agreed with the President that the economy was on a more stable basis than ever before and that there was no longer need to fear the recurrent cycles of depression which had heretofore characterized the nation's history. The report of the President's Commission on Recent Economic Changes emphasized in 1929 the new "dynamic equilibrium" in the country's industrial structure, happily stating that "our situation is fortunate, our momentum remarkable." But with the advantage of hindsight, those widening cracks in the economic structure that made for collapse are readily apparent. There will never be full agreement in evaluating the causes of the depression, but certain of them have become very clear.

The gradual decline of agriculture is a case in point. As the foreign market for staple crops contracted with increased production of wheat and cotton in other lands, and domestic consumption was restricted by changing dietary habits and new clothing styles, the agricultural surpluses forced prices downward. The farmer was again experiencing the troubles of the 1890's, caught in the old squeeze of having to sell his products in an open market while he bought his machinery, tools, and equipment in a protected market. This meant reduced buying power for a large segment of the population whose purchases of manufactured products were essential for full industrial production.

The existence of certain "sick industries" within the framework of otherwise general business prosperity was also a dangerous factor. Coal mining was in the doldrums throughout the greater part of the 1920's; the immensely important construction industry began gradually to decline in the mid-1920's, and the textile trades were never able to keep pace with the advances made on other sectors of the industrial front. In another sphere of economic activity, foreign trade was buoyed up very precariously by loans and credits, often advanced on a very insecure basis, which alone enabled European importers to obtain the exchange to pay for their purchases of American goods.

A more general and more important consideration was the fact, realized in later years as it was not realized in the 1920's, that the unequal distribution of the national income severely restricted the over-all purchasing power of the nation in terms of the continued growth of productive capacity. Too much money was being diverted into corporate investment or savings, too little going into the hands of consumers. This meant that excess funds were being used not only for enlarging the industrial plant beyond effective needs, but for unrestrained speculation in the security markets, while the public lacked the resources to buy, at prevailing prices, the expanded output of factory and mill. Purchasing power, it is true, was increasing. A growing volume of consumer goods was being absorbed, but not at the rate necessary to assure a balanced economy.

Innumerable statistics might be cited to illustrate this unequal distribution of income. One or two comparisons may suffice. While corporate dividends had increased, between 1923 and 1929, by 65 per cent, the real income of workers had gone up by only 11 per cent. At the close of the decade, 36,000 families in the upper income brackets received a share of the national income approximating that of 11,000,000 in the lowest group. Over half of those in the latter category had earnings of less than $1,000 a year. Entirely apart from the effect upon individual families of such relative poverty, industry needed their purchases to maintain full production and a high rate of employment.

Once the influence of such adverse factors began to make itself felt, a chain reaction was set off in bringing industrial advance to a halt. As the demand for goods slackened, manufacturers necessarily cut production schedules. This meant the progressive lay-off of workers, and a still further decline in consumer income. Industry was then forced to curtail operations even more substantially; additional workers were dismissed and wages severely cut. The cumulative effects of such general economic dislocation steadily intensified the depression. And at that time there were no wage laws to provide a floor under the workers' earnings, no unemployment insurance to help sustain the purchasing power of the jobless.

The real significance of the warning implicit in the break in the stock market was not at first understood. The illusion of prosperity had too strong a hold upon the imagination—the imagination of economists as well as of political leaders and the general public—for the dangers in the situation to be properly appreciated. Not until nationwide wage cuts, the rising tide of unemployment, and the lengthening bread lines starkly revealed that something much more fundamental was wrong with the country than an overinflated security market did the American people fully realize what had happened.

★ THE STOCK MARKET CRASH

The sudden and spectacular collapse in security prices nevertheless shook the entire country. Speculation had become the order of the day as the paper value of common stocks spiraled upward. Prices were already high in 1927, but in the next two years General Electric rose from 128 to 396, American Telephone and Telegraph from 179 to 335, Montgomery Ward from 132 to 466, and Radio from 94 to 505. Bank presidents and college professors, midwestern dirt farmers and urban factory workers, clerks, stenographers, and office boys appeared to be following the tip to invest in common stocks that John J. Raskob, vice-president of General Motors and Al Smith's campaign manager, had graciously given the public in an inviting article in the *Ladies' Home Journal* entitled "Everybody Ought To Be Rich." There seemed to be no limit to the speculative frenzy in 1929, and every hint of caution was brushed aside in those feverish, hectic days of the great bull market.

A few premonitory qualms cast their shadow in September; then came "Black Thursday"—the twenty-fourth of October. A tremendous wave of liquidation inexplicably hit the stock market on that particular day, and within a few hours the precipitate downward plunge of stocks swept away hundreds of millions of dollars in paper profits. Complete collapse was narrowly averted by the hurried organization of a banking pool, but five days later the market crashed again. Selling orders swamped the brokers, the tickers could not keep pace with market transactions, and over 16,000,000 shares changed hands amid the wildest confusion the stock exchange had ever known. The liquidation was not even then halted. It continued spasmodically until November 13. By that date the recorded loss in stock values was over $30,000,000,000 with the average price of leading securities more than halved.

Solemn statements from every possible quarter sought to reassure a nervous public that panic on Wall Street was not a matter of fundamental concern. President Hoover summoned a meeting of business employers to win their promise that there would be no wage cuts or dismissal of employees, and upon its conclusion stated his firm conviction that this move had re-established public confidence. In comparable reassuring statements the Secretary of the Treasury forecast a complete revival of business activity in the spring, and the Secretary of Commerce said that there was nothing in the situation to be disturbed about. Again and again public officials declared, in a phrase which would haunt men's minds for a decade, that "conditions are fundamentally sound."

The promised recovery failed to materialize; economic conditions grew steadily worse. There could be no blinking the harsh fact that prosperity was not just around the corner and that the country faced a dire domestic crisis. In every previous period of depression the forces making for recovery had in time automatically asserted themselves. It had not proved necessary for government to intervene in helping to restore economic stability. But the situation that developed in the early 1930's gave little hope for such natural readjustments. There was forced upon a reluctant administration the unhappy realization that the powers of government had somehow to be invoked to try to stem the tide of economic disaster. Confident reliance upon a laissez faire philosophy and the spirit of rugged individualism was no longer possible when forces seemingly beyond men's control threatened the paralysis of business, trade, and agriculture, and unemployment figures were rising upward as rapidly as prices, production, and wages were plunging downward.

President Hoover recognized and accepted the new responsibility of government under these circumstances. The policy of drift that had appeared for a time to mark his attitude was abandoned, once it was clearly seen that nationwide depression rather than a stock market panic confronted the country. A series of measures carefully designed to restore economic stability were gradually adopted. In so doing Hoover broke with all past precedent and pioneered in entirely unknown areas of governmental activity. By acknowledging that under existing circumstances the reserve powers of the federal government had to be used for the protection of its citizens, this conservative Republican president in many respects laid the basis for the New Deal.

Nevertheless, the steps that Hoover took did not adequately meet the national emergency. In the phrase used on the occasion of later war crises, they were "too little and too late." The backward pull of nineteenth-century economic and political concepts, at least partly blinding the President to the realities of the changed society of the twentieth century, prevented him from implementing his policies with sufficient vigor or on an adequately broad front. Hoover continued to think almost exclusively in terms of assistance for business, largely ignoring the need for direct aid to distressed farmers, impoverished workers, and the army of unemployed.

★ HERBERT HOOVER

When he had taken office in 1929 great things were expected of Herbert Hoover. His background and experience appeared to fit him admirably for the presidency in a period that had led Coolidge to declare with assurance that the business of America was business. His career was in the Horatio Alger tradition of success. Born on an Iowa farm and orphaned at the age of ten, he worked his way through college and became a mining engineer. Once launched on this profession, he had climbed rapidly, gaining unusual worldwide experience and amassing a very considerable personal fortune. His profitable handling of his extensive business interests appeared proof of outstanding executive and administrative ability.

Since 1914, moreover, Hoover had not only further demonstrated administrative skills in public affairs, but he had revealed a strong humanitarian interest and social conscience. First coming into prominence through his work with the Belgian Relief Commission, then serving with outstanding distinction as wartime Food Administrator, he was appointed after the close of hostilities the director of the American Relief Administration. This task involved feeding Europe. Hoover won a worldwide renown to which John Maynard Keynes, among many others, attested when he said that "never was a nobler work of disinterested goodwill carried through with more tenacity and sincerity and skill."

Even then considered presidential timber, Hoover's subsequent activities as Secretary of Commerce under both Harding and Coolidge further strengthened popular belief in his capacity to direct national affairs. He was "the great engineer" who would bring to government the pragmatic ideals of his profession, tempered by his humanitarian outlook, and thus be able to further the economic progress that was the glory of the 1920's. It was a perverse and ironic fate that where his far less able predecessors had sowed the wind, Herbert Hoover should reap the whirlwind.

However, the new President lacked almost completely the political aptitude that is far more essential for a chief executive than are the most expert administrative skills. He had never held elective office and had no experience whatsoever in the rough-and-tumble of American politics. He did not know how to get on with Congress, how to work with

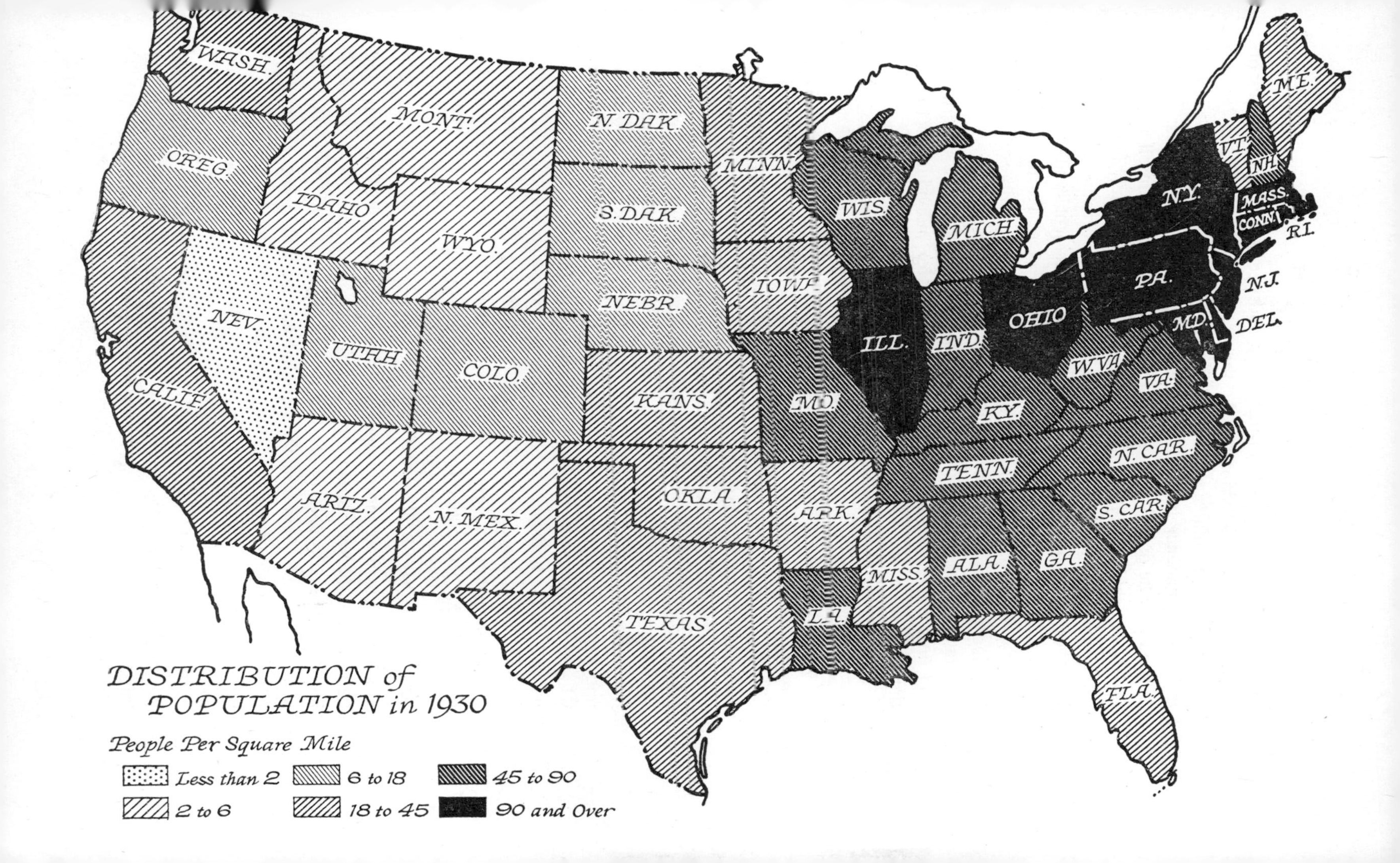
DISTRIBUTION of POPULATION in 1930
People Per Square Mile
Less than 2
2 to 6
6 to 18
18 to 45
45 to 90
90 and Over
WASH.
OREG.
CALIF.
NEV.
IDAHO
MONT.
WYO.
UTAH
COLO.
ARIZ.
N. MEX.
N. DAK.
S. DAK.
NEBR.
KANS.
OKLA.
TEXAS
MINN.
IOWA
MO.
ARK.
LA.
WIS.
ILL.
MICH.
IND.
OHIO
KY.
TENN.
MISS.
ALA.
GA.
FLA.
S. CAR.
N. CAR.
VA.
W. VA.
MD.
DEL.
PA.
N.J.
N.Y.
VT.
N.H.
ME.
MASS.
CONN.
R.I.

men who were not his subordinates but independent representatives of another branch of government. As this inability to provide the leadership in national affairs which the country expected gradually became manifest, confidence in the Great Engineer was badly shattered.

Whatever he did, Hoover seemed unable to present himself in a very favorable light before the general public. He was completely incapable of establishing friendly relations with the Washington correspondents whose influence in forming the popular image of a president is all-important. There was no natural give-and-take about the man. He did not sense public opinion, as had Harding and Coolidge, and sometimes gave needless and tactless affront. When he refused on principle to encourage a program of direct relief for the unemployed, he gave the unfortunate and false impression of lacking any sympathy for individual victims of the depression.

Hoover was to be the scapegoat for many things for which he could not be held directly responsible, but it was often his own fault in that he did not clearly explain his attitude. He said the wrong thing at the wrong time. His natural sympathy was so buried beneath a cold, forbidding exterior, that people ceased to believe he had any real understanding of their distress.

His personal appearance was against him. He had a broad, rather pudgy face. His neat blue serge suits and stiff white collars became a symbol of conservatism. In later years he was to mellow a great deal, but during the critical period of his presidency, he was stiff, unbending, and stuffy. He rarely smiled in public, had no light touch or humor whatsoever, and was unable to communicate any feeling of personal warmth to the audiences which heard his campaign speeches or public addresses. His associates and co-workers from earlier days had not only deep respect but also great fondness for him; they were to remain intensely loyal. The public found him sadly wanting.

★ THE HOOVER PHILOSOPHY

Hoover's ideas were more important than his personality, however, and he remained the spokesman for a philosophy of government that proved increasingly inadequate under the impact of continuing depression. In spite of his realization that the national administration had to exert its influence in trying to restore some sort of balance to the economic system, he continued throughout his administration to move too slowly and too cautiously.

The ground for his refusal to countenance direct aid for farmers or the unemployed was his conviction that it would undermine individual initiative and create a dangerous dependence upon Washington. Whatever validity there may have been for such fears, however, the public felt that there was a cruel paradox in his reluctance to help the common people and his willingness to aid the banks, railroads, and insurance companies—whose individual initiative he apparently felt was proof against any undermining influence.

The distinctions Hoover drew in the development of such relief measures as circumstances finally forced him to adopt were, indeed, sometimes hard to understand. When drought assailed the Southwest, for example, he approved federal aid in the form of contributions of feed for the farmers' livestock and of seed for the replacement of their crops, but withheld his support from any more direct aid for the farmers themselves. There were bitter complaints that while he was willing to feed starving mules, he had no concern for starving men and women.

Another instance of apparent indifference to human suffering was his attitude in dealing with the Bonus Expeditionary Force which marched on Washington in the summer of 1932 to demand the immediate payment of the adjusted service certificates owed the veterans of World War I. Its members were for the most part jobless, homeless, and poverty-stricken. They commanded a good deal of public sympathy, even though there was general approval of Congress' refusal to grant their demands. Hoover, however, considered their march on Washington an attempt to coerce the government by mob rule and ordered the military to disperse them. It fell to the lot of General Douglas MacArthur to carry out this assignment, and troops under his command, equipped with machine guns, tanks, and tear gas, summarily disbanded the B.E.F. and burned its encampment to the ground. The public saw in such drastic action only a shocking lack of understanding for the unemployed veterans' pitiful plight.

It was never want of sympathy that caused Hoover to adopt such a seemingly callous attitude. He was rigidly adhering to principles that he felt all-important. He would continue to believe that for the federal government to provide direct relief would break down our traditional concepts of community responsibility and subject the people to control of a remote bureaucracy. Loans might be tolerated, not gifts. The latter "would have injured the spiritual responses of the American people. . . . A voluntary deed is infinitely more precious to our national ideals and spirit than a thousandfold poured from the Treasury."

In spite of those measures ultimately taken to promote recovery, Hoover also continued to maintain a stubborn opposition to any move that could possibly be interpreted as injecting government into business. A single step along this dangerous path, he apparently believed, would almost certainly lead to state socialism.

His point of view on this general issue was set forth most forcefully on a matter involving government and water power. Throughout the 1920's there had been debates and dispute over such matters. Neither Harding nor Coolidge was very much concerned with the effective operation of a Federal Power Commission set up by Congress in 1920, and they also hoped to transfer to private interests controlled by Henry Ford a power development project that had been planned in connection with a nitrate plant set up during the war at Muscle Shoals on the Tennessee River. Congress had other ideas on Muscle Shoals, however. At the instigation of Senator Norris of Nebraska it passed a bill for government operation of these properties. Coolidge let the bill die with a pocket veto, but Congress repassed it in 1931 and presented it to President Hoover. He opposed completely this program which was the forerunner of the T.V.A., and in a ringing veto message made clear just where he stood:

> This bill would launch the federal government upon a policy of ownership and operation of power utilities upon a basis of competition instead of by the proper government function of regulation for the protection of all the people. I hesitate to contemplate the future of our institutions, of our country if the preoccupation of its officials is to be no longer the promotion of justice and equal opportunity but is to be devoted to barter in the markets. That is not liberalism. It is degeneration.

His critics were to point out that Hoover failed to admit either the extent to which individual economic freedom was largely an illusion in an industrial society, or the role government might play in giving it greater reality. He shut his eyes, they declared, to the vital importance of some assurance of reasonable security as the basis for any sort of freedom. His views were not changed by such arguments. Hoover continued to oppose what he termed the basic alterations in our American system inherent in such projects as the Muscle Shoals development.

Hoover was not a conservative in the sense that both Harding and Coolidge were conservatives. He was no stand-patter. His claim that his policies represented the "true liberalism" can hardly be substantiated, however, in the light of the circumstances produced by the depression. In spite of his own innovations in meeting the crisis of economic collapse, he constantly appeared to be trying to re-create a world that no longer existed and could not be revived. If not an advocate of the laissez faire state, nothing seemed to frighten him more than the concept of a welfare state.

Whatever Hoover and those who agreed with him might say, the fearful consequences to which intervention in the economic sphere might conceivably lead did not seriously alarm a people already suffering so severely from the failure of government to adopt more adequate relief measures. They were willing to take such risks. Had Hoover's own program proved successful, the popular attitude might have been quite different. But his repeated assurance that prosperity would be reestablished by continuing his measures and policies was hardly enough in the light of what was actually taking place.

★ AGRICULTURE AND THE TARIFF

The first important measure of the Hoover administration—one that actually antedated the depression—was the Agricultural Marketing Act, adopted in 1929, with its provisions for stabilizing farm prices by holding surplus crops off the market. A Federal Farm Board was set up to handle this program, with a revolving fund of $500,000,000, and immense quantities of wheat and cotton were bought up and stored in government warehouses. For a brief time the downward trend in prices appeared to be halted by this "freezing" of the surplus crops, but after the stock market break the decline was rapidly accelerated. The wheat and cotton kept off the market created new uncertainties, and with no purchasers for the huge government stocks, a further drop in prices simply left the Federal Farm Board holding the bag. Its funds were virtually exhausted, and with storage charges beginning to run higher than the value of the crops stored, the Board was soon forced to withdraw from the market. Wheat plunged to fifty-seven cents a bushel, the lowest price since 1896; cotton fell to five cents a pound.

The Agricultural Marketing Act was a complete failure. Without any provision for limiting production, it had not even touched the heart of the farm problem and only served to point up the need for a much more comprehensive program. Hoover had no idea of going any further along such lines. It was to be left to the New Deal to develop a general policy which has apparently made direct agricultural aid, in one form or another, a permanent function of government.

The tariff revision that was so closely linked with farm relief was no more successful. After long debate Congress passed the Hawley-Smoot Act in June 1930. The increases rather than decreases it decreed in existing import duties almost immediately brought about the results that its critics feared. Other countries took prompt retaliatory action. The world-wide adoption of import quotas, exchange restrictions, and other measures impeding the normal interchange of goods helped to dry up all foreign trade. The new American tariff simply accentuated the forces making for world-wide economic depression.

It has already been noted that in the area of intergovernmental financial transactions, Hoover finally undertook to mitigate the adverse effect of our insistence upon war debt payments by initiating a general moratorium. Had this been done earlier, and carried through more effectively, it might have proved to be of some value. But again the breakdown had gone too far for a temporary palliative to solve any basic problem.

★ PUBLIC WORKS AND THE R.F.C.

Of greater significance than these measures were two important steps taken even more directly as a consequence of the depression in the hope of stimulating domestic industrial activity and thereby promoting recovery. The first was an expansion of the public works program, and the second assistance for financial institutions through the agency of the Reconstruction Finance Corporation.

As early as January 1930 recommendations were made for priming the industrial pump and increasing employment by way of federal construction projects; a little less than two years later, Hoover anticipated the New Deal by specifically recommending the creation of a Public Works Administration. The building of highways, new river and harbor improvements, and such large-scale undertakings as the Boulder Dam across the lower reaches of the Colorado River, were vigorously encouraged. Governmental expenditures were stepped up to what at the time was the large figure, however inconsequential it may appear in an age of tremendously expanded budgets, of $600,000,000 a year.

The Reconstruction Finance Corporation was established in January 1932. Within a year it had advanced nearly $2,000,000,000 to banks, agricultural credit associations, insurance companies, railroads, and state governments. It was to be charged that in some instances these loans were made to institutions so greatly overcapitalized that it might have been better if they had been allowed to fail. Yet there can be no question that the Reconstruction Finance Corporation helped to forestall a demoralizing wave of bankruptcies, and to some extent served as a brake against even more serious economic collapse. Its activities were not only continued when Roosevelt came into office, but greatly extended.

A few cautious steps were also taken to provide direct relief in spite of Hoover's stand against any general program along these lines. The surplus wheat and cotton stocks held by the Federal Farm Board were made available, through distribution by the American Red Cross, to the victims of the drought of 1931. Federal loans to the states ultimately provided funds—some $300,000,000—for the immediate relief activities of local governments. Otherwise, however, the President remained true to his conviction that any obligation to help the needy rested with individuals, local communities, or at the most state governments, rather than the federal government.

As his term of office drew to a close, Hoover became involved in incessant wrangling with the Democratic Congress that had been elected in 1930. He refused to approve its proposals for a really vast public works program and for direct relief, declaring that the Democrats were playing politics with human misery. He was later to claim that the measures his administration did promote constituted "the most gigantic program of economic defense and counter-attack ever evolved in the history of the Republic." This was true—no earlier administration had done anything to meet the problems of depression—yet the harsh fact remained that the Hoover program was not sufficiently imaginative or effective to bring back prosperity. Economic paralysis became even more widespread; the army of unemployed continued to grow.

★ PARTY PROGRAMS IN 1932

As the time approached for the national political conventions in the summer of 1932, there were surprisingly few signs of the social unrest that might have been expected under such adverse economic conditions. Incensed farmers protested low prices on occasion by burning crops and dumping milk cans or sought to foment agricultural strikes with the slogan, "Be Pickets or Peasants." The unemployed in the larger cities created disturbances in a few scattered instances. The communists were doing what they could to stir up trouble and a considerable number of intellectuals and writers became party members or fellow travelers. But radical propaganda made little headway among the great mass of workers and while there was some talk in timorous circles of "the coming revolution," the American people showed no signs of seeking to take matters into their own hands. Contemporary observers were struck by the apathy with which the unemployed appeared to accept their fate.

"They just sit at home and blame prohibition," wrote one magazine contributor. "Like the Republican administration, they are awaiting nothing more drastic than the return of prosperity." Mocking the fears of the timid, the religious leader Reinhold Niebuhr declared that there was not even "a hand-sized revolutionary movement on the political horizon."

Yet this did not mean that the people were content with the Hoover policies. Far from it. There was a mounting feeling of resentment toward an administration that seemed to be so impervious to the human factors in the situation, to the misery and want that were breaking the spirit of individuals. As the election results were to demonstrate, the American people were insistent upon a change in government. It was a change that was to be brought about, however, by the normal exercise of political power rather than by any violent attack upon the established order.

The Republicans knew their position was difficult, but they had no alternative other than to renominate Hoover for the presidency and defend the policies he had been following. Any other course would have been an abject admission of failure. The line they adopted, therefore, was to reiterate that conditions were actually on the mend and that recovery was being delayed only by the impact of foreign developments on the national economy. Any attempt to change domestic policies at such a critical juncture, according to this thesis, would court disaster. Hoover stood his ground. "If there shall be no retreat, if the attack shall continue as it is now organized," he asserted, "then this battle is won."

The Democrats were quick to take advantage of the most favorable opportunity for their return to office that had presented itself since the war. Their platform let out the stops in assailing the Republican administrations of the previous twelve years for all the ills with which the country was faced. Economic isolationism, the encouragement of monopoly, and the manipulation of public credit for private profit were declared to be the chief causes of the nation's unprecedented economic and social distress. The only hope for bringing the country back to its proud position of world leadership lay "in a drastic change in economic governmental policies."

The Democrats were nevertheless extremely cautious about proposing any specific changes. They placed a major emphasis in their platform on the reduction of governmental expenses, which had begun to exceed governmental income under the impact of depression, on the restoration of a balanced budget, and on the maintenance "at all hazards" of a sound currency. They called explicitly for the repeal of the Eighteenth Amendment. Other planks conformed to established tradition in urging tariff revision, enforcement of the antitrust laws, and the regulation of public-utility holding companies. On the new issues confronting the country the Democrats went no further than to urge effective control of crop surpluses, unemployment and old-age insurance under state laws, and the extension of federal credit to the states for immediate relief. It was a highly conservative platform—"not one wild nostrum or disturbing proposal in the whole list," proclaimed the *New York Times*. In the opinion of many liberal critics of the Hoover administration, it offered little more than did the Republican program and held out no real hope of an effective attack upon the depression. "A puny answer to the challenge of the times," the *New Republic* commented caustically.

★ THE ROOSEVELT CAMPAIGN

Far more important than the adoption of the platform, was the nomination of a presidential candidate. On the fourth ballot the convention named Franklin D. Roosevelt, then governor of New York. His preconvention campaign had cleared the way for his selection, but he was none too well known to the general public, and the country as a whole had little idea of what might be expected of him. As informed a political observer as Walter Lippmann found little more to say about Roosevelt in the summer of 1932 than that he was "an amiable man, with many philanthropic impulses . . . who without any important qualifications for the office, would very much like to be President." But the Democratic nominee at once gave a striking demonstration of the energy, initiative, and self-confidence that were so markedly to characterize his career. Disregarding all precedent he flew to Chicago to accept the Democratic nomination in person, dramatically proclaiming a policy that foreshadowed the major political development of this period in American history: "I pledge you, I pledge myself, to a new deal for the American people."

As the campaign developed, Roosevelt did not provide any too clear an indication of what his "New Deal" actually meant. He attacked what he called the false economic policies of the Hoover administration—"it delayed relief, it forgot reform"—and declared war upon "the 'Four Horsemen' of the present Republican leadership: The Horsemen of Destruction, Delay, Deceit, Despair." He strongly supported the Democratic platform, with its contradictory promise of reduced expenditures and expanded credit for unemployment relief. He emphatically stated that far from seeking to alter the basic principles of our economic system, his aim was to put them into effect. But there were only vague suggestions as to the specific policies he expected to pursue should he be elected.

A few of his speeches did throw somewhat more light on his underlying political philosophy. Even before his nomination he had called for a "wiser, more equitable distribution of the national income," and emphasized the need for greater consideration of the interests of the common people. The aid which Hoover sought to provide in meeting the depression, Roosevelt declared, was restricted to banks and industry. He entered a powerful plea for "the forgotten man at the bottom of the economic pyramid."

Thirty-six years earlier William Jennings Bryan had stated that there were two ideas of government: the theory that if you legislated to make the well-to-do prosperous, their prosperity would leak through on those below; and its counterpart, that if you made the masses prosperous, their prosperity would find its way up through every class that rested on them. In attacking the Republican "trickle-down" theory and upholding a policy to strengthen the bases of the economic pyramid, Roosevelt clearly took a leaf directly out of Bryan's book.

The Democratic candidate's ideas were most expressly stated in a campaign talk before the Commonwealth Club of San Francisco. The new century had marked a turning point in national history, Roosevelt declared, and with the disappearance of the frontier and free land, there was necessary a complete reappraisal of social values. The country needed an economic declaration of rights, a new economic constitutional order. The fundamental principles of democratic capitalism remained completely sound, according to this view, but government had to face the challenge in the current emergency by seeking to adapt "existing economic organizations to the service of the people."

Going on from this premise, Roosevelt stated that the right every man has to life means also the right to make a comfortable living, and that the right of every man to his own property means also the right to be assured of the safety of his savings. Government, in other words, had a direct responsibility for safeguarding the economic interests of all classes in a nation sorely beset by the critical problems of overproduction, underconsumption, inequitably distributed wealth, and vast unemployment.

The public paid little attention to the Commonwealth Club speech, and not much more to Roosevelt's elaboration in other talks of his more general ideas in regard to relief, social security, and agricultural aid. William Allen White declared that for the first time since 1912, "a candidate of one of the major parties sounded an unterrified liberal note in the formal clarion call to his party," but there were few commentators to echo so emphatic an interpretation of Roosevelt's stand in 1932. The *Literary Digest* reported that editorial opinion as examined through a nationwide survey found little reason to see any promise of better times in the adoption of his program. The anti-Democratic forces were said to be delighted with the turn of events. They were happily hailing Roosevelt —in one of the most ironic of all political forecasts—as "God's greatest gift to the Republican party."

Hoover sensed far more keenly than the public the potential differences between his own political philosophy and that of his rival. A new approach to governmental responsibilities in providing for the general welfare had almost certainly become inevitable by 1932, regardless of election results or what party was in office, but Hoover was entirely correct in finding in what Roosevelt called the New Deal a doctrine that meant the final overthrow of laissez faire and rugged individualism. Answering Roosevelt, Hoover declared:

> My countrymen, the proposals of our opponents represent a profound change in American life. . . . Dominantly in their spirit they represent a radical departure from the foundations of one hundred and fifty years which

have made this the greatest nation in the world. This election is not a mere shift from the ins to the outs. It means deciding the direction our nation will take over a century to come.

★ ELECTION RESULTS

In seeking to arouse the public to such fundamental considerations of national policy, Hoover could make little headway. Entirely apart from the possible validity of his thesis, the country was too absorbed in the immediate problems of the depression. "Of what avail were his long speeches and his car-end harangues," the *New York Times* asked, "against the more eloquent oratory of farm prices at the lowest ever known and 10,000,000 unemployed?"

The American people saw the failure of Hoover's policy on every hand, and they heard from Roosevelt the promise of a new deal. Theirs was not to reason why. Without any deep concern over what a new deal might actually bring in its train, they were prepared to repudiate the old deal. They went to the polls in 1932 to vote against Hoover rather than to vote in favor of Roosevelt.

Looking back on the election, there would seem to have been slight reason ever to doubt its outcome. The depression was the all-compelling issue. When the ballots were counted, Roosevelt had received a popular vote of 22,822,000 against his rival's 15,762,000, carrying all but six states with an electoral college majority of 472 to 59. The repudiation of Republican policy was clear and decisive.

The country's newspapers took the prospective return of the Democrats to power philosophically; they little anticipated the exciting events just over the horizon. They were impressed, as one editorial writer put it, by "the tidal wave of popular emotion demanding a change," but even the most conservative Republican organs saw no reason to believe that Roosevelt would introduce any radical or upsetting proposals. "We think he will be swayed hither and thither," commented the New York *Evening Post,* "and then end up on some kind of a middle course." While this was not actually too wide of the mark, there were many contemporary observers who were fearfully to describe the early days of the new administration as the Roosevelt Revolution.

CHAPTER XXII

Advent of the New Deal

★ THE INAUGURATION OF ROOSEVELT

On March 4, 1933, a worried country waited expectantly for the inaugural address of its new president. The rank and file of the Democratic party had gathered excitedly in Washington to usher in the administration, but the mood of the country as a whole was far from one of celebration. It was tense and nervous. The crisis confronting the nation could only be compared to that of war.

Economic conditions had not improved during the four months that intervened between Roosevelt's election and inauguration. Factories, mills, and workshops throughout the country were either closed down or operating with greatly restricted production; the continued paralysis of trade and commerce was graphically portrayed by the empty freight cars that packed railway yards and the idle ships tied up at a hundred wharfs. Agrarian distress had mounted with the failure of any price recovery, and embittered farmers were now taking the law in their own hands to prevent further mortgage foreclosures. The ranks of the unemployed had swollen to somewhere near fifteen million, and a new restiveness was demonstrated in sullen hunger marches and bread riots.

In the week just before the inauguration, a culminating wave of bank failures had added a new element of confusion to the troubled scene. State after state had been forced to close its banks to stave off complete financial chaos. The prospect could hardly have been more bleak as a frightened people turned to Washington to discover what the President could offer them in the way of hope for the long-delayed recovery.

Roosevelt's address was a ringing appeal for the restoration of national confidence. It was a summons to apply a new set of social values for those that had led the country into such deep distress. It was a promise of determined leadership and immediate and effective action.

The keynote was sounded in the opening paragraph as the President confidently proclaimed that the nation would endure as it had always endured, would revive and prosper: "The only thing we have to fear is fear itself—nameless, unreasoning, unjustified terror which paralyzes needed efforts to convert retreat into advance."

The national distress came from no failure of substance, Roosevelt declared, but through the failure of the "rulers of the exchange of mankind's goods" who knew only the motives of profit-making and self-seeking. Their practices were indicted in the court of public opinion, and the measure of the restoration that the nation now sought would lie in the extent to which social values more noble than mere monetary profit were applied in carrying forward reconstruction.

The new President outlined in general terms a program to put his ideas and principles into effect. It embraced additional public works, support for higher agricultural prices, a halt to mortgage foreclosures, the unification of all relief activities, national planning and supervision for transportation and public utilities, greater control over banking and security exchanges, a balanced budget, and an adequate and sound currency. Action along these lines was entirely feasible within the framework of a constitution that had met every stress of national emergency, Roosevelt stated emphatically, but if the normal balance of powers between executive and legislature proved inadequate to meet the unprecedented task he faced, a temporary departure from that balance might prove necessary:

> I am prepared under my constitutional duty to recommend measures that a stricken Nation in the midst of a stricken world may require.
>
> These measures, or such other measures as the Congress may build out of its experience and wisdom, I shall seek, within my constitutional authority, to bring to speedy adoption.
>
> But in the event that the Congress shall fail to take one of these two courses, and in the event that the national emergency is still critical, I shall not evade the clear course of duty that will then confront me.
>
> I shall ask the Congress for the one remaining instrument to meet the crisis—broad executive power to wage a war against the emergency as great as the power that would be given to me if we were in fact invaded by a foreign foe.
>
> For the trust reposed in me I will return the courage and devotion that befit the time. I can do no less.

The calm assurance of this address and its spirited call to action awoke a nationwide response that changed the temper of the American people. Roosevelt was perhaps to perform no greater service in all his long career than in making this confident assertion that the crisis facing the country could and would be successfully resolved. He somehow conveyed his own resolute courage and glowing faith to a people that had lost its courage and faith, arousing them overnight from the somber depths of their despair.

Popular approval crossed party lines. The New York *Herald Tribune* declared that the President had conducted himself "like a true leader, who realizes the difficulties before him, and faces them unafraid"; the Chicago *Tribune* said that the speech struck "the dominant note of courageous confidence"; the Washington *Post* stated that "the determination to act, and to act heroically, strikes a popular chord," and the Los Angeles *Times* agreed that the stand taken was "well calculated to inspire confidence." A public statement by a group of national leaders drawn from the ranks of business, labor, and agriculture spoke enthusiastically of the "spontaneous and spiritual uprising of confidence and hope in our chosen leader."

★ THE NEW PRESIDENT AND HIS PHILOSOPHY

The inaugural address reflected the character and strength of Franklin D. Roosevelt. In the momentous years that lay ahead, he was to make mistakes in policy and in the administration of policy. He was to lose the well-nigh universal support he commanded in 1933 and arouse the embittered opposition of a powerful minority. Yet there was to be no denying his leadership, his unfaltering courage, or his buoyant confidence. As time went on, it was clear that he had no very well-defined program for either economic recovery or social reform. Expediency often dictated the measures he proposed, and he happily confessed that, like a football quarterback, he could not plan ahead rigidly because "future plays will depend on how the next one works." However, he stood steadfastly by the general principles that he had outlined in taking over the presidency. For all his shifts and turns in policy, his basic approach to the problems of his era had a hard core of consistency.

Once when he was asked about his views by a reporter, the following exchange took place, as told by Frances Perkins in her revealing book *The Roosevelt I Knew:*

"Mr. President, are you a Communist?"

"No."

"Are you a capitalist?"

"No."

"Are you a Socialist?"

"No," he said, with a look of surprise as if he were wondering what he was being cross-examined about.

The young man said, "Well, what is your philosophy then?"

"Philosophy?" asked the President, puzzled. "Philosophy? I am a Christian and a Democrat—that's all."

Miss Perkins, who served throughout his administration as his Secretary of Labor, has herself borne eloquent testimony—as, indeed, have many others who knew him well—to Roosevelt's intense religious faith and conviction. His strong party feeling, though it would not prevent him from making a number of notable Republican appointments, was always fully apparent. His social attitudes were a blend of an innate idealism and the exigencies of politics.

The period, however, was ripe for the reforms in which he believed. The goal that he once set as the primary objective of the New Deal—"the security of the men, women, and children of the nation"—conformed to the prevailing attitude of mind of the country as a whole. Roosevelt expressed the spirit of his age. He was a born leader and greatly influenced his generation, but history decreed that the times should be made for the man quite as much as the man was made for the times.

★ HIS BACKGROUND AND CHARACTER

Roosevelt's background—aristocratic forebears, inherited wealth, Groton and Harvard—gave him a natural interest in preserving a free enterprise system that in his eyes made for the good life. He was thoroughly convinced, however, that it could be saved only by ruthlessly attacking the abuses which threatened to undermine public confidence in its beneficent working. "The true conservative," he said, "seeks to protect the system of private property and free enterprise by correcting such injustices and inequalities as arise from it." He placed first and foremost in his thinking the forgotten man whom he saw bearing the brunt of the depression. Only so far as the farmers, the workers, the small businessmen, and tradespeople believed that they were getting fair treatment, he was convinced, could democratic capitalism survive in a world in which fascism and communism were winning such wide support. Their interests were considered paramount as the New Deal swung into action. It was in their behalf that Roosevelt would proudly boast, in 1936, that his administration had "saved the system of private property and free enterprise."

His first introduction to politics had been his election, against overwhelming odds, as a state senator in New York in 1910. He stood as an independent, liberal Democrat and became an advocate of social reform more because of his humanitarian instincts than through any reasoned doctrine. Attracted to Woodrow Wilson by the latter's championship of progressive principles, the young Roosevelt worked for his election in 1912 and was rewarded by appointment to the post his distant cousin Theodore Roosevelt, whose career he was so closely to follow, once held—Assistant Secretary of the Navy. He served in this position with distinction, demonstrating high administrative capacity, and was nominated by the Democrats as the running mate of James M. Cox in the latter's unsuccessful bid for the presidency in 1920.

It was shortly after this defeat that Franklin Roosevelt suffered an attack of infantile paralysis and entered upon his long, valiant struggle to win back his health. The effect of this attack on the future president's character has ever since been a topic of endless conjecture. Yet there can be little doubt that his triumph over an illness which would have led almost anyone else to give up all thought of politics, accounted in considerable measure for the courage and optimism with which he faced the national crises of depression and war. His personal ordeal steeled his spirit against any further buffetings of fate. He is reported as saying that "if you had spent two years in bed trying to wiggle your big toe, after that anything else would seem easy!"

There was high drama when Roosevelt, called back into politics to aid Alfred E. Smith in 1924, dragged himself on crutches to the rostrum at the Democratic convention that year and nominated the "Happy Warrior" for the presidency. And four years later, again upon the insistent urgings of Smith, he reluctantly agreed to run for the New York governorship in order to bolster the party ticket. Contrary to all expectations, Roosevelt was elected in that unhappy Democratic year and was chosen for a second gubernatorial term in 1930. His record was a sound one but in no way phenomenal. However, in his advocacy of agricultural aid, unemployment insurance, conservation, the regulation of public utilities, and other reform measures there were significant intimations of what was to become the New Deal.

Roosevelt's radiant personality was an asset of overtowering proportions. He brought something fresh and dynamic into the stale atmosphere of contemporary politics. His personal magnetism would have been notable at any time, but in contrast with Coolidge and Hoover it could hardly have been more striking. It reached out not only to the people that directly heard his speeches but to the vast radio audience which always listened to him. He had a marvelous voice. From the moment he began one of his Fireside Chats with the familiar phrase, "My friends," Roosevelt was able to hold millions of listeners in the palm of his hand. For all the help he received in their preparation, his speeches always bore the mark of his own personality. They could be forceful and dynamic, cleverly persuasive, witty, and disarming. The phrases he coined became political propaganda against which his foes fulminated helplessly.

The country has perhaps never had a more handsome man as its representative in the White House. Roosevelt's head and shoulders were massive, giving an impression of great strength, and few people realized how seriously crippled he was and what a great strain every public appearance made on his energy. Not that he did not enjoy campaigning and public speaking. He delighted in the political battle. But he could not stand by himself; he had always either to lean on the rostrum or have someone take his arm. His smile was infectious—it was usually a happy grin—and the invariable long cigarette holder, held at such a jaunty angle, was the delight of cartoonists.

Like Theodore Roosevelt, this Democratic scion of a famous family was warmhearted, gregarious, insatiably curious, interested in anything and everything. No great thinker, no intellectual, he often borrowed his ideas. He was said to play by ear rather than by note. "Roosevelt's background of economic innocence," one not unfriendly historian has written, "was dappled by only occasional traces of knowledge." The energy that might have gone into sports went into talk and into his collections—books, ship models, stamps. He made the atmosphere of the White House, with the sympathetic co-operation of Eleanor Roosevelt, one of friendly informality, and his political critics were often afraid of being beguiled by their host's soothing influence. There was one thing on which everybody who came in personal contact with Roosevelt appears to have been completely agreed: he had almost irresistible charm.

There were other sides to his highly complex character. He was an opportunist; he often lacked candor, and he seemed sometimes to take an almost wicked delight in doing by indirection things that might better have been done more straightforwardly. He was not the best of administrators, sometimes being too soft-hearted to take the drastic steps necessary to keep peace in his official family, and he often tended to play favorites. There were occasions when his subordinates, or members of Congress, were convinced that Roosevelt agreed with them, only to discover that he took an exactly opposite tack. His administrative approach has been defended as stimulating competition, calling forth his assistants' best efforts, but his critics declared that he could not be trusted. The most bitter attacks made on him were by those who felt that he was dishonest. However, none of the men and women who really knew him—or the country as a whole—ever questioned his basic integrity.

Franklin D. Roosevelt will always remain a highly controversial figure. He held office so long, dealt with so many issues and with so many men in such a critical period, that there could never be full agreement on his personality, his philosophy, or his policies. Yet there can be little question that he will hold an assured and commanding position in American history, and will always be considered one of our great presidents.

★ THE HUNDRED DAYS

The promise of action, and action now, that he made on that raw March day in 1933 when he was for the first time inaugurated President, was quickly fulfilled. The next three months, which were to become known as the Hundred Days, saw a mass of legislation rushed through Congress under circumstances for which there was no parallel in all American history. So far-reaching were many of these new measures, and so rapidly were they adopted, that it was not altogether surprising that many people thought in terms of peaceful revolution. Although virtually every new law had its antecedents deeply rooted in the American tradition, the breathtaking speed with which the program went into effect sometimes gave the appearance of a complete overturn in the old order.

Roosevelt at once proclaimed a national banking holiday, closing every single bank in the country, and called Congress into special session. It met on March 9 and before the day was over, an Emergency Banking Act was passed enabling the Treasury to call in all gold and providing for reopening banks judged by federal inspectors to be sound, with the appointment of "conservators" for those whose condition appeared to demand such protection. The next day a second presidential message called for enactment of an economy measure reducing the salaries of federal employees by 15 per cent and substantially cutting veterans' benefits. This move was promptly followed by a request for immediate repeal of the Volstead Act, pending final action on prohibition whose failure the country now accepted, in order to open up a new source of federal revenue through taxes on beer. And finally, in this first burst of energy, a proposal was made for a relief scheme which took form as the Civilian Conservation Corps.

The Congress responded with alacrity to these messages. Before the month was out, every one of the presidential recommendations had been adopted. An aroused public realized that when Roosevelt had promised "direct, vigorous action," he had meant exactly what he said.

Yet this was only a beginning. In the weeks that followed, Roosevelt took the first steps leading to devaluation of the dollar as a means to stimulate price recovery, proposed the establishment of a Federal Emergency Relief Administration, together with adoption of concrete measures to relieve distressed farmers and urban home owners from the pressing burden of mortgage payments, called for effective regulation of the stock market through the Truth-in-Securities Act (later supplemented by creation of the Securities and Exchange Commission), introduced a farm relief program to be operated under a new Agricultural Adjustment Administration, gave effective support to the creation of what became the

Tennessee Valley Authority, and as the capstone of his fast-moving program, introduced the National Industrial Recovery Act, with its comprehensive scheme of self-governing industrial codes, labor regulations, and the appropriation of $3,300,000,000 for a vast expansion of public works.

Congress continued to follow the President's dynamic leadership: every one of the proposed bills had become law before the end of June. Here was the substance of what has sometimes been called the First New Deal. Sporadic opposition flared up to some features of the program. There were those who passionately declared that the National Recovery Administration was "the most sweeping and perilous experiment in economic revolution since the Soviet regime was set up in Russia." But the country as a whole applauded enthusiastically Roosevelt's dramatic fulfillment of his inaugural pledges.

"Never in the history of the nation," Henry I. Harriman, president of the Chamber of Commerce of the United States emphatically stated, "has an Administration more courageously and fairly attempted to deal with so many and such far-reaching problems."

The New Deal was in many respects not to make good the early promise of these exciting days. Its inner contradictions, its overly ambitious objectives, mistakes due to haste and inexperience, the tremendous cost of new governmental operations, had to be reckoned with as time went on. Increasing opposition developed as dismayed business leaders, cautiously emerging from the cyclone cellars to which they had retreated under the impact of depression, tried desperately to save what they could of special privilege from such sweeping change and reform. The Hundred Days, however, restored national confidence, reversed the downward trend of depression, and led to a measure of immediate recovery that appeared to promise the restoration of economic stability.

"We have shown the world," Roosevelt felt justified in stating, "that democracy has within it the elements necessary to its own salvation."

★ THE RELIEF PROGRAM

The twofold purpose inspiring this first phase of the New Deal was relief and recovery. It did not represent any long-range plan, and as already suggested, some of the President's proposals were hard to reconcile with any consistent, underlying objective. It is highly significant, for example, that Frances Perkins has reported that even in April 1933 the President's mind "was innocent as a child's of any such program as NRA." Different features of Roosevelt's policy were suggested by different advisers. Members of the "Brain Trust" which had first helped him during the presidential campaign enthusiastically descended on Washington to work for the fulfillment of their glowing dreams of a reorganized society. Every record of those days bears witness to the feeling of excitement, urgency, and great things underway which animated the nation's capital. The wonder is not that the New Deal program had so many contradictory features, but that it held together at all.

Relief was an immediately vital need, and from the very first Roosevelt's approach to this problem differed sharply from that of Hoover. He accepted, as his predecessor had never been willing to accept, a primary obligation to do whatever could be done through direct assistance to the unemployed. "Whether or not it is written in the Constitution," Roosevelt declared, "it is the inherent duty of the Federal Government to keep its citizens from starvation." Moreover, he did not think of relief in terms of charity or as a dole. What he had in mind was work-relief. Every person willing to work had a right to a job, according to this thesis, and when private enterprise failed to provide one, it was incumbent on government to fulfill what was in effect a debt of society to its members.

An immediately successful application of this principle was the Civilian Conservation Corps. It enrolled young men and boys needing work and set them to tasks that only government could undertake and which were of general social value. These activities included reforestation, with the planting of hundreds of millions of small trees, erosion and flood control projects, the building of countless check dams, and the construction of thousands of miles of forest roads. Available funds made possible the employment of only some 300,000 men and boys at one time, but eventually a total of nearly 3,000,000 went through the CCC camps scattered from Maine to California, from Washington to Florida.

The Federal Emergency Relief Administration, also set up in these early days, was designed to meet the broader needs of the country. It provided direct aid for the unemployed, through grants to the states, and had at its disposal $500,000,000. To establish work-relief as contrasted with such emergency assistance Congress then created, in October 1933, a further national agency known as the Civilian Works Administration. Operating within the framework of the general relief program, which had been placed under the direction of Harry L. Hopkins, a former state relief administrator in New York, the CWA soon had 3,000,000 jobless on its rolls.

This undertaking was not, however, a success. The available appropriations—$400,000,000—did not provide adequately for the purchase of building materials or equipment. The CWA was consequently unable to furnish many jobs other than those which involved making minor improvements on public property, landscaping parks, or doing general repair work. This was the leaf-raking era of relief, the sorry days in which the country seemed to be wasting its substance on "boondoggling," and the effect of such inconsequential made-work appeared to be even more demoralizing than an outright dole. The CWA was liquidated in April 1934 and the entire relief burden fell back on the FERA.

In line with the New Deal belief in really effective work-relief, it consequently became clear that a thorough reorganization of the entire program was essential. This was finally brought about in 1935. The men and women out of work were placed in two distinct categories. Those who because of age or physical disability were unemployable became eligible for direct relief administered primarily by the states with funds supplemented through federal grants-in-aid. The needs of the employable, on the other hand, were met through bona fide jobs on worthwhile projects, instituted and carried forward by the federal government itself. The agency to promote the second part of this new program was the Works Progress Administration, created in May 1935 with an initial appropriation of nearly $5,000,000,000.

★ THE WPA

The WPA was designed to give work not only to unemployed wage earners, but to unemployed salaried personnel, other white collar workers, and professional men and women. Going even further in developing the philosophy that work-relief should be adapted to the aptitudes and skills of the unemployed, the WPA set up its special projects for writers and artists, musicians and actors. At the same time a related activity for offering various part-time work opportunities that would enable students to carry on their college and even postgraduate education was developed through the National Youth Administration.

The WPA was a gigantic and entirely unprecedented undertaking. Before its final liquidation during war days, its multifarious projects provided jobs for over 8,000,000 persons, with aggregate expenditures totaling $13,000,000,000. The tremendous cost, which contributed materially to the annual deficit with which the federal government operated during these years, may be placed on the debit side of the ledger. There was no question that direct relief would have been far more economical. But the gains for the morale of the unemployed implicit in work-relief, and the community value of the great majority of WPA projects, far outweighed the immediate savings in dollars and cents that any other approach to unemployment aid would have realized.

What most caught the imagination about the WPA was the wide scope of its activities. Over 650,000 miles of surfaced roads were built under its aegis, and some 35,000 school houses, post offices, and other public buildings. Thousands of tennis courts, swimming pools, golf courses, and recreational centers were constructed. At the same time, a series of admirable state guide books was issued by the Writers' Project; plays produced by the Federal Theatre were staged for nationwide audiences totaling 22,000,000, and countless miles of murals were painted by unemployed artists to adorn federal buildings. As one contemporary summed up WPA achievements:

> From the construction of highways to the extermination of rats; from the building of stadiums to the stuffing of birds; from the improvement of airplane landing fields to the making of Braille books; from the building of over a million privies to the playing of the world's great symphonies. . . . One might contrast sewing garments and rip-rapping levees; draining swamps and painting murals; repairing wharves and mending children's teeth; seeking abandoned mines and teaching illiterate adults to read and write; planting trees and planting oysters.

At one time the records of the WPA, the FERA, and other agencies of the federal government showed that nearly 7,000,000 individuals or families were simultaneously on government payrolls. It was estimated that nearly one-fifth of the entire population of the United States, directly or indirectly, received some form of federal assistance during the 1930's. If this was a measure of the astounding extent to which the government was prepared to fulfill its responsibilities in taking care of its citizens, it was also a less happy indication of the failure of economic recovery to provide the means whereby private enterprise could take up the unemployment slack. In spite of the steadily increasing burden for the nation's taxpayers, relief measures had to be continued on an extensive scale until the eve of American entry into World War II. The continuing impact of unemployment—still estimated at some 8,000,000 in 1941—left a hardpressed government no alternative unless it were entirely to abandon its assumed responsibilities.

★ EARLY RECOVERY MEASURES

The failure to lessen the relief load was not for want of a myriad of recovery measures, and this legislation helped to bring about a substantial measure of economic improvement even if it never succeeded in restoring full employment. Indeed, every index of industrial activity began to register a sharp rise after Roosevelt came into office. The New Deal was popularly supported in the midterm elections in 1934 largely because of the gains made in almost every segment of the national economy. The President was able to make his most telling appeal for votes by simply asking his nationwide radio audience, "Are you better off than you were last year? Are your debts less burdensome? . . . Are your working conditions better?" But this recovery did not carry through. For all the progress made under the New Deal in comparison with the situation when Roosevelt came into office, the fact remained that economic stability was not really restored until the war created those artificial demands which led to a new and booming prosperity.

This may perhaps be most clearly seen by taking as an illustration the estimated totals of national income. In 1932 the reported figure of approximately $40,000,000,000 was less than half that recorded in 1929. For four years there was steady rise to a total of $71,000,000,000, followed by a decline to $63,000,000,000, and then a further increase in 1939 to $70,829,000,000. Even without taking into consideration price rises and the increase in population, this meant that recovery had not in 1939 brought the country back to the levels of ten years earlier. On any relative basis the nation was not as well off as it had been in the 1920's.

The interrelation of the various measures seeking to promote economic recovery, and their relative success or failure, raise questions that the historian can hardly hope to answer satisfactorily. The devaluation of the dollar, finally effected in January 1934 through the abrogation of the gold clause in all public and private contracts, and reduction in the dollar's gold content by approximately 40 per cent, would appear to have had no basically important effect on the national economy. It did not bring about the healthy rise in price levels that its proponents envisioned, nor did it lead to the disasters that its critics so freely predicted. Perhaps the best that can be said of devaluation—"the gold nobody knows"—is that it served to head off insistent agrarian demands for a more radical program of currency inflation, which would have started the printing presses turning out a flood of greenbacks.

The public works program, undertaken as a vast pump priming operation to encourage industrial production, appeared at least for a time to be much more successful. It originally called for the expenditure of $3,300,000,000, as appropriated under Title II of the National Industrial Recovery Act, for the construction of highways and public buildings, the development of water power resources, the transmission of electric energy, the improvement of rivers and harbors, and the promotion of slum clearance and low-cost housing. The Public Works Administration was authorized to allocate the necessary funds directly for federal projects and to provide assistance for nonfederal projects through grants-in-aid to local governments.

The preparation of the blueprints for these large-scale undertakings, to say nothing of making arrangements with local communities and letting out the contracts to private builders, consumed a great deal of time. Nevertheless, Secretary of the Interior Harold Ickes, appointed

Public Works Administrator, approved allotments for over 13,000 federal projects and 2,500 nonfederal projects by the close of 1933. As actual construction then got underway, orders for materials poured in to the capital goods industries, especially steel and cement, and work was furnished some 650,000 men. The PWA was ultimately to account for the completion of more than 34,000 public works at an aggregate cost of $6,000,000,000.

But what was its contribution to recovery? Once again no definite answer can be given. That it helped both directly and indirectly to stimulate industry may be taken for granted, but this stimulation did not enable industry to get back completely on its own feet. The program was severely criticized for its cost, but it was also argued that considerably larger appropriations were necessary on the theory that if pump priming is to be effective, it must be continued until the pump is operating under its own power. When PWA appropriations were cut off before this goal was fully realized, the proponents of the program maintained that its basic purpose was automatically defeated.

The recovery that was ultimately realized through the far greater expenditure of government funds on national rearmament in part substantiated this argument. But the inflationary effect on the economy of continued deficit financing may have discouraged investment in private industry under the circumstances prevailing in the mid-1930's, and thereby blocked essential plant expansion. The capital goods industries, in any event, showed no such improvement during these years as the consumer goods industries.

Whatever the role of the PWA in such economic recovery as was finally realized, it had a further significance. As in the case of WPA undertakings, the country received a valuable heritage in the schools, post offices, court houses, roads, bridges, dams and power projects built under PWA auspices. The nation's wealth, as reflected in the development and utilization of its natural resources, was substantially increased.

★ AGRICULTURAL AID

More significant than dollar devaluation or public works were the measures adopted by the Roosevelt administration to furnish direct assistance to farmers, businessmen and industrial workers. The Agricultural Adjustment Administration and the National Recovery Administration were the main pillars of the New Deal recovery program. They also reflected, as did the President's general attitude, a basically nationalistic approach to the whole problem of depression. Tariff reciprocity would later be promoted as a means to stimulate foreign trade, but in 1933 Roosevelt was not interested in the international aspects of the depression problem. He refused at the London Economic Conference in May to agree to either currency stabilization or any international agreement for lowering of tariffs. He concentrated entirely on domestic problems. "I shall favor as a practical policy," he had said in his inaugural address, "the putting of first things first."

The AAA embodied a highly complicated program. It was constantly being modified in practice under the impact of altered circumstances, Supreme Court decisions, and new developments on the agricultural front. There was no end to the shifts and changes in administration. The principal purpose of the original plan, as adopted in May 1933, however, was to raise agricultural prices, and then maintain them on a parity with industrial prices (taking 1909 to 1914 as a base period), through a measure of government control which would restrict production in staple crops. For so limiting their output the farmers would be subsidized through benefit payments derived from taxes levied on all processors of agricultural commodities. Although this meant an economy of scarcity, graphically demonstrated in the subsequent plowing under of cotton and the slaughter of little pigs, no other alternative presented itself. The distribution of surplus crops through government relief, except on a very limited scale, would have undermined the bases of the farm economy in a system of free enterprise. Restricted production appeared to be the only practical way whereby agricultural prices could be increased, the purchasing power of the farmer restored, and some sort of balance reestablished in the nation's economic structure.

The adoption of some such drastic form of agricultural relief could certainly not have been avoided much longer. Roosevelt was thoroughly convinced of the necessity for prompt action in meeting an immediate emergency, and at the same time he realized that the depressed status of agriculture presented long-range problems of even deeper significance. Assistance for the nation's farmers had become essential if a way of life, as well as agrarian purchasing power, was to be preserved. "The American farmer, living on his own land," the President stated, "remains our ideal of self-reliance and spiritual balance—the source from which the reservoirs of the nation's strength are constantly renewed." Moreover, it was hoped through the AAA to promote the conservation of natural resources. Marginal land would be taken out of cultivation, crop rotation and the planting of soil-building legumes encouraged, and a program of control instituted which would help to preserve the fertility of farming areas for the long future.

Something like 10,000,000 acres of land were taken out of production under this system in 1933, but more intensive cultivation of the land actually planted resulted in a much larger harvest than had been anticipated. Definite production quotas were then imposed upon growers of certain staple crops, and due to this procedure and even more to the effect of a severe drought, marketing supplies were the next year greatly reduced. Farm prices rose substantially and by 1936 agricultural cash income for the country as a whole had increased some 50 per cent. The ratio between the prices the farmer received for his crops and the prices he paid for manufactured goods, moreover, showed that he was (on the average) a third better off than he had been four years earlier.

The Supreme Court then broke in on this program, outlawing the first Agricultural Adjustment Act under circumstances to be taken up in another chapter, and various new approaches were tried to gain the same ends. Ultimately, a second Agricultural Act, passed in 1938, provided direct benefit payments for those farmers who agreed to use part of their land for soil-building crops as part of an expanded conservation program, and additional parity payments if they also accepted specified acreage allotments for growing wheat, cotton and other staples. Should overproduction still take place, special marketing controls could be applied with imposition of a penalty tax on all farmers who exceeded their quotas. But this was subject to approval by two-thirds of the growers of the commodities affected. The AAA also undertook to extend commodity loans to provide "an ever normal granary," and set up a system of crop insurance against bad harvests.

Nearly 6,000,000 farmers, whose land represented about three-fourths of all crop lands, participated in this new program, and by the close of the 1930's the total farm income had risen to a figure nearly twice as high as it had been at the opening of the decade. Outstanding farm indebtedness had been reduced by almost a fourth, and farm bankruptcies had declined by over 70 per cent.

The cost to the public, however, remained high. Under the second AAA, all farm payments were drawn out of the general treasury and they amounted to about $500,000,000 annually. Moreover, there was continuing criticism of any program that restricted crops while there were still people in want, and the AAA was also said to be working out primarily to the advantage of the large farmer. The problems of small farmers, southern sharecroppers, and agricultural labor appeared in many instances to have been actually accentuated.

Two things may perhaps be said of the New Deal agricultural program as it had developed prior to the outbreak of World War II. First, need for some form of farm relief, involving subsidies, had been clearly demonstrated, and the Agricultural Adjustment Administration specifically and concretely met this need. Second, constantly changing conditions and the stubborn individualism of the American farmer made agreement on any permanent program highly difficult, if not impossible. There could be no foretelling when the 1930's ended, just what shape or form future agricultural aid might take, but it had become an accepted responsibility of the national government.

★ THE NRA

If there were intimations of immortality in the program of the AAA, the NRA enjoyed but a brief and inglorious life. Seldom has a governmental project been launched with such fanfare or enthusiasm and then passed to oblivion with so few mourners. In June 1933 Roosevelt described its enabling act as "the most important and far reaching legislation ever enacted by the American Congress." Within a year it was being almost universally attacked, and when the Supreme Court gave it the final *coup de grâce* in 1935, even the staunchest adherents of the New Deal breathed a long sigh of relief.

The National Recovery Administration, in whose development representatives of industry had played a major role, with some assistance from labor, in effect shelved the antitrust laws by permitting business to draw up its own codes of self-government and fair competition. All codes, however, were to contain certain restrictive provisions applying to labor. Maximum hours and minimum wages were set up for industrial workers, child labor was abolished, and most importantly, all employees were guaranteed "the right to organize and bargain collectively through representatives of their own choosing."

The underlying purpose of this drastic economic legislation was to aid business by permitting it to brake the downward course of industrial prices through co-operative action, and at the same time encourage employment and maintain consumer purchasing power through enforcement of hour and wage controls. The codes had the force of law and were to be administered by code authorities. The ramifications of the program were immense. Entirely apart from the opposition that in time developed from every quarter—big business, little business, and labor—a basic reason for the NRA's failure was that it attempted to do far too much.

Under the dynamic administration of Hugh S. Johnson, NRA got off to a flying start in the summer of 1933. Over five hundred codes were drawn up, and business appeared to be enthusiastically ready to enter upon this new era of government-fostered industrial co-operation. Parades were held in city after city to dramatize the NRA. Thousands of firms proudly displayed the Blue Eagles formally awarded them as a sign of their acceptance of the codes and their willingness to co-operate in their execution.

The honeymoon was shortlived. Big business made the most of its virtual freedom to fix prices and set up monopoly controls. Little business consequently found itself being squeezed to the wall, and the consuming public saw living costs rapidly rising all along the line. But big business was not entirely happy. Even though mounting industrial profits were getting the larger companies out of the red, they soon grew resentful of the obligations imposed upon them in respect to their dealings with labor. They had little inclination to accept the principle of collective bargaining and see their rising profits whittled away by having to pay higher wages. When the code authorities appeared ready to support what rapidly developed into a powerful industrial counterattack on the unions, organized labor lost faith in the NRA. It became convinced that the guarantees safeguarding the right to organize were illusory and brushed off the entire program as the "National Run Around."

A survey of current operations in May 1934 by a specially appointed review board added further fuel to the fires of popular discontent. Its report officially concluded that the new economic setup was fostering monopoly, bearing down unfairly on small manufacturers and distributors, allowing big business to dictate consumer prices, and promoting industrial unrest. The NRA found itself very much on the defensive. Code provisions were openly violated; the unions increasingly resorted to strikes to uphold labor interests. Hugh Johnson resigned as administrator. There was general confusion, and no denying the impracticability of the entire program. Such lingering doubts as still remained were then completely resolved when in May 1935 the Supreme Court decreed in *Schechter Corporation* v *U.S.*—the famous "sick chicken" case—that the National Industrial Recovery Act was unconstitutional.

The New Deal was later to pick up some of the broken pieces of the NRA through enactment of the National Labor Relations Act and the Fair Labor Standards Act. No attempt would be made, however, to revive the shattered system of business self-government through industrial codes. On the contrary, a new campaign was soon launched to enforce the antitrust laws, with an entirely fresh approach to basic economic problems suggested by the creation of a Temporary National Economic Committee to study monopoly, price fixing, and trade associations.

★ PROGRESS OF RECOVERY

The New Deal recovery program as developed under the impetus of dollar devaluation, expanded public works, agricultural relief, and especially the NRA was a most important undertaking. But in spite of such gains as were recorded, the failure of the capital goods industries to match the advances made by manufacturers of consumer goods, as already noted, provided from the outset a shaky foundation for continued progress. While there were actually to be greater gains in the two years following the collapse of the NRA than had already been made, the sharp recession that set in late in 1937 showed that there was as yet no sound basis for full recovery.

Additional appropriations for public works proved necessary to meet the new emergency in 1937. They once again stimulated production, and economic advance was recorded all along the line, but again not to the extent anticipated. The government was forced to carry the heavy burden of continuing unemployment relief, with an actual increase in the WPA rolls, and federal expenditures once again rose alarmingly. There seemed to be no escaping deficit financing, and the year-by-year failure to balance the budget led to a steady increase in the public debt. Between 1933 and 1939 it nearly doubled, rising to a total of about $42,000,000. Whatever might be said on other counts, indebtedness and unemployment clearly revealed the uncertain nature of such economic recovery as had been attained.

In the meantime the New Deal had long since shifted its ground in certain important respects. While its program for relief and recovery was naturally of continuing and vital importance, Roosevelt had become increasingly concerned with more fundamental adjustments in the economic system designed to provide a stronger basis for national well-being in the long future. After 1935, he placed an increased emphasis upon reform—the regulation of business, protection for organized labor, and social security.

CHAPTER XXIII

Reform and Social Security

★ THE SHIFT TOWARD REFORM

While the shift toward reform—sometimes called the Second New Deal—became particularly pronounced in 1935, legislation looking toward removal of capitalistic abuses and otherwise promoting the interests of the people as a whole had not been neglected even during the Hundred Days. Roosevelt showed his very deep interest in conservation in the AAA, boldly tackled the problem of regulating the security exchanges in urging establishment of the Securities and Exchange Commission, and, in an imaginative approach to the whole problem of control of water and power resources, gave his support to the many-sided TVA. Nevertheless, it was not until he had been in office for two years that he really came to grips with the need for permanent readjustments in the economic system.

The collapse of the NRA, with its reliance upon business co-operation, was a primary cause for this new attitude. Since the more conservative policy that the original recovery program represented had not paid off, Roosevelt was compelled by circumstance to seek a fresh approach to the unsolved problems still facing the country. Political pressures from the left, which could not be ignored, were also building up. In his annual message to Congress in January 1935 the President strongly asserted that reform was inseparable from recovery and that the long-term goal of the New Deal was a greater measure of social justice.

The population was suffering from grave inequalities, Roosevelt declared, and for all the measures that had been taken to combat the depression, these inequalities had not been eliminated. "In spite of our efforts and in spite of our talk, we have not weeded out the overprivileged and we have not effectively lifted up the underprivileged." He called upon the country to look toward the longer future and strongly reiterated that the New Deal sought "the security of the men, women, and children of the Nation."

The reform program, as gradually developed, had many facets. Conservation was increasingly stressed as part of the agricultural aid program, with a new Resettlement Administration undertaking to remove families from unproductive marginal lands which could then be set aside as grazing ranges, forest territory, or wildlife preserves. The WPA strongly emphasized social and economic factors in coping with unemployment and played a significant role in promoting education, broadening the people's recreational opportunities, and otherwise contributing to the general welfare.

The WPA, indeed, had a significant cultural impact on the life of the entire nation. The encouragement given students to carry on their work through college and postgraduate courses helped to make education more generally available, with an upward trend in university enrollments. As already noted, the aid given writers, painters, sculptors, and musicians had an effect that outlasted the WPA projects themselves. The new awareness of the American scene and of the American past, so greatly stimulated when unemployed writers and artists turned to native subjects, had profound psychological implications for the American people as a whole.

The funds made available for the WPA and the PWA were also drawn upon to further the slum clearance and low-cost housing projects which the New Deal consistently tried to develop. Just as agricultural reform envisioned better living conditions for farmers, these undertakings had as their goal a higher standard of living for industrial workers. When progress lagged under existing agencies, a United States Housing Authority was set up in 1937 with a substantial borrowing authority, ultimately totaling $1,600,000,000, to provide "decent, safe, and sanitary dwellings for families of low income."

The reform impetus also led to a renewed assault upon the citadels of big business and high finance in order to break up monopolistic controls and bring about a more equitable distribution of income. Antitrust activities were resumed by the Department of Justice, public utility holding corporations were subjected to regulation through the strongly contested Holding Company Act of 1935, and firms and individuals with excessively high incomes were penalized by a new wealth tax, currently described as a "soak the rich" program.

Though the various moves were all significant, they were in no instance entirely successful. The AAA and the WPA were more effective in providing relief than in assuring permanent rehabilitation; low-cost housing developed very slowly, and the new income taxes met such strong opposition that the rates were materially scaled down. Where the New Deal reform program proved to be far more effective was in another series of measures renewing and extending the safeguards for the nation's workers that had first been written into the National Industrial Recovery Act, and in new legislation setting up a comprehensive, nationwide system of social security.

The laws guaranteeing labor's right to organize, establishing floors under wages and ceilings over hours, providing unemployment insurance and old-age pensions stand out conspicuously (together with TVA) as the New Deal's most lasting achievements. While they left the system of private enterprise intact, they substantially altered the entire structure of the national economy.

What such legislation, together with the AAA and the WPA, most clearly demonstrated was the complete abandonment of the old concept of the laissez faire state, which at least in theory postulated a governmental hands-off policy in the economic sphere, and acceptance of the new idea of a social welfare state wherein government assumed responsibility for promoting the well-being of the people as a whole. The origins of such activities may of course be traced back to the beginnings of the Republic. They had received an important impetus during the Progressive era and were further advanced under Hoover. The New Deal was prepared, however, to go much further than had ever before been contemplated in adopting a social security philosophy and implementing it through federal legislation.

★ AN ECONOMIC BILL OF RIGHTS

If the function of government in an earlier day had been primarily, if not exclusively, the protection of political rights, the New Deal argument ran, there could no longer be any escaping the obligation to safeguard economic rights. The twentieth-century citizen found his actual liberty far more gravely endangered by business domination, monopoly, and economic forces beyond his control than by any governmental encroachments on his freedom of action. If he were to realize his right not only to life and liberty but to the pursuit of happiness, he needed protection which only the national government could offer.

Roosevelt had first suggested this theory when he called in 1932 for a new economic constitutional order. He developed it much more explicitly twelve years later when in the midst of war, he cogently set forth a specific Economic Bill of Rights as a new basis for national security and prosperity. As he was to outline these rights to Congress in January 1944, they embraced:

The right of a useful and remunerative job in the industries, or shops or farms or mines of the nation;

The right to earn enough to provide adequate food and clothing and recreation;

The right of every farmer to raise and sell his products at a return which will give him and his family a decent living;

The right of every business man, large and small, to trade in an atmosphere of freedom from unfair competition and domination by monopolies at home or abroad;

The right of every family to a decent home;

The right to adequate medical care and the opportunity to achieve and enjoy good health;

The right to adequate protection from the economic fears of old age, sickness, accident and unemployment;

The right to a good education.

The attempt to carry out this program was attacked from its first conception. The New Deal was not only charged with seeking to create a welfare state that would undermine the entire system of private enterprise, but with betraying the fundamental ideas of American democracy. In line with his earlier statements, former President Hoover solemnly declared in 1936:

In the last campaign we charged these men with the intention to introduce these foreign creeds of Regimentation, Socialism and Fascism into America. They denied it. No proof is needed after three years of these attempts at so-called Planned Economy; this government in business; this breaking down of constitutional safeguards; this reduction of Congress to a rubber stamp; this substitution of personal government of men for government of laws; and these attacks upon the Constitution.

Roosevelt stuck to his guns. Far from borrowing from foreign creeds, he stated, the New Deal was actually seeking "a fulfillment of old and tested American ideals." He accepted what he considered the imperative need to adjust and adapt national policies to the new circumstances of twentieth-century life. He stoutly declared, "We are not going to turn back the clock."

★ TVA

The Tennessee Valley Authority, which was first set up in 1933, falls only partly within the general framework of the reform program. Like so many undertakings during this period it was compounded of those three original New Deal aims—recovery, relief, *and* reform. It was hoped that the TVA would stimulate recovery in the Tennessee Valley and afford some measure of practical relief for its inhabitants; a more fundamental objective, however, was the rejuvenation of the entire area through government control and utilization of its water-power resources. While TVA was a regional project, its implications as a bold experiment in social planning were nationwide.

The program was the end result of those persistent efforts Senator Norris of Nebraska had been making for over a decade to establish government ownership and operation of the wartime nitrate plant at Muscle Shoals. While Hoover's emphatic veto of the Norris-sponsored measure that finally passed Congress had underscored the conservative approach to control of water power, Roosevelt's willingness to sponsor such a program illustrates the completely different attitude of the New Deal.

The TVA was a federal agency set up to build a series of great dams and then produce, distribute, and sell electric power from the impounded waters of the Tennessee River. But this only suggested the broad scope of its activities. It was concerned with flood control, the irrigation of submarginal lands, reforestation, the prevention of erosion, and the production of fertilizers as contemplated in the original Muscle Shoals project. It also undertook to promote rural electrification, land improvement, low-cost housing, and public recreation. As President Roosevelt stated in explaining a project that covered an area of 40,000 square miles embracing parts of seven states:

> What we are doing there, is taking a watershed with about three and a half million people in it, almost all of them rural, and we are trying to make a different type of citizen out of them from what they would be under their present conditions. . . . TVA is primarily intended to change and improve the standards of living of the people of that valley.

The TVA was launched on this ambitious program with broad authority and the allocation of large funds from the Public Works Administration. It built the contemplated dams on the Tennessee River (ultimately twenty), constructed power stations, extended transmission lines throughout the valley, and by providing cheap electricity for both farm and household uses, went far toward achieving the aims Roosevelt had set forth. It also made power available for new industrial undertakings which became of outstanding importance during later war years. The epochal developments at Oak Ridge that were to lead to the atomic bomb might not have been possible without TVA water power.

Private industry could not have undertaken this far-reaching program whose total costs had mounted by the mid-1950's to over a billion dollars. Only the national government was able to carry through plans that called for such a huge investment, embraced so large an area, crossed state lines, and had so many ramifications. The TVA was to be vigorously criticized, reflecting the opposition that Hoover had originally voiced, and it became involved in a continuing quarrel with the private utility industry. In the sale of its own power a "yardstick" was set up for the regulation of electric rates in other areas, and this yardstick was attacked as entirely unreasonable in view of the federal agency's freedom from taxation. However, TVA was more generally judged on the basis of its general services to the community. As time advanced, its over-all success was increasingly acknowledged. It has been called "the greatest peacetime achievement of twentieth-century America."

This success was in considerable measure due to the policies followed by its first director, David E. Lilienthal, whose approach was to avoid overcentralization, and by following democratic methods, to invite the support and the participation of the people of the Tennessee Valley themselves. It was his constant aim to develop the TVA on a "grass roots" basis. His concept of the project as putting a river to work, with community co-operation all along the line, was eloquently set forth in a ten-year report to the public which he significantly entitled, *Democracy on the March.*

Roosevelt's attempt to establish comparable agencies to develop power resources in other river valleys, most notably in the Missouri Valley, was nevertheless combatted successfully by public utility and other business interests. TVA stood alone as a remarkable experiment in over-all planning for community welfare.

★ THE SOCIAL SECURITY ACT

A far more general program than that of the Tennessee Valley Authority was outlined in the Social Security Act. This epochal measure, becoming law in August 1935 was perhaps more than any other New Deal project dear to Roosevelt's heart. He considered it "the cornerstone of his administration," and his sustained interest, more than any other single factor, accounted for its adoption. "In his own mind," one of his colleagues has written, "it was *his* program."

Social security in the form of old-age and unemployment insurance was not of course a new idea; it had long since been accepted in many European countries. But the United States had lagged far behind both Great Britain and Germany in making such an adjustment to the new conditions of industrial society. The principles of laissez faire had too strong a hold. Even the American Federation of Labor, under the conservative leadership of Samuel Gompers and William Green, for long opposed unemployment insurance for fear of its effects on union organization. The depression accentuated the need for provision for the unemployed, however, and the whole concept of social security as a governmental obligation rapidly gained both labor and popular support.

Roosevelt initiated economic studies of the problem early in 1933, talked often with his advisers upon the need for "cradle to the grave" insurance (a phrase perhaps first used by Edward Bellamy in the 1880's), and finally set up among his cabinet members a Committee on Economic Security to prepare the necessary legislation. The bill this committee drew up was placed upon his "must list," and after long debate, considerable delay, and extensive amendment, Congress finally accepted it.

There were three major parts to the Social Security Act as adopted in 1935. The first provided for unemployment compensation to be handled through the states. The federal government placed a tax on all payrolls, and then agreed to remit 90 per cent of the revenue to the states upon their adoption of compensation programs that met federal standards. The second section set up an old-age pension scheme that was directly administered from Washington, with funds made available through equal taxes upon both employers and employees. Finally, aid to certain special categories of the needy was provided through federal grants to the states. These categories included the aged who were ineligible for pensions, the blind, the crippled and disabled, and dependent children. In addition, there were special grants to the states for child health services, rehabilitation of the disabled, and general public health.

The Social Security Act was a belated gesture in the light of the depression. It was still inadequate in some respects in meeting the nation's needs, for its benefits were limited and they did not extend to the entire labor force. The adoption of the program it embodied was, nevertheless, a tremendously significant milestone in the economic and social progress of the United States. And in spite of inevitable diehard opposition to any such new departure, and much sound criticism of certain administrative shortcomings, there was never any question of the popular acceptance of social security. From the time of passage of the act the only question asked was how the program could be most effectively administered and in what ways its benefits could be reasonably extended. Even the Republicans were driven to acknowledge that "society has an obligation to promote the security of the people, by affording some measure of protection against involuntary unemployment and dependency in old age," and since 1936 they have consistently held this principle.

Two basic considerations led to what became universal support for social security. The first was a humanitarian sense of obligation to provide for the unemployed as victims of circumstances beyond their control; and the second, the immense importance of sustaining purchasing power by giving the unemployed some income in times of future depression. Roosevelt strongly emphasized the latter consideration in signing an act which he declared would flatten out the peaks and valleys of inflation and deflation. "It is, in short," he stated, "a law that will take care of human needs and at the same time provide for the United States an economic structure of vastly greater soundness."

★ THE WAGNER ACT

Even before the National Industrial Recovery Act was declared unconstitutional, a strong movement was underway to provide more explicit guarantees for labor's right to organize and bargain collectively than had been incorporated in the industrial codes. The Supreme Court decision, completely removing the NRA safeguards for labor, gave a final and decisive push to the newly proposed legislation. The National Labor Relations Act—better known as the Wagner Act—became law on July 5, 1935. Its enactment was a watershed in the history of organized labor. Heretofore, government had at best tolerated the unions; now it actively encouraged them. In the general area of industrial relations the New Deal was heavily weighting the scales in favor of organized labor.

The Wagner Act had no place in Roosevelt's original program. He had not particularly liked its implications when it was first described to him. The collapse of the NRA, however, meant that something had to be done to protect labor's rights, and Raymond Moley has reported that in 1935 the President "flung his arms open" to embrace Senator Wagner's bill. Moreover, he continued to support it even though the new law was acknowledgedly onesided. "By preventing practices which tend to destroy the independence of labor," Roosevelt said in reference to the prohibition of certain anti-union policies formerly followed by industry, "it seeks, for every worker within its scope, that freedom of choice and action which is justly his."

The Norris-La Guardia Act, passed by a Democratic Congress at the close of Hoover's administration, had first given expression to what was to become the new governmental attitude toward labor. It specifically outlawed both yellow dog contracts and the use of injunctions in industrial disputes, and its preamble stated that the worker should have full freedom to organize and bargain collectively without interference, restraint or coercion from his employer. The latter right had then been incorporated in the industrial codes of the short-lived NRA. It was now explicitly reaffirmed in the Wagner Act with emphatic proscription of those "unfair" practices whereby employers might still try to block union activities.

The new law prohibited them from restraining or coercing their employees in the exercise of their rights, from seeking to dominate any labor organization by financial support, from encouraging or discouraging union membership by discrimination in hiring and firing, and from refusing to bargain collectively. In still further encouragement of unions it provided that the representatives chosen for collective bargaining by a majority of the workers in any appropriate unit, whether an employer, craft, or plant unit, were to have exclusive bargaining powers for all employees in that unit.

A National Labor Relations Board was set up to administer the law. It had sole authority to determine the appropriate bargaining unit in every case at issue, and to supervise the elections in which the employees chose their representatives. It was empowered to hear complaints of unfair employer practices and to issue "cease and desist" orders where such action was found to be justified. The NLRB was entirely concerned with the practical encouragement of collective bargaining; it had nothing to do with the substance of industrial disputes or settlement of strikes.

The importance of the Wagner Act was universally recognized and no other New Deal measure awoke more powerful opposition. Its one-sidedness was defended as redressing a balance that had always been in favor of management, but the business community vehemently condemned such restraints upon the employer without any corresponding restraints upon unions. While there was widespread public sympathy for labor's aspirations at this time, and the Wagner Act may be said to have won general popular approval, business and industry could never accept the New Deal's labor program. For a long time many employers stubbornly refused to obey the law on the ground that it was unconstitutional, and they continued to fight union organization and collective bargaining with every weapon at their disposal. Even when the Supreme Court upheld the Wagner Act, there was little let-up in the attacks made upon it. The demand for at least revision of the law was eventually to gain wide support. It finally led in 1947, under circumstances to be discussed later, to passage of the Taft-Hartley Act, with its prohibition of certain unfair union practices to compensate for the bans already imposed upon unfair employer practices.

In spite of all criticism and subsequent revisions, the Wagner Act had once and for all established the basic principle of governmental responsibility in industrial relations. The need for intervention in the public interest was now no longer disputed. There was to be no return to the day when government stood completely aside until open industrial warfare forced it into action to maintain law and order. A responsibility to support collective bargaining as a part of the nation's economic structure was fully accepted in the hope that such a policy would successfully promote labor peace.

★ WAGE AND HOUR LEGISLATION

While the Wagner Act had been originally passed in order to re-establish the safeguards for union labor thrown out by collapse of the NRA, Roosevelt was also concerned with the wage and hour legislation that had also been a part of this early recovery measure. He strongly urged passage of a new law that would sustain wages and spread employment as a means of sustaining purchasing power, and in the face of very considerable opposition, he repeatedly called upon Congress for action. To a special session in November 1937 he said:

> I believe that the country as a whole recognizes the need for congressional action if we are to maintain wage increases and the purchasing power of the nation against recessive factors in the general industrial situation. The exploitation of child labor and the undercutting of wages and the stretching of the hours of the poorest paid workers in periods of business recession has a serious effect on buying power. . . . What does the country ultimately gain if we encourage businessmen to enlarge the capacity of American industry to produce unless we see to it that the income of our working population actually expands sufficiently to create markets to absorb that increased production?

There was a good deal of delay, with the redrafting of the original administration bill many times to meet objections from both industry and labor, before Congress acted. But the next summer—July 1938—at last saw passage of the Fair Labor Standards Act. It established for all employees in trade or industry affecting interstate commerce a minimum wage of twenty-five cents an hour, rising to forty cents in seven years; and a maximum forty-four-hour week, to be reduced within three years to forty hours. The new bill also included prohibition of the labor of children under sixteen in industries whose products entered into interstate commerce.

Perhaps no other New Deal measure went further in breaking down the old concepts of laissez faire. The national government, supplementing its legislative support of collective bargaining, had moved on to direct control of wages and hours. While the states had started upon such a path during the Progressive era, in the interest of public health and morals, there would have been no support for such federal legislation from any quarter before the depression. Labor was opposed to even state minimum wage laws in the 1920's. The federal law was now generally approved as an economic measure essential for the maintenance of consumer purchasing power as well as for being highly beneficial to the workers themselves.

★ THE NEW ECONOMIC ORDER

Those aspects of the New Deal program that related primarily to relief and recovery were temporary in nature. They were designed to meet the emergency of the depression and did so with varying but never entirely complete success. Only the demands of a wartime economy, as previously noted, created the nationwide prosperity that eluded the Roosevelt administrations throughout the 1930's. The permanent achievements of the New Deal were in the field of reform. They provided the basis for the expanded functions of government which later administrations could hardly fail to accept, however much they might try to modify practice and application.

The growth of federal agencies is perhaps the most significant key to what was happening during the 1930's, furnishing telling evidence of the responsibilities newly assumed in promoting the welfare state. Prior to the depression the Interstate Commerce Commission, the Federal Trade Commission, the Federal Power Commission, the Federal Communications Commission, and, in a somewhat different category, the Federal Reserve Board made up what has sometimes been called "the fourth arm of government." To these commissions were added in the days of the New Deal a plethora of agencies whose operations affected almost every phase of national life. The Agricultural Adjustment Administration, the Federal Security Board, the National Labor Relations Board, the United States Housing Authority, the Securities and Exchange Commission, and the Tennessee Valley Authority do not by any means exhaust the list. They merely illustrate a trend which sometimes appeared to have no stopping place.

For better or for worse, a new economic constitutional order had been created under Roosevelt's dynamic leadership. The federal government was intervening, directly or indirectly, in almost every phase of the country's economic activity. Without seeking in any way to undermine private enterprise, Roosevelt stated in his second inaugural address, the New Deal was carrying forward an expansive program "to erect on the old foundations a more enduring structure for the better use of future generations."

A year or two later, when the reform program began to slow down, he again defended New Deal policy and reverted to the idea he had earlier expressed in respect to its role in restoring confidence in democratic capitalism:

> Democracy has disappeared in several other great nations, not because the people of those nations disliked democracy, but because they had grown tired of unemployment and insecurity, of seeing their children hungry while they

sat helpless in the face of government confusion and government weakness through lack of leadership in government. Finally, in desperation, they chose to sacrifice liberty in the hope of getting something to eat. We in America know that our democratic institutions can be preserved and made to work. But in order to preserve them we need . . . to prove that the practical operation of democratic government is equal to the task of protecting the security of the people. . . . The people of America are in agreement in defending their liberties at any cost, and the first line of that defense lies in the protection of economic security.

This statement came directly to grips with that basic issue which set apart those New Dealers and anti-New Dealers who were trying to look beyond their own immediate political or economic interests. If it be admitted that there can be neither absolute liberty nor absolute security in the modern world, there is a point where individual freedom may be safely sacrificed—indeed, must be sacrificed—to assure that degree of security without which liberty is a meaningless fiction. "Necessitous men are not free men." The opponents of the New Deal would continue to believe that the restrictions imposed upon individual freedom of action by legislation governing agricultural production, labor organization, the regulation of business, and social security would ultimately lead to the destruction of all freedom. They were obsessed with the idea that the nation was embarked "on the road to serfdom." New Dealers held no less firmly to the conviction that so long as the American people maintained democratic control over their government, the policy represented by Roosevelt's Economic Bill of Rights would protect rather than endanger their liberties. Here lay the real challenge of the times in a world where security and liberty had become two facets of the basic human need for self-development and the good life.

"The only sure bulwark of continuing liberty," Roosevelt said, "is a government strong enough to protect the interests of the people, and a people strong enough and well informed enough to maintain its sovereign control over its government."

CHAPTER XXIV

The Rise of Labor

★ LABOR AND THE NRA

While the New Deal had a vivifying influence on every segment of the national economy and was to stimulate a new feeling of social consciousness among the people as a whole, nowhere was its effect greater than on American labor. When Roosevelt was inaugurated in 1933, less than 3,000,000 workers were union members and the influence of organized labor was almost nil. A decade later, total union membership exceeded 12,000,000. More important than numbers, the employees in the great mass production industries had been organized for the first time. The new industrial unions were forging ahead as the C.I.O. came to rival the A.F. of L. There was a dynamic drive about the labor movement that was to have a profound influence on the national economy and on national politics.

On the eve of Roosevelt's election there had been little evidence of the powerful forces that were to be let loose by the sympathetic attitude of the New Deal. "Today labor stands patient and hopeful," the Cleveland *Plain Dealer* commented during the grim summer of 1932. "Never has there been a period of depression so free from labor strife. Unemployment has harassed it. Closed factories have taken away its livelihood. But, in the face of enormous hardship, labor has showed its good citizenship and sturdy American stamina. Labor deserves a salute." While it may well be doubted that labor was altogether satisfied with this generous salute in place of jobs and satisfactory wages, the generally passive attitude of the workers was a notable phenomenon of the dire days of depression.

The promise of protection for organized labor activity first contained in the National Industrial Recovery Act, upon which the A.F. of L. leadership had always vigorously insisted, immediately and drastically changed the entire situation. Labor organizers promptly took up the task of restoring moribund locals, setting up new unions, and moving into territory from which they had heretofore been barred. "Millions of workers throughout the nation," William Green declared, "stood up for the first time in their lives to receive their charter of industrial freedom." When the American Federation of Labor met at its annual convention in the autumn of 1933, the announcement was made that union membership had already increased by 1,500,000, making up the losses of the past decade. A total of 4,000,000 would soon be raised to 10,000,000, the A.F. of L. chieftain further stated, and he confidently forecast an eventual figure of 25,000,000.

Large numbers of the new recruits to the ranks of organized labor came from the mass production industries—100,000 in automobiles, 90,000 in steel, 90,000 in lumber yards and sawmills, and 60,000 in rubber. The A.F. of L. chartered hundreds of so-called federal unions among these industrial workers. The whole set-up of organized labor appeared to be changing as government for the first time actually encouraged the formation of unions and the use of collective bargaining.

But the mounting opposition of industry to this program soon began to make itself felt. The *Commercial and Financial Chronicle* warned of the danger of organized labor becoming so powerful as to threaten the State; the *Iron Age* referred alarmedly to "collective bludgeoning," and the magazine *Steel* called upon industry to uphold the Open Shop. In spite of the clear intent of the new legislation, many employers refused to deal with the new unions, and when the workers then resorted to strikes to protect their rights, every weapon in the industrial armory was used in vigorous counterattack. Subsequent disclosures by a Senate civil liberties committee, headed by Senator Robert M. La Follette, Jr., of Wisconsin, revealed that between 1933 and 1937, more than 2,500 corporations were hiring labor spies, bringing in strikebreakers, and furnishing plant management with machine guns, rifles, revolvers, ammunition, and tear gas equipment. The Republic Steel Corporation and the Youngstown Sheet and Tube Company alone were reported to have amassed "adequate equipment for a small war."

It was in the midst of this growing industrial unrest that the NIRA was declared unconstitutional and labor militantly insisted upon the more comprehensive safeguards of what was to become the Wagner Act. "I do not mind telling you," Green truculently informed a congressional committee, "that the spirit of the workers in America has been aroused. They are going to find a way to bargain collectively. . . . Labor must have its place in the sun." Even after the new bill became law, however, the fight for recognition of labor's rights continued. A wave of strikes came to a dismaying peak in 1937 as industry refused to accept its obligations under the Wagner Act on the ground that it was unconstitutional.

★ INDUSTRIAL UNIONISM

In the meantime unexpected problems had developed within the ranks of labor itself. The great burst of activity in the mass production industries had subsided, not only because of management's aggressive counterattack but as a result of an inherent weakness in labor policy. The A.F. of L. was highly reluctant to encourage industrial unionism —the policy of bringing all workers in a single industry into one union —even though this form of organization was the only practical approach to unionizing employees in such industries as steel or automobiles or rubber. A conservative leadership brought up on the theory and practice of craft unionism, and also fearful of the influence of a powerful group of new industrial unions on their own position in the A.F. of L. hierarchy, did not want to grant new charters for the mass production workers. They took the position that all wage earners should be brought into "the respective national and international unions where jurisdiction has been established."

A militant minority within the A.F. of L. combatted this traditional approach to unionization and demanded more vigorous action. In spite of half-way promises, the old-line leadership did not change its policies. When the Federation met at its annual convention in 1935, the insurgents again insisted bluntly that only industrial unionism could meet the needs of the great bulk of unskilled workers, but after a stormy debate the majority rejected their demands. The proponents of craft unionism remained in full control, with adoption of a resolution declaring it to be a primary obligation of the A.F. of L. "to protect the jurisdictional rights of all trade unions organized upon craft lines."

The industrial unionists refused to accept this decision. They set up their own Committee for Industrial Organization and declared their intention to launch an independent campaign of unionization in the mass production industries. The executive committee of the A.F. of L. promptly called for the dissolution of this committee, castigating its activities as promoting dual unionism and fomenting insurrection within labor's ranks. When its order was ignored, the executive committee suspended the ten unions that had become affiliated with the C.I.O.

The angry controversy continued throughout 1936, without any healing of the breach in labor's ranks, and the A.F. of L. finally took the decisive step of permanently expelling the dissident unions. Their response was to press even more intensively their independent organizing drive, and early in 1938 all remaining ties with the A.F. of L. were broken when the original C.I.O. was transformed into a permanent Congress of Industrial Organizations. With every effort at conciliation and peace failing, the labor movement was divided into two opposing camps.

★ JOHN L. LEWIS

The leader of the insurgents was John L. Lewis, head of the United Mine Workers, and his outstanding lieutenants were such men as Charles P. Howard of the Typographical Union, Sidney Hillman of the Amalgamated Clothing Workers, David Dubinsky of the International Ladies' Garment Workers, and Philip Murray, second in command of the United Mine Workers. These men were able and militant unionists, but Lewis stood out as the dominating figure in the C.I.O. Aggressive, determined, ruthless, he was to loom more importantly on the national stage in coming years than any other public figure except President Roosevelt. He belligerently attacked the world of industry ("They are striking me hip and thigh . . . right merrily shall I return their blows"); assailed no less strongly his foes within labor's own ranks, and he was in time to challenge the government itself in angry defiance of any authority other than his own.

Lewis performed an immense service for organized labor in building up the strength of the C.I.O. That could no more be gainsaid than could his contribution to the welfare of his own miners through his stubborn defense of their interests on all and every occasion. However, his overweening personal ambition, dictatorial attitude, and scornful dismissal of public opinion during the coal strikes of war days were a disheartening denial of the constructive leadership that had been the promise of his early career.

Lewis was always a contradictory figure. "What makes me tick?" he was once reported asking. "Is it power I am after, or am I a Saint Francis in disguise, or what?" Public opinion became increasingly convinced that power was the answer to this question. His melodramatic attitude ("My life is but a stage," he once said), and a bull-dog aggressiveness emphasized by his glowering scowl, bushy eyebrows, and jutting jaw at least gave little support to the idea that he might be a Saint Francis.

Lewis had come to the crucial convention of the A.F. of L. in 1935 determined on action. He eloquently called upon the delegates to heed the cry from Macedonia of their less fortunate co-workers in the mass production industries. He declared that industrial unionism would make the federation into the greatest instrument that had ever been forged to befriend the cause of humanity. Should this great opportunity be lost, Lewis somberly warned the convention in the flowery language he always affected, "high wassail will prevail at the banquet tables of the mighty." When the final vote went against his proposals for industrial unionism, Lewis threw himself determinedly into the formation of the C.I.O. and became the driving force behind its organizing campaigns.

★ THE LITTLE STEEL STRIKE

The C.I.O. chose the steel industry, so long an apparently unassailable redoubt of the anti-union forces, as the first objective of its attack. With funds made available by the unions which had seceded—or had been expelled—from the A.F. of L., it sent hundreds of organizers into the mills to persuade the employees to join the Steel Workers' Organizing Committee, later to become the United Steelworkers. In an industry where wages still fell as low as some $560 a year, the response to this drive was immediate. By the close of 1936 membership in the new union was already more than 100,000. The industry fought back aggressively, inserting full-page advertisements in newspapers throughout the country declaring that communist influences were at work in the C.I.O., but the appeal of the new union was well-nigh irresistible.

Lewis warned big business that there could be no withstanding the C.I.O. campaign to organize not only the steel workers but all industrial workers:

> Let him who will, be he economic tyrant or sordid mercenary, pit his strength against this mighty upsurge of human sentiment now being crystallized in the hearts of thirty million workers who clamor for the establishment of industrial democracy and for participation in its tangible fruits. He is a madman or a fool who believes that this river of human sentiment . . . can be dammed or impounded by the erection of arbitrary barriers of restraint.

The stage appeared set for a nationwide steel strike, when suddenly and unexpectedly there came a joint announcement from the C.I.O. chieftain and the board chairman of United States Steel that the steel workers' union had been recognized and an agreement reached which provided for a 10 per cent wage increase and a forty-hour week. "Big Steel" had dramatically surrendered. A corporation that had adamantly refused throughout its history to accept collective bargaining now acknowledged without further struggle the rising power of industrial unionism and undertook to come to terms with it.

This sensational victory for the C.I.O. was not to be immediately carried through for the industry as a whole. While scores of small independent companies promptly followed the lead of "Big Steel," a group collectively known as "Little Steel"—Republic, Youngstown Sheet and Tube, Inland, and Bethlehem—stubbornly refused any concessions whatsoever to the triumphant steel union. The latter's answer was to call a strike in the spring of 1937, and some 75,000 workers walked out of the plants of "Little Steel." The companies (except for Inland Steel) immediately called in strikebreakers, protecting them with special guards, and when the workers fought to maintain their picket lines, violence flared in a score of steel towns in Pennsylvania, Ohio, and Illinois.

The bloodiest clash occurred in South Chicago on Memorial Day. Without provocation—as later revealed by moving pictures—the police opened fire on a peaceful march of some three hundred pickets. The workers frantically fled for cover, leaving ten of their number dead on the street and over a hundred injured. Twenty-two police were also hurt in the melee, but not one suffered a critical injury.

This "Memorial Day Massacre" awoke widespread public sympathy for the strikers, but local sentiment in the closely controlled steel towns remained strongly against them. They could make no headway in the face of organized propaganda and organized force. In spite of recognition by "Big Steel," the workers were not yet in a position to hold out against the anti-union companies. The strike was broken. It was not until four years later in 1941 that "Little Steel" was finally compelled through the intervention of the National Labor Relations Board to recognize the union and accept collective bargaining. By then the entire industry had been organized, and the membership of the United Steelworkers had grown to 600,000.

★ THE AUTO WORKERS' STRIKE

Before the outbreak of the "Little Steel" strike, equally violent developments had taken place in the automobile industry. The C.I.O. was no less anxious to organize the auto workers than workers in the steel mills, and throughout 1936 it had been busily engaged in building up the strength of the United Automobile Workers, a small union that had broken its A.F. of L. affiliations to join the C.I.O. The giants of the automobile industry—General Motors, Chrysler, and Ford—did not have any intention of accepting collective bargaining, the Wagner Act notwithstanding, and the battle lines were drawn. An open struggle was precipitated when General Motors flatly refused to deal with the union on any basis whatsoever. The workers in its plants, over 100,000 strong, went out on strike in January 1937.

There was something new about this strike. In the General Motors plants at Flint, Michigan, the employees resorted to the sit-down. They did not walk out; they remained at their work benches. The management declared that this move was an unlawful invasion of property rights and called upon local authorities to eject the men from the plants by force. The workers refused to budge. With their friends and families bringing in food and supplies, they were prepared to sit out the strike until management capitulated to their demands.

When the police tried to rush one plant, they were met by such a hail of coffee mugs, pop bottles, iron bolts, and automobile door hinges that they were forced to beat a hasty retreat. Returning to the attack with tear gas bombs, they were once again repulsed as the strikers turned the plant fire hoses against them. The victory won in what the workers joyfully called "the battle of the running bulls" strengthened the determination of the beleaguered strikers to hold the fort no matter what happened.

As the struggle dragged on under these dramatic circumstances, General Motors obtained a court order for the ejection of the strikers as trespassers, and called upon Governor Murphy of Michigan to order the state militia to clear the plants. "We the workers," the strike leaders promptly wired Murphy, "have carried on a stay-in strike over a month to make General Motors Corporation obey the law and engage in collective bargaining. . . . Unarmed as we are, the introduction of the militia, sheriffs or police with murderous weapons will mean a bloodbath of unarmed workers. . . . We have decided to stay in the plant."

As the zero hour for the execution of the court order approached, the sit-downers barricaded the factories, and outside the company grounds thousands of sympathetic workers and members of women's emergency brigades milled about as sound trucks blared forth "Solidarity Forever."

Governor Murphy refused to send the militia into action. Unwilling to make a move that might well have caused widespread violence if not social revolt, he summoned officials of General Motors and the C.I.O. to Detroit, and with the full support of President Roosevelt insisted upon negotiations. After an agonizing delay, success finally crowned his efforts. General Motors agreed to recognize the United Automobile Workers as the bargaining agent for its members—although not for all company employees—and to suspend legal action against the union. It was not a complete victory for the U.A.W., but a breach had been successfully made in another powerful anti-union stronghold. The first step had been taken toward establishing collective bargaining throughout the whole automobile industry. The workers were soon to win a comparable victory in their dealings with Chrysler, and while Ford was to hold out for another four years, even this company had eventually to recognize the growing power of organized labor.

★ FURTHER C.I.O. GAINS

The successful use of the sit-down by General Motors employees brought on a flood of comparable C.I.O. strikes in the spring and summer of

1937. Hundreds of thousands of men and women in the new unions—from rubber workers to department store clerks, from electricians to janitors—sat down on the job and enthusiastically sang the new song of labor revolt:

> When they tie the can to a union man,
> Sit down! Sit down!
> When they give him the sack, they'll take him back,
> Sit down! Sit down!
>
> When the speed-up comes, just twiddle your thumbs,
> Sit down! Sit down!
> When the boss won't talk, don't take a walk,
> Sit down! Sit down!

These strikes created nationwide alarm. Responsible labor no less than industry opposed the use of a weapon which invaded property rights and held out such a dangerous threat of violence. Upton Sinclair commented happily that "for seventy-five years big business has been sitting down on the American people, and now I am delighted to see the process reversed." Public opinion, however, never condoned a strike technique that court decisions ultimately decreed to be unlawful trespass. Its only possible justification was that in refusing to obey the Wagner Act, industry had made the first move in violating the law and labor was therefore entitled to use comparable tactics. When the Supreme Court upheld the constitutionality of the Wagner Act and the National Labor Relations Board began to enforce compliance with its provisions, this somewhat dubious argument lost all validity and labor abandoned the sit-down strike completely.

Through its strenuous organizing activity in steel, automobiles, rubber, textiles, and other mass production industries, the C.I.O. had built up by the close of 1937 a total membership of 3,700,000. It had successfully breasted the ramparts that had previously blocked the organization of the great mass of unskilled workers and given a new dynamic force to the entire labor movement. It had shattered the lines of the traditional craft unionism upheld by the A.F. of L., and also demonstrated a much broader organizing approach by welcoming to its ranks, without discrimination, all classes of labor—immigrants, Negroes, and women.

The success of the C.I.O. soon led to more aggressive activity on the part of the A.F. of L. The latter organization was forced to recognize the necessity of approaching the unionization of workers in the mass production industries from a new direction. Thousands of unskilled workers were now admitted into such multiple-craft or semi-industrial A.F. of L. unions as the machinists, boilermakers, meat cutters, restaurant employees, teamsters, and common laborers. Going even further along the road plotted by the C.I.O., the federation also began granting charters to completely new industrial unions. In spite of the defections from its ranks when the C.I.O. was first organized, the A.F. of L. consequently succeeded in making up its losses and by 1937 its membership of 3,400,000 was only slightly under that of its rival. With the encouragement of government protection through the Wagner Act, a veritable revolution had taken place in labor's ranks. Both the A.F. of L. and the C.I.O. would continue to drive ahead with steady membership gains for the next ten years.

Frequent attempts were made to bring the two organizations together. President Roosevelt urged peace negotiations on several occasions, and they were periodically undertaken. But while the original cause for disagreement had largely disappeared, with the A.F. of L. compelled to accept the validity of industrial unionism, and the C.I.O. in its turn recognizing that in some instances craft unionism was more effective, no progress was made during these years in getting together. The mutual rivalries engendered at the time of split continued to bar any reconciliation.

In the heat of the controversy in 1935 and 1936, Green and Lewis had filled the air with noisy charges and countercharges. The A.F. of L. president accused his rival of disrupting the entire labor movement to establish his own dictatorship—"consumed with personal ambition, he gave the lie to the democratic process after it had rejected his leadership." The C.I.O. leader struck back savagely with the charge that the organizing efforts of the federation were twenty-five years of unbroken failure. "Alas, poor Green," Lewis told reporters, "I knew him well. He wishes me to join him in fluttering procrastination, the while intoning *O tempora, O mores!*"

The intralabor battle no longer concerned principles. It had become a struggle for power in union politics, centering about the personal ambitions and personal security of rival labor leaders. There appeared to be no formula that would enable Lewis and Green, to say nothing of the heads of individual unions, to take the steps necessary to bring dual unionism to an end and restore labor unity.

★ LABOR AND POLITICS

A further development growing out of industrial unionism was the broadened interest of organized labor in national politics. While the A.F. of L. clung to its established policy of nonpartisanship, the C.I.O. was prepared to exert all possible political pressure in supporting Roosevelt and the New Deal. Government intervention in the sphere of industrial relations, as represented by the important role of the National Labor Relations Board in supervising union elections and proceeding against unfair employer practices, obviously gave a new importance from the unions' point of view to the maintenance in office of an administration sympathetic with labor's aims and aspirations. The C.I.O. fully recognized this new situation, and also the broader interest of the workers in such aspects of the New Deal program as social security, wage and hour controls, and unemployment relief. John L. Lewis early spoke to this point (although he was later to revert to a more laissez faire attitude) in discussing C.I.O. activity in the mass production industries:

> With the guarantee of the "right to organize," such industries may be unionized, but, on the other hand, better living standards, shorter working hours and improved economic conditions for their members cannot be hoped for unless legislative or other provisions be made for economic planning and for price, production and profit controls. Because of these fundamental conditions, it is obvious to industrial workers that the labor movement must organize and exert itself not only in the economic field but also in the political arena.

Support for Roosevelt and the New Deal was natural under these circumstances. Whatever may have been his original attitude toward organized labor, the President had become increasingly sympathetic with the union cause as time went on, and he had also come to accept labor as a political ally. Stating on one occasion that "collective bargaining must remain the foundation of industrial relations for all time," he declared his intention not only to help labor maintain gains already won, but to seek their further advancement. First through Labor's Non-Partisan League, and then through a special Political Action Committee, the C.I.O. consequently supported Roosevelt in each of his election campaigns and made every effort to swing the labor vote into the Democratic column. The A.F. of L. unions were also drawn to the New Deal, but in this period the federation itself did not declare its official support or work as importantly for Roosevelt as did the C.I.O. It would later more directly follow the political lead of its rival.

A strange incident related to labor political activity was to take place in 1940. John L. Lewis withdrew his support from Roosevelt and unsuccessfully tried to swing the labor vote to the Republican candidate, Wendell L. Willkie. The most valid explanation for this shift in his attitude was thwarted personal ambition. The story is told of Lewis suggesting that as a powerful labor leader, he should have a place on the Democratic ticket as vice-presidential candidate, and then being greatly affronted when Roosevelt made no move to take up his proposal. Whatever actually happened, there was a notable cooling-off in the onetime close relations between Roosevelt and Lewis.

The latter, indeed, would appear to have been harboring well before 1940 a feeling of resentment toward the President growing out of his failure to intervene more directly in the automobile and steel strikes of 1937. Roosevelt had flared out during those critical days with a "plague on both your houses" statement, and the burly chieftain of the C.I.O. was incensed. "It ill behooves one who supped at labor's table and who has been sheltered in labor's house," he said, "to curse with equal fervor and fine impartiality both labor and its adversaries when they become locked in deadly embrace."

By 1940, in any event, the split was complete. Frustrated and ill-tempered, Lewis finally came out with a dramatic statement that Roosevelt's re-election "would be a national evil of the first magnitude." Going even further, he declared that since a Democratic victory at the polls would clearly mean that the members of the C.I.O. had rejected his advice, he would accept such an election result as an expression of lack of confidence in his leadership and retire from the C.I.O. presidency.

On Roosevelt's re-election, Lewis made good his pledge to step down and resigned his post with the C.I.O. His role as a national spokesman for labor, however active he remained as head of the United Mine Workers, would never again be quite what it was in the 1930's. Philip Murray replaced him at the C.I.O., and soon quarreling with his successor as he had formerly quarreled with the A.F. of L. leaders, Lewis then took the United Mine Workers out of the C.I.O. and back into the A.F. of L. He would later repent this move and again walk out of the A.F. of L. —but not to return to the C.I.O.

It may have been Lewis' ambition to make over the Democratic party into a labor party, or even to try to create a third independent party dedicated to the workers' interests. In no other quarter, however, was there any idea of seeking to change the nation's traditional political alignments. Except for establishment of the state American Labor party in New York, the new unions steered clear of any possible third-party activity. Their backing of Roosevelt was based upon the premise that the New Deal was sympathetic toward labor's aims; there was no thought of trying to follow along the socialistic path of the British Labour party. In keeping with American labor's traditional support for the free enterprise system, the workers in the 1930's were concerned with the reform of capitalism rather than its overthrow.

There were frequent charges that the C.I.O. was communistic. It is true that Lewis, ready to accept help from whatever quarter it was offered, knowingly used communists in the early period of organization in the mass production industries. Under such circumstances, a number of unions fell under communist control including the electrical workers, the seamen, and the West Coast longshoremen. In other instances communists or communist sympathizers attained posts of authority or influence. But very few important labor leaders, and only a tiny minority of workers, ever actually embraced communism. The rank-and-file of industrial union members, as of craft union members, would have none of it. The clamor of the communists was out of all proportion to their numbers, and responsible labor leadership was no less anxious to eliminate their influence than political or industrial leadership.

★ POPULAR REACTIONS

There was widespread public sympathy for labor in its struggles with industry in the 1930's. The right to organize and bargain collectively, as upheld in New Deal legislation, was generally acknowledged to be one which management should be obliged to recognize. The aggressive tactics of the C.I.O. and the mounting power of industrial unionism, however, soon caused something of a change of heart. The ability of the new unions to stage industrywide and nationwide strikes, sometimes threatening the economic paralysis of the entire country, led to a growing demand for some sort of restrictions on labor.

The great majority of individual unions were pursuing constructive policies. The area of collective bargaining, to the mutual advantage of labor and management, was greatly expanded with substantial progress in allaying industrial strife in many segments of the national economy. Nevertheless, these aspects of the labor situation were often overshadowed by those violent outbreaks of industrial strife that seriously threatened the public interest. Jurisdictional disputes between rival unions, flagrant instances of labor racketeering, wholly arbitrary action on the part of a number of unprincipled union leaders added fresh fuel to popular discontent. Popular anger mounted against what often appeared to be a growing irresponsibility on the part of both the A.F. of L. and the C.I.O.

Even the friends of labor felt that the new industrial unions sometimes ignored the public interest in the belligerent assertion of their rights. So liberal a journal as the *New Republic* severely criticized both national organizations. "The union movement in this country is no longer an infant requiring protection," it editorialized. "It has grown up physically, and if it is to conduct itself like a responsible adult it must be controlled by the same social discipline which governs the rest of the community."

On the eve of American entry into World War II, a new outbreak of industrial strife led to more strikes than in any previous year in labor history except 1937. Several of them, especially one called by John L.

Lewis in the country's coal mines, gravely endangered the national defense program. With an outraged public insisting that something be done, thirty bills to curb the unions were introduced in Congress.

Some modification of the Wagner Act was clearly in order, and under normal circumstances Congress might then and there have amended it. But American entry into the war postponed any immediate action. It was not until after the conclusion of hostilities that Congress again took this issue up.

As the period of the New Deal drew to a close in 1939, the membership in labor unions, including those affiliated with both the C.I.O. and the A.F. of L., had attained a total of some 10,000,000. It is again important to emphasize, however, that far more significant than numbers was the fact that the unskilled workers in the mass production industries had for the first time become an integral part of the organized labor movement. The greater economic strength of these wage earners, and their growing political awareness, had consequences importantly affecting every phase of national life. While the foes of labor remained fearful of these developments, its friends were confident that stronger unionism would substantially bolster the whole structure of democratic capitalism.

"Only in free lands," President Roosevelt told the International Brotherhood of Teamsters, "have free labor unions survived. When workers assemble with freedom and independence in a convention like this, it is proof that American democracy has remained unimpaired; it is a symbol of our determination to keep it free."

CHAPTER XXV

Close of a Decade

★ THE STATUS OF THE NEW DEAL: 1936

The midterm elections of 1934 had given the public a first opportunity to express its attitude toward the New Deal. The real test, however, came in 1936. The presidential election of that year invited a full dress debate on the philosophy and purpose of the Roosevelt program, led to a division of opinion along class lines that the country had not experienced since 1896, and aroused in some quarters a shocking degree of bitterness. The business-organized American Liberty League spearheaded a venomous attack on "that man in the White House"; the President struck back no less viciously at those whom he called "economic royalists." Here was a battle royal in the making which aroused the country as it had not been aroused in years.

Conditions were highly propitious for a New Deal victory in 1936. The people as a whole were distinctly better off than they had been at any time since the depression first struck the country. The recession that would the next year bring new setbacks was hardly foreseen. The pertinent economic facts seemed clear: business profits were up, farm income had materially risen, and higher wages and shorter hours had been won by a great majority of industrial workers. There were still millions of unemployed, but they were being cared for as they had not been four years earlier through the government's vast unemployment relief program.

The cost of New Deal operations had already proved to be staggering. The concept of economy and a balanced budget, on which Roosevelt had originally placed such emphasis, had long since been abandoned in meeting current expenditures for public works and relief. The successive deficits of these years were increasing the national debt at an average of something like $5,000,000,000 a year. But while business and financial leaders were gravely concerned over the dangers of this continued deficit financing, the general public was not very much worried about the rising debt. It did not look beyond the surface indications of what seemed to be returning prosperity.

There was strong popular support for the reform program instituted the year before. Stimulated by the safeguards for collective bargaining written into the Wagner Act, organized labor viewed with enthusiastic approval an administration that had so directly encouraged union organization. As its inherent value to the nation as a whole was more widely recognized, the social security program attracted additional New Deal converts. Many people whose imagination had been caught by Roosevelt's castigation of the "rulers of the exchange of mankind's goods" were won over by such developments as the "soak-the-rich" program. In shifting its emphasis from recovery through co-operation with industry to drastic reform of the economic system, the New Deal was successfully appealing to the most numerous elements in the body politic. It had created for its support a new political coalition of which farmers, workers, and the unemployed provided the most numerous components.

Still another feature in the existing situation aroused the general public. New Deal policies had run up against the opposition of the Supreme Court. Measures that Congress had passed on Roosevelt's insistence were being repeatedly struck down on the ground of unconstitutionality. While the Court had somewhat reluctantly upheld the gold devaluation program and the legislation establishing the TVA, it declared the National Industrial Recovery Act unconstitutional in *Schechter Corporation* v *United States* and invalidated the Agricultural Adjustment Act in *United States* v *Butler*. These laws, the Court stated, exceeded any reasonable interpretation of the powers that Congress exercised over interstate commerce, invaded the powers of the states, and in the case of the NRA, constituted an unwarranted delegation of power to the president. In other almost equally important decisions in 1935 and 1936 the Court nullified the New Deal laws dealing with mortgage and bankruptcy relief, pensions for railway workers, stabilization of the coal industry, and also a state minimum wage law. Its attitude brought into question the constitutionality of both the Wagner Act and the Social Security Act.

Roosevelt had burst out angrily against what he termed "horse-and-buggy" interpretations of the Constitution, and he largely succeeded in identifying the Court's position with reactionary opposition to the New Deal's social theories. The general public hardly considered the possible validity of the Court's constitutional scruples; its concern was with the mounting threat to the entire New Deal reform program. Although this issue was not greatly emphasized during the presidential campaign, it underlay the contest and added to the vehemence with which both New Dealers and anti-New Dealers fought out their battles.

★ THUNDER ON THE LEFT—AND RIGHT

Although the New Deal thus appeared to command massive popular support—and in fact did—there was nevertheless sharp criticism not only from the Right but from the Left. While the business community voiced its alarms over attacks on free enterprise, there were rumblings in other quarters that the New Deal had abjectly surrendered to Wall Street. A number of dissident movements had arisen that called for more sweeping reform, flirting with various inflationary panaceas that might have proved highly dangerous to the economy. These movements were neither socialistic nor communistic—they were only vaguely radical.

In California Upton Sinclair, the socialist muckraker of the Progressive era, had a program of high taxes and generous pensions under the name End Poverty in California, or EPIC; another Californian, Dr. Francis E. Townsend, had a system for monthly payments of $200 to all persons over sixty that had led to the rapid formation of thousands of Townsend clubs throughout the country; a Catholic priest and radio commentator in Detroit, the Reverend Charles E. Coughlin, was persuasively advocating a vast inflationary program and claimed countless members for his National Union for Social Justice; and Governor Huey Long of Louisiana, the "Louisiana Kingfish," was stridently demanding adoption of a share-the-wealth program that would make every man a king.

These demagogic agitators commanded several million followers. The political pressure they were able to exert had been in part responsible for Roosevelt turning to a "soak the rich" policy on his own account, and their combined influence in creating leftwing opposition to the re-election of the President was for a time of very real concern to New Deal political strategists. Huey Long, whose program had its fascistic undertones, appeared to be an especially alarming threat.

Fortunately for the New Deal—and for the country—such thunder on the Left was largely stilled before the election. Huey Long was killed by an assassin's bullet in September 1935, and there was no one to succeed him as a really strong leader of the radical anti-New Deal forces. The other dissident groups tried to form a third party, nominating as their presidential candidate Representative William Lemke, a farm leader from North Dakota, but deprived of Long's leadership, they could get nowhere.

The rightwing attacks on the New Deal, however, increased in intensity with the approach of the election, and they were given the widest publicity because of conservative control of the press. Some two-thirds of the nation's papers had consistently assailed what they termed Roosevelt's inept bungling ever since the honeymoon of the Hundred Days. They now condemned the New Deal out of hand for reckless waste and extravagance, flagrant disregard of constitutional restraints, and dictatorial interference with the life of the people.

The Liberty League sought to marshal bipartisan support for its impassioned anti-New Deal drive. Such onetime Democratic leaders as Al Smith and John W. Davis, former presidential candidates, were in the forefront of this extreme conservative movement, but its real support came from the big business interests generally identified with the Republican party. The sinews of war were provided by the executives of Du Pont, General Motors, Republic Steel, and other big corporations whose instinctive opposition to economic reform had been accentuated by New Deal labor policies.

★ THE ELECTION OF 1936

As the time came to nominate a candidate to oppose Roosevelt, the Republicans found themselves in a difficult position. To condemn the New Deal was easy enough—their platform was to declare "America is in peril"—but in seeking constructive alternatives to Democratic policy, little help was available from either the leftwing or the Liberty League. The country clearly favored reform, and that was the New Deal program—only slightly left of center. From the point of view of practical politics there seemed to be little the Republicans could do other than offer a watered-down version of the very things that the Democrats were proposing. Their only forthright and explicit pledge was repeal of reciprocal trade agreements and a return to protection, and their platform's general condemnation of the New Deal was largely nullified by its oblique endorsement of unemployment relief, social security, safeguards for labor's right to organize, and agricultural aid.

For their standard bearer the Republicans named Governor Alfred M. Landon of Kansas. He had a reputation for liberalism and represented the more progressive midwestern wing of his party. Lacking a very assertive personality, however, he was to allow the Republican extremists largely to control his campaign and virtually repudiate the party platform. The charges of demagogy, dictatorship, and even communism leveled against the New Deal were not of Landon's making, but they became Republican stock-in-trade and grew almost hysterical in tone as the campaign progressed.

The Democrats were obviously ready to renominate Roosevelt and stand on the record. They confidently proclaimed that the issue was clearly drawn between a Republican administration that would seek to regiment the American people into the service of privileged groups, and a Democratic administration dedicated to the establishment of equal opportunity. The program on which they had embarked would be continued, the party leaders declared, and touching upon the vexed constitutional issue, the Democratic platform called for a clarifying amendment should such action prove necessary to keep the road open to social advance.

The campaign was increasingly to become a struggle between conservative big business and the President himself. Landon was almost forgotten. Big business, directly represented in the Liberty League, drew its support from the more wealthy and prosperous elements in the community, while Roosevelt succeeded in identifying himself with the great masses of the people. Replying to the charge that he was trying to overthrow national institutions and establish a dictatorship, the President counterattacked by declaring that what really aroused the economic royalists was that the New Deal was seeking to take away their power. He emphatically denied that he had any quarrel with big business as such and asserted that the New Deal program was directed only against private monopoly and uncontrolled wealth.

Class lines steadily hardened as the campaign progressed—subsequent analyses of the vote would clearly show a division according to income groups—and political exchanges took on increasing virulence. Roosevelt was assailed for trying to curry favor with the mob, for seeking personal power, for betraying his class. What was said in public went far enough, but his foes spared no epithets in their private denunciation of his policies and personal character.

For a time the President tried to ignore the personal charges, but he was finally driven to strike back with angry vehemence. In a speech at Madison Square Garden that brought his campaign to a close, he said defiantly:

> We had to struggle with the old enemies of peace—business and financial monopoly, speculation, reckless banking, class antagonism, sectionalism, war profiteering. They had begun to consider the Government of the United States as a mere appendage of their own affairs. We know now that Government by organized money is just as dangerous as Government by organized mob. Never before in all our history have these forces been so united against one candidate as they stand today. They are unanimous in their hate for me—and I welcome their hatred.

It was a bitter end to a bitter campaign. With the lines so clearly drawn between the privileged and the underprivileged, however, the results remained a foregone conclusion. Yet few realized how great an appeal the New Deal had made to the country as a whole. The farmers guaranteed agricultural aid, the workers promised union protection, the unemployed given relief, were expected to support Roosevelt, but even their totaled votes could not wholly account for the massive landslide the radio reported on election night. The electorate not only gave Roosevelt 27,477,000 votes to Landon's 16,680,000, but returned immense Democratic majorities to both houses of Congress. Only Maine and Vermont remained stubbornly in the Republican column.

There could be only one interpretation of the election results. The nation had overwhelmingly endorsed Roosevelt's leadership and given its emphatic sanction to the general program represented by the New Deal.

★ F.D.R. AND THE SUPREME COURT

Roosevelt's second inaugural address reaffirmed the goals that the New Deal had set itself and called for further social reform. "I can see one third of a nation ill-housed, ill-clad, ill-nourished. . . . The test of our progress is not whether we add more to the abundance of those who have much; it is whether we provide enough for those who have too little." There was no mention in his speech, however, of what was to become within the next two months the burning issue of the day. How could the New Deal program be promoted so long as the Supreme Court threatened to declare unconstitutional all its most important legislation?

The President hurled his challenge at the Court, without forewarning, early in February 1937. In a special message to Congress he called for a drastic reorganization of the federal judiciary which would provide (with an over-all limitation of fifty, and of six in the case of the Supreme Court) an additional appointee to the bench for every judge over the age of seventy who did not voluntarily retire. The excuse for such a proposal was that the incumbent judges could not handle an overloaded docket, but its clear intent was to allow the President to make such appointments to the Supreme Court, six of whose members were over seventy, as to secure a majority which might be expected to uphold New Deal legislation. What soon became called "the court-packing plan" immediately involved Roosevelt in the fiercest struggle of his political career.

There was nothing unusual in American history about a contest between the executive and the judiciary. Since Jefferson declared in 1801 that the Federalists had retreated to the courts as to a stronghold to beat back the further assaults of the Republicans, every powerful President had sooner or later found himself at odds with the Supreme Court.

Roosevelt was convinced that its opposition to the New Deal was not based upon legitimate constitutional reasons, but upon the majority's outmoded economic and social philosophy. He would have appealed from the Supreme Court to the Constitution itself, stating that only through invigorating the judiciary with new blood could interpretation of the law be brought in line with modern needs. His plan would save the Constitution, he was to tell the country, from "hardening of the judicial arteries."

Roosevelt appeared to have a sound basis for much of his criticism of the Supreme Court. While certain of its adverse rulings, notably that invalidating the NRA, reflected a unanimous or nearly unanimous judgment, the others revealed a very narrow majority. And it was always the same justices who made up these five-to-four, or at best six-to-three, anti-New Deal majorities. The Supreme Court split along conservative and liberal lines appeared to reflect a rigid economic bias in regard to the competing concepts of the laissez faire and social welfare state. Moreover, the dissenting opinions in several cases gave Roosevelt fuel for his attack on the Court. On one occasion Justice Stone referred to the majority's "tortured construction of the constitution"; on another, Chief Justice Hughes bluntly characterized a majority decision as "unwarranted" and "a departure from sound principles."

Among various proposals made to overcome this impasse before Roosevelt introduced his court-packing plan were the clarifying amendment suggested in the Democratic platform, a proposal that Congress under certain conditions could re-enact a law invalidated by the judiciary, thereby purging it of its unconstitutionality, and a plan for requiring at least a two-thirds court majority in nullifying congressional laws. The President, however, took the bull by the horns in his direct attack upon the Supreme Court itself, and the consequent political storm swept through New Deal ranks quite as fiercely as through the Republican opposition. Roosevelt was accused of trying to upset the traditional balance of power in our constitutional system, seeking to impose executive control over the judiciary, undermining the constitutional liberties of the American people, and taking the first step toward establishment of a dictatorship.

He bent before the storm, but adamantly refused to withdraw his plan. Going to the people in a Fireside Chat, he again assailed the obstructive role that the conservative judges had assumed. Quoting Chief Justice Hughes' dictum that the Constitution is what the judges say it is, he declared that the Supreme Court had improperly set itself up as a superlegislature, reading into the Constitution words and implications that were never intended to be there. He brushed aside the possibility of meeting the issue through more traditional methods on the ground that immediate action was essential and every delay heightened the danger of intervening events making solution of the country's problems more difficult. Answering directly the charge that he was trying to pack the Supreme Court, Roosevelt said:

> If by that phrase "packing the Court" it is charged that I wish to place on the bench spineless puppets who would disregard the law and would decide specific cases as I wished them to be decided, I make this answer: that no President fit for his office would appoint, and no Senate of honorable men fit for their office would confirm, that kind of appointment to the Supreme Court.
>
> But if by that phrase the charge is made that I would appoint and the Senate would confirm Justices worthy to sit beside present members of the Court who understand these modern conditions, that I will appoint Justices who will not undertake to override the judgment of Congress on legislative policy, that I will appoint Justices who will act as Justices and not as legislators—if the appointment of such Justices can be called "packing the Courts," then I say that I and with me the vast majority of the American people favor doing just that thing—now.

★ THE DEFEAT OF JUDICIAL REORGANIZATION

Roosevelt nevertheless lost out. Too many members of his own party deserted him; he could not control Congress. His overconfidence had led him to make the gravest political miscalculation of his career in failing to realize the storm of opposition that any idea of tampering with the constitutional system would create. The Senate Judiciary Committee, bluntly characterizing his plan as an invasion of judicial power such as had never before been attempted in this country, overwhelmingly rejected it. There was to be no authority for the appointment of additional judges, whether to the Supreme Court or to any other federal court. Congress later adopted a greatly emasculated version of the President's proposed bill, but it went no further than the most minor judicial reforms. For the first time since his election in 1932 Roosevelt suffered a complete and decisive political defeat.

Yet even as he was losing this battle, he was winning his war. Without a single addition or change in its membership, the Supreme Court reversed its position in the very midst of the reorganization struggle, upholding in a new series of cases the extension of governmental powers that it had formerly rejected. Its changed attitude was first revealed on March 29 in *West Coast Hotel* v *Parrish,* in which it accepted a minimum wage law in the state of Washington. Two weeks later it sustained the validity of the Wagner Act in *National Labor Relations Board* v *Jones and Laughlin,* and then on May 24 upheld the Social Security Act in *Steward Machine Company* v *Davis.* These decisions amounted in effect to approval of the constitutional basis of the entire New Deal program. Congressional laws coming up for review were henceforth to be sustained just as persistently as for a time they had been nullified.

What had happened? The new decisions were again almost invariably by a five-to-four vote, but the dissenting minority had been transformed almost overnight to an approving majority because one key man had changed his mind. Justice Roberts swung over from the conservative position he had formerly maintained to agree with the more liberal members of the Supreme Court on a broad interpretation of both the police power of the state and of the authority of Congress under the commerce clause. In sharp distinction to its earlier attitude this meant that the Supreme Court as a whole, by however narrow a margin, was now prepared to allow Congress the power to control labor relations, agricultural production, and wages and hours wherever interstate commerce was directly or indirectly affected, and also to impose taxes which were designed, as in the case of the Social Security Act, not to raise revenue but to promote the general welfare.

While the immediate cause of the Court's change was the shift in the opinion of Justice Roberts, there were other factors in the situation. Chief Justice Hughes, deeply disturbed by what might happen if the majority rejected the labor and social security laws, is said to have had a decisive influence on court deliberations; it has also been maintained that the new laws were so much more carefully drawn that there were no longer valid grounds for rejecting them. Yet it remains true that between 1936 and 1937 a fundamental change had taken place in the Supreme Court's attitude that has been aptly called *Constitutional Revolution—Limited.*

Roosevelt was later to declare that his ultimate victory in winning constitutional acceptance of the New Deal was one of his greatest achievements in the field of domestic policy. He took major credit for this turning point in modern American history. "I feel convinced," he wrote four years after the court struggle, "that the change would never have come, unless the frontal attack had been made upon the philosophy of the majority of the Court." He admitted that he had made a mistake in the way he had first presented his plan, evading as he did the real issue of Supreme Court decisions, but he staunchly defended his general policy.

Critics maintained then—and have ever since—that no such direct assault upon the judiciary was necessary to bring about a change in its views. The Supreme Court was bound, sooner or later, to adjust itself to the new circumstances of the times and give a broader construction to the powers of Congress under the Constitution. This argument was bolstered by the historical record that in the long run the Court almost invariably does respond to popular pressure for new forms of social action; that is, in Mr. Dooley's sage comment in the early 1900's, it follows the election returns. If the President could have been a little more patient, according to this thesis, he could have achieved his objectives without stirring up such a hornet's nest of angry criticism and suffering such a sharp political setback.

The Supreme Court was, indeed, under the heaviest sort of pressure even before Roosevelt proposed his packing plan. The popular mandate that the public had given the New Deal in 1936 could not help but affect the thinking of those justices who were more concerned with maintenance of the constitutional system than with the furtherance of their own economic views. The question may still be raised, however, whether the country would have quietly awaited a gradual change in the Court's point of view in the circumstances of the time. For 1937 was a year of industrial unrest, widespread strikes, and impending recession. There was a clear danger that if the Supreme Court continued, even temporarily, to block measures on which so great a part of the people were agreed, popular opinion would have demanded immediate and radical changes in the entire system of judicial review. This would have been a far more serious blow to our constitutional system than Roosevelt's proposal. It is now known that Justice Roberts was prepared to shift his position before the court-packing plan was announced, but of this the President was ignorant.

In any event the change in the attitude of the Supreme Court took place, as has already been said, before any change was made in its membership. The justices who handed down the decisions upholding the Wagner Act and Social Security Act were the same "nine old men" who had found the NIRA and the AAA invalid. This shift in policy, however, was soon to be given a more substantial basis than one justice's altered views. Roosevelt finally was given the opportunity, through normal retirement or death, to appoint sufficient new members to the Court to make the dominance of a liberal majority uncontestably certain.

One of the conservative bloc, Justice Van Devanter, announced his intention of retiring at the end of the term while the judiciary battle was still raging. Roosevelt named Senator Hugo Black, a strong New Deal supporter from Alabama, to fill this vacancy. This was the beginning of a rapid succession of new appointments. Within four years, six new associate justices and a new chief justice had completely made over the bench.

While the new Supreme Court was much more friendly than its predecessor to New Deal philosophy, there was a still more basic difference in its attitude. It was prepared to exercise a pronounced measure of judicial restraint in dealing with congressional laws. Some years earlier, Justice Brandeis had somberly warned his brethren on the bench of the necessity of being constantly on guard "lest we erect our prejudices into legal principles." The old Court appeared to have let itself be maneuvered into a position of doing just that; the new Court was to follow a much more careful policy.

★ ROOSEVELT'S ENTOURAGE

Throughout the entire period of the New Deal, not only during such exciting weeks as those of the judiciary struggle, the dominating figure of Roosevelt eclipsed all others in Washington. He was the undisputed leader of his party and the acknowledged leader of the country. His practice of talking directly to the people in his Fireside Chats introduced him into every home in the land, and his friendly persuasiveness gained millions of devoted followers. The New Deal policies, conforming as they did to the felt needs of the time, commanded extraordinary popular support, but Roosevelt's warm personality also won the hearts of most of his countrymen.

To combat the repeated charge that he was trying to build up a personal dictatorship, he at one time felt obliged to go out of his way to deny that he had any such intention. The record bore him out. Yet there was no gainsaying his ambition, and it was almost inevitable, for a man in his position, to have a growing sense of importance and even indispensability. The idea was spread about, perhaps not altogether without warrant, that he was seeking to keep anyone else from attaining a position that would rival his own political prestige and power, and there were some withdrawals from his official family of men who thought he was giving undue weight to his own personal role in government.

One of the men who early broke away was Raymond Moley, the leading member of the Brain Trust which had played such an important role during the election of 1932. After serving for a time as an assistant secretary of state, he began to disapprove more and more of Rooseveltian policies, resigned in something of a huff, and then became an increasingly severe New Deal critic. Another associate departing—although not until a good deal later—was Postmaster General James A. Farley, the large, jovial, handshaking politician who had managed Roosevelt's first campaign. Farley found himself less and less in sympathy with the New Deal as time went on and increasingly absorbed in his own political ambitions.

Only two cabinet members were to go the full course. Frances Perkins, who had been an industrial commissioner in New York, remained Secretary of Labor throughout the entire Roosevelt period, and Harold Ickes, one-time Bull Mooser and always an insurgent, stayed on as Secretary of the Interior. The former served ably and well, in spite of some criticism, and remained generally in the background of public affairs. The latter comment hardly applied to Ickes. His stubborn individualism, constant tendency to feud with other officials, and gift for trenchant, outspoken language made him a conspicuous figure throughout his stormy but effective Washington career.

Secretary of State Hull remained in office almost until Roosevelt's death. He played a secondary role to that of the President in determining foreign policy, but was always highly useful because of his political influence and ability to deal with Congress. Dignified and restrained, although occasionally given to sharp outbursts that betrayed his Tennessee mountaineer background, Hull commanded widespread respect for his tenacious promotion of trade reciprocity, one of the New Deal's important programs, and somewhat later for his patient if ultimately unsuccessful efforts to maintain friendly relations with Japan.

Henry Wallace, a conspicuous and highly controversial figure throughout New Deal days, served as both Secretary of Agriculture and Secretary of Commerce, with a vice-presidential term intervening in 1941–45. In spite of efficient administrative work, he was always identified with what were considered the more extreme or visionary elements within the New Deal, and he bore much of the opprobrium for the unpopular features of the AAA. Roosevelt consistently supported him and only with great reluctance withdrew his support from his renomination for the vice-presidency in 1944. There was always an erratic quality about Wallace, however; for a time after the war he appeared to have let himself become the dupe of leftwing radicals.

One of the most interesting members of the Roosevelt entourage was Harry Hopkins, head of FERA and WPA, and subsequently Secretary of Commerce. With a background of wide experience in the Red Cross and in social work generally, he devoted himself to the development of the New Deal work-relief program with impassioned zeal. Like Roosevelt, to whom he was intensely loyal, Hopkins was a man of courage, confidence, and infectious optimism. He was also brilliant and impulsive, highly idealistic, and imbued with a warm humanitarianism. In the minds of all anti-New Dealers, he was completely visionary and unrealistic; in short, they considered him an irresponsible crackpot who took a huge delight in spending the government's money. But for all the criticism of extravagance and political favoritism, Hopkins actually administered the immense sums—some $9,000,000,000—allocated for the relief projects under his control with a high measure of disinterested efficiency.

Hugh Johnson, the explosive director of the NRA, once described Hopkins as "a doer of good deeds, executor of orders, go-getter, Santa Claus incomparable, and privy-builder without peer." He was one of the most influential men in Washington; for a time Roosevelt even appeared to be grooming him as his successor. The war and Hopkins' increasing ill-health broke up all such plans, but the glorified privy-builder was to go on to win new triumphs as an unofficial presidential adviser and special wartime envoy to Churchill and Stalin.

Rexford G. Tugwell, who became Assistant Secretary of Agriculture in 1933, was another central figure for a time in the Roosevelt circle. An impassioned reformer, his great dream was to make America over into a new land—"a land in order, wisely used, with the hills green and the streams blue." He evoked a great deal of criticism for some of his schemes, but labored strenuously for agricultural reform and conservation. Somewhat later two protégés of Justice Frankfurter, Thomas Corcoran and Benjamin Cohen, won high favor with the President, were conspicuously active in governmental circles, and played an influential role in drawing up the reform measures of 1935.

While Roosevelt never had a "kitchen cabinet" in the sense in which some of his predecessors had, there was a changing group that commanded his confidence and upon whom he often relied heavily for advice. After the death of his earliest adviser and assistant, Louis Howe, his closest confidants on policy matters were probably—in succession—Moley, Tugwell and Hopkins. The President always, however, remained master of his household.

★ POLITICAL REVERSES

Taking up again the story in 1937, Roosevelt found himself very much politically weakened by the defeat he had suffered on the court-packing plan. The very size of the Democratic majorities in both House and Senate also made them difficult to control. Summoning a special session of Congress in October, he succeeded in winning passage of the second Agricultural Adjustment Act and the Fair Labor Standards Act. Congress balked, however, at his requests for additional reform legislation. It would have none of his plan for extending the idea behind the TVA to other parts of the country; it rejected a scheme for reorganization of the executive branch of the government on which the President set great store. Opposition to further government planning accounted for the defeat of the first measure, while the suspicions of presidential dictatorship aroused by the attack on the Supreme Court was a decisive factor in blocking executive reorganization.

The decline in Roosevelt's influence over Congress was paralleled by wavering popular support. This was due as much to economic as political causes. The sharp recession that set in during 1937 appeared to cast doubt on the validity of the whole recovery program, and for a time seemed to endanger the national economy very seriously. Under spirited prodding Congress appropriated an additional $3,000,000,000 for an expanded public works and pump-priming program, and conditions began to improve, but for the first time the Roosevelt administration found itself on the defensive. Attacks again were from both the Right and the Left. The former was still concerned with curbing New Deal reforms by whatever means possible. The latter had become impatient over what it considered the slow pace of reform and held it responsible for the recession. The political pot was boiling.

Roosevelt was prepared to accept the challenge to his leadership and at the midterm elections of 1938, he called not for a Democratic Congress but for the return of "liberal" candidates of whatever political affiliation. They were defined as those men who recognized that new conditions throughout the world called for new remedies, but what Roosevelt clearly and unmistakably meant was men who would always, and no matter under what circumstances (as in the court fight), be ready to support the New Deal. The President strongly attacked what he termed the "yes, but . . . fellows" and directly sought to purge the Democratic party of such lukewarm followers of his own program.

The result of the midterm elections was a Roosevelt reverse. While the Democrats retained nominal control in both the Senate and the House, the Republicans and the conservative wing of the Democratic party recorded substantial gains. From this time on, an anti-New Deal coalition cutting across party lines stood as an imposing obstacle to any further reform measures. Roosevelt was not again to command anything like the support on domestic issues he had enjoyed during his first administration.

He accepted the handwriting on the wall. While he would seek to maintain his longterm goals of greater security for the men, women, and children of the nation, Roosevelt recognized in his annual message to Congress in 1939 that there was no further urgent demand for reform. He declared that the past three Congresses had met in whole or in part the pressing needs of the new order and that the time had arrived for consolidating the gains already made.

"We have now passed the period of internal conflict in the launching of our program of social reform," Roosevelt said. "Our full energies may now be released to invigorate the processes of recovery in order to preserve our reforms."

The New Deal to all practical purposes had come to an end.

★ THE NEW DEAL IN RETROSPECT

With the perspective of years certain aspects of this era, in which Roosevelt was grappling with domestic issues brought to the forefront by depression, begin to stand out more clearly. While the New Deal failed to bring about complete recovery, it succeeded in raising the standard of living for the people as a whole, and, more importantly, its willingness to exert all the powers of government in seeking to restore a better balance in the national economy revived faith in democratic capitalism. Existing institutions were given a new life and vitality. Where other nations turned to much more radical experiments, with both fascism and communism making terrifying gains, the United States held true to the ideals and traditions that had made it great. With the passage of years, indeed, the basically conservative nature of the New Deal has been increasingly recognized. Whether a system of private enterprise may be permanently maintained is necessarily a question for the long future. The New Deal, however, clearly demonstrated that for the time being at least, democratic capitalism had the inherent strength to meet the challenge of the times.

The essential factor in this re-establishment of confidence in the American way of life, as already suggested, was the federal government's assumption of its new responsibilities in doing things, as Lincoln once phrased it, which private citizens, either separately or together, could not do by themselves or could not do as well as government could do them. The recognition of those obligations set forth in the Bill of Economic Rights was of tremendous significance. It held out the promise that henceforth all the energies of government would be marshaled to promote equal opportunity in "the pursuit of happiness" without sacrifice of those basic liberties that other political systems had so ruthlessly suppressed. It was all too clear that the problems created by the growth of an industrial civilization were incredibly difficult of solution, but the national government was prepared to face up to them.

While extravagance had all too often seemed to mark federal expenditures for relief and public works during the depression days, the increase in the nation's physical wealth as a result of the New Deal's reconstruction and conservation program offset much of this apparent waste. The great projects undertaken for the harnessing of water power, thousands of miles of paved highways, new bridges, culverts, drainage systems, and harbor improvements, the modern school buildings that everywhere dotted the land—all this was an important addition to the nation's economic and social potential.

The over-all expansion in governmental activities, with that increase in federal agencies, the federal bureaucracy, and federal expenditures, for which there was no parallel in earlier history, had its dangers. It meant that government was more centralized than ever and that there had been a distinct shift in the traditional relationship between the states and national authority. While government was modernized and made effective, it was in a position to impose controls over economic enterprise almost at will and thereby drastically restrict individual freedom. The power of the executive was also enhanced, as a result both of the national emergency and Roosevelt's own character, and a new emphasis placed upon the President's role as a national leader. Although in the context of the times this appeared not only inevitable but also to have had highly salutary results, there again could be no denying its potential hazards.

For all their apparent departures from precedent, however, these developments in the field of political power and economic responsibility grew out of the past, conformed to American traditions, and had been brought about within the framework of the Constitution. There was no essential alteration in the methods and practices that enabled the people, through their elected and responsible representatives, to make the ultimate decision on just how much control or regulation they were willing to accept. They remained the guardians of their own liberties.

The New Deal had its faults quite as much as its virtues. It could not finally resolve the age's fundamental problem in reconciling the competing demands of security and individual freedom. It was in essence, however, a reaffirmation of faith in the nation's ability to meet through democratic action whatever domestic difficulties or problems might confront it.

CHAPTER XXVI

Neutrality

★ ROOSEVELT'S FOREIGN POLICIES

When Roosevelt was inaugurated in 1933, he referred to a "stricken Nation in the midst of a stricken world." Yet it was not only economic distress that marked the international scene. The tides of political security were running out both in Asia and in Europe. Having already struck at Manchuria, Japan was biding her time to strike again at China and ultimately plunge all eastern Asia into war. Germany was stirring restlessly, and this same year saw Adolph Hitler come into power, ready to start on the reckless course that was soon to engulf Europe in tragic conflict. Everywhere old fears were rising to eclipse the hopeful dream of collective security.

Throughout the 1930's, however, the United States believed that even should war come in Europe or Asia, it would be able to maintain a separate peace. Roosevelt's only reference to foreign affairs in his first inaugural address was to dedicate the country to the policy of the Good Neighbor. He made no mention of the international situation whatsoever in his second inaugural. With national policy almost entirely concentrated on the domestic problems growing out of the depression, the country as a whole was even more isolationist in its thinking than it had been during the 1920's.

The renewed emphasis upon setting our own house in order was revealed in Roosevelt's torpedoing of the World Economic Conference held in London in the spring of 1933. For a time there had appeared to be some prospect that this meeting might lead to a solution of the interrelated problems of international currency stabilization, debt payments, and tariff barriers. But when Roosevelt instructed the United States delegation that there could be no stabilization of the dollar under existing circumstances, and no commitment to any program "for freeing the flow of world trade," all such hopes collapsed. After the failure of the conference, each of the attending nations went its own way in trying to cope with a depression which was the common problem of them all.

Along more strictly political lines Roosevelt generally followed the course already plotted by Hoover. The United States continued to participate in the disarmament talks held under League auspices in Geneva and still refused to make any definite pledge in support of a collective effort for the maintenance of peace. In the Far East the Stimson Doctrine of nonrecognition of territorial changes effected by force was reaffirmed, and in Latin America the bases laid by Hoover for a more cordial understanding with the countries of the Western Hemisphere were further broadened.

Roosevelt indeed took a number of specific steps to give practical application to his Good Neighbor doctrine, and Latin American policy was far more effective than policy in any other part of the world. The old right under the Platt Amendment to intervene in the affairs of Cuba was abandoned, the marines still stationed in Central America were entirely withdrawn, issues at stake in Mexico were amicably adjusted, and reciprocal trade agreements concluded to strengthen American economic ties with the countries south of the Rio Grande. After attending in person the Inter-American Conference for Peace, held in Buenos Aires in 1936, the President told Congress:

> Among the nations of the Western Hemisphere the policy of the good neighbor has happily prevailed. At no time in the four and a half centuries of modern civilization in the Americas has there existed—in any year, in any decade, in any generation, in all that time—a greater spirit of mutual understanding, of common helpfulness, and of devotion to the ideals of self-government than exists today in the twenty-one American Republics and their neighbor, the Dominion of Canada. The policy of the good neighbor among the Americans is no longer a hope, no longer an objective remaining to be accomplished. It is a fact, active, present, pertinent and effective.

Only in one respect did Roosevelt depart directly from the precedents established by his predecessor. In November 1933 after protracted negotiations with Foreign Commissar Litvinov, he extended diplomatic recognition to Soviet Russia. A more realistic appraisal of the stability of the communist regime, developments in eastern Asia, and the desire to promote Russian-American trade combined to bring about this shift in the policy of the previous sixteen years. For a time it was hoped that the renewal of diplomatic contacts would make possible a real *rapprochement* between Russia and America in spite of their political and ideological differences. Such expectations were never fully realized—not even during the alliance of 1941–45. The issue of Russian-American relations was to be projected into the future as the most formidable problem of the postwar world.

★ BACKGROUND OF NEUTRALITY

More important than any of these developments was the mounting crisis in European affairs. The rise of fascism in Italy was supplemented by the rise of Nazism in Germany; there was a steadily widening rift between these two powers and the democracies of western Europe. A succession of startling events soon gravely underscored the danger of a new war—or the renewal of the old war—as the upstart dictators, drawing ever closer together until they defiantly set up their Berlin-Rome axis, challenged any interference with their aggressive designs. Hitler embarked upon a program of active rearmament in flagrant disregard of the Versailles Treaty, boldly marched German troops into the Rhineland, and shrilly asserted Germany's right to expansion in Central Europe. Demanding recognition of Italy's dominant position in the Mediterranean, Mussolini took a first step toward war itself when he cynically invaded Ethiopia and annexed that little African nation as part of a greater Italian Empire.

In the face of these frightening developments in 1935–36, the United States sought to maintain a proud aloofness from what were generally regarded as solely European quarrels. Its answer to the danger of war was a newly conceived neutrality policy which undertook to insulate the country against any risky involvement in foreign affairs. There would be no entangling alliances; there would be no support for collective security. The oceans by which the nation was surrounded would be transformed from avenues for trade into barriers against war.

The explanation of the popular attitude which supported this policy is largely found in the disillusionment born of the failure to achieve the goals for which the nation believed it had taken up arms in 1917. The world had not been made safe for democracy. Even more tyrannical totalitarian powers had arisen on the ruins of the fallen empires. There had been no end to wars. The spirit of aggression was everywhere threatening new hostilities. The American people forgot Wilson's solemn warning that in turning their backs on international co-operation, they had cravenly renounced their opportunity for world leadership and would soon be "witnessing the tragedy of it all." They were prepared to compound their past errors in the illusory hope that neutrality was still possible in the twentieth century.

The popular sense of disillusionment was also heightened by the current belief that the United States had been dragged into the European conflict in 1917 solely because of the machinations of international bankers and munitions makers. A senatorial investigation committee disclosed the supposed intrigues of these "merchants of death," and a short-memoried people readily accepted this grossly oversimplified explanation of American policies twenty years earlier. It pointed to an easy way to avoid once again being caught in the same trap. All that the United States had to do, it was plausibly argued, was to make sure that the international bankers and munitions makers were this time prevented from forging those economic ties with belligerent nations that had drawn us into war in 1917.

Abandoning the traditional doctrine of freedom of the seas, Congress consequently adopted a legislative program which banned the sale of munitions to any belligerent nation, refused loans to any belligerent nation, and prohibited American citizens from traveling on belligerent vessels. Regardless of the possibility that such a policy would actually encourage aggression, by serving notice that its victims would get no assistance from the United States, the general public was content that it appeared to promise our own security.

There was opposition to this policy. Advocates of collective security strongly felt that the United States had a vital stake in the developing conflict between fascism and democracy and could not possibly stand aside should war break out in a world even more interdependent than the world of the early 1900's. The only way to safeguard this country's peace, they declared, was to throw American influence behind every movement to forestall aggression, warning Hitler and Mussolini that any nation which they attacked would have the support of the United States. But for all such highly vocal criticism of the neutrality legislation and insistence upon the need for concerted action against all disturbers of the peace, isolationism continued to command decisive support.

★ NEUTRALITY LEGISLATION

The first neutrality law was enacted in 1935 to meet the crisis created by Italy's attack on Ethiopia. Roosevelt tended to favor a more moderate policy that would at once preserve American neutrality and yet penalize an aggressor, but Congress was fearful that any attempted distinction between belligerents would give the impression of taking sides, bringing about the charge of interference that it was most anxious to avoid. The ban upon munitions sales was therefore made absolute in the case of any nation that found itself at war.

When civil war broke out in Spain a year later, with nationalist forces under General Franco attacking the republican government, this rule was to be extended to both contesting factions. Even though this was not an international conflict in the accepted sense, and the United States had the friendliest relations with republican Spain, Roosevelt himself urged such action even though in this instance it would bear most heavily upon the defenders of democracy. On January 6, 1937, Congress consequently adopted with near unanimity a resolution applying an arms embargo to Spain, and it was strictly enforced in spite of attacks from many quarters upon what seemed to be a paradoxical shift in the President's attitude.

What had happened was that the Spanish civil war had taken on a distinctly international character. Both Italy and Germany were directly aiding the fascist-oriented Spanish rebels, and Soviet Russia was assisting the republican loyalists. Fearful of the spread of the war, England and France had formed a Non-Intervention Committee and were seeking, though without success, to prevent supplies from reaching either rebels or loyalists. Roosevelt was no more than bringing American policy, rightly or wrongly, in line with that of the European democracies.

Among liberals this policy was both at the time and in later years considered an irretrievable blunder in that it not only gravely weakened the capacity of the Spanish republic to resist fascist aggression, but afforded encouragement to both Mussolini and Hitler to push their own plans of conquest. But while there was vociferous controversy in this country between supporters of the Spanish loyalists, who identified the loyalist cause with that of democracy, and conservative—especially Catholic—sympathizers with the rebels, who believed the issue was the suppression of communism, the American people as a whole remained largely indifferent to what was happening in Spain. The returns of a Gallup poll in 1936 revealed that 40 per cent of the persons questioned simply had no opinion at all in regard to either the loyalists or the rebels. There was actually little Roosevelt could do other than conform to Anglo-French policy.

The neutrality measures so far adopted were on a temporary basis. On May 1, 1937, Roosevelt signed the bill which constituted the so-called permanent neutrality legislation. It retained the mandatory bans upon all shipments of munitions and upon all loans to belligerent nations, together with the prohibition of American travel on belligerent vessels, but it incorporated a new provision with respect to wartime trade in supplies other than munitions. This trade was now placed on a cash-and-carry basis. The President was empowered to prohibit at his discretion the sale of all non-embargoed goods to belligerents, unless such supplies were fully paid for before leaving this country and were transported overseas in other than American vessels.

This provision represented a compromise between the President's desire for discretionary power in applying the ban upon munitions, so as to use it as a weapon to discourage aggression, and the bitter-end isolationists' insistence that under no circumstances should neutrality legislation differentiate between nations at war. The cash-and-carry program was mildly in the interest of England and France: they controlled the seas, and while buying freely in American markets (except for munitions), they could cut off any attempted trade on the part of Germany or Italy. So highly controversial was this feature of the law that its application was limited to a two-year period.

The neutrality legislation had been passed with European war in mind. It was rigorously enforced, as has been seen, in both the Italian-Ethiopian conflict and on the occasion of civil strife in Spain. The question of its possible application in the Far East then arose when Japan renewed her attack upon north China in 1937. Here was a challenge to the entire American position in the Pacific, but the wisest course was judged to be complete inaction. The neutrality legislation was not enforced on the pretext that there had been no formal declaration of war.

In answer to criticism of this stand, the Roosevelt administration could more successfully defend its policy than it had been able to do in the case of Spain. While neither Japan nor Nationalist China could have obtained any American munitions if the legislation adopted in 1937 had been applied to war in eastern Asia, Japan's control of the seas would have enabled her to purchase whatever other supplies she needed on a cash-and-carry basis and at the same time cut off China from all trade whatsoever. Failure to apply the neutrality law was thus in the interest of a China which almost all Americans felt to be the victim of a wholly unprovoked attack.

Regardless of the details of the neutrality legislation or of the differing circumstances of its enforcement, the final effect of American policy in the mid-1930's was strongly to re-enforce isolationism. The United States was unwilling to take a stand anywhere to prevent the wars already breaking out from spreading still further. In spite of Ethiopia and Spain and China, the public would not be convinced that there really was any great danger of general war. And the conviction persisted that even in the event such optimism was misplaced, war would not endanger American security if the United States continued to maintain a strict neutrality by refusing to sell munitions to any of the belligerent powers.

★ ROOSEVELT'S POSITION

As European tension increased in spite of popular skepticism in this country over the likelihood of war, Roosevelt began to give increasing attention to foreign affairs. He had accepted the neutrality legislation with misgivings—"I regret . . . that I signed that Act," he was later to say—and he soon became convinced that the United States should reverse its policy and take a positive and forthright stand against aggression wherever it threatened. There were to be repeated charges that in trying to arouse the public to perils overseas, he was seeking to divert attention from the failures of the New Deal at home. Even after the outbreak of European strife in 1939 his warnings of the danger to the United States were often passed off as politics. Yet events were to demonstrate that he saw far more clearly the implications of world developments than those who accused him of warmongering.

Roosevelt's first important plea for a policy that might more constructively meet the threat of war than continued reliance on neutrality was made in an address delivered in Chicago on October 5, 1937, which was to become known as his "quarantine speech." Declaring that the high aspirations expressed in the Kellogg-Briand Pact had given way to "a haunting fear of calamity," he drew attention to the undeclared wars raging in so many parts of the world, stating emphatically that should such attacks on freedom persist, there could be no escape for America. The peace-loving nations, he insisted, should stand together in concerted efforts to forestall the international anarchy and instability from which there could be no escape through mere isolation or neutrality. He then made his famous analogy:

> The peace, the freedom and the security of ninety per cent of the population of the world is today being jeopardized by the remaining ten per cent who are threatening a breakdown of all international order and law. Surely the ninety per cent who want to live in peace under law and in accordance with moral standards that have received almost universal acceptance through the centuries, can and must find some way to make their will prevail. . . .
>
> When an epidemic of physical disease starts to spread, the community approves and joins in a quarantine of the patients in order to protect the health of the community against the spread of the disease.

Other than to emphasize that America was actively engaged in a search for peace that was not necessarily contrary to the observance of neutrality, the President gave no concrete suggestion of how the aggressor nations might be quarantined. He had in mind, it has since become known, some idea of calling an international conference, but he was to have no chance to develop any such plans. The popular reaction to his speech was generally hostile. It was again dismissed as warmongering, or as a red herring drawn across the trail of domestic discontent. A poll taken that same October by *Fortune* found 60 per cent of the people interviewed stating that their feelings toward Germany, Italy, and Japan were entirely neutral.

During the next two years, such further efforts as the President made to win support for a policy that would in some way deter aggressor nations rather than encourage them to believe they had nothing to fear from the United States proved equally unavailing. There was to be no change in the neutrality legislation. Public opinion polls continued to reveal the general complacence of the American people, with majorities as large as 70 per cent expressing their satisfaction with the stand that had been taken. A striking illustration of isolationist and pacifist sentiment was the near passage in January 1938 of a resolution introduced in Congress by Representative Ludlow. It called for a constitutional amendment that would make any declaration of war dependent upon a popular referendum.

★ THE MOUNTING CRISIS

In the meantime the international situation was rapidly deteriorating. Japan continued on her course of conquest in China, Italy consolidated her hold over Ethiopia, and Germany occupied Austria. With Asia already plunged in war and all Europe feverishly rearming, only the Americas could boast of anything resembling peace. There, an important development occurred when the United States joined forces with the Latin American countries to transform the Monroe Doctrine from a unilateral to a multilateral undertaking for their mutual security. At a conference at Lima agreement was reached for immediate consultation in the event that the peace of the Western Hemisphere should be threatened. Further strengthening of the Good Neighbor policy and of Latin American goodwill was important, but was a very minor gain for world security in the light of events in Europe.

A first frightening crisis took place in the fall of 1938, when Hitler called for the return to German rule of those parts of Czechoslovakia—the Sudetenland—populated by Germans. Would England and France, their attitude stiffening in the face of Germany's peremptory demands, take a decisive stand in support of Czechoslovakia? Would Germany defy all opposition and carry out her threat of seizing the territory by force if it was not surrendered peacefully? Every device of diplomacy was hurriedly employed to avert the outbreak of the gathering storm.

The result of this crisis is all too well-known: the frantic conferences among Great Britain, France, Germany, and Italy—with the significant omission of Soviet Russia; the somber journeyings of Prime Minister Chamberlain to negotiate with Hitler at Berchtesgaden and Godesberg, and the final denouement when at their conference at Munich in late September, the western Allies bowed to Germany's demands and forced Czechoslovakia to cede the disputed territory. In the vain expectation that appeasement—a word that thereafter enjoyed a sinister and unhappy connotation—had satisfied Hitler's lust for power, Chamberlain returned to London to announce the establishment of "peace in our time."

The entire world, including the United States, breathed easier with the apparent resolution of the Munich crisis. Those convinced that appeasement could not halt Germany on the dangerous path along which Hitler was leading her felt that the betrayal of Czechoslovakia was the betrayal of democracy. In general, however, hope persisted that fascist aggression would be content with its triumphs and that war could now be avoided.

Roosevelt did not succumb to this illusion. He recognized the mounting danger—"it has become increasingly clear that peace is not assured" —and he continued to try to arouse the American public to the necessity of more effective action in its own interest. In his annual message to Congress in January 1939 he took up again the theme of his quarantine speech of two years earlier: "All about us rage undeclared wars—military and economic. All about us are threats of new aggression—military and economic. . . . There are many methods short of war, but stronger and more effective than mere words, of bringing home to the aggressor governments the aggregate sentiments of our own people."

The popular response to this appeal was once again apathetic, and Roosevelt was unable to develop any positive program for employing "methods short of war" which would call Germany, Italy, and Japan to account. The sympathy of the American people had clearly swung to the democratic as opposed to the fascist powers, but any concrete expression of such sympathy was blocked by the pervasive threat that the United States might be drawn into their surging conflict. When the President proposed that our neutrality laws be amended to permit the sale of arms and munitions to the victim of any unwarranted attack, Congress was not moved. Every suggestion of direct aid for the western democracies was greeted with an alarmed isolationist outcry.

Munich did not uphold "peace in our time" for very long. Hitler tore up the pledges he had made in his negotiations with Chamberlain and in March 1939 sent his armies marching into Czechoslovakia. A few weeks later Mussolini profited from his partner's success in defying the Anglo-French Allies and forcibly seized Albania. "I'll be back in the fall if we do not have war," was Roosevelt's revealing commentary on his own fears when he left Warm Springs, Georgia, on April 9 to return to Washington. Once more the cry of warmonger was raised by his opponents, who refused to ponder his prophetic statement that "peace by fear has no higher or more enduring quality than peace by the sword."

The final signal for conflict was given in August when Germany and

Soviet Russia concluded their notorious nonaggression pact. Free to maneuver without worrying about the U.S.S.R., Hitler now called on Poland to surrender the Polish Corridor. England and France were faced with their final crisis. This time they did not hesitate: there could be no further surrender to Nazi ruthlessness. They supported Poland in rejecting Hitler's new challenge to the peace and security of Europe and when German troops crossed the Polish border on September 1, 1939, they countered with a declaration of war.

It was still hard for the American people to realize what had happened. Yet in spite of their reluctance to abandon hopes for peace during the last fateful weeks of August, they were at least better prepared for the actual outbreak of hostilities than they had been in 1914. The crisis in European politics had been followed with avid interest, and radio reports gave an immediacy to these events that had not been felt in any comparable way twenty-five years earlier. Moreover, there was no question where national sympathies lay in 1939. The general public could not have been more anxious to avoid any involvement in the conflict, but it almost universally condemned Germany as the aggressor and ardently hoped for an allied victory.

Speaking to the people in a Fireside Chat on September 3, 1939, Roosevelt stated:

> This nation will remain a neutral nation, but I cannot ask that every American remain neutral in thought as well. . . . I hope the United States will keep out of this war. I believe that it will. And I give you assurance and reassurance that every effort of your government will be directed toward that end. As long as it remains within my power to prevent it, there will be no black-out of peace in the United States.

★ REVISION OF NEUTRALITY

The provisions of the existing neutrality legislation went into immediate effect upon the outbreak of European war. The expiration of the two-year cash-and-carry clause adopted in 1937 somewhat fortuitously left the door open to trade in nonmilitary goods, but shipments of arms and munitions to any belligerent remained automatically banned. Within less than two months, however, sympathy for the Allies led to a first breach in the wall that had been erected to prevent America taking sides in the conflict. On November 4 Congress repealed the arms embargo and placed all belligerent trade, whether in munitions or other supplies, on a cash-and-carry basis.

Roosevelt took the lead in urging this revision of the law. He declared that such action would represent a return to America's traditional defense of freedom of the seas and that the stimulus afforded national production by developing the trade in munitions would help the United States in building up its own national defense. And so long as all trade of any sort was kept on a cash-and-carry basis, he added, American lives and American property would be protected. There would be no risk, as there had been in 1914, of becoming involved in any hostilities. "There," Roosevelt stated, "lies the road to peace!"

What the President did not point out, but what was clearly in his mind and that of all proponents of repeal of the arms embargo, was the extent to which the cash-and-carry trade in American exports would strengthen the allied cause. England and France would be able through their control of the seas to obtain in this country all the necessary materials of war—whether airplanes, tanks, or foodstuffs—from which Germany would be completely cut off. The basic idea behind the new policy was to provide all possible aid short of war to England and France, in the belief that only Germany's defeat could in the long run keep the United States out of war.

Whatever might have been the consequences of trying to maintain the more strict neutrality originally envisaged in the legislation of the mid-1930's, revision of the existing law placed the nation not on the road to peace, but on the road to war. There is little likelihood that the United States could have in any way permanently avoided hostilities. But when it took the stand that it was willing to provide economic support for the Allies, on the implicit theory that their victory was essential to American security, only the collapse of Germany could have prevented the eventual repeal of the neutrality legislation as a whole, and consequent direct involvement in Europe's conflict.

The former advocates of collective security strongly supported Roosevelt's policy; it was violently opposed by the isolationists. The country became sharply divided along lines that would become steadily intensified during the next two years. While a considerable majority in both houses of Congress approved neutrality revision, the vote nevertheless was significant. In the Senate it was 55 to 23; in the House 242 to 172. So far as the President was already committed to promoting an allied victory, this relatively close decision made it clear that he would have to move cautiously in taking any further steps.

★ "THE PHONY WAR"

The war in the meantime followed an unexpected course. While Hitler's armies rapidly overran Poland and in a matter of weeks inflicted a devastating defeat on that unfortunate country, little or nothing happened on the western front. Neither Germany nor the Allies made any attempt to launch a full-scale offensive, and it began to appear as if the deadlock might become permanent. The fears aroused by the first outbreak of hostilities subsided as Americans joked over "the phony war." For a time it was widely believed that the German and Anglo-French armies might be locked indefinitely behind the defensive fortifications of the opposing Siegfried and Maginot lines.

Attention was diverted to Russian activities in eastern Europe. With the protection of the agreements that had been reached with Germany in August, the Soviet Union occupied the eastern half of Poland, forcefully annexed Estonia, Lithuania, and Latvia, and demanded territorial cessions of Finland. Only the latter country could resist Russian pressure, and throughout the winter of 1939–40, bitter warfare raged between the greatly outnumbered Finnish forces and the Red armies. Public opinion in the United States, already deeply stirred by what was regarded as the Soviet Union's betrayal of the democratic cause through its nonaggression treaty with Hitler, turned savagely against the communists. The "dreadful rape of Finland" was judged to be even more flagrant aggression than the German onslaught against Poland. The hope once maintained that Russia would be found on the side of peace and security, Roosevelt declared in February 1940, "is today either shattered or put away in storage against some better day."

The Russo-Finnish war ended in Soviet victory about a month later. An ominous quiet then settled over eastern Europe, and there was still no break in the apparent stalemate in the West. The isolationists seemed to be confirmed in their belief that if the United States carefully avoided any overt act, it could escape being drawn into a war which would probably be settled by the mutual exhaustion of the contesting powers.

A British visitor, Robert Bruce Lockhart, author of *British Agent* and other books, gave this opinion of America's attitude toward England and France during the period of the phony war: "We Americans went into the last war to save democracy. We pulled you out of a hole and we received very grudging thanks. At Versailles and after Versailles you trampled on democratic ideals. Now, largely through your own fault, you are in trouble again and you want our help. Well, we've learnt our lesson."

There were nevertheless many observers who felt that the United States was being lulled into a false sense of security. Should the war end in a stalemate as a result of American failure to pull the Allies out of a hole—few foresaw how close England and France were to come to complete and catastrophic defeat—they believed that fascism would become an intolerable threat to democracy everywhere. Robert E. Sherwood is authority for the statement, made in his *Roosevelt and Hopkins,* that Roosevelt was deeply concerned at this time over the possibility of a negotiated peace that would actually strengthen Hitler's position. Yet he felt his hands were completely tied in respect to offering any further aid or encouragement to the Allies. "It was one crisis in Roosevelt's career," Sherwood wrote, "when he was completely at a loss as to what action to take—a period of terrible, stultifying vacuum."

★ THE FALL OF FRANCE

It was against this confusing background that Germany suddenly and dramatically shattered not only the uneasy truce of the western front, but every illusion of the phony war and a negotiated peace. In a series of lightning-like blows in the spring of 1940, Hitler's armies invaded Norway, overran Denmark, broke through the meager defenses of Holland and Belgium, conquered northern France, and drove the British expeditionary forces reeling back to the British Channel, where they were saved only by the miracle of Dunkirk. In a brief three months, the Wehrmacht—with the aid of paralyzing air attacks and the subversive intrigues of fifth columnists—had completely overwhelmed the opposing armies of the western democracies. Hitler stood astride half the continent. His armies were poised on its western shores with only the British Channel serving as a final rampart in defense of England.

France's surrender and the immediate threat to Great Britain jerked the United States out of its complacency overnight. Nothing could have been more devastating than the astounding triumphs of the blitzkrieg. Whatever differences of opinion existed as to the measures that should be taken to build up American security—and such differences were acerbated rather than lessened—even the isolationists could no longer ignore the possible threat to the United States in any further German triumphs. It was not the outbreak of European war that made national defense the predominant concern of the American people; it was the fall of France and imminent threat of Hitler's invasion of Great Britain.

In September 1939 Roosevelt had declared a limited emergency, but in doing so had carefully pointed out that there was no need to do all the things that such a situation might seemingly call for. "There is no thought in any shape, manner or form," he stated, "of putting the Nation, either in its defenses or in its internal economy, on a war basis. That is one thing we want to avoid. We are going to keep the Nation on a peace basis, in accordance with peacetime authorizations." Nine months later an emergency that could no longer be considered quite so limited launched the country on what was to be an all-out program of industrial mobilization, rearmament, and military conscription. Moreover, Roosevelt committed the nation to further aid for the forces still continuing the fight against Nazi aggression with a tacit promise to England that she could count on continuing American support.

Speaking at Charlottesville on June 10, the very day that Italy entered the war ("the hand that held the dagger has plunged it into the back of its neighbor"), the President outlined American policy in the fearful crisis now confronting the world:

> In our American unity, we will pursue two obvious and simultaneous courses; we will extend to the opponents of force the material resources of this nation; and, at the same time, we will harness and speed up the use of those resources in order that we ourselves in the Americas may have the equipment and training equal to the task of any emergency and every defense.

CHAPTER XXVII

Pearl Harbor

★ NATIONAL DEFENSE

The series of special messages that Roosevelt sent to Congress to meet the needs of national defense after the fall of France had an impact upon the country comparable to that of the messages with which he had bombarded Capitol Hill during the crisis of the depression. And Congress responded with the same alacrity as it had in 1933.

Before the summer of 1940 came to an end, it had passed a series of separate bills appropriating the money to build up the army, obtain essential supplies and mechanized equipment, increase the strength in ships of war so as to provide for an effective two-ocean navy, and establish an adequate air force. The immediate appropriations for national defense amounted to $13 billion; and within a year they had totaled $37 billion. This was more than the entire bill for American participation in World War I.

"At this time, when the world—and the world includes our own American hemisphere—is threatened by forces of destruction," Roosevelt told the nation, "it is my resolve and yours to build up our armed defenses. We shall build them to whatever heights the future may require. We shall build them swiftly, as the methods of warfare quickly change."

To carry forward this program, every effort was made to mobilize the industrial strength of the nation and win over wholehearted public support. To give it a nonpartisan character, the President summoned two Republicans to key positions in his cabinet. Henry L. Stimson, former Secretary of State under Hoover, became Secretary of War, and Frank Knox, the Republican nominee for the vice-presidency in 1936, was made Secretary of the Navy. Representatives of both industry and labor served on the various national defense agencies. For a time there was much confusion in the allocation of responsibility for procurement, allocation, and the determination of priorities in military supplies, and not until early 1941 was even a part way satisfactory system worked out. Roosevelt then established the Office of Production Management, jointly headed by William S. Knudsen, the president of General Motors, and Sidney Hillman, chief of the Amalgamated Clothing Workers.

An even more important step had meanwhile been taken with adoption of a peacetime draft to build up the nation's armed forces. Congress passed the Selective Service Act in September 1940. It required the registration of all men between the ages of twenty-one and thirty-five, and provided for the induction of 900,000 men annually for a year's military training. National guardsmen were called into service and voluntary enlistments in both the army and navy continued, but as in World War I, the main reliance was to be placed upon a national draft.

The President had spoken of the threat Hitlerism represented for all the Americas, and every possible measure was taken to strengthen hemispheric solidarity. Through the Act of Havana, adopted in July 1940, the American republics agreed to take immediate action in mutual self-defense should the status of any European colony in the Western Hemisphere appear to be threatened, a move further strengthening the new concept of the Monroe Doctrine as a collective guarantee against European aggression. Canada had already been brought within the scope of hemispheric action, and for the further development of such plans the United States and Canadian military authorities created a Permanent Joint Board on Defense.

Roosevelt not only was convinced of the necessity of these measures, but was also determined to do everything possible to aid those European countries still fighting Nazi aggression. The cause of Britain, standing virtually alone against almost hopeless odds, was to be made America's cause in the belief that here lay this country's first line of defense. Only so far as the United States could succeed in bolstering up whatever forces continued to resist Hitlerism, the President was to declare again and again, could it hope to prevent a triumphant Germany from some day carrying the war to our own shores.

The vital decision to back Great Britain with everything that the United States could possibly offer her in the way of material and moral encouragement, Robert Sherwood has written in his *Roosevelt and Hopkins,* was basically the President's own. He faced strong opposition from within his own official family, and his position with the public was less secure than at any time since he had first come into office in 1933. But both strategic and moral considerations, according to Sherwood, led Roosevelt in spite of strong criticism to adopt the policy of all aid to the Allies short-of-war, and he was prepared to exert all his powers of national leadership to persuade the country that this was the course to be followed.

The risks of such a policy were clear. Unless material aid succeeded in enabling Great Britain to defeat Germany, the logic of events was almost certain to bring the United States into increasingly active participation in the war. Roosevelt was prepared to run such risks rather than invite the greater danger of allowing the United States to become isolated from all potential allies. His repeated assertion that his goal was peace was completely justified, in his own mind, because he was acting on the premise that a Hitler permitted by default to conquer all Europe would be certain to make the United States the next object of direct or indirect attack. "I have one supreme determination," the President stated emphatically, "to do all that I can to keep war away from these shores for all time." The significant phrase was "these shores."

The most important move made in 1940 to aid Great Britain was the destroyer-naval base deal. England was in dire need of destroyers to help fend off threatened German invasion, and the United States had available fifty over-age destroyers from World War I. The United States lacked the means to defend the security zone, three hundred miles wide, that had been set up off the coast of the Americas, and England controlled the potential air and naval bases that could be used for its protection. After protracted negotiations the United States transferred the destroyers to England, and England leased or otherwise granted the naval and air bases to the United States.

Roosevelt concluded this momentous transaction, so clearly modifying the original concepts of American neutrality, on his own responsibility. It was announced to Congress on September 2, 1940, as a *fait accompli* which the President characterized as "the most important action in the reinforcement of our national defense that has been taken since the purchase of Louisiana." The methods employed, officially upheld on the ground that the transaction was a legitimate exercise of the President's powers to provide for the national defense, were severely criticized, but the obvious advantages to the United States resulted in general popular approval for what had been done.

★ INTERVENTIONISTS VS ISOLATIONISTS

In spite of acceptance of the destroyer-naval base deal, public opinion was still anything but united behind Roosevelt's general policy of aid to the Allies. The split that had long since been apparent between the advocates of intervention and the proponents of isolationism was if anything widened under the impact of Germany's conquest of western

Europe and the crucial Battle of Britain. Although there would always be strong general support for national defense, the two extremist wings in American thought battled ceaselessly over every other phase of foreign policy. The one urged active intervention in the war before the Allies were conquered; the other opposed every move in their support as needlessly dragging the country nearer participation in a conflict that was considered none of its concern.

The interventionists argued that the time for temporizing and halfway measures was over. America could not let the democratic nations of Europe be one by one overwhelmed by the ruthless power of Nazi aggression. National security was immediately at stake. If the United States stood supinely by while Hitler conquered all Europe, it would eventually find itself fighting alone. It should throw its full force into the conflict while England still stood as a European bastion of the democratic cause and the British fleet controlled the seas. The interventionists supported Roosevelt, but they were constantly prodding him to take more drastic measures.

The isolationists, on the other hand, maintained just as stoutly that the United States had no direct interest in the European quarrel and that even a Hitler victory would not represent any real threat to American security. The war was no more than another chapter in the senseless duel between British and German imperialism. The United States had no need to fear foreign attack unless the American people brought it on themselves by meddling with affairs abroad. Should there actually be any danger of such an assault materializing, it was all the more important that the United States should not dissipate its strength by aiding Great Britain. It should concentrate upon its own national defenses behind the protective barrier of the Atlantic Ocean.

As time went on the conflict between these two groups, which were represented by the Committee to Defend America by Aiding the Allies and the America First Committee, became intensified, and the debate over intervention or nonintervention raged ceaselessly throughout the land. The general public, standing between the two extreme factions, was uncertain and confused. There was no question of what the overwhelming majority wanted: a democratic victory over fascism *and* peace for the United States. But if these objectives became irreconcilable, as the course of the war in Europe so perilously suggested they would, should peace be sacrificed for the defeat of fascism? And if this question were answered affirmatively, at what point and in what manner should the United States intervene? The American people floundered hopelessly amid their conflicting hopes and fears.

Public opinion polls reflected this indecision. They repeatedly showed substantial popular majorities favoring such assistance for Great Britain as would assure her survival, and at the same time opposing any measures that seemed to invite war. Until Pearl Harbor itself, this attitude persisted. The temper of the people compelled Roosevelt to move with increasing caution in order to command the popular support that an effective foreign policy, whatever line it followed, necessarily demanded. Accused by the interventionists of being too timid, and by the noninterventionists of being too daring, he walked a narrow and dangerous tight rope.

Both at the time and in later years he was criticized for not taking a position of more decisive leadership. Roosevelt was keenly aware, however, of the terrible danger of seeking congressional authority for some direct move against Germany, and then having Congress withhold such authority. He was carefully to refrain from "the irrevocable act." In the long run national unity was the all-important consideration, and the incontrovertible fact remained that in 1940–41 the country was too divided for the President to dare move in any direction without the greatest circumspection.

How sharp the cleavage in public opinion had become was graphically revealed when, late in 1941, Roosevelt finally asked for the repeal of the already badly battered neutrality act. Congress followed his lead, but the vote in the Senate was 53 to 37, and that in the House 212 to 194.

★ THE ELECTION OF 1940

In the meantime, a presidential election had taken place in 1940, and shattering all historical precedent, the American people had elected Roosevelt to a third term.

He had originally had no intention whatsoever of again running for office. Sometime during the spring of 1940, however, the mounting international crisis convinced him that it was his duty to do so, if his party chose to name him again. He made no public announcement of his position, but his possible availability blocked too serious consideration of any other candidate. Renomination became an almost foregone conclusion. Named on the first ballot at the Democratic convention, Roosevelt thereupon stated: "My conscience will not allow me to turn my back upon a call to service."

The Republicans, actually meeting before Roosevelt's renomination was fully certain, first faced the old problem of formulating a program that would acknowledge the popularly accepted concept of government's broadened role in economic affairs, and yet effectively call the Democratic administration to account for its domestic failures. Their platform accepted the general goals of social security, even while it declared that for seven long years the New Deal had "whirled in a turmoil of shifting, contradictory, and overlapping administrations and policies." Foreign affairs presented even greater difficulties. The Republicans were highly critical of Roosevelt's policy, but their own ranks were split on what should be done. Moving cautiously, they declared their support for national defense and condemned any move toward war.

The nomination of the presidential candidate struck a new and positive note. Passing over the claims of the expected political aspirants, including both Governor Dewey of New York and Senator Taft of Ohio, the Republicans named Wendell L. Willkie, a wealthy public utility executive and onetime Democrat, who was best known at the time for his stubborn fight against the TVA and government control over industry. On the face of things Willkie could not have been a less likely candidate; he was closely associated with Wall Street and without political experience of any sort. His dynamic and forceful personality, however, won him a host of backers who believed that a plain, commonsense businessman, typifying efficiency, could bring new life to the Republican party and successfully challenge Democratic rule. While the professionals within his own party never looked with much favor on Willkie's candidacy, growing grass-roots support brought him the nomination amid enthusiasm that recalled the Bull Moose convention of 1912.

In the course of the campaign the Republican nominee showed himself to be an independent liberal and an internationalist. He assailed the New Deal's failure to carry out its own domestic program successfully, rather than quarreling with its underlying principles, and in much the same way he accepted the basic concept of a foreign policy based on aid short-of-war for the nations fighting Hitlerism. While the party's isolationist wing cried out that Roosevelt had reached secret agreements with England and was trying to take the country into war in contemptuous disregard of both Congress and the people, Willkie himself approved the destroyer-naval base deal and refused to make foreign affairs a campaign issue. His principal attacks upon his opponent centered about the third term, and he vigorously condemned the idea that any one man should be considered indispensable in a democratic system of government.

As in every one of Roosevelt's campaigns there was a scurrilous undercover attack upon his integrity. A reflection of the attitude which many people continued to maintain was caught in a cartoon (later hung in one of the White House rooms), showing a little girl protesting to her mother about a little boy who was chalking something on the sidewalk.

The caption under the picture was, "Look, Mother—Wilfred wrote a bad word!"—and the word was ROOSEVELT.

The President stayed for a time on the sidelines in 1940, declaring that he was too busy to campaign. However, the charges of the isolationists finally drove him to refute what he said were deliberate falsifications of fact and to declare angrily that the Republicans were "playing politics with national security." Disclosing what he considered their obstructive record on national defense, he defended his own policies and declared that foreign aid was the road not to war but to peace. His position was much that of Wilson in 1916, and his attempts to assure the country that he opposed war led him to make statements something less than forthright in view of his belief that intervention could not be long avoided. "Your President says this country is not going to war," he stated unequivocally on one occasion; and again: "Your boys are not going to be sent into any foreign wars." The reservation in his own mind was that the United States would not fight unless attacked, but it was becoming increasingly clear that his policy openly ran the risk of inviting attack.

A greater number of people voted in the election of 1940—nearly 50,000,000—than ever before in American history, and the election was closer than in any presidential race since 1916. The final count gave Roosevelt 27,243,000 votes and Willkie 22,204,000. A reluctance to change national leadership in the face of the international crisis, and restored popular faith in the man himself, appeared to be the decisive reasons for Roosevelt's third triumph.

★ LEND-LEASE AND THE ATLANTIC CHARTER

The Battle of Britain, so heroically displaying the determination and fortitude of the British people, had been fought and won before Roosevelt's re-election, but the position of England still remained perilous. With a renewed popular mandate for his policy, the President was all the more determined to meet Prime Minister Churchill's urgent request for help—"Give us the tools"—in beating back the Nazi onslaught. In a Fireside Chat on national security in December 1940, Roosevelt said:

> Thinking in terms of today and tomorrow, I make the direct statement to the American people that there is far less chance of the United States getting into war, if we do all we can now to support the nations defending themselves against attack by the Axis than if we acquiesce in their defeat, submit tamely to an Axis victory, and wait our turn to be the object of attack in another war later on.
>
> If we are to be completely honest with ourselves, we must admit that there is a risk in any course we take. But I deeply believe that the great majority of

our people agree that the course I now advocate involves the least risk now and the greatest hope for world peace in the future.

Calling for the full mobilization of all the nation's resources and a greatly stepped-up program of industrial production, the President declared that "we must be the great arsenal of democracy."

In order to make munitions and war supplies more easily available for the Allies, he now presented to Congress a plan for lend-lease aid. To avoid the pitfalls of foreign loans and yet meet the problem of the Allies' exhausted credit, he proposed that the United States lend or lease to any nation whose defense the President deemed vital for the defense of the United States such materials of war as the nation under attack needed to resist aggression. Roosevelt used a homely analogy to support his plan. If one's neighbor's house was burning down and one had a length of garden hose, he said, one would hardly argue over terms for making the hose available to put out a fire so dangerous to one's own house. American resources, the President declared, should in the same way be made available to help put out the conflagration in Europe.

The proposal aroused long and stormy debate, in and out of Congress. However on March 11, 1941, the Lend-Lease Act became law with the President's signature, and shortly afterwards Congress appropriated $7,000,000,000 (with a quarter of this sum earmarked for airplanes) to get the program underway. Harry Hopkins was placed in charge of it.

As the war continued to spread throughout Europe during these fateful months, finally leading to the climactic attack of Germany upon Soviet Russia in the early summer of 1941, the energies of the American people were more and more absorbed in making the nation over into the arsenal of democracy. Still nominally at peace, the country was virtually placed on a war footing as the Roosevelt administration built up the army, navy, and air force, amassed munitions and equipment, and speeded up the transatlantic flow of the airplanes, tanks, artillery, and other supplies so urgently needed by Great Britain, Soviet Russia, and the other nations fighting Germany. "All our domestic problems," the President stated, "are now a part of the great emergency."

In August a further move startled the country. President Roosevelt secretly met Prime Minister Churchill in a conference at sea off the Newfoundland coast, and the two statesmen agreed upon a joint declaration of their nations' common aims in any future settlement of peace. The President had already touched upon his hopes for the future in calling for the realization of the four freedoms—freedom of speech, freedom of religion, freedom from want, freedom from fear—and the Atlantic Charter, which would subsequently become the foundation stone for the grand wartime alliance of the United Nations, now set forth eight basic principles to govern a future peace. They included no territorial aggrandizement, respect for the right of peoples to choose their own form of government, equal access on the part of all nations to the raw materials of the world, full economic collaboration, a peace that would assure the fullest freedom from fear and want, and abandonment of the use of force in international relations.

An idealistic expression of world aspirations for collective security, comparable in many respects to Wilson's Fourteen Points, the Atlantic Charter aroused both favorable and unfavorable repercussions. Its significance and implications entered into the furious debate still being waged in the United States between isolationists and interventionists, and in some quarters it brought down a storm of abuse on Roosevelt. The question would again and again be raised as to how far he had gone in promising support for Great Britain. It is true that he had officially authorized military discussions between the general staffs of the two countries, but they were on a basis of "if or when" the United States became engaged in hostilities. The President at no time made any binding commitments other than those involved in the destroyer-naval base deal and the lend-lease program.

★ THE UNDECLARED WAR

Even though no pledges had been made to Great Britain except those which were public knowledge, the President's policy was rapidly wearing away the thin veneer of American neutrality. The consulates of the Axis powers had already been closed down, with the freezing of the financial assets of both Germany and Italy, and far more important, measures were already underway not only to provide more economic aid for Great Britain, but to make certain that such aid reached her. It was only logical that with the country committed to the lend-lease program, efforts should be made to help England parry the increasingly dangerous submarine attacks on the ships that were bringing her the American-made airplanes, tanks, guns, and ammunition. On the ground that the protection of the waters off our own coasts was essential for national defense, Roosevelt was ready to re-enforce the security zone in the north Atlantic as a way of reducing Great Britain's burden in guarding the sea lanes.

Through agreement with Denmark, air bases were established in Greenland in April, and three months later American troops were stationed in Iceland. Roosevelt had already announced that "our patrols are helping now to insure delivery of the needed supplies to Britain. . . . This can be done; it must be done; it will be done." He now stated, reasserting the traditional doctrine of freedom of the seas, that in fulfillment of its pledges of aid to Great Britain, the United States would take such further measures as might prove necessary to carry out this policy: "We in the Americas will decide for ourselves whether, and when, and where, our American interests are attacked or our security threatened. We are placing our armed forces in strategic military position. We will not hesitate to use armed force to repel attack."

In spite of official denials that such steps represented a violation of neutrality, Germany strongly protested American policy. She could no more afford to allow the free flow of supplies across the Atlantic in 1941 than in 1917, and the inevitable consequence was the beginning of submarine attacks on American vessels. The first sinking of a merchant ship occurred in the south Atlantic rather than north Atlantic; soon afterwards two American vessels operating under Panamanian registry were torpedoed in the northern security zone. Then in early September a German submarine attacked the destroyer "Greer," albeit under provocation that was not at the time revealed.

The situation still differed somewhat from that which had developed just a quarter of a century earlier because the United States did not as yet claim the right to send American vessels into the war zone. But so far as the greatly expanded North Atlantic security zone was concerned, Roosevelt was prepared, as Wilson had been, to accept this challenge of submarine warfare whatever the risk to peace. In a worldwide radio broadcast on September 11, he explicitly warned Germany:

> These Nazi submarines and raiders are the rattlesnakes of the Atlantic. They are a menace to the free pathways of the high seas. They are a challenge to our sovereignty. They hammer at our most precious rights when they attack ships of the American flag—symbols of our independence, our freedom, our very life.
>
> It is no act of war on our part when we decide to protect the seas which are vital to American defense. The aggression is not ours. Ours is solely defense. But let this warning be clear. From now on, if German or Italian vessels of war enter the waters, the protection of which is necessary for American defense, they do so at their peril. The orders which I have given as Commander-in-Chief to the United States Army and Navy are to carry out that policy—at once. The sole responsibility rests upon Germany. There will be no shooting unless Germany continues to seek it.

With specific instructions to the commanders of naval vessels to carry out this general policy by attacking submarines in the security zone on sight, Roosevelt now went to Congress—on October 9—to ask authority for the single remaining act short-of-war which would make aid to Great Britain still more effective: permission for armed American merchant ships to trade directly with belligerent nations. The time had come for final and complete repeal of the neutrality legislation.

"We Americans," the President declared, "have cleared our decks and taken our battle stations . . . standing ready in the defense of our nation and the faith of our fathers to do what God has given us the power to see as our full duty."

Congress debated the President's proposal furiously, but with German submarines attacking two more destroyers, the "Kearny" and the "Reuben James," with heavy loss of life, it finally fell in line. Early in November it voted away the last restrictions of the original neutrality legislation and by the close vote already noted authorized the arming of American merchantmen to carry supplies to Great Britain.

As the United States plunged into this undeclared war the country still remained divided over the wisdom of the steps that had been taken. The proponents of intervention had cast off all pretense of the United States remaining neutral. They more insistently than ever demanded immediate entry into the war as the only way of averting the Nazi menace to this country. The United States, they reiterated, could no longer stand aside. Unless it came promptly to its potential allies' help, with more than economic assistance, this country would soon be left alone to fight a Germany victorious over both England and Russia.

At the same time, the ranks of the isolationists had been solidified. They had opposed each successive step taken by the President since the neutrality laws were first modified, and they now called for an immediate halt to the mad course on which they believed the country was embarked. They particularly resented aid to the Soviet Union and would have left Germany and Russia mutually to exhaust each other in continued combat. Such unexpected bedfellows as former President Hoover and John L. Lewis, Senator Wheeler and Colonel Lindbergh, agreed that there was no danger of a German attack on the United States, whatever happened in Europe, unless this country asked for it. They also continued to insist that even should the perils conjured up by Roosevelt become an actuality, the United States could defend itself alone. Although isolationism in the country as a whole appeared to be waning, and had indeed suffered a finally decisive defeat in the repeal of the neutrality legislation, its individual spokesmen were becoming almost hysterical in their attacks on presidential policy.

The debate went on in Congress, in the press, over the radio, and in meetings and discussions throughout the country. Yet at the same time a fatalistic feeling developed that the nation was being drawn ever closer to the abyss whatever it did. Events were getting beyond control. As the year drew to a close the decision for war or peace appeared to many observers to be entirely out of American hands.

At this point the die was cast, suddenly and unexpectedly, by direct enemy attack on American territory. The blow came, however, not from across the Atlantic, but from across the Pacific. On December 7, 1941, Japanese planes roared in with the early dawn over the peaceful shores of Hawaii to bomb Pearl Harbor.

★ BACKGROUND IN THE PACIFIC

The dangers of a crisis in relations with Japan, even while the shooting war in the Atlantic grew every day more menacing, had not been completely ignored by the American people. Japanese aggression in eastern Asia was clearly forcing a situation where the United States faced the hard alternatives of appeasement or war. But the immediacy of the danger was certainly not fully realized, and there was no forewarning whatsoever that Japan might strike directly at the United States. Shocked and stunned surprise, a strange feeling of utter unreality, was the almost universal reaction as radio programs were interrupted that fateful Sunday afternoon in early December with the announcement that American warships had been destroyed and American lives lost by enemy action.

The split in Japanese-American relations had nevertheless been steadily widening since Japan had renewed her assault upon Nationalist China in 1937, embarking on a campaign of military conquest that was to bring nearly a third of China under Japanese control. While the failure of the United States to apply its neutrality legislation in "the China incident" had left American markets open to both countries, a growing sympathy for China as the victim of unprovoked aggression soon led to demands for a special ban on any further shipments of munitions to Japan. The administration recognized this point of view, going so far as to place a moral embargo on the sale of airplanes and aviation gasoline, but for the time being, it refused to intervene any more directly in the Far Eastern conflict.

Roosevelt was determined to follow a very cautious policy in this part of the world. In keeping with the precepts of the Stimson nonrecognition doctrine, there was at no time any disposition to recognize Japanese conquests, but any overt act that might endanger Japanese-American relations was studiously avoided until the summer of 1939. As a sign of the growing concern of the United States over Japanese claims to a coprosperity sphere throughout eastern Asia, announcement was then made that the existing Japanese-American commercial treaty would be terminated in six months. This was the most popular move Roosevelt made during these years in foreign policy. On the basis of Gallup polls a majority of some 80 per cent of the people favored the abrogation of this treaty as a protest against Japanese imperialism.

The outbreak of war in Europe soon followed. Japan's seizure of the opportunity provided by the fall of France in the spring of 1940 to send troops into northern Indo-China, the pressure exerted upon the Dutch East Indies to bring those important islands within the sphere of Japanese influence, and finally the adherence of the Tokyo government to the Berlin-Rome Axis drastically changed the entire situation. Japanese imperialism no longer threatened China alone. In co-operation with fascism, it menaced the rights and interests of all western nations in eastern Asia. But while more than ever opposed to Japanese expansion on the Asiatic mainland, the United States was re-enforced in its determination to move very cautiously because of the dangerous potentialities of the alliance between Tokyo and Berlin. Long since convinced that the principal foe of American democracy was Hitlerism, Roosevelt wished above all else to avoid any involvement in the Pacific that would impair the effectiveness of American aid to Great Britain.

★ RESTRAINING JAPAN

Nevertheless, various forms of economic pressure were adopted in the hope of restraining Japan without inviting retaliation. Among other measures the government withheld export licenses for any further shipments of materials of war, including iron and steel scrap. At the same time the President extended lend-lease aid to China and assigned military advisers to the Nationalist president, Generalissimo Chiang Kai-shek.

These moves proved to be completely ineffective in halting Japan's creeping advance, and the Roosevelt administration found itself under severe criticism for not taking more decisive measures. There was very much the same confusion in public thinking on Far Eastern issues as on European affairs. The American people wished to block Japanese aggression, and yet were unwilling to run the risks of war in so doing. When Japan brazenly occupied southern Indo-China in July 1941, however, Roosevelt became convinced that the time had arrived for a step which he had long hesitated to take—the application of all-inclusive economic sanctions.

It was a fateful decision. It in effect forced Tokyo to choose between abandoning its imperialistic advance or attempting to break through economic sanctions by war. For Japan was highly vulnerable, especially in respect to oil supplies, and the militarists in control of her government viewed economic isolation as national suicide. While the State Department fully realized the dangers in this situation, informed opinion held that Japan would not dare challenge the United States unless—or until—Germany defeated Great Britain.

The seeming contradiction between Roosevelt's reluctance to force the issue with Japan at any earlier period and his willingness to run this risk in the summer of 1941 is explained by Japan's persistent advance in southeastern Asia. The threat to American interests, including the Philippines, could no longer be ignored. It appeared impossible to allow Japan to consolidate her position in this part of the world by default. Prime Minister Churchill hoped that the United States would go even further than its economic boycott. At his Atlantic conference with Roosevelt, he urged announcement of a joint policy which would have warned Japan that any further advance meant war. The President refused to make any such firm commitment—indeed, he had no constitutional authority to do so—but he was now ready for at least economic sanctions.

In spite of these developments in midsummer 1941 there was still a faint hope that negotiations with Japan might produce some formula that would bring about a peaceful solution of Pacific problems. Even as this hope grew dimmer, moreover, the advantages of prolonging negotiations, and thereby postponing possible conflict, appeared to be all-important. The United States was not yet prepared for war; both military and naval authorities urged the State Department to exhaust every possible diplomatic resource before giving up. Every month, every week, and ultimately every day that could be gained was considered worth winning.

The conflict with Japan could have been at least temporarily resolved at any time if the United States had been willing to accept Japan's conquest of China. This was the fundamental demand of the Tokyo government, and the basic concession that the United States refused to make. Even if there had been no moral obligation to uphold traditional American policy in support of Chinese independence and the Open Door, it was felt that only an illusory peace could have been obtained by selling China down the river and conceding Japanese overlordship on the Asiatic continent.

This point of view was almost universally supported. Innumerable editorials in the nation's press declared that American interests in Asia were closely involved in the maintenance of China's independence and that from a broader point of view the defense against Nazi aggression in Europe would be frustrated if the United States passively allowed Japan to make a clean sweep in the Pacific. The dangers of the American position were recognized. There seemed, however, to be no alternative other than to stand fast in upholding the principle of Chinese territorial integrity while seeking through every means possible to persuade Japan that only a modification of her imperialistic ambitions could avert Pacific war.

★ THE WASHINGTON NEGOTIATIONS

Throughout the summer and fall of 1941, negotiations continued between Secretary of State Hull and the Japanese envoys in Washington. At no time did they make any headway. There was some discussion of a meeting at sea between President Roosevelt and Premier Konoye but it came to nothing. Japan kept repeating her demand that the United States in effect acknowledge Japanese control over China, and the United States insisted just as strongly that Japan recognize the Nationalist government and withdraw her troops from Chinese territory. Other issues involving the status of Indo-China, the renewal of Japanese-American trade, and the relations between Japan and the Axis powers entered into the discussions; the crux of the dispute remained always the status of the Chinese Republic.

On November 20 the Japanese delivered a note to Secretary Hull that in effect set forth their final position. It embodied the usual insistence upon a free hand in China, and while giving vague reassurances about Indo-China and general peace, made no real concessions to the American point of view. For a time the State Department considered answering it with a proposal for some temporary *modus vivendi,* but the objections of our allies—especially China—and also the impracticality of such a plan finally led Secretary Hull to forward to Tokyo a direct and uncompromising answer. This American note, of November 26, 1941, has sometimes been described as an ultimatum. Actually, it went no further than to reiterate the terms which the United States had set forth from the very first as the only possible basis for accommodation with Japan. The recall of Japanese troops from both China and Indo-China, Tokyo's acceptance of Chinese sovereignty, and withdrawal of Japan from the tripartite pact with Germany and Italy were the fundamental conditions for the renewal of normal Japanese-American trade relations and Pacific peace.

These negotiations in Washington had an unusual feature, unknown at the time to the public. The Japanese code had been broken by a secret process known as "magic," and every time the Japanese diplomats conferred with Secretary Hull he had advance notice of their instructions. At the time of the November note giving Japan's final terms, a deciphered message from Tokyo revealed that the Japanese Premier regarded this communication as Japan's last word. Two days later the Japanese envoys were further told—as Secretary Hull again knew through "magic"—that unless a favorable reply was received from the United States by November 29 negotiations would come to an end. "This time we mean it," the order from Tokyo stated explicitly. "The deadline absolutely cannot be changed. After that things are automatically going to happen."

There was no inkling of what was going to happen, but as subsequently made known through the Tokyo war trials, the Japanese had already definitely decided on their course of action. It was actually on November 25, the day before Secretary Hull answered Japan with his final statement of American policy, that the task force ordered to attack Pearl Harbor sailed for its secret rendezvous in the Kurile Islands.

While Hull did not know of this move, he was convinced that further negotiations with the Japanese had become futile. "I have washed my hands of it," he told Secretary Stimson, "and it is now in the hands of you and Knox, the Army and the Navy." He had come to the unhappy realization that the resources of diplomacy were exhausted.

The concluding conversations with the Japanese envoys, and the dispatch by Roosevelt of a personal peace appeal to the Japanese Emperor, had no relevancy so far as the issues of peace and war were concerned. The die had been cast. But while responsible officials in Washington realized that some overt act on Japan's part was imminent, the general public necessarily remained in ignorance of the revelations of "magic." The American people blindly continued to hope that some basis for mutual accord might still be discovered to ease Pacific tensions. It was only the Japanese attack on Pearl Harbor that finally disabused them of all such hopes.

★ WAR

The shocked surprise of the American people on December 7 was no greater than that of Washington officialdom, for all its forewarnings of possible attack. The belief was well-nigh universal, in the most informed quarters, that if or when Japan struck, it would be in the southwest Pacific. While there had been vague rumors, including one relayed from Tokyo by Ambassador Grew early in the year, that Pearl Harbor might be the Japanese objective, apparently no one in either diplomatic or military circles seriously contemplated any such rash move on Japan's part. While general instructions were sent out to all Pacific outposts to be on guard against the outbreak of war, no explicit special warning was given to the commanders in Hawaii.

The failure to order an emergency alert at Pearl Harbor was not due to any sinister intention to invite attack, as has sometimes been wildly charged against the Roosevelt administration. However, the military and naval authorities at Pearl Harbor, and through the chain of command their superiors in this country and the commander-in-chief himself, cannot be absolved of all responsibility for being caught off guard. While their individual negligence reflected a universal conviction that Japan would not risk direct attack upon American territory, and from that point of view was perhaps understandable, the fact remains that they were directly charged with maintaining the national defenses against attack from any quarter and at any time. They should have been more on the alert, but there was no "secret of Pearl Harbor" suggesting a Rooseveltian conspiracy for war.

The news that Pearl Harbor had been bombed reached the White House that fateful Sunday of December 7 just before a conference that the Japanese envoys had requested of the State Department for delivering Tokyo's answer to the last American note. Secretary Hull was informed of what had happened. Nevertheless, he calmly received the Japanese and read through the communication they presented to him. It was a flat rejection of the American proposals, stating that the plan put forward by the United States "ignores Japan's sacrifices in the four years of the China affair, menaces the empire's existence itself, and disparages its honor and prestige." After reading the note, Hull bluntly said that it was "crowded with infamous falsehoods and distortions on a scale so huge that I never imagined until today that any Government on this planet was capable of uttering them." He then summarily dismissed the Japanese envoys.

There were hurried conferences in the White House that evening as Roosevelt met with his cabinet and congressional leaders to prepare measures for meeting the national crisis. He no longer needed to hesitate or equivocate over foreign policy. The next day he appeared before Congress and delivered his war message:

> Yesterday, December 7, 1941—a date which will live in infamy—the United States of America was suddenly and deliberately attacked by naval and air forces of the Empire of Japan. . . . It will be recorded that the distance of Hawaii from Japan makes it obvious that the attack was deliberately planned many days or even weeks ago. During the intervening time the Japanese Government has deliberately sought to deceive the United States by false statements and expressions of hope for continued peace. . . . I ask that Congress declare that since the unprovoked and dastardly attack by Japan on Sunday, December 7th, a state of war has existed between the United States and the Japanese Empire.

Congress responded by declaring war with only a single dissenting vote.

Three days later, Germany and Italy resolved any lingering doubts about the role those countries intended to play in this new conflict by declaring war on the United States. No more than in the Pacific theater was there to be any further temporizing in the European theater. The United States was arrayed beside Great Britain, the Free French, Soviet Russia and Nationalist China in a gigantic global conflict that would be waged in the four quarters of the world until the complete downfall of Germany, Italy, and Japan was finally encompassed.

CHAPTER XXVIII

Total War

★ ROOSEVELT AND WARTIME STRATEGY

"We are now in this war. We are all in it—all the way. Every single man, woman and child is a partner in the most tremendous undertaking of our American history."

Speaking over the air two days after Pearl Harbor, President Roosevelt called upon the country to meet the challenge of the concerted attack of Japan, Germany, and Italy with all its resources and confidently declared his faith that in spite of initial setbacks the United States would ultimately win complete victory. He knew that he could count upon a universal response. Whatever the mistakes of foreign policy, whatever misgivings had been in the minds of the people, every doubt was now swept away. Japan had struck a heavy blow at the nation's naval power in the Pacific through her successful attack upon Pearl Harbor; far more important, she had overnight forged a new national unity among all elements of the American people.

Had Japan moved southward instead of striking across the Pacific, there would almost surely have been continued differences over foreign policy. She had done the one thing that could most effectively have brought down on her the full might and power of an aroused America. Prime Minister Churchill, fearful of divided counsels in the United States and desperately hoping for our full participation in the war against both Japan and Germany, greeted the news of Pearl Harbor with somber joy. His immediate reaction was, "The Lord hath delivered them into our hands."

Roosevelt had already made his major decision on strategy should the United States become involved in war. Early in 1941 it had been settled that no matter what happened in eastern Asia, Hitler was the chief enemy. As the British Prime Minister hurried across the Atlantic to consult with the President, he was nevertheless concerned whether the Japanese attack might force some shift in the projected American policy. Roosevelt stood firm. Although bitter defeat followed bitter defeat in the vast reaches of the Pacific—the destruction of the "Prince of Wales" and the "Repulse," the fall of Singapore, surrender in the Dutch East Indies, the Japanese investment of the Philippines—the plans went forward to marshal the nation's greatest forces for action in Europe.

The over-all strategy at this time and throughout the war was worked out in the closest co-operation between the United States and Great Britain. The Combined Chiefs of Staff drew up the blueprints for every campaign, and in both the European and Pacific theaters Anglo-American forces fought under a common command. "It was the most complete unification of military effort," General Marshall wrote, "ever achieved by two Allied nations."

Roosevelt bore an immense burden of responsibility. Again and again his judgment was decisive. The suggestion came from the Philippines in February 1942 that due to the helplessness of the islands, they should surrender and seek a Japanese guarantee of their neutrality for the remainder of the war. The President at once radioed the American commander there, General MacArthur, "American forces will continue to keep our flag flying in the Philippines so long as there remains any possibility of resistance." There was later protracted debate within Anglo-American military circles over the issue of whether the Allies should strike first at North Africa, or immediately attempt a cross channel invasion of the European continent. Roosevelt made the final decision, upholding British views as against those of both Secretary Stimson and General Marshall, that gave priority to the North African campaign and postponed what was to become Operation Overlord until 1944. And again it was Roosevelt, largely on his own initiative, who set forth the war aims of the Allies as the "unconditional surrender" of the enemy powers.

These were both strategic and political decisions. As with others made at the series of wartime conferences—Quebec, Casablanca, Teheran, Cairo, and Yalta—they represented hard choices. In some instances they were subject to justifiable criticism, especially with the hindsight of postwar years. But they maintained the solidarity of the Grand Alliance and paved the way to final victory. Whatever mistakes Roosevelt may have made during these perilous years he demonstrated an immense capacity for both national and international leadership. The calm confidence that he so successfully conveyed in his spirited appeals for national support of the war effort had an incalculable influence in sustaining the faith and courage of all the peoples fighting Hitlerism.

Secretary of War Stimson, a Republican and no friend of the New Deal, paid eloquent tribute to his chief as a great war leader:

His vision of the broad problems of strategy was sound and accurate, and his relations to his military advisers and commanders were admirably correct. In the execution of their duties he gave them freedom, backed them up, and held them responsible. In all these particulars he seems to me to have been our greatest war President. And his courage and cheerfulness in times of great emergency won for him the loyalty and affection of all who served under him. Lastly and most important, his vision and interpretation of the mission of our country to help establish a rule of freedom and justice in this world raised a standard which put the United States in the unique position of world leadership which she now holds.

★ THE OVER-ALL PATTERN OF WAR

The scope and extent of the war activities conducted by the United States, both at home and abroad, were so extensive and so far-reaching that the complete story cannot possibly be told. In mobilizing its economic resources the country produced ships and airplanes, tanks and guns, in quantities that completely dwarfed production figures of World War I and went far beyond estimates of what had been thought possible. Existing industries were transformed to turn out the materials of war; entirely new industries were created to produce goods normally obtained through imports.

The number of troops ultimately in the Armed Forces rose to some 15,000,000, of which two-thirds were in the Army. Included among them were more than 200,000 women—"Wacs," "Waves," "Wasps," and "Spars." The equipment, maintenance, and eventual transportation overseas of this huge force presented more formidable problems than the comparable ones of a quarter century earlier. Training was also far more elaborate. The functions of air crews, engineer battalions, service forces, and all the other specialized branches of Army, Navy, and Air Corps called for experts; the infantrymen had to be taught the use of a wide range of new weapons and how to conduct themselves in street fighting, jungle warfare, and close combat.

Overseas operations girdled the globe. American troops fought on the sands of North Africa, in the rugged hills of Italy, amid the hedgerows of Normandy, and in the valley of the Rhine. They battled the Japanese on Guadalcanal, in the jungles of New Guinea, in the Philippines, and on the shores of Okinawa and Iwo Jima. They built railroads in Iran, opened up the Burma road to China, and defended Alaska.

The Navy patrolled the Atlantic and convoyed merchant ships on the suicidal Russian supply route to Murmansk. On the opposite side of the world it challenged and defeated the fleets of Japan at Coral Sea, Midway, and Leyte Gulf. The Air Transport Command flew by way of Dakar, Accra, and Khartoum to the Near East and carried supplies from India to China over the "Hump." American bombers roared out from bases in North Africa to attack Romanian oil fields and daily crossed the Channel from Great Britain to break up the transportation system and shatter the industrial potential of Hitler's European fortress. They struck at Japan from mid-Pacific bases in the Marianas and finally carried to Hiroshima and Nagasaki the devastating destruction of the atom bomb.

The war in which the United States was engaged from 1941 to 1945 was total war and global war. The tremendous industrial strength of the nation, the valiant fighting capacity of the Armed Forces, the skillful and imaginative leadership of the high command, and the confident support of the entire nation were the co-ordinating factors that made possible the final victory. Yet it was not just an American victory. The war was waged by a great coalition, in the closest co-operation, and the contributions of Great Britain, Soviet Russia, and the other countries that made up the Grand Alliance were no less essential than those of the United States in bringing about the successive defeats of Italy, Germany, and Japan.

★ INDUSTRY AND SCIENCE

In the mobilization of resources on the home front, a key role was played by Donald Nelson, Sears-Roebuck executive, who was put in charge of a streamlined War Production Board, replacing the Office of Production Management. "Debating societies are out," Nelson stated when he took over his job in January 1942. "We are going to have action." The WPB promptly brought passenger automobile assembly lines to a halt, banned the manufacture of radios for civilians, drastically curbed the production of hundreds of other articles from lawnmowers to girdles, from typewriters to zippers, restricted the use of cloth by decrees limiting the length of women's skirts and eliminating the cuffs on men's trousers. The major production facilities of the entire country were converted to meet the imperative and pressing needs of national defense.

President Roosevelt set first production goals at 60,000 airplanes, 45,000 tanks, 8,000,000 tons of merchant shipping. Even Nelson thought such goals impossible; they were attained and passed. By the close of the war nearly 300,000 airplanes had been produced, 86,000 tanks, and 55,000,000 tons of shipping. At the same time, 71,000 new naval ships —from airplane carriers to landing craft—were built. The American Navy became "the greatest sea-air power on earth."

To furnish the basic materials for these and other manufactures, the nation's steel production was nearly doubled, that of aluminum increased sixfold, and the output of copper, bauxite, and petroleum all showed tremendous gains. An entirely new industry produced over 700,000 tons of synthetic rubber annually. There was also a great increase in agricultural production with farm acreage expanded to supply more wheat, corn, livestock, cotton, and other staples. All previous records were broken as the nation's farmers, as well as its industrial workers, bent their energies to satisfy apparently insatiable demands.

Continued shipments to our Allies under lend-lease absorbed a good part of American manufactures. Thousands of airplanes, tanks, and other motorized equipment were sent to Russia; even greater numbers to Great Britain. The United States equipped the forces of the Free French, the armies of Nationalist China, and the fighting legions of Europe's exiled governments. It built harbor works in the Persian Gulf, laid oil pipe lines in France, set up aluminum factories in Canada, and constructed air fields throughout the world—from North Africa to Burma, from the British Isles to New Guinea.

An even greater task was to furnish the sinews of war for the nation's own armed forces. There were always bottle necks, a good deal of waste, and extravagance. At times serious deficiencies threatened interference with overseas operations. The job, however, was done. On Labor Day, 1944, General Eisenhower expressed in behalf of the army under his command his "grateful thanks to the workers of America for having made this the best equipped force in history."

A fascinating and almost unbelievable war chapter was written by invention and technology. In 1941 the President set up an Office of Scientific Research and Development under the joint chairmanship of President Conant of Harvard and Dr. Vannevar Bush of the Carnegie Institution of Washington. The scientists it enlisted, always working in close co-operation with both the armed services and the universities, were to make contributions without which the war almost certainly could not have been won. For a time the race to victory between American scientists and those of Germany was perilously close, and it is possible that the greater freedom given in this country to research marked the difference between Allied or Axis victory.

The imperative demands of antisubmarine war, and then of air warfare, stimulated intense activity in the development of radar. When its use by the enemy in detecting bombers threatened the failure of the air attack on Germany, research then worked on methods of radar jamming. The proximity fuse was to prove of vital importance in artillery fire. Other contributions to aerial warfare were rocket guns, incendiary bombs, guided missiles, and jet propulsion. In the field of military medicine, there were no less significant scientific developments. The part played by the sulfa compounds, penicillin, and other drugs in reducing battlefield deaths can hardly be evaluated. Yet even more impressive in its life-saving record was the use of plasma, which General Eisenhower declared was "the most important single advance in surgical treatment of the wounded in this war." Plasma injections were held largely responsible for holding down the death rate among the wounded to just half what it had been during World War I.

Far and away the most dramatic achievement of science and technology was the production of the atomic bomb. The original suggestion for experimentation in atomic fission had come in 1939 from a group of physicists including Albert Einstein. The work was promptly entrusted to the Office of Scientific Research and Development, and soon thereafter President Roosevelt made the epochal decision—kept absolutely secret—to go ahead with every available resource to make the bomb. As early as midsummer 1941, success was predicted if a way could be found to secure a sufficient quantity of uranium 235. There were further successful experiments, and then the vast group of plants known as "the Manhattan District" was set up in eastern Tennessee, with power made available by the TVA, to carry forward the engineering phase of the project. The first atomic bomb was set off on July 16, 1945, in a remote section of the New Mexico desert.

"We were reaching into the unknown and we did not know what might come of it," said one of the responsible scientists. The first answer to this statement was Hiroshima and Nagasaki; there was little likelihood that it was the last. No one could foretell the ultimate consequence of the momentous experiments ushering in a new age.

★ LABOR, PRICE CONTROLS, COSTS

The conversion of the economy to meet wartime needs created a host of problems on the home front. There were shortages of manpower and shortages of civilian goods. The government faced the incredibly complicated task of maintaining a reasonable balance in the nation's economic life, controlling inflationary pressures, and raising the funds to finance wartime operations. Scores of interlocking agencies, staffed by experts from every walk of life, were created to handle these manifold issues.

In spite of the withdrawal of 15,000,000 men to serve in the Army, Navy, and Air Corps, the nation's civilian labor force rose from 47,000,000 to 53,000,000 persons. The return of older men to work and the recruiting of over 6,000,000 women largely accounted for these gains, and their services obviated the need for any general draft of manpower. Such a step was only narrowly averted, however, and for a time Congress seriously considered some form of conscription to meet the constantly recurring need for additional workers in critical areas. The increased production of labor, stepped up not only by the incentive of high wages and overtime pay but by loyalty to the cause for which the entire country was working, saved the day.

With both the A.F. of L. and the C.I.O. giving no-strike pledges immediately after Pearl Harbor, the President created a War Labor Board to handle all disputes between workers and management. Yet there were a number of work-stoppages that for a time gravely endangered the national defense program. On two occasions John L. Lewis led his half million coal workers out on strike, defying the government even when it seized the mines. He ordered the men back to work only after substantial concessions had been made to his demands. A threatened railway strike also forced the government to assume temporary control of the railroads, but unlike the situation during World War I, it did not prove necessary to continue to run them. Other sporadic outbreaks of industrial strife sufficiently disturbed Congress so that it passed in June 1943 a War Labor Disputes Act giving the President authority to seize any industry in which a serious work stoppage was threatened. It was a bungling and badly drawn law. The subsidence of unrest was due to increasing labor-management co-operation rather than this congressional attempt to legislate industrial peace.

When the war period as a whole is considered, the actual number of strikes was very small and the total man-hours lost through work stoppages proved to be only an infinitesimal fraction of the total working time. The strikes reflected an urgent need for wage increases that would compensate for the rise in wartime living costs. The War Labor Board recognized the justice of such demands through its authorization of limited increases and of generous allowances of so-called fringe benefits. While organized labor insisted upon its right to preserve the gains that had been made under friendly New Deal legislation, its participation in the war effort compared favorably with that of any other group in American society. Its part in making possible the continued shattering of production records was strongly attested by all those in a position to know how great labor's contribution really was.

The inflation responsible for rising living costs was combatted by strenuous efforts to hold down prices under the direction of an Office of Price Administration and Civilian Supply—the OPA. They were far more effective than anything done during World War I, in spite of the difficulties arising from an inflationary gap of nearly $20,000,000,000 between national consumer income and the production value of civilian goods. An Emergency Price Control Act, adopted in January 1942, provided the original basis for the program, but later that same year it had to be supplemented by a new Anti-Inflation Act, giving the President authority to stabilize wages as well as prices at their prevailing levels. Further threats to the economy then led Roosevelt in April 1943 to issue a "hold-the-line" order and call upon the country for greater co-operation in bringing about as equitable a distribution as possible of all scarce goods.

These various economic controls made new automobiles, typewriters, bicycles, and many other such manufactures almost completely unavailable for civilians, and it soon proved necessary for the OPA to ration an increasing number of other things. Gasoline first fell under its restrictions, and then coffee and sugar. By March 1943 a long list of food-stuffs was included, and then shoes. Eventually, the OPA established community price ceilings on over a thousand grocery-store items which could be bought only on the presentation of coupons from the ration books distributed to every family throughout the land.

Perhaps no other government agency had a more difficult task or was subject to more severe criticism than the OPA. It rapidly expanded into an unwieldy organization of 50,000 employees and some 200,000 volunteer workers. The nation was bewildered by the flood of orders, directives, questionnaires, licenses, and special regulations it issued. No other phase of wartime activity so directly affected so many people. Once the original price rise was checked, however, the line was held reasonably well. The close of the war found living costs no more than about 30 per cent above prewar levels.

An important factor in the fight against inflation was the influence of wartime taxes in drawing off excess purchasing power. The government took this into consideration even when more immediately concerned with financing the war effort. All taxes were stepped up and something like 40 per cent of the war costs were met on a pay-as-you-go basis. This left huge amounts to be borrowed, and the necessary funds were obtained through the sale of war bonds to both financial institutions and the public.

The total cost of the war amounted to an estimated $350,000,000,000—or nearly ten times the cost of participation in World War I—and the government had to borrow around $50,000,000,000 a year. By the end of hostilities, the national debt had consequently risen to the astronomical height of $250,000,000,000. The increase in the national income, stimulated by wartime production, did not make this as onerous a burden as such a figure would by itself suggest. On the other hand, it was a striking symbol of the lasting costs of total war.

In spite of all the problems of a wartime economy—high prices, rationing, increased taxes, regulations, and restrictions—civilian life in the United States was not nearly so much affected as civilian life in either allied or enemy countries. The fear—and actuality—of losses among the troops overseas was a constant shadow over the country, but no battles were fought or air raids experienced in the continental United States. The American people continued to enjoy a measure of security and also high living standards which were in marked contrast with conditions in England, to say nothing of those on the continent. Yet public participation in the war effort exceeded by far that of 1917–18; there was at once a greater degree of unity among the people and less intolerance of inconsequential dissent. Neither the flamboyant patriotism nor the hysteria of the war years a quarter century earlier were very much in evidence. The spirit of the nation was one of steady determination to carry through an unwanted but necessary job.

Millions of people enrolled for civilian defense, served as volunteers on draft and rationing boards, took part in the war bond drives, enlisted in campaigns to salvage essential materials, cultivated victory gardens, worked with the Red Cross, and donated blood—some 13,000,000 pints—for shipment overseas as plasma. The home front stood solidly behind the fighting front.

★ THE ATLANTIC TRANSIT

If industrial production and the determination of the American people to meet every demand upon them were basic factors in the defeat of the enemy powers, it was nevertheless the Army and the Navy that fought the battles. Everything done at home was a means to an end—victory on the field. And there were dark, discouraging days before such victory appeared to be assured and the tide of battle, so long running in favor of Germany and Japan, finally turned.

The opening months of 1942 found the United States, in co-operation with Great Britain, fighting two critical battles where the odds were for long heavily against them—the Battle of the Atlantic and the initial Battle of the Pacific. In both instances, the primary demand made upon this country, still unprepared for war and feverishly building up its naval and military forces, was maintenance of its overseas communications to prevent the enemy from dangerously dividing the Allies. The intense submarine warfare launched by Germany in the Atlantic for a time threatened to cut off England from American aid entirely, while the sweep of Japanese forces in the Pacific led not only to the conquest of southeastern Asia, but imperiled Australia, India, and the British lines to the Middle East.

During the first four months of 1942 submarines sank some eighty-two cargo ships in the Atlantic sea lanes. When measures were taken to provide additional protection for Britain-bound convoys, this German attack was shifted with frightening success to the southern waters of the Atlantic, crowded with vessels carrying essential supplies of iron, steel, cotton, sugar, coffee, and oil to and from the Atlantic ports. A devastating toll was taken among coastwise shipping, especially tankers. Vessels were sunk within sight of the New Jersey beaches, and at least two were attacked only a few miles off the channel entering New York harbor. Ships were being lost at a far faster rate than they could be built, while countermeasures led to the sinking of only some twenty submarines in the first half of the year, or less than Germany's monthly production.

Desperate efforts were necessary to save the situation. The whole protective system had to be overhauled and naval vessels of every kind —destroyers, corvettes, armed trawlers, minesweepers, converted yachts —were pressed into service to provide escorts for the merchant ships. Even so there was no way to guarantee that the convoys could get through as the Germans now began hunting them down with submarine packs. One convoy on the dangerous route to North Russia, made up of thirty-three merchantmen and a fleet of escorting vessels, was attacked again and again by dozens of U-boats. A running battle was fought for days on end; only eleven of the merchant ships arrived safely. At the close of 1942 the number of submarines operating in the Atlantic had doubled, and they were now concentrating on cutting laggard ships out of the convoys with such success as again to threaten the severance of supply lines.

The move which finally enabled the Allies to swing ahead in the Battle of the Atlantic was the establishment of sea-air patrols. Working in close conjunction with the fleet, both Army and Navy air forces concentrated heavily upon antisubmarine warfare. New airfields were built, bombers were equipped with radar and depth bombs, and aviators specially trained in the immensely difficult task of hunting down submarines on the high seas. By late 1943 the Allies' combined air and sea attack was taking a greater toll of submarines than the submarines were taking of merchant ships.

"One thing is certain," Samuel Eliot Morison, naval historian, has written, "it was air power, properly co-ordinated with the United States navy and the British Admiralty, that gave the Allies their advantage; without it, they would have lost the war."

★ WAR IN THE PACIFIC

The dangers confronting the United States in the Pacific were even more dramatic. For a time after Japan's bold stroke at Pearl Harbor, which temporarily succeeded in immobilizing the American fleet with the sinking or disabling of eight battleships, there appeared to be no way of stopping her victorious advance. The conquest of southeastern Asia, including Burma and Thailand as well as Malaya, the Dutch East Indies, and the Philippines, completely upset the balance of Pacific power. China was isolated except for the air route over the "hump" from Burma. While the heroic defense of the American forces in the Philippines, holding out desperately at Bataan and then at Corregidor until May 1942, delayed the timetable of Japanese operations, Australia and India soon lay open to possible invasion. With its own forces deeply engaged in the Battle of the Atlantic the United States could not afford to throw too much strength into the Pacific struggle.

But the Japanese failed to take full advantage of this weakness, or were unable to do so because they had extended their lines too far, and once the immediate threat to India and Australia was averted the day was saved. Time was with the Allies. The United States gradually built up its forces, eventually sending into the Pacific a fleet so powerful that it could not be withstood. Had the Japanese been able to carry forward the momentum of their first successful advance in southeastern Asia, they would not necessarily have won the war, but their defeat would have been long postponed.

The first check to the calamitous string of Japanese victories was the Battle of the Coral Sea early in May 1942. It was primarily an engagement between carrier planes—the ships of the opposing forces were never in sight of each other—and neither side won a complete victory. However, the result of the battle was a Japanese withdrawal and an end to any immediate threat to Australia. Less than a month later, Admiral Nimitz brilliantly won the far more decisive Battle of Midway. Such heavy losses—including the sinking of four carriers—were inflicted on the enemy by a numerically inferior American fleet that Japanese plans for further advance in the central or south Pacific were completely foiled. Admiral Yamamoto ordered a general retirement; the American flag remained flying at Midway.

Even though primary attention was centered upon the European phase of the war, the United States was now enabled to embark upon limited offensive-defensive operations in the southwest Pacific. The long, grueling, bloody Solomons campaign got underway in August, and soon afterward the first steps were taken to win control of New Guinea, where the Japanese had thrust forward toward Port Moresby. American land forces were being slowly built up in Australia with the longterm objective of enabling General MacArthur to fight his way back to the Philippines. For any such operation it was essential to capture or neutralize the islands that had been seized by the Japanese and recover both naval and air control over the surrounding area.

Guadalcanal was selected for the first landing of American troops. Although it was an initially successful operation, the enemy struck back viciously. The United States suffered a serious defeat at the Battle of Savo Island, and for six long months the embattled marines on Guadalcanal fought a fierce jungle war against overwhelming odds. The outcome was grimly in doubt until the air-naval Battle of Guadalcanal in mid-November finally tilted the scales. Two months later the American forces finally compelled the Japanese to evacuate the island.

Guadalcanal was a relatively minor victory against the background of the vast reaches of the Pacific, but it was a highly significant one. The Japanese had already been set back at Coral Sea and at Midway. With this first land advance the opportunity was at hand to drive them entirely out of the Solomons and to win control of New Guinea. The way back was long. There were desperate encounters still ahead for the embattled forces in the southwest Pacific, but Japan was on the defensive.

★ NORTH AFRICA AND ITALY

While the battle for Guadalcanal was still underway, the United States launched its initial campaign in the European theater. In the debates over military strategy when Roosevelt and Churchill first met in Washington in December 1941, the Americans favored a cross-Channel invasion of the continent early in 1943, while the British insisted that the risks for such an operation were far too grave until allied forces had been greatly strengthened. The North African campaign was accepted as a compromise which did not go so far as to set up the "second front" which Roosevelt believed necessary to relieve pressure on the Russians, but it had immense potentialities for throwing the enemy off balance. If control of North Africa could be secured by the eastward advance of a new allied force landing in Algeria, and a breakthrough by the British Eighth Army battling General Rommel's Afrika Corps in Libya, Spain would be immobilized, the Mediterranean brought under allied domination, and a springboard provided for further attack upon Italy.

It was on the morning of November 7, 1942—just eleven months after American entry into the war—that combined British and American forces under General Dwight D. Eisenhower landed at Casablanca,

Oran, and Algiers. Operation Torch, as the campaign was called, was a first experience with amphibious attack and involved preparations that were still something new in the history of war. But the landings were made with clocklike efficiency; the Germans and Italians were taken completely by surprise. French troops under the control of the Vichy government headed by Marshal Pétain, which had been established after the German occupation of France, put up stiff resistance for a time at Casablanca. The Allies found themselves involved in an immensely complicated diplomatic tangle until negotiations with Admiral Darlan, the French commander in North Africa, were finally successful in persuading him to issue a cease-fire order. When he was shortly afterward assassinated, a further agreement was reached with General de Gaulle, leader of the Free French, for the full co-operation of his forces in the further stages of the campaign. The way was opened for an advance into Tunisia and ultimate juncture with the British Eighth Army, which was now driving westward from El Alamein.

The Germans were nevertheless prepared to put up a determined struggle for North Africa, flying thousands of troops into Tunisia. There was to be hard and arduous fighting, marked by one critical American setback at Kasserine Pass, before the gigantic pincers of the Anglo-American forces advancing from east and west began to close in on the German and Italian armies. But Rommel was being forced steadily back toward Tunis and Bizerte, and as those cities fell before the allied onslaught early in May, half a million British and American troops had victory within their grasp.

The German army now retreated in a gathering rout to the beaches of Cape Bon, and when all means of escape were cut off, unconditionally surrendered. It was the first great Anglo-American victory of the war. North Africa was cleared of enemy troops and the bag of prisoners totaled some 300,000. The Allies held an initiative which would never again be lost. As in the Pacific, the road to final victory would prove to be long and bloody, but the succession of defeats had come to an end.

Little time was lost in taking advantage of this success in North Africa. Meeting at Casablanca in January 1943, while the enemy still held Tunisia, Roosevelt and Churchill had agreed upon their general strategy, and subsequent conferences of the combined chiefs of staff worked out the necessary plans. The conquest of Italy was to be the immediate allied objective, and as soon as practical the next year there would be invasion of western Europe. The reluctance of the British to undertake a cross-Channel attack was finally overcome, and once this decision had been reached, there were no further differences over future policy. While the Mediterranean campaign was prosecuted with the utmost vigor, Operation Overlord loomed more and more importantly over the horizon.

An attack upon Sicily, preliminary to invasion of the Italian peninsula, was made early in July. The landings were successful, but over a month of hard fighting was necessary before the island was finally conquered. Over 100,000 prisoners were taken, although approximately the same number of enemy troops escaped to fight another day, and allied casualties totaled 31,000. The stage was set for the further landings in Italy, and on the very eve of this next advance a sudden political development appeared to promise quick and easy results. Mussolini was deposed on July 25, 1943, and a new government under Marshal Badoglio soon agreed to Italy's surrender. But hopes for a peaceful occupation of the Italian peninsula were quickly dashed, for despite the new government the country had been occupied by the German army. When the Americans landed at Salerno, there was no quick victory but rather a hard-fought fight against a strongly entrenched foe.

Nevertheless, the Germans were forced to retreat. The American Fifth Army under General Mark Clark joined with the British Eighth Army, which had landed farther to the south, and Naples was in allied hands by October 1. While the gains from this operation were immense, especially in the occupation of airfields for bombing northern Italy and Germany, there still lay ahead of the allied forces a long and almost unendurable campaign up the Italian boot against ever-stiffening German resistance.

The war in Italy was fought in rugged mountain country where the enemy took every advantage of the terrain to slow the allied advance. One heavily fortified line across the peninsula was no more than cracked than the doggedly advancing troops found themselves blocked by one even harder to breach. A diversionary operation, when the Americans landed behind the German lines at Anzio, failed to force the anticipated enemy retreat, while for three months the Allies vainly tried to storm the monastery-city of Cassino, which the Germans had made the key to their Gustav Line. A grimly popular song of the hard-slugging G.I.'s ran:

> Yes, we have no Cassino
> We have no Cassino today.
> We have Aversa, Caserta, Mignano, Minturno
> And dear old Napolii,
> But, yes, we have no Cassino
> We have no Cassino today.

The Italian campaign was a secondary operation, often lost to sight as the invasion of western Europe got underway, but it entailed heavy losses and great hardship. During 1943–44 it was for the most part a bitter, unending struggle in freezing weather, cruel sleet, and downpours of rain—a war of attack and counterattack, constant air raids, artillery bombardments, and savage fighting amid the rubble of destroyed villages. Rome was not captured until June 4, 1944, and even this victory still left all northern Italy in German hands.

★ OPERATION OVERLORD

As Rome finally fell, the greatest armada of ships and men that had probably ever been assembled in all history was preparing to strike across the British Channel and invade France. The long-awaited D-Day was on hand, and Operation Overlord was to eclipse all else that had happened in five years of European conflict. In many ways everything that had gone before was but a preparation for this stupendous blow aimed directly at Hitler's European fortress.

Final victory in the Battle of the Atlantic had enabled the United States to build up its forces in Great Britain, the staging area for continental invasion, with great success. Under the supervision of General Eisenhower, given over-all command of the entire operation, men and materials had been collected and final plans for the assault worked out to the last minute detail. The allied forces totaled nearly 3,000,000 soldiers, sailors, and fliers; the stockpiles of supplies amounted to an aggregate 2,500,000 tons. Thirty-nine divisions were marked for the channel crossing and 11,000 planes made available for air support. The fleet assembled to protect and transport the troops was made up of 600 warships and 4,000 supporting craft.

Just as important as these preparations was the steadily intensified air war that was being waged against Germany by American and British bombers. The first thousand-plane raid had struck Cologne on May 30, 1942; during the next two years attacks on German munitions factories, submarine pens, oil and gasoline depots, and finally transportation had been stepped up steadily month by month. The general strategy of this campaign was for the British to concentrate on night saturation bombing, while the Americans engaged in daytime precision bombing. For a time American operations were restricted to cities in France, Holland, and Belgium, but they were soon extended to the Saar and Ruhr, to Hamburg, Bremen, Cologne, Düsseldorf, and Berlin itself. Liberators and Flying Fortresses more than proved their effectiveness as instruments of deadly destruction. On the eve of the invasion of France, General Arnold, commander of the A.A.F., announced that they had dropped nearly 500,000 bombs.

The total weight of bombs dropped by Anglo-American planes was to increase even more phenomenally as the war went on. By May 1945 several million sorties had loosed on enemy targets the incredible total of 2,700,000 tons. Yet until the last year of the war, according to the subsequent reports of the United States Strategic Bombing Survey, these raids caused no serious breakdown in German munitions production. Cities might be destroyed, but the factories somehow restored their assembly lines. In spite of heavy and greatly publicized attacks on the ball-bearing factories at Schweinfurt, for example, German output of this essential item in the production of military weapons reached its peak in September 1944. The areas in which bombing finally proved to be highly effective were oil and gasoline production and transportation. Before the war came to an end much of the Luftwaffe was grounded for lack of fuel, and the German railway system was virtually paralyzed, perhaps the most important single cause of Germany's ultimate economic collapse.

The effect of American bombing was not really known as D-Day approached—its results were actually very much exaggerated—but the preparations for the invasion were all made, the day and hour set. "The mighty host," General Eisenhower was to write in *Crusade in Europe,* "was as tense as a coiled spring, and indeed that is exactly what it was—a great human spring, coiled for the moment when its energy should be released and it would vault the English Channel in the greatest amphibious assault ever attempted."

The moment was the early morning hours of June 6, 1944. With the guns from hundreds of warships raking the beaches of the Normandy coast, British and American troops drove in on LST's and other landing craft through a high surf and fought their way ashore. The Germans were taken unawares. A feint in the general direction of Calais, simulated by radio transmission, had thrown them off guard. While they were still able to pour a withering fire on the beaches and take a heavy toll of lives as the allied troops struggled through barbed wire entanglements and mine fields, the landings were successful. By the end of the day over 120,000 men had been brought ashore, parts of three airborne divisions had parachuted behind enemy lines, and tanks, armor, and supplies were flowing across the Channel in ever-increasing quantity.

"The history of war," the Russian dictator, Marshal Stalin, was to state admiringly, "does not know any such undertaking so broad in conception and so grandiose in its scale and masterly in its execution."

★ THE LIBERATION OF FRANCE

The war now rose to a frightening crescendo as the Allies clung to their precarious foothold and the Germans sought to compress their lines within a tightening ring of steel. One vital objective was the capture of the port of Cherbourg, and it was taken on June 26, but even more important was the winning of sufficient territory to provide a base for the breakthrough that alone would make the invasion successful. The fighting amid the Normandy hedgerows lasted until late July, but the Allies gradually extended their lines, brought over more men and supplies, and were soon ready to strike out.

The British captured Caen, hinge of the German line, the Americans crashed through stubborn opposition at St. Lô, General Patton swung out with his armor into Brittany, and the Battle of Normandy became the Battle of France. Hitler ordered a counterattack at Avranches, but his Seventh Army was destroyed in the Falaise gap and a general retreat soon turned into a rout. The Allies swept across northern France in an advance that was the real turning point of the European war. As the American First Army neared Paris the underground forces in the French capital rose in revolt. The Germans withdrew; on August 25 Paris was once again free.

Additional landings in the south of France between Toulon and Cannes had in the meantime posed a new threat to the Germans. Moving up the valley of the Rhone the American Seventh Army raced to a juncture with the American Third Army, which had pushed on through Orleans and Troyes. All southeastern France was effectively sealed off. The Americans destroyed two German armies and took 80,000 prisoners.

The thrilling excitement of these days of August 1944 can hardly be recaptured. As the *New York Times* told the story:

> The succession of triumphs made dazzling reading, a flashing roll call of names carved on many battle-monuments. In a line reaching in from the Channel coast the Canadian First Army captured Rouen, drove straight to Dieppe and Abbeville; the British Second Army raced through Beauvais, took Amiens, crossed the Somme, captured historic Vimy Ridge, struck for Arras, sealed off the robot coast; the American First Army roared through Belleau Wood, Chateau Thierry, Soissons, Laon, Rheims, to the fortress of Sedan; the American Third Army hammered through Chalons, across the Marne and Aisne, into the fortress of Verdun, on toward Metz, southward into St. Mihiel.

Nowhere could the Germans make an effective stand. Their demoralized troops retreated pell mell to the protective barrier of the Westwall, leaving behind them immense quantities of materials and losing in all 500,000 men. France was liberated, in Churchill's phrase, "as if by enchantment"; Belgium and Luxemburg were freed, and early in September the surging allied armies from Holland to Switzerland were ready to throw themselves against the Siegfried Line. Then German resistance stiffened. The Allies had outrun their supplies and a halt was necessary before any further assault could be made. "All along the front," General Eisenhower was to write, "we felt increasingly the strangulation on movement imposed by our inadequate lines of communication."

A confused series of battles was fought during the next two months while the Allies regrouped their forces and prepared for the next major attack. There was fierce fighting to win control of the Scheldt Estuary, following the defeat of a British airborne division landed at Arnhem, deadly combat in the Hurtgen Forest, and after General Patton's Third Army had captured Metz, invasion of the Saar. In mid-December Hitler took the immense gamble of an all-out counteroffensive in the Ardennes, and for a time the Allies were compelled to give way in the desperate Battle of the Bulge. Successful defense of the key center of Bastogne blocked what might have been a disastrous enemy breakthrough, and finally the Germans were once again pushed back and the bulge sealed off. Not until the end of January 1945, however, was General Eisenhower able to resume his interrupted advance toward the Rhine.

★ ADVANCE IN THE PACIFIC

Other great events had meanwhile occurred on the kaleidoscopic scene of global war. The entire picture can hardly be kept in focus. There were not only the final capture of Rome, and a renewal of the slow, dogged Anglo-American advance in northern Italy, but on the great eastern front, the massive armies of Soviet Russia were everywhere on the march. They had won a decisive victory at Stalingrad in February 1943, and ever since that memorable battle there had been no stopping their relentless advance. As 1944 gave way to 1945 the drive of the Red armies into Poland threatened Warsaw, a northern campaign was overrunning the Baltic countries, and steady progress in the Balkans had already brought about the capitulation of Romania and Bulgaria.

On the opposite side of the globe, there had been no letup in the fighting, and the promise of the first American offensive against Japan was being slowly fulfilled. The war there was distinguished by two major operations: a naval advance to break through the island ramparts of the central Pacific, and the amphibious campaign in the southwest Pacific. This is not the whole story of the struggle against Japan. American forces recaptured the Aleutian Island outposts Japan had occupied in 1942; under as different conditions as can be imagined, they were fighting an unremitting war in the fever-infested jungles of Burma to reopen communications with China, and they were occupying scores of islands throughout the Pacific—the Fijis, New Caledonia, Tahiti, Galapagos, Palmyra. However, the double-pronged advance in the Pacific was the decisive campaign.

For the thousands of men stationed in the widely separated island outposts where military strength was massed for each successive strike at the Japanese, life was constant exposure to steaming jungle heat, soddening tropical downpours, malaria, strange skin diseases, jungle rot. And always, loneliness and boredom. "Our war was waiting," James Michener wrote in his *Tales of the South Pacific,* "You rotted on New Caledonia waiting for Guadalcanal. Then you sweated twenty pounds away in Guadal waiting for Bougainville. There were battles, of course. But they were flaming things of the bitter moment. A blinding flash at Tulagi. A day of horror at Tarawa. . . . Then you relaxed and waited. And pretty soon you hated the man next to you, and you dreaded the look of a cocoanut tree." The waiting at last drew to an end, however, as the men and ships and planes were gathered for final and decisive action.

Admiral Nimitz, commanding the Pacific fleet, was entrusted with the naval operations that were designed to win control of the Gilbert and Marshall Islands, and then the Carolines and Marianas. An immense fleet set forth on this task early in November 1943. After fierce fighting at Makin and Tarawa, the Gilberts fell into American hands, and in February 1944 the island of Kwajalein in the Marshalls. The next attack was centered on the Marianas. The Japanese could not afford to lose these essential bases, including Guam, and a large fleet moved out to challenge the American advance. It tangled with forces under Admirals Spruance and Mitscher in the first Battle of the Philippine Sea. After repeated attack and counterattack—involving ships, submarines, and planes—the Japanese suffered such heavy losses that they beat a swift retreat; the way was cleared for landings on Saipan, Tinian, and Guam. Last-ditch resistance, especially at Saipan, had to be overcome before these islands were secure, but their capture gave the American fleet vital naval bases and also provided air fields for bombing raids on the Japanese homeland.

The campaign in the southwest Pacific had by this time brought the Solomons and the northern coast of New Guinea completely under American control. Working closely together, naval forces under Admiral Halsey and ground forces under General MacArthur pushed forward to New Britain, Bougainville, and the Admiralty Islands, sealing off the important Japanese base at Rabaul, and advancing up the New Guinea coast to Lae, Aitape, and Hollandia. These amphibious assaults have been variously described as "island-hopping" and "leap-frogging." They secured essential bases and, bypassing Japanese positions that could be effectively hammered from the air, left over 130,000 Japanese troops to wither on the vine.

By midsummer 1944 the Americans were a thousand miles nearer Japan, but the final strategic decisions as to the next steps in the Pacific war had not yet been made. There were still various schools of thought as to the most effective way of carrying the war home to Japan. It had been hoped that China might become the base for such an assault. The difficulties encountered in the Burma campaign and the failure of the Chinese Nationalists to hold their positions against Japanese counter-attack had created seemingly insurmountable obstacles to any landing on the China coast. The feasibility of occupying Formosa was also considered and then discarded. The decision ultimately reached was to combine General MacArthur's project for reconquest of the Philippines with an advance toward Japan itself up the ladder of the Bonin Islands. Mounting successes in the southwest and central Pacific not only held out an encouraging promise for the fulfillment of such plans, but led to a speedup in the timetable for attack on the Philippines. It was decided to attempt in October a landing in force on the island of Leyte.

Ships and planes heavily pounded all enemy bases in preparation for this action and inflicted tremendous damage with relatively little loss. The Japanese claimed they had sunk the American carriers—to which Admiral Halsey retorted, "Ships reported sunk by Tokyo have been salvaged and are now retiring toward the enemy." Not one of them was hit. As a landing force of over 150,000 men, embarked upon transports and LST's protected by battleships, cruisers, and escorts, steamed into Leyte Gulf, the Japanese were unable to put up effective resistance. A twenty-mile beachhead was quickly secured and General MacArthur dramatically announced: "People of the Philippines, I have returned."

But the enemy were determined to challenge this perilous invasion and made the crucial decision to risk their entire fleet in a final bid to recover control of the Pacific. The Battle of Leyte Gulf was the finally decisive naval engagement of the Pacific war. The intricate maneuvering is too complicated to describe, but the losses sustained by the Japanese—battleships, cruisers, and carriers—were so heavy that they could not again hope to contest American naval and air supremacy. Here was a blow from which there was no possibility of recovery. While much hard fighting still lay ahead in the Philippines, at Iwo Jima, and at Okinawa, victory at Leyte was the beginning of the end in the war against Japan.

So it was that with the opening of 1945, as the allied armies stood poised on the left bank of the Rhine for the climactic invasion of Germany, preparations were also being made in the Pacific for the final assaults upon the Japanese Empire. The world was tense with expectancy as on opposite sides of the globe the Allies mounted all their strength for the last great pushes of the war.

★ ROOSEVELT'S RE-ELECTION AND DEATH

In the fall of 1944 another presidential election had been held in the United States. It was a significant triumph for democracy that at the very height of such a critical phase of the war, the American people did not allow the hostilities to interfere with their elections, nor their elections to divert their energy from carrying on the war. They went to the polls as they had at four-year intervals since the founding of the Republic, casting their votes without fear or favor.

The renomination of Roosevelt, even though it was for a fourth term, was generally conceded under such emergency conditions; the only contest at the Democratic convention was for the vice-presidency. The incumbent, Henry Wallace, had lost much popular support. After a good deal of confused and controversial maneuvering, the nomination finally went to Senator Harry S. Truman of Missouri.

The Republicans were as usual in a difficult position. Wendell Willkie had withdrawn from possible candidacy after a sharp defeat in the Wisconsin primaries, and the convention's choice finally fell upon Governor Thomas E. Dewey of New York, young, energetic, and of demonstrated vote-getting ability. Their program called for full support of the war effort. Their chief attack on the Democratic administration was centered on what was declared to be its inability to meet the problems that would inevitably rise with the cessation of hostilities. Roosevelt and his colleagues were repeatedly described as "tired old men," with Dewey and other Republican orators insistently repeating that it was "time for a change."

The electorate was not yet convinced that such a time had arrived; it appeared willing to entrust future problems to an administration that had been so successfully waging war. Roosevelt's popular plurality was about 3,500,000 votes; he carried thirty-six states with an electoral college majority of 432 to 99. The Democrats also made slight gains in Congress.

The President interpreted his re-election as a mandate not only for the vigorous prosecution of the war to final victory, but for the realization of his declared objective of setting up at its close a new world organization that would guarantee future peace. "We have learned that we cannot live alone, at peace; that our own well-being is dependent upon the well-being of other nations far away," he declared in his fourth inaugural. "We have learned to be citizens of the world, members in the human community."

His plans for postwar organization had first begun to take shape late in 1943 at a foreign ministers' conference at Moscow and had been further advanced when he met Churchill and Stalin at Teheran in November of that year. During the following summer representatives of all the nations at war with the Axis powers met at Dumbarton Oaks to draw up the blueprint for what was to become the charter of the United Nations. A little more than a month after his fourth inauguration, in February 1945, Roosevelt went to Yalta for the last and most momentous of the wartime conferences among the Big Three, and there final agreement was reached for an all-inclusive conference on the new world organization to be held in San Francisco in April. These developments in the story of the peace will be taken up more fully in another chapter. In the meantime, even though the end was clearly in sight when Roosevelt went to Yalta, neither Germany nor Japan had yet surrendered.

The President returned from this final trip worn and tired from the immense and overburdening responsibilities that he had borne for twelve years. Although he was a sick man, the public only dimly realized how much the strain had told on him. In the hope of winning back his strength, he went to Warm Springs, Georgia, where he had fought his first battles against paralysis. But his days were numbered. On April 12, 1945, he died of a cerebral hemorrhage without warning or premonition.

The American people, deeply shocked by the suddenness of his death, were also benumbed by a sense of personal bereavement that was quite as telling as their feeling of public loss. Nor was this country the only one to be plunged into mourning by the passing of Franklin D. Roosevelt. In Great Britain and in France, in the Soviet Union and in Nationalist China, in all the allied nations, the widespread expressions of universal grief dramatically reflected the pre-eminent role he had played as the world leader of democracy. He had indeed proved himself to be an even greater figure in war than in peace. His place in history was assured.

Roosevelt was succeeded by Vice-President Harry S. Truman, and on his shoulders fell the burden of leading the nation through the final phase of the war and along the uncharted course of postwar reconstruction. His immediate pledge to the country was that there would be no letup in the drive toward final victory in Europe and the Pacific, no relaxation in the efforts to secure a peace that would banish from the earth the age-old spectre of war.

★ THE FINAL VICTORY

German resistance was beginning to crumble when Roosevelt died. Recovering from the setback of the counterattack in the Ardennes, the regrouped forces under General Eisenhower had advanced to the Rhine by mid-March, and already such cities as Cologne and Bonn were in allied hands. An unexpected chance to seize a bridge at Remagen afforded a first opportunity to cross the river itself and helped pave the way for large-scale operations that soon had allied troops firmly ensconced on the Rhine's eastern bank. The American First and Ninth Armies closed in about the Ruhr, where 325,000 Germans were trapped in what has been called the largest envelopment in the history of warfare, and other British and American armies plunged ahead deep within Germany on the heels of the fleeing and badly disorganized enemy troops.

The debacle was becoming complete. As the Allies swept ahead on the western front toward the Elbe, the Russians successfully broke through the last German resistance on the eastern front and surrounded Berlin. At long last the Anglo-American forces cracked the enemy lines in northern Italy, and a victorious American Fifth Army joined the American Seventh Army which had swung down from a liberated Austria. The end of April saw the Germans everywhere surrendering by the hundreds of thousands, and in spite of fears that they might somehow rally for a last stand they never did so.

Then came the news that Italian partisans had killed Mussolini, and that Hitler had committed suicide amid the flaming ruins of his capital city. With the allied and Russian armies meeting at the Elbe, all Germany was conquered. The final step of unconditional surrender was effected when on May 7, 1945, General Jodl signed the articles of capitulation at allied headquarters at Rheims.

There was still no peace. On the other side of the world, none could say how long the final stages of the war would take. But plans were put into execution for the deployment to the Pacific of all American troops in Europe not needed for the occupation of Germany, and in the meantime rapid progress was being made in the steady advance toward Japan.

The Philippines were fully liberated by the time Germany surrendered, Manila having fallen in February, and after the bloody battles of Iwo Jima and Okinawa the American forces successfully advanced through the Bonins and Ryukyus to the threshhold of the Japanese home islands. The resistance on Iwo Jima and Okinawa had been as stubborn as in any engagements throughout the war, with suicidal attacks by *kamikaze* planes and bloody hand-to-hand fighting on the rocky shores. The Americans suffered some 20,000 casualties at Iwo and twice this total at

Okinawa, but overwhelming sea and air support gave them a decisive advantage over the enemy.

Japan was now virtually isolated. Her navy was destroyed, all communications severed, and her cities were under constant and increasingly heavy assault by American bombers based on the Marianas. Moreover, Soviet Russia was prepared to enter the war against Japan once Germany had surrendered, and did so on August 8. Nevertheless, the American military believed that actual invasion of the home islands would be necessary to force Japan's final surrender, and they were preparing two separate operations—an invasion of Kyushu in the fall of 1945 and of Honshu in the spring of 1946. While the strategic bombing continued the commanders in the field were to ready their final plans.

There was, however, another factor in the situation. The experiments secretly conducted in the New Mexican desert with an atomic bomb had demonstrated the practicality of this awful engine of destruction. In a message from Potsdam, where he was meeting with the other members of the Big Three on postwar plans, President Truman presented Japan on July 26 with a final demand for capitulation. "The alternative to surrender," he declared warningly, "is prompt and utter destruction."

Japan hesitated and temporized. Truman made his fateful decision. An American plane dropped an atomic bomb on Hiroshima on August 6, and three days later another fell on Nagasaki. The destruction in the two cities was catastrophic, the loss of life overwhelming. Over the protests of some few diehard, fanatical militarists, the emperor insisted on surrender. On August 14, 1945, the Japanese government accepted the allied terms.

Whether surrender could have been obtained at this time without dropping the atomic bomb can never be known with absolute certainty. It would appear with all the advantages of hindsight that Japan's complete collapse was imminent. But the decision to employ this most terrible of all weapons of destruction was taken in the conviction that the bomb would save countless American lives—estimated at a million—that might otherwise have been lost in the invasion of Japan itself. The military authorities feared that the enemy might fight on his home islands as he had fought at Iwo Jima and at Okinawa—to the last man.

Twelve days after the Japanese cease fire, an American fleet steamed into Tokyo Bay and on September 2 representatives of the United States and Japan signed aboard the battleship "Missouri" the official documents of surrender. Militarism in the Far East had been overthrown as had fascism in the West. World War II had come to an end. The forces of the United Nations were everywhere victorious over their enemies.

CHAPTER XXIX

The Postwar Scene

★ DEMOBILIZATION AND RECONVERSION

The end of war was not to mean settled peace for the people of the United States or for those of any other country in a still troubled world. It was not enough that the Axis powers had been defeated. New rivalries and new conflicts soon arose. The bright hopes of the "One World" to be realized through the effective operation of the United Nations gave way to a sharp division between the western democracies and communist Russia. Mid-century found the world confronted with a "cold war" that held out the all too dangerous possibilities of developing once again into global conflict.

Yet in spite of somber intimations of possible future trouble even as the guns fell silent in Europe and Asia, the American people turned eagerly to the tasks of reconversion and reconstruction at home. Believing that somehow their wartime aims of an enduring peace would be realized, they let themselves become increasingly absorbed in immediate domestic issues. And as such problems were gradually resolved, the country rejoiced in a measure of prosperity and stability that surpassed all expectations.

The demobilization of the country's armed forces, the liquidation of wartime agencies, and the reconversion of industry to the production of civilian goods took place with speed and dispatch. The desire to shake off the controls of the past five years was irresistible, and nothing could have more graphically demonstrated the unmilitary character of the American people than this rush to disarm. "Bring Daddy Back Home" was a popular slogan carrying far more weight than serious consideration of how rapidly the nation could really afford to strip its defenses. The number of men in uniform was cut to 3,000,000 within a year, and another twelve months saw this figure halved, with the peacetime total for Army, Navy, and Air Force theoretically stabilized at 1,500,000. The discharged G.I.'s were rapidly absorbed in the domestic economy. Special provisions for job reinstatement, unemployment pay, and business or farm loans eased this process, while several million veterans were able to resume interrupted educations through the allowances granted under the G.I. Bill of Rights.

The War Production Board almost at once lifted its controls over industry, $35,000,000,000 in war contracts were canceled, Army and Navy surplus goods offered for sale, and taxes sharply reduced. Although the price controls of the OPA were for a time maintained, popular pressure soon forced their relinquishment under confused circumstances in which politics rather than the public interest played the major role. The cycle of events in 1919 appeared to be repeating itself in 1946: the country wanted to forget the war and return to the customary ways of peace.

An immediate consequence of such a precipitate removal of wartime restrictions was dangerous inflation. Prices, which had been held down relatively well under President Roosevelt's wartime hold-the-line orders, soared upward when the OPA was disbanded. The increase in living costs during the latter half of 1946 was more than 25 per cent, or approximately twice the rise of the previous three years. Before costs showed any signs of becoming at least temporarily stabilized in mid-1948, the consumers' price index, which had by V-J Day risen from its 1939 base point to about 130, shot up to 175. An apparently insatiable demand for consumer goods, supported by increasing national income, exercised a pressure on the price structure that could not be withstood.

The most notable aspect of the economic scene, in spite of inflation, was the spectacular resumption of industrial progress. There had been widespread fears of unemployment, hard times, and depression. The sharp decline that had struck the country in 1921, three years after the Armistice ended World War I, was very much in the minds of the leaders of government, industry, and labor. But nothing of the kind took place in the 1940's. Replacement needs in industry, continued overseas shipments for relief and reconstruction, and especially the pent-up consumer demand for automobiles, radios, electric refrigerators, and scores of other goods that had been off the market for four years stimulated production all along the line. Expanding manufactures were largely responsible for the full employment—60,000,000 jobs—that was the most significant index of postwar prosperity.

Heavy government expenditures also contributed to economic advance as well as to inflationary pressures, and the simultaneous reduction of taxes meant a continuation of deficit financing. It was not until 1948, and then only briefly, that the federal budget was balanced. Annual outlays for military costs, various forms of veterans' aid, interest on the public debt, social welfare services, and current administrative expenses averaged as much as $40,000,000,000 annually (four times the total for even the depression years), and the federal debt remained over the $250,000,000,000 mark.

There were obvious dangers in this situation, and the soundness of a prosperity shored up by government expenditures at home and abroad could well be questioned. Yet the fact remained that far from experiencing economic collapse, the United States was taking reconversion and reconstruction in its stride. Between 1945 and 1950, the national income rose more than twenty-five per cent—to a total of $226 billion. It was more widely distributed than ever before in history. While business was making record profits, wages were rising and the farmers doing so well that both mortgages and farm tenancy were substantially reduced. It was estimated in 1948 that three-fourths of the families in the United States had incomes of more than $2,000 a year.

★ THE CHALLENGE OF LABOR

The most important domestic issue of the immediate postwar years concerned the status of labor. The total union membership, largely concentrated in the A.F. of L. and the C.I.O., had risen to about 15,000,000. The workers generally had observed their no-strike pledge during the war, but they were now prepared to defend their interests, whether in the matter of union recognition or wage increases, by every means within their power. They were determined, especially those in the mass production industries, to prevent any recurrence of the setback labor had experienced at the close of World War I. When industry showed itself reluctant to meet postwar demands for higher pay, in some instances appearing ready to challenge the basic concept of collective bargaining, a wave of strikes threatened to paralyze the entire reconversion program. They were not the violent, bloody strikes of earlier periods, but gruelling endurance contests between two well-organized forces.

The wage issue was the immediate cause for these outbreaks of industrial strife in 1945 and 1946. The workers had received about a 15 per cent increase during the war, and with prices up nearly a third over prewar levels, they demanded raises that would bring their income in line with mounting living costs. More fundamental than wages, however, was the whole question of the status of organized labor and the place of collective bargaining in the national economy. The leaders of the C.I.O.

—such men as Philip Murray and Walter Reuther—were especially concerned that industry should not whittle away the longterm gains that labor had made under the friendly protection of the New Deal.

The successes the unions achieved in winning the first round of postwar wage demands, and then going on to further victories in collective bargaining, were of the utmost significance. Organized labor had consolidated the position built up since passage of the Wagner Act and could compel industry to accept collective bargaining as the basic means for settlement of industrial disputes. Postwar developments on the labor scene, even more than those of the 1930's, clearly revealed that the rise of organized labor, as represented primarily through the immense economic power wielded by such unions as those in coal and steel, automobiles, electrical equipment, railroading, and shipping was the outstanding development in the domestic economy since the inauguration of the New Deal.

Nearly 500,000 workers were on strike within a month of the war's end, but the organized campaign to assure labor's position and win new wage adjustments was really initiated by the United Automobile Workers in December 1945. Under Walter Reuther's militant leadership, they demanded a 30 per cent wage increase and when it was refused first struck against General Motors and walked out en masse from the company's plants throughout the country. While this strike was still in progress the meat packers, and wage earners in seventy-eight plants of the electrical equipment industry walked out, and the steel workers struck. The number of men on picket lines throughout the nation spiraled to over 2,000,000. As additional workers faced the loss of their jobs and industry everywhere slowed down, the public clamored for government intervention to forestall a complete economic breakdown.

President Truman subscribed to the prolabor policies of the New Deal. He flatly stated that wage increases were imperative "to cushion the shock to our workers, to sustain adequate purchasing power and to raise the national income." Moreover, he was convinced that rate increases could be granted without upsetting the stable price structure which his administration was still trying to maintain. When his hopes that postwar wage disputes would be peacefully settled by collective bargaining were disappointed with the failure of industry and labor to come to terms, he consequently established fact-finding boards in the various industries. Their general conclusion, as first set forth in the case of the steel industry, was that increases were in order of around eighteen cents an hour, or as much as 20 per cent, because of the rise in living costs since adoption of wartime wage controls.

The steel industry accepted this figure, after assurance of some price relief, and it became the generally accepted basis for new wage contracts throughout the business world. The General Motors strike, after dragging along wearily for four months, was settled on this general formula. By mid-March 1946 industrial unrest had so substantially subsided that the number of men on strike had fallen from 2,000,000 to less than 200,000. As the nation resumed the interrupted task of reconversion the natural resiliency of the economy rapidly reasserted itself.

This was not the end of industrial strife. John L. Lewis, whose wartime strikes had led to government seizure of the coal mines, was determined to do even better for his coal workers than other labor leaders had done for their union members. A weary succession of strikes in this basic industry plagued the country, and there appeared to be no way to combat successfully the arbitrary, ruthless tactics of a labor dictator who never hesitated to defy either the government or public opinion. Repeated seizure of the coal mines, injunctions, and contempt of court proceedings seemed unavailing. While the coal strikes were ultimately settled, Lewis in each instance won notable concessions for his miners.

A national emergency was also threatened for a time when the Railroad Trainmen and Locomotive Engineers went on strike in May 1946. Truman acted promptly in this crisis, taking over the railroads, and when the trainmen and engineers still refused to return to work, he went before Congress to ask authority to draft them into the Armed Forces. As he was actually delivering his message he was handed a note that the strike had been settled on the terms he had suggested. Under the circumstances the proposed legislation was not adopted. As the trainmen and engineers returned to work the nation breathed a long sigh of relief.

Prices continued to rise after the settlement of this first round of wage demands, and the unions were soon insisting on further increases. In most instances satisfactory agreements were worked out through collective bargaining, but there were disturbing strikes on the part of seamen, longshoremen, telephone workers, and coal miners. The tremendous economic power of the unions, and the constant danger of national strikes threatening public health and safety, increasingly alarmed the public. A feeling grew that some way had to be found to prevent arbitrary domination over the country's economic life by any organized minority, even as representative as labor. The government was called upon to meet the challenge of big labor as it had once been called upon to assert its authority over big business.

★ THE TAFT-HARTLEY ACT

The Truman administration opposed the adoption of any restrictions weakening the rights secured for the unions by the Wagner Act, but with the election of a Republican Congress in the midterm elections of 1946, the way was cleared for new legislation. What was to become the Taft-Hartley Act was approved by Congress in June 1947. Vetoed by President Truman on the ground that it was "bad for labor, bad for management, bad for the country," it was promptly re-enacted over his objections to become law.

The clear purpose of the Taft-Hartley Act was to redress a balance in industrial relations which seemed to have swung too much in favor of the unions and thereby restore equality of bargaining between employers and employees. The unions were to be barred from certain unfair practices, compelled to give sixty-day notice of termination of any contract, and prohibited from making political campaign contributions. The closed shop was outlawed and restrictions placed about the union shop. In the case of strikes imperiling national health or safety, the government was empowered to seek an injunction restraining all strike activity for eighty days.

The Taft-Hartley Act did not solve the problem of organized labor's role in American society. Fulfilling neither the hopes of its advocates nor the fears of its critics, it would not in succeeding years appear to have any really important influence in allaying industrial strife. Its most significant aspect was that, far from reversing the principles incorporated in the Wagner Act, it actually broadened government's role in dealing with industrial relations. While it restored a greater measure of equality between employer and employee through the prohibition of unfair practices on the part of unions as well as on the part of management, it could not guarantee the success of collective bargaining.

Taft-Hartley was to remain a controversial issue for a decade and more. Organized labor vehemently opposed its passage, characterizing the measure as "a slave labor bill," and continued to insist on its repeal. Management was hardly less satisfied with it and worked assiduously for more stringent amendments. It remained political dynamite. Congress wanted to have no more to do with it.

★ SOCIAL DEVELOPMENTS

Other aspects of the social scene did not suggest such a sharp postwar reaction as had generally marked the 1920's. There was no comparable revolt of the younger generation, jazz grew in popularity but there was no "jazz age," prohibition no longer remained to stimulate defiance of the law, and no spectacular revolution occurred in morals and manners. In politics a Fair Deal was to succeed the New Deal—as will be discussed later—without any such break in continuity as that between Progressivism and normalcy. The 1950's were in some ways to resemble the 1920's, but the atmosphere of the immediate postwar period was quite different. It was partly perhaps that the American people had gone to war in 1941 in a far more practical spirit than they had in 1917 and did not experience the sense of disillusionment that had characterized the 1920's.

This matter-of-fact attitude was as true of the veterans as of other groups. Returning to the farm, the factory, the business office, or professional pursuits, they were soon indistinguishable from their co-workers who had not served in the Armed Forces. Those who went back to schools and colleges worried about classroom assignments and examination grades with little suggestion that a few months before they had been daily confronted with the somewhat graver issues of life or death on the battlefields of Europe and Asia.

Still, there were always some critical problems of social adjustment. For many G.I.'s the resumption of civilian jobs was not as easy as had been anticipated, and women leaving war work to pick up former family obligations sometimes found the transition highly difficult. The war had led to many hurried marriages, and far more of them than would have been the case under ordinary circumstances broke up with the return of peace. The rate of one divorce for every four marriages reported in 1946 seemed to have ominous implications. Family life for many young people, including the thousands of married veterans in colleges and universities, was often made extremely complicated because of the great scarcity of homes and apartments. Temporary G.I. villages and trailer camps helped out, but housing continued to be a problem throughout the 1940's.

Education had necessarily suffered during the war days, and as the school population increased at all levels—especially in the colleges as a result of the influx of veterans—an appalling lack of school buildings, equipment, and teachers became apparent. Overcrowding and a lowering in teaching standards could hardly be avoided. Less than one half the country's teachers in grade schools and high schools, to cite but one revealing statistic, had college degrees. Every effort was made to remedy such conditions with increased state appropriations, and the demand was voiced—but not met at this time—for some form of federal aid for education.

One of the factors that led to proposals for federal aid was the marked difference in some parts of the country between the educational facilities available for white and Negro children. This was but part of the larger and highly sensitive problem of racial equality. A long compaign against such discrimination in the employment area, as applied to Jews and other minority groups as well as Negroes, had found support during the war days in the establishment of a Fair Employment Practices Commission, and President Truman was to press vigorously for its permanent continuation. While every proposal for such action on a national basis was blocked by the filibustering tactics of southern senators, a number of states set up their own FEPC's. Neither these commissions nor other legislative action completely eliminated discrimination, but they encouraged further progress along the difficult road to racial equality.

The Supreme Court helped to promote this democratic cause. A series of significant decisions nullified existing white primary laws in the southern states, did away with Jim Crow restrictions in transportation so far as they affected interstate commerce, outlawed the enforcement of discrimination clauses in real estate transactions, ordered the acceptance of Negroes in southern universities where other comparable educational facilities were not available, and generally upheld racial equality as a fundamental principle in a democratic society. To this story we must return; the point here is that in the 1940's the public conscience was already becoming aroused over what a decade later would become such a vital, all-important issue.

The Supreme Court also rigorously safeguarded other civil rights. An exception was its decision in *Korematsu* v *United States* upholding the wartime evacuation of citizens of Japanese ancestry from California, but otherwise the court record of the entire 1940's was far more liberal than that of the 1920's. Judicial support for freedom of speech, freedom of the press, freedom of association, and freedom of religion was a distinguishing characteristic of the decade in spite of all the stress and strain of war.

As the menace of communism began to develop in the late 1940's, however, a wave of popular intolerance, as distinguished from the attitude of the courts, began to sweep the country. Congressional investigations nominally directed against communists and subversive activity, but often embracing in their scope anyone remotely suspected of radical or even liberal views, became the order of the day. The tactics of the House Un-American Activities Committee, set up almost a decade earlier, were often far more un-American in their disregard of civil liberties than anything disclosed about the people being investigated. The Department of Justice drew up a long list of supposedly subversive organizations; many states passed laws requiring loyalty oaths of civil servants and school teachers. Guilt by association became a widely accepted popular, if not legal, concept, and many instances of persecution and suppression gravely prejudiced the safeguards for individual freedom embodied in the Constitution.

While loyalty investigations and charges of subversive activity in many ways recalled the Red Scare of 1919, they were given even greater weight because of current fears not only of communism, but of the military power of Soviet Russia arrayed in support of communism. In contrast with the situation thirty years earlier, when the Soviet Union had been far too weak to threaten the Western World, the Russia of mid-century was powerful and aggressive. But whatever the need to assure patriotic loyalty in a time of international crisis, grave dangers for democracy were reflected in sensationally headlined witch hunts and hysterical public accusations of sympathy with communism. An atmosphere of fear and suspicion was created which provided the basis for the even uglier manifestations of intolerance in the 1950's that were associated with McCarthyism.

Whatever may be said of the strength or weakness of democratic principles, material well-being remained the phenomenon that most forcibly struck observers in the first postwar years. Economic progress and a more equitable distribution of the national income meant more things for more people—automobiles, electric refrigerators, washing machines, deep freezes, power mowers, radios, and television sets. The last named was of course something new—a spectacular symbol of both the march of science and of general prosperity. The rapid development of television was quite as amazing as that of the radio a quarter of a century earlier. The world may have entered upon the atomic age, with all its dread possibilities of death and destruction, but TV had a far more immediate effect on the daily life of the citizens of the United States.

★ HARRY S. TRUMAN

As the nation sought to adjust itself to the ways of what it still hoped would be an enduring peace, domestic politics followed a highly erratic course. Upon his succession to the presidency, Truman had stated in April 1945 his determination to maintain and extend the program of social reform associated with the New Deal. It was widely expected that mounting criticism of the policies of the Roosevelt administration, reenforced by the sort of postwar reaction that had marked the early 1920's, would lead to popular repudiation of this program and the return of the Republicans to political power. Such expectations seemed to be fully confirmed in the results of the midterm elections of 1946. Winning control of the House and Senate, the Republicans prepared to sit it out until their anticipated victory in the 1948 presidential election also put them in charge of the executive branch of government.

A virtual deadlock between Congress and the President consequently characterized the first postwar years, with Truman's position further weakened by the divisions within his own party. The southern Democrats had completely turned against the New Deal program, and on many issues the President could count upon the support in Congress of only northern Democrats and a few maverick Republicans. In many ways it was an impossible situation, not unknown in earlier political eras, and it was hardly helped by what appeared for a time to be Truman's faltering leadership. His intentions often appeared to be of the best, but during these first days he seemed to lack the forthright grasp of affairs, the independence of mind, the creative imagination that the times demanded.

His presence in the White House was a strange political accident. There had been nothing in his earlier career to foreshadow such eminence for this inconspicuous man from Missouri. After serving in World War I as an artillery captain, he had unsuccessfully tried the haberdashery business and then drifted into politics under the wing of the notorious Pendergast machine in Kansas City. A number of terms as a county judge made him eligible for political advancement (although Truman was never charged with making any deals with Pendergast), and he was somewhat casually offered the opportunity to run for the Senate. Swept into office in the Democratic landslide of 1934, he served out his six years and was then re-elected, again not because of any outstanding record but because he was the incumbent and it was another Democratic year.

Truman faithfully and consistently supported the New Deal while a member of the Senate, but he made no effort to play a significant role in legislative activities. He seldom spoke on the floor and gave no indication of having very firm convictions on any of the issues that came up for consideration. It was not until the war period that he did anything to distinguish himself in any way. His efficient and able conduct of a Senate committee's investigations of wartime industrial contracts then won him considerable recognition, but there was still little idea that he had an important political future. His nomination for the vice-presidency in 1944 was largely due to his last moment availability as a compromise candidate in the contest over Henry Wallace, and it was as a surprised and rather reluctant nominee that he ran for office. Modest, unpretentious, friendly, Truman seemed more than anything else just a typical example of the average man.

When Roosevelt's death elevated him to the presidency, he took over the immense responsibilities imposed upon him with appealing humility. Truman recognized his own limitations and lack of experience. But as he gradually learned he grew more self-assured; he sought to take over the role of national leadership. A number of early appointments, however, appeared to show a tendency to rely upon old political friends rather than to seek out men of broad experience. The public began to look more critically at his policies than it had when he first took office during the war. Confronted not only with a determined Republican opposition, finally freed from the self-imposed restraints of wartime, but meeting also at every turn the obstructive attitude of conservative southern Democrats, a far stronger chief executive than President Truman would have found the going very hard.

The impasse that developed between the White House and Congress did not mean that Truman's first administration was a failure. The reconversion program was carried through successfully, in spite of both inflation and labor disputes, and the country prospered. The progressive reform ideals of the New Deal were reflected in administration support for slum clearance and low-cost housing, an increase in minimum wage standards, health insurance, and a program of full employment. The latter interest led to passage in February 1946 of an Employment Act which established a Council of Economic Advisers to investigate, plan, and advise on all matters affecting the national economy. The armed services were unified through passage of the National Security Act, and civilian control over atomic energy was affirmed with the creation of an Atomic Energy Commission. But Truman quarreled with Congress over the labor legislation that eventuated in the Taft-Hartley Act, over health insurance, over anti-inflation measures, and over civil rights bills. Politics appeared to be blocking the development of any long-range, broadly constructive program in meeting postwar issues. The country impatiently looked to the next election to give a clearer view of the shape of things to come.

★ THE ELECTION OF 1948

The Republicans were superbly confident in 1948 that their long awaited day had arrived. They again nominated Thomas E. Dewey, in spite of his defeat four years earlier, and in the belief that their old slogan "Had Enough?" could now evoke only one possible response, they hardly bothered to be more explicit on their own policies. Dewey gave his hearty adherence to the vague proposition of "re-establishing liberty at home," but on other issues he studiously avoided taking a stand that might create any dissension within the ranks of his supporters. He too was certain that this time the Republicans could hardly fail, and with what was to prove unjustified complacency, simply waited for election day.

There appeared to be every reason for Republican confidence. The Democrats adopted an almost defeatist attitude, and Truman was nominated to succeed himself with singularly little enthusiasm. He was opposed by the extreme left and right wings of his own party, and the rank-and-file Democrats appeared largely uninterested. Soon after the convention the conservative southern bloc revolted to form a new states' rights party, the Dixiecrats, and named their own presidential candidate, Governor J. Strom Thurmond of South Carolina. At the very opposite end of the political spectrum Henry Wallace, whom Truman had dismissed as Secretary of Commerce for his interference in foreign policy matters, broke away to form a new Progressive Party with leftwing, radical support. The Democrats seemed to be splitting apart entirely, with their presidential candidate the helpless and hopeless victim of internecine strife and popular apathy.

Harry Truman refused to be defeated. He carried his fight for re-election to the people with complete faith that in spite of the defection of Dixiecrats and Wallace Progressives, and virtual desertion by party leaders, he could win. He waged an aggressive, cocky campaign. Boldly reaffirming the basic principles of the New Deal he attacked the "do-nothing" record of the Republican Congress and vehemently declared that its leaders were obstructive and reactionary. He emphasized these issues in scores of carefully prepared speeches, but his most effective campaigning—although few realized at the time how very effective it was—proved to be his informal talks at hundreds of "whistle-stops" along the route of his special train. No matter how briefly the train paused, Truman appeared on the back platform with his family—unassuming, folksy, friendly—and told the villagers and townspeople what he was trying to do in Washington.

The nation could not have been more astounded at the election results. Never had what was almost universally accepted as a foregone conclusion been so completely upset. Truman not only won the presidency, with a popular plurality of over 2,000,000 votes, but he carried his party to control of both houses of Congress. Wallace did not win a single state; the Dixiecrats only four. The margin of victory was small—the narrowest in many years—but the incontrovertible fact remained that Truman had confounded all the prophets and in the face of every informed prediction except his own had been re-elected President.

Interpretations of the election results differed widely. The failure of the Republicans to take the campaign more seriously, Truman's folksy appeal in contrast to Dewey's cold and reserved manner, popular sympathy for the underdog, the strong labor vote, the unexpected support of midwest farmers, and continuing loyalty to Roosevelt were all advanced to explain the phenomenon. Generally, it was agreed that the election was a great personal victory for Truman; less universally, that the country was far more liberal-minded than the politicians realized.

Truman was in any event ready to interpret his election as a mandate to carry forward the policies he had taken over from Roosevelt. In a fighting inaugural address he called for enactment of a program which he now called the Fair Deal, designed to meet the needs of the common people and promote the general welfare. Continued support for labor and agriculture, higher taxes in the upper income brackets, expanded social security, health insurance, and the protection of civil rights were the goals of his administration. The President called for congressional and popular support for policies which would carry out the aims of progressive democracy.

When Truman was inaugurated in 1949, however, the lowering clouds of international strife had long since begun to darken the horizon. Foreign affairs were becoming of increasing concern, and for all the importance of domestic issues popular attention was diverted to an ever-greater extent to the implications of communist imperialism. Truman succeeded in making only very limited progress toward achieving the goals of his domestic policy, suffered a severe political setback in the midterm elections of 1950, and was compelled almost entirely to subordinate any further reform legislation to the exacting demands of national defense in the face of war in Korea. This narrative must consequently now turn to an account of those foreign developments that led to the new crisis in international affairs.

CHAPTER XXX

The Mirage of Peace

★ BACKGROUND OF CONFLICT

The achievement of lasting peace rather than victory alone had been a primary purpose of President Roosevelt during the war. Convinced that the United States could no longer avoid its compelling responsibilities as a world power, he labored incessantly to persuade the American people that this time there could be no such renunciation of leadership as had taken place in the 1920's. From the proclamation of the Atlantic Charter in 1941, with its call for "the establishment of a wider and permanent system of general security" to the specific reaffirmation at Yalta of the principles underlying world organization, the line of advance was straight and undeviating.

"We seek peace—enduring peace," Roosevelt wrote in a last speech which he was destined never to deliver. "More than an end to war, we want an end to the beginning of all wars. . . . Today, as we move against the terrible scourge of war—as we go forward toward the greatest contribution that any generation of human beings can make in this world—the contribution of lasting peace—I ask you to keep up your faith."

A few months after his death, the formal establishment of the United Nations at the San Francisco Conference of April-June 1945 appeared to hold out every hope that this bright dream might be realized. "You members of this conference," President Truman, who was fully dedicated to the Roosevelt program, told the delegates of the fifty nations assembled at San Francisco, "are to be the architects of a better world." Germany was about to collapse, Japan would soon follow her in unconditional surrender, and on the ruins of these fallen empires it was hoped to erect a free society of all peace-loving nations.

How these hopeful expectations came to be overshadowed by the deepening tension between Soviet Russia and the democratic nations of the West is a tragic story. Before its telling, some general considerations may help to set the stage for postwar developments on the international scene. Almost every great war has led to a collapse of the coalition that won the victory. The circumstances surrounding the triumph of the Great Alliance in World War II made such an eventuality even more likely than in the past.

There were two distinct aspects of postwar conflict in the 1940's. The principles of communism as championed by the Soviet Union were sharply at variance with the democratic concepts of the Allies. While there continued to be some optimism over the possibility that these differences could be submerged in a common search for peace, any sort of friendly co-operation between communist and capitalist states became every year more difficult. Socialist doctrinaires declared their permanent coexistence to be impossible. At the same time more strictly political causes of friction grew up to separate the eastern and western worlds. A revived imperialism which saw the Soviets embracing the historic ambitions of czarist days presented an even more concrete challenge than communism itself to international peace and security. Nor were the United States and the other western powers free from their own ambitions for power and influence. Ideological and political rivalries were at once separate and closely interwoven.

Circumstance accentuated the perils of this twofold clash. As the United States and Soviet Russia emerged from war as the world's two outstanding powers, both of them young, strong, dynamic nations, they were irresistibly drawn into a struggle for position in the power vacuums that had been created by the downfall of Germany and Japan. And everywhere new revolutionary forces, in the Far East and the Middle East as well as in Europe, had been let loose by the general upheaval. The contest whether in eastern Europe or eastern Asia was for men's minds as well as for political domination, and the danger of such contests leading to war was intensified by the fact that neither the United States nor Soviet Russia was prepared by experience to deal with the responsibilities imposed by their new-found power.

It had been Roosevelt's conviction that peace could be maintained. He was ready to make concessions that he hoped would convince Soviet Russia that the United States was not her enemy and that communism and democracy could avoid a fatal clash. The necessity for making every possible effort at conciliation, whatever the risks involved, was in his estimation a moral imperative. Any other policy was to accept the inevitability of a third world war in a defeatist spirit that was completely foreign to his nature. And certainly it may be said, in spite of everything that has happened since, that the co-operation proffered by the United States, and refused by Soviet Russia, in the mid-1940's, strengthened America's world position as the leader of those nations which have been unwilling to surrender their liberties and accept communist domination.

The bitter irony of the early negotiations in 1945 is found in the American policy-makers' confidence that they had laid the foundations for a peaceful world. "We really believed in our hearts," Harry Hopkins has been quoted as saying after the Yalta conference, "that this was the dawn of the new day we had all been praying for and talking about for so many years. We were absolutely certain that we had won the first great victory for peace—and by 'we,' I mean all of us, the whole civilized race." Had the United States adopted from the first a "tough" attitude toward Russia, there is no assurance that its position would actually have been any stronger in later years. What might conceivably have been gained from the point of veiw of strategic expediency would have been at the expense of moral principle. The attempt to collaborate on the assumption that a way of peace existed, was the least that could be done to justify the immense sacrifices already made in the hope of saving succeeding generations from war's terrible scourge.

★ THE EARLY ALLIED CONFERENCES

The foreign ministers of the United States, Great Britain, and Soviet Russia, meeting in Moscow late in 1943, had for the first time agreed upon the need to establish "a general international organization, based on the principle of sovereign equality of all peace-loving nations, open to membership by all such states, large and small." Shortly afterwards, Roosevelt, Churchill, and Stalin met in conference at Teheran. It represented the high water mark of wartime collaboration, leading to full agreement on common measures for the prosecution of the war, and as already noted, confirmation of the foreign ministers' pronouncement in support of world organization. The Big Three stated in a joint declaration that their countries were not only prepared to work together in war, but would co-operate "in the peace that will follow."

Public opinion in this country was by no means unanimously in favor of American membership in a world organization. The attitude of mind that had rejected the League of Nations a quarter of a century earlier still persisted in some quarters. But as the war progressed, the concept of international co-operation gathered increasing support and the tides of isolationism receded ever further into the background. Popular polls in mid-1944 showed that at least seven out of every ten persons believed that the United States should take the lead in promoting collective security; the nation's leading business, labor, and farm associations went officially on record as favoring a new international league.

In the light of Woodrow Wilson's experiences in 1919, Roosevelt was very much in favor of setting up the proposed world organization before the war ended, divorcing it completely from the actual peace-making. Instead of being designed to uphold any particular settlement, its primary function would be the prevention of future aggression from any quarter through united international action. The President consequently urged a preliminary conference as soon as possible at which the United States, Great Britain, and Soviet Russia would be joined by Nationalist China in drawing up tentative plans. So far as this country was concerned, he was also determined to develop policy along bipartisan lines. Again learning from Wilson's mistakes, he was prepared to consult with Congress at every step along the way and to have American delegates representative of both parties at all international conferences.

In June 1944 the President set forth his ideas in very specific terms and some two months later, with Congress expressing its approval, the proposed conference was held at Dumbarton Oaks, just outside Washington, with representatives of the four major powers in attendance. They agreed tentatively upon the general outlines of what was to become the United Nations. Not all points of difference were settled, but sufficient progress was made to give every assurance that future negotiations could iron out the points still in dispute.

These moves toward world organization looked to the long future. Their implementation, as well as consideration of the more immediate problems of peace-making with Germany and Japan, then came up for review in February 1945 at the most important of all wartime meetings —held by the Big Three at Yalta in the Crimea. With the war drawing to an end the circumstances of this meeting were highly dramatic, and the decisions reached were to have incalculable consequences. They were based, as previously suggested, on the fundamental premise that peacetime co-operation between the western democracies and Soviet Russia was possible. Concessions were made by the United States to the Russian point of view; the Soviet Union in turn made concessions to American policy. It is easy to forget, in retrospect, that the apparent spirit of compromise was mutual.

★ YALTA

Roosevelt, Churchill, and Stalin agreed at Yalta upon a program for the joint occupation of a defeated Germany, in which France too would participate, with destruction of Nazism and the trial of war criminals, and they also accepted the principle of reparation payments so limited as not to destroy Germany's productive capacity. They promised a reconstitution of the government in Poland, and free elections both there and in the other liberated countries of eastern Europe in order to allow the peoples of those nations to set up their own democratic regimes. Turning to eastern Asia, they agreed that in compensation for Russian fulfillment of an earlier pledge to enter the war against Japan within two or three months of Germany's surrender, the Soviets would be awarded the Kurile Islands, the southern half of Sakhalin, extensive privileges in Darien and Port Arthur, and control over the Manchurian railways. These concessions were made without consulting China, but Stalin pledged recognition of the sovereignty of the Chiang Kai-shek government over Manchuria, and shortly afterward a treaty of friendship, incorporating the Yalta agreements, was concluded between Nationalist China and the Soviet Union.

On the broader issue of world organization, the Big Three also came to an accord on the questions left unsettled at Dumbarton Oaks. While the United States and the Soviet Union had both insisted at this earlier meeting on a veto power in the Security Council of the United Nations, they differed in the way in which it should be used. The United States was much more concerned than Russia over safeguarding the interests of the small powers from arbitrary domination by the great powers. The compromise accepted by Roosevelt and Stalin at Yalta provided that the veto should be used, and then sparingly, only on questions of substance. It would not be applied to procedural matters. The general qualifications for membership in the United Nations were also settled by mutual concessions respecting the status of White Russia and the Ukraine, the composition of the new Polish government, and the admission of Latin American nations.

In spite of justified criticism of certain of the Yalta decisions, especially perhaps those involving China, full consideration of the circumstances of the time clearly absolves Roosevelt from the extremist charge of complete surrender to Russia. The war was not yet over; the practicality of the atomic bomb had not yet been demonstrated. In no event could Russian interests, supported by the presence of huge armies in the field, have been ignored whether in eastern Europe or eastern Asia. Military opinion strongly emphasized the vital importance of assuring full Russian aid in the final defeat of Japan. Moreover, in return for the concessions the United States made, it must be remembered that the Soviet Union agreed, on what then seemed to be very reasonable grounds, both to free elections in eastern Europe and to continued cooperation with Nationalist China.

"Our hopeful assumptions were soon to be falsified," Churchill has written in what might be taken as a definitive interpretation of Yalta. "Still, they were the only ones possible at the time."

The tragedy of Yalta lay not in the nature of the accords concluded, but in the failure of Soviet Russia to carry them out. It was heightened by Roosevelt's confidence, not unlike that of Wilson at the Paris Peace Conference, that entirely apart from the settlement of any immediate issues, a basic understanding had been reached which assured the success of the United Nations as a guarantor of future world security.

"I come from the Crimea Conference," the President reported on his return home, "with a firm belief that we have made a good start on the road to a world of peace. . . . a turning point—I hope in our history and therefore in the history of the world."

★ THE UNITED NATIONS

Only three months later the conference at San Francisco wrote the final chapter in the organization of the United Nations. The fifty governments which signed its Charter mutually agreed to refrain from the use of armed force, save in the common interest, and to employ the machinery of peaceful negotiation in all future international disputes. The General Assembly was authorized to investigate, discuss, and advise on any issues imperiling international peace, and the Security Council was empowered to meet any threat of actual war through the adoption of such measures "by air, sea, or land forces" as might prove necessary. A permanent Secretariat, an International Court of Justice, and an Economic and Social Council were also created, with additional agencies to handle problems involving relief and rehabilitation, food and agriculture, world health, and international labor.

The United States Senate approved the United Nations Charter (with only two dissenting votes) on July 28, 1945; it came into effect three months later after some twenty-eight other nations had also ratified it. In many ways like the old League of Nations, it had two distinct advantages over that organization. Its authority to take action in the event of any threat to peace was far broader, and both the United States and Soviet Russia were original members. There appeared to be valid grounds for the hopes of its founders that the bases for world peace had been greatly strengthened.

The failure of the United Nations to fulfill these expectations was the result of factors beyond its control. No world organization—let alone one as yet so untried—could have hoped to meet successfully the stresses and strains created by so basic a conflict as that which developed between Soviet Russia and the West. The entire concept of the United Nations was predicated on the willingness of the major powers to co-operate. When Russian postwar policy was reversed, as illustrated by increasingly arbitrary use of the veto power to block measures on which other members of the Security Council were agreed, a situation was created that could not possibly be resolved solely through the machinery of the UN. Yet during its early years the United Nations had a number of signal achievements to its credit which may well have served to avert minor clashes from developing into war, even though it could not settle all underlying issues.

The role of the United Nations was highly important in bringing about settlement of a threatening dispute between Soviet Russia and Iran, safeguarding Greece from the inroads of communist guerillas from neighboring states, helping to establish Israel as an independent nation, preventing further strife in Indonesia, and arousing public sentiment in support of the peaceful settlement of a number of other seemingly critical issues. There was also encouraging progress in the work of the United Nations' many nonpolitical agencies, and in the growing awareness of the need for concerted effort to promote the economic and social welfare of the peoples of the world as a whole. In spite of failure to solve the problem of control of atomic energy, largely due to Russia's refusal to accept the American plan, drafted by a committee headed by Bernard M. Baruch, for creation of an International Atomic Development Authority, continued discussions on other aspects of disarmament at least kept alive the idea that the United Nations had responsibilities in this broad area of international action which would some day have to be met.

For all its apparent weakness the UN remained operative. It continued to serve as a great forum for international debate. So long as its meetings continued the possibilities of peace were not exhausted. Finally, in 1950, under circumstances to be discussed later, it took the unprecedented step of actively intervening in Korea to repel aggression against the government that had been set up under its auspices in South Korea.

★ THE GROWING RIFT

The deepening international conflict that was responsible for the weakness of the United Nations and the disappointment of all hopes of a secure peace, first found expression in the inability of the United States, Great Britain, and France to agree with the Soviet Union upon policy toward Germany. Immediately after V-E Day, a further conference had been held in July 1945 at Potsdam among the Big Three—now President Truman, Premier Stalin and Prime Minister Attlee as successor to Churchill. They agreed upon provisional boundaries between

Germany and Poland, occupation zones in Germany which were subject to the provision that the country as a whole would be treated as an economic unit, procedures for disarmament, denazification, and the promotion of democracy in Germany, and the creation of an Allied Control Council to handle all problems of her military administration. They charged a new Council of Foreign Ministers with responsibility for the negotiation of peace treaties with Italy, Austria, the former Axis satellites, and ultimately Germany. On the surface these Potsdam agreements appeared to reaffirm the unity of purpose manifest at Teheran and Yalta, but there were already intimations that Soviet policy was swinging toward the harsh assertion of wholly Russian interests and the broad extension of a communist sphere of influence.

In succeeding months Moscow showed no disposition whatsoever to treat Germany as an economic whole, began recklessly stripping the Soviet occupation zone of raw materials, and refused to co-operate with the western powers on other matters of common interest. Having brought its government fully under communist control, Russia then encouraged Poland to take over permanently territories whose final disposition was yet to be settled by treaty, and stubbornly blocked the free elections to which she was pledged in Hungary, Romania, and Bulgaria. Although Czechoslovakia would not be brought behind what became the Iron Curtain until 1948, Soviet policy was already clearly directed toward communist domination of all eastern Europe in flagrant disregard of the Yalta accords. Behind this policy stood the immense force of the Red armies, not yet demobilized.

The United States was in the meantime experiencing its own difficulties in developing a constructive policy toward a defeated Germany. The dismantling of war industries, maintenance of a level of production that would prevent a complete collapse of German economy, denazification and the war criminal trials at Nurenberg, and the exercise of administrative authority gave rise to a host of incredibly complicated problems. And all these problems were aggravated by lack of co-operation on the part of the Russians and mounting evidence of their intention to rule their occupation zone in east Germany entirely in their own interests. The United States was compelled to recognize what was happening and adjust its policy to meet these new and unhappy realities.

The shift in American attitudes first became apparent in a speech delivered by the new Secretary of State, James F. Byrnes, at Stuttgart, in September 1946. Sharply criticizing Soviet policy Byrnes declared that the United States could not accept responsibility for a program that was blocking Germany's recovery. He called for a return to the principles agreed upon at Yalta and Potsdam and a revision of the reparations agreements to protect the well-being of all the German people.

The implied warning of the United States went unheeded. Soviet Russia continued to go her own way. As the chances of being able to work out a co-operative policy for Germany as a whole faded, the western Allies consequently proceeded to take their own steps to bring about the economic merger of their occupation zones regardless of what Moscow might do. The country was to be divided into a separate East Germany and West Germany.

Other aspects of Russian policy were by now causing equally great concern. While the Council of Foreign Ministers finally succeeded in concluding peace treaties with Italy, Romania, Hungary, and Bulgaria, which were signed in February 1947, no progress was being made on any permanent settlement with either Austria or Germany. The complete subjection of the governments of eastern Europe to Soviet control was every day more apparent. Additional instances of interference in the internal affairs of neighboring countries were reported in the Middle East, with steady pressure being exerted on Greece and Turkey. The issue facing the United States was whether it could afford to stand aside while the sphere of communist influence steadily broadened and the threat of communist aggression imperiled the security of all Europe.

★ THE TRUMAN DOCTRINE AND THE MARSHALL PLAN

President Truman felt compelled to take a firm stand and on March 12, 1947, laid down the general lines of a policy to "contain" further Russian advance. Its immediate cause was the growing danger that Greece and Turkey might be compelled to surrender to Soviet pressure and Russia score what would for the West be a disastrous breakthrough into the Mediterranean. Truman specifically called on Congress to provide economic and military aid for these two countries. The implications of what was to become known as the Truman Doctrine, however, went far beyond this proposal for strengthening the defenses against communism in the Middle East.

"One of the primary objectives of the foreign policy of the United States," the President declared, "is the creation of conditions in which we and other nations will be able to work out a way of life free from coercion. . . . I believe that it must be the policy of the United States to support free peoples who are resisting subjugation by armed minorities or by outside pressures."

The United States was taking the initiative. There would be no further retreat before Soviet pressure, whether in the Middle East, in Germany, or on other issues coming up before the United Nations. It was not a policy immediately or universally approved by the American people. Sharp debate developed in both Congress and in the country at large over the advisability of the Truman Doctrine. Danger was seen in foreign commitments that might carry the United States too far afield. Nevertheless, Congress approved the initial request of $400,000,000 for aid to Greece and Turkey in May, and in spite of criticism and controversy, the new "get tough" policy steadily gained increasing popular support.

The containment of possible communist aggression would continue to be the ultimate basis of American foreign policy. The Truman Doctrine initiated a national program of profound importance. As the hopes of postwar international co-operation receded into a dim and distant background and "the cold war" between West and East became an incontrovertible fact, the United States had taken its stand in vigorous support of the free world.

A month after adoption of the program to aid Greece and Turkey the first authoritative suggestion was made of an even more comprehensive move to combat communism in Europe, where it was making dangerous gains, especially in France and Italy, as a result of chaotic economic conditions. General Marshall, who had replaced Byrnes as Secretary of State, proposed in a speech at Harvard University on June 5, 1947, a joint undertaking for recovery in which the European nations would be assured of all necessary aid and assistance from the United States. This country had already shown a lively concern in European postwar reconstruction. It supported both the International Monetary Fund and the International Bank for Reconstruction, advanced credits totaling $3,750,000,000 to Great Britain, and generously aided in the relief and rehabilitation of a shattered continent through its contributions to UNRAA. What was to become the Marshall Plan had far broader implications and led to an unparalleled extension of economic help at tremendous cost to the American people.

"Our policy is not directed against any country or doctrine," Marshall stated in outlining his proposals, "but is directed against hunger, poverty, desperation, and chaos. Its purpose should be the revival of a working economy in the world so as to permit the emergence of political and economic conditions in which free institutions can exist."

Europe responded enthusiastically, and preliminary negotiations for working out a joint program were promptly started in Paris. Invitations to this conference were extended to Soviet Russia and her satellites, but it quickly became apparent that Moscow would have no part in any co-operative approach to European recovery. Communism throve on economic distress. The countries of western Europe then went ahead and proceeded to draw up plans which were designed, at an estimated cost of some $22,000,000,000, to restore normal trade and production within a period of four years. In mid-December 1947 President Truman submitted the whole gigantic project to Congress with a request for supporting appropriations of $17,000,000,000.

The debate as to whether such action should be taken was prolonged and acrimonious, once again bringing out the traditional division over American policy toward Europe which had been reflected in the contest between internationalists and isolationists in the 1930's. The advocates of the Marshall Plan stressed its humanitarian aspects, but it was universally recognized that the real question was how far the United States should go in supporting western Europe against the inroads of communism. Should the American people ignore what was happening abroad or should they intervene through enlightened self-interest? Senator Vandenberg, a onetime leader of the Republican isolationists but now a convinced internationalist, put the issue bluntly: "The greatest nation on earth either justifies or surrenders its leadership. We must choose. . . ."

An event which helped to tilt the scales was the startling coup which brought Czechoslovakia into the Soviet camp while the debate was still in progress. Congress knew it had to act to stem any further communist advance. In April 1948 it finally approved the Marshall Plan as a whole, authorized an initial appropriation of $5,300,000,000, and set up the Economic Co-operation Administration to carry the program into effect.

The program to aid Greece and Turkey had already proved successful; the results of the Marshall Plan were even more so. The promise of financial assistance at once stimulated European production, and with actual aid under the ECA ultimately totaling $12,000,000,000 the continent was getting firmly back on its feet by 1950. Moreover, important steps were taken to integrate the economy of West Germany with that of the other European countries, encouraging progress was made in the re-establishment of financial and monetary stability, and the dangerous "dollar gap" in the balance of international payments to the United States was progressively narrowed. Western Europe attained a measure of economic recovery that in 1947 had seemed almost impossible. These improved conditions had a significant consequence in weakening the hold of the European communist parties and in building up a better morale in all classes of society.

★ THE BERLIN AIRLIFT AND NATO

The adoption of the Marshall Plan did nothing to lessen the tension between the East and West. It not surprisingly accentuated the quarrel over policy in Germany, the focal point of immediate controversy, and Europe almost immediately faced a new crisis.

As the western powers completed the merger of their occupation zones in Germany, with final collapse of the Allied Control Council, and laid their plans for what was to become the Bonn government, the Soviets took a drastic retaliatory step. In the summer of 1948 they imposed a blockade on Berlin, in the Russian occupation zone but by agreement under four-power control, and sought to shut off all allied access to the former German capital. The American authorities realized that this move to isolate Berlin was a challenge which could not be allowed to go by default. "If we mean to hold Europe against Communism," declared General Clay, commander of the American occupation forces in Germany, "we must not budge." Nor did President Truman hesitate. His answer to the suggestion that the United States might withdraw was unequivocal: "We are going to stay, period."

The answer to the Russian challenge was the miraculous improvisation of an airlift that from June 1948 until May 1949 provided besieged Berlin with food, coal, and all other essential supplies. Planes of the United States Air Force and the British R.A.F. flew from West Germany to Berlin, on a close round-the-clock schedule, in a delivery service that had no parallel in the history of air transport. They made in all nearly 300,000 flights, carrying almost 2,500,000 tons of supplies.

In the face of such determination to hold Berlin the Soviet Union had no alternative other than surrender unless it wished to invite actual war. It lifted the blockade on May 12, 1949. This victory for the western Allies did not resolve the conflict over Germany, but it dramatically demonstrated a readiness to uphold their interests at whatever risk.

In the meantime the gathering evidence of Russian aggression on other sectors of the worldwide front as well as in Germany had led the United States to take an even more important step than that represented by the Marshall Plan in organizing Europe to resist possible Soviet attack. After congressional passage of a bipartisan resolution introduced by Senator Vandenberg which called for support of regional agreements for self-defense, Dean Acheson, the new Secretary of State, responded to overtures from the Western Union organized by the European nations and commenced negotiations for what became the North Atlantic Treaty. This important pact was concluded in April 1949, just as the blockade of Berlin was about to be lifted. While it fell within the framework of the United Nations Charter, which authorized regional agreements for self-defense, it involved a commitment for action in the European theater which this country had never before even remotely contemplated in time of peace. The twelve signatories of the North Atlantic Treaty mutually agreed that "an armed attack against one or more of them shall be considered an attack against them all." Three months later, on July 5, the Senate approved this epochal pact by a vote of 82 to 13.

The bolstering of western defenses against both communism and Soviet imperialism through the Marshall Plan and the North Atlantic Treaty won increasing popular support. Debate continued in Congress and in the press; criticism of the broad commitments made in the name of national security was sometimes vehement. But the American people generally accepted the realities of the cold war in Europe and the vital importance of checking further Soviet advance. Moreover, the new American policy seemed to be winning measurable gains. If there was no sense of permanent security on the European continent, the clearcut decision of the United States to continue active support—economic and military—for all countries resisting communist aggression, had succeeded in maintaining a balance of power that for the time forestalled war.

★ JAPAN AND CHINA

Events in eastern Asia were following a quite different course from those in Europe during these troubled postwar years. American policy in this area of the world was vacillating and confused, largely lacked the bipartisan support that had been built up for policy in Europe and seemed completely incapable of stemming communist advance. The effectiveness of the measures adopted in the West was in the minds of many people counterbalanced by glaring failure in the Far East.

The United States was the sole occupying power in Japan. Under the direction of General MacArthur, who was only nominally subject to the advice of an Allied Council, a far-reaching program was instituted to break down the forces of Japanese militarism, introduce democratic procedures in government, and encourage economic restoration. Japanese war criminals were tried and the old industrial trusts broken up. At the same time the United States continued to occupy the Ryukyu and Bonin Islands, and under the authority of the United Nations it administered a strategic trusteeship over the Caroline, Marshall, and Mariana Islands. In agreeing to these arrangements Soviet Russia had admitted a primary American interest in the western Pacific. While there were occasional complaints against MacArthur's policies, the military and naval position of the United States precluded any direct Russian-American clash over Japan. A peace treaty was ultimately signed, although without Russian adherence, on September 8, 1951.

China, however, was to become the critical issue in eastern Asia, as it had been in the prewar rivalry between the United States and Japan, and developments in that unhappy country were to provide an increasingly serious—seemingly insoluble—problem for American foreign policy.

After Japan's surrender the conflict between Chinese Nationalists and Chinese Communists that had seriously impeded allied military operations in Asia, threatened to erupt into civil war. In the hope of averting such strife, President Truman sent General Marshall to China on a special mission early in 1946 to try to arrange a truce between the opposing forces and encourage establishment of a coalition government, on broadly democratic lines, under Generalissimo Chiang Kai-shek. It was an impossible task; the Marshall mission was a complete failure. The United States then abandoned any idea of further direct intervention in Chinese politics, in effect retiring to the sidelines to await further developments.

The expected civil war promptly materialized. The reactionary nature of the Chiang Kai-shek regime, which failed to institute the land reforms demanded by the Chinese people, appeared to have largely alienated popular support. The Communists made startling gains in extending the territory under their control, first driving the Nationalists out of Manchuria and then from all north China. By 1949 they were in control of virtually the entire country, having set up the People's Republic of China with its capital at Peking, and Chiang Kai-shek fled with a remnant of his former forces to Formosa.

American policy could hardly have been more ambiguous as these events unfolded. The United States was at once fearful of the extension of Soviet influence in Asia, belatedly realizing that Russia was prepared to collaborate with the Chinese Communists, and highly critical of the Chinese Nationalists whose failure to command popular allegiance appeared to demonstrate the complete bankruptcy of the Chiang Kai-shek government. In this situation it was unwilling to give the Nationalists any direct military support, and yet it continued to advance them economic aid that amounted to some $2,000,000,000. This policy appeared to be predicated on the hope that in spite of the close ideological ties between Moscow and Peking, Communist China would assert its independence of Russian influence, but it may well have actually encouraged the new Chinese government's Soviet orientation by continuing aid to the Nationalists.

No phase of postwar policy was more vehemently criticized, and the whole China issue became a topic of furious partisan debate. Could the Nationalist cause have been saved by more timely assistance, or was it so discredited among the Chinese people that a communist victory was in any event inevitable? If the United States had intervened directly in support of the Nationalists, would it have found itself involved in possible war with Soviet Russia? Would recognition of the Chinese Communists serve to weaken their ties with Moscow or merely strengthen their position? There could be no definitive answer to these vital questions. The State Department was nevertheless widely accused of being "soft" toward communism because of its failure to recommend more active measures in support of Chiang Kai-shek. Secretary Acheson, the fourth man to head the department since the war, bore the brunt of these attacks and was subjected to political pressures that made an incredibly difficult task all the harder. Confusion was twice confounded.

The status of the Chinese Communists then became a subject of international controversy as a result of differing policies on their recognition, and the consequent problem of China's representation in the United Nations. The Soviet Union insisted that representatives of the Nationalist Government, now exiled in Formosa, should be replaced on the Security Council by representatives of Communist China. The United States took the lead in opposing any such move and continued to uphold the Nationalist cause. The impasse grew until the Russians took the drastic step in January 1950, of walking out of the Security Council in angry protest against the American attitude. The entire structure of the United Nations seemed to be seriously endangered.

★ WAR IN KOREA

It was some five months after this development that war suddenly broke out in Korea. Its background was again highly complex. There had been agreement among the Allies, at a conference held in Cairo in 1943, to recognize the freedom of this former Japanese colony and establish a unified and independent Korean government. Upon the surrender of Japan Soviet forces had occupied north Korea and American forces south Korea pending nationwide elections under the auspices of the United Nations. But the refusal of Russia to co-operate in this task led to division of Korea along the thirty-eighth parallel and the establishment of rival governments: North Korea under the aegis of Moscow and South Korea under United Nations sponsorship. The occupation forces of both the United States and Soviet Russia were withdrawn by 1949, but the two rival Korean governments confronted each other across the thirty-eighth parallel with ill-concealed hostility. These were the circumstances when on June 25, 1950, the North Koreans crossed the border in massive invasion of South Korea.

This act of flagrant aggression was a direct challenge to the authority of the United Nations. President Truman asked for condemnation of the attack and the employment of force to restore peace. The Security Council, freed from the restriction of a possible Russian veto by the Soviets' absence, at once fell in line with American policy. It declared the action of North Korea a breach of peace and called upon the member nations of the United Nations to furnish such support as was necessary to repel the armed attack. Land and sea forces of the United States, soon followed by ground troops drawn from the occupying forces in Japan, went into immediate action under the command of General MacArthur.

War in Korea—the operation rapidly went beyond the limited police action originally intended—was to impose a terrific burden upon the United States for in spite of the co-operation of other UN members, it supplied the great bulk of the troops and bore the major costs of the entire operation. There was never any question of the support the North Koreans were receiving from Soviet Russia; they were well equipped for modern warfare. The American troops first dispatched to the scene to back up the South Koreans were almost driven off the peninsula before sufficient re-enforcements became available to swing the tide of battle in their favor. The North Koreans were then driven back, but instead of halting at the thirty-eighth parallel, the American and South Korean forces, now supplemented by other United Nations' contingents, pressed on in the late autumn of 1951 against a fleeing foe and were soon approaching the Manchurian border. General MacArthur promised an end to hostilities by Christmas.

Intervention by the United Nations in Korea had electrified the democratic world. Here was proof positive that action could be taken to repel aggression, and a somber warning to Soviet Russia that the strategy of attack through satellites would not be tolerated. Comparisons were drawn between the failure of the League of Nations to resist aggression in this same part of the world twenty years earlier, and the prompt and vigorous measures taken by the United Nations. There was a feeling in some quarters, both in this country and abroad, that the United States rather than the United Nations was the agent of intervention in Korea, yet the fact remained that the Security Council had made the critical decision, and American troops in the field—as well as those of South Korea and other nations—were operating under its authority.

The hope that the defeat of the North Koreans would open the way to a peaceful restoration of national unity, however, was doomed to tragic disappointment. As the United Nations forces continued their advance toward the Manchurian border, Chinese Communist "volunteers" unexpectedly came to the aid of the Korean Communists. Both General MacArthur and the administration were taken completely by surprise. Here was a new war, and one with even more explosive possibilities. And its first phase was a sharp reversal for General MacArthur's command. The United Nations forces were driven down the peninsula and the enemy recaptured Seoul. Only after the most narrow escape from catastrophe was General MacArthur able to halt the retreat and in January 1951 establish a new defensive line in the general area of the thirty-eighth parallel.

While public attention was centered on the seesaw course of battle in Korea during the winter of 1950–51, it was always realized that behind the North Koreans and Chinese Communists loomed the aggressive forces of Soviet imperialism. Every attempt on the part of the United Nations to institute negotiations for a peaceful settlement of the issues at stake in Korea was blocked by Russia, which had now resumed her place in the Security Council. The entire western world was alarmed by a new pattern of aggression which appeared to threaten the security of all free nations. The question everywhere being asked was whether Asia was to furnish the tinder that would light the flames of another world war.

★ THE GREAT DEBATE

The reaction in the United States, not unlike that following the fall of France in 1940, was universal support for a tremendously stepped-up program of national defense. Recognizing that Korea was not the real issue—nor any other problem of eastern Asia in itself—public opinion was generally agreed that dangerous as the immediate situation might be in the Far East, it was still Europe that held the real clue to peace or war on any world scale.

President Truman called for drastic measures to meet the emergency, both at home and abroad. They included the mobilization of national resources, price and wage controls to combat inflationary pressures, huge appropriations for building up the nation's military strength, new draft laws to increase the size of the armed forces, and other steps vividly recalling the preparations for war which the United States had twice before undertaken when faced with the threat of becoming involved in world conflict. The President also proposed the dispatch of additional American troops to western Europe to meet our commitments to the North Atlantic Treaty Organization, to which continued support in troops and military supplies had been pledged in September 1949 through the first Mutual Defense Assistance Act. He recalled General Eisenhower to command NATO's combined military forces and assigned to him the immense responsibility of co-ordinating the defenses of all western Europe against possible Soviet attack. The clear intent of American policy was to impress on the Russians just where the United States stood in its determination to resist aggression against any peace-loving nation.

There was vigorous debate over these measures, in which partisan politics often played a noisy role, and vehement criticism of every phase of past and present foreign policy. President Truman and Secretary Acheson came under repeated attack. There was condemnation in some quarters both for intervention in Korea and for the dispatch of troops to western Europe; and on the other hand, clamorous demands for a more aggressive, all-out campaign in Korea even at the risk of war with Russia.

In the meantime the Truman administration, caught off guard by the intervention of the Chinese Communists in Korea, had adopted what appeared to many persons an equivocal policy in the further pursuit of the war. It instigated a United Nations resolution condemning Communist China as an aggressor, but sought to limit actual operations on the Korean front so as to prevent any further spread of the conflict. Discontent with this policy came to a head when General MacArthur, chafing under the restraints imposed upon him by this concept of limited war, particularly his inability to bomb the Chinese Communist bases in their "privileged sanctuary" of Manchuria, openly defied presidential authority in publicly insisting on broader operations on the ground that there was "no substitute for victory."

Convinced that such tactics would invite full-scale hostilities with the Chinese, and possibly the Russians—that in the words of General Bradley, Chairman of the Joint Chiefs of Staff, it would be "the wrong war at the wrong place, at the wrong time and with the wrong enemy"—President Truman stood firm and finally, on April 11, 1951, relieved General MacArthur of his command. The vituperative attacks upon Truman inspired by this move—though he was warmly upheld by perhaps more people than condemned him and the criticism gradually died down—were a measure of the discontent and sense of frustration over a tragic situation from which there seemed to be no escape.

The Korean stalemate soon afterwards led, in July, to the initiation of armistice negotiations. Fighting continued on a somewhat moderated scale, however, and the talks dragged on interminably for what proved to be nearly two more years. As the casualties mounted, ultimately reaching for the American forces alone a total of 144,000, including 25,000 dead, popular sentiment grew increasingly outraged, but short of all-out war or surrender, there was no alternative to holding the established lines.

The debate on the more general aspects of foreign policy continued through the winter of 1951–52. The general area of agreement was actually of greater significance than the points in dispute. How far the United States should go in dispersing its forces overseas, what reliance should be placed upon ground troops as opposed to sea and air contingents, and how the co-operation of the countries of western Europe could be most effectively guaranteed were the questions most widely discussed. There were few signs of the old isolationism of the 1930's. The United States had taken its stand at long last in support of collective security. Having assumed the leadership of the nations of the free world, the American people were ready, in spite of continued differences over immediate policy, to carry out the responsibilities that history, geography, and the nation's own great resources irrevocably imposed upon them.

At this critical juncture—actual war in Korea, impassioned debate over almost every phase of foreign policy, and feverish preparations for national defense under the fearful shadow of a possible third world war—the American people faced a presidential election. They were to go again to the polls, as they had in such other periods of foreign war or threatening war as 1916, 1940, and 1944, to decide into whose hands they were willing to entrust national leadership.

CHAPTER XXXI

The Eisenhower Era

★ THE ELECTION OF 1952

There was a spirit of unrest as well as anxiety abroad in the land in 1952. While the war in Korea and the fear that increased tension might lead to a major conflict with Soviet Russia were of first concern, domestic difficulties also appeared to be piling up. The apparent ineffectiveness of foreign policy was matched by a number of minor but unhappy scandals in Washington that suggested an unfortunate laxity in the conduct of public affairs. Perhaps more than anything else, the long succession of Democratic administrations—for the party of Roosevelt and Truman had been in office for just short of twenty years—seemed to have convinced the American people of the need for a change.

The Republicans were persuaded that their hour had at last come and they were determined this time, after the unhappy experience with Dewey in 1948, to nominate a winning candidate. A new name had been entered in the presidential sweepstakes—that of General Dwight D. Eisenhower. He had made an immense reputation in the war, not only as a military leader but perhaps even more as a skillful diplomat who had somehow been able under intense stress and strain to maintain allied unity. President Truman had made him chief of staff in succession to General Marshall, and then after a brief interlude when this career soldier acted as president of Columbia University, the President summoned him back into service in 1950 to take over supreme command of the unified forces of NATO. While he was still overseas, the more liberal, internationalist wing of the Republican party persuaded him to let his name go before the Republican convention.

It was only after a hard-fought battle, however, that he won the nomination. His chief rival was Senator Robert A. Taft, a staunch defender of conservatism and "Mr. Republican" in the eyes of the party's rank-and-file. General Eisenhower, however, was a national hero, a symbolic figure of allied victory, and standing somewhat above the party battle he seemed to have the greater possibility of winning the popular support that the Democratic coalition had so successfully received since 1932. The convention chose him on its first ballot, although he was closely pressed by Taft, and then named Richard M. Nixon, senator from California, as his running mate.

The Democrats also chose a newcomer to national politics. The field was wide open with the withdrawal of President Truman, and the party was still badly divided as a consequence of the splits that had taken place in the election of 1948. In these circumstances Adlai E. Stevenson, serving his first term as governor of Illinois, had an unusual appeal because he was not identified with any party faction and could symbolize a new Democratic unity. He repeatedly disclaimed any desire for the nomination, but his support piled up steadily. After a sharp struggle the convention in effect drafted him as its candidate with Senator Sparkman of Alabama as its vice-presidential nominee.

Stevenson's background was Princeton University, law practice in Chicago, and a number of government posts during the 1940's, including membership on the American delegation to the United Nations. He had been elected governor of Illinois in 1948. A convinced liberal and internationalist, his campaign was to be uniquely distinguished by the high level he maintained in the discussion of both foreign and domestic issues and by the quality of his idealism. His speeches were like a fresh wind blowing across the arid plains of American political life. Stevenson was modest and urbane, with a rare felicity of expression and a flashing wit. His popular appeal, his eloquence, his skillful use of television won him wide support, but more particularly he built up a devoted following among college graduates and liberal intellectuals.

General Eisenhower also campaigned effectively. He made every effort to heal the breach that the rejection of Senator Taft had caused in party lines, and by advocating a moderate, middle-of-the-road "modern Republicanism," he succeeded in winning the backing of both liberals and conservatives. He vigorously attacked what the Republicans were happily calling "the mess in Washington," found fault with the Truman administration's social and economic policies, and emphatically criticized (in spite of his own role with NATO), what he termed the "appalling and disastrous mismanagement of our foreign affairs." He heavily stressed the unhappy stalemate in the Korean war and dramatically pledged that if he were elected, he would at once go to Korea and seek out every means to bring hostilities to an early and honorable end.

More important than anything Eisenhower said or did, was the impact upon the country of his open, friendly, wonderfully engaging personality. His rather pedestrian approach to the discussion of high policy actually proved to be an asset. There appeared to be something about "Ike's" natural simplicity and his broad grin, no matter what he said, that inspired greater confidence than his rival's more sophisticated manner and his sometimes baffling brilliance.

The election was a Republican triumph. An unusually heavy popular vote gave Eisenhower a substantial majority—33,824,000 to 27,315,000—and an electoral college vote of 442 to 89. The Republicans also won control of Congress but by a majority so narrow that it heavily underscored the extent to which the election was a personal victory for Eisenhower rather than one for his party.

★ THE REPUBLICANS IN POWER

Back in power for the first time since Hoover had glumly handed over the reins of office to Franklin Roosevelt in 1933, the Republicans found themselves confronting a world that could hardly have differed more from that of two decades earlier. The United States had experienced all the bitter travail of depression and global war. Rugged individualism had given way to the welfare state; political and economic isolationism had been succeeded by a new internationalism. And a nation immediately involved in hostilities in Korea faced the vital challenge of communist imperialism both in Asia and in Europe. The United States had become the leader of the free world under conditions and circumstances that could hardly have been foreseen in the era of Republican supremacy in the 1920's.

There was to be no attempt on the part of the Eisenhower administration to turn back the clock or try to retreat to so dim and distant a past. The new President accepted the broad implications of both the New Deal and the Fair Deal; he was prepared to acknowledge the responsibilities of the United States as a world power. No basic change was contemplated in the nation's broad long-range objectives in either domestic or foreign policy.

Yet there was to be a difference in tone and a difference in the implementation of policy. The Eisenhower administration represented a moderate shift toward conservatism, and it was ready to accept a greater measure of business influence over government. This was soon to be revealed in certain aspects of domestic policy, but it was immediately apparent in the composition of the new cabinet. President Eisenhower brought to Washington a number of outstanding business leaders who would hardly have found a place in the cabinets of Roosevelt or Truman. Charles E. Wilson, formerly head of General Motors, became Secretary of Defense; George M. Humphrey, a Cleveland industrial magnate, was appointed Secretary of the Treasury. So conspicuous were the men of wealth in the cabinet, with the exception of the Secretary of Labor, Martin P. Durkin of the Plumbers' Union, that the popular quip of the day was that it was made up of "eight millionaires and one plumber."

The general domestic program of the new administration was directed toward greater economy in government, a balanced budget, the transfer of electric power development to private industry, a moderate extension of social security benefits, an increase in the minimum wage, and a more flexible system of price supports for agriculture.

In the field of foreign policy the President was prepared to seek peace in Korea and elsewhere while building up and strengthening both at home and abroad the defenses against possible communist aggression. He appointed as his Secretary of State a New York lawyer, John Foster Dulles, who had already served the State Department in an important advisory capacity, having been largely responsible for the negotiations of the peace treaty with Japan. In his campaign Eisenhower had called for a more dynamic foreign policy than Truman had pursued, and he had accepted the idea of the man who was to become his Secretary of State that the United States should seek the liberation of the captive peoples of eastern Europe.

This was the first of a number of pronouncements that reflected a hope that foreign policy would be made more effective in rolling back Soviet power. Secretary Dulles subsequently threatened on one occasion an "agonizing reappraisal" of policy in regard to the role of the United States in Europe, declared that communist aggression at any point would be met by "massive retaliation," and spoke of proceeding when necessary to the very "brink of war" in meeting Russian threats. These assertive pronouncements invariably succeeded in frightening the allies of the United States more than its enemies. In the final analysis the Eisenhower administration was to carry forward the policy whose major lines had already been laid down by President Truman. Its basis remained the attempt to contain communism. The President repeatedly affirmed his wholehearted support for a "coherent global policy" that would at once safeguard the national interest and provide the basis for lasting peace.

★ SETTLEMENT IN KOREA

The first business of the new administration was Korea. Eisenhower carried out his pledge to visit that unhappy country, flying there in December before taking office, and the armistice negotiations that had been intermittently proceeding for so long were vigorously pressed. By the spring of 1953 encouraging progress was finally reported with both sides prepared to accept the military stalemate that had developed along the thirty-eighth parallel. The other issues involved were immensely complicated. One of the most important was arrangements for the exchange of prisoners, since the United Nations negotiators were unwilling to hand back to communist control North Koreans who preferred to remain in South Korea. At one time the negotiations seemed certain to break down completely. President Syngman Rhee, of South Korea, on his own authority released some 25,000 anti-communist North Koreans in arbitrary defiance of the enemy's demand that they be repatriated.

The negotiations continued, however, and a final truce agreement was concluded on July 27, 1953. It provided in effect for the continued division of North and South Korea along the general lines of the thirty-eighth parallel, and the exchange under carefully drawn conditions of the remaining prisoners of war. The question of the ultimate union of North and South Korea was left for a future conference. What had originally started as a limited police action by the United Nations to repel aggression, but had turned into a three-year war with immensely heavy casualties, had finally come to an end.

The results were hardly conclusive. North and South Korea remained divided. But it could at least be said that the United Nations had taken a decisive stand in defense of the principles which it espoused and had firmly upheld them. President Eisenhower did say just this. "We have shown, in the winning of this truce," he declared, "that the collective resolve of the free world can and will meet aggression in Asia—or anywhere in the world."

There was obviously no solution to the major problems of foreign policy in this inconclusive truce on what was but one of the worldwide fronts where the democratic forces of the world faced the threat of communist aggression. In succeeding years the free world was repeatedly challenged in other parts of Asia, in the Middle East, and in Europe. Soviet policy appeared to be based upon the highly successful technique of keeping the United States and its allies constantly off balance, never pressing to a final breaking point but steadily building up tension and forever threatening to break down allied unity. This story will be taken up later. In the meantime, the repercussions of the war in Korea and other events led to a number of important developments within the United States itself.

★ THE RISE AND FALL OF MC CARTHYISM

It has already been noted that during the Truman regime the growing fear of communism had greatly magnified popular suspicions of any persons who could be remotely suspected of radical or leftwing sympathies, let alone possible involvement in the communist conspiracy. The Korean war, following so closely upon the debacle in China which had brought the Chinese Communists into power, was still further to intensify such suspicions. Moreover, a succession of disclosures of subversive activities and actual communist espionage within the United States seemed to substantiate the mounting alarm.

Under the terms of the anti-communist Smith Act originally adopted in 1940, the government had proceeded against a group of communist leaders, and in a long, widely publicized trial in 1949 they were found guilty of conspiring to teach the overthrow of the government. Other investigations revealed the activities of an Anglo-American spy ring that had sold atomic secrets to the Soviets, arousing new suspicions of further espionage. And most dramatically, Alger Hiss, a onetime member of the State Department and the president of the Carnegie Endowment for International Peace, became involved in a sensational trial for perjury after he had denied charges by Whittaker Chambers, an admitted former Soviet agent, that he had turned over classified documents to him in 1937. Hiss could not be tried directly for treason because of the statute of limitations, but after a second trial on the perjury account, the first having resulted in a hung jury, he was found guilty of this offense and sentenced to prison for five years.

Against this background of suspicion and mistrust, extending to official circles in Washington, the junior senator from Wisconsin, Joseph R. McCarthy, further shocked and alarmed the country by stating early in 1950 that he had the names of a number of members of the State Department (his actual count varied from 205 to 57) who were communists. He was unable to prove his charges in a single instance, but they strengthened the belief in other quarters that the State Department had been "soft" on communism. With the outbreak of the Korean war, the country was consequently swept by a wave of hysteria over possible communist subversion and infiltration, often wholly irrational, that went far beyond anything in its previous history. Congress responded with passage of the McCarran Internal Security Act, tightening up existing security regulations, and both House and Senate committees launched a series of further investigations.

There seems to be little question that Senator McCarthy, in his capacity as chairman of the Senate Committee on Government Operations, was seeking to make all possible political capital out of the public fear of communism. He continued to make reckless and ill-founded charges, completely ignored the civil rights of the persons summoned to testify before his committee, browbeat witnesses whoever they might be, and turned a legitimate effort to safeguard national security into a sensational witch hunt. His tactics violated the basic principles of a democracy which cherished free speech and individual freedom and added to the suspicious attitude so generally prevailing a new element of fear. What soon became known as McCarthyism spread its evil influence throughout the country.

After the election of 1952 McCarthy showed that he was quite as willing to attack the Eisenhower administration as the Truman administration for being too lenient with communists, and with amazing arrogance took it upon himself not only to criticize but to interfere directly with foreign policy. For long the President, anxious to maintain peace between the divergent factions within his own party, ignored the entire issue. Matters came to a head, however, when after his frequent pillorying of the State Department, McCarthy began to make charges of communist infiltration in the army. The Department of the Army then struck back at him with the countercharge that he had sought to obtain special privileges for one of his protégés who had been inducted into the armed services. The consequence of this new furor was a public investigation by a Senate committee in the spring of 1954.

The hearings were nationally televised, and they created a sensation. In effect McCarthyism was on trial before the public and the brutal, domineering, intolerant attitude of its chief spokesman led to its popular indictment. For while the results of the hearings were in themselves inconclusive, the critics of this un-American approach to what was admittedly a very real problem now dared raise their voices in defense of individual liberties. Shortly afterward the Senate moved directly against McCarthy himself, and while it ignored the civil rights issue it adopted a resolution by a vote of 67 to 22 censuring the senator from Wisconsin for conduct unbecoming a senator.

McCarthy did not recover from these successive blows. His influence, once so powerful, was completely undermined. It can also be said that McCarthyism, so much more important than the man himself, now gradually gave way to a return to common sense and greater respect for individual rights. It had been an unlovely phenomenon, posing the basic question of whether a democracy could hope to defend itself against communism if in the process it sacrificed its own principles of civil liberty and free speech.

★ THE SEGREGATION ISSUE

Not unrelated to the struggle to maintain civil rights in the face of McCarthyism was the continuing liberal effort, carrying over from the pre-Eisenhower days, to sustain the fight against discrimination and segregation in the case of Negroes. Once again it was widely felt that the United

States could not hope to stand before the world as the champion of democracy and deny so basic a democratic principle as equal rights for all its citizens. The Supreme Court had already played a notable part, as previously mentioned, in declaring a number of discriminatory laws unconstitutional. In May 1954 it struck a resounding blow at the whole policy of discrimination against the Negro by declaring in a unanimous decision, *Brown* v *Board of Education of Topeka,* that segregation in any state school system could not be reconciled with the principle of equal protection of the laws as guaranteed by the Fourteenth Amendment. Its decision in effect reversed one made a half century earlier, *Plessy* v *Ferguson,* which had maintained that "separate but equal" facilities conformed to the spirit of the Constitution. The Court did not demand immediate compliance with its startling decision, but it was to insist that all affected communities desegregate their public schools with reasonable speed.

The District of Columbia, and such states as Delaware, Tennessee, and Kentucky undertook gradual desegregation, but the greater part of the South was at once up in arms against the Supreme Court ruling, bluntly refusing to accept what it declared to be a perversion of principles long established and an unwarranted invasion by the federal government of states' rights. The legislatures of a number of states went emphatically on record as refusing to countenance desegregation, and in some cases enacted laws designed to circumvent in one way or another the Supreme Court's decision. The National Association for the Advancement of Colored People—the NAACP—sought every legal means to compel the southern states and communities to comply with the court ruling; hastily formed White Councils undertook just as vigorously to prevent any school integration whatsoever.

The most dramatic of the early incidents growing out of this embittered conflict—and one which attracted not only nationwide but worldwide attention—took place in the fall of 1957 in Little Rock, Arkansas. Its Central High School had drawn up plans for gradual integration of its students in compliance with the Supreme Court ruling, but when the school authorities sought to implement them and admitted nine Negro students, Governor Faubus suddenly interfered. On the ground that the admission of Negroes to the high school threatened the peace and safety of Little Rock, he sought a temporary state court injunction against this move, and calling out the national guard to maintain order, he instructed it to turn the Negroes away. This was a clear challenge to national authority. After a federal court overruling of the state injunction, President Eisenhower ordered troops to Little Rock to enforce compliance with court orders.

The students returned to school under guard. But while a principle had been upheld, the local attitude remained dangerously hostile. When the federal troops were withdrawn it was considered necessary to replace them by federalized national guardsmen, and the Negro students remained in school under military protection. Governor Faubus still had no intention of surrendering, and as his subsequent re-election demonstrated he had the general support of the community. At his instigation the Arkansas legislature passed laws to set up a private school system in order to avoid forced integration, and the next year after the most complicated legal maneuvering had failed to bring about any solution of the problem, the Central High School in Little Rock was closed.

The Little Rock incident was only the most sensational among many developments illustrating the South's determination to maintain its segregated school system. State legislature after state legislature in the deep South enacted what were in effect anti-desegregation measures, and Virginia also adopted a series of massive resistance laws (later declared unconstitutional by its own courts) that were to lead to the temporary closing of schools in several cities. The legal involvements—suits, countersuits, injunctions, appeals, court decrees—multiplied with each passing month. There were few signs that the more obdurate states had any intention of surrendering to federal authority. They continued to resent what they termed northern interference with their rights, insisting upon being left alone to solve the problem of the status of Negroes in their own way. They were not moved by constitutional arguments in respect to equal rights or by the contention that the Supreme Court's dictum made desegregation the law of the land.

There was substantial progress toward integration in some areas. The picture was perhaps not so bleak as these dramatic instances of opposition to the Supreme Court decision might suggest. Moreover, there was no question that integration posed immense difficulties in many communities which would have liked to develop a gradual program of educational reform. Early in 1959 developments in Virginia, and even in Arkansas, held out some hope that opposition to closing the schools might encourage a slowly expanding movement for compliance with the Supreme Court rulings.

★ DEVELOPMENTS IN ORGANIZED LABOR

On quite a different segment of the domestic front during the first years of the Eisenhower era were a number of highly important developments affecting organized labor. President Eisenhower was pledged to seek new legislation modifying the Taft-Hartley Act, as both labor and management had been demanding from their different points of view ever since

1947, but Congress was as unwilling as ever to act. The important event for labor was something entirely of its own doing—the merger of the A.F. of L. and the C.I.O. This long-projected move was finally completed in February 1955, and the unified organization could then boast of a total membership of some 15,000,000 workers in a broad array of both industrial and craft unions.

In spite of voices of alarm in some quarters public comment was generally favorable to the merger, and newspaper editorials widely hailed it as a great feat of labor statesmanship that demonstrated the growing muturity of the organized labor movement. There was praise both for George Meany, the A.F. of L. leader who became president of the new organization and for Walter Reuther, of the C.I.O., who became its vice-president.

The formation of the A.F. of L.–C.I.O. did not by any means provide a solution for the continuing problems of labor. The opposing union and management forces continued to spar over proposed modifications of Taft-Hartley and, even more acrimoniously, over the so-called right-to-work laws that a number of states enacted to outlaw the union shop. While the processes of collective bargaining were successful in the great majority of cases in settling wage disputes, strikes were sufficiently numerous to keep the public gravely concerned over the effect of such apparently needless work stoppages on its own convenience and on the national welfare. At one time or another almost every major industry was affected by strikes during the 1950's which were ultimately settled by substantial wage increases that in effect split the difference between the employer's offer and the union's demand.

Also disturbing in the labor picture was the gathering evidence of widespread corruption on the part of some union leaders in the handling of union funds, especially the large amounts being built up in pension funds. A few unions, two or three of them very important, had fallen under the dominant control of completely irresponsible leaders who not only followed fraudulent practices in union finances, but countenanced gangsterism, violence, and whatever strong-arm methods seemed necessary in upholding their organizations. Such conditions were most widely prevalent among the dockyard workers in New York and San Francisco, and in the powerful, nationwide Teamsters' Union.

Investigations initiated in 1957 by a senatorial committee headed by Senator McClellan of Arkansas dramatically revealed this gangsterism and corruption, and they inspired the new A.F. of L.–C.I.O. to undertake a vigorous housecleaning campaign which led to the expulsion from the merged labor movement of the Longshoremen's Association and the International Brotherhood of Teamsters. The government also prosecuted the leaders of the latter union on charges of the misuse of funds and its president, Dave Beck, was given a prison sentence for embezzlement. The McClellan committee subsequently recommended—in 1958—new legislation to curb the abuses in union management, but as in the case of the continued controversy over Taft-Hartley, the consideration of almost any phase of the labor problem touched off political fireworks. A closely divided Congress was hesitant to take any conclusive action.

Apart from strikes and corrupt practices, the public was also critical of labor unions for the pressure they exerted in forcing wages upward. This was considered one of the basic causes for the period's inflation and President Eisenhower himself was to appeal to the unions to moderate their attitude in the interests of a more stable economy. The leaders of the A.F. of L.–C.I.O. denied labor responsibility for inflation, insisting on the need for continued wage increases to build up purchasing power and encourage further expansion in the national economy.

★ POLITICS AND THE ELECTION OF 1956

While such broad issues as McCarthyism, segregation, and the position of organized labor largely overshadowed party politics during the first Eisenhower administration, the President was having difficulties. He found himself constantly battling Congress even during the brief period when the Republicans held their slight majority, let alone after the Democrats had recaptured control of both houses in 1954. He finally succeeded in achieving a balanced budget for the fiscal year 1956–57 (there had been only three years in the past quarter century that this had proved possible), but he faced a constant struggle in trying to reconcile the immensely increased expenditures for national security with available income. Taking this year of a balanced budget as an example of the astronomical sums that had now become commonplace even in peacetime, total expenditures of the federal government were $69,300,000,000 and total income $71,000,000,000. By far the greater part of the expenditures, some 60 per cent of the total, were for defense. The total national debt had at this time risen to $270 billion.

In regard to other issues Congress followed a somewhat erratic course. On one side of the ledger it allocated offshore oil rights to the states and turned over certain power development projects to private industry; on the other, it extended federal aid for slum clearance and low cost housing, broadened social security coverage, and raised minimum wages. It also renewed the reciprocal trade agreements, initiated a huge highway program involving the ultimate expenditure of some $34,000,000,000, and perhaps most importantly, authorized the building of the St. Lawrence Seaway.

This was a respectable but not too exciting record. It did not satisfy the hopes of liberals, who were offended by the administration's stand on electric power and offshore oil rights; it aroused the criticism of conservatives who saw in the support for social security and public housing, only surrender to the principles of the New Deal.

Whatever the record, the continued personal popularity of President Eisenhower made him an almost inevitable candidate to succeed himself in the election of 1956. He had suffered a heart attack the previous year, which for a time threatened to take him out of the running, but his quick recovery and the favorable reports on his health made him again available and the Republicans did not hesitate to renominate him. The situation was a good deal more confusing for the Democrats, but after the elimination of other potential candidates, they again chose Adlai Stevenson.

The country was generally prosperous in this election year. Inflation remained a perennial problem, but a booming national economy had given rise to further expansion in trade and industry, with a progressive advance in the standard of living for the great majority of the people. Although there had been no actual alleviation of the tensions of the Cold War, at least in the summer of 1956 no immediate crisis seemed to threaten the nation. Even the eruption of trouble in the Middle East before the campaign was over did not seem to affect the domestic situation. Eisenhower did not need to have any issues. He campaigned soberly and seriously on the hardly original platform of peace, prosperity, and progress.

Stevenson took the aggressive, as he had to do. He strongly attacked the Eisenhower administration for what he charged was its conservatism in domestic affairs and irresponsibility in foreign affairs. He rang the changes on basic themes with the persuasive eloquence of his earlier campaign, but without making very much impression. The novelty of his approach to politics had worn off. The real disadvantage that Stevenson suffered—probably the decisive one—was that he was not campaigning against a mere Republican candidate or even president. The years of his first administration had greatly enhanced the stature of Dwight D. Eisenhower. He had become something of a folk hero, projecting the image of a kindly father whose help and protection the American people deeply craved in an uncertain world.

The election results graphically revealed his immense popularity. Eisenhower was victorious by a popular majority of over 9,300,000 votes, nearly a million larger than in 1952. At the same time the Democrats retained control of both houses of Congress. One had to go back a full century in American history to find a similar instance of a party electing its candidate to the presidency and yet failing to win control of either house of Congress. There could have been no more emphatic demonstration of Ike's personal hold on the emotions of his countrymen, or of their almost mystical faith—in spite of his party—in his ability to bring them continued peace and prosperity. For once a campaign slogan—"We like Ike"—appeared to have expressed an indubitable national sentiment.

To leap somewhat ahead of the chronological account of these years, the country would express its skepticism about the President's party even more decisively in the midterm elections of 1958 when throughout the country Republican candidates for Congress went down to disastrous defeat. In spite of Eisenhower's election in 1952 and 1956, the Democrats were still the majority party. But by 1958 something had also happened to the President's own stature and to the popular veneration in which he had been held. There was a wide feeling of disenchantment with his leadership.

★ SOCIAL PROGRESS

The most characteristic feature of the years marking Eisenhower's first term, other than the impact of the Cold War to which this narrative must later turn, was continuing prosperity. Against this fortunate background the social scene was constantly changing. In some ways the 1950's even appeared to resemble the 1920's. The difficulties of the earlier decade's "lost generation" had their counterpart in the restlessness of a new "beat generation"; the spirit of revolt and lawlessness in the 1920's was paralleled by a new outbreak of gangsterism and the violence associated with juvenile delinquency. In other ways the popular crazes and extraordinary fads of the two decades, from jazz to women's fashions, sometimes seemed to reflect the same erratic impulses. The parallels may be easily forced, but the 1950's had something in common with the 1920's even beyond a Republican president in the White House and a surging prosperity.

Among many other social developments something of a crisis in education aroused the country in the 1950's. It has already been noted that the depression of the 1930's and then World War II had severely curtailed support for public schools and universities, as well as private institutions, and that the immediate postwar period had revealed an appalling lack of trained teachers, entirely inadequate school buildings, and a great scarcity of up-to-date equipment. The increase in the school population in mid-century, however, greatly accentuated these problems.

Between 1950 and 1956 public school enrollment rose from 25,000,000 to 31,000,000, and that at colleges and universities from 2,600,000 to nearly 3,000,000. The projection of these figures into the future underscored even more heavily the imperative need for more teachers and further expansion of plant.

The means whereby sufficient funds could be obtained to keep up proper educational standards all along the line, ways of attracting more men and women into the teaching profession, the pros and cons of new methods of instruction from the kindergarten to the graduate school, provided topics for endless debate in educational circles. Toward the close of the decade the progress being apparently made in the schools of the Soviet Union, especially as reflected in that country's scientific and technological achievements, added new fuel to the burning fires of academic controversy. For the first time sufficient pressure was built up to persuade Congress to develop a moderate program of federal aid for education in the hope of raising general standards and, even more specifically, of encouraging the more brilliant students in the sciences to continue their work through college and graduate school.

In an area somewhat comparable to popular education, the continued expansion of television was phenomenal: the number of sets in use was estimated in 1958 at 50,000,000. In its impact on the recreational patterns of American life, the world of salesmanship and advertising, national politics, and, at least potentially, popular education, televison was playing an even greater role than radio. The entertainment it provided struck heavily at all other forms of amusement, especially moving pictures, and its wide use as an advertising medium had a great deal to do with the expansion of sales in the products that it advertised. The effect upon politics was revolutionary: it was no longer enough to have a good speaking voice, an effective TV personality was essential. It was a television show, as already noted, that helped to expose the dangers of McCarthyism.

If the great bulk of television programing was soap operas, westerns, movie reruns, and (at least for a time) quiz shows that had no cultural value whatsoever and even incredibly low entertainment standards, this was not the whole story. Other programs such as the "Arthur Godfrey Show" and the "Ed Sullivan Show" were more deservedly popular, interesting experiments were made with television theater, both news and sports were given wide coverage, and there were "Omnibus," "Face the Nation," "Meet the Press," and Edward R. Murrow's "Person to Person."

A distinctive cultural phenomenon of these years was the rapid growth of paperback books. They had been first introduced in 1939, with Pocket Books the original pioneers, but it was not until after World War II that they began to flourish. The paperbacks first featured westerns, mysteries, and crime stories (with Mickey Spillane an all-out leader), but new publishers in the field gradually broadened the lists. They included everything—classics, philosophy, poetry, history, popular fiction, detective stories, do-it-yourself manuals. In the spring of 1958 over 6,000 titles were thus in print; it was estimated that an eager public had bought some 2,600,000,000 paperbacks. They were being increasingly used by students, but their circulation nevertheless indicated a tremendous growth in reading on the part of the general public—radio and television notwithstanding.

As to the literary quality of what was being more generally published in the 1950's, there was no renaissance comparable to that which had enlivened the postwar period thirty years earlier. A number of the writers of the 1920's and 1930's—most conspicuously Faulkner, Hemingway, Steinbeck—were still in the literary spotlight, but critics were generally agreed that their current writing, with some few possible exceptions, hardly sustained the standards of an earlier day. Moreover, in spite of all the encouragement of a broadening audience and immense book sales, it was hard to discover new writers who seemed assured of a permanent place in literary history.

The status of the other arts was more encouraging. Theater was flourishing and reaching a broader public. The off-Broadway theaters in New York, summer theaters in many parts of the country, and Shakespearean revivals attested to growing popular interest. The ballet and the dance also won new audiences, and music continued to build up its role in the national culture. The tradition of popular musicals was successfully carried forward with *West Side Story* and *My Fair Lady*. Music for the former show was written by Leonard Bernstein, who became the conductor of the New York Philharmonic. He was also the composer of a number of serious orchestral pieces.

Further artistic endeavor in painting and sculpture was perhaps overshadowed by the new achievements of modern American architecture. The trends already noted for the years between the wars were carried forward, with the functional being progressively modified by new decorative and romantic elements. The work of such modernists as Erro Saarinen, Buckminister Fuller, and Edward D. Stone exemplified the new styles, and in such buildings as Lever House in New York, the RCA Building, the Air Force Academy, and the M.I.T. chapel American architecture was winning real triumphs.

Even broader in its implications for American society than the postwar phenomena already touched upon was the accelerated expansion of the suburbs. It was estimated in the late 1950's that the number of people living in what was neither country nor city but suburbia had reached a total of approximately 47,000,000. This movement from the city had innumerable ramifications, both reflecting and influencing the whole course of the country's social development. It emphasized the middle-class nature of American society and accentuated middle-class manners and morals; it suggested a more conservative political and economic orientation as workers moving to the suburbs accepted their prevailing mores. Suburbia set the standards of a society that flourished on new style, split-level ranch houses with highly mechanized kitchens, mammoth shopping centers and supermarkets, ever larger automobiles, elaborate television sets, vacation trips to Florida if not the Caribbean and Europe, and an ever-wider range of expensive amusements.

From this point of view the problems of society in the 1950's were not those of the quest for social justice that characterized the early 1900's, or of the revolt against convention that marked the 1920's, or of the battle against poverty and unemployment that dominated the 1930's. They revolved about what appeared to be the increasing uniformity and conformity in American social life. The "white collar class," the "man in the grey flannel suit," the "organization man," the "lonely crowd," —to borrow the phrases from contemporary book titles that entered immediately into the language—became the symbols of the malaise of mid-century society in the United States.

Here were social problems—significant and important—but they were often eclipsed by a more immediate and desperate issue. There had been no letup in the challenge of communism since the inconclusive truce which ended the Korean war. Over the world there still hung the dread shadow of "the bomb." The United States appeared to be confronted by a chronic crisis in its foreign policy. Before the 1950's drew to a close the world in general had entered upon a new era as the atomic age gave way to the age of space.

CHAPTER XXXII

America and the World

★ SOUTHEASTERN ASIA

In their consideration of foreign policy, neither President Eisenhower nor Secretary of State Dulles harbored any illusions about the Korean truce. It was clear that this agreement with the communists had solved nothing and that the entire situation in eastern Asia remained highly dangerous. Yet neither Eisenhower nor Dulles perhaps anticipated that even before the projected conference to consider the possible unification of Korea could be held, there would be a further crisis. This time it was the result of the inability of the French to defend their position in Vietnam, one of the three associated states of Indo-China, against the communist Vietminh forces in the north. The latter were being actively supported by the Chinese Communists, with consequent threat of a further extension of the power and influence of Communist China throughout southeastern Asia.

The United States had no direct interest in this situation in itself, but such an expansion of communist influence appeared to endanger all the free nations in that part of the world. Secretary Dulles feared that if Vietnam fell, the others would topple over "like dominoes." He was prepared to intervene actively in support of the French, but opposition both at home and among the British to running such a grave risk of conflict with Communist China forestalled any action. Meanwhile, agreement was reached among the powers involved in the affairs of eastern Asia, including Communist China, for a meeting of their foreign ministers at Geneva to consider possible settlements in both Korea and southeastern Asia.

This Geneva conference, meeting in the spring of 1954, made no headway whatsoever on the Korean problem. There could be no agreement on unification. It surprisingly concluded an accord on the conflict in Indo-China between France and Vietnam on the one hand, and the

Vietminh and Chinese Communists on the other. The latter agreement was brought about, however, because of the defeat of the French forces in the field and the consequent decision of a new French government under Premier Mendès-France to recognize the realities in the situation and agree to a division of territory, not unlike that in Korea. The settlement bifurcated Vietnam into a communist-controlled state in the north, and a democratic-controlled state in the south. France was now ready to withdraw its own troops from Indo-China, acknowledging the independence of South Vietnam and leaving it to fend for itself against any possible further aggression.

The United States ostentatiously took no part in this settlement; it hardly approved what was considered a further retreat before communist aggression in Asia. There was, nevertheless, nothing it could do other than reluctantly acquiesce in the French decision. At the same time it was ready to strengthen and aid the South Vietnam government, and Secretary Dulles also completed his plans for building up the defenses of the other free nations in Asia against Communist China. After a conference which met in September 1954 in Manila the United States, Great Britain, France, Australia, New Zealand, the Philippines, Thailand, and Pakistan formed the Southeastern Asia Treaty Organization.

While the purpose of this organization was to safeguard the security of Southeastern Asia against attack from any quarter, SEATO lacked the effectiveness of NATO. It did not have the specific guarantees of the European security treaty nor any practical provisions for military cooperation. More important, the major countries of Asia, most notably India, refused to have anything to do with it. Little could be said for SEATO as of the time of its formation other than that it dramatically illustrated the ever-broadening scope of the commitments that the United States was making in seeking to uphold the free world against the communist world. Mutual security agreements had already been concluded with Japan, South Korea, the Philippines, Australia, and New Zealand, and one was shortly to be signed with Nationalist China; financial and economic aid was being extended not only to these nations but to many other Asiatic countries. SEATO was a still further projection of this expansive policy.

★ THE SPIRIT OF GENEVA

Even as these developments were taking place in Asia, new troubles were brewing for American foreign policy in Europe. The American position was based firmly upon NATO, which had been greatly strengthened since the Korean War, but there were additional plans to integrate the defenses of western Europe through the creation of a European Defense

Community in which West Germany as well as Great Britain, France, Italy, and the Benelux countries would fully participate. In August 1954 France suddenly withdrew its support from the projected European Defense Community and the collapse of this scheme to work out a common program with West Germany created what Secretary Dulles called "a crisis of almost terrifying proportions." The entire American policy in Europe appeared to be jeopardized, but there was nothing the United States could do other than hope that the European powers themselves would resolve their problem.

Fortunately, they succeeded in doing so. After a hectic series of negotiations in September and October, they set up a new Western European Union to replace the European Defense Community and signed a set of protocols providing for the restoration of complete sovereignty for West Germany, its admission to NATO, and its controlled rearmament as a full partner in the western alliance. The United States emphatically approved the new accords which Secretary Dulles characterized as marking a shining chapter in history. There was something ironical about this eager welcome of Germany into NATO within less than a decade of the close of the war, but it dramatically illustrated the shifts and changes in the world balance of power since the lowering of the Iron Curtain over eastern Europe.

While seeking to strengthen the defenses of the free world, the United States was simultaneously striving to lessen international tension and promote disarmament. No progress had so far been made in United Nations conferences and negotiations toward either international control of the atomic bomb or any phase of disarmament. The deadlock appeared insoluble. The advent of Eisenhower to the presidency had almost coincided with the death of Stalin on March 5, 1953, however, and there was a revived hope as time went on that Soviet Russia's change in leadership might provide a more favorable atmosphere for renewed negotiations between the West and East. The hydrogen bomb had by now superseded the atomic bomb in the case of Soviet Russia as well as that of the United States, and the potential destructiveness of nuclear warfare underscored more heavily every day the imperative need to find a way to avert war.

The possibilities of a conference at "the summit," which would bring together the new leaders of the United States and Soviet Russia, as well as those of Great Britain and France, began to be widely discussed. A more conciliatory attitude on the part of Stalin's successors, Bulganin and Khrushchev, as reflected in final conclusion of an Austrian treaty early in 1955, suggested there might indeed be a real shift in Soviet policy; there also appeared to be greater receptiveness in the United States to the possibilities of peaceful co-existence. Addressing Congress in December 1954, President Eisenhower had not attempted to minimize the dangers in the world situation, but he emphatically stated "that we owe it to ourselves and to the world to explore every possible peaceful means of settling differences before we even think of such a thing as war."

As a consequence of these developments, agreement was reached for a summit conference, and in July 1955 the heads of state of the United States, Great Britain, France and Soviet Russia met in Geneva. The atmosphere was cordial. President Eisenhower strongly affirmed the deep desire of the United States for international accord; Premier Bulganin reciprocated with a strong expression of the Russian desire for peace. There was discussion of possible ways to resolve the basic problem of German reunification, for the continued existence of a democratic West Germany and a communist East Germany precluded any general peace treaty, and of other means to re-establish Europe's security and open the way to disarmament. The most dramatic proposal advanced at the conference was President Eisenhower's suggestion for the exchange between the United States and Soviet Russia of the blueprints of their military establishments, with agreement for mutual aerial reconnaissance of one another's territories. This bold plan which it was thought might lead to some limitation of arms hardly appealed to the Russians, but the atmosphere of the conference continued to be friendly. While the heads of state did not reach any specific agreements in spite of their genial good will, they assigned to their foreign ministers the task of seeking definite accords at a further meeting to be held in October.

The conference seemed to relax the tension under which the world had been laboring, but unhappily the "Spirit of Geneva" proved to be of very short duration. By the time the foreign ministers met, Soviet Russia had reverted to its intransigent position of previous years. Bluntly rejecting the western proposal for popular elections to form an all-German government, Moscow appeared to be no more willing than in the days of Stalin to make any concessions on the major problems underlying the Cold War. The lines were drawn ever more sharply across a divided Europe. On the one side were the democracies, including West Germany, bound together in NATO, on the other Soviet Russia and its communist satellites, including East Germany, linked by their opposing Warsaw Pact.

★ RELATIONS WITH COMMUNIST CHINA

Continuing deadlock in Europe remained always in the background during these years in the mid-1950's, but more immediate crises developed periodically in both eastern Asia and in the Middle East as the communist powers made every effort to advance their designs and undermine the unity of the western world. In trying to meet these successive challenges the United States was repeatedly thrown off balance. On occasion its policy aroused the deepest fears on the part of its allies that precipitate action might plunge the world into war. There seemed to be no way to wrest the initiative from a shrewd and astute foe.

The unsatisfactory truces concluded in Korea and Indo-China had brought no relaxation of tension in eastern Asia, and the United States found itself more and more at odds with a resurgent Communist China. It still refused to recognize the Peking government and began to increase its support for the Nationalist government that Chiang Kai-shek maintained on Formosa. During the Korean war, President Truman had ordered the American Seventh Fleet to enforce the neutrality of Formosa and prevent any possible move on the part of the Chinese Nationalists to attack the Chinese Communists. Eisenhower had "unleashed" the Nationalists in 1953, however, by withdrawing the Seventh Fleet from patrol duty in the Formosa Straits.

This situation first took on ominous aspects when—even as conversations in Europe were paving the way for the Summit Conference—the Chinese Communists began concentrating forces on the mainland adjacent to the Nationalist-held islands of Quemoy and Matsu, threatening their capture in what was interpreted as a possible first step toward the conquest of Formosa. In this emergency President Eisenhower went before Congress early in 1955 to seek authority, under the terms of the mutual assistance treaty with Nationalist China, to use the armed forces of the United States to repel any assault on Formosa, without specifically stipulating whether this included attack on Matsu and Quemoy. Congress granted him such authority by an overwhelming vote of 85 to 3 in the Senate, and 409 to 3 in the House. In the face of such clear-cut evidence of the determination of the United States to defend Formosa, the Chinese Communists stopped shelling Quemoy and Matsu and did not launch the feared assault on either the off-shore islands or Formosa.

The crisis had appeared to be a very real one and the policy of the United States had won little support from its allies. War for a time had seemed imminent. Secretary Dulles was to assert that "we walked up to the brink and looked it in the face. We took strong action." But his statement was hardly reassuring to either the American public or the peoples of western Europe. Nor had American policy in any way succeeded in resolving the underlying conflict in the relations between Nationalist and Communist China.

Three years later a comparable crisis arose. Once again the Chinese Communists began shelling Quemoy and Matsu, where the Nationalists had in the meantime strengthened their military forces, and posed anew the threat of an attack on Formosa. The Seventh Fleet was ordered—in August 1958—to safeguard the delivery of supplies from Formosa to the beleaguered islands, but there was very little public support for any policy which might let this new emergency once again lead the country to the brink of war. President Eisenhower asserted in a radio address on September 11 that there would be no appeasement of the Chinese Communists, but strong pressure was exerted upon Chiang Kai-shek not to take any action that might lead to hostilities. Although it was denied, amid conflicting and ambiguous pronouncements from the State Department, that there had been any change in American policy, it appeared that official envoys from Washington had finally made plain to the Nationalist leader that he should give up any hopes he might still have of being able to return to the mainland in an attempt to overthrow the Communist regime. The United States steadfastly refused to concede the Chinese Communist claims to Quemoy and Matsu, let alone Formosa, but it was ready also to hold the Nationalists in check.

This second crisis of the Straits of Formosa finally subsided as had the first without precipitating active hostilities. Yet the situation remained tense and could easily blow up again at any time. Communist China insisted that Formosa was an integral part of China and declared its determination to liberate it from what it termed American control exercised through the puppet Nationalist government; the United States appeared equally determined as a matter of principle and military security to defend it against any attack. There was no resolving the problem of "the two Chinas."

The situation was the more dangerous because of the growing strength—industrial and military—of Communist China and the mounting evidence of the power that it was beginning to exert in the communist bloc. The continued American refusal to consider diplomatic recognition appeared completely unrealistic to critics of the Eisenhower-Dulles policy. They maintained that in no other phase of postwar diplomacy had the United States more notoriously blundered than in its entire China policy.

A principal argument against recognition was that it would be interpreted throughout Asia as surrender to communism. India and other of the free nations in that part of the world were nevertheless strongly opposed to American policy and considered it a continuing threat to peace. The attitude of this neutralist or uncommitted group of countries was demonstrated by their unwillingness to join SEATO and by their resentment of the military aid being extended to Nationalist China, the Philippines, Thailand, and Pakistan. The position taken by Prime Minister Nehru of India was that the best defense against the spread of communism in Asia was effective technological and economic assistance for the underdeveloped countries—assistance that would enable them to demonstrate to their peoples that there was another way to economic stability and a higher standard of living than communism.

The United States had long since been extending such aid to an impressive extent. The policies initiated by President Truman, who had originated the so-called Point Four program, were continued under President Eisenhower. There were generous grants of assistance to the countries in Asia as to those in other parts of the world. However, the greater emphasis on military assistance made the maintenance of economic aid highly difficult. Congress appeared to be growing increasingly reluctant to appropriate the necessary funds to expand this program, although President Eisenhower emphatically stressed its importance.

★ THE MIDDLE EASTERN CRISES

During this same period of alarms and excursions in the Far East the world was also periodically agitated by a series of crises in the Middle East. While the part played by Soviet Russia in these developments was highly significant, they grew more directly from the rising tide of Arab nationalism. A spirit of revolt against the West spread throughout the countries of both the Middle East and North Africa. It was compounded of many and highly complex elements. The Arab states resented foreign control and exploitation of the immense oil reserves of the region (there had been an earlier flare-up over this issue in Iran), and also what they considered the unjustified support given to the new state of Israel, toward which they had remained implacably hostile ever since its creation in 1948. The leader among these restive nations was Egypt. Colonel Gamal Abdul Nasser came into power in that country in the spring of 1954, and riding high on a wave of intense nationalism he threatened all foreign interests. Here was a boiling cauldron of troubles which provided the Soviet Union with an unique opportunity to spread communist propaganda and further confuse and confound the West.

Ironically enough, the first major crisis in the Middle East, which led to Anglo-French intervention over the Suez issue in November 1956, coincided with a Soviet crisis in eastern Europe. The crosscurrents operative on the international stage were more complex than at any time since the war. And the week that found these separate events at their most critical juncture was the week of the presidential election in which the American people awarded Eisenhower his second term of office.

The Soviet Union's difficulties in eastern Europe grew out of the demands of the peoples of Poland and Hungary, following Premier Khrushchev's denunciation of Stalin early in 1956, for greater freedom. The

Poles succeeded in winning certain concessions from the Soviet Union, with the accession to power of Wladyslaw Gomulka, but while the Hungarians for a time also appeared to have set up a more independent regime under Imre Nagy, their uprising took on such an anti-Russian character that Moscow deviously maneuvered to crush it by force. After apparent acceptance of the new regime, the Red armies were sent into Hungary with orders to arrest Nagy and stamp out every vestige of revolt.

The dramatic and ultimately tragic story of Hungary created greater excitement for a time than perhaps anything that had happened since the war. Did this uprising mean the communist satellites were about to follow the example of Yugoslavia, where Tito had long since broken with Moscow, and throw off the Russian yoke? Did it foreshadow a climactic weakening of the whole communist system in eastern Europe? Such hopes as the heroic Hungarian struggle aroused were cruelly shattered by the brutal and ruthless tactics whereby the Red army completely crushed the revolutionaries.

The United Nations took up the issue when Soviet Russia forcefully intervened in the affairs of a supposedly independent country. The General Assembly condemned Russia's action as a breach of peace. But Moscow completely ignored the United Nations and in the circumstances there was nothing it could do. The West was paralyzed unless it wished to interfere with force and thereby invite, almost certainly, the big war.

In the meantime the events transpiring in the Middle East were also brought before the United Nations. The quite different circumstances surrounding this concurrent crisis, however, had enabled it to take action which in the Hungarian affair the Soviet Union so successfully blocked.

The Suez affair was the direct consequence of the maneuvering of Nasser to build up Egyptian nationalism and eliminate all western influence in his country. American policy was undoubtedly a contributing factor in the final denouement: It wavered between sympathy for Israel and support for the Arab nations, it sought to safeguard the region as a whole from possible Soviet penetration through promoting (but not actually joining) the Bagdad pact, and it first sponsored and then withdrew economic aid for Egypt itself.

The crisis first began to build up when Secretary Dulles, concerned over Nasser's flirtations with Moscow and his purchase of arms from Czechoslovakia, suddenly canceled in July 1956 a previous offer for large-scale assistance in building the Aswan Dam, an ambitious project for impounding the waters of the Nile. Partly in consequence of this abrupt act Nasser moved to nationalize the Suez Canal. Alarmed by this direct blow at both their economic interests and their national security, England and France thereupon reverted to the imperialistic tactics of an earlier day. In probable conjunction with Israel, which had already seized the opportunity to attack Egypt in projection of their perennial border warfare, the two western democracies launched an invasion of the Suez area on November 5, stating that their forces would occupy the canal zone to assure freedom for international traffic.

This was aggression in terms of both France's and England's commitments to collective security. When Egypt immediately took the issue to the United Nations, the Assembly condemned the Anglo-French move, called for an immediate cease-fire, and agreed to dispatch a United Nations police force to Egypt to ensure compliance with its order. The startling aspect of this action was that the United States and Soviet Russia, in spite of Anglo-French opposition, stood together in upholding it. In the face of such unusual collaboration—and also Moscow's threat to send "volunteers" to support the Egyptians—England and France, reluctantly and bitterly, agreed to withdraw their forces and accept the mediation of the United Nations.

The United States had not been informed in advance of the Anglo-French plans, and found itself in a critical dilemma. President Eisenhower fully realized the grave risks to the whole western alliance in siding against England and France. Yet he felt a strong obligation to uphold the principles for which the United Nations stood and which the United States had itself professed so often. There was also no telling what the long-range effect of this western resort to force might be on the explosive situation in the Middle East, or what policy Soviet Russia might adopt if the United Nations took no action. In the past, the affairs of the Middle East had often seemed so remote that the American people cared little what might happen there. This could no longer be the case if they threatened to bring on war. The wages of world power was inescapable responsibility.

In spite of Russian threats to intervene, unhappy rumblings from England and France (and also from Israel), and further nationalist agitation in Egypt something like calm settled over the Middle East after the United Nations' intervention. The foreign troops were withdrawn from Egypt, a United Nations Emergency Force took over supervision of the truce, and salvage crews were rushed to the Suez Canal which the Egyptians had blocked by sinking ships. Nasser had if anything strengthened his position; he became more than ever the leader and spokesman of Arab nationalism.

The United States still remained deeply troubled over the whole situation. It was hardpressed to renew the shattered unity of the western allies and in spite of its temporary collaboration with the Soviet Union was more than ever fearful of communist subversion in the Arab states.

The administration felt it imperative to seek some more effective way to assure stability in such a critical area of the world—a region on which western Europe remained so greatly dependent for essential oil supplies.

Early in 1957 President Eisenhower announced a new policy, to which Congress subsequently gave its support, wherein it was stated that the United States would come to the assistance of any country in the Middle East that found itself threatened by communist aggression and invited such aid. What became known as the Eisenhower Doctrine promised also economic support for the Middle East, but its most significant aspect was its direct pledge of military assistance to block communist penetration.

Within little more than a year, as the still unsettled conditions in the Middle East grew steadily worse in the light of Nasser's attempts to build up Egyptian nationalism with Moscow's open encouragement, the United States felt compelled to put the Eisenhower Doctrine to the test. Nasser had already brought about the union of Egypt and Syria in the United Arab Republic, and new disturbances among the Arab nations culminated in a *coup d'état* in Iraq which installed a radical and vehemently nationalistic government. For fear that such disturbances would spread to the one strongly western-oriented country in that part of the world, the little Republic of Lebanon, the United States in July 1958 landed troops at Lebanon's request to safeguard its existing government. It was a tangled situation, and in no way clarified by the American action or the simultaneous intervention of British troops in Jordan. The United Nations was once again seized with an occasion for possible condemnatory action, and amid even more confused crosscurrents than at the time of the Suez crisis, it took up this new problem. The Arab nations and Soviet Russia vigorously protested American intervention; the United States sought to uphold its action as entirely within its rights and as a move for peace.

The situation finally resolved itself, if again only temporarily, when the United States and Great Britain, after a personal appearance by President Eisenhower before the Assembly, made clear their intention to recall their troops. The Arab nations accepted such pledges after long debate, and themselves introduced the final resolution, passed unanimously, which provided for the United Nations, through its Secretary-General, making such arrangements as would "facilitate the early withdrawal of the foreign troops from the two countries."

The crisis was over. There still remained the question of Nasser's further intents and purposes, the nature of the relationship between the United Arab Republic and Soviet Russia, and future Anglo-American policy. The United States' forceful intervention in Lebanon had evoked widespread criticism both at home and abroad; it appeared to have proved very little. As once again an uneasy quiet settled over the Middle East, the interrelated problems of Soviet-American rivalry, Nasser's own ambitions, Arab nationalism in the region as a whole, communist intrigue and propaganda, Israel's hopes and aspirations, the ambiguous status of Iraq, and western oil interests were no nearer solution than ever.

★ EISENHOWER'S SECOND TERM

In some measure the problems of eastern Asia and the Middle East, for all their potential dynamite, were peripheral to the major conflict between the democratic West and the communist East. The decisive battlefield remained Europe, and the status of Germany remained the key to Europe. So long as this basic problem remained unresolved, and there were still no signs of a weakening of the opposing positions held by the West and the East on German unification, there seemed to be no escape from the two sides' endless maneuvering to build up political and military power.

The arms race was indeed taking on more and more ominous overtones with the continued stockpiling of bombs, the dangerous testing of new nuclear weapons, the development of intermediate and intercontinental ballistic missiles in both the United States and Soviet Russia. No way presented itself, in spite of all the conferences and negotiations, to bring this mad rivalry to a halt. Every hopeful move, and an anxious world was quick to seize upon any hint of a possible thawing of the Cold War, collapsed in complete failure.

Starting his second term in January 1957, President Eisenhower did not appear to have any plan to give a more affirmative, positive cast to a foreign policy that often seemed to be little more than a frantic reaction to Soviet Russia's more calculated moves on the international chess board. He reiterated his deep and sincere desire for peace and stressed the need to build up and strengthen the military forces of the United States and its allies. But when new crises arose in eastern Asia and the Middle East, as we have already seen, they were handled on an emergency basis that did not provide any long-term answer to the underlying problems.

The administration was also plagued by problems on the home front. The President had no sooner been inaugurated than the economy began to falter badly, and before the year was out the country found itself in the midst of a sharp recession. A Republican administration and a Democratic Congress quarreled fiercely over what measures should be taken, and with unemployment mounting to some 5,000,000, conditions for a time went from bad to worse. But the recession actually proved to be as brief as it was temporarily acute. Even before such antirecession measures as Congress adopted could have any real effect things began to improve, and by the summer of 1958 the country was well on the road to recovery. The safeguards built into the economic system through agricultural aid, minimum wages, and unemployment insurance proved their value as the nation righted itself and industry once again began to forge ahead.

In the meantime, the recession had thrown the budget badly out of balance, and in spite of unemployment there was no relief from the continued pressure of inflation. A sharp conflict developed between the need for governmental economy and the pressing demands of national defense. At one and the same time President Eisenhower proposed the largest budget in peacetime history for the next fiscal year and called for greater economy all along the line. Congress adopted at his urging a bill for the reorganization of the Department of Defense and accepted some reductions in defense expenditures, but it refused to accept all of the President's proposals and its Democratic majority accused the administration of taking an ambiguous and contradictory stand in its basic fiscal policies and of endangering national security.

The year 1957 was in every way a difficult one for Eisenhower. The public showed itself highly critical of his leadership, or rather what was judged a lack of leadership. The inadequacies of foreign policy so clearly demonstrated in both the Formosa Straits and Middle Eastern crises, appeared to be matched by indecision in meeting the domestic problems posed by the recession, continued inflation, and the conflict over segregation and civil rights. The political reaction to this situation was to be demonstrated by the Democratic sweep in the midterm elections in 1958. Meanwhile, the debate over fiscal and defense policies continued. There were increasingly acrimonious exchanges between Congress and members of the administration over whether the United States was behind or ahead of Soviet Russia in such vital areas as strategic bombing, the development of nuclear weapons, and experimentation with ballistic missiles.

★ SPUTNIK AND THE AGE OF SPACE

In the midst of these debates and controversies there occurred, in the autumn of 1957, an event that shattered any sense of complacency the American people or their government might have had as to where the United States really did stand in the arms race with Soviet Russia. Moscow dramatically announced on October 4 that Russian scientists had succeeded in launching an earth satellite. As the Sputnik circled the globe emitting a staccato beep-beep-beep while it whirled through space, the American people, shocked and bewildered, were forced to recognize that Russian science and Russian technology had stolen a march on their own scientists and technologists in breaking the barriers of space. The implications of Sputnik were breathtaking. Here was a new age—the Age of Space.

The administration, Congress, and the American people were at once aroused to meet this new challenge from Soviet Russia. Did this tremendous scientific triumph herald a decisive shift of power from the free world to the communist world? As 1957 gave way to 1958 Congress undertook on the urging of both the President and its own leaders to revitalize the whole program of scientific research. It was all too clear that everything possible had to be done to speed up the development of missiles and antimissiles and press forward with a more ambitious satellite program. There was a new sense of urgency in the air. It influenced not only the drive to strengthen the nation's military posture but inspired, for a time at least, a movement to do something about scientific education in the United States on the theory that Soviet Russia was getting far ahead in the training of scientific personnel.

Soon after the launching of the first Sputnik, the Russians sent a second satellite—carrying a dog—into space. Their experiments were to prove to be the beginning of a whole series, but the United States was soon to enter this startling competition. Beginning slowly, with some well-publicized failures, it went on in 1958 to win its own triumphs and launched a satellite equal to any that the Russians had yet attempted which went into orbit relaying a recorded radio message from President Eisenhower. Then before the year was over, the Soviets announced they had sent a great rocket hurtling through space which had passed beyond the moon and entered into orbit around the sun. The seemingly fantastic imaginings of the science fiction writers of an earlier age were coming true. Amid predictions of space ships circling the earth, shots at the moon, and man-carrying rockets the layman hardly knew what to believe of the age's unpredictable future.

There were other developments on the national stage as the 1950's drew to a close. Further conflicts developed out of the acute segregation problem, the drive to do something about labor corruption was renewed, and on a more positive note, Alaska and Hawaii were admitted to the Union as the forty-ninth and fiftieth states. The issue overshadowing all others, however, was the rivalry with Soviet Russia in maintaining in this new age America's world leadership in industry, scientific developments, and military might.

The progress in missile and satellite experimentation at the same time emphasized rather than lessened the imperative necessity for trying to discover some way to reduce the risk of international conflict inherent in the Cold War. There were once again proposals for a new summit conference, or at least renewal of negotiations on some other level for the settlement of the problems of European security which still hinged on the divided status of Germany. The continued exchange of notes between Eisenhower and Khrushchev, the alternate backing-and-filling of the spokesmen of both the western democracies and of the communist bloc, the inconclusive nature of such talks as were initiated on the suspension of nuclear tests and prevention from surprise attack, did not appear to be making much headway as 1958 drew to an end. But with the next year prospects for a high-level conference appeared to improve with some signs of a greater resiliency on the part of both the Soviet Union and the Western powers.

At this juncture of affairs the United States suffered a sharp blow in the death of Secretary of State Dulles, but his replacement by Christian A. Herter brought an able and experienced man to head the State Department. It fell to his lot to participate in the conference of foreign ministers which had already been arranged to pave the way to the summit, and it duly met in Geneva during the late spring of 1959. This meeting was not held under the happiest auspices. The Soviet Union's apparent determination to try to force the democratic powers out of West Berlin was countered by the equally adamant refusal of the United States, Great Britain, and France to surrender their position in this important enclave within communist-dominated East Germany. As a consequence the conference was a complete failure: no progress whatsoever was made in resolving the impasse over Berlin or in settling the larger related question of the possible unification of Germany. This failure was, however, overshadowed at the last moment by the dramatic announcement on August 3, 1959, that President Eisenhower and Premier Khrushchev had agreed upon an exchange of personal visits.

This startling new development did not of itself mean any change in the basic positions of either the United States or Soviet Russia. But it was generally felt that so long as talks and discussion continued, there was still valid ground to hope that actual war could be averted. It was unrealistic to expect any definitive solution of the world's problems, whether those posed by the threat of international communism or those arising from the strident nationalism and basic economic needs of the underdeveloped countries of Asia, Africa, and the Middle East. Nevertheless, the avoidance of war at least kept open the opportunity for dealing with them through peaceful negotiation and mutual adjustment rather than force of arms.

★ THE CLOSE OF THE 1950's

At the close of the 1950's, the American people faced as paradoxical and contradictory a situation as they had ever before confronted in their entire history. The nation was almost unbelievably strong, wealthy, and powerful. The growth of its industries and manufactures, sustained by the most amazing technological achievements, had created a more affluent society than the world had ever known, and had made possible, in spite of some continuing pockets of poverty and unemployment, a generally high standard of living for which all history had no parallel. Yet at the same time there existed an apparent threat to everything for which the country stood—democracy, liberty, and peace—that ironically made for intense anxiety and even fear.

This threat—international communism—was twofold. First, communist principles and ideology had an undoubted appeal to the minds of men throughout the world, especially in those countries where the West was still associated with imperialism and white supremacy, which might endanger democracy everywhere. Second, the possible resort to military aggression by the communists, whether emanating from Soviet Russia or Communist China, held out the dread prospect of a world war that could destroy western civilization.

In this new age of space, dramatically heralded by the Sputnik which Russia had launched so successfully, the dangers of the possible subversion of democratic values or even physical annihilation were nevertheless counter-balanced by potentialities for the most tremendous material and social advances mankind had ever experienced. Civilization could move in either direction. The horizons were limitless if only a divided world could somehow agree to marshal its resources for constructive rather than destructive purposes.

Upon the United States rested the responsibility of seeking how best it could exercise its great influence—moral as well as material—in establishing a peace that would not only assure mankind of the opportunity for further social and economic advance, but one that would also sustain and uphold freedom. This was the ultimate challenge facing the American people.

SUGGESTED READINGS

The most useful, and indeed indispensable, bibliography for books dealing with American history is *The Harvard Guide to American History* (1954). These notes, which will make no attempt to rival that extensive reference work, are limited to highly selective lists, on a chapter by chapter basis, of studies that should appeal to both the general reader and the student. Attention might also be called at this point, however, to a number of collections of contemporary documents or other writings that often give a more vivid impression of the passing scene than any later analysis or description. Among the best are Henry S. Commager, *Documents of American History* (1958), W. Thorp, M. Curti, and C. Baker, *American Issues* (2 vols., 1941), and (available in paperback) Richard Hofstadter, *Great Issues in American History, 1864–1957* (1958).

CHAPTER I. THE AFTERMATH OF WAR

Two standard studies of this period are W. A. Dunning, *Reconstruction, Political and Economic, 1865–1877* (1907), and W. L. Fleming, *The Sequel of Appomattox; a Chronicle of the Reunion of the States* (1919), but a more recent volume embodying later interpretations of Reconstruction is J. G. Randall, *The Civil War and Reconstruction* (1937). Also valuable are Howard K. Beale, *The Critical Year: A Study of Andrew Johnson and Reconstruction* (1930) and the highly readable Claude G. Bowers, *The Tragic Era; the Revolution after Lincoln* (1929).

Further books on Reconstruction and the South's recovery are noted under the next chapter heading. The following biographies might be mentioned here: G. F. Milton, *The Age of Hate; Andrew Johnson and the Radicals* (1930), R. N. Current, *Old Thad Stevens: A Story of Ambition* (1942), G. H. Haynes, *Charles Sumner* (1909).

On more general economic and social aspects of the postwar scene, see Allan Nevins, *The Emergence of Modern America, 1865–1878* (1927).

CHAPTER II. RECONSTRUCTION AND RECOVERY

Apart from books already noted, excellent accounts of the developing situation in the South that in some instances go beyond the Reconstruction era itself are E. M. Coulter, *The South During Reconstruction* (1947), Paul H. Buck, *The Road to Reunion, 1865–1900* (1937), F. D. Simkins, *The South Old and New* (1947), C. Vann Woodward, *Reunion and Reaction* (1951) and also his *The Origins of the New South, 1877–1913* (1951), and W. J. Cash, *The Mind of the South* (1941). The most recent study, popularly written, is Hodding Carter, *The Angry Scar: The Story of Reconstruction* (1959).

For the evolving position of the Negro in American society one should have reference to the classic study by Gunnar Myrdal, *An*

American Dilemma: The Negro Problem and Modern Democracy (2 vols., 1944) and the very penetrating account of John Hope Franklin, *From Slavery to Freedom: A History of the American Negroes* (1947).

CHAPTER III. THE LAST FRONTIER: GOLD, CATTLE, AND WHEAT

The most comprehensive study of the westward movement is Ray A. Billington, *Westward Expansion* (1943), but fundamental for an understanding of the influence of the frontier is Frederick Jackson Turner, *The Frontier in American History* (1920) and particularly his essay "The Significance of the Frontier in American History." For the phase of settlement which its title suggests, W. W. Webb, *The Great Plains* (1936) is highly interesting and important, and also James C. Malin, *The Grasslands of North America* (1948).

Other more specialized studies include R. E. Riegel, *America Moves West* (1947), Everett Dick, *Vanguards of the Frontier* (1941) and *The Sod-House Frontier, 1854–1890* (1937), and Fred A. Shannon, *The Farmer's Last Frontier, 1860–1897* (1945).

On policy toward the Indians, Helen Hunt Jackson, *A Century of Dishonor* (1881) is of continuing interest while a more recent and general account of Indian life is John C. Collier, *Indians of the Americas* (1947). A standard study of the mining country is T. A. Rickard, *A History of American Mining* (1932), while among the many books on the cattle country are Ernest S. Osgood, *The Day of the Cattleman* (1929), Edward E. Dale, *The Range Cattle Industry* (1930), and Louis Pelzer, *The Cattleman's Frontier* (1936).

Such contemporary writing as Mark Twain, *Roughing It* (2 vols., 1872), and Andy Adams, *Log of a Cowboy* (1903), make fascinating reading as well as do the novels of Willa Cather, *O Pioneers!* (1913) and *My Antonia* (1918), and Ole Rølvaag, *Giants in the Earth* (1929).

CHAPTER IV. THE GROWTH OF INDUSTRY

There is a wealth of material on this topic but two of the best general books are T. C. Cochran and William Miller, *The Age of Enterprise* (1942) and Ida Tarbell, *The Nationalizing of Business, 1878–1898* (1936). A more recent brief study is Samuel P. Hays, *The Response to Industrialism, 1885–1914* (1957). A very readable but sometimes extravagant account of the great entrepreneurs of this period is Matthew Josephson, *The Robber Barons* (1934); a more recent and more objective study is William Miller, *Men in Business* (1952).

There are not many satisfactory individual biographies of these industrialists but Burton J. Hendrick, *The Life of Andrew Carnegie* (2 vols., 1932) is helpful, and in a class by itself is Allan Nevins, *Study in Power: John D. Rockefeller* (2 vols., 1953).

CHAPTER V. AGRICULTURE AND LABOR

On the situation facing the farmers a number of the books cited under the sections dealing with the New South and the West are important, especially F. Shannon, *The Farmer's Last Frontier* and E. Dick, *The Sod-House Frontier*. For the beginnings of Populism, the best book is still John D. Hicks, *The Populist Revolt* (1931), but there are also many more specialized accounts of the movement in different states. An excellent biography dealing with one phase of the movement is C. V. Woodward, *Tom Watson, Agrarian Rebel* (1938). A fascinating study of the "myth" of the West is Henry Nash Smith, *Virgin Land* (1950). See also, for this entire period and later, Richard Hofstadter, *The Age of Reform* (1955).

Contemporary writing is again most illustrative of actual conditions on the farms. In addition to the novels by Willa Cather and Ole Rølvaag, already mentioned, there are the short stories, *Main-Travelled Roads* (1891) and autobiography, *A Son of the Middle Border* (1923) by Hamlin Garland.

The standard history of American labor is the monumental study of John R. Commons and Associates, *History of Labour in the United States* (4 vols., 1918–35), but the entire story is more briefly related in Foster Rhea Dulles, *Labor in America* (1949). A more detailed study of the period now under review is Norman Ware, *The Labor Movement in the United States, 1860–1895* (1929).

Two accounts of the labor leaders themselves are highly interesting: *The Path I Trod: The Autobiography of Terence V. Powderly* (1940) and Samuel Gompers, *Seventy Years of Life and Labor* (2 vols., 1925). One of the best biographies is Ray Ginger, *The Bending Cross: A Biography of Eugene Victor Debs* (1949). Two excellent accounts of labor strikes are Henry David, *The History of the Haymarket Affair* (1936) and Almont Lindsay, *The Pullman Strike* (1942).

CHAPTER VI. THE CHANGING PATTERN OF AMERICAN LIFE

For the period from 1865 to the close of the century, much interesting material is available in the three volumes of *The History of American Life* series: Allan Nevins, *The Emergence of Modern America*, and Ida Tarbell, *The Nationalizing of Business*, already noted, and Arthur M. Schlesinger, *The Rise of the City, 1878–1898* (1933).

On more specialized topics there may be recommended for further reading Robert Bremner, *The Discovery of Poverty in America* (1956), Arthur Mann, *Yankee Reformers in the Urban Age* (1954), Bernard Jaffe, *Men of Science in America* (1944), Henry F. May, *Protestant Churches and Industrial America* (1949), Dixon Wecter, *The Saga of American Society* (1937), Foster Rhea Dulles, *America Learns to Play, A History of Popular Recreation, 1607–1940* (1940), James D. Hart, *The Popular Book: A History of America's Literary Taste* (1950), E. P. Cubberly, *Public Education in the United States* (1934), Frank L. Mott, *American Journalism* (1950) and *A History of American Magazines* (4 vols., 1930–57).

CHAPTER VII. LITERARY AND INTELLECTUAL TRENDS

There is no substitute for reading the authors themselves—especially Walt Whitman, Emily Dickinson, Mark Twain, William Dean Howells, Henry James—as an introduction to the literature of this period. But there are innumerable literary histories or critical studies that are very helpful for an understanding of literature's significance. There is a great deal of interesting material, for example, in the appropriate sections of

Robert E. Spiller and others, *Literary History of the United States* (3 vols., 1948), Vernon Louis Parrington, *The Beginnings of Critical Realism in America, 1860–1920* (1930), Van Wyck Brooks, *New England: Indian Summer, 1865–1950* (1940) and *The Confident Years, 1885–1915* (1952). Among other studies that might be mentioned: Everett Carter, *Howells and the Age of Realism* (1954) and Bernard De Voto, *Mark Twain's America* (1932).

On aspects of social thinking and reform there are a number of excellent books that would include, although the period they cover is longer than that treated in this chapter, Eric Goldman, *Rendezvous with Destiny* (1952), Richard Hofstadter, *Social Darwinism in American Thought, 1860–1915* (1944) and *The Age of Reform* (1955), and Daniel Aaron, *Men of Good Hope* (1951).

The intellectual currents of the day—again in respect to a broader canvas than this immediate period—are discussed in Merle Curti, *The Growth of American Thought* (1951), Ralph H. Gabriel, *The Course of American Democratic Thought* (1940), and Henry S. Commager, *The American Mind* (1950)—three indispensable books.

CHAPTER VIII. THE POLITICAL SCENE

Many of the books previously noted have their bearing on the material in this chapter. It is generally covered in such a study as Matthew Josephson, *The Politicos, 1865–1896* (1938), but a far more objective and scholarly record is found in Eugene H. Roseboom, *A History of Presidential Elections* (1958) which goes much beyond its title.

The most interesting reading is biographies. Among those which stand out are W. B. Hesseltine, *Ulysses S. Grant, Politician* (1935), H. J. Eckenrode, *Rutherford B. Hayes* (1930), R. G. Caldwell, *James A. Garfield* (1931), G. F. Howe, *Chester A. Arthur* (1934), J. A. Barnes, *John G. Carlisle* (1931), David S. Muzzey, *James G. Blaine* (1934), Allan Nevins, *Grover Cleveland* (1932), and Ray Ginger, *Altgeld's America* (1958).

A very colorful, although now outdated, political account of the closing years of the century is H. T. Peck, *Twenty Years of the Republic, 1885–1905* (1907).

CHAPTER IX. POPULISM AND THE ELECTION OF 1896

John D. Hicks, *The Populist Revolt,* has already been cited as the standard account of its subject. It may be supplemented by C. M. Destler, *American Radicalism, 1865–1901* (1946), and R. B. Nye, *Midwestern Progressive Politics: A Historical Study of Its Origins and Development, 1870–1950* (1951).

There is no good biography of McKinley, but a laudatory and uncritical study is by Charles S. Olcott, *The Life of William McKinley* (2 vols., 1916). Nor are either of the two lives of Bryan, M. R. Werner, *Bryan* (1929), or Paxton Hibben, *Peerless Leader* (1929), very satisfactory. There is more interesting material in William Allen White, *Masks in a Pageant* (1928) and Herbert Croly, *Marcus Alonzo Hanna* (1912).

CHAPTER X. IMPERIALISM

There is a vast literature on the origins and development of American imperialism. It is discussed in such general diplomatic studies as Thomas A. Bailey, *A Diplomatic History of the American People* (1950), Samuel F. Bemis, *A Diplomatic History of the United States* (1950), Foster Rhea Dulles, *America's Rise to World Power* (1955), and more particularly the latter author's *The Imperial Years* (1957). A useful collection of documents on foreign policy generally is Ruhl J. Bartlett, *The Record of American Diplomacy* (1947), and a still more recent history is Robert H. Ferrell, *American Diplomacy* (1959).

Contemporary books of both interest and importance are the works of Alfred Thayer Mahan, especially *Lessons of the War with Spain, and Other Articles* (1899), and Josiah Strong, *Our Country* (1885). Underlying factors in the growth of imperialism are discussed in Albert K. Weinberg, *Manifest Destiny* (1935), and Hofstadter, *Social Darwinism in American Thought*. One of the most important scholarly studies of the immediate period is Julius W. Pratt, *Expansionists of 1898* (1936), and the same author has dealt with the decline of imperialism in *America's Colonial Experiment* (1950). A popular and fascinating account of the Spanish War itself is Walter Millis, *The Martial Spirit* (1931). The naval aspects of the subject are taken up in Harold and Margaret Sprout, *The Rise of American Naval Power, 1776–1918* (1939).

Among books dealing with the Open Door are A. Whitney Griswold, *The Far Eastern Policy of the United States* (1938), Paul Varg, *Open Door Diplomat—The Life of W. W. Rockhill* (1952), and Tyler Dennett, *John Hay* (1933).

An especially stimulating and provocative book analyzing foreign policy in this and other periods is Robert E. Osgood, *Ideals and Self-Interest in America's Foreign Relations* (1953).

CHAPTER XI. THE SPIRIT OF PROGRESSIVISM

An excellent one-volume study of the entire Progressive period is by George E. Mowry, *The Era of Theodore Roosevelt* (1958), and it is covered from somewhat more specialized angles in two books by Harold U. Faulkner, *The Quest for Social Justice, 1898–1914* (1931) and *The Decline of Laissez Faire, 1897–1915* (1951). Both the previously noted Goldman, *Rendezvous with Destiny*, and Hofstadter, *The Age of Reform*, also discuss the period with unusually keen insights. Two important background studies of the social ferment of these years are Louis Filler, *Crusaders for American Liberalism* (1939) and C. C. Regier, *The Era of the Muckrakers* (1932). From the point of the depression era, John Chamberlain has written of progressive thought in his *Farewell to Reform* (1932). Attention may also be called to the interesting journalistic series, Mark Sullivan, *Our Times, 1900–1925* (6 vols., 1926–35).

Among the many contemporary or autobiographical books that stand out are Lincoln Steffens, *The Shame of the Cities* (1904) and *The Autobiography of Lincoln Steffens* (2 vols., 1931), Ida Tarbell, *The History of the Standard Oil Company* (2 vols., 1904) and her autobiographical

All in the Day's Work (1939), Ray Stannard Baker, *American Chronicle, The Autobiography of Ray Stannard Baker* (1945), and *The Autobiography of William Allen White* (1946). Equally interesting and revealing in their discussion of contemporary ideas are Herbert Croly, *The Promise of American Life* (1909), Walter Weyl, *The New Democracy* (1912), and Walter Lippmann, *Drift and Mastery* (1914).

There are also the social novels of Theodore Dreiser, Winston Churchill, Frank Norris, and Upton Sinclair.

CHAPTER XII. THE ROOSEVELT ERA

Many of the books noted under the previous chapter, especially Mowry, *The Era of Theodore Roosevelt,* apply equally to this chapter. The best biography of Roosevelt is still by Henry F. Pringle, *Theodore Roosevelt* (1931), but it is interestingly supplemented by George E. Mowry, *Theodore Roosevelt and the Progressive Movement* (1947), and J. M. Blum's, *The Republican Roosevelt* (1954). A still more recent biography is Carleton Putnam, *Theodore Roosevelt* (vol. I, 1958). There are also Roosevelt's *Autobiography* (1913) and his always fascinating letters, edited by Elting E. Morison, *The Letters of Theodore Roosevelt, 1868–1919* (8 vols., 1951–54).

Among other political biographies or autobiographies are Henry F. Pringle, *The Life and Times of William Howard Taft* (2 vols., 1939), Robert La Follette, *Autobiography* (1919), and Belle Case and Fola La Follette, *Robert M. La Follette* (2 vols., 1953), George W. Norris, *Fighting Liberal* (1945), John A. Garraty, *Henry Cabot Lodge* (1958), Claude Bowers, *Beveridge and the Progressive Era* (1932), N. W. Stephenson, *Nelson W. Aldrich* (1930), and the first volume of Arthur S. Link's continuing and definitive biography of *Woodrow Wilson: The Road to the White House* (1947).

CHAPTER XIII. THE NEW FREEDOM

Woodrow Wilson's own book on his program, *The New Freedom* (1913), is a brilliant synthesis of his ideals. The early stages of his administration are covered in the second volume of Arthur S. Link's biography, *Wilson, The New Freedom* (1956), and his entire domestic program in the same author's *Wilson and the Progressive Era* (1954). Two recent and briefer Wilson books are J. M. Blum, *Woodrow Wilson and the Politics of Morality* (1956), and John A. Garraty, *Woodrow Wilson* (1956). A still newer biography is that of Arthur Walworth, *Woodrow Wilson* (2 vols., 1958), of which volume I deals with domestic policy. Among more special studies might be noted William Diamond, *The Economic Thought of Woodrow Wilson* (1943).

The best of the autobiographies of his contemporaries is Josephus Daniels, *The Wilson Era: Years of Peace, 1910–1917* (1944).

CHAPTER XIV. SOCIAL AND CULTURAL CHANGE

Many of the books cited for the previous three chapters, as well as a number of those under Chapter VII, bear upon social and cultural change in this period. This is especially true of Faulkner, *The Quest for Social Justice* and *The Decline of Laissez Faire,* Mowry, *The Roose-*

velt Age, Link, *Wilson and the Progressive Era,* and Chamberlain, *Farewell to Reform.*

On labor there are also the books on this topic already noted which may be supplemented by Herbert Harris, *American Labor* (1938), P. F. Brissenden, *The I.W.W.; A Study in American Syndicalism* (1919), L. L. Lorwin, *The American Federation of Labor* (1933), and R. H. Harvey, *Samuel Gompers* (1935).

The best books on immigration are perhaps Oscar Handlin, *The Uprooted* (1951), Carl Wittke, *We Who Built America* (1939), and Marcus Lee Hansen, *The Immigrant in American History* (1940). The story of the automobile is told by David L. Cohn, *Combustion on Wheels: An Informal History of the Automobile Age* (1944), but with far more detail and exposition in Allan Nevins, *Ford, the Times, the Man, the Company* (1954). On moving pictures there is Lewis Jacobs, *The Rise of the American Film* (1939).

The best of many literary studies covering this period is Alfred Kazin, *On Native Grounds* (1942), and in the field of art, Oliver H. Larkin, *Art and Life in America* (1949).

CHAPTER XV. THE ROAD TO WAR

The standard texts on diplomacy are naturally worth-while reading on this topic, but there are numerous special studies. On foreign policy during the Progressive era a comprehensive and scholarly account is Howard K. Beale, *Theodore Roosevelt and the Rise of America to World Power* (1956), while later policy toward Mexico is best reviewed in Harley Notter, *The Origins of the Foreign Policy of Woodrow Wilson* (1937). There might also be noted for this period J. Fred Rippy, *The Caribbean Danger Zone* (1940), Dwight C. Miner, *The Fight for the Panama Route* (1940), and for material on the Algeciras Conference, Allan Nevins, *Henry White, Thirty Years of American Diplomacy* (1930).

On entry into the war two books highly sympathetic to Wilson's policy are Charles Seymour, *American Diplomacy during the World War* (1934) and *American Neutrality, 1914–1917* (1935), while quite different interpretations are presented in Charles C. Tansill, *America Goes to War* (1938), and Walter Millis, *The Road to War* (1935). The most recent and authoritative study, based on many heretofore unavailable documents, is Ernest R. May, *The World War and American Isolation, 1914–1917* (1959). A further book on a broader but related topic which might be noted is Forrest Davis, *The Atlantic System: The Story of Anglo-American Control of the Seas* (1941).

CHAPTER XVI. THE GREAT CRUSADE

The actual prosecution of the war is comprehensively treated in Frederic L. Paxson, *American Democracy and the World War* (3 vols., 1936–48). Other studies on special topics include J. G. Harbord, *The American Army in France, 1917–1918* (1936), Elting E. Morison, *Admiral Sims and the Modern American Navy* (1942), Harold Lavine and James Wechsler, *War Propaganda and the United States* (1940), and Zachariah Chafee, *Free Speech in the United States* (1941).

In the vast array of books dealing with peacemaking, the most illuminating is probably Paul Birdsall, *Versailles Twenty Years After* (1941). There are also two critical studies by Thomas A. Bailey, *Woodrow Wilson and the Great Betrayal* (1945) and *Woodrow Wilson and the Lost Peace* (1944); and a more pro-Wilson account by D. F. Fleming, *The United States and the League of Nations, 1918–1920* (1932). Highly interesting both because of author and subject matter is Herbert Hoover, *The Ordeal of President Wilson* (1958).

Note should also be made of the original material available in Ray Stannard Baker, *Woodrow Wilson and World Settlement* (3 vols., 1922), Charles Seymour, *The Intimate Papers of Colonel House* (4 vols., 1926–28), Robert Lansing, *War Memoirs* (1935) and *The Peace Negotiations* (1921), and Josephus Daniels, *The Wilson Era: Years of War and After, 1917–1923* (1946).

CHAPTER XVII. FOREIGN POLICY IN THE 1920's

On the special topics treated in this chapter, there are excellent studies apart from the more general diplomatic histories.

On relations with Soviet Russia there is Foster Rhea Dulles, *The Road to Teheran: The Story of Russia and America, 1781–1943* (1944); policy in Latin America may best be followed in Samuel F. Bemis, *The Latin American Policy of the United States* (1943); J. C. Vinson has written the best account of the Washington Conference in *The Parchment Peace* (1950), but it should be supplemented by Harold and Margaret Sprout, *Toward a New Order of Sea Power: American Naval Policy and the World Scene, 1918–1922* (1940); and two excellent studies dealing primarily with the attempted outlawry of war and crisis in Manchuria are Robert H. Ferrell, *Peace in Their Time: The Origins of the Kellogg-Briand Pact* (1952) and *American Diplomacy in the Great Depression* (1957).

Other important books include Dana F. Fleming, *The United States and World Organization, 1920–1933* (1938), B. H. Williams, *The United States and Disarmament* (1931), Herbert Feis, *The Diplomacy of the Dollar: First Era, 1919–1932* (1950), Leo Pasvolsky, *War Debts and World Prosperity* (1932).

There is fascinating material in Henry L. Stimson and McGeorge Bundy, *On Active Service in War and Peace* (1947), and some discussion of the Washington Conference in Merlo J. Pusey, *Charles Evans Hughes* (2 vols., 1951).

CHAPTER XVIII. A BUSINESS CIVILIZATION

Five general books deal interestingly with the decade of the 1920's. They are Harold Faulkner, *From Versailles to the New Deal* (1950), George Soule, *Prosperity Decade* (1947), Karl Schriftgiesser, *This Was Normalcy* (1948), Samuel H. Adams, *Incredible Era* (1939), and William E. Leuchtenberg, *The Perils of Prosperity, 1914–1932* (1958). They emphasize respectively politics, economics, the Republican administration, the Harding scandals, and general history. A more journalistic and always fascinating record is Frederick Lewis Allen, *Only Yesterday* (1931), and again interesting, Mark Sullivan, *Our Times*.

On more specialized topics are F. A. Shannon, *America's Economic Growth* (1951), Herbert Harris, *American Labor* (1939), S. Perlman and Philip Taft, *History of Labor in the United States, 1896–1932* (1935), Theodore Saloutos and John D. Hicks, *Agricultural Discontent in the Middle West, 1900–1939* (1951), R. K. Murray, *The Red Scare* (1955), and Zachariah Chafee, Jr., *Free Speech in the United States* (1941).

There is no biography of Harding, but an excellent one on Coolidge is by William Allen White, *Puritan in Babylon* (1938). For the election of 1924 there is Kenneth C. MacKay, *The Progressive Movement of 1924* (1947), and for that of 1928 R. V. Peel and T. C. Donnelly, *The 1928 Campaign* (1931). See also Oscar Handlin, *Al Smith and His America* (1948).

CHAPTER XIX. SOCIAL DEVELOPMENTS

The more general books noted under Chapter XVIII treat many of these issues. To these may be added R. L. Garis, *Immigration Restriction* (1927), supplementing the books already noted on this topic; Herbert Asbury, *The Great Illusion* (1950), Charles Merz, *The Dry Decade* (1931), and Peter H. Odegaard, *Pressure Politics: The Story of the Anti-Saloon League* (1928)—studies of prohibition—and Roger Burlingame, *Peace Veterans* (1932).

On recreation, popular reading, newspapers, and magazines the most easily available sources are books already noted: Dulles, *America Learns to Play*, Hart, *The Popular Book*, Mott, *A History of American Magazines* and *American Journalism*.

A brilliant analysis of American society in the 1920's by a foreigner is André Siegfried, *America Comes of Age* (1927), and a careful sociological study is Robert S. and Helen M. Lynd's *Middletown* (1929).

CHAPTER XX. LITERATURE AND THE ARTS BETWEEN WARS

The writers themselves provide the best material on the literary scene, and both in themselves and as social history such novels as Scott Fitzgerald, *The Great Gatsby*, Sinclair Lewis, *Main Street*, John Dos Passos, *U.S.A.*, and John Steinbeck, *The Grapes of Wrath* give a fascinating picture of the period.

The climate of opinion is further revealed in such contemporary books as Joseph Wood Krutch, *The Modern Temper* (1929), Harold E. Stearns, *Civilization in the United States: An Inquiry by Thirty Americans* (1922), Walter Lippmann, *A Preface to Morals* (1929), and Malcolm Cowley, *Exile's Return* (1951).

Once more attention may be called to such significant volumes as Kazin, *On Native Grounds* and Commager, *The American Mind*. On art see again, Larkin, *Art and Life in America*.

CHAPTER XXI. PROSPERITY TO DEPRESSION

A recent and brilliant study of this period is the first volume of Arthur Schlesinger Jr.'s projected full-scale work on the Roosevelt era, *The Crisis of the Old Order* (1957). Also good but more largely concerned with the 1930's are Dixon Wecter, *The Age of the Great Depression,*

1929–1941 (1948), and Broadus Mitchell, *Depression Decade: From New Era to New Deal, 1929–1941* (1947). A highly readable account of the market crash is John K. Galbraith, *The Big Crash* (1955), and on the depression itself there is Gilbert Seldes, *The Years of the Locust* (1933).

Herbert Hoover has left an extensive record of his ideas and activities in his collected speeches and in his *Memoirs.* The most pertinent volumes for this chapter are *The New Day* (1928), *The Cabinet and the Presidency, 1920–1933* (1952), and *The Great Depression, 1929–1941* (1952). Among accounts of his administration, the most detailed is W. S. Myers and W. H. Newton, *The Hoover Administration: A Documented Narrative* (1936). A more recent volume is Harris G. Warren, *Herbert Hoover and the Great Depression* (1959).

For Franklin D. Roosevelt during these years there are the first volumes of the biography by Frank Freidel, especially *The Ordeal* (1954) and *The Triumph* (1956), which carry the account through 1932.

CHAPTER XXII. ADVENT OF THE NEW DEAL

A number of the books cited for the last chapter, such as those by Dixon Wecter and Broadus Mitchell, also cover the New Deal period, and it will be further examined in the continuing studies of Arthur Schlesinger, Jr., another volume of which, *The Coming of the New Deal,* appeared in 1959, and also in those of the multivolume Roosevelt biography by Frank Freidel. Somewhat in the same category as Wecter and Mitchell, brief and readable, are D. W. Brogan, *The Era of Franklin D. Roosevelt* (1950), and Dexter Perkins, *The New Age of Franklin Roosevelt* (1957). An earlier but still interesting study is Basil Rauch, *History of the New Deal, 1933–1938* (1944).

While Freidel's biography of Roosevelt promises to be outstanding among such books, J. M. Burns's *Roosevelt: The Lion and the Fox* (1956) is an excellent political narrative, and John Gunther's *Roosevelt in Retrospect* (1950) a highly interesting anecdotal study. Among the mounting stream of reminiscent studies by people close to the President, the best remain those by Robert Sherwood, *Roosevelt and Hopkins* (1948), Frances Perkins, *The Roosevelt I Knew* (1946), and Samuel I. Rosenman, *Working with Roosevelt* (1952). A more critical view is Raymond Moley, *After Seven Years* (1939).

Among other books by persons closely associated with the New Deal are Eleanor Roosevelt, *This I Remember* (1949), James A. Farley, *Jim Farley's Story: The Roosevelt Years* (1948), *The Secret Diary of Harold Ickes* (3 vols., 1953–54), James F. Byrnes, *Speaking Frankly* (1947), and *All in One Lifetime* (1958), Rexford G. Tugwell, *The Democratic Roosevelt* (1957), and William D. Hassett, *Off the Record with F.D.R.* (1958).

On more specialized topics note may be made of H. L. Ickes, *Back to Work: The Story of the WPA* (1935), H. S. Johnson, *The Blue Eagle from Egg to Earth* (1935), Arthur Moore, *The Farmer and the Rest of Us* (1945), and Harry L. Hopkins, *Spending to Save; the Complete Story of Relief* (1936).

CHAPTER XXIII. REFORM AND SOCIAL SECURITY

The reading heretofore noted for Chapter XXII relates also to this chapter. It may be supplemented by a number of more specialized studies bearing more directly on reform and social security.

Such books include Abraham Epstein, *Insecurity, a Challenge to America* (1938), Nathan Straus, *The Seven Myths of Housing* (1944), Joseph Rosenfarb, *The National Labor Policy* (1940), and, especially, David Lilienthal, *TVA: Democracy on the March* (1938).

CHAPTER XXIV. THE RISE OF LABOR

The most interesting study of labor during the New Deal is perhaps Herbert Harris, *Labor's Civil War* (1940), but other treatments of the subject are J. R. Walsh, *C.I.O.: Industrial Unionism in Action* (1937), Benjamin Stolberg, *The Story of the CIO* (1938), Edwin Levinson, *Labor on the March* (1938), and Robert R. R. Brooks, *Unions of Their Own Choosing* (1939). Of the biographies of labor leaders the most valuable are Saul D. Alinsky, *John L. Lewis* (1949), Matthew Josephson, *Sidney Hillman; Statesman of American Labor* (1952), and Irving Howe and B. J. Widick, *The U.A.W. and Walter Reuther* (1949).

For the development of labor in its historic setting, reference may be made to such previously noted books as Herbert Harris, *American Labor,* and Foster Rhea Dulles, *Labor in America.*

CHAPTER XXV. CLOSE OF A DECADE

Again, many of the books heretofore noted bear on this chapter but there is also extensive literature on the Supreme Court struggle. A first reference, because of the author's own role in the Justice Department, is Robert H. Jackson, *The Struggle for Judicial Supremacy* (1941), but it should be supplemented by the more objective accounts of Edward S. Corwin in *Constitutional Revolution Ltd.* (1941) and *Court Over Constitution* (1938). A very lively account is Joseph Alsop and Robert Kintner, *The 168 Days* (1938).

Among biographies of members of the Supreme Court in this period are Merlo J. Pusey, *Charles Evans Hughes* (2 vols., 1951), which deals more with its subject's earlier career, and Alpheus T. Mason, *Harlan F. Stone* (1957) and also his *Brandeis, A Free Man's Life* (1946).

CHAPTERS XXVI AND XXVII. NEUTRALITY AND PEARL HARBOR

The wealth of material—including public documents, official speeches, diaries and memoirs, monographic studies, general books—dealing with the neutrality policy of the United States and the events leading up to American entry in World War II is overwhelming. The whole record is set in a broad context in such general books as George F. Kennan, *American Diplomacy, 1900–1950* (1951), a challenging interpretive account, Samuel F. Bemis, *The United States as a World Power* (1950), an authoritative text, and Foster Rhea Dulles, *America's Rise to World Power* (1955).

The period 1937–41 is most authoritatively treated in two massive volumes by W. L. Langer and S. E. Gleason, *The Challenge to Isola-*

tion, 1937–1940 (1952) and *The Undeclared War, 1940–1941* (1953). There are, however, a number of other excellent and shorter accounts including Basil Rauch, *Roosevelt: From Munich to Pearl Harbor* (1950), Allan Nevins, *The New Deal and World Affairs* (1950), and, with special reference to the Pacific, Herbert Feis, *The Road to Pearl Harbor* (1950), and Walter Millis, *This Is Pearl! The United States and Japan—1941* (1947). A more popular general account is Forrest Davis and E. K. Lindley, *How War Came* (1942).

These studies are generally sympathetic with the Roosevelt policy. Attention should be called to a "revisionist school" that is highly critical. A first such book is Charles Beard, *President Roosevelt and the Coming of War, 1941* (1948), while among many later studies the most significant is Charles C. Tansill, *Back Door to War—Roosevelt Foreign Policy, 1933–1941* (1952).

Other books on the New Deal already noted, particularly Sherwood, *Roosevelt and Hopkins,* also have material bearing on the diplomacy of these days. The struggle over the neutrality policy is treated in Walter Johnson, *The Battle Against Isolation* (1944), Wayne S. Cole, *America First: The Battle Against Intervention, 1940–1941* (1953), and Selig Adler, *The Isolationist Impulse* (1957). *The Memoirs of Cordell Hull* (2 vols., 1948), Joseph Davies, *Mission to Moscow* (1941), Joseph C. Grew, *Ten Years in Japan* (2 vols., 1944), and *Ambassador Dodd's Diary, 1933–1938* (1941), are of uneven merit but are all interesting.

CHAPTER XXVIII. TOTAL WAR

The story of American participation in the war is told in a number of the period histories already noted, but more interesting reading is found in the contemporary accounts and memoirs. Among such books may be particularly noted Dwight D. Eisenhower, *Crusade in Europe* (1948), Omar N. Bradley, *A Soldier's Story* (1951), Mark W. Clark, *Calculated Risk* (1951), Joseph W. Stilwell, *The Stilwell Papers* (1948), and Henry H. Arnold, *Global Mission* (1949). Comparable books on the home front include Donald M. Nelson, *Arsenal of Democracy: The Story of American War Production* (1946), and E. R. Stettinius, Jr., *Lend-Lease, Weapon for Victory* (1944).

The War Department has published a long series of volumes on the war; the Navy Department a less ambitious but more readable series written by Samuel Eliot Morison. A brief comprehensive account is Fletcher Pratt, *War for the World* (1950), and Eliot Janeway, *The Struggle for Survival* (1951). The classic of World War II remains Winston Churchill, *The Second World War* (6 vols., 1948–53).

CHAPTER XXIX. THE POSTWAR SCENE

The return to peacetime conditions and problems of the next decade are most interestingly discussed in Eric Goldman, *The Crucial Decade: America, 1945–1955* (1956). On the labor situation two important studies are H. C. Millis and E. C. Brown, *From the Wagner Act to Taft-Hartley* (1950), and Joel Seidman, *American Labor from Defense to Reconversion* (1953).

On politics above everything else are the candid story of Harry S.

Truman, *Memoirs* (2 vols., 1956) and *Mr. President: The First Publication from the Personal Diaries, Private Letters, Papers and Revealing Interviews,* edited by William Hillman (1952). A general and penetrating study is Samuel Lubbell, *The Future of American Politics* (1952).

CHAPTER XXX. THE MIRAGE OF PEACE

The *Memoirs* of Truman, noted for the previous chapter, provide fascinating—if somewhat controversial—material for the foreign affairs of the postwar decade. Also James F. Byrnes, *Speaking Frankly* (1947), *The Private Papers of Senator Vandenberg* (1952), *The Forrestal Diaries,* edited by Walter Millis (1951), Edward R. Stettinius, Jr., *Roosevelt and the Russians: the Yalta Conference* (1949), William D. Leahy, *I Was There* (1950), and Lucius Clay, *Decision in Germany* (1950). On Eastern Asia see particularly Herbert Feis, *The China Tangle: The American Effort in China from Pearl Harbor to the Marshall Mission* (1953), John King Fairbank, *The United States and China* (1958), and Albert C. Wedemeyer, *Wedemeyer Reports* (1958).

There has been a plethora of books on what lines our foreign policy should have followed in these immediate postwar years. A few that have continuing interest are John Foster Dulles, *War or Peace* (1950), George F. Kennan, *Realities of American Foreign Policy* (1954), Thomas K. Finletter, *Power and Policy* (1954), and Robert A. Taft, *A Foreign Policy for Americans* (1951).

CHAPTER XXXI. THE EISENHOWER ERA

This period is too recent for significant historical treatment. Such books as have appeared, for example, on Dwight D. Eisenhower and John Foster Dulles, are of very slight value, and in spite of his special sources for the record of the Eisenhower administration, R. J. Donovan's *The Inside Story* (1956) obviously lacks perspective.

There are numerous rewarding studies of contemporary American society, including David Riesman, *The Lonely Crowd* (1950), C. Wright Mills, *White Collar* (1951) and *The Power Elite* (1957), W. H. Whyte, Jr., *The Organization Man* (1956), Alan Barth, *The Loyalty of Free Men* (1951), Bernard Barber, *Science and the Social Order* (1952), Russell Lynes, *The Tastemakers* (1954), John K. Galbraith, *The Affluent Society* (1958), and perhaps most importantly, the monumental and brilliant study of Max Lerner, *America as a Civilization* (1957). In a somewhat different category, relating to military history, there may also be recommended Walter Millis, *Arms and Men* (1956), and Robert E. Osgood, *Limited War: The Challenge to American Strategy* (1957).

This list could be greatly extended, but from their various points of view, the writers of these books provide a very penetrating analysis of the contemporary scene. For a highly optimistic account of the changes that have occurred since 1900, there is also the brief and readable account of Frederick Lewis Allen, *The Big Change: America Transforms Itself, 1900–1950* (1952).

CHAPTER XXXII. AMERICA AND THE WORLD

The actual record of American foreign policy in the 1950's may be found in State Department reports, newspaper records (especially those of the *New York Times*), such magazines as *Foreign Affairs, The Reporter, The U.S. News and World Report,* and other contemporary publications.

There should also be noted such very recent books discussing policy as Dean Acheson, *Power and Diplomacy* (1958), Thomas K. Finletter, *Foreign Policy: The Next Phase* (1958), Henry A. Kissinger, *Nuclear Weapons and Foreign Policy* (1958), and William A. Williams, *The Tragedy of American Diplomacy* (1959), a highly provocative historical analysis.

INDEX